THEMES ON THE NIGERIAN LEGAL SYSTEM

THEMES ON THE NIGERIAN LEGAL SYSTEM

Edited by

Chijioke Chris Ohuruogu

malthouse

Malthouse Press Limited

Lagos, Benin, Ibadan, Jos, Port-Harcourt, Zaria

ISBN 978-978-60203-2-7

Published by Malthouse Press Limited
Lagos Jos Port Harcourt Zaria

43 Onitana Street, Off Stadium Hotel Road,
Off Western Avenue, Lagos Mainland
E-mail: malthouselagos@gmail.com
Facebook:@malthouselagos
Twitter:@malthouselagos
Instagram:@malthouselagos
Tel: 0802 600 3203

International Distributors
African Books Collective, Oxford, UK
Email: abc@africanbookscollective.com
Website: http://www.africanbookscollective.com

ACKNOWLEDGEMENTS

We acknowledge and appreciate the various contributors who spared time to research and write and waited patiently for the publication to see the light of the day.

PREFACE

The idea to produce this text was conceived in 2014 as Nigeria prepared to mark the 100th year of the amalgamation of the North and South Protectorates to form what is now Nigeria. The idea was to produce a text to tell the *legal history* of Nigeria from 1914 to 2014. The task was commenced, but along the line, due to the difficulties in getting contributors to meet the editorial deadlines, there was a need to restructure the book and also change its original title.

Contributors have written in areas they have competence and understanding. They, therefore, bear responsibility for any error or omission in the chapters contributed.

What is here presented as *Themes on the Nigerian Legal System* constitutes a revised edition.

Professor Chijioke Chris Ohuruogu
Ado-Ekiti, Nigeria.
March 2015, 2023

FOREWORD

This book is presented as a contribution to the growing texts on the Nigerian legal system. The beauty of it lies in the fact that it is a contribution from learned authors writing in specified areas of Nigerian Law. The authors have written in simple easy to understand language, and we hope this will help.

Nigerian Legal System is taught to students in the LLB programme in Nigerian universities as a compulsory course. It is also taught at the Nigerian Law School to foreign-trained students studying for the Bar Examination.

The book offers additional reading in areas not covered by existing texts on Nigerian Law and will be useful not only to students but to practitioners and researchers seeking information on aspects of Nigerian Law.

This book is highly recommended.

ABBREVIATIONS AND ACRONYMS

AGF Attorney General of the Federation
AJA Admiralty Jurisdiction Act
AJA Admiralty Jurisdiction Act
AJPR Admiralty Jurisdiction Procedure Rules
AJPR Admiralty Jurisdiction Procedure Rules
ATP's Awaiting Trial Persons
AU African Union
CA Court of Appeal
CAA Court of Appeal Act
CAC Corporate Affairs Commission
CAMA Companies and Allied Matters Act
CC Criminal Code Act
CCTV Closed Circuit Televisions
CD Campaign for Democracy
CDHR Committee for the Defence of Human Rights
CEDAW Convention on the Elimination of All Forms of Discrimination Against Women
CFRN Constitution of the Federal Republic of Nigeria, 1999
CJN Chief Justice of Nigeria
CLO Civil Liberties Organisations
CPA Criminal Procedure Act
CPC Calabar Port Complex
CPC Criminal Procedure Code
CRP Constitutional Rights Project
DPC Delta Port Complex
DPP Directors of Public Prosecution

EFCC	Economic and Financial Crimes Commission
FA	Factories Act
FCT	Federal Capital Territory, Abuja
FHC	Federal High Court
FIDA	International Federation of Women Lawyers
GIS	Government Inspector of Shipping
GRT	Gross Registered Tonnages
IAP	Industrial Arbitration Panel
IBA	International Bar Association
ICAN	Institute of Chartered Accountants of Nigeria
ICCPR	International Covenant on Civil and Political Rights
ICESCR	International Covenant on Economic Social and Cultural Rights
ICPC	Independent Corrupt Practices Commission
ILO	International Labour Organisation
IYC	Ijaw Youth Congress
JJSC	Justices of the Supreme Court
JSC	Judicial Service Committee
JTF	Special Joint Military Task Force
LAC	Legal Aid Council
LPC	Lagos Port Complex
LUA	Land Use Act
MA	Marriage Act
MCA	Matrimonial Causes Act
MEND	Movement for the Emancipation of the Niger Delta
MOSOP	Movement for the Survival of Ogoni People
MSA	Merchant Shipping Act
NAJUC	National Association of Judicial Correspondence
NBA	Nigerian Bar Association
NCWS	National Council of Women Societies
NDDC	Niger Delta Development Commission
NDVF	Niger Delta Volunteer Force
NEPAD	New Partnership for Africa's Development
NGOs	Non-Governmental Organisations
NIC	National Industrial Court
NIMASA	Nigerian Maritime Administration and Safety Agency

NIPC	Nigerian Investment Promotion Commission
NLRC	Nigerian Law Reform Commission
NMA	National Maritime Authority
NNPC	Nigerian National Petroleum Company
NSCDC	Nigeria Security and Civil Defence Corps
NSE	Nigerian Society of Engineers
NULAI	Network of University Legal Aid Institutions
NWLR	Nigerian Weekly Law Report
NYSC	National Youth Service Corps
OAU	Organisation of African Unity
OPC	Onne Port Complex
OSIJI	Open Society Justice Initiative
PC	Penal Code
PCA	President of the Court of Appeal
RPC	Rivers Port Complex
SCA	Sharia Court of Appeal
SPDC	Shell Petroleum Development Corporation
SRI	Shelter Rights Initiative
SSSCE	Senior Secondary School Certificate Examination
STR	Subject To Regularisation
TCIPC	Tin Can Island Port Complex
TDA	Trade Disputes Act
TUA	Trade Union Act
TWP	Temporary Work Permit
UDD	Universal Defenders of Democracy
UDHR	Universal Declaration of Human Rights
UN	United Nations
UNCLOS	United Nations Convention on Law of The Seas

EDITOR

Chijioke Chris Ohuruogu, educated at the Obafemi Awolowo University Ile-Ife and the University of Lagos, also a Barrister and Solicitor of the Supreme Court of Nigeria, is a Professor of Law ;had served as Dean of Law at Baze University Abuja and Benson Idahosa University of in Benin city. He was one-time Head of Department of International Law, Enugu State University of Science and Technology, among others.

CONTRIBUTORS

Abdulhakeem A. Tijani is a Lecturer in Faculty of Law, Ambrose Alli University, Ekpoma.

Akingbehin, E. O., LL.B (Hons) Ife, LLM, Ph.D (Lagos) BL, Senior Lecturer, Department of Public Law, University of Lagos, Akoka, Yaba, Lagos, Nigeria.

Akpoghome, T. U. (Mrs), LL.M, LL.B, BL. Lecturer, Department of Public Law, Faculty of Law, Benson Idahosa University, Benin City, Edo

Ambrose, O. O. Ekpu, Professor and the Dean, Faculty of Law, Ambrose Alli University, Ekpoma, Edo State, Nigeria.

Anya, A. K., Associate Professor of Law-Dept. of Public & International Law, Igbinedion University College of Law, Okada Nigeria

Asada, Dominic is a professor of law of the Faculty of Law, University of Jos and the current Deputy Dean of Law.

Asogwah, Frank is a Professor of Law and Dean, Faculty of Law at the Enugu State University of Science and Technology, Agbani

Bello, Bamidele Joseph, LLM, LL.B, BL, Barrister & Solicitor of the Supreme Court and lecturer Faculty of Law, Benson Idahosa

University, Benin City.

Edeh, K.N. Esq., LL.M (Ife), LL.B (Ife), Senior Lecturer, Faculty of Law, Enugu State University of Science and Technology, Enugu.

Erugo, **Sam,** PhD (Ibadan), Reader, Faculty of Law, Abia State University, Uturu, Nigeria.

Fabamise, **Sesan,** LLM. Senior Lecturer, College of Law, Afe Babalola University.

Gbadebo, Anthony Olagunju, LL.B, LL.M, Ph.D, Solicitor and Advocate of the Supreme Court of Nigeria. Senior Lecturer in the Department of Jurisprudence and International Law, Faculty of Law, Lagos State University, Nigeria. Formerly Visiting Research Fellow at the Max Planck Institute for Comparative Public Law and International Law, Heidelberg, Germany, and Fellow, Salzburg Global Seminar, Austria.

Ibanga, **Michael,** Reader, Faculty of Law,University of Calabar.Nigeria.

Igwe, Chinedu Akam (LL.B, LL.M, BL), Lecturer, Department of Public and Private Law, Faculty of Law, Ebonyi State University, Abakaliki.

Iheme, Emeka, a Nigerian citizen, studied law at the University of Nigeria, Nsukka (LL.B., Hons., 1986), the Nigerian Law School, Lagos (B.L., 1987) and the University of Lagos (LL.M., 1998). He was called to the Nigerian bar in 1987. He is a legal practitioner and development consultant with substantial experience in legal and institutional reform as well as project cycle management in Commonwealth African countries. He has written and edited several books and papers on law and development.

Ine, Nnadi (Mrs) (PhD), Senior Lecturer, HOD, Commercial Law, Faculty of Law, Imo State University, Owerri, Imo State.

Inegbedion, Nathaniel A., LL.B; LL.M; Ph.D; Associate Professor, Department of Public Law, Faculty of Law, University of Benin. Member, Council of Legal Education; Notary Public.

Madubuike-Ekwe, **Joseph Ndubisi,** S.J.D (GGU, San Francisco, USA), LL.M (Ile-Ife); BL.; LL.B (Hons) (UNN); Senior Lecturer and HOD, Public Law, Faculty of Law, Benson Idahosa University, Benin-City, Edo State Nigeria.

Njoku, **Nduka C.,** Lecturer, School of Law, National Open University of Nigeria, Lagos, Nigeria

Nwano, Theophilious Chinedu, LL.M, LL.B, BL, Barrister & Solicitor of the Supreme Court and lecturer Faculty of Law, Benson Idahosa University, Benin City.

Obeagu, Chukwuma C., Lecturer, Faculty of Law, Enugu State University of Science and Technology, (ESUT) Enugu.

Obi-Okoye, Chineze S., LLM Lecturer, Faculty of Law Nnamdi Azikiwe University, Awka, Anambra State

Ogbodo, S. **Gozie,** is a Senior Lecturer at the Faculty of Law, University of Benin. He also serves as the Assistant Co-ordinator of the Post-Graduate Programme of the Law Faculty. Taught as an Adjunct Professor at the prestigious Golden Gate University in San Francisco, California, United States of America. Dr. Ogbodo holds the Fellowships of the Public Policy Institute of the University of California, Davis, as well as that of the Annenberg School of Communication, University of Southern California.

Oguno, P.E.O. Ph.D, Senior Lecturer, Faculty of Law, Anambra State University Igbariam campus.

Ojogbo, Samuel E., LL.M (Western Ontario) B.L, Lecturer Faculty of Law, Benson Idahosa University, Benin City, Edo State, Nigeria.

Okani, Juliana Omolegho, LL.M (Benin), Lecturer, Faculty of Law, Benson Idahosa University, Benin city.

Okoro, Celestine Chukwuemeka, LL.B (Hons. Nig.), LL.M (Benin), D.C Lorca, Lecturer, Faculty of Law, Enugu State University of Science and Technology, Enugu

Okoye, Chukwudumebi, Legal Practitioner and formely Lecturer in Law at Benson Idahosa University Benin city

Sokefun, Justus, Professor of Law National Open University of Nigeria, Lagos, Nigeria.

Taiwo, Elijah Adewale, LLB, LLM, MPhil (OAU, Ile-Ife, Nigeria), LLD (NMMU, Port-Elizabeth, South Africa), BL (NLS, Lagos); Research Associate, Department of Public Law, Nelson Mandela Metropolitan University, South Africa; Professor of Laws & Head of Department of Private and Business Law, Afe Babalola University, Ado-Ekiti, Nigeria; Fellow of the Netherlands Institute for Advanced Study (NIAS), Wassenaar, the Netherland.

Umahi, Okechukwu Timothy, PhD (Manchester), LL.M (Manchester), LL.M (LASU), LL.B (Enugu), BL., Lecturer Faculty of Law, University of Nigeria, Enugu Campus.

TABLE OF CASES

Eguamwense *v.* Amaghizemwen (1993) 9 NWLR (pt 315) 1, 20; 226
Egwu *v.* Ike (1999) 3 NWLR (pt.594) 189; 463
Ehigie *v.* Ehigie (1961) 1 ALL NLR 871; 97
Ehigie *v.* Ehigie (1961) All NLR 842
Ehuwa *v.* Ondo State (2006) 8 NWLR (pt. 1012) 544; 456
Ekependu *v.* Erika (1959) 4FSC 79; 603
Ekpenkhio *v.* Egbadon [1993] 7 NWLR (pt. 308) 717 CA; 315
Elbinger A.G. *v.* Armstrong [1874] L.R. 9 Q.B. 473; 238
Elegushi *v.* Oseni (2005) 14 NWLR (pt. 945) 348; 611
Eliochin (Nig) Ltd. *v.* Mbadiwe (1986) 1 NSCC 42; 14
Emeakuana *v.* Umeojiako, Suit No. AA/1A/76 (unreported) High Court Awka October 15, 1976; 632
Emerieru *v.* Ovirie & Ors (1977) 2 SC 31
Emezi *v.* Osuagwu & Ors. [2005] 30 WRN 1 (SC); 188
Emmanuel Ahmed *v.* Federal Republic of Nigeria, [2009] 13 NWLR (pt. 1159) 536 CA; 492, 494, 508
Emmanuel Chijioke Orlu *v.* Chief (Dr.) Mpakaboari Gogo-Abite (2010) 41 (pt. 1) NSCQR 458
Emmanuel Ogbe *v.* Chief Justice, East Central State & Ors. (1972) 1 All NLR (pt. 2) 153; 230
Emmanuel Ojo Wey *v.* Lagos Executive Development Board (1959) LLR 20; 228
Enderby Town Football Club Ltd *v.* Football Association Ltd, (1971) 1 Ch. 591; 21
Entick *v.* Carrington (1765)19 St Tr 1030; 36
Erhahon *v.* Erhahon (1997) 6 NWLR (pt. 510) 667; 648
Eshugbayi Eleko *v.* Govt. of Nigeria (1931) AC 662; 76
Eshugbayi Eleko *v.* The Officer Administering the Government of Nigeria (1931) AC 662; 79, 80
Eshugbayi Eleko *v.* Frank Morrish Baddelely (1925) 6 NLR 56; 228
Essan *v.* Faro (1947)12 WACA 135
Estisione H. (Nig.) Ltd & Anor *v.* Osun State Government & Anor [2012] 14 NWLR (pt. 1321) 540; 319
Etuk *v.* Isemin (1992) 4 NWLR (pt. 236) 402; 457
Eugene Meribe *v.* Joshua Egwu (1976) 6 ECSLR 208

TABLE OF STATUTES

NATIONAL

REGIONS / STATES

EASTERN REGION

NORTHERN NIGERIA

WESTERN REGION

ANAMBRA STATE

BENDEL STATE

EBONYI STATE

IMO STATE

LAGOS STATE

PAKISTAN

SOUTH AFRICA

UGANDA

UNITED KINGDOM

UNITED STATES

INTERNATIONAL

CONTENTS

PART B: LAW MAKING: STATUTORY LAW AND DELEGATED LEGISLATION

PART C: LAW ENFORCEMENT, SANCTIONS, AND REMEDIES

PART D: JUDICIAL AND QUASI-JUDICIAL SYSTEM

PART E: LEGAL PROFESSION AND LEGAL EDUCATION IN NIGERIA

PART F: SOME CONTEMPORARY ISSUES

PART G: OUTLINE OF PROCEDURAL/ADJECTIVAL LAWS

PART A

GENERAL THEMES

Chapter 1

NATURE AND FUNCTIONS OF LAW IN NIGERIA

Chukwuma C. Obeagu*

INTRODUCTION

A critical look at Nigeria's legal system from the pre-colonial era to date reveals a unified system encompassing our local customs on the one hand and others on the other hand. The others include the received English laws, local legislations, judicial precedents, and international laws. This is because these other laws, including local legislations made by Nigerian legislative bodies patterned after the British Legal System, are all foreign to our local customs. Islamic or Sharia Law is often classified as the written aspect of our local customs, and rightly too.

In this united structure of the Nigerian legal system, the Supreme Court sits at the top, while at the base is the customary court or Area Court in the Southern part and Northern parts of Nigeria, respectively. Between these basic courts and the Supreme Court are such other courts as the Magistrate Courts, High Courts, and Court of Appeal, as well as other tribunals and courts established by law, all operating in the administration of justice.

It is noteworthy that the Supreme Court, composed of mainly Muslims and Christians, hears appeals arising from customary courts that border on traditional beliefs, as we shall soon see. Consequently, we are going to discuss the nature of the pre-colonial and contemporary

* Chukwuma C. Obeagu, Lecturer, Faculty of Law, Enugu State University of Science and Technology, (ESUT) Enugu.

legal systems in Nigeria, their roles thereof, and consequently, draw a conclusion.

THE PRE-COLONIAL LEGAL SYSTEM (LOCAL CUSTOMS)

Pre-colonial Nigeria possessed informal legal systems, and the machinery through which justice was dispensed in the different communities, which formed part of the hallmark of human civilization, substantive law was recognisable, binding, and obligatory, although it was unwritten. There were arrest and trial procedures. The trial process was quick, cheap, effective, open, and participatory. The courtroom was known often under a big tree in the village squares. What to do with a convict was defined. Penal measures were non-custodial and restitutive, the philosophy was reconciliatory (present-day reformation and rehabilitation) and restoration of distorted equilibrium to the society. The personnel of the legal systems ranged from kings, chiefs, and elders to linguists, orderlies, messengers, town criers, age-grade and secret cults, diviners, oracles, and witch doctors. If there were differences at all between the legal systems existing in pre-colonial Nigeria and those in all the societies of Western Europe, such differences were more of degree than kind.[1]

Nigeria undoubtedly had a pre-existing level system (local customs) prior to the coming of the white man – Europeans as traders, missionaries, and colonialists alongside their legal system.

This pre-existing legal system was comprehensive, as far as maintenance of law and order was concerned, and effective in the administration of justice in society. Ranging from lawmaking, and execution of the laws to the interpretation of such laws as well as beliefs in traditional oath-taking to determine cases, the pre-colonial Nigeria State functioned and existed in a cohesive and orderly form.

Since the pre-colonial legal system, the whole gamut of our indigenous local customs, traditions, beliefs, and practices is essentially

---

[1] Justus A. Sokefun (ed), *Nigerian Legal System II*, National Open University of Nigeria (Lagos: Adesola Prints & Co. Ltd., 2009) pp. 15 – 16.

the same as our contemporary local customs administration; the focus will now be on local customs.

LOCAL CUSTOMS/CUSTOMARY LAW LEGAL SYSTEM

Local custom or customary law refers to the amalgam of the Nigerian indigenous people's traditions, customs, beliefs, and practices from generation to generation that regulates and binds the people in their whole living in any given society.

In *Aku* v. *Aneku,*[2] the Court of Appeal defined custom or usage as:

> The unrecorded tradition and history of the people which has 'grown' with the 'growth' of the people to stability and eventually become an intrinsic part of their culture. It is a usage or practice of the people, which, by common adoption and acquiescence and by long and unvarying habit, has become compulsory and has acquired the force of law with respect to the place or the subject matter to which it relates.

In the same vein, in *Oyewummin & Anor* v. *Ogunesan,*[3] Obaseki JSC defined customary law as follows:

> The organic or living law of the indigenous people of Nigeria regulates their lives and transactions. It is organic in that it is not static. It is regulating in that it controls the lives and transactions of the community subject to it. It is said that custom is a mirror of the culture of the people. I would say that customary law goes further and imports justice to the lives of all those subject to it.[4]

The Evidence Act[5] provides for the admission of customs as part of the Nigerian legal system as well as enjoins judicial notice by superior courts.

Section 16(1) provides what customs are admissible:

[2] (1991) 8 NWLR (Pt. 209) p. 280
[3] (1990) 3 NWLR (pt. 137) p. 187
[4] At p. 207
[5] 2011, which took effect on 3rd day of June, 2011.

A custom may be adopted as part of the law governing a particular set of circumstances if it can be judicially noticed or can be proved to exist by evidence.

Section 17 on judicial notice of customs provides thus:

> A custom may be judicially noticed when it has been adjudicated upon once by a superior court of record.

The above legal authorities go to show very firmly that local customary law remains an integral part of the Nigerian legal system.

SCOPE OF CUSTOMARY LAW OPERATION

The operation of Customary Law covers virtually every aspect of law and other matters, especially those matters that are directly relevant to the lives of the people. Areas of coverage include Environmental Law, Family Law, Land Law, Law of Contract/Commercial transactions, political and social organizations, religion, customs and traditions, and general administration of law and justice. A notable exception today is the trial of the alleged commission of crimes, undertaken exclusively under English Law.

To demonstrate environmental consciousness under customary law, the case of *Bale of Idona* v. *Abuodun Kova* [6] becomes relevant. There, the defendant was alleged to have entered a sacred groove in the community and cut down some trees. The native court held that although the defendant's farmland was adjacent to and, in fact, formed part of the groove, he was nevertheless ordered to vacate the whole land. This was aimed toward conserving and preserving the ecosystems.

FEATURES OF CUSTOMARY LAW SYSTEM

Customary Law administration possesses some unique features distinct from the English legal system and even Islamic law.

The operation of customary law is highly informal. The substantive law is essentially unwritten, personnel of the legal system consist mainly

[6] (unreported) Ilegun Native Court 85/1956

of kings, elders, chiefs, town-criers, diviners, and age-grade organizations. However, efforts are being made now to enhance the productivity of the administration of customary law as trained lawyers are presiding judges in some localities with newly constructed or refurbished court buildings.

Also, the trial process is speedy, cheap, and aimed toward reconciling the parties and ensuring social cohesion. An instance of the informal nature of customary law operation is in the area of traditional oath-taking, a practice that has received approval from our Superior Courts in settling disputes.

In the old case of *Chuku Obaji & 2 ors* v. *Nwali Nweke Okpo & 2 ors,*[7] Uche J. held as follows:

> In this part of the country, swearing on juju to assert a right is very much in vogue even in these modern days among the native population. This native jurisprudence shows a belief that regulates the rural life of the people. A man staking his life to assert his right is the highest appeal to conscience. A decision of the elders embodying this is pure and simple arbitration by native customary law. The swearing on the juju to determine the ownership of the land in dispute and the arrival of the minding period of the plaintiff's representative operate as *res judicata* in favour of the plaintiff against the defendant.

Also, in a very recent case of *John Onyenge & Ors* v. *Chief LoveDay Ebere & Ors,*[8] the Supreme Court firmly and unmistakeably affirmed the validity of oath-taking before the Ogwugwu Akpu juju deity in Okija, Anambra State over title to land situate in Ukwa Local government Area of Abia State.

The respondents filed a suit at the Customary Court, Ukwa, against the appellants and claimed a declaration that they, the respondents, were entitled to the Customary right of occupancy in and over a piece of land situated at Ukwa. They also claimed damages for trespass and a perpetual injunction restraining the appellants from further acts of trespass on the land in dispute on the basis that they (the respondents)

---

[7] (1978) IMSLR p. 258

[8] (2004) 13 NWLR (pt. 889) p. 20

were the descendants of the person who deforested the land in dispute and that the first son of their ancestor pledged the land in dispute to the appellants' ancestors. They further claimed that when the 1st respondent's father sought to redeem the pledge and tendered the redemption money, the appellants refused to accept the money and counter-claimed that the land in dispute was not on a pledge to the appellants but belonged to them (appellants) as original owners.

There was evidence that the appellants summoned the respondents before the "*Ogwugwo Akpu*" *juju* in Okija, Anambra State, which was subsequently brought on the land in dispute, and the respondents took an oath to assert their title. They survived the customary one-year of the oath-taking and celebrated it in accordance with the custom of the Ukwa people to which both parties belonged and, thereafter, became entitled to exclusive possession of the land in dispute by the custom of the parties.

In its judgments, the Customary Court granted all the reliefs of the respondents. The Customary Court of Appeal reversed this judgment and entered judgment in favour of the appellants. The respondents, being dissatisfied, appealed to the Court of Appeal, which restored the order of the Customary Court and held that since the respondents were the owners of the land, they acted properly by not suing for the redemption of the pledge denied by the appellants before commencing their suit.

The appellants were dissatisfied and again appealed to the Supreme Court where it was contended on their behalf that the respondents did not prove their title to the land by credible evidence and that the Court of Appeal erred by upholding the customary court decision that the appellants were liable in trespass when they were in possession.

Upon these facts, the apex court held, while approving the conclusions of the Court of Appeal on the issue of trespass, per Niki Tobi, JSC (as he then was) thus:

> Once the fact of such arbitration and oath-taking and survival has been successfully established, the oath taker acquires the rights of full ownership and possession. If the other party remains in possession, he does so as a

> trespasser if such possession is not with the consent of the owner. In the circumstance of this case, the lower court was clearly wrong to hold that the plaintiffs should have sued for redemption first. It was because the defendants refused to take the redemption money that arbitration became necessary. The evidence before the trial court, confirmed by the defendants, was that the plaintiffs were to swear that the defendants held the land for them as pledges and (not) to take the land. There was evidence also that the plaintiffs did take the oath and survived. Right of ownership and possession, therefore, automatically became vested in them. After one year of the oath, the defendants could not be said to be in possession as against the plaintiffs. What they had was mere physical occupation. The plaintiffs had a legal right of possession, which was better than the defendants' occupation. The plaintiffs could, therefore, maintain an action in trespass against the defendants. The trial court was perfectly justified in so holding.

Tobi, JSC, further clarified the position on the applicable law when he stated:

> The situation, in this case, is different from the point made by learned Senior Advocate for the appellants. The issue was based on the oath-taking and the after-effect of the exercise on the parties. In view of the fact that the respondents survived after taking the oath, the parties were not bound by the niceties of the law as submitted by Learned Senior Advocate that possession is nine-tenths of ownership. That may be so under the common law but certainly not the position in the customary law under which the oath was taken. It is my view that where parties decide to be bound by traditional arbitration resulting in oath-taking, common law principles in respect of proof of title to land no longer apply. In such a situation, the proof of ownership or title to the land will be based on the rules set out by the traditional arbitration resulting in oath-taking. I think it is a good law that in arbitration under customary law, the applicable law is customary law and not common law principles with their characteristic certainty and ossification.

THE ISLAMIC LEGAL RULE

Under the Nigerian legal system, the Islamic legal practice is regarded as part of our customary law in written form. The basic legal document here is the Koran. The Islamic attitude to traditional oaths is relative.

Muslims are totally forbidden from swearing juju oaths.[9] In some states in northern Nigeria, where the scope of Islamic law was enlarged in the post-1999 democratic era, it is a serious offence for a Muslim to invoke the *juju.*[10]

However, in pre-colonial and colonial eras, Islamic courts accepted traditional oaths in cases between non-Muslims where customary law applied.[11] In the contemporary era, Islamic Courts no longer have jurisdiction over customary law matters. The point must be made that Islamic law governs the civil aspect of personal law between Muslim faithful to the exclusion of any other law, especially local customary law and English-type law. Thus such issues as adoption, custody of a child, intestate dispositions, and marriage cannot be effectively determined based on any other source of law except the relevant Sharia Law.

An instructive case is *Alhaji Zana Bukar Mandara* v. *Haroun Ahmed Amin & 2 Ors.*[12] There, M. S. Muntaka-Commasie, JCA, in his leading judgment held as follows:

> I must state that the subject-matter is not within the jurisdiction of the High Court, it being a claim of inheritance of property subject to Islamic personal law as provided by Section 242 (2) (c) of the 1979 Constitution, now section 277 of the 1999 Constitution, especially section 277 (2) (a), (b), (c), and (d) ... The issue of Islamic personal law has transcended the State law. It is now governed by the provisions of the constitution.

To demonstrate in clear terms the difference in content and applicability of Islamic law with other sources of Nigerian law, *Mandara* v. *Amin*[13] is relevant again. His Lordship Munkata-Commasie, JCA, unequivocally stated:

---

[9] At pp. 40-41

[10] At p. 41 (emphasis mine).

[11] The prophetic tradition is: "He who has to take an oath, he must not take oath but by Allah, related one Muslim, Sahjh Muslim (rendered into English by ALL sickligi undated, Dara-Arnbiyyali Vol. 11 hadith No 4040 at 875.5 cited in Ikejiani, C.C. "Customary Arbitration as an Alternative Dispute Resolution Mechanism in Nigeria: A case study of Enugu State" (Unpublished LL.B Project, NOUN, 2013) p.37.

[12] See for example, Section 405 of Sharia Penal Code, No. 10, 2000 provides the worship or invocation of any juju shall be unlawful and makes Presiding over and presence at such invocation liable to capital punishment (SPC 406(d)).

[13] (2004) JELR 54732 (CA)

> The issue of the sale under Islamic law cannot be divested from Islamic law...It is to be noted with respect that the whole proceedings in English law are at variance with that of Islamic Law. For instance, under Islamic law procedure, it is the judge, based on the dictates of Sharia, that decides who is to be the plaintiff and which of the two parties to be called the defendant.

THE RECEIVED ENGLISH LAW

Arising from Nigeria's colonial experience under Britain, the bulk of the Nigerian Legal System rests on the Received English Law introduced into Nigeria. The received English Law essentially consists of the common law, the doctrines of equity, and the statutes of general application in force in England as of 1 January 1900.

Ever since the reception of this English-type law in Nigeria, it has remained an integral and essential component of Nigeria's legal system alongside customary law comprising our local customs and Islamic law.

THE NATURE OF NIGERIA'S LEGAL SYSTEM

In the light of the preceding discourse, it is undoubtedly clear that the nature of our legal system is characterised by the plurality of laws, including Local Customs, Islamic Laws, and English-type Laws. The plurality of laws permits a situation where one system applies to one transaction and another system to another as has been shown above.

However, it must be stated that our legal system is anchored on Nigeria's basic legal document – the constitution, which is the yardstick for determining the validity or invalidity of any other Law. At the same time, the Supreme Court sits atop the hierarchy of courts in Nigeria, which adjudicate legal disputes on all points of law in Nigeria, to which its decision is final and binding.

It is also necessary to state that the objective or main function of our law is to administer and promote the interest of justice among the generality of the citizenry.

CONCLUSION

Efforts have been made to show that Nigeria's legal system is pluralistic in nature embodying customary laws and English law side by side. That each type of law applies to specific subject matters at a time whether as local custom, Islamic law or the English law.

This plurality of our legal system is most appropriate considering our heterogeneous nature as well as Nigeria being, at present, a federation of thirty-six states and a Federal Capital Territory, Abuja.

Furthermore, the plural nature of our law does not hamper, but rather enhances the due administration of law and justice for an orderly and progressive society.

Chapter 2

SOURCES OF NIGERIAN LAW

Celestine Chukwuemeka Okoro*

INTRODUCTION

"Sources of Nigerian law" refers to the materials through which a legal practitioner or a court or judge would find reliable authorities for a particular legal question.[1] The origin or sources of Nigerian law can be classified into two aspects, namely, primary and secondary sources.

The primary sources include English law, customary law rules, legislation, International law, and judicial precedent.[2] The secondary sources of Nigerian law are law reports, textbooks, legal periodicals, law digests, legal dictionaries, newspapers,[3] etc.

THE PRIMARY SOURCES

The English Law

The received English law remains a veritable source of Nigerian law. This is understandably so because of Nigeria's colonial heritage, as English law was introduced into different parts of this country following the establishment of the English colonial administration in the nineteenth century.[4] The various legislatures in Nigeria have thereafter made enactments which received English law directly into

* Okoro Celestine Chukwuemeka, LL.B (Hons. Nig.), LL.M (Benin), D.C Lorca, Lecturer, Faculty of Law, Enugu State University of Science and Technology, Enugu;*

[1] Olowu D. & Lasebikan F, "Sources of law in Nigeria" I*ntroduction to Nigerian Legal Method,* (second and enlarged edition), Ile-Ife, Obafemi Awolowo University Press Limited 2006) P 245.

[2] Custom, judicial precedent and legislation are the main sources of law in common law jurisdictions

[3] It is important to note that only the primary sources could have binding force on a court of law in Nigeria whereas the mentioned secondary sources can merely serve persuasive purposes, and are usually relied upon where no primary source is available or applicable.

[4] Tobi, N, *Sources of Nigerian law* (Lagos, MIJ Publishers Ltd, 1996) P. 6

their jurisdictions or extended the force of English statutes into Nigeria. For example, section 45 (ii) of the Interpretation Act[5] provides:

> Subject to the provisions of this section and in so far as another provision is made by any Federal law, the common law of England and the doctrines of equity, together with the statutes of general application that were in force in England on the 1st of January, 1900, shall be in force in Lagos and in so far as they relate to any matter within the exclusive legislative competence of the Federal legislature, shall be in force elsewhere in the Federation.

The "statutes of general application"[6] which were in force in England on the *1st day of January 1900"* have been received into all the jurisdictions in Nigeria with the exception of Edo, Delta, Ekiti, Osun, Ondo, and Ogun states of Nigeria, where these statutes have not been received in so far as such statutes deal with matters within the legislative competence of those states.

Similarly, section 14(1) of the Supreme Court Ordinance, 1914, provides that:

> Subject to the terms of this or any other ordinance, the common law, the doctrines of equity, and statutes of general application which were in force in England on the 1st of January 1900 shall be in force within the jurisdiction of this court.

Thus in the case of *Attorney General Federation* v. *Attorney–General Abia State,*[7] it was held Per Uwais, CJN:

> Historically, the British ruled their colonies by introducing English laws to the colonies. Most of the colonies in Africa, including Nigeria, were either

---

[5] Cap 123 LFN, 2004

[6] Commonly referred to among law students as SOGA

[7] (2002) FWLR (Pt. 102) 1

conquered or ceded colonies or protectorates and trust territories. English law was introduced in those colonies by express enactment. The legislation provided for the introduction and observance of English law... In this case, the authority for the application of English law is to be found in such enactment as the Supreme Court Ordinance of Nigeria, Court Ordinance of Gold coast (now Ghana), the amount of law received was the "common law, doctrines of equity and statutes of general application."

Furthermore, it was held that:

Common Law has been received law in this country since 1863 when it was applied to Lagos and 1914 when by the Supreme Court Ordinance of that year, it was applied to the colony and protectorate of Nigeria.[8]

WHAT IS A "STATUTE OF GENERAL APPLICATION"?

The Supreme Court Ordinance, the Interpretation Act, and other enactments on the subject of the statutes of general application do not define what constitutes a statute of general application. We are therefore compelled to rely on case law. Thus, the case of *Dede* v. *African Association Ltd*[9] Weber, J, ruled that statutes of general application must mean:

Those statutes were applicable throughout the United Kingdom and not those in force in England only. This would have been an unfortunate decision had the judge not said that the Supreme Court ordinance expressly mentioned "the statutes of general application that were in force in England" and not the United Kingdom.

The following English statutes have been held to be statutes of general application with reference to Nigeria:

(a) Infant Relief Act, 1874;
(b) Trustees Act, 1888;
(c) Limitations Act (Real Property), 1874;

---

[8] Supra note 9 per Ogundare J.S.C see also *Charlie King Amacheree* v. *Daniel Kalio,* 2 NLR 108; *Att. Gen. of southern Nigeria* v. *John Holts & Co. (Liverpool) Ltd (*1915) AC 599; 2 NLRI *and Chief Brande* v. *Chief Adoki,* 10 NLR 15, etc.

[9] (1910) 1 All NLR 130, see also the following cases; *Attorney General* v. *John Holt & Co Ltd supra* note 9; *Lawal* v. *Younan* (1961) All NLRI; *Braithwaite* v. *Folarin,* (1938) 4 WACA 76 *and Young* v. *Abina, (1940)* 6 WACA 180

(d) Statute of frauds, 1677.

It is important to note that such statutes of general application are still in force in Nigeria even if they have been repealed in England. What we are saying here is that the application of English common law and principles of equity are not barred or limited by time in Nigeria.[10] See the case of *Braithwaite* v. *Folarin*[11] where it was held that:

> The statute in question is, in our view, a statute of general application applying as it does quite generally to ordinary affairs and dealings of men without any qualification or specialty restricting its application. The statute was simply a declaration of the common law at the time. And the statute was in force in England on 1st January 1900. The repeal in 1925 does not therefore affect its application in Nigeria as the repealing Act was subsequent to 1st January 1900.

Also, the common law principles and the doctrines of equity are still applicable in the development and continued development of our legal system in Nigeria. See the case of *B.J. Export & Chem. Co. Ltd* v. *Kaduna Refining & Petro-chemical Co. Ltd.*[12] where it was held that:

> Having regard to the history of this great nation, Nigeria and its legal system, the common law principles of law are not only still applicable in the development and continued development of our legal system but will also continue to be so applicable.

It is useful to note that Nigeria being an independent and sovereign state, foreign laws, including the English law, do not have any binding force on our courts but may only serve as persuasive authorities.[13] See the case of *Ali* v. *Okulaja*[14] where Beckley, J. held that:

> The High Court in Nigeria cannot be bound by a decision of the court of Appeal of England, this country now being an independent sovereign state but judgment of an independent sovereign state but judgment of an eminent judge would certainly be of the most persuasive authority and

---

[10] Asein J.O, *Introduction to Nigerian Legal System,* (Ibadan, Sam Bookman Publishers, 1998), P. 102

[11] (1938) 4 WACA 76

[12] (2003) FWLR (Pt. 165) 445

[13] English laws are mere guide to the Nigerian court and not of binding authorities.

[14] (1970) 2 All NLR 35, *also see Eliochin (Nig) Ltd.* v. *Mbadiwe* (1986) 1 NSCC 42

would be followed except the court feels otherwise strongly about the *ratio decidendi* of such decision.

From the above, it is safe to conclude that though the English laws remain a very important source of Nigerian law, they are mere guide to the Nigerian court and not of binding authorities.

LEGISLATIONS OR STATUTES

Legislation is the laying down of legal rule by a sovereign or subordinate legislator.[15] Also, legislation or statute is a law enacted by a legislature, and it is usually in a written form or code.[16]

Nigerian legislation consists of statutes and subsidiary legislation. The legislative branch of the Federal government of Nigeria has the power to make laws for the peace, order, and good government of Nigeria.[17] By virtue of legislation or statutes, successive governments have affected more and more positively the political, economic, and social aspects of national life. In short, there is universal agreement that deliberate lawmaking of this kind is indispensable to the efficient regulation of the modern state.[18]

During the nineteenth and twentieth centuries, a huge increase in the use of enacted law has taken place, and it is clear that legislation has now become by far the most important source of law. Legislation is made by a legislature that is elected by the people. Thus, statutes made by the legislature enjoy a direct democratic legitimacy.

It is important to note that all federal statutes in Nigeria up to 31st January 1990 were revised and consolidated in what is now known as the Laws of the Federation of Nigeria (LFN) 1990.[19]

The Laws of the Federation of Nigeria (LFN) 1990 were revised up till 2002 and now published as laws of the Federation of Nigeria in June 2004. The revised Laws of the Federation of Nigeria are printed in

---

[15] Egwummuo J.N, "Legislation as a source of law," *Focus on Law and Jurisprudence* (Enugu, Academic Printing Press, 2007) p. 282

[16] Are therefore called written laws.

[17] Constitution of Federal Republic of Nigeria 1999 (2011) Amended S. 4(2) and (7)

[18] *Op. cit.,* note 19

[19] The LFN, 1990 consists of 491 chapters in 21 volumes

loose-leaf format ostensibly to ensure easy incorporation of future published amendments or revision of the present laws.

Legislations are called various names; Ordinances, Acts, Decrees, Laws, Edicts, or bylaws. Subsidiary legislation is delegated legislation. Examples of these are: statutory instruments such as regulations, rules, orders, and directives:

- Orders in council;
- Bye-laws of local governments;
- Rules of court, etc.

ORDINANCE

When the British first came to Nigeria, legislative councils were created in the colony of Lagos and in other parts of Nigeria. Legislative councils made local legislations called ordinances. In 1954, when the country was divided into regions, each region published ordinances which dealt with matters within Federal competence and were then regarded as Acts of the Federal legislature. Thus, ordinances are laws passed by the Nigerian central legislature before 1st October 1954, when federalism became a constitutional phenomenon in Nigeria.[20]

However, the question of whether a pre-1954 ordinance is now to be regarded as a federal Act or a regional law, or both is to be decided by the court. This is so since no foolproof way of deciding which ordinance deal with exclusive, residual, or the concurrent list has been worked out.

ACT AND LAWS

In Nigeria, any statute enacted by the elected federal legislature in a civilian regime, otherwise known as the National Assembly, comprising of both the senate and the House of Representatives, is known as an Act. For statutes enacted by the National Assembly to be valid, they

---

[20] "Federalism" as a constitutional concept was introduced into Nigeria by the Lyttleton Constitution which came into force on 1st October, 1954. The constitution was named after Sir Oliver Lyttleton, then Governor-General of Nigeria.

have to be passed according to the prescribed legislative procedure.[21] After the required number of readings, usually three, and debate, some of the laws require at least two-thirds votes of the total members of the legislature to become law, whilst others require only a simple majority of votes.

After a bill has been passed, it has to be sent to the president for his assent. This he does by appending his signature to it, and it becomes law. Where assent is withheld, the legislature may, on its own by the required majority of votes, pass the bill into law.[22] The national assembly can enact statutes within the ambit of the legislative list assigned to it by the constitution.[23]

Acts of Parliament is said to be supreme to all other laws. By virtue of section 1 of the Constitution of the Federal Republic of Nigeria, 1999 (Amended in 2011), the Constitution is supreme and above all other laws in Nigeria, as it constitutes the *grundnorm*. Any law which is inconsistent with the constitution (Acts of Parliament) will be declared void to the extent of its inconsistency.[24] It should be noted that Acts of Parliament is the highest law in the land from which other laws derive their validity. The House of Assembly of the various states of the Federation has the power to make laws for the governance of the state. An enactment made by the elected state legislature in a civilian regime is known as the law.

DECREES AND EDICTS

When a military government is in power, a statute passed by the Federal Military Government of Nigeria through the military law-making bodies (variously called a supreme military council, armed forces ruling council, provisional ruling council) is called a decree. While an enactment made by the Military Governor/Administrator of a state during a military regime is known as Edict. However, a government

[21] *Op. cit.*, note 21, sections 58, 59, 60, 100 and 101. *A.G. Bendel State* v. *A.G. Federation 827 others* (1982) 3 NCLR 855C

[22] *Op. cit.,* note 21, sections 58(5), 59(4), 100(5)

[23] Ibid., Exclusive Legislative List and Concurrent Legislative List in Part 1 and Part 11, of the second schedule

[24] See the following cases: *Maji Yagbe* v. *A.G. 8, ORS* (1957) NRNLR 158; *African Continental Bank PLC v. Lasoda (Nig) Ltd* (1995) I NWLR (pt. 405) 26; *Tony Momoh* v. *Senate* (1981) I NCLR 21

may by law convert and deem specified decrees and edicts to be Acts or laws, and from the date of such legislation, making the conversion, the affected decree or edicts may be properly called and referred to as an Act or Law.[25]

Similarly, decrees and edicts which are not repealed by the constitution are automatically converted to Acts and Laws when civil rule is installed. Under military rule, decrees take precedence over Acts. Section 5 of the Constitution (suspension and modification) Decree No. 107 of 1993 provides that no question as to the validity of any decree made during the period 31st December 1983 to 26th August 1993 or made thereafter shall be entertained by any court of law in Nigeria.

BYE-LAWS

Bye-laws are legislations made by local government councils in areas within their competence, like markets, motor parts, collection of rates, naming of streets or roads, registration of birth, deaths, marriages, shops, sale of liquor,[26] etc.

DELEGATED LEGISLATION

These are the enactments made by persons or bodies other than the legislature pursuant to express powers conferred on such persons or bodies by the competent legislature. These delegated law-making are known as delegated, subsidiary, or subordinate legislations. The use of these species of legislation has become very important because of the increase in governmental functions and the dynamics involved in modern-day governance. Examples of administrative lawmakers are:

- The President;[27]
- Governor;
- Chief Justice of Nigeria[28] and the Chief Judges[29] of the states;
- Ministers;

---

[25] All decrees included in the laws of Nigeria 1990 edition are therein converted and deemed to be Acts
[26] *Op. cit.*, note 21, Fourth schedule, see also *Akingbade* v. *Lagos Town Council* (1955) 21 NLR 90
[27] For instance, *op. cit.*, note 21, Section 32
[28] Ibid., section 46(3)
[29] Ibid., section 248, 254, 264, and 274

- Commissioners;
- Governmental ministries;
- Departments; and
- Public corporations, agencies, statutory bodies, etc.

The legislature merely provides the general framework of principles that would regulate human conduct and administration of public affairs, leaving specialists, technocrats, and those who are involved in specific activities to deal with particular and subjective cases.

Any legislation made pursuant to a delegated power must not exceed the limits of the power so granted otherwise, the wrongful exercise of power may render it *ultra vires* (beyond power), null and void.[30]

It must also be noted that any legislation made pursuant to delegated power is also an integral part of sources of law. In fact, all the delegated legislation made pursuant to Federal statutes was also consolidated with their principal statutes under the LFN 1990.

CUSTOMARY LAW

Custom is the oldest source of law in Nigeria. Customary law consists of customs accepted by members of a community as binding among them. In Nigeria, customary law may be divided in terms of nature into two classes, namely ethnic or non-Muslim customary law and Muslim law. Ethnic customary law in Nigeria is indigenous. Each system of such customary law applies to members of a particular ethnic group. Muslim law is religious law based on the Muslim faith and applicable to members of the faith. In Nigeria, it is not indigenous law; it is received customary law introduced into the country as part of Islam.[31]

Ethnic customary law is unwritten. There are several such customary law systems in the country; each ethnic group has its own separate system. Unlike ethnic customary law, Muslim law is principally in written form. The sources of Muslim law are the Holy Koran, the

[30] See Owoade, T.O., *Jurisdiction in Administrative Law* (Ibadan: Caltop Press, 2001) p. 44 *et seq.*
[31] Obilade A.O, Customary Law, *The Nigerian Legal system,* (Ibadan, Spectrum Law publishing 2000) p. 83

practice of the prophet (the *Sunna*), the consensus of scholars, and analogical deductions from the Holy Quran and from the practice of the prophet.[32] Muslim law is alternatively called "Islamic Law" or "the Sharia" (the Sacred Law of Islam). The version of Muslim in force in Nigeria is the Muslim law of the Maliki School.[33]

THE CHARACTERISTICS OF CUSTOMARY LAW

One of the main features of customary law is its acceptance as an obligation by the community. A customary law rule must be in existence at the relevant time and must be recognized and adhered to by the community. This point has been noted by Speed A.G. CJ at the first instance in *Lewis* v. *Bankole*[34] when he said:

> Their Lordship entertains no doubt that the more barbarous customs of earlier days may, under the influence of civilization, become milder without losing their essential character as custom. It would, however, appear to be necessary to show that in their milder form, they are still recognized in the native community as custom, so as in the form to regulate the relations of the native community *inter se*.

Another striking feature is its flexibility and adaptability to changing social trends. According to Osborne, C. J. in *Lewis* v. *Bankole*,[35]

> One of the most striking features of West African native custom is its flexibility; it appears to have always been subject to motives of expediency, and it shows unquestionable adaptability to altered circumstances without entirely losing its character.

For instance, formerly, any transaction involving the use of writing was considered to be outside the province of ethnic-group customary

---

[32] See Fyzee A. A., *Outline of Mohammadan Law* (3rd ed. 1964) pp. 18-21

[33] See e.g. section 14 of the Sharia Court of Appeal Law (N.N Laws 1963, Cap 122 which empowers the Sharia Court of Appeal of each of the Northern states to administer Muslim law of the Maliki school as customarily interpreted at the place where the trial at first instance took place

[34] (1908) 1NLR, 81 at pp. 100-101, see also *Kimderg & ors* v. *Military Gov. of Gongola State,* (1988) N.S.C.C. vol. 19 pt. 1 at 827

[35] *Supra* note 38

law. But that position has changed. Thus, a written agreement may be governed by such customary law.[36]

THE VALIDITY OF CUSTOMARY LAW

It must be noted that rules of customary law are subject to tests of validity. The test is laid down in the Supreme Court Act, the various high court laws of all the states[37] of the Federation, and the evidence Act. Before a customary law rule is applied by Nigerian courts, it must have passed the three prescribed tests of validity:

a. repugnancy test;
b. incompatibility test;
c. public policy test.

For a customary law to be enforced by the courts, it must pass the validity test. In the first place, it must not be repugnant to natural justice, equity, and good conscience. See the case of *Edet* v. *Essien*[38] where the appellant was married to his wife under native law and custom. His wife left him and went to live with the respondent. Two children were born of the union between the respondent and the wife. The respondent did not pay the appellant the money which the appellant had paid as dowry on the wife. The appellant, therefore, claimed that the children were his.

It was held that it was contrary to natural justice, equity, and good conscience to allow the appellant to claim the children of another man merely because the other man had deprived the appellant of his wife without paying dowry for her.

A custom or customary law which is also incompatible with any existing law for the time being in force will not be enforced. See the case of *Re: Adadevoh*[39] furthermore, for customary law to be enforceable, it must not be contrary to public policy. Thus in *Enderby Town Football Club Ltd v Football Association Ltd,*[40] it was held that the FA rule 38(b)

---

[36] See *Alfa* v. *Arepo* (1963) W. N. L. R. 95

[37] Section 13(1) of the High Court law of Bendel State, section 44 High Court law, Oyo state, 1978, section 34(1) High Court Law, Plateau state, 1981 and section 14(3) evidence Act

[38] (1932) 11 NLR 47*, also see Re: Effiong Okon Ata* (1930) 10 NLR 65. *Mariama* v. *Sadiku Ejo* (1961) NRNLR 81.

[39] (1951) 13 WACA 304, see also *Rufai* v. *Igbira N.A* (1957) NRNLR 178

[40] (1971) 1 Ch. 591

was not invalid as being contrary to natural justice. But FA rule 40(b) purporting to prevent legal proceedings without the consent of their council is contrary to public policy and invalid. It is safe to state that custom is the oldest source of law in Nigeria, but for it to be a valid legal source, it must pass the validity tests.

INTERNATIONAL LAW

International Law is generally formulated by international agreements,[41] which creates rules binding upon the signatories, and customary rules[42] which are basically state practices recognized by the community at large as laying down patterns of conduct that have to be complied with.[43]

It must be noted that by virtue of the constitutional system in Nigeria, Nigeria is one of the nations where a treaty does not become operative until it has been domesticated by National Assembly.[44] It is prudent to note that because the world has become a global village more than ever before, there is, to a greater extent, interdependence of Nations, and the Law of Nations has become a very important source of law to regulate the conduct of Nations.

CASE LAW OR JUDICIAL PRECEDENT

Judicial precedent means the process whereby judges follow previously decided cases where the facts are of sufficient similarity. The doctrine of judicial precedent involves an application of the principles of *stare decisis* i.e., *'to stand by the decided.'*

---

[41] Thus we have the United Nations Charter, the International Covenant on Civil and Political Rights, International Covenant on Economic, Social and Cultural Rights, the African Charter on Human and Peoples Right … etc.

[42] It is regarded as an authentic expression of the needs and values of the community at any given time. It is a dynamic source of law. For example, the Universal Declaration of Human Rights of 1948 from a declaration intended to have moral persuasion and representing a common standard to one where many of the provisions are binding upon all states as customary law.

[43] Malcom N. Shaw, Development of International Law, *International Law*, (Fourth edition, United Kingdom; Cambridge University Press, 1997) P. 6.

[44] See Section 12(1), Constitution of the Federal Republic of Nigeria with Fundamental Rights 1999 (Amended in 2011) where it states that no treaty between the Federation and other country shall have the force of law except to the extent to which any such treaty has been enacted into law by the National Assembly.

It is an English judicial tradition to follow their previous decisions within certain defined limits. In practice, this means that inferior courts are bound to apply the legal principles set down by superior courts in earlier cases. This provides consistency and predictability in the law. However, this is subject to the condition that such a decision has not been overruled by another court higher in the hierarchy.[45]

The doctrine of precedent postulates that cases must be decided the same way when their material facts are the same.[46] As a common law doctrine, it applies only to those courts which are empowered to administer adjective common law of which the doctrine forms part.[47] Judicial precedent is legal experience and, in effect, is nothing but reliance by a judge deciding a case today on the experience of yesterday.

Precedents can be binding or persuasive. A precedent that must be applied or followed is known as a binding precedent. For example, decisions of lower courts are not binding on courts higher in the hierarchy. Precedents are persuasive when the court is not under obligation to follow them.

Under the Nigerian legal system, persuasive precedents may arise out of the following contextual situations:

(a) decisions of lower courts are not binding on higher courts but, at best, are persuasive;
(b) decisions of a high court are the persuasive authority for later cases in the high court;
(c) recent decisions of the Supreme Court of United Kingdom.
(d) Decisions of other courts within the Common Law World.

To facilitate a better understanding of this concept, it is necessary to explain the meaning of some phrases which are inherently linked to the subject under discussion.

Ratio Decidendi

The decision of a court may fall into two parts: the reason for the decision and that which is said by the way. The *ratio decidendi* of a case

---

[45] For example, the Supreme Court of Nigeria which is the highest court in Nigeria and is conferred with the power of finality by virtue of Section 235 of the 1999 Constitution (as amended)

[46] Williams, G,. *Learning the Law* (4th edition), (London, Stevens and Sons, 1982) p. 67

[47] Obilade, A.O. *The Nigerian Legal System,* (Ibadan, Spectrum Books Ltd, 2005), p. 114.

is the principle of law on which a decision is based. When a judge delivers judgment in a case, he outlines the facts which he finds have been stored on the evidence. Then he applies the law to those facts and arrives at a decision for which he gives the reason (*ratio decidendi*).

Goodhart[48] defined the *ratio decidendi* of a case as the material facts of the case plus the decision thereon. Determining the ratio of a case is sometimes fraught with difficulties, especially where a judge gives more than one reason for his decision.

Obiter Dictum

The judge may go on to speculate about what his decision would or might have been if the facts of the case had been different. This is called *obiter dictum.*[49] It does not form part of the *ratio decidendi* of the case and therefore creates no binding precedent but may be cited as persuasive authority in latter cases. However, the value attached to *obiter dictum* depends on the court from which it emanates and the eruditeness of the judge who made it.

Distinguishing

A binding precedent is a decided case that a court must follow. But a previous case is only binding in a latter case if the legal principle involved is the same and the facts are similar. Distinguishing a case on its facts or on the points of law involved, is a device used by judges usually in order to avoid the consequences of an earlier inconvenient decision which is, in strict practice, binding on them.

What is reasonably distinguishable depends on the particular cases and the particular court – some judges being more inclined to distinguish disliked authorities than others. In *Jones* v. *Secretary of State for Social Services,*[50] Lord Reid stated:

> It is notorious that where an existing decision is disapproved but cannot be overruled, courts tend to distinguish it on inadequate grounds. I do not

---

[48] See "Determining the *Ration Decidendi* of a Case", *Essays in Jurisprudence and the Common Law* (1931) 1, cited in Obilade, *op. cit.*, note 51, p.113

[49] *Oxford Dictionary of Law,* 5th edition, defined *obiter dictum* (a Latin jargon meaning remark in passing) as something said by a judge while giving judgment that was not essential to the decision in the case.

[50] (1972) AC, 944.

> think that they act wrongly in doing so; they are adopting the less bad of the only alternatives open to them. But this is bound to lead to uncertainty...

At the other extreme, Buckley LJ in *Olympia Oil* v. *Produce Brokers*[51] stated:

> I am unable to adduce any reason to show why that decision which I am about to pronounce is right...but I am bound by the authority which, of course, it is my duty to follow...

OVERRULING

A higher court can overrule a decision made in an earlier case by a lower court, e.g., the Court of Appeal can overrule an earlier High Court decision. Overruling can occur if the previous court did not correctly apply the law or because the latter court considers that the rule of law contained in the previous *ratio decidendi* is no longer desirable. An example of the former is the overruling of *Anderton* v. *Ryan*[52] by the House of Lords in *R.* v. *Shivpuri*[53] concerning the Criminal Attempts Act 1981, and an example of the latter is the House of Lord's decision in *Miliangos* v. *George Frank Ltd,*[54] which overruled previous authority that judgments could not be given in foreign currency.

Reversing

Reversing is the overturning on appeal by a higher court of the decision of the court below that heard the appeal. The Appeal Court will then substitute its own decision.

Per incuriam

A decision that is reached *per incuriam* is one reached by carelessness or mistake and can be avoided. In the case of *Morelle* v. *Wakeling,*[55] Lord Evershed MR. stated that:

---

[51] (1914) 3 KB, 1262.
[52] (1985) *2* All ER *355.*
[53] (1986) 2 All ER 334
[54] (1975) 3 All ER 801.
[55] (1955) 2 QB. 379.

> The only case in which decisions should be held to have been given *per incuriam* are those of decisions given in ignorance or forgetfulness of some inconsistent statutory provision or of some authority binding on the court concerned.

In *Secretary of State for Trade and Industry* v. *Dersai,*[56] Scott L.JJ said that to come within the category of *per incuriam*, it must be shown not only that the decision involved some manifest slip or error but also that to leave the decision standing would likely inter alia, produce serious inconveniences in the administration of justice or significant injustice to citizens.

However, this rule does not permit the Court of Appeal to ignore the decisions of the Apex Court. In *Cassell* v. *Broome,*[57] Lord Denning MR held the House of Lords' decision in *Rookes* v. *Barnard*[58] to be *per incuriam* on the basis that it ignored previous House of Lords' decisions. He was rebuked sternly by the House of Lords' who considered that the Court of Appeal really only meant "that it did not agree" with the earlier decision. *Per incuriam* does not simply mean the earlier Court got things wrong. It only means there was a significant oversight and failure to take account of relevant authorities, which may have affected the reasoning in the case as well as the outcome.

THE HIERARCHY OF AUTHORITY

For the doctrine of *stare decisis* and judicial precedent to be meaningful, there must be a defined judicial hierarchy. The courts in Nigeria are stratified as follows:

1. Supreme Court;
2. Court of Appeal;
3. High Courts (Federal and States);
4. Magistrates' Court.

Other courts include the Sharia Court of Appeal, Customary Court of Appeal, Sharia Courts, and Customary Courts. The common law

---

[56] (1991), *The Times* 5 December.
[57] (1972) AC, 1027.
[58] (1964) AC 1129.

doctrine does not apply to these courts as there is no organized system of Law reporting covering their decisions.[59]

There are other specialized courts like the National Industrial Court, Investment and Securities Tribunal, and Court Martial from which appeal lies to the Court of Appeal.

Supreme Court

The Supreme Court is the highest in the hierarchy of Courts in Nigeria. The decision of the Supreme Court binds all other Courts in Nigeria[60]. The Supreme Court once pronounced that: *"...it is not proper for a lower court to defy the decided authority of a higher court otherwise it may border on or amount to judicial impertinence."*[61] One problem that arises from here is, what should the lower courts do to conflicting decisions of the Supreme Court on one question of law? In other words, which of the two conflicting decisions should they follow?

In *G.T.B. Plc.* v. *Fadco Industries Limited,*[62] the Nigerian Court of Appeal stated as follows:

> I am being faced with two conflicting decisions of the Supreme Court of Nigeria, one supporting the respondent, the other supporting the position of the appellants. I am fully aware of the fact that I am bound by the decision of the Supreme Court, but it is also the law that, in this kind of situation, I am allowed to choose which to follow between the two decisions.

However, this dilemma of the lower courts was resolved in *Osakue* v. *Federal College of Education Asaba,* where the Supreme Court held that where the Court of Appeal is faced with two conflicting decisions of the Supreme Court, it must follow the latter or last. It is also pertinent to note that the Supreme Court of Nigeria is not bound by its own decision in contra-distinction to the English position in which the

---

[59] Obilade, A.O. *op. cit.*, note 51, p.111
[60] Section 230(1) of the 1999 Constitution of Nigeria (as amended) (2011)
[61] *Daira* v. *U.B.N. Plc.* (2007) 16 N.W.L.R. (Pt. 1059) 99 at 159.
[62] (2007) 7 N.W.L.R (Pt. 1033) 307

House of Lords from 1898[63] to 1966[64] considered itself not free to depart from its previous decision.

The Nigerian Supreme Court is entitled to depart from or overrule its previous decisions in the interest of justice, where the decisions are shown to be:

1. vehicles of injustice;
2. given *per incuriam;*
3. clearly erroneous in law;
4. impeding the proper development of the law;
5. having result which is unjust, undesirable, or contrary to public policy;
6. inconsistent with the provisions of the Constitution; or
7. capable of fettering the exercise of judicial discretion by a court.[65]

Nigerian Court of Appeal

The Court of Appeal is next to the Supreme Court in the hierarchy of Courts in Nigeria. The Court of Appeal was established by Section 237 of the 1999 Constitution of Nigeria (as amended). This Court is bound by the decision of the Supreme Court even if it was given *per incuriam.* And all other courts below the Court of Appeal must loyally abide by the decision of the Court. The affected court includes the High Court's (Federal and States) and the Magistrates Court.

As a general rule, the Court of Appeal is bound by its previous decision. However, the case of *Young* v. *Bristol Aeroplane Co. Ltd*[66] provides three exceptions to this general rule, that is, circumstances in which the court may not follow its previous decisions. These are namely:

1. Court of Appeal can choose between its own conflicting decisions;
2. Court of Appeal must refuse to follow its own decision, which though has not been expressly overruled by the Supreme Court but

---

[63] *London Trainways* v. *London Country Council* (1898) AC, 375.
[64] Practice Statement (Judicial Precedent) 1966 1 WLR 1234.
[65] *See Adisa* v. *Oyinwola* (2000) 10 NWLR (Pt. 674) 116.
[66] (1944) K.B. 718 at 723, Per Lord Greene MR.

which, in its opinion, cannot stand with a decision of the Supreme Court;

3. Court of Appeal is not bound by its own decisions found to have been made *per incuriam*. Though the Nigerian Court of Appeal ordinarily adheres to the principle of *stare decisis* but in criminal matters, it seldom does follow its decision which it considers to be wrong.[67]

High Court

High Courts are bound by the decision of the Supreme Court and the Court of Appeal but are not bound by the decisions of other High Courts. This is because all the High Courts in Nigeria are courts of co-ordinate jurisdiction, and as such, they are not bound by the decision of one another though such decisions are of strong persuasive authority and are usually followed in the High Courts.[68] The magistrates' courts are normally bound by the decision of the Supreme Court, the Court of Appeal, and the High Court.

MERITS AND DEMERITS OF JUDICIAL PRECEDENT

Merits

1. Judicial Precedent makes for certainty in the law. By looking at existing precedents, it is possible to forecast what a decision will be and then plan accordingly.
2. The doctrine also fosters uniformity in law, thereby making it possible for similar cases to be treated in the same way. This is really important to give the system a sense of justice and the nature of acceptability to the public.
3. Judicial precedent is flexible. There are a number of ways to avoid precedents, and this enables the system to change and adapt to new situations.

a. Judicial precedent is practical in nature; it is based on real facts, unlike normal legislation.

4. Judicial precedent is detailed. There is a wealth of cases to refer to.

---

[67] See *R.* v. *Taylor* (1950) 2 K.B. 368; *Motayo* v. *Commissioner of Police* (1950) 13 W.A.C.A. 114.

[68] See *Barclays Bank* v. *Hassan* (1950) WNLR 293

Demerits

1. Difficulties can arise in deciding what the *ratio decidendi* is, particularly if there are a number of reasons.
2. There may be a considerable wait for a case to come to court for a point to be decided.
3. Cases can easily be distinguished on their facts to avoid following an inconvenient precedent.
4. There is far too much case law, and it is complex.

Lord Denning had argued that the rigidity of *stare decisis* might lead to injustice in some particular cases.[69]

JUDICIAL ACTIVISM / ROLE OF THE JUDGES IN LAW MAKING

All courts essentially apply rules (statutes/laws) promulgated by the legislative bodies though the procedures for doing this vary from country to country. The application of these rules by the courts involves interpreting them and applying them to specific situations. Sometimes the courts may have to fill gaps to cover unforeseen situations which never came to the contemplation of lawmakers while drafting the laws. This, simply put, is judicial activism. "As courts decide disputes in individual cases, they create an important by-product beyond peaceful settlements by which they develop rules for deciding future cases."[70] The court's decision containing these interpretations will later become controlling points of reference for future cases, sometimes to the extent that they become laws, giving rise to what is known as Judicial-Law making.

To the extent, the judiciary plays a vital role in the development of the law through judicial activism. But then, what is judicial activism? The concept of judicial activism has been variously defined at different times by different authors.

Bryan[71] defined judicial activism as:

---

[69] See The Rt. Hon. Lord Denning, *The Discipline of the Law* (London: Butterworth, 1979) p. 292.

[70] http://www.britannica.../Judicial-lawmaking (accessed 23/7/2012).
HYPERLINK "http://www.britannica.../Judicial-lawmaking" http://www.britanni

> A philosophy of judicial decision-making whereby judges allow their personal views about public policy, among other factors, to guide their decision, with the suggestion that adherents of this philosophy tend to find constitutional violations and are willing to ignore precedents.

One learned author, Dava,[72] sees judicial activism as:

> The phenomenon of the courts dealing with those issues which they have traditionally not touched or which were not in the contemplation of founding fathers.

However, one fundamental understanding of the concept of judicial activism is that it is a liberal method of interpreting statutes and judicial precedents in favour of progressive social policies, which ensures equity and egalitarianism in the social engineering process.[73]

A foremost proponent of the concept of judicial activism is Lord Denning, who argued in *Packer* v. *Packer*[74] that the judges should not only be proactive but innovative in their judicial functions in order to develop the law and society ultimately. Judicial activism is a call for judges to be pragmatic in the exercise of their functions.

Though the concept of judicial activism provides a platform for the judiciary to make a robust contribution to the development of the law, unrestrained activism of the judges will certainly contravene the principle of separation of powers. One cardinal rule of interpretation, as was upheld by the court in *Olowu* v. *Abolore & Ors,*[75] is that the traditional custodians of the power of legislative interpretation (judiciary) should avoid judicial legislation and making nonsense of a statute or constitution in order not to defeat the manifest intention of the legislature. Under the system of separation of powers, the judiciary is the third arm of government which is vested with the powers to interpret, construe and apply the law. It is globally accepted that where there is a gap in the law, it is not for the courts to lay down the law but

---

ca.../Judicial-lawmaking (accessed 23/7/2012).

ical Preview of Judicial Activism" (*Delhi Journal of Politics,* Vol. 1, 1997), – www.indlaw.com/publicdata/articles pp.30-40

73 Suleiman Ismaila Nchi, *The Nigerian Law Dictionary,* Green World Publishing Company, 1996, p. 296.

74 *Packer* v. *Packer* (1954) AC, 22

75 *Olowu* v. *Abolore & Ors* (1993) 6 SCNJ (Pt. 1) 19-20.

for the legislature to amend and reform the law. The role of judges in Nigeria is essentially to apply the law as made by the legislature.[76]

Furthermore, an interpreter of the law is not to assign meanings to the clear, plain, and unambiguous provisions of a statute so as to make it conform with the court's own view of the meaning or of what it ought to be.[77]

In performing its functions, a court must be careful so that a statute made by the legislature with the best intention does not become an instrument of injustice and confusion.[78]

A court, as a temple of justice must, however, balance equally the delicate scale of justice so that justice, truth, and judicial boldness or radicalism to do justice are not jeopardized. In other words, the courts must resist any attempt to use them as tools for the implementation of manifestly unjust statutes.[79]

CONCLUSION

To have a good grasp of the concept of law, it is desirable that we understand the origin from which rules of human conduct come into existence and derive legal force or binding characters. A true conception of the rudimentary nature of law would be greatly hampered if we do not have any insight into the sovereign substructure from which the law derives its force or validity. The knowledge of the sources of law gives an insight into the antecedent past, which enhances the understanding of the present and then ultimately creates a platform for proper planning for the future. Every legal jurisdiction has a history, and the explanation of such history remains the function of a study on the sources of law.

---

[76] *See Ransome-Kuti* v. *A.G. Federation & Ors* (1985) 2 NWLR (Pt. 6) page 211; *Bisi Onabanjo* v. *Concord Press of Nigeria Ltd* (1981) 2 NCLR 399.

[77] *Okumagba* v. *Egbe* (1965) 1 A.N.L.R., 62 at 65.

[78] *Okumagba* v. *Egbe* (*supra*).

[79] *Guardian Newspaper Ltd.* v. *A.G. Federation* (1995) 5 NWLR (Pt. 398) 703.

Chapter 3

CLASSIFICATION OF LAWS

Bello Bamidele Joseph*

INTRODUCTION

Laws can be classified into various branches. Such branches may be municipal in nature or international. Similarly, the historical origin of some laws may play a major factor in their global application. To this extent, therefore, this topic shall make a foray into various laws and their origin and their jurisdictional application.

INTERNATIONAL LAW

In every community of persons, there are bound to be laws, rules, and guidelines to regulate behaviors, conduct, commerce, etc. Similarly, in every society or nations, laws do exist. These laws regulate the conduct of such society or nation: *ubi societas ubi jus.*

International laws therefore consist of rules and principles governing the relationship and dealings of nations with each other.[1] International law, also called the law of nations, evolved partly from understanding among nations of the world to accept certain rules of conduct which have customary coverage as standard rules to be observed. These are generally called bilateral or multilateral agreement. International law is founded upon international custom, conventions, treaties and general principles of law.[2] Norms forming the basis of international law derive their strength from universal acceptance.

---

*LL.M, LL.B, BL, Barrister & Solicitor of the Supreme Court and lecturer Faculty of Law, Benson Idahosa University, Benin City. Email: jbello@biu.edu.ng

[1] Edeko, S.E., *Foundation of International Law*,(Benin City: Tide Publishing, 2003), 1.

[2] http://legal-dictionary.thefreedictionary.com/international-law Assessed 10th August 2012]

International law was defined by Jeremy Bentham (1748-1832) as the body of legal rules, norms, and standards that apply between sovereign states and other entities that are legally recognized as an international actor.[3]

However, the scope of international law has been redefined to include relations between states and individuals, and relations between international organizations. International law exists on the legal theory of equality based on consent. Once consent is given, it cannot be withdrawn in the case of fundamental principles. A withdrawal will constitute a breach of the principle of *pacta sunt servanda.*[4]

DIVISION OF INTERNATIONAL LAW

International law is subdivided into public international law and private international law. Public international law deals with questions of rights between several nations or nations and the citizens or subjects of other nations. Private international law concerns itself with disputes between private persons, whether natural or juridical, emanating out of issues having significant relationship to more than one nation.[5]

PRINCIPLES OF INTERNATIONAL LAW

International law emphasizes three main legal principles that are recognized on the basis of courtesy and respect:

(a) principles of comity - this permits one nation to submit to the laws and judicial decrees of another state where the two nations share common public policy ideas;

(b) act of state doctrine- this doctrine recognizes the sovereignty of a nation within its own territory, such that its official action may not be questioned by the judicial body of another nation;

(c) doctrine of sovereign immunity - this doctrine postulates that where an action is brought by one sovereign state against another sovereign state, that other foreign sovereign state cannot be bound in court without its consent.

---

[3] http://www.britanica.comEBChecked/topic/291011/international-law [Assessed 10th August 2012]

[4] Rufus . O. Olaoluwa., *Introduction to International law*, (Ikeja: Silk Communications ltd: 2000) p4

[5] Ibid.

INTERNATIONAL COURT OF JUSTICE

The International Court of Justice (ICJ) which succeeded the Permanent International Court of Justice was established in 1945. The ICJ is the permanent international court. It is seated at The Hague.

MUNICIPAL LAW

Municipal laws are laws of a nation. These are laws that are operative within any nation as distinct from international law, that is, laws that operate outside and between states, international organizations, and similar entities. In some domains, they are laws that pertain solely to citizens and inhabitants of a town, cities, villages, and their local government. In that context, they are seen as bylaws. They are legislations made in a municipal council with application within that town council.[6]

Authority

A municipality may pass bylaw within the authority conferred on it through the instrumentality of the constitution. Where a constitution does not support a law legislated by a municipal authority, that bylaw is *ultra vires* the municipality.

Application

More basically, municipal laws in a council cover taxes, levies, and fines relating to violations of bylaws covering such areas as markets, parks, abattoirs, public conveniences, etc.

Enforcement

Municipal laws usually provide for modalities for enforcement. A violator of a municipal law is brought before a competent court of law for trial. Such courts in the case of a town council may be a mobile court and sentences are usually light either in the form of fines or light prison sentence.

---

[6] http://hirealawyer.findlaw.com.choosing-the-right-lawyer/municipal-law.html [Assessed 11th August 2012]

PUBLIC LAW

Public law is the area of law governing relationship between individuals i.e., citizens or corporations, and the state. Public law includes such laws as constitutional law, administrative law and criminal law etc. These laws demand strict observance or compliance from the citizens. Any violation has a penal consequence.

Constitutional law as a part of Public law regulates relations between the state and individual and relation between the various branches of government such as the executive, legislature and the judiciary.[7] In countries operating a written constitution, such as Nigeria and US, this relationship is spelled out in the constitution. However, in countries such as Great Britain, its constitution is not found in one single document but scattered in various documents such as *Magna Carta,* the Petition of Right, Bill of Right, the Act of Settlement 1700, and the Parliament Act 1949. Its constitution is also found in case law, such as landmark decisions in *Entick* v. *Carrington;*[8] *M* v. *Home Office.*[9] However, in Nigeria, the 1999 Constitution (as amended) is the *grundnorm.*

Administrative law as a body of public law is the aspect of public law which refers to the body of law that governs bureaucratic managerial procedures and it defines the powers of administrative agencies. Enforcement of administrative law is basically done by the executive i.e. Government. However where there appears to be an abuse, infractions or acts *ultra vires,* the court can inquire into such cases.

PRIVATE LAW

This is that part of the law that regulates relationship or legal rights of private persons whether natural or juridical.[10] Private law is that body of law that defines, regulates, enforces and administers relationship among individuals, associations and corporations. Private law, as used

---

[7] http://dictionary.reference.com/browse/public+law[Assessed 12th August 2012]
[8] (1765)19 St Tr 1030
[9] [1994] 1 AC 377; [1992] QB 270.
[10] http://dictionary.reference.com/browse/private+law (assessed on 12th of August 2012)

in distinction to Public law, means that part of the law that is administered between citizens and citizen, or that is concerned with the definition, regulation, and enforcement of rights in cases where both the person in whom the right inheres and the person upon whom the obligation rest are private individuals. It is, therefore, the body of law governing private persons, their properties, and relations with other private persons, which do not concern the state.

SUBSTANTIVE LAW

Substantive laws are the legislations that define the principles, objectives, circumstances, limitations, etc. governing the society and the rights of the individual. For example, an individual has a right to expression, but this is not without limitation, particularly where national integrity is concerned. A substantive law establishes the principles, whereas procedural law defines the procedure for establishing the right. Substantive law is the written law that defines rights and duties such as crimes and punishment in criminal law, civil rights, and responsibility in civil law. These laws are the result of legislation or judicial pronouncements.[11] Substantive law refers to all categories of public and private law, including laws of Tort, Contract, Real Property, and Criminal law. Substantive law is the legislation that defines the principles, objectives, circumstances, limitations, etc., governing the society and the rights of the individual.[12]

PROCEDURAL LAW

Procedural law is that aspect of the law that defines the procedure for bringing and enforcing substantive law. It is the body of legal rules that govern the process of determining the right of parties. Procedural law sets the rules and methods employed to obtain one's rights and, in particular, how the courts are conducted. Impliedly, procedural law is the machinery for enforcing those rights and duties. It comprises the rules by which a court hears and determines what happens in a civil or

---

[11] Abumere , P. I., *Fundamentals of Legal Method*, (Onitsha: Roberts Printers ltd: 1999), page 102.

[12] http://legal-dictionary.thefree dictionary.com/substantive+law [Assessed 12th August 2012]

criminal proceeding, as well as the methods and means by which substantive law is made and determined.

CRIMINAL LAW

Criminal law is the body of public law that imposes penal sanctions on crimes committed by individuals or corporate organizations so as to attain a peaceful and well-ordered society. Criminal law is that part of a state law that defines acts constituting offenses and stipulates sanctions attached to them. It is the law that penalizes offenses committed against the state.[13] Acts or omissions that have penal consequences, whether they be acts or omissions arising from infractions against a person or his property or that are defined as crimes or they are infractions against the state. Criminal law is the extant law of the land that defines an act or omission as a crime or criminal in nature that must be punished by the state.[14] Major enactments in Nigeria covering criminal offenses are the Criminal code and the Penal code.

Offenses are classified as simple offenses, misdemeanours, or felonies. Two major elements of a crime are the *actus reus,* i.e., the physical element constituting the offense and the *mens rea,* which means the mental element. The mental element is often expressed as an intention to do the act or make the omission. The establishment of an intention to commit an offense is a major requirement in a criminal trial, except the offense is one that is a strict liability offense. Criminal offenses are tried in any of the established courts in the land. Enforcement of the decisions of the courts, which may be either fines or imprisonment or both, are done by the instrumentality of the state apparatus such as the police, the Army, State Security Service, etc.

UNWRITTEN LAW

These are the laws that are observed among the people as binding yet were not formally enacted as statutes or case laws. Laws are said to be unwritten when they are either wholly unwritten or partly unwritten.[15] The English common law of England is generally acknowledged as

---

[13] http://www.law.cornell.edu/wex/criminal-procedure [Assessed 14th August 2012]

[14] http://legal-dictionary.thefreedictionary.com/procedure+law [Assessed 14th August 2012]

[15] Ese, Malemi., *The Nigerian Legal Method,* 1st ed., (Lagos: Princeton Publishing Co: 2010), page160

unwritten. Similarly, the Nigerian Customary law is largely unwritten. Case laws are also unwritten.[16] The fact of their unwritten characteristic has not impugned their efficacy and obedience among the people.

WRITTEN LAW

Written laws are laws that are enacted and codified in the statute books. These are laws that are the outcome of a legislative exercise. The legislation may be by the National Assembly, State House of Assembly or the Legislative Arm of the Local Government. Such laws are the Constitution, Criminal code, Penal code, Edicts, bylaws, treaties, decrees, etc.[17]

STATUTORY LAW

Statutes are laws that evolve as a result of legislation. Their existence is facilitated by the instrumentality of a legislative process. They are codified and compiled into book. The various parliamentary bodies, including the local government parliamentary arm, are empowered by the constitution to make laws within their legislative competence. Similarly, the State Legislative Assembly is empowered to make legislation called edicts with the application within the state,[18] while the national assembly is empowered to legislate for the entire nation.[19] All these various legislation can be referred to as statute having been evolved through a parliamentary procedure.

CUSTOMARY LAW

Customary laws are laws that evolve out of the customs among the people. Such customs having existed among the people for a long time and having an accepted usage may metamorphose into law among its adherents.[20] These are traditional common law rules or practices that have become an intrinsic part of the accepted and expected conduct in a community, profession, or trade and are treated as legal requirements. Customary law is recognized not because it is backed by the power of

---

[16] Ibid.. 161
[17] Ibid.. 161
[18] S. 4 (7) 1999 Constitution of the Federal Republic of Nigeria (as amended)
[19] S. 4 (1) ibid.
[20] *Op. cit.,* note 16 p 165

strong individuals or institutions but because each individual recognizes the benefits of behaving in accordance with other individual's expectations, given that others also behave as he expects.[21] Under customary law, offenses are treated as civil wrongs or injuries and not as crimes.[22] Customary law in Nigeria varies from tribe to tribe. For instance, the custom of the people of Edo, as it affects the right to inheritance, may vary from what is obtainable among the people of Imo. Similarly, the custom of the Ashanti may differ from that of the Kumasi people when you talk of burial rites.

However, the custom of a group of people is legally recognized or given accepted usage if it has been given judicial recognition. A customary law is only recognized as enforceable if it is not repugnant to natural justice, equity, and good conscience. It must not be unfair, unjust, and unconscionable.

ENGLISH LAW

English law refers to the law as it evolved in England through the English common law process and a host of English legal norms established by parliament, the crown, and the judiciary. English law has also made an incursion into countries of the Commonwealth heritage basically by reason of their colonial history with England. In Nigeria's legal system, there is a profound presence of English law. Part of the sources of Nigeria's legal system is the received English law applicable in England as of 1900, which are referred to as statutes of general application. It is noteworthy to mention that the English common law system is judge-made law, and by the doctrine of *stare decisis,* where such laws are made by superior courts, lower courts are bound to follow them on the principle of precedence.

COMMON LAW

The common law is a legal system developed in England. It is judge-made law. Judge-made in the sense that decisions were reached based

---

[21] *Op. cit.*, note 11 page 131
[22] Ibid.. 161

on common sense and the custom of the people. These decisions, which were not majorly codified, developed over the years on the doctrine of judicial precedence and so are binding on lower courts. The principle holds the position that it is unfair to treat similar facts differently on different occasions.[23] One major problem of the common law was encoding the decisions for the purpose of uniformity.

EQUITY

Equity as a legal term may be used in the general juristic sense or equity in the narrow sense. Equity, in the general sense, is a mollifier of the rigors of common law, that is to say, finding a way to give substantive justice to the parties. Equity in the narrow sense is that stream of law developed immediately before the *Judicature Acts* of 1873-75 in England. In the early stages of the English legal system, the common law Justices designed a standard writ system in which all litigants must pigeonhole their complaints to be able to access justice. In most cases, these were not possible as certain wrongs were novel and so could not find existing standard forms.[24] Those who could not find access to the common law courts due to the narrow nature of the writ system then petitioned the King for remedy. This prompted the King to empower the Lord Chancellor to hear and resolve these cases purely on grounds of merit and justice without following any formal procedure. This system of civil hearings grew to become the court of Chancery. The court of Chancery and the common law court became the two court systems in England before the Judicature Act of 1873, which later merged the two courts into one and empowered any sitting Judge to apply the principles of equity and the common law where necessary.[25]

PUBLIC INTERNATIONAL LAW

Public International law concerns the structure and conduct of sovereign states, analogous entities such as the Holy See, and

---

23 *Op. cit.*, note 11, p 24

24 Ibid.

25 *Op. cit.*, note 14 p162

intergovernmental organizations.[26] Public international law cover laws of nations (*jus gentium*) and international treaties, agreements, and conventions (*jus inter gentes*). Public International law has three sources; treaties, customs, and general principles of laws. Public International law recognizes the concept of the acquisition of territory, state immunity, and legal responsibility of the state in their conduct with each other. Public International law is also concerned with the treatment of individuals within state territory. Its focus also covers international crimes, treatment of aliens, prisoners of war, refugees, nationality problems, and human rights generally.

CONFLICT OF LAWS OR PRIVATE INTERNATIONAL LAW

Conflict of laws, also called Private international law, is a set of rules of procedure for determining which legal system or jurisdiction applies to a given dispute. Where a legal dispute has a cross-boundary or foreign element, i.e., a multi-jurisdictional character, the legal rules that are used to resolve it is referred to as conflict of laws.

There are three branches of conflict of laws: jurisdiction, choice of law, and foreign judgment. The term conflict of laws is used in the jurisdictions of the common law legal tradition, such as the United States, England, Canada, Nigeria, Australia, etc., while Private international law as a term is used in non-common law jurisdictions.

PRIMARY LAWS

These are laws enacted by the parliamentary process. They are statute laws of any nation. They are the general legislations forming the leading laws of any nation. Also categorized as primary laws are case laws, particularly landmark decisions of the apex courts, particularly the decisions of the Supreme Court on such major issues affecting the national interest.

SECONDARY LAWS

These are secondary sources of law such as legal writings of scholars, analysis of the law, commentaries or publications which tend to

[26] *Op. cit.*, note 3 p. 40

highlight the law, Ministerial regulations, and directives. Secondary sources are sometimes referred to as delegated legislation. To these, we can add treaties, bilateral agreements, conventions, etc.

AUTONOMOUS OR AUTONOMIC LAWS

These are a class of subsidiary legislations mainly made by professional bodies, such as the Nigerian Bar Association (NBA), the chartered professional bodies such as the Institute of Chartered Accountants of Nigeria (ICAN), Nigerian Society of Engineers (NSE). These are subsidiary legislations in the form of ethical regulations and control of the mode of practice.

Chapter 4

INTERNAL CONFLICT OF LAWS IN NIGERIA

P. E. O. Oguno* & C. S. Obi-Okoye**

INTRODUCTION

The courts, everywhere and always, are inclined to apply the law of their own state or region unless they have a compelling reason why they should do otherwise. The opposing party to a case would have to convince the court to apply a law that it considers foreign to the jurisdiction that it operates in. It is always this foreign element of a case that gives rise to the conflict of law rules that have been developed in many legal systems in order to deal with issues of conflict of law situations. Such foreign element may be the domicile, nationality, and the customary or personal law of one of the parties to the suit. In that situation, the court is therefore faced with a choice of law situation and analysis in order to meet the justice of the case.

Conflict of laws may be evident where it involves parties from different nationalities or a case where the *res* is located in a different legal system or where for instance, in a case of tort, the injury occurred in another foreign country different from the nationalities of the parties. However, it may not be that simple in situations where parties have affiliations with variant ethnic and customary laws in the same legal system. This is the subject of internal conflict of laws. Nigeria, with its peculiar pluralistic legal system comprising of received English law,

* Oguno, P.E.O. Ph.D, Senior Lecturer, Faculty of Law, Anambra State University Igbariam campus

** Chineze S. Obi-Okoye, LLM., Lecturer, Faculty of Law Nnamdi Azikiwe University, Awka.

federal law, state law, and customary law, showcases the legal geography that is readily amenable to bringing about internal conflict of laws.

The objective of this work is to look beyond the understanding of most common examples of conflict of law, which the courts are ordinarily faced with in suits between persons of different nations, one of which is foreign to the court, and look inward into the legal geography of Nigeria in order to bring to the light the current problems and the potential problems the court in Nigeria are wont to face as a result of internal conflict of law.

The thesis that this research puts out is that there are more cases of internal conflict of law in Nigeria than we can imagine. However many they are, the courts in Nigeria and the current legal system still need to do a lot of work in the area of conflict of law subject in order to churn out clear rules to guide the courts when faced with such conflict.

The peculiar legal geography of Nigeria has for so long been taken for granted. Unless the peculiar legal problems associated with the pluralistic legal structure of Nigeria are given proper attention, the law on the Conflict of Law will continue to be left to the whims and caprices of the sitting judge. The result will then be that our system will continue to lack the certainty expected in a rule of law environment, which we, unfortunately, claim as a democratic society.

In order to achieve this objective, I have chosen to look at some of the literatures for a general understanding of the conflict of law and as it applies to Nigeria. Some Nigeria cases will be analysed to show how rife the internal conflict of law is and how uncertain the rules are in resolving cases of internal conflict of law in Nigeria.

The work is divided into four parts. Part one takes a look at the Conflict of Laws in general. Part two attempts to make a distinction between international, inter-state, and internal conflict of law. In part three, I will conduct a cursory inquiry into the legal history and geography of Nigeria and how it has occasioned internal conflict of laws. Part four will deal with a demonstration of the Internal Conflict of laws in Nigeria.

Having showcased situations of internal conflict of laws in Nigeria, In part five, I will conduct an analysis of how the courts in Nigeria have tried to resolve cases of internal conflict of law using many known principles of Conflict of Laws. Thereafter, the conclusion of the essay will ensure to demonstrate that a lot of work is needed in this area of law. The courts, state legislature, and the federal legislature have to take another serious look into this area of our law since the peculiar legal and political structure of Nigeria cannot do without incidences of internal conflict of law. Some measure of certainty is needed if we are to measure up to a Rule of Law country that we claim to be.

CONFLICT OF LAWS IN GENERAL

The *Black's Law Dictionary* defines conflict of laws as "A difference between the laws of different states or countries in a case in which a transaction or occurrence central to the case has a connection to two or more jurisdictions."[1]

As a branch of law, the law dictionary further defines it as "that body of jurisprudence that undertakes to reconcile such differences or to decide what law is to govern in these situations; the principles of choice of law"[2] in other words, conflict of law contemplates a situation wherein a part of the domestic law of a country or state deals with a case that cannot be properly decided without a consideration given to the foreign element contained in that case.

In other words, for a case to invoke the prevailing rules of the conflict of laws, there must exist the ingredient of domestic law having to grapple with a foreign element that presents to the adjudicator with a choice of law to apply or to make a decision about jurisdiction. By a foreign element, it simply means a context or case, or transaction that involved systems of law other than the domestic or internal law of the place or country or state, or community. Alternatively, it is also called Private international law because the relevant facts of the case, in addition to the foreign element, are directly or indirectly connected with the domestic law by virtue of the persons involved or by territorial links.

---

[1] Garner Bryan (ed), *Black's Law Dictionary*, (7th ed), West Group: St Paul, Minnesota 1999, p.295

[2] Ibid.

The foreign element may be one of the parties whose residence or domicile is in some territory other than the territorial jurisdiction of the court involved, or it may be the location of the subject matter of the dispute, for example, in a case of contract where the contract was made or performed or breached or in a case of tort, where the tortious act occurred or in a land matter where the land is situated.

The foreign element may also be in regard to the law governing the substantive matter differs from the law applicable in the jurisdiction of the court which claims jurisdiction; in that case, the court may be called to entertain the foreign law. In some absolute sense, as Nnamdi Nwabueze puts it, "It is the foreign element that gives conflict of laws its distinctive character because it brings to question the application of another system of law. Without at least a foreign element, a case would not qualify as a conflict of law case."[3]

Another author who chose to regard "the conflict of laws subject" as the Law of choice of law corroborating the above-named principles elucidates that: "It is a body of rules which determine the law applicable to situations containing relevant foreign element. Such elements as mentioned previously are the foreign domicile or nationality of a relevant person, the occurrence abroad of a relevant event or the foreign *situs* of a relevant thing."[4]

In the light of this clear elucidation, the author insists that the subject of conflict of laws seeks to answer such questions as: Is it the foreign law with whose applicability we are concerned with or with individual foreign rules? Is it the foreign rules that we purport to apply or our domestic law incorporating the foreign law? Will domestic or foreign law remain unchanged, or will it be adapted for purposes of conflict law?[5] Etc.

Scholars like Albert Ehrenzweig noted that the history of conflict of laws reflects a clash between two mainstream conceptions, namely the universalist or internationalist conception and the pluralist or

---

[3] Nwabueze, R. N, The History and Sources of Conflict of Laws in Nigeria with Comparison to Canada, A thesis submitted to the Faculty of Graduate Studies in Partial Fulfilment Of the Requirements for the degree of Master of Laws, October, 2000

[4] Ehrenzweig Albert A. *Conflicts in a Nutshell*, (3rd Ed) St Paul, Minn: West Publ Co,1974, p.8

[5] Ibid.

nationalist conception. The former sees conflict as a potentially all comprehensive system or rules which would allocate to each state clearly defined legislative jurisdictions or powers to create rights and obligations entitled to recognition elsewhere,[6] while the former refuses to assume jurisdiction or powers in the absence of such jurisdictions or powers in the absence of such positive super laws as treaties and constitution…[7]

It is necessary to note that whenever a court is called to make a decision in any case in which a foreign element is involved, conflict of laws comes in to perform a number of functions, namely above all, to indicate whether a court has jurisdiction to entertain a particular suit containing one or more foreign elements and in the event of an affirmative answer to indicate which one or more of the several possibly relevant laws will be applied to reach a decision in the suit and then to indicate when and subject to what conditions another court will be prepared to recognize and enforce a judgment rendered in a foreign court. In the light of the above, scholars are generally agreed that a given conflict situation generally involves four basic issues, namely:

1. choice of jurisdiction;
2. choice of law;
3. recognition of Foreign Judgment;
4. time factor in the spatial application of law.

INTERNATIONAL, INTERSTATE, AND INTERNAL CONFLICT OF LAWS

No nation, so to speak, is an island. There is a need for continuous cooperation among nations, people, and communities. Moreover, the ever-changing social and economic interests of people of every tongue and nation have necessitated more business and social transactions among peoples of varied languages, legal systems, and cultural affinities. As a result of these interactions among people beyond their nation or state or cultural boundaries, there is a need to formulate rules to govern

[6] Ibid., p.14
[7] Ibid.

day today activities and transactions that go across legal, social, and cultural boundaries.

International conflict of law: On the international level, the main purpose of the conflict of law is to protect and ensure the peaceful interaction of private persons in different countries. Thus international business transaction may be difficult if there do not exist a legal system or structure for promoting, guiding, and protecting international human activities.

Agbede highlights the importance of an established legal structure for resolving conflicts of an international nature when he says that "this basic principle is predicated on the desire to protect the reasonable expectation of parties in their out-of-state legal transactions. Otherwise, a person would not be able to sue a Nigerian for a tort committed against him or for a contact that took place abroad.[8]

An instance of an International conflict of law would be a Nigerian who goes to China and orders a container of various articles of a certain quality. In processing his order, the Chinese businessman packages another set of goods for him of lower quality and has it shipped to Nigeria. The conflict of law questions are: which country has jurisdiction to entertain the suit secondly, whose law of contract would be applied - China or Nigeria or Common Law? Which nation's applicable law/judgment on breach of contract would be applied - the Nigerian or the Chinese?

What if the statutory bar to the action in breach of contract has kicked-in in Nigeria but not yet in China? Which of the conflicting laws would the court adopt, supposing the case is tried in Nigeria? The essence of the conflict of law on the international scene is to highlight that there are occasions when courts in one country must take account of the laws that are obtained in another when such rules relate to issues performed outside those areas. Thus in some circumstances, a foreign court will abandon her municipal law and apply foreign law in order to get to the justice of the case.

---

[8] Agbede I. O. (ed), Unpublished Lecture Notes, Laws 513, Conflict of Laws, National Open University

INTERSTATE CONFLICT OF LAWS

In a federal constitution such as Nigeria, Canada, or the United States of America, the legal system of each federating unit may well differ in many respects from the legal system of another federating unit. The foreign element, in this case, may be the different set of divorce laws wherein two persons of different states of origin are involved or in succession laws where two sets of succession laws are contemplated in a case where the deceased has a domicile different from his state of origin. This may also be seen in child custody laws that sometimes conflict among themselves.

The conflict of law situation poses a question of choice of law between the legal systems of the two states since the facts of the case have contacts with two or more of the states. A typical example of the interstate conflict of law is as follows: "A was a passenger in a car driven by B and was injured in an automobile accident in the Abia state of Nigeria as a result of B's negligent driving of the car. A and B are residents of Imo state, where B's car was insured and registered. C, another car owner involved in the accident, was a resident of Rivers State of Nigeria, where his car was registered and insured. The laws of the three states have conflicting provisions in respect of the issues arising from the accident.[9] The question that would arise is, which of the three state laws will provide the rule for a decision in action in tort for negligent driving and for damages.

INTERNAL CONFLICT OF LAWS

Although interstate conflict of law and internal conflict of law seems to be very similar in meaning and structure, there are a few issues peculiar to the internal conflict of law, strictly speaking. For Nwabueze Remigius, internal conflicts of laws arise because of different aspects of the local legal system.[10] We find these different aspects in local laws respecting succession, divorce and marriage laws, etc. For the purpose of this, I would treat internal conflict of law in a loose sense to include

---

[9] Nwabueze, N., *op. cit.*, p.
[10] Ibid.

interstate conflict of law, i.e., states as may be found in the federal system of government like Canada or Nigeria.

THE NIGERIAN LEGAL GEOGRAPHY AND INTERNAL CONFLICT OF LAW

In 1863, the English law of general application and doctrines of common and equity was received into Lagos and in 1900 for the rest of the country. There was no serious adaptation work done before the reception. It was presumed that the Nigeria pre-colonial legal regime did not conflict with any local laws or laws in force in the country at that time. Until Nigerian peoples of diverse socio-cultural ties began to cross boundaries and intermarry among themselves, the question of internal conflict of law did not arise because the conflict between diverse legal regimes had not been entertained as the subsequent intermixture between people of different legal backgrounds was at its lowest ebb. Aside from the reception of English law into Nigeria in 1900, there was also the apparent variant socio-religious culture that characterizes Northern and Southern Nigeria.

While the greater part of Northern Nigeria was earmarked by Islamic socio-cultural stamp, southern Nigeria, for the most part, was developed both in its religious and sociological character under the auspices of the native law and custom and, later in history, Christian culture.

Thus, the introduction of Islam in Northern Nigeria meant the regime of Islamic law. Till date, in Northern Nigeria, Islamic law remains the personal law of most Muslims. The application of Muslim law in Northern Nigeria left not much room for choice of law conundrum. It is apposite to say that even before the reception of English law in Nigeria, Islamic law had already pervaded the life of every person in that part of Nigeria as far back as the 1080 A.D when the trading contract was already present among tribes in the Northern part of Nigeria.

While the problem of Conflict of Law in the Northern part of Nigeria was the Islamic law being the personal law of Muslims, the problem of the conflict of law in southern Nigeria, for the most part, arose from the incidence of deep cultural heritage, which was indispensable among tribes and ethnic groups in the south, notably the Ibos and the Yorubas. Kayode rightly said: "Nigeria did have laws before the advent of the British despotism. The despots did not meet Nigeria in a state of Anarchy. The laws consisted principally of the customs focusing upon the nature and background of the people."[11] Thus we have customary laws in the south. These customary laws of various ethnic groups exist independent of each other and they were used and applied on a territorial basis to regulate various aspects and activities of the people in a given area. These customary laws/Islamic laws now operate side by side with the received English law and the other statutory laws in Nigeria.

It is no surprise then that Nigeria running under a federal constitution and subject to a dual legal system, namely the Islamic /customary law vis-à-vis the positive law enacted by the elected assemblies of states, remains very fertile soil for conflict of law problems. It is important to observe that Islamic law that was operational in the North was largely documented and set down in the Islamic holy book- the Quran, while the native law and custom were, for the most part, kept by oral tradition.

Most recently, we are beginning to see the codification of these customary laws by various ethnic and territorial groups. In today's Nigeria jurisprudence, the constitution of Nigeria duly restricts the application of Islamic law to personal law, and the sharia court is given the competence to try matters relating to Islamic personal law, while the customary law, although not limited to the southern states of Nigeria admits of no limitation in respect of matters which the customary courts would entertain.[12] Thus be it noted, as Kayode Eso puts it, that "while one part of the country had been entrenched in customary law, the other has its entrenchment in Islamic law."[13]

[11] Eso Kayode, *Further Thoughts on Law and Jurisprudence*, Lagos: Spectrum Law Publishing 2003,p.117
[12] S. 244 & 245 of Nigeria Constitution of 1999
[13] Eso Kayode, *op. cit.*, p.125

DEMONSTRATION OF INTERNAL CONFLICT OF LAWS IN NIGERIA

Be it as it may, we will endeavour in this section to conduct an exposition into the peculiar particulars of the internal conflict of laws in Nigeria. We shall be guided by the definition we have provided for internal conflict of laws and interstate conflict of laws, for which we ascribed both as analogue to each other.

We would like to borrow the statement of Agbede to highlight the background for proper understanding of this unit as follows "It is worth mentioning that most of internal conflict of Laws particularly in relation to which jurisdiction of customary law courts, which choice of laws between systems of customary laws are most found in state laws."[14] For the purposes of a systematic approach to the topic, the investigation will be conducted in this order:

- Islamic Law as applicable in the North;
- Customary Laws of Marriage, Succession, and Capacity;
- Other Internal Conflicts of law.

In *Tapa* v. *Kuka*,[15] the deceased, A Nupe man, died interstate in Bida, leaving a house in Lagos. The question was whether his domestic law should apply or the law of the place where the property was located, which is the *lex situs*? In that case, the deceased's personal law was applied, which is Mohammedan Law prevailing among the Nupe people. The case clearly concerns the law on succession to the property of a person whose personal law is the Mohammedan law.

Herein, the foreign element is the location of the property of the deceased, which happened to be in a place where Islamic law is not operational. In resolving the conflict, the court gives due consideration to the personal law of the deceased as well as to the law applicable in his place of domicile in order to do justice to the case and give effect to the intention of the deceased.

A brief history of the Conflict of laws engendered by the application of Islamic law in Nigeria might be necessary here in order to

---

[14] Agbede I. O. (ed), Unpublished Lecture Notes, Laws 513, Conflict of Laws, National Open University Agbede I. O. (ed)

shed better light on the topic. The Sharia legal system is of great antiquity in Nigeria. Islam as religion got to Nigeria via Kanem Borno in 1085 (eleventh century). However, it is not certain when Sharia was introduced into Kanem Borno. But it is at least clear that in 1805 with the Jihad of Uthman Dan Fodio (which brought into being the Sokoto caliphate, which overthrew the Hausa kings who already were Muslims but not ruling according to Sharia), the Sharia came to be applied as a legal system.

As the Jihad set into motion by Uthman Dan Fodio was yet to dwindle of its simmering effects, the caliphs organized further raids with an aim to expand the house of Islam. Thus by the quarter of the 19th century, when the Royal Niger Company came to explore Northern Nigeria for business, "Sharia had become the way of life."[16] Ikenga Ozigboh exposing a similar line of thought, said, "Under the caliphate, the Sharia came to its full flower in Northern Nigeria. All Islamic, social, political, and judicial processes and institutions were emphasized."[17] With the proclamation of the protectorate of Northern Nigeria on 1st January 1900 by Sir Lugard (the first High Commissioner), the British began to administer the North. When Lugard took over the administration, an assurance was given to the ruling emirs that the Islamic religion would not be tampered with, and this was concretized in a treaty.

Against this backdrop, Sharia law continued to be administered, and the British authorities came to recognize the Sharia in the North as a native law and custom, and new emirs were installed who imposed their Islamic authority and law on the Hausa folks of Northern Nigeria. In 1914, the Northern and Southern protectorates and the Lagos colony were amalgamated into what is today called the Federal Republic of Nigeria, and thus began the interaction between the North and South.

With amalgamation, the 1904 Criminal Code that previously applied in southern Nigeria was extended in 1916 to the whole country.

, Unpublished Lecture Notes, Laws 513, Conflict of Laws, National Open University Publications), 2001, p.93

[17] Ikenga Ozigbo, Sharia in the Multi- Religious Nigeria Society (being a paper delivered at a Symposium organized by the Spiritan School of Theology Enugu), 23rd March, 2001.

However, the Sharia law, regarded as native law and custom, continued to be applied in the North as interpreted by *Maliki School* hence a situation of two systems of law existing side by side. This *Maliki law* contained many rules, which were unacceptable to those trained in English law. In a series of legislation and proclamation, the British colonial authority tried to overhaul the law and subjugate the Islamic legal systems under the British/English common law.

While the colonial masters were making efforts to streamline the two legal systems from the civil angle, there were also beginning to appear some issues related to criminal law and prosecution. At that time, there was in existence one criminal code for the entire country. Thus the existing law is that while a native court may charge a person for offences under native law and custom, the punishment which may be inflicted where the offence is also a criminal code offence must be in accordance with the punishment laid down in the criminal code.

In the year 1957, after the leading case of *Maizabo* v. *Sokoto N. A*[18] the position was settled that the correct law was that Native or Customary courts were empowered to apply customary criminal law, even if there was a provision in the Criminal Code on the subject. But they must not pass sentences in excess of the maximum that could have been imposed if the case had been tried under the Criminal Code. However, the unsatisfactory result of this was that cases in native courts would, in effect, require an examination of two different sets of law: First, Native law and custom, and second, to ascertain sentence. The situation needed to be re-examined. In 1958, the Northern Government set up a panel of Jurist to consider the problem.

The panel recommended that the Sharia law (Maliki law) should be confined to the personal and family law of Muslim litigants, and criminal law, both in its substantive and procedural aspects, should be codified. Since the criminal code at that time was not drafted for the Muslim community, it was unacceptable and not adopted. The code which eventually emerged in 1959 was the Penal code, which was

[18] (1957) N.R.N.L.R 133

drafted based on a code that had been working successfully in the Sudanese Muslim community.

In the penal code, traditional Muslim crimes such as adultery, drinking alcohol, and insult to the modesty of a woman were preserved. On account of the enactment of the Penal Code for Northern Nigeria, the sharia law and its application was clearly restricted to Muslim personal and family law, hence the establishment of the Sharia Court of Appeal.

The current legal environment, although better streamlined, did not succeed in cleaning out incidences of conflict of laws, especially as it presents itself in the daily interaction of Nigerians in the north as it impacts their civil and criminal activities since some states in the North came close to enacting sharia as a form of law in those states notably the Zamfara state. Although some of these efforts are deemed unconstitutional, no invasive energy has been spent to repeal those laws as they continued to regulate the civil activities of the person in those regions.

A very common example of the conflict of law in the area of criminal law is undeniable when one reflects that the Penal Code in its section 3(2), provides as follows "No person shall be liable to punishment under any native law or custom,"[19] yet the Sharia law of the Zamfara state and other states in the region which have adopted the sharia legal system continues to try and sentence people using the various tools of the newly enacted sharia legislations. This is a clear case of the internal conflict of law within the region.

On a broader level, the details of the punishment as set down in Sharia law of some of these states conflict with the details of human rights provisions of the 1999 constitution. It is understood that for some crimes like the *Had* crimes[20] under Islamic law, the punishment is as recommended by the Quran, not the Penal Code.

---

[19] S. 3(2) The Penal Code, 1959

[20] Had crimes according to Islamic principles are crimes against God's law. They have fixed punishment because they are set by God. And they are also found in the Quran. A judge can only impose the 'Had punishment' when a person confesses to the crime and when there are enough witnesses to the crime. The judge has no discretion with respect to the punishment for any had crimes. The Quran must strictly be followed. Had crimes include Murder, Apostasy, theft, Adultery, Robbery, Alcohol drinking etc.

Some of the crimes under sharia law are clearly opposed to the dictates of human rights; for instance, the crime of apostasy punishable by death under sharia law is nowhere found in either the criminal code not the penal code runs and, at the same time, violates the fundamental right to freedom of religion and conscience as provided in the human rights section of the 1999 Constitution.[21]

It must be seriously argued that not only is the sharia law on apostasy unconditional; it should not never be applied in any court of law as it is clearly opposed to the fundamental rights as enshrined in the Nigerian constitution. The sharia law of some of these Northern states outlines some of the crimes like adultery, fornication, and Alcohol drinking and prescribes punishment for them. It should be noted that these crimes have no place either in the Penal Code or Criminal Code, and it is important to note that sharia courts (creature of the state legislature) that try these offences do so without proper jurisdiction or, to say the least, ultra vires as the current Nigeria constitution specifically restricts the jurisdiction of sharia courts to Islamic personal law.

If the legislator had wanted to extend that jurisdiction to criminal law, it would have done so by inserting "criminal law" into the wording of s.277 of the 1999 Constitution, just like it did in s.272, where it provided for the jurisdiction of the High Court.

CUSTOMARY LAWS WITH RESPECT TO MARRIAGE, SUCCESSION, ETC.

Every society with its different cultural trappings has a concept of marriage which might be slightly different from the others. Consequently, customary laws of marriage differ from culture to culture. In addition to the customary laws that govern the marriage institution, the Marriage Act (to regulate the formal validity of marriage) and Matrimonial Causes Act 1970 (to govern causes where

[21] S.38(1) of the 1999 Constitution(As amended)- provides as follows: "Every person shall be entitled to freedom of thought, conscience and religion including freedom to change his religion or belief..."

the validity of the marriage is not in issue) were enacted to deal with peculiar issues common to statutory marriage.

The Matrimonial Causes Act confers original jurisdiction to High courts to entertain legal action in case of marriages contracted under statutory law. At the same time, customary law courts are also conferred with original jurisdiction in matrimonial causes and matters between persons married under customary law arising from or connected with a union contracted under customary law.[22]

Given that the application of some aspects of the customary law might procure unreasonable results, the Evidence Act provides a stratum for the validation of customary law in Nigeria. Thus, Obilade noted, "Rules of customary law are subject to test of validity prescribed by statute. An applicable rule of customary law is not to be enforced by courts unless it passes the test."[23] The evidence Act presents the statutory position for testing the validity of customary law.

It provides that a given customary law to be enforced must not be contrary to public policy and must be in accord with natural justice and good conscience.[24] Nwaogugu adds that: "Such customary law is applicable in so far as it is neither repugnant to natural justice, equity and good conscience nor incompatible either directly or by necessary implication with any written law for the time being in force."[25]

That being said, it is important to note that in spite of these legislative efforts to pre-empt any foreseeable conflict of law in the application of customary law, there still exists a flurry of conflict of law situations, especially in matrimonial cases and causes. The most common problems do not usually arise from the repugnancy test or conflict with any law in force but rather with the applicability of two customary laws apparently contrary to each other.

The foreign element arises either on account of clash between the custom of one of the spouses differing from that of the other spouse

---

[22] Nwaogugu E. I., *Family Law in Nigeria* (Ibadan: Heinemann Books, 1999), p.117, see also S. 12 (2) of the Customary Court Law, 2010 of Anambra State

[23] Obilade A. O. *The Nigeria Legal System* (Ibadan: Spectrum Book, 1979), p.101

[24] S. 18(3) Evidence Act 2011- In any judicial proceedings where any custom is relied upon, it shall not be enforced as law if it is contrary to public policy or is not in accordance with natural Justice, equity and good conscience.

[25] Nwaogugu, *op. cit.,* p. 120

such that the courts will be faced with the choice of law in that given circumstance. In many cases, the options available to the court to choose (either in a case where the issue concerns the formal validity of marriage or causes arising from marital contracts like divorce or custody or maintenance) varies from the law of the place where the marriage was celebrated (*Lex loci celebrationis*) to the law of the place where the husband is domiciled (by origin or in fact) to the law of the place where the matter was instituted (*Lex fori*), in which case here, the foreign element is totally disregarded.

A classic example of conflict of law involving marriage under customary law might be in respect to the capacity to marry, where the age of capacity might differ from culture to culture. For some customs, the age of capacity is 14 years for girls and 18 years males, while in others, it is 15 years for girls. Where a girl who is 14 years in a culture where the capacity to marry is fixed at 14 years gets married to a man whose custom as to capacity is 15 years old, the question then is: what choice of law will be obtainable in order to determine the validity of that marriage?.

Under the culture from where the girl was married from, she possesses the capacity, but under the choice of law of her spouse, she is deemed to be incapable. Other factors where respecting the capacity to contract a valid marriage might bring about internal conflict of laws include prohibited degrees of consanguinity, parental consent, and consent of the parties. Some customs would consider the consent of the parents less important than the consent of the parties.

Conflict of law situation for marriages contracted under customary law might also arise in action for dissolution of marriage or alimony, legitimacy, and custody of the children, for instance, where in action for alimony, for instance, the customary laws of the concerned spouses might differ from each other. In such a situation, a judge is faced with the option of the choice of law to apply to meet the justice of the situation.

The law of succession under customary law also poses another problem for conflict of law. Succession to land or property may either be testate or intestate. A person is said to have died testate if he has given directions for the disposition of his property after his death in the manner prescribed by law. If he has not given any such directions, he is said to have died intestate. Where a person dies testate and is domiciled abroad, which customary law would be invoked - the Law of domicile or the law of origin - to determine whether his testament would be the guiding post for the disposition of his property.

In *Adesubokan* v. *Yinusa*,[26] the court was invited to pronounce on a will of Muslim which was at variance with the Maliki law of Muslims, alleged to be binding on the testator. The testator was a Yoruba man from Lagos and he died in Zaria, Northern Nigeria, where the property affected was situated and where Muslim Law applied as part of the customary law. The alleged ground of invalidity was that the testator had discriminated against the plaintiff, one of his children.

The court of first instance held that the will was invalid and set aside the probate, which had already been granted. On appeal to the Supreme Court, the will was upheld on two main grounds. First, there was no evidence that the Muslim law of Maliki was part of the customary law of Lagos, which was the law binding on the deceased. Second, where the Muslim law is to be applied, such Muslim law is incompatible directly or by implication with the provisions of the Wills Act, 1837, an English statute incorporated by reference in s.33 of the High Court Laws of Northern Nigeria.

The extended result of this is that any rule of customary law, which denies a Nigerian full testamentary capacity, will not be enforced. Similarly, in cases where of intestate succession, the customary laws vary from place to place. Judges are often forum shopping as to the law to apply where the law of domicile and the law where the property is situated (*lex situs*) conflict. Often the law of domicile is often preferred over the *lex situs.* Sometimes the conflict of law may arise in a situation where the subject of controversy is the position of these illegitimate children where the deceased had children outside marriage, which was acknowledged by him before his death. Some customs recognize such children as the full-fledged children of the deceased, while some do not.

---

[26] Unreported Suit No. SC 25/70 of 17/6/71

Where it happens that the customary law of the mother to those children admits of full rights to children outside wedlock, while that of the man does not, the judge will be left with no option but also consider the customary laws and circumstances obtainable in the place where and when the children were born in order to arrive at the actual intention of the parties and be able to do justice to the case.

RESOLVING INTERNAL CONFLICT OF LAWS: BASIC PRINCIPLES AND ATTITUDE OF THE COURTS

Courts will usually respond to the internal conflict of laws in one or more possible ways. First, it can treat the case as a strictly domestic one and apply its own law or the law of the place, technically called the *lex loci*, to the resolution of the conflict regardless of the foreign element. By so doing, it may just ignore and make no concessions to the foreign dimension of the litigation.

A court could also take the position that its laws and procedures are inadequate for a particular case with a foreign element and refuse to entertain it or adjudicate it, technically declining jurisdiction. Herein, the assumption is that there is another more appropriate and more equipped court somewhere to handle the case. Another possibility or approach is that the court admits that cases with foreign elements cannot be refused. However, it recognizes in this approach that the case with a foreign element poses some critical problems, which demand critical and commensurate attention; otherwise, there would be no justice in the matter.

The court adopts any of these approaches based on the nature of the foreign element. The nature of the foreign element occasioning the conflict could be based on any of the following factors that define the personal law of individuals and determine, in some situations, the choices open to the court for proper adjudication of matters in situations of internal conflict of law namely: *lex domicile, lex situs, lex celebrationis, lex fori, lex loci, lex succesionis.*

In all of these, in connection to internal conflict of laws, the court is being guided by two fundamental legal principles, namely the issues of jurisdiction and choice of law.

It must be noted that on account of the pluralistic nature of the legal system and the recognition of customary law in Nigeria, the incidence of internal conflict of law comes as no surprise. Attempting to draw some boundaries to the admission of customary law as law and to limit the incidences of conflict of laws in general occasioned by customary law in our courts, the high court laws of states and the evidence act law introduces the repugnancy doctrine, which disallows the admission of any given customary law where it is contrary to natural justice, equity and good conscience.[27]

Although the repugnancy test has its jurisprudential problems (like inquiring into whether the standard of natural justice, equity, and good conscience is universal to all cultures or is it relative to the whims and caprices of the sitting judge or a given society against another?), it does draw a line so as to avoid the admission of any antiquated custom as law in our court. The repugnancy test was applied successfully in the case of *Edet* v. *Essien*[28] to resolve the apparent internal conflict of laws. In that case, the plaintiff had paid the dowry for a woman and married her.

She later left him and married another man by whom she subsequently had two children. The plaintiff alleged that under the native law and custom, he was entitled to the custody of these children since his dowry had not been repaid to him. It was held that such a line of customary law was repugnant to natural justice, equity, and good conscience. To reflect the dynamic character of the customary law as it applies in Nigeria, it was therefore well stated that "A conduct that might be acceptable a hundred years ago may be heresy these days and vice versa.

The notion of public policy ought to reflect the change. That a local custom is contrary to public policy and repugnant to natural justice, equity, and good conscience necessarily involves a value judgment by the court. But this must objectively relate to contemporary mores, aspirations, expectations, and sensitivities of the people of this country

27 Evidence Act, *supra*

28 (1932) 11, Nigeria Law Report, 47

and to consensus values in the civilized international community which we share....Full cognizance ought to be taken of the current social conditions, experiences and perceptions of the people. After all, the custom is not static,"[29] in the same vein, *Ehrenzweig* also reasserts: "If a choice of law rule is found to refer to a foreign law which is considered as less capable of doing justice than the law of the forum, the court may reject the foreign law as violating the forums' public policy."[30]

While there may be more to be said in respect of the preceding point, I intend to direct my attention to principles the courts have applied to resolve issues of internal conflict of law.

Regarding the issues of personal law of litigants, especially as it connects to succession rights, courts are not definitive as to the law that must be applied – *lex domicile*- (which is the law of the person's domicile) or personal customary law of the person. Sometimes the customary law of inheritance may conflict with the English law where the deceased is married under statutory law; what then determines which choice of law to be applied? An illustration may help to clarify the conundrum.

For instance, which law of succession, English or Customary law, would govern the estate of an Ibo Native, for example, who went through a Christian form of marriage and died intestate? To decide that it is English law of succession without proper consideration of the customary practices totally castigates the application of Customary Law.

The jurisprudence among Nigerian courts reveals a flurry of different approaches, and this leads one to conclude that the applicable law depends on the facts and circumstances of each case. In another illustration, the courts may be called to decide the choice of law to be applied where a woman is married under statutory law to two men successively, and it happens that she died intestate, being survived by her last husband and children from both marriages. In her culture, that is her domicile of origin,

> Conflict of Laws may arise if the Customary law posits that a husband's succession rights to the estate of his wife are inferior to that of

[29] Nwabueze Nnamdi, Op. cit

[30] Ehrenzweig Albert, *Op Cit.* p. 79

her children, while under English law, his succession rights are superior to that of the children. Similarly, under Customary law, a wife has no succession rights beyond that of the actual abode in her late husband's house, sometimes even qualified if she has a male child for the deceased, but under English law, the wife has well-defined rights of succession. It is instructive to assert that no well-informed decision can be made without looking at all the circumstances of the case.

The court would not ignore the application of the English law, nor would it cast aside the customary law that apparently differs from the applicable English law or any Customary law applicable to the parties in the case. The Court of Appeal was called to decide on the inheritance by a surviving spouse in the case of *Motoh* v. *Motoh*. Aboki, JCA stated categorically thus, "the position of the law is that where a man who marries under the statute dies intestate, his estate is only inheritable by the wife legally married under the Marriage Ordinance, or Marriage Act."[31]

Following the principle adopted in the case of *Salubi* v. *Nwariaku,*[32] Ezeonu opines that:

> The test to be adopted in determining the applicable law of Succession in each case is whether an intestate was married in accordance with the marriage Act or customary law. If the intestate married under customary law, his properties shall devolve in accordance with his native law and custom; if the intestate married under the Marriage Act, the relevant provisions of the applicable Administration and Succession Law shall apply.[33]

Sometimes in resolving internal conflict of laws, the court pays attention to the *lex loci* - which represents the law of the place where the infraction took place. For instance, in action in Tort, the applicable law is usually the law of the place where the negligence occurred. The law of Domicile of the parties cannot be called into question; thus, none of the parties can make a claim under any other law but the '*lex loci*.'

The *lex situs* is another principle that is sometimes given due consideration in resolving internal conflicts of laws. *Lex situs* is simply

---

[31] (2011) 42 W.R.N, Per Aboki JCA

[32] (1997) 5 NWLR

[33] Ezeonu Obumneme, *Probate Practice In Nigeria, A Practical Approach*, (Enugu: Snaap Press Ltd), 2012, p.55

the law that is applicable in the place where the subject matter- '*the res*' of the litigation is located, for example, in a case of sale of real property, where the property being sold is located.

Thus where the personal laws of the persons involved in the transaction conflict, the *lex situs* is applied to resolve the conflict unless, in the given case, the parties agree to have the Customary law of one of the parties apply or to suspend the application of Customary law and have English law become the norm for regulating the transaction. In such cases, the courts would readily resolve the incidence of conflict of laws following the express agreement of the parties to suspend the application of a given customary or personal law regime, be it Islamic or Christian personal law.

Personal law covers most matters of status, which may vary from culture to culture. It, therefore, regards all questions concerning marriage, conjugal rights, divorce, the capacity of a person's right to succession, etc. Domicile has traditionally been regarded as the principal determinant of personal law. Domicile is understood as the correlation between a person and a particular territory. Sometimes, the residence is often confused with domicile.

To highlight the difference between residence and domicile, Lord Westbury, in the case of *Bell* v. *Kennedy* delineated:

> Residence and domicile are two perfectly distinct things. It is necessary in the determination of the law that the idea of domicile should exist and that the fact of domicile should be ascertained in order to determine which of the two municipal laws may be invoked for the purpose of regulating the rights of the parties...Domicile is an idea of law. It is a relation that the law makes between an individual and a particular locality or country.[34]

The individual first acquires a domicile of birth, and that domicile does not change until an actual change is made, at which time the personal status of another domicile is acquired. In furtherance, Lord Westbury clarified that "the domicile of origin adheres until a new

[34] (L.R) 1 Sc. & Div. 307

domicile is acquired."[35] A new domicile could be acquired by choice or intention, at which point it alters the personal law of the individual. A noted principle of domicile is that no one can simultaneously have more than one operative domicile.

The justification for that is that domiciles being the sole determinant of the personal law, must by its nature be exclusive; otherwise, a further determinant is needed. This is why in most cases, nationality cannot be taken as the sole determinant of personal law, as some people have dual nationality. In simple language, domicile means someone's permanent home.

A person is said to have a home in a place where he resides permanently without any intention of moving. However, a person does not cease to have his permanent home in a country merely because he is temporarily residing elsewhere. Domicile is, therefore, to be understood as a place of habitual residence. In the 'Conflict of Law' jurisprudence, domicile is often used as a prerequisite for the assumption of jurisdiction by the forum or for recognition and assumption of a foreign court's jurisdiction. Domicile, therefore, connects a person with a legal system, the purpose of which is to regulate his legal relationships.

Law distinguished three types of domicile, namely: domicile of origin, domicile of choice, and domicile of dependency. The domicile of origin is the form of domicile imposed on every person at the moment of birth. This form of domicile attaches to a person until he acquires another domicile. It may be removed but never destroyed since the possibility of its being revived is real. In the case of domicile of dependency, it can only be acquired by children and mentally ill persons.

The next form of domicile is domicile by choice. In *Udny* v. *Udny*, Lord Westbury described domicile of choice as "... a conclusion or inference which the law derives from the fact of a man fixing voluntarily his sole or chief residence in a particular place with the intention of continuing to reside there for an unlimited time."[36] Two elements are

[35] Ibid.

[36] (1869) LR 1 Sc & Div 441

therefore considered essential for the acquisition of this domicile, namely the *animus manendi* (the intention to remain) and the *factum* (the very fact of residence).

There cannot be a good discussion of Internal Conflict of Laws in Nigeria without highlighting how the doctrine of Domicile impacts on it in modern-day pluralistic Nigerian society. In a federation like Nigeria, a citizen must be domiciled in a particular part of the territory of Nigeria, and it is the characterization of a person's domicile that forms the basis for the ascertainment of his personal law for the purposes of conflict of law discourse.

For instance, where the domicile of an accused is Kano, and an offence is committed in Kano, the northern city of Nigeria, where the penal code applies, even though the person happens to have a domicile of origin in Enugu, a southern city of Nigeria, where the criminal code is applicable, the court in Kano would for the purpose of the conflict of laws based on the principle of Domicile apply the penal code for the determination of the guilt of accused.

Sometimes there are other factors that determine the designation of domicile in Nigeria. An example of this is that in an ethnic society like Nigeria, membership to an ethnic group like an Ibo or Yoruba ethnic group attaches to a person in such a way that it determines the person's personal law and, in fact, follows the person wherever he or she goes irrespective of her domicile.

Similarly, membership to a particular religion like Islam attaches to the person and characterizes his or her personal law. It has therefore become increasingly difficult for courts to resolve cases where the dynamics of the composite structure of Nigeria, with the peculiar application of the systems of customary law and the insufficiency of the concepts of domicile as touchstones of personal law are present at the same time. Such a situation is, for example, when an Ibo man establishes a permanent home in Lagos and acquires a domicile of choice there, he becomes affixed with the laws of Lagos state.

However, since he is not Yoruba by birth, he is not subject to Yoruba customary law, which is part of the legal system of Lagos state.

He would only be subject to the laws enacted by the Lagos state legislature and Federal enactments applicable in Lagos state.

One may, however, raise a question as to whether the Ibo Customary law being his personal law, would still attach to regulate some of his capacities and the validity of his actions? Where the Ibo Customary law of inheritance conflicts with the Lagos state law of succession, what likely direction would the courts follow to resolve the conflict, given that the two legal systems attach to the same person, one on the basis of Domicile by choice, and the other on the basis of membership to the relevant ethnic group?

Although there are no cases on all fours to attend to the questions raised above, the closest jurisprudence we can find is in the case of *Olowu* v. *Olowu.*[37] In that case, the appellant were the children of one Adeyinka Ayinde Olowu, whose intestate estate was the subject matter of the action. The deceased was a Yoruba man of Ijesha extraction. He lived from childhood to his death in Benin City and married Benin women, and acquired substantial immovable property in Benin City. During his life, he applied to naturalize in Benin to the Oba, and it was granted.

His entire estate was distributed in accordance with Benin Customary law of succession. The appellants were dissatisfied and brought an action contending that Yoruba customary law was applicable since their father was of Yoruba origin. The respondents, some of his children, argued otherwise and maintained that Benin customary law was applicable because their father was a naturalized Benin man. Both the High Court and the Court of Appeal held for the respondents.

On appeal to the Supreme Court, the judgment of the lower court was upheld, and the appeal was struck out. It needs to be stated that upon reflection on the case, it is not as if the court was not minded to consider the application of the Yoruba customary law of succession, but because the onus of proving that their father who had naturalized as a Benin but had not abandoned his Yoruba personal law and

[37] (1985) 3 NWLR 378

consequently the law of succession was placed on the appellants and unfortunately they failed to discharge that burden.

One appreciates in the instant case the issues arising from an internal conflict of laws in Nigeria that attaches to the understanding of domicile and the attendant doctrine of personal law. There is, therefore, no hard law to guide the courts in making a decision in situations of similar internal conflict of law. Every case has its own facts and circumstances, and the court must be minded to make a decision applying the basic principles we have outlined but not without considering the peculiar circumstances of each case.

CONCLUSION

In this essay, we have discussed some elements of Conflict of Laws in general and, subsequently, the internal conflict of Law in Nigeria. We have basically established that the composite structure of Nigeria, its peculiar legal history, its federal system, and peculiar application of customary law at various levels of state and ethnic affiliations made possible the unhindered problem of internal conflict almost a daily occurrence.

However, we must admit that the jurisprudence on the internal conflict of laws in Nigeria is not as copious as one would have expected it. Perhaps part of the problem is that many Customary or local communities where these internal conflicts arise or want to arise are not litigious communities, hence the lack of many decided cases attempting to resolve issues of internal conflict of law. It can also be argued that our courts, in many instances, have chosen to avoid any analysis around that area of law, given the sensitive nature of inters ethnic, inter-religious, and inter-cultural discourse in the Nigeria polity.

Thus, it is enough to admit that as the polity struggles with inter-cultural and inter-religious, and inter-ethnic crises, it is not prudent to arouse another conflict or struggle on the legal front. A typical case in point is the issue of the constitutionality of the sharia legal system as enacted in many Northern states of Nigeria, for which the Supreme Court has refused to make a pronouncement on.

The last point that we must add is that our courts, the state legislature, and the Federal House of Assembly must wake up to their civic duties to help the development of this area of law which is as important to the country, Nigeria as its unity. It must not be left to the whims and caprices of the sitting judges alone; if we do, we are forestalling uncertainty in our legal system.

Chapter 5

NATURE OF CUSTOMARY LAW IN NIGERIA

Chris Chijioke Ohuruogu* & Chukwudumebi Okoye**

INTRODUCTION

It is established that every society, primitive or civilized, is governed by a body of rules which members regard as the standard of behaviour. The nature and structure of these rules are often rooted in the history and culture of the people concerned. Prior to the advent of colonialism, the geographical area now known as Nigeria was made up of several settlements (societies), each having its own distinct identity, administrative techniques, method of governance, and indigenous (customary) laws, by which they regulated their affairs.

Those laws consisted of customs accepted by members of the communities and enforced by them; those laws were derived from customs[1] being the embodiment of those principles which commend themselves to the natural conscience as principles of truth, justice, and public utility. The conscience is the true base of customs; the origin of custom lies in the invisible, internally assimilated, and deeply seated beliefs that propel man to act in the way he does.[2]

The true basis of customary law has its existence, its reality, in the common consciousness of the people. This existence is an invisible

* Chris Chijioke Ohuruogu is a Professor of Law at the College of Law, Afe Babalola university,Ado-Ekiti.

** Chukwudumebi Okoye,Legal Practitioner and formely Lecturer in Law at Benson Idahosa University Benin city

[1] Customs, according to New Webster's Dictionary, is a generally accepted practice or habit. It can be classified into two: (a) abstract and (b) real custom.

[2] Salmond J: On Jurisprudence, 11th edn. cited in Aboki, Y "Are some Nigerian Customary Law Really Repugnant" (1991) 9-10 *Ahmadu Bello University Law Journal*, P. 2

3. Salmond, ibid.

thing. By what means can we recognize it? We do so when it reveals itself in an external act when it steps forth in usage, manners, and custom.[3]

With the advent of British colonial rule, the applicability of customary Law was subjected to certain "tests of validity" determined and implemented by the English judges, who considered that some of the customs that formed the basis of the customary laws were "barbaric" and "unfit for civility." Some were regarded as retrogressive, while others were considered "inhumane" and "degrading to human dignity."

This chapter examines the general nature of customary laws and the validity tests, the application of the tests, and the effect on the consciousness and convictions of the people. It will be divided into six sections, including the introduction, which is Section I; section II will examine the general nature of customary laws and their attributes; Section III will examine the validity and application of customary laws in Nigerian Courts with particular reference to the repugnancy doctrine, the public policy test, and the incompatibility test; Section IV will deal with the influence of Natural Law theories in the application of the validity tests, and Section V will consider issues of proof of a valid customary law in the law courts and Enforcement while Section VI is the conclusion.

THE GENERAL NATURE OF CUSTOMARY LAW AND ITS ATTRIBUTES

A. Customary Law: A Distinction between Bare Customs and Customary Law

T. O. Elias in *Kharie Zaidan* v. *Fatima Khalil Mohssen* [4] described customary law as:

---

[4] 1973) 1 SC. This is almost in all fours with the definition contained in section 2 of the customary courts law of the former Eastern region which provides that customary law is "...A rule or body of rules regulating rights and imposing correlative duties being a rule or body of rules which obtain and is fortified by established usage and which is appropriate and applicable to any particular matter, dispute issue or question."

> A rule or body of rules regulating rights and imposing correlative duties is a rule or the body of rules not enacted by the legislature but fortified by established usage and which are appropriate and applicable to any particular cause, action, suit, matter, or dispute.

It is the system of law not being a law enacted by any competent legislature in Nigeria, but which is enforceable and binding within Nigeria as between the parties subject to its sway.

This definition was adopted in *Joseph Ohai* v. *Samuel Akpoemonye Ler.*[5]

The Evidence Act[6] defined custom as a rule which in a particular district has from long usage obtained the force of law.

There is some form of consensus among jurists[7] that customs become law by the common will of the people. However, not all forms of customary practices culminate into law or customary law. For example, customs such as annual "yam eating" festivals, annual or seasonal masquerade festivals, and others, vividly portray the non-law quality of these customs; thus, with regards to masquerade festivals, if a man invites the public to the celebration of a masquerade and fails to fulfil his obligation on the appointed day, no one can coerce him to do so, and there is no sanction for his failure; also whereas it is customary among the Igbo to offer kola nut to visitors and to present kola nut at occasions and ceremonies, failure or omission to do so, does not attract punitive actions.

What, then, is it that distinguishes customary law from bare customs? The term "law" has been defined by several jurists from different points of view:[8] one major distinctive element of law from the definition proffered by jurists is that it has a coercive order, and it is binding.[9] Customary laws stem from practices that have the force of law (coercion) and are, therefore, binding and enforced. This is

---

[5] (2011) S.C.161, Per Uthman JSC. ...any system of Law not being the common law and not being a law enacted by any competent legislature in Nigeria but which is enforceable and binding within Nigeria as between the parties subject to its sway.

[6] 2011,Section 258(1)-the interpretation section

[7] Falc N, Puchla J.F. Gusta Hugo cited in Okogeri, *Fundamental Issues in the Philosophy of Law* (Benin: Ashat Publishers; 2005)

[8] Such as the positive view, historical view, realistic view etc.

[9] Adaramola F., *Basic Jurisprudence* (Lagos: Mayce Publishing Company Ltd; 2002) 107

distinguishable from bare customs, which do not have the force of law.[10]

A customary practice does not enjoy the status or force of law unless and until such practice fulfilled certain conditions: the practice must have endured a length of practice sufficient to constitute it a norm; it must additionally have been practiced continuously by the community in question; it must have been accorded the status of law, exerting obligations rather than an expression of socio-cultural habits; its content and ambit must be certain, and the practice must exhibit consistency with practices in the surrounding communities.

Variants of Customary Law in Nigeria

Customary laws in Nigeria are of two kinds:

1. Ethnic, indigenous, or non-Muslim customary law[11]
It must be appreciated that there is no single customary law in Nigeria though there may be noticeable resemblances; there are as many customary rules as there are tribal and indigenous communities. As observed by AEW Park[12]

> ...the use of the single term 'customary law' does not indicate that there is a single uniform set of customs. It is used rather as a blanket description covering the very many different systems. These systems are largely tribal in origin and usually operate only within the area occupied by the tribe...there may be local variations within such an area.

This observation was also echoed by Obilade that indigenous customary law is extremely varied; its diversity is a true reflection of the atomistic nature of the ethnocultural setting in Nigeria, with about 400 identifiable linguistic groupings and probably as many internal sub-ethnic micro-groups speaking divergent dialects.[13]

---

[10] Ibid.

[11] This operates within the different ethnic or ethno-cultural areas. Each system of such customary law applies to members of a particular ethnic group

[12] *The sources of Nigerian Law* (London: Sweet & Maxwell, 1964), page 65,cited in Ngwakwe, EC., *African Customary Law: Jurisprudence, Themes and Principles*(Abakaliki: Ave Maria Academic Publishers,2013) 104.

[13] Obilade,O. A., *The Nigerian Legal System* (Ibadan: Spectrum BooksLtd,1979)

This diversity and variance of customary laws is a major obstacle to a uniformity of customary law systems in each state and ethnic group; they also lead to the internal conflict of laws; Non-ethnic or non-indigenous or Islamic law[14]

Attributes (Characteristics) of Customary Law

Over the years, attempts have been made by scholars and judges to extract the various attributes of customary law. Thus it is generally acknowledged that customary law:

1. Reflect the generally accepted usages within the ethnic or sub-ethnic group where they operate. Customary law mirrors accepted usages.[15] It is the consent of the community that gives customary law its binding force.
2. As a consequence (direct result) of being mirrors of accepted usages, they are flexible,[16] evolutionary, and ever-changing, reflecting the changing social and economic conditions of the society wherein it operates.[17] This does not mean that it lacks precision or that its provisions are unclear. Rather it means that customary law responds to social developments; it is dynamic and capable of growth to accord with changes in time[18]. They usually operate according to the principles of expediency and adaptability to altered circumstances without entirely losing their character.[19]
3. Unlike other laws which are statutory, it is proper to say that customary law is unwritten, especially in its pristine pre-colonial

[14] These operate in certain parts of northern Nigeria as customary law where people adopted Islamic tenets as such. It is not indigenous law because it is received customary law introduced into the court as part of Islam.

[15] *Owonyin* v. *Omotosho* (1961) 1 ALL NLR 304,309; see also *Bello* v. *Gov. Kogi state* 1997 7 NWLR(Pt.521),496 CA; *Osolu* v. *Osolu* (1998) 9 NWLR (Pt.535),532 CA; *Okene* v. *Orianwo* (1998) 9 NWLR (Pt.566),408 CA. In *Agbai* v. *Okogbue* (1991) 7 NWLR (Pt.24) 391 the Supreme Court declared that "Customary laws were formulated from time immemorial. As our society advances, they are more removed from its pristine social ecology. They meet situations which were inconceivable at the time they took root."

[16] *Alfa* v. *Arepo* (1963) WNLR 95

[17] *Alfa* v. *Arepo* (1963 WNLR 95

[18] See: *Pam* v. *Gwom* (2000) 1 SC 56;*Ogolo* v. *Ogolo* (2003) 18 NWLR (Pt.852),494 SC

[19] *Lewis* v. *Bankole* (1908) 1 NLR 81 at 83

state.[20] However, a good number of them may now be found in various judicial decisions and pronouncements.

4. They evolve among the local community and are recognized as having the binding force of law on the particular members of that community;[21]this endogenous evolution of customary law is strengthened by the acceptance of the community concerned. Customary law is developed and accepted by the community themselves and not imposed upon them. This attribute of customary law 'finds a pedigree in the historical school of legal jurisprudence.'[22]

Islamic customary law, on the other hand, is a written law (*lex scriptum*) having its sources from the Holy Quran, the practices of the Prophet Mohammed, and the consensus of Islamic scholars and analogies from these sources. Arguments exist as to whether Islamic law is customary law properly so-called. Those who express reservation argue that it is not.[23] Among the reasons for the argument to exclude Islamic Law as customary law are the facts that it is basically a system of codes; also, it was not endogenously evolved.

APPLICABILITY AND ENFORCEMENT OF CUSTOMARY LAW: THE VALIDITY TESTS

Prior to the establishment of the modern legal system, customary law was the only law in the communal legal system, and it enjoyed respect. The communal courts acted on the basis of customary law and their sanctions which were backed by coercion, all derived from customs.[24] However, customary law today does not have the privilege of automatic enforcement in the modern court system, as was the case in the days when communal and village courts held sway.[25]

[20]Ngwakwe, E C., *African Customary Law: Jurisprudence, Themes and Principles* (Abakaliki: Ave Maria Academic Publishers,2013) 107

[21] *Eshugbayi Eleko* v. *Govt. of Nigeria* (1931) AC. 662 673

[22] Ngwakwe, E C.*supra* note 20 @116.

[23] See for example, Badaiki, A,D. *Development of Customary Law* (Lagos: Tiken Publishers,1997),p.12; the dictum of Bello, CJN in *Usman* v. *Umaru* (1992)7 NWLR (Pt.254)372@377

[24] Malemi, E, *The Nigerian Legal System* 3rd edn. (Ikeja: Princeton Publishing Co; 2009) 63

[25] Ibid.

Before a custom can be applied or enforced as customary law in our modern court system, the custom must satisfy or pass some validity test prescribed by statutes.[26]

The validity Tests for Customary Law in Nigeria

An applicable rule of customary law is not to be enforced by the courts unless it passes the tests called "validity tests." They are:

the Repugnancy test; the custom must not be repugnant to natural justice, equity, and good conscience;[27]

1. the Incompatibility test;[28] and
2. the Public Policy test.[29]

According to Adaramola,[30] the essence of these validity tests was not to abolish customary law but to ensure the dynamism, survival, preservation, and retention of the best customary laws for an emerging, modern, forward-looking and progressive Nigerian nation. The validity tests are thus viewed as necessities of modern times and enabled customary law to adapt and survive; this enabled society to preserve only customs which are considered just, humane and progressive and which held the community together, whilst customs that were selfish, discriminatory, objectionable and unjust were deservedly disallowed by the validity test and were not enforced.[31]

Lending support to the above view, Sir John Marshall, a director of the Royal Niger Company, had this to say:

> My own experience of the West Coast of Africa is that Government has, for the time, succeeded best with natives who have treated with consideration for their native laws, habits, and customs instead of ordering all these to be suppressed as nonsense and insisting on...submitting to the British Constitution and adopting our ideas of life and civilization. What I wish to say is that the natives of the Gold Coast and the West Coast of Africa have

[26] See the proviso to S. 18(3) Evidence Act, 2011.

[27] Proviso to S. 16(3) Evidence Act 2011; State High Court Law, e.g. S.26 High Court of Lagos State Law 2003 etc.

[28] Ibid.

[29] Ibid.

[30] *Supra* note 9.

[31] Malemi, E., *supra* note 24

> a system of laws and customs which it will be better to guide, modify and amend rather than destroy by ordinance or force.[32]

The relevance of the validity test was also enunciated in the case of *Agbai* v. *Okogbue*[33] thus:

> Customary laws were formulated from time immemorial. As our society advances, they are more removed from its pristine social ecology. They meet conditions that were inconceivable at the time they took root. The doctrine... affords the courts the opportunity of fine-tuning customary laws to meet changed social conditions where necessary, especially as there is no forum for repealing or amending customary laws. When, however, customary laws are confronted by a novel situation, the courts have to consider the applicability under the existing social environment.
>
> The validity test, therefore, affords the court the opportunity of fine-tuning customary laws to meet changing social conditions. It can be argued that the Colonialists did not come to destroy customary law but to make sure that what was fair, just, and good were retained, whilst customs that were retrogressive were abolished.[34]

The Repugnancy Test

The repugnancy test requires that a customer can only be applicable if it is *not contrary to Natural Justice, Equity, and Good Conscience*. This was succinctly expounded in *Ojiogu* v. *Ojiogu* (per Chukwuma-Eneh JSC).[35] The court held that the repugnancy principle means that there are provisions which set down tests to which customary law must be subjected before it is observed and even enforced by the courts.

There are specific enactments containing the repugnancy clause. They demonstrate the criteria for enforcing native law and custom. Currently, this principle is clearly provided for in the proviso to section 18(3) of the Evidence Act. The subsection has even widened the criteria by adding that the native law and custom must also not be against public policy.

---

32 Cited by Pats-Acholunu, JCA "The Relevance of Customary Law in the Nigerian Legal System" (1988) *The LASU Jurist*, vol. 1 No. 7 p. 38

33 (1991)) 9 NWLR (pt. 368) p. 301

34 For example which required the killing of twins supra note 210

35 (2010) 3-5 SC. (pt11)

Adaramola noted that the phrase "natural justice, equity, and good conscience" is a term used to note a single ideal, the ideal of civilized conduct[36] or reasonable behaviour to which rules of customary law must conform to in order to be accepted as valid by the courts.

Repugnancy means "contrary to" or "contradictory to"; "inconsistent" or "incompatible with"; "distasteful" or "objectionable to"[37] ideal civilized conduct. The question then is, 'what is the standard of an ideal civilized conduct?' Whose conscience is in reference? Is it those of lawyers and judges trained in English law? Is it the conscience of those in the communities where the practice is accepted as a way of life and who are indifferent to and unperturbed by the court's declaration?

From cases decided in courts presided by English Judges, it seems that the conscience of the British men was the determinant factor in administering the repugnancy clause. One cannot but question the morality of this approach. For instance, in *Lewis* v. *Bankole*,[38] Osborn C.J held that because a customer did not form part of the English doctrines of equity.[39] It was invalid by virtue of the repugnancy test.[40] However, from a plethora of decided cases, it is obvious that in the application of the repugnancy test, recourse is not to English laws but to natural law and to changing social conditions.

The repugnancy test has been applied to various issues of customary law, such as matters involving widows' inheritance[41] woman to woman marriages: marriage to a dead person,[42] paternity and custody of children;[43] Adultery;[44] inheritance and succession;[45]

[36] See the *locus classicus* of *Eshugbayi Eleko* v. *Officer Administering The Government of Nigeria* (1931) A.C. 662 at p. 673

[37] Ejinkeonye O "A woman who is a husband and father, An essay in customary law" Faculty of law lecture series No.5 (2005) 30

[38] (1908) I NLR 81 at pp.99-102. See also *Dawodu* v. *Danmole* (1958) 3 F.Sc. 46;

[39] The trial judge considered the clause as there separate units' namely (a) repugnant to natural justice (b) repugnant to equity (c) repugnant to good conscience. But the courts usually considered the clause as a whole

[40] However, the full court of the Supreme Court, in 1909, rejected the view

[41] *Okonkwo* v. *Okagbue* (1994) 9 NWLR (pt 368) p. 301

[42] *Chawere* v. *Aiheru* v. *Ejo* (1935) 12 NLR 4

[43] *Chawere* v. *Aihenu & Anor* (1935) 12 NLR 4

[44] *Cole* v. *Cole* (1998) 1 NLR 15; *Re Effiong Okon Ata* (1930) NLR 65 *Nzekwu* v. *Nzekwu* (1989) 2 NWLR (pt 104) p. 373 SC. *Agidibi* v. *Agidibi* (1992) 2 NWLR (pt 221), p.89 SC

[45] *Iwuchukwu* v. *Anyanwu* (1993) 8 NWLR (pt 311) p. 307

customary tenancy;[46] alienation of family, land;[47] customary tort of disgrace;[48] and so forth. Whilst some customs passed the repugnancy test, others actually did not. In *Eshugbayi Eleko* v. *The Officer Administering the Government of Nigeria*, the Court illuminated the attitude of courts when faced with issues of customary law as follows: "The court cannot itself transform a barbarous custom into a milder one if it still stands in its barbarous character it must be rejected as repugnant to natural justice equity and good conscience."[49]

In *Guri* v. *Hadejia Native Authority*,[50] a rule of Maliki law was declared null and void because it prohibited an accused person who is standing trial for highway robbery from defending himself. In *Edet* v. *Essien,*[51] the plaintiff claimed title to the custody of three children born to a native man because the bride price he had paid on the woman had not been refunded to him. The court held that this customary law was repugnant to natural justice, equity, and a good conscience, and it would not be enforced. In *Meribe* v. *Egwu*,[52] the Supreme Court held that a customary law that permitted the marriage of one woman by another woman was repugnant to natural justice, equity, and good conscience. However, in *Agidigbi* v. *Agidigbi*,[53] the Supreme Court reaffirmed that the Bini customary rule of inheritance which allows the eldest son to exclusively inherit the deceased father's personal living house, is not repugnant to natural justice equity and good conscience. In *Nzekwu* v. *Nzekwu*,[54] a custom which permitted that the head of a deceased husband's family could single-handedly alienate the deceased's property while his wife was alive was held uncivilized and therefore repugnant to natural justice, equity, and good conscience.

In summarizing the thoughts of judges with respect to the application of the repugnancy doctrine, Niki Tobi JCA, as he then was

---

46 *Odusoga* v. *Ricketts* (1997) 7 NWLR (pt. 511), P.L.S.C.

47 *Ugboko* v. *Ani Kaonye* (1971) 1 UILR. 8

48 *Agbai* v. *Okogbue* (1991) 7 NWLR (pt 204), p.391 at 417

49 (1931) AC 662

50 (1959) 4 FSC 44

51 (1932) 11 MLR 47

52 *Meribe* v. *Egwu* (1978) 3 SC 23

53 (1992) 2 MLLR (pt. 221) p. 98 SC. *Ogiamen* v. *Ogiamen* (1967) NMLR 245 (1989) 2 NMLR 245

54 (1989) 2 NWLR (pt. 104), p. 323. *Lawal-Osula* v. *Lawal-Osula* (1993) 3 NWLR (pt. 274), p.158

stated thus: "We need not travel all the way to Beijing to know that some of our customs are not consistent with our civilized world in which we all live today, including the appellant."[55] Frowning at the custom that discriminates against the female gender, he asserted thus:

> It is the monopoly of God to determine the sex of a baby and not the parents. Although the scientific world disagrees with this divine truth, I believe that God, the Creator of human beings, is also the final authority of who should be male and female. Accordingly, for a custom or customary law to discriminate against particular sex is, to say the least, an affront on the Almighty God Himself. Let nobody do such a thing on my part. I have no difficulty in holding that the custom is repugnant to natural notice, equity, and good conscience.[56]

Reiterating the above, the court, in the case of *Motoh* v. *Motoh*,[57] held that native law and custom of Umuanagu Awka which discriminates against female children of the same parents and favors the male children who inherit all the estate of their father to the exclusion of their female siblings was repugnant to natural notice, equity and good conscience.

In conclusion, it is important to note from the decision in *Rufai* v. *Igbirra Native Authority*[58] that a rule of customary law is not necessarily repugnant just because it deprived a litigant a right that he/she would have had under English common law.

The Incompatibility Test

For a set of customary laws to be enforceable, it must not be incongruous or incompatible either directly or by implication with any Nigerian enactment or Law "for the time being in force."[59] It is required that a rule of customary law should not clash with "written laws," which include all ordinances, proclamations, and rules of Courts

---

[55] *Mojekwu* v. *Mojekwu (*1997) 7 NWLR (pt. 512) p. 283
[56] Ibid. *at* P.283-305. See also *Ukeje* v. *Ukeje* (2001)
[57] (2010) 9 NWLR (part 1198) p.5
[58] [1957] NRNWLR 178
[59] S. 26(1) High Court of Lagos State; S. 24 (1) High Court of Northern States

made by any person or body having authority under any statutory or other enactments to make the same; the Constitution,[60]etc.

The Courts have applied this test differently from case to case based on the facts of each case. In *Mojekwu* v. *Mojekwu*,[61] a rule of customary law that precludes daughters from inheriting their father's property was held repugnant to natural justice, equity, and good conscience *and also null and void for being incompatible and contrary to the fundamental right to freedom from discrimination guaranteed in the Nigerian Constitution*. In this case, the provisions of the Constitution implicitly abolished the discriminatory rule of customary law on inheritance. Where a customary law is expressly or impliedly abolished or modified by statute, it becomes automatically incompatible with that statute wholly or to the extent of that modification.

Apart from the 1999 Constitution (as amended in 2011), which implicitly abolished all discriminatory practices and practices against human dignity,[62] other laws abound that expressly abolished well-practiced customs, such as the Abolition of Osu System Law of Eastern Region 1956, Abolition of Child Marriage Law 1993, Slavery Abolition Ordinance (No. 35) of 1916, etc. A clear case of express abolition of customary law practice is the *Re Effiong Okoh Ata*.[63] In that case, a custom that granted the head of a house the right to administer the personal estates of a former slave who died intestate was declared incompatible with the Slavery Abolition Ordinance No. 35 of 1916. It was also declared to be contrary to natural justice, equity, and good conscience.

Similarly, in *Nwachukwu* v. *Nnoremde*,[64] the issue was the *Osu Caste* System practiced in the Eastern region. The Osu Caste system regards certain persons as outcasts, slaves, or descendants of slaves and, as such, are denied certain rights that should ordinarily accrue to them.

---

[60] However, the list excludes any act of the U.K. Parliament extending either expressly or by implication to Nigeria and also orders of the Queen-in-council, Royal Charters or royal letters, Patent which are not "written law: within the meaning of the provisions of the various laws. See also *Re Adadevoh* (1951) 2 WACA 304, 310.

[61] (1997) 7 NWLR pt. 512 p. 282 CA

[62] See chapter IV of the 1999 Constitution (as amended, 2011); also s 315 of the 1999 Constitution.

[63] (1930) 10 NLR 65

[64] (1957), 1 ERLR. 50

Declaring the system incompatible with the Abolition of Osu Caste Law of Eastern Region 1956, Mbanefo J (as he then was) stated that:

> the aim of the Ordinance was to abolish all forms of social and legal disabilities attached to the Osu Caste system as obtained in some parts of the region. It makes it an offence to deny a person the right due him because of the system.[65]

Generally, in construing the term "any law for the time being in force," the courts have been divergent: In *Adesuboka* v. *Yinusa*,[66] the court construed the term "any law for the time being in force" to include English Laws – Wills Act of 1837, an English Statute of General Application which applied in Nigeria.[67]

However, in *Rotibi* v. *Savage*,[68] it was held that the phrase "any law for the time being in force meant only local statutes, that is, Nigerian Statutes. From this case, it can be argued that it is not the intent of the lawmakers in stipulating the validity test to replace customary law with English laws. The Nigerian legal system being an integrated system of multiple systems of laws made up of customary laws, statutes, and foreign systems of laws.[69]

Obilade rightly submitted thus: "Customary law is so inconsistent with English law that prescribing any reference to English law would result in a virtual abolition of customary law."[70] Therefore, customs which are incompatible with Nigerian statutes are regarded as unenforceable. Such customs are not difficult to recognize. They include such that involves slavery; discrimination, treating others as outcasts or less human, customs that lead to a breach of the peace, etc.

The question of which Statute or Law should govern a given situation is a question of fact to be gathered from the circumstances of the case.

---

65 Ibid.

66 (1971) All NLR 227

67 See also *Re Adadevoh* (1951) 13 WACA 304 which declared that "any law" includes English statutes of general application.

68 (1944) 17 NLR 77

69 Malemi, *supra* note 24

70 Obilade, *supra* note 13.

The Public Policy Test

Section 18(3) of the Evidence Act states thus: "...In a case of any custom relied upon in any judicial proceedings it shall not be enforced if it is contrary to public policy..."

The term "public policy" defies precise definition. Malemi defines it as public welfare, public good, and public interest. It means the security and welfare of the individual and the state in general[71]. Public policy is the decisions, laws, programs, and actions of governments usually expressed in plans, pronouncements, policies, manifestos, programs, actions and projects of government, and, most importantly, the constitution of the country.

The Preamble of the 1999 Constitution declares some of the public policies of the government of Nigeria thus: "…promoting the good government and welfare of all persons in the country on the principles of freedom, equality and justice and…consolidating the unity of our people…"

There are very few reported cases in which reference has been made to public policy in relation to customary law.[72]

In *Helen Odigie* v. *Iyere Aika,*[73] a custom of woman-to-woman marriage was held to be odious, outrageous, and contrary to public policy. The practice will not promote the security and welfare of the parties involved nor that of society. In this case, a woman had married a young girl to bear children for her. The learned trial judge held that the customary practice was contrary to public policy.

The learned trial judge stated that:

> It is an odious custom to permit a woman to marry a woman. It is equally atrocious and against public policy to deprive unwilling biological parents for any reason of their child and vest the same on childless parents or childless man or woman as if the child was a chattel. This ugly custom is distinguishable from the system of child adoption, which primarily is for the welfare of the child.

---

[71] Section 14 (2) (b) of the 1999 Constitution (as amended 2011).

[72] However, see *Re Adadevoh* (1951) 13 WACA. 304; *Alake* v. *Pratt* (1955) 15 WACA.20.

[73] Suit no.4/24A/29,unreported Judgement of the Ubiaja High Court of the former Bendel state of Nigeria presided over by Ohiwerei J and delivered on the 23rd of March 1982; cited in *Nigerian Bulletin of Contemporary Law,* (1985) p.5

In *Okonkwo* v. *Okagbue*,[74] an alleged custom whereby a woman married a dead man nominally in order to bring forth children for him in his name was held to be contrary to public policy. In *Re Adadevoh*,[75] the Yoruba customary law states that the acceptance of paternity of a child born outside wedlock by a man during his lifetime conferred legitimacy on the child and entitles him to share in his estate with the children born to the man in a marriage contracted under the Marriage Act.

The West African Court of Appeal, refusing to uphold the custom, held that it was contrary to the public party to recognize a rule that would encourage sexual promiscuity and pervert society.

Legal Basis for the Validity Test for Customary Law

Section 315 of the 1999 Constitution (as amended 2011) requires that as existing law, customary law should conform to its provision. Thus, the Constitution provides for the continued existence of customary law provided it is not at variance with other provisions of the Constitution (especially the Fundamental Human Rights guaranteed in chapter 4).

Other statutes that validate the continued enforcement of customary law, subject to the requirements of the validity tests, include:

1. Supreme Court Ordinance (No. 4), 1876; S. 19 (No. 6), 1900; S. 13. (No. 6), 1914; S. 20, and No. 23 of 1943; S. 17; now Supreme Court Act;[76]
2. Native Courts Ordinance No. 9, 1990, and the Native Courts Ordinance 1914 and 1948;
3. Court of Appeal Act;
4. High Court Laws of the states;
5. Customary Courts Laws of the relevant states;[77]
6. Area Court Laws of the relevant states;
7. Evidence Act 2011 and Evidence laws of the states;
8. Interpretation Act and laws, among other laws, etc.

---

[74] (1994) 9 NWLR pt. 368, p. 304
[75] (1951) 13 WACA 304
[76] Cap S15, LFN 2004
[77] See for instance S. 20 Customary Court Law, Lagos State 2003

The proviso to Section 18(3) of the Evidence Act and Section 26 of the High Court of Lagos State, respectively, put the validity test succinctly as follows:

> In any judicial proceeding where any custom relies upon it shall not be enforced as law if it is contrary to public policy or is not in accordance with natural justice, equity, and good conscience.[78]

> Section 26 of the High Court of Lagos provides:

> The High Court shall observe and enforce the observance of customary law, which is applicable and is not repugnant to natural justice equity and good conscience nor incompatibility either directly or by necessary implication with any law for the time being in force.[79]

We have noted earlier that the application of customary law is subject to three tests: repugnancy, incompatibility, and public policy test. It is noteworthy that these tests are not applied separately but are applied jointly in the determination of the cases that are before the court.

THE INFLUENCE OF NATURAL LAW THEORIES IN THE APPLICATION OF THE VALIDITY TEST

Natural law theorists[80] believe that there is law, not written, but born within us, which we have not learned or received by tradition or read but which we sucked in and imbibed from nature itself, which we were not trained in, but which is ingrained in us.

It is immutable, eternal, undying, absolute, and universal; the same exists in all societies and often to the understanding of everyone in the society through the reasoning faculty.[81] It is the measure of true law and, indeed, customary laws. Any rule (customary) which is not in

[78] Provision to section 18(3) Evidence Act 2011.
[79] Section 26 of the High Court of Lagos State
[80] Hugo Grotius (1583-1645), Cicero (106-43BC) Thomas Aquinas, etc.
[81] Okogeri G.O., *Fundamental Issues in the Philosophy of Law.* 2nd Ed (Benin: Ashart Publishers: 2005) 86

conformity with the precepts of natural law is no longer a law but a perversion of the law. Natural Law refers to a normative system of law which is eternal and outside humanity. It is deemed to lay down general principles of behaviour for the guidance of the human race.

The Discovery of the Values and Precepts of Natural Law

The truths of natural law, according to Marcus Aurelius,[82] are ascertainable by man through the exercise of the reason which he is by nature endowed. To discover the content or principles of natural law, man must be observant, sober, and reflective. In this regard, he stated thus:

> We do not find that the heaven opens and a hand comes through clouds, passing down to mankind, a table of stone on when the truths of natural law are inscribed even when it was done in the old, he still went ahead to inscribe it in the hearts of men, in their conscience, if the power of thoughts is universal among mankind, so likewise the possession of reason, making us rational creatures. It follows, therefore, that this reason speaks no less universally to us all with its "thou shall" or "thou shall not." So then there is a world law, which in the term, means that we are all fellow citizens and share common citizenship and that the world is a single city.

Noteworthy in this theory is the assertion that the precepts or values of natural law are ingrained in us (our conscience) and are deducible when a man is sober and reflective.

However, several scholars[83] have questioned the claim of the absolutism of values based on our common citizenry. To them, values vary from place to place, age to age, and generation to generation according to societal perceptions.

They opined that the claim to absolutism and universality of values was a scheme used to keep Africans perpetually mentally enslaved. It was an attempt to impose their ideas and moral conviction as eternal, ultimate, and absolute truth. The basis of their argument is that although natural law is eternal, God ordained, its transmission from God and its receipts by a human being is ultimately reduced to a

[82] Meditations Book 4:4

[83] Okogeri, *supra* note 80

process of either mental or sensual experience which is influenced by the socio-economic conditions of a place. These influences, therefore, according to Okogeri,[84] defy any claim to absolute and universal values.

Nevertheless, whatever the criticisms are, it is agreed that natural law, which is the law of God (eternal), is ingrained in all humans, and its principles are known intuitively. For example, the principles of preserving life, to live with others in society without discrimination, to love your neighbour as yourself, the preservation of the dignity of all human beings, both male and female, are all well-settled principles of Natural law and are adopted in the Constitutions of many nations of the world and also recognized internationally as fundamental human rights.[85]

It is no gain-saying the fact that some of our customary practices are in opposition to these eternal principles, for instance, inheritance and succession under customary laws[86] which discriminates against widows and female children; the *Osu* caste system in eastern Nigeria[87] a system whereby a person dedicated to a god is seen as a thing set apart, a taboo forever and his children after him. He could neither marry nor be married by the freeborn. He was, in fact, an outcast living in a special area of the village close to the great shrine. An Osu could not attend an assembly of the free-born, and they, in turn, could not shelter under his roof and a host of other obnoxious practices.

From the *ratio decidendi* of courts, the enforcement of customary law was subject to general principles of natural law and not English law. The factor that has always guided their approach was whether the custom relied upon by parties was for the good of the given Nigerian society; whether it would advance the interest of the Nigerian society or not; whether it was unjust, oppressive, and discriminatory, or otherwise a step in retrogression? All of these principles were general principles of

[84] Ibid.

[85] Universal Declaration of Human Rights (1948), International Covenant on Civil and Political Rights (1966); International Covenant on Economic, Social and Cultural Rights (1966).

[86] *Akunibi* v. *Grace Akunibi* (1997) 2 NWLR (pt. 486) at 159

[87] Achebe C. "Things Fall Apart" in Nigerian Democratisation and Culture, Socio-political and Civil Right Implicationshttp://www.afbis.com accessed 27/7/12.

natural law and not English law and were the principles that guided the judges in administering and enforcing customary law.

Civilized Laws Governing Uncivilized People

As earlier noted, in applying the validity tests, the factor that has always guided the judges faced with an issue on customary law is the socio-economic issues of the country: Whether the custom is for the good of the given Nigerian society or whether it would advance the interest of the Nigerian society or not? There is a list of interests which are legally protected in any society, such as the protection of one's person, freedom of action, belief and reputation, etc. Although not exhaustive, Adaramola[88] opined that what these interests are, depended largely on certain political, economic, and cultural beliefs/convictions of the people in that society. Therefore "Any law that fails to take the society wherein it operates into consideration has failed in its function.[89]

The conviction, the beliefs of the people in the society is what Eugene Ehilch[90] regards as the "living law" and is different from the law in the books, "formal law" (e.g., validity test: the repugnancy clause, incompatibility clause, and the public policy clause).

The aim of the repugnancy doctrine, as enunciated by judges, is to "obliterate the primitive and obsolete customary practices." To what extent has it achieved its aim? Are not these practices still operating effectively among the people (living law) even where there are formal laws (e.g., validity tests in the statutes)? What amounts to this disparity between living laws and formal laws?

According to Eugene's postulations, none of these formal laws succeeded in bringing about the desired changes in society as they sought to because they did not conform to the social aspirations and consciousness of the people. The law (the validity tests) is seen as higher than the way of life and belief systems of the people. Is it the function of formal laws to stamp out such retrogressive customary practices merely because they are the "living laws" of the people? Is the law not supposed

---

[88] *Supra*, note 9
[89] Ibid.
[90] An American Sociological Jurist quoted in Adaramola *supra* note 9

to be a catalyst of progress and positive change in society, as posited by the sociological school?[91]

According to H.L.A. Hart, stamping such retrogressive practices would certainly retard social progress.[92] What then can be done to bridge the gap between the consciousness of the people (living law) and the formal laws (the validity tests) to bring about development, progress, and civilization?

It is arguable that if this dichotomy keeps on existing, the desired changes in society would be only an illusion as it is today in many parts of the country. To bridge the gap, it is suggested that judges who are saddled with the responsibility of interpreting the law, the provisions of the repugnancy clause, should bend over backward to carry the people along. They do so by appealing to their consciences and educating them (in their *ratio decidendi*) as to the barbarous nature of the custom and to the necessity of abolishing them.

Niki Tobi JSC did so when he reasoned thus: "it is the monopoly of God to determine the sex of a child…" By so doing, the belief system and consciousness of the people is influenced in the direction of the law.

Certainly, when people regard certain practices and beliefs as naturally pre-ordained and essential for society, nothing but a fundamental change in their values can abolish such practices.[93]

The obvious reason for this is that conducts and practices are akin to trees which never die permanently unless their root is killed. The root of all practices is "belief" or "conviction."[94]

From the foregoing, it is obvious that the validity tests of customary law cannot be intelligently employed without regard to the social needs and requirements of the people. These needs change and are modified through process of time. For example, most of the objectionable rules of customary laws have fallen out of use today.

---

[91] Ibid.

[92] Adaramola, ibid..

[93] O. O. Omorogbe, (1994),"Women and the Family in Nigeria" *African Journal of International Comparative Law.* P. 201

[94] Aboki, Y, (1991) "Are Some Nigerian Customary Law Really Repugnant" (1991) *Ahmadu Bello University Law Journal*, Vol. 9-10, p. 2

However, certain other obnoxious practices are still operational among the peoples of the nation; female disinheritance, widow's subjugation, etc., even with the prevalence of the repugnancy doctrine. To bring about the desired change, obliterating retrogressive practices, certain machineries must be put in place.

Ways to Abolish Repugnant Customs

Education/Mass Enlightenment Programmes

According to Omorogbe,[95] changes in beliefs or attitudes and convictions can be effected through mass enlightenment campaigns and programs, the efficacy of which can themselves depend on an appreciable rise in the literary levels and in the standard of living of the people. In this regard, emphasis must be placed on the vital role of the educated minority to educate, enlighten, persuade and teach both by precepts and examples. By this approach, the values, belief systems, and convictions of the people can be changed.

The mass enlightenment programs must be designed in such a way as to show the listener why the practices are unjust. That for instance, there is no rational reason for believing that women are innately inferior to men or that the gods would hurt anyone who associates with an "*Osu*" and that society as a whole will benefit from a system where there is mutual respect and equality. Such programs should involve dialogues with members of society from different communities.

Improved Standard of Living of the People

This includes improvement of road facilities, water, electricity supply, grass root education, and an improvement on technological devices, e.g., the internet, media, etc. All of these have the capacity to expose people to a civilized way of living.

---

[95] *Supra*, note 94

PROOF OF CUSTOMARY LAW IN COURT

The existence of customary law is generally a matter of fact. It is to be specifically pleaded and proved by leading evidence. The onus rests on the person claiming the existence of such.[96]

Section 16 of the Evidence Act provides thus:

> (1) A custom may be adopted as part of the law governing a particular set of circumstances if it can be noticed judicially or can be proved to exist by evidence;
>
> (2) The burden of proving a custom shall lie upon the person alleging its existence.

There are two methods of establishing customary law in Court:

A. by Evidence;

B. by Judicial Notice.

Proof by Evidence

Customary law is an issue of fact and has to be proved before the court can act on it. The onus of proof of customary law rests on the person claiming its existence.[97] It has to be proved by calling witnesses who have such personal knowledge of the particular custom, and it is only when such custom becomes notorious as a result of frequent proof in courts that judicial notice of it is taken without further proof.[98]

In *Motoh* v. *Motoh*, the respondent sued the original defendant claiming, amongst others declaration that he is the Okpala and the only male issue of late Jeremiah Anagor Motoh and as such entitled to hold and manage the property of late Jeremiah Anagor Motoh, according to the custom of Umuanagu Village, Awka. The respondent's case was that he is the only son of late Jeremiah Anagor Motoh, who died intestate in January 1962 and was subject to the native laws and customs of Umuanaga Awka.

---

[96] *Egbuta* v. *Onnuna* (2007)10 NWLR (Pt. 1042) 298

[97] *Motoh* v. *Motoh* (2011) 16 NWLR (Pat 1274) pg. 483

[98] *Ogolo* v. *Ogolo* (2003) 18 NWLR (pt. 852) 494; *Egbuta* v. *Onuna* (2007) 10 NWLR (pt. 1042) 298

The respondent averred that late Jeremiah Anagor Motoh married two wives, the defendant, and the respondent's mother. While the defendant's mother had six female children for the deceased, the respondent's mother had the respondent and his sister. The deceased owned many landed properties, and the respondent claimed that by the native law and custom of Awka, a man's only son is entitled to inherit the estate of his deceased father on intestacy and to maintain his sisters and wives of the deceased father from the proceeds of the estate until the sisters are all married.

The Court of Appeal held that although witnesses testified on behalf of the respondent that his mother married late Jeremiah Motoh under customary law, the fact of that marriage was not sufficiently proved before the court. The Court further held that the onus of proof of customary law rests on the person claiming its existence.[99]

This case was decided in line with other prior cases. For instance, in *Giwa* v. *Erimolokun*, Taylor FJ explained that:

> It is a well-established principle of law that native law and custom is a matter of evidence to be decided on the facts presented before the court in each particular case unless it is of such notoriety and has been so frequently used that it would be taken without evidence required in proof.[100]

Modes of Proving Customary Law by Evidence

According to Evidence Act Proof by evidence of customary is in three modes:

1. witnesses;
2. expert evidence or opinion;
3. textbooks, documents, and manuscripts.[101]

Witnesses

Section 18(1) of Evidence Act[102] states:

---

[99] *Egbuta* v. *Onuna* (2007) 10 NWLR (Pt. 1042) *Balogun Agbai & ors* v. *Samuel Okogbue* (1991) 9-10 SCNJ 49 at 80-81; (1991) 7 NWLR (Pt. 204) 391
[100] (1961) All NLR 294
[101] Section 16, 70, 59, and 62 of the Evidence Act 2011
[102] 2011

> Where a custom cannot be established as one judicially noticed, it must be proved as fact by calling evidence to show that persons concerned in the particular area regard the alleged custom as binding upon them.

One way of doing that is either by the party claiming the existence of a custom, adducing oral evidence to establish the custom he alleges, or calling another person or persons as witness to collaborate his evidence on the existence of an alleged custom. Usually, the evidence of a party being a person interested in the outcome of the case is not usually enough to prove the existence of a custom.

As Ademola CJF rightly stated in the *Queen, Ex partes Lewis Ekpanga* v. *Ozogula II*, that: "it was of the greatest importance that native law and custom be strongly proved. It is correct that a custom is not proved by the number of witnesses called, but it is not enough that one who asserts the custom should be the only witness."[103]

If a party is interested in the outcome of a suit alleges a custom, they usually call an expert witness to adduce evidence in support or proof of the alleged custom.

While the success of a plaintiff's case as a general rule does not depend on the number of witnesses called, it is desirable that a person or persons other than the claimant give evidence to the existence of the customary law and tradition which forms the basis of the claim.

It is unsafe to accept the statement of a single person asserting the existence of a custom as conclusive.[104] However, the courts have noted that the quality of evidence required has nothing to do with the multiplicity of witnesses. The witnesses must be those who have knowledge of the existence of the custom in the issue.

Expert or Opinion Evidence

Section 18(2) of the Evidence Act 2011 provides thus:

---

[103] (1962) 1 ALL NLR 264 at 268: See also *Osolu* v. *Osolu* (1998) 9 NWLR (Pt535)532; *Okene* v. *Orianwo* (1998) 9 NWLR (Pt.566) 408; *Bello* v. *Gov. Kogi State* (1997) 9 NWLR (pt.521) 496; *Adeogun* v. *Ekunrin* (2004) 2 NWLR (Pt.856)52.

[104] *Adeogun* v. *Ekunrin* (2004)2 NWLR (Pt.856) 52,CA

> Where the existence or nature of a custom applicable to a given case is in issue, there may be given in evidence the opinions of persons who would be likely to know of its existence...

Such evidence can emanate from "native chiefs or other persons having special knowledge." They can be called upon to express their opinion as evidence on a point of customary law. Experts include Native chiefs, other persons having special knowledge of native laws and customs, for instance, by virtue of their experience, position, or role in society, and authors of any book, document, or manuscript of legal authority on their customs, and so forth.[105]

The challenge is always how to measure the veracity of the opinions so rendered. Mudiaga Odje speaking in relation to the customary law of succession said:

> How can we be sure that the magistrate and judges, some of whom may not be well acquainted with the customary law, would be furnished with evidence of the correct rules of the applicable customary law? This is a real problem that has been pointed out in several cases in which the rules of customary law have been deliberately twisted by parties and their witnesses or stated in genuine ignorance.

Osborn CJ pointed out that the so-called experts are usually faster in coming to bear testimony that corresponds exactly with the views put forward by the side on whose behalf they appear.[106] However, when the opinion comes up, they are also subjected to the rigorous exercise of cross-examination by the opposite party, who is under the duty by law to rebut or counter such evidence by expert evidence to the contrary.

Books and Manuscripts

The Evidence Act permits the reliance by judges on books, documents, and manuscripts presented by a party to establish the existence or otherwise of a custom[107]subject to prescribed conditions. For a party to

---

105 Malemi,E, *supra* note 20

106 *Lewis* v. *Bankole* (1908) NLR at P. 100

107 Section 70, Evidence Act 2011.

successfully rely on books and manuscripts, he must lay the necessary foundations before tendering such books as exhibits; the necessary foundations are as follows:

i. The book or manuscripts must form part of the evidence given in the case.
ii. It must be shown that the book or manuscript is recognized by the people of the relevant community as legal authority or a true and authentic or authoritative statement of the given native law and custom.

After laying the above foundation, the party must thereafter:

1. Call persons versed in the knowledge of the customs of the community, by virtue of their position in the community, to testify that the books or manuscript is recognized by the community as a legal authority on their customs or the particular custom in the story.
2. Call the author of the book or writing to give evidence and avoid the hearsay rule, or where the author cannot attend courts, his absence is sufficiently explained, and the necessary foundation laid to tender the writing as documentary evidence.[108]

In spite of some constraints in reliance on books and manuscripts to establish a custom, the cases of *Olusesi* v. *Ojelusi*[109] and *Oyelowo* v. *Oyelowo*[110] reveal that the judges have successfully relied on books and manuscripts in determining customary law. In the former case, the Court of Appeal relied on the book titled "the Nigerian Land Law by T. O. Elias, while in the latter case, the court relied on Nigerian land law by Ben Nwabueze.

Judicial Notice

Judicial notice of customary law is governed by Section 17(2) of the Evidence Act. It provides that:

> A custom may be judicially noticed when it has been adjudicated upon by a superior of record.
>
> The phrase "may be judicially noticed" shows that the court is not under compulsion to take judicial notice of a

[108] *Adedibu* v. *Adewoyin* (1951) 13 WACA 191
[109] (1986) 3 NWLR (Pt. 31) P. 634
[110] (1981) 2 NWLR (Pt. 56) P. 239

custom. Rather it is discretionary. However, this discretion is exercised where the rule of customary law had been previously proved before the court or is so clearly established, well settled, or is common knowledge.[111]

A customary court presided over by either a legal practitioner or by a non-legal practitioner is deemed to know the customs of their area of jurisdiction, and proof of a custom by evidence may be dispensed with if the custom is a common knowledge and the court has taken judicial notice of it.[112] However, this presumption of knowledge does not apply to an upper Area court as it is not deemed to be well versed in the custom of its area of jurisdiction. This is because of its wide area of jurisdiction and the diversity of tribes or communities often within such jurisdictions.[113]

CONCLUSION

Customary laws are, no doubt, part of laws applicable in Nigeria. The introduction of English laws and subsequent enactments of statutes did not in any way alter the validity of customs save in circumstances where it was adjudged repugnant to natural justice, equity, and good conscience, incompatible with any written law for the time being in force and where it is contrary to public policy. The jurisprudence of the courts of Nigeria reveals that judges are wary of the fact that indigenous customs be preserved as much as possible and would only rule that they are inapplicable where it fails the validity tests. Judges are also mindful of the fact that reference to "natural justice, equity and good conscience" is not a reference to English notions of justice but to generally acceptable and civilized conduct. The continued application of customary law is also made subject to proof as evidence except where it is of such notoriety as it should be judicially noticed. Despite the

---

[111] This is the exception to the general rule on proof of customary law which stipulates that every customary law has to be proved in the first instance by calling witnesses who are acquainted with the custom.

[112] *Ehigie* v. *Ehigie* (1961) 1 All NLR 871.

[113] *Pam* v. *Gyang* (1969) MNLR Pt. 29, P. 460 C.A

rigorous tests to which customary law is subjected to, it remains part of the "living law" of the people and is not easily eradicated without engaging the conscience and reasoning processes of the people.

PART B

LAW MAKING:
STATUTORY LAW AND DELEGATED LEGISLATION

Chapter 6

LEGISLATIVE PROCESS IN NIGERIA

Sesan Fabamise *

Military rule accounts for about-thirty years of the country's existence as an independent nation.[11] Under the successive military governments, the law-making organ of government – the legislature – had always been abrogated. Only the Executive and Judicial arms of government were allowed to function. The legislative functions of government were undertaken by the executive as constituted in the various armed forces' highest ruling bodies. Laws made by the military then were called Decrees, and there were specifically no processes or procedures followed for lawmaking.

However, with the advent of civilian rule and under the presidential constitution under which Nigeria operates, there is a clear division of roles assigned to each of the three arms of government. The legislative powers of the federal government are vested in the National Assembly, which is made up of the Senate and the House of Representatives.[2] While those of the states of the federation are vested in the Houses of Assembly of the States.

These institutions are vested with powers to make laws "for the peace, order and good government of the federation or any part thereof with respect to any Matter.[3]

---

*Sesan Fabamise, LLM. Senior Lecturer, College of Law, Afe Babalola University.

[1] Nigeria became independent on October 1, 1960. The Military ruled between Jan 15, 1966 and October 1979 and handed over to a civilian government headed by Alhaji Shehu Shagari but struck and took over power again on December 31 1983 before handing over power to a civilian administration on May 29, 1999.

[2] S 4 (1) of the 1999 Constitution of the Federal Republic of Nigeria 1999 (As amended).

[3] S 4 (6), ibid.

The Executive branch comprises of the President, the Vice-president, Ministers, and Special Advisers. They implement the programs and policies of the government and enforce the laws made by the legislature, while the Judiciary is empowered by the constitution to adjudicate and interpret the laws. Even though there is a separation of powers among these branches of government, they ensure that no branch abuses its power through the institution of checks and balances.

TYPES OF LAWS

Constitution

The constitution is the supreme law of the land that guides the process of governance. It sets forth the duties and obligations of the different branches of government and delineates the fundamental rights and obligations of citizens.

It is the supreme law of the land, and it declares its supremacy by stating that the constitution is the ground norm or the ultimate law of the land. No law may contravene any of the provisions of the constitution, and any law that contravenes any of the provisions is void to the extent of the inconsistency.

Statutes

Statutes are laws passed by the National Assembly, the State's Houses of Assembly, and the legislative Houses of the Local Governments. They have the power to amend or repeal existing laws. Laws made by the National Assembly are called Acts of the National Assembly. Those made or enacted by the Houses of Assembly of the states are called Laws, while statutes enacted by the legislative Houses of the Local Governments are called Edicts.

Customary Law

The Nigeria customary law system is the law of the different communities in the country. Basically, every community has its own law, which is largely unwritten. It is derived from the customs of the people, and these laws are applied and interpreted by the customary courts presided over by community leaders and traditional chiefs.

Customary law specifically deals with such issues as marriage, divorce, inheritance, and so on.

The Penal and Criminal Codes

The penal code is in force among the sixteen Northern states and the Federal Capital Territory. The penal code was adapted substantially from the Sharia (Islamic Legal System), but the punishments are modified as against that which Islam prescribes. The criminal code is operated among the southern states of the country. It contains the criminal code, which is fashioned after British law. The criminal procedure Act prescribes the procedure for punishing a breach of the codes.

THE INSTITUTIONS FOR LAW MAKING

The highest law-making body in the country is the National Assembly. Nigeria operates a bicameral system of legislature. That is, the National Assembly has two legislative chambers. The first chamber is referred to as the Senate, and the second one is referred to as the House of Representatives.

These houses are given the power by the Nigerian constitution to make laws for peace and security as well as the good and orderly administration of the country. Laws made by the National Assembly are superior to laws made by any State's House of Assembly. In other words, if a state makes a law that contradicts that one made by the National Assembly, such a law is null and void to the extent of the inconsistency.

The National Assembly has exclusive power to make laws on all the subjects under the exclusive legislative list. In general, there are three legislative lists. These are the Exclusive, the Concurrent, and the Residual lists. While only the National Assembly is empowered by the constitution to make laws in all three areas, the state and local governments cannot make laws on the Exclusive list. Equally, a local government cannot make laws on the concurrent list as it is reserved for only the National and State Assemblies.

The Exclusive legislative list, among other things, includes subjects like currency, foreign policy, petroleum, military and paramilitary forces, space, aviation, etc. Subjects contained in the concurrent list are education, transport, communication, health, and so on. Residual list on which local government councillors make their laws include subjects like land, chieftaincy matters, road, health, etc. The state can also make laws on the Residual list, not, unlike the local government. However, no law made by the state or the local government may contravene the constitution or any law made by the National Assembly.

The Senate

The Senate has a total of one hundred and nine (109) members. Each of the present thirty-six states of the federation is divided into three (3) senatorial districts. Each of the senatorial districts and the Federal Capital Territory, Abuja, has a senator in the senate. The idea of equal representation in the senate is to promote equality among the states regardless of population and size.

Members of this chamber, called Senators, are elected for a four-year term and are expected to represent the interest of their people. Section 69 of the 1999 Nigerian constitution empowers the people in any constituency to recall a Senator whose conduct they consider unsatisfactory or not representing their interests adequately.[4]

For any person to qualify for election to the senate, she/he must be a citizen of Nigeria and must have attained the age of thirty-five years. She/he must possess a minimum educational qualification of school certificate and must be a member of a registered political party. From among the elected senators, an election is conducted to elect the President and Deputy President of the Senate. The President of the Senate presides over the business of the Senate.

The House of Representatives

The House of Representatives consists of three hundred and sixty members. Unlike the Senate, each member is elected to represent one of

[4] However, the procedure for this recall is not so simple. See section – of the Electoral act.

the three hundred and sixty federal constituencies of the country. Constituencies are divided in such a way that each has the same size and possibly the same number of people. Unlike what obtains in the senate, states do not have equal representation in the House States are represented according to their population. In other words, states with more population have more representatives than those with less population.

The speaker of the House of Representatives, who is elected by the members, heads the House. His/her Deputy, who is elected among others in the House, assists him/her. Anyone seeking election to the House of Representatives must have attained the age of thirty (30) years.

SOURCES OF BILLS

These are the three major sources of the bill.

Executive Bills

A number of bills are often initiated by the Executive branch of government. This is due to the fact that the Executive comprises the President and the Ministers who formulate policies. These policies must be enacted for the President and Ministers to carry out their responsibilities. Hence, any bill initiated by a Minister or the President himself falls under this category of an Executive Bill. All executive bills are initiated and presented by the President of the Federal Republic of Nigeria via a letter to the speaker of the House of Representatives and the President of the Senate.

Members Bills

The primary duty of members of the legislature is to make laws. So, any bill introduced by a Senator or a Member of the House of Representatives falls under this category.[5]

---

[5] Often times, more than one senator or member may team up to introduce a bill on the floor of the Senate/House. The idea is to carry as many as possible lawmakers along and get their support.

Private Bills

These are bills initiated by individual citizens and professional bodies in the country. However, such bills need to be sponsored by either a member of the House of Representatives or a Senator, as the case may be, before they can be presented on the floor of the House or Senate.

HOW LAWS ARE MADE

Generally, in presidential systems of government, the process which a bill goes through before becoming law is essentially the same. The process of law-making generally requires a long period of deliberation and consideration of the many interests and implications of the Bill.

Stage 1

The first stage is the identification of the need for a bill. This can be a new one, introducing a new idea not yet covered by existing law. It can also be an amendment to an existing law.

A bill can be initiated by anybody, but only a member of the House or a Senator can introduce it on the floor of the House or the Senate. Bills are grouped into three categories: Executive, Member, and Private Bills. A bill is like a proposal or an idea that has to be deliberated upon and passed into law by the National Assembly. Before a bill is introduced, a compendium of its financial costs must be calculated and attached. In other words, the amount that would be needed in executing specific aspects of the law when it is passed must be computed or calculated so as to know whether the government would be able to accommodate it in the budget.[6]

When a bill is prepared by the Executive, it has to be forwarded to the Speaker of the House and the Senate President with a cover letter from the President. A bill from members of the House of Representatives is presented to the Speaker, while the one from Senate is presented to the Senate President. Bills from the Executive branch of government can, at times, be discussed concurrently, i.e., at the same

---

[6] For example, in passing the Niger Delta Development Commission (NDDC) Bill, the government gave a breakdown of what it would take to make the commission function in terms of staff, transport, accommodation and other facilities that would assist or enhance the work of the Commission. It also stated the sources of such funds the Commission would receive.

time in both the Senate and the House of Representatives. Bills from the member and private individuals are always discussed in the chamber of its origin first before it is sent to the other for passage.

All bills are numbered or marked according to their chamber of origin.[7] On the receipt of the bill, the Speaker or the Senate President forwards it to the Rules and Business Committee of the respective chamber. These committees then look at the bill to determine whether it meets all standards in draft and presentation.[8] After this, the committee sends the bill for gazetting.[9]

The Rules and Business Committee of the two chambers determine the day and time it is to be discussed in the House/Senate. All bills must receive three readings before they can be passed into law, and the readings must be on different days.[10]

Stage 2

First Reading

The clerk of the House/Senate usually does the reading of the bills scheduled on the House/Senate order of proceedings paper. She/he reads the short title of the bill for the first time and then proceeds to table it.[11] Normally, at this stage, there is no debate on the bill on the floor of the House/Senate. The reading simply informs the members that a particular bill has been introduced from there, the bill moves to the next stage.

Second Reading

This period is when debate occurs on the bill. Debate commences with a motion by the Senate or House Leader that the bill be read the second

---

[7] A bill from the House of Representatives is marked HB (House Bill) while the one from the Senate is marked SB (Senate Bill). An Executive Bill is marked with "Executive" printed on the title page of the bill. It is printed tiny and to the right- hand side of the page.

[8] If not, the bill will be forwarded to the legal department of the National Assembly for re-drafting and further advice.

[9] Executive bills are gazetted or published in the House/Senate Journal once, while those introduced by members are published three times before they can be presented to the House/Senate for consideration.

[10] Some bills can receive accelerated consideration it on the same day based on their urgency and significance for government policy. Bills that are needed to enable the President to take urgent action on matters relating to national security fall under fens.

[11] The word "table" is used to mean the action by which the clerk places the bill on the table.

time. The motion must be seconded (supported) by any of the other parties' leaders. When it is not seconded, the bill cannot be debated.[12]

However, if the bill is by a member, the sponsor of the bill would move that it be read the second time. The motion must be seconded by another member.[13] The person moving the motion, whether in the case of the Executive or Member bill, is expected to highlight the objectives, general principles, and subject matter of the bill. He is also expected to highlight the benefits of the bill if passed into law. If the motion is agreed upon, the clerk will read the long title of the bill. Immediately after this, members must signify their intention to speak on the bill. Two things can occur at this stage:

1. the bill may receive the support of the majority of the House/Senate and be allowed to move to the next stage. Once it gets the needed support, it moves to the committee stage;
2. the bill may be 'negative' if it does not get the support of the majority of the House/Senate members.[14]

After the debate on the general principles of the bill, it is referred to the appropriate standing committee. The Senate President/Speaker of the House is empowered by the rules of both the Senate and the House to determine the relevant committee(s) to which the bill is referred.

Committee Stage

This is the period when the committee assigned to deliberate on a bill examines it more critically. The House and the Senate have two types of committees. The first one is the Committee of the Whole House, and the second is the Standing Committee.

If the Committee of the Whole House is to discuss a bill, the Speaker of the House acts as the chairperson. The Speaker would leave his or her seat and sit at the clerk's seat. The mace, too, will be taken to the lower table for the committee of the whole House deliberations to

---

[12] Executive bills are allowed, as a matter of courtesy to proceed to a second reading.

[13] When a bill by a Member cannot get the support of another Member, it cannot be debated and hence stands rejected.

[14] When a bill is "negative" or "killed", it is taken off the table and cannot be discussed until it is re-introduced at a later date.

commence. In the case of the Senate, the Senate President acts as the chairperson of the Committee of the Whole House and thus presides. She/he stops being addressed as the Deputy Speaker or the Senate President. Rather, she/he is to be called "Mr Chairman Sir" or 'Chairperson Ma' for the period of the committee session. As for the standing committee, the chairperson presides over the committee, or in his/her absence, his deputy stands in for him or her. The committee examines all aspects of the bill clause-by-clause and point by point. They also organize public hearings on the bill. This may take place at the National Assembly complex or any other area or location the committee deems appropriate.

Any member of the public or expect(s) having an interest in the bill may be allowed to attend the public hearing and make contributions to the public debate of the bill. A member of the public can make suggestion(s) on any aspect of the bill, but only a member of the committee can propose an amendment to the bill. All amendments must be in line and relevant to the principle and the subject matter of the bill as agreed to at the second reading stage. Sometimes, however, a bill may touch on areas of two or more standing committees. When this happens, the committee with the dominant issues will take the bill while others will form sub-committees to consider areas relating to them and report to the main committee.[15] The main committee will collate all suggestions and amendments of the "sub-committees" and report to the House or Senate.

Committee of the Whole House

After the committee has concluded its work, it will report back to the whole House/Senate in plenary with or without amendments. It must beforehand ask the Rules and Business Committee to put the bill on the "Order Paper". It is important to note that the Committee of the Whole

[15] For example, all committees are always involved in the "Appropriation Bill" (Budget) but they act as sub-committees to the Appropriation Committee in the House/Senate. In other words, they report back to the Appropriation committee with their changes or amendments.

House must report back to the House/Senate. When it is reporting back, the Speaker or the Senate President goes back to his or her former seat, and the mace, too, returns to its original position. Whether it is the Standing Committee or the Committee of the Whole House that considers a bill at the committee stage, the chairperson is expected via a motion to report progress on the bill.

Third Reading

After the report of the committee and the deliberation of the committee of the Whole House, a motion may be moved that the bill be read the third time either immediately or at a later date and passed after each chamber has certified the contents of the clean copy to be accurate.

Generally, no amendment can be entertained after the third reading stage. However, if a member wishes to amend or delete a provision contained in the bill or to introduce a new provision, she/he must give notice of his or her intention "that the bill be re-committed" before the motion for the third reading is moved. If the motion is agreed upon, the House/Senate will dissolve itself into a committee of the Whole House/Senate immediately or at a later date to discuss the amendments. After all necessary amendments, the House/Senate will then proceed to the third reading and pass the bill.

Stage 3

The Clerk Prepares the Clean Copy of the Bill

When a bill has been read the third time and passed, a clean copy of it, incorporating all amendments, will be produced, signed by the clerk, and endorsed by the Speaker/Senate President. The copy will then be forwarded to the Clerk of the House or Senate as the case may be. The copy will be accompanied by a message requiring the concurrence (passage of the bill or agreement) of the receiving chamber. In the case of the Executive bill, both chambers will just exchange copies of the bill since they both received copies and discussed the bill almost at the same time.

When a bill is sent to either chamber for concurrence, three things may happen;

i. The receiving chamber may agree with the provisions of the bill and hence pass it;
ii. The chamber may not agree to some parts of the bill and hence make amendments;
iii. The chamber may not agree with the bill at all and therefore reject it entirely. However, this situation is rare.

In the event of the second situation, the chamber from which the bill originated may agree with the amendments or recommendations. But if the amendments are not agreeable to the chamber, then a Conference Committee of the two chambers will be constituted to work out any disagreement.

Joint Conference Committee

The Joint Conference Committee is normally constituted when there are differences in a bill passed by both legislative chambers. Membership of the committee is based on equality, usually six members from each chamber with a Senator acting as chairperson.

The mandate of the committee is to harmonize the differences between the two chambers on the bill. They cannot introduce any new matter into the bill. The decision of the committee on those areas of difference is binding on the chambers. Failure to accept the decision of the Joint Conference Committee may lead to a joint sitting of both the Senate and the House, with the Senate President presiding on the area of contention.

At the conference committee stage, members or select members of the committees which considered the bill originally meet and deliberate only on the areas of disagreement between the two chambers. The sitting of the Joint Committee may be open or closed to the public. This will depend on the subject matter under discussion and the view of the majority of the Joint Conference Committee members. The report of the Joint Conference Committee is presented in both chambers for consideration. If both chambers adopt the report, all the original papers are sent to the Clerk of the chamber where the bill originated. The Clerk puts together all the amendments and produces a clean copy of the bill, which is sent to the Clerk of the National Assembly, who then sends it to the President for his signature.

Stage 4

Presidential Assent

Another way in which the President is involved in the act of law-making is by signing bills into law. A bill does not become law until the President signs it. The Clerk of the National Assembly will "enrol"[16] the bill for the President. The Clerk of the National Assembly produces the clean copy, certifies it, and forwards it to the president.

The President has thirty (30) days to sign a bill sent to him or her by the National Assembly. If she/he disagrees with the provision of the bill or some aspects of it, she/he can veto it by withholding his or her signature. Within the thirty days, the President must communicate to the National Assembly his or her feelings and comments about the bill. The President must state the areas she/he wants to be amended before she/he signs the bill. If the National Assembly agrees with the President, the bill can be withdrawn for deliberation on the amendments suggested by the president.

However, the National Assembly is empowered by the constitution to overrule the veto of the President. If, after thirty (30) days, the President refuses to sign the bill and the National Assembly is not in support of the President's amendments, the two chambers can recall the bill and re-pass it. If the bill is passed in the form it was sent to the President by a two-thirds majority vote in both chambers, the bill automatically becomes a law even without the signature of the President.[17]

---

[16] Enrolment is the production of the clean copy for the assent of the President

[17] This happened in the case of the Niger Delta Development Commission Bill. The two chambers passed the bill into law after the president failed to sign it within the time that is prescribed for him to so do.

Chapter 7

LEGISLATION AS LAW IN NIGERIA

Sam Erugo*

INTRODUCTION

There is no argument that legislation is law in Nigeria. In fact, the legislation appears to be the most powerful source of Nigerian Law. The other sources of law include the received English common law and doctrines of Equity, customary law, and case law. By its nature, legislation has been the most dynamic, wide-ranging, and all-inclusive formal source of law. It has the character of abrogating and changing the tenor of all other laws, including itself. Legislation comprises laws as legislated, promulgated, or passed by the legislature or other law-making authority of a government. In most civilized nations, the legislature is the arm of government charged with the very critical role of legislating and making laws. The other arms of government are the executive and judiciary. Centuries ago, Alexander Hamilton considered the moot question: "Why has government been instituted at all?" In candour, he retorted that it was "because the passions of men will not conform to the dictates of reason and justice without constraint."[1] This statement made as far back as 1787 is certainly relevant today. The constraint requiring reason and justice is provided by the government essentially through laws made by the legislature, which are interpreted by the judiciary and enforced by the executive. Thus, legislation is critically important because it provides some form of order by setting acceptable standards of conduct in society.

Sam Erugo, PhD (Ibadan), Reader, Faculty of Law, Abia State University, Uturu, Nigeria.

[1] See, A. Hamilton, "The Federalist Papers", Federalist No. 15, December 1, 1787: http://www.westillholdthesetruths.org/quotes/513 -accessed 16 November 2013

But the crucial question is what exactly constitutes legislation given its intrinsic character as law in Nigeria. This chapter makes a critical assessment of legislation as law in Nigeria and concludes that it is the most powerful source of law in this jurisdiction and very dynamic, it has always been, and efforts must be made to ensure the best quality of legislation.

DEFINITION OF TERMS AND CONCEPTUAL FRAMEWORK

Legislation is defined as: "1. the process of making or enacting a positive law in written form, according to some type of formal procedure, by a branch of government constituted to perform this process; 2. the law so enacted; 3. the whole body of enacted laws."[2]

Thus, legislation is all about enacting or making a positive law or substantially the positive law made by a law-making authority. There is no generally accepted definition of law. The divergent views on the meaning of law crystallized into what is better known as the schools of jurisprudence or law. The natural and positivist schools are the dominant schools very relevant to the present discussion. To the naturalists, the law is predicated upon the assertion that there are objective moral principles that depend upon the nature of the universe and which can be discovered by reason.[3]

Thus, it is dependent on reasoning and morals independent of man-made enactment. According to Cicero, for instance, "True law is right reason in agreement with nature. It is of universal application, unchanging and everlasting."[4] This means there is a moral order in the universe that is perceptible to man through his rational faculty - so this school draws inspiration from nature. The Universal Declaration of Human Rights and other international bills of rights are said to find support from this school. But these declarations have also been the basis of some formal laws.

On the other hand, positivists insist that natural or moral prescriptions are not law until they are enacted or created and

---

[2] *Black's Law Dictionary*, Bryan .A Garner, (ed.) (7th Ed, West Group Minn 1999)

[3] Lloyd, *et al.; Introduction to Jurisprudence*(ELBS, London,1985) 22a

[4] Cicero, *The Republic*, Chapter 3, Section 33, cited by Osita Nnamani Ogbu, *Modern Nigerian Legal System*, (CIDJAP Publishers, Enugu 2002), 12

sanctioned by an authority, which only is the source of its validity. In other words, however morally right and sound a rule may be, until it is codified and enacted by the State, it is not recognised by the positivists. This is the basis of legislations-Acts, Laws, By-laws, and Regulations. In this wise, "Positive law" has been defined as

> a system of law promulgated and implemented within a particular political community by political superiors, as distinct from moral law or law existing in an ideal community or in some non-political community. Positive law typically consists of enacted law, the codes, statutes, and regulations that are applied and enforced in the courts....positive law literally means law established by human authority.[5]

Legislations are positive laws established, written, and enforced by a recognized authority of the state. It is different from the unwritten moral codes of the natural school of law.

The scope of legislation in Nigeria is comprehensive and broad, covering virtually every aspect of government and private life of citizens. One discovers that there are laws:

a. Constituting the government itself, for example, the Constitution of the Federal Government of Nigeria, ostensibly the *grundnorm.* This prescribes the organs of state, defining and restricting their powers and relationship with each other, as well as the rights of citizens;
b. Prescribing minimum acceptable standard of conduct and actions of citizens at the risk of sanctions and penalties for failure to conduct so. This is aimed at maintaining social equilibrium. For example, the Criminal Codes;
c. Prescribing framework of government and private relations;
d. Prescribing all other relations.

TYPES OF LEGISLATION

There are different types of legislation in Nigeria. These include Acts, Laws, By-laws, and Regulations, which expressions tacitly refer to the legislative authority of legislations.

[5] *Black's Law Dictionary, op cit*

Acts

Section 37(1) of the Interpretation Act[6] defines "Act" to mean "an Act of the National Assembly, whether passed before or after the commencement of this Act..." So, an Act is legislation passed by the National Assembly or the legislative arm of the Federal Government of Nigeria. The defunct Federal Military Government had ruled by Decrees. Suffice to state that those Decrees promulgated by the Federal Military Government of Nigeria during the military era and found in our statute books today are referred to as Acts supposedly as legislation by the legislative arm of the Federal Government.

By section 47 of the Constitution of the Federal Republic of Nigeria, 1999,[7] as altered, there are established "a National Assembly for the Federation which shall consist of a Senate and a House of Representatives." Section 58 of the Constitution prescribing mode of exercising general Federal legislative power provides that:

> (1) The power of the National Assembly to make laws shall be exercised by bills passed by both the Senate and the House of Representatives and, except as otherwise provided by subsection (5) of this section, assented to by the President.
>
> (2) A bill may originate in either the Senate or the House of Representatives and shall not become law unless it has been passed and, except as otherwise provided by this section and section 59 of this Constitution, assented to in accordance with the provisions of this section.
>
> (3) Where a bill has been passed... it shall be presented to the President for assent...
>
> (4) ...he shall within 30 days thereof signify that he assents or that he withholds assent.
>
> (5) Where the President withholds his assent, and the bill is again passed by each House by a two-thirds majority, the bill shall become law, and the assent of the President shall not be required.

---

[6] Cap I 23, Laws of the Federation of Nigeria, 2004

[7] Cap C23, Laws of the Federation of Nigeria, 2004

Once a bill is passed by the National Assembly and assented by the President or passed again under section 47(5) where the President withheld his consent, it becomes an Act or legislation of the Federal Government.

This type of legislation by the National Assembly applies throughout the territory of Nigeria or any part of it as may be circumscribed by the legislation. For the purpose, the legislative powers of the Federal Republic of Nigeria are vested in the National Assembly for the Federation by section 4 of the Constitution. Section 4(2) thereof provides that "the National Assembly shall have power to make laws for the... good government of the Federation or any part thereof with respect to any matter included in the Exclusive Legislative List set out in Part 1 of the Second Schedule to this Constitution." The power to make laws under this subsection (2) shall be "to the exclusion of the Houses of Assembly of States."[8]

The National Assembly shall also have powers to make laws with respect to any matter in the concurrent list,[9] and if any law enacted by the House of Assembly of a State is inconsistent with any law validly made by the National Assembly, the law made by the National Assembly shall prevail, and that other law shall to the extent of the inconsistency be void.[10] It is our humble submission here that it is only the courts that can declare the invalidity of a law made by the National Assembly.

Laws

These are legislations passed by a State House of Assembly or the legislative arm of a State Government in Nigeria. Section 18(1) of the Interpretation Act[11] defines "Law" as "any law enacted or having effect as if enacted by the legislature of a State and includes any instrument having the force of law which is made under a Law."

The Military Governors and Administrators had ruled by Edicts. All the Edicts promulgated by Military Governors and Administrators

[8] Ibid, Section 4(3)
[9] Ibid, Section 4(4)(a)
[10] Ibid, Section 4(5)
[11] *Op. cit.*

of States in Nigeria during the military era and currently found in the statute books are referred to as laws, supposedly as legislation by the legislative arm of the relevant State Government.

Section 90 of the Constitution of the Federal Republic of Nigeria, 1999, as altered, establishes a House of Assembly for each State of the Federation. By section 100 of the Constitution, the mode of exercising general State legislative power is prescribed. This section provides that:

> (1) The power of a State House of Assembly to make laws shall be exercised by bills passed by the House of Assembly and, except as otherwise provided by this section, assented to by the Governor.
> (2) A bill shall not become law unless it has been duly passed and, subject to subsection (1) of this section, assented to in accordance with the provisions of this section.
> (3) Where a bill has been passed by the House of Assembly it shall be presented to the Governor for assent.
> (4) ...he shall within 30 days thereof signify that he assents or that he withholds assent.
> (5) Where the Governor withholds his assent, and the bill is again passed by the House of Assembly by a two-thirds majority, the bill shall become law, and
> (6) the assent of the Governor shall not be required.

When a Bill is passed by the House of Assembly and assented by the Governor or passed again under section 100(5) where the Governor withheld his consent, it becomes a law or legislation of the relevant State Government. This type of legislation applies and has force of law within the territory of the relevant State only. For this purpose, the legislative powers of the State is conferred by section 4(6) of the Constitution on the House of Assembly of a State. A State House of Assembly shall have the power to make laws for the good governance of the State or any part thereof with respect to any matter included in the

Concurrent Legislative List but not in any matter included in the Exclusive list.[12]

Byelaws

Byelaws are legislations made by Local Government Councils that constitute the third tier of government in Nigeria. The Councils legislate at the local level in matters reserved for them pursuant to section 7 of the Constitution.

Byelaw can also refer to subordinate or subsidiary legislation issued by an administrative body, agency, or office deriving power from principal legislation or enabling statute. This category of legislation is sometimes referred to as administrative rulemaking[13] or legislation.

Rulemaking is the "issuance of regulations or the making of determinations which are addressed to indicated but unnamed and unspecified persons or situations..."[14] There is no argument that these administrative rules have a force of law just like the enabling legislations. The "analogy between administrative rule-making and a legislature's enactment of statutes is plain. In laying down rules to be followed in the future, the administrator simply exercises a power that had originally been lodged in the legislature and that had been delegated to it."[15]

Thus, the Legislature delegates its legislative powers to make subordinate or administrative legislation subject only to the doctrine of *ultra vires* for unconstitutional and improper delegations.[16] However, a "By-law cannot permit what the statute expressly forbids, and *vice versa*, though it can forbid what would otherwise be lawful at common law."[17] From enabling statutes, the usual delegates of these legislative powers include the President,[18] the Federal Executive Council,

---

[12] Section 4(7), ibid.

[13] B.O Iluyomade and B.U. Eka, *Cases and Materials on Administrative Law in Nigeria* (University of Ife Press, 1980) 34

[14]Ibid.

[15]Ibid., 40

[16]*Doherty* v. *Balewa* [1961]All N L R 604

[17]*Powell* v. *May* [1946] K B.330 Lord Goddard, CJ.

[18]See section 305(1) of the 1999 Constitution enabling the President to issue a Proclamation of a state of emergency in the Federation or any part thereof, by instrument published in the Official Gazette. The President is required thereafter to transmit copies of the official Gazette to the National Assembly for

Ministers,[19] Chief Justice,[20] Professional Bodies,[21] Commissions, and Regulatory Agencies.[22]

These subordinate or administrative legislations are found published as subsidiary legislations in Government Gazettes or in published volumes of laws of the Federation and various States. For instance, the Supreme Court Rules, Rules of Professional Conduct, Civil Service Rules, and Proclamations of State of Emergency.

Regulations

A Regulation is a specie of subsidiary legislation, defined as "the act or process of controlling by rule or restriction."[23] Section 18 of the Interpretation Act defines "regulations" to include "rules and By-laws." Regulation in this right-wide context is discussed later under subordinate legislation.

Generally, Legislation in Nigeria could also be classified into Supreme, principal, subsidiary, ancillary, and subordinate legislation:

Supreme Legislation

Supreme legislation is defined as "legislation that derives directly from the Supreme or sovereign power in a state and is therefore incapable of being repealed, annulled, or controlled by any other legislative authority."

Probably there is presently no such supreme legislation in Nigeria from a Supreme or sovereign power in view of the source of our present Constitution, but the Constitution is supreme legislation. Section 1(1) of the 1999 Constitution, as altered, proclaims that "this Constitution is

---

approval within days in recognition of fact that it is a legislation function. Example here can be found in the current proclamation of state of emergency in Borno, Yobe and Adamawa States by President Goodluck Ebele Jonathan.

[19]See section 16 of Companies and Allied Matters Act, Cap C20, Laws of the Federation of Nigeria, 2004 conferring power on the Minister to make regulations for the purposes of the Act.

[20]See for example sections 236 and 42(3) of the 1999 Constitution, as altered, respectively delegating legislative power to the Chief Justice of Nigeria to make Rules for the Supreme Court and the Fundamental Rights Enforcement Procedure.

[21]The Rules of Professional Conduct for Legal Practitioners is made by the Attorney General and Minister for
Justice/Chairman of General Council of the Bar enabled by section 12(4) of the Legal Practitioners Act, 2004

[22] See sections 160 and 204 of the Constitution, for Federal and State Commissions respectively.

[23]*Black's Law Dictionary, loc. cit.*

supreme and its provisions shall have binding force on all authorities and persons throughout the Federal Republic of Nigeria." To emphasize the supremacy of this legislation, subsection (3) states the obvious that "If any other law is inconsistent with the provisions of this Constitution, this Constitution shall prevail, and that other law shall to the extent of the inconsistency be void."

Supremacy of the Constitution in this sense translates to something akin to a *grundnorm*. *Grundnorm*, also called basic norm,[24] is best described in terms of "the legal theory of Hans Kelson, the law from which all other laws in a society derive. Kelson's 'pure theory of law' maintains that laws are norms. Therefore, a society's legal system is made up of its norms, and each legal norm derives its validity from other legal norms. Ultimately, the validity of all laws is tested against the 'basic norm,' which may be as simple as the concept that all pronouncements of the monarch are to be obeyed. Or, it may be an elaborate system of lawmaking, such as a constitution. The Constitution is the *grundnorm* of the Nigerian State, and other legislation is tested by its standard.

It has long been established that "laws must be made in strict accordance with the provisions of the constitution or risk being set aside by a court of competent jurisdiction: *William Marbury* v. *James Madison*[25]. In this case, the American Supreme Court ruled that Congress cannot pass laws that are contrary to the Constitution and that it is the role of the judiciary system to interpret what the Constitution permits.

Principal Legislation

The principal legislation is the primary or basic statute passed on any subject of legislation by the Legislature at federal or state level, as opposed to the subsidiary or ancillary legislations. In the recent case of *NNPC & Anor* v. *FAMFA Oil Ltd*,[26] the Supreme Court rightly observed that the Petroleum Act is the substantive or principal law

---

[24] *Black's Law Dictionary, loc cit*

[25] 5 US 137(1803) a land mark case, now *cause celebre* in the United States of America.

[26] (2012)5 SC Part II) 38

while the Bank-in-Right Regulation made by the Minister is the subsidiary legislation. The Court went on to hold that it is the principal law that provides the subsidiary legislation, the source of its existence. Without the principal law, there can be no subsidiary legislation.

Subsidiary or Ancillary Legislation

Subsidiary or ancillary legislation is defined as "legislation that is auxiliary to principal legislation."[27] The Interpretation Act elaborately defines "subsidiary instrument" as meaning "any order, rules, regulations, rules of court or By-laws made...in exercise of powers conferred by an Act." And "enactment" means any provision of an Act or subsidiary instrument.[28]

Subordinate Legislation

Subordinate legislation is "Legislation that derives from any authority other than the sovereign power in a State and that therefore depends for its continued existence and validity on some superior or supreme authority."[29] Also, Regulation:[30] "The act or process of controlling by rule or restriction 2. By-law... 3. A rule or order, having legal force, issued by an administrative agency or a local government. Also termed in sense three-agency regulation; subordinate; delegated legislation."

Subsidiary and subordinate legislations, as well as byelaws, rules, orders, and regulations are generally delegated legislations. These are legislation made by a person or body other than the legislature by virtue of powers given to such person or body by an enabling statute.[31]

Learned writers Iluyomade and Eka[32] rightly observe that: "the validity of the subordinate legislation may be challenged on the ground that it is in conflict with the enabling statute or any other statute. The subsidiary legislation may be declared invalid if it is inconsistent with that statute: *NNPC & Anor* v. *FAMFA Oil Ltd.*[33] Again, a delegated

---

[27] *Black's Law Dictionary, loc cit*
[28] Section 37, *op cit.*
[29] Ibid.
[30] Ibid.
[31] C.O Ajah, *A Digest of Nigerian Case Laws,*(FIAC Press, Enugu,2003),97
[32] *Op. cit.,* 83
[33] *Supra*

legislation that is inconsistent with the provisions of the enabling statute is invalid. But a delegated legislation is not invalid simply because it deals with something which the enabling statute does not expressly deal with. However, a delegated legislation cannot make unlawful what the enabling statute expressly makes lawful.[34]

USE OF SUBORDINATE LEGISLATIONS

Subordinate legislations are useful in cases "requiring some measure of flexibility so as to take care of future contingencies and unforeseen supervening developments in the execution of government policy"[35] or filling technical details that the legislature may not have the capacity or time to fill, as well as details in "statutes passed in skeleton form."[36] But "these so-called details," it has been argued, "are those that affect the rights of the common man most, and it is undesirable that these details are not filled in by the elected representatives of the people."[37]

Legislative Bodies

From the foregoing discussion, the main legislative bodies in Nigeria are:

i. The National Assembly exercises the legislative power of the Federal Government of Nigeria. It comprises the Senate and House of Representatives;
ii. The State Houses of Assembly exercises the legislative power of States in Nigeria;
iii. Local Government Councils are vested with the legislative power of Local Government Areas in Nigeria;
iv. Administrative legislative authorities exercise subordinate legislative powers delegated by the principal legislative bodies.

---

[34] C.O. Ajah, *op. cit.*, 97-98
[35] Ibid., 27
[36] See J.F Garner, *Administration Law*(1974) 50 cited by B.O Iluyomade and B.U Eka, *op. cit.*,27
[37] Ibid., see also Iluyomade, B.O and Eka B.U, *op. cit., 27*

HIERARCHY OF LEGISLATIONS

For purposes of determining the hierarchy of legislations, there are basically three substantive types of legislation in Nigeria-the Acts, Laws, and By-laws, respectively, made by the legislative arms of the Federal, State, and Local governments. Subsidiary legislations derive powers from these substantive legislations.

Of course, the Constitution is the grundnorm and most important and supreme legislation in Nigeria. As the supreme law, any legislation or law in conflict or inconsistent with any provision of the constitution is invalid, unconstitutional, null, and void to the extent of its inconsistency[38].

In a similar way, all Acts of the National Assembly are superior to Laws and By-laws passed by the States, Local Government Councils, or other subordinate legislative bodies.

Of course, the By-laws by Local Government Councils bow to the laws.

Since the three tiers of government can make laws, the Constitution determines in what areas these tiers of government can legislate. As between the Federal and State governments, the Constitution prescribes three Legislative Lists-the Exclusive, Concurrent, and Residual contained in schedules to the Constitution. While the Federal legislature has exclusive power to legislate on matters in the exclusive list, the States can legislate on the matters in the Residual List and may make laws on the Concurrent Legislative List. Although both Federal and State governments can make laws on matters in the Concurrent List, if there is any conflict, the Federal law will take precedence: Section 4(5) of the Constitution.

The Exclusive Legislative List has 67 items, including Accounts of the Government of the Federation; Arms, ammunition, and explosives, aviation, including Airports, Awards of national titles of honour, bankruptcy and insolvency, banks, banking, bills of exchange, and promissory notes, census, citizenship, naturalization, and aliens, copyright, creation of states, currency; customs and excise duties, defence, diplomatic, consular and trade representation, drugs and

[38] See sections 1 and 4(5) of the Constitution

poisons, evidence, exchange control, external affairs, insurance, labour, military, maritime shipping and navigation, national parks, mines and minerals, meteorology; passports and visas, nuclear energy; patents, trademarks, pensions, police, prisons, railways, stamp duties, etc.[39]

AMENDMENT OF LEGISLATIONS

Legislations can be amended, altered, or repealed by the appropriate legislative body.

Although the supreme law of the land, the Constitution, would seem to be sacrosanct, Section 9 of the Constitution provides for the mode of altering provisions of the Constitution. It states that:

> (1) The National Assembly may, subject to the provisions of this section, alter any of the provisions of this Constitution.
>
> (2) An Act of the National Assembly for the alteration of this Constitution...shall not be passed in either House of the National assembly unless the proposal is supported by the votes of not less than two-thirds majority of all the members of that House and approved by resolution of the Houses of Assembly of no less than two-thirds of all the States.
>
> (3) An Act of the National Assembly for the purpose of altering the provision of this section, section 8, or Chapter IV of this Constitution shall not be passed by either House of the National Assembly unless the proposal is approved by the votes of not less than the four-fifths majority of all the members of each House, and also approved by resolution of the Houses of Assembly of not less than two-thirds of all the States.
>
> (4) ...

Thus, Section 9 of the Constitution empowers alteration, not amendment, of the provisions of the Constitution. However, alteration of

[39] See Second Schedule, pursuant to section 4 of the Constitution, as altered.

the Constitution is made somehow more difficult by generally requiring more than a simple majority of members present and voting[40]. Again, the alteration is made quite rigorous and difficult by requiring the support of higher majority votes and of all members of each House as well as approval of two-thirds of State Houses of Assembly. Alteration of certain provisions, including Section 9 enabling alteration, requires much more in terms of approval and four-fifths majority. Suffice to state that alteration is possible, and three alterations[41] have been made to the 1999 Constitution to date.

In every other case, any legislation may be amended by the appropriate legislative body in the exercise of the general legislative power conferred by the Constitution.[42] Section 56 of the Constitution provides, in part:

> (1) Except as otherwise provided by this Constitution, any question proposed for decision in the Senate or House of Representatives shall be determined by the required majority of the members present and voting; and...
>
> (2) Except as otherwise provided by this constitution, the required majority for the purposes of determining any question shall be a simple majority.

A similar provision is made in section 98 for the State Houses of Assembly.

REVIEW OF LEGISLATION

Although legislations can be reviewed by the legislative bodies for purposes of alteration or amendment,[43] the common review is by the judiciary. Judicial review of legislations is one appropriate check and balance created by the doctrine of separation of powers. There are known criteria for judicial review of legislations, and the court can in

[40]Generally decisions of the National Assembly is by simple majority of members present and voting: see Section 56 of the Constitution

[41]The latest being the Constitution (Third Alteration) Act No.3 2010 assented to on 4 March 2011

[42]Section 58 for the National Assembly and section 100 for the State Houses of Assembly

[43]For instance, the 1999 Constitution has continued to be reviewed by the National Assembly: The outcome of previous reviews have seen three alterations to the Constitution, ostensibly amendments to the legislation.

fact, set aside legislation for good reasons. This power of the Court is recognized by Section 4 of the Constitution, which confers legislative powers on the National Assembly and the State Houses of Assembly. Section 4(8) provides that "Save as otherwise provided by this Constitution the exercise of legislative powers by the National Assembly or by a House of Assembly shall be subject to the jurisdiction of courts of law..."

Firstly, legislation or law generally must be made strictly in accordance with the provisions of the Constitution or risk being set aside by a court of competent jurisdiction based on the *ultra vires* doctrine.[44] The defect could be in terms of procedure or substance: *A.G. Bendel* v. *A.G. Federation*;[45] *Attorney General of Abia State* v. *Attorney General of the Federation & Ors.*[46] No legislative body is allowed to enact or pass a law that is contrary to the provisions of Constitution. It is acknowledged that it is the role of the judiciary to interpret the laws made by the legislature and determine what the constitution permits: *N.E.M.G.I.A Ltd.* v. *Uchay*.[47]

In Nigeria, not much action has been seen from the courts striking down on substantive legislations,[48] but there are many reported cases of setting aside subordinate legislations for being *ultra vires* the powers conferred. An unconstitutional or unlawful exercise of a lawfully delegated power will be struck down.[49] As earlier mentioned, delegated legislation that is inconsistent with the enabling statute or any other statute will be set aside.[50] Furthermore, a delegated legislation could also be set aside if it is substantively *ultra vires*. The test is whether the delegate of legislative power has performed only those acts that the enabling statute specifically authorized or those which "may fairly be

---

[44] *William Marbury* v. *James Madison, supra*
[45](1981) 10 S C 1
[46](2002) 95 LRCN 407
[47](1974)4 S C 1
[48]But see the old case of *Balewa* v. *Doherty* [1963] 1 WLR 949 where the Commissions and Tribunal of Enquiry Act, 1961 passed by the Federal Parliament was declared null and void by the Privy Council, on the ground inter alia, that it was beyond the constitutional powers of parliament
[49] *Williams* v. *Majekodunmi* [1962]All N L R 413
[50] *Powell* v. *May, supra*

regarded as incidental to or consequential upon those things which the legislature had authorized."[51]

CONCLUSION

The ambit of legislation as law in Nigeria is very wide. It comprises not just Acts, Laws, and Byelaws but also numerous administrative subordinate legislations enabled by a delegation of legislative functions under substantive legislations. For several reasons, these subordinate legislations are very important for the day-to-day running of government, supplying necessary details, filling vital gaps, and responding to exigencies of governance. Legislations are dynamic and cover the field, particularly the legal, economic, social, and political spheres. This law is also most effective and powerful and obviously superior to other sources. Legislation supersedes customary law and easily overrides received English law and even annuls former legislation.

[51]See Iluyomade, B.O and Eka B.U, *op cit.*, 83; *Attorney General* v. *Great Eastern Railway* [1880]5 Appeal Cases 473, at 478

Chapter 8

INTERPRETATION OF STATUTES IN NIGERIA

Michael Ibanga*

INTRODUCTION

Judges have the duty of declaring the common law on issues brought to them by litigants. Where provisions of statutes are relevant to claims brought before the court, the judge has the duty to decide on the meaning of words or clauses in the statutes.[1] The role of the courts is to apply the statutes made by the legislature to the facts of cases before them. This task will be simple and straightforward in some cases but will not be so in situations where the. In such circumstances, the court is imposed with the responsibility of finding out what the legislature really meant to say by what is expressed in a legislative provision or words in it. In such cases, the court is said to be interpreting the statute.[2]

It is not the entire statute that is being interpreted; rather, it is a particular provision of it, or a word, or a clause in a particular provision. In every instance of interpretation of a statute is the tacit desire by the court to ensure fairness of its decision to the parties in dispute. Equally implicit in the exercise is the yearning of the court to

---

*Reader, Faculty of Law, University of Calabar, Nigeria.

[1] Denis Keenan, *Smith and Keenan's English Law 8th ed.* (London: Pitman, 1986) p.141.

[2] Michael E. Ibanga, *Learning Legal Theory and Legal Method* (Calabar; Associated Publishers Ltd. 1996) p.231.

discover and give effect to the *intention of the legislature* – an issue that has generated a lot of debate among theorists.[3]

In this chapter, our purpose is not merely to discuss the known principles of interpretation of statute; the scope of the paper will necessarily extend to a consideration of the attitude of the Nigerian court when faced with the delicate task of balancing the scale of justice in difficult situations of interpretation of the statute. The issue of concern in this regard is whether the Nigerian court is inclined to the view that the duty of the court is merely to apply the law made by the legislature and no more, or is ready in appropriate circumstances to adopt a liberal attitude of interpretation and "fill the gap" in the statute where necessary. As a necessary background, the chapter briefly discusses the factors that give rise to the interpretation of the statute by the court.

FACTORS THAT NECESSITATE INTERPRETATION OF STATUTE

Statutory provisions embody social policies expressed in legal terms.[4] Adoption of statutes involves communication between the law-maker (the legislature) on the one hand, and the "law-subjects" (whose conducts and interactions have to be regulated by the statutory provisions), the implementers (the Executive), and interpreters of the law (the court), on the other hand. The problems experienced in ordinary life in the process of communication also apply to situations in which policies are communicated to the citizenry through statutory provisions. Some statutory provisions or words in them, because of being vague or ambiguous, may not be easily understood by the court in the judicial process. When this happens, it amounts to a failure to communicate the "message" in the statutory provisions in clear terms.

Ambiguity and Vagueness

Statutes embody legal rules and principles in their provisions, and it is the rules and principles that the courts apply in the resolution of

---

[3] M. D. A. Freeman, *Lloyd's Introduction to Jurisprudence 8th ed.* (London: Sweet & Maxwell, 2008) p.1557.

[4] Michael Ibanga, note 2 *supra.*

matters brought before them. If a word found in the provision of a statute is capable of two or more meanings, this will occasion ambiguity concerning the application of the provision. If it is difficult to say what a particular provision in a statute really means, it can be said that the provision is vague.[5] The problems of ambiguity and vagueness in statutory provisions distort the meaning of the words or clauses in them, thus causing a kind of "semantic blurs". When this occurs in the process of adjudication, it becomes difficult for the court to say what the legislature "intended" to communicate through the medium of the word or clause in focus.

Statutory provisions are subject to the imperfections of every linguistic message, which are inherent in every language; such imperfections make it difficult for a man to express his thought clearly. When the court is faced with the problem of ambiguity or vagueness of statutory provision in the process of trying to apply it to the case in hand, the court has to "interpret" it, that is, find out what the legislature "intended" to say by what is expressed in the statutory provision or a word in it.

Open Texture of Statutory Provisions

One of the factors that lead to the interpretation of the statute is the lack of sufficient details in a statutory provision as to the range of matters to be covered by it. The legislature often uses general words intentionally in the belief that judges are the most adept in filling the details.[6] And ordinarily, statutory provisions embody general rules and principles which are intended for certain circumstances. That is, statutory provisions are pitched at a convenient level of generality so that they can cover as much as possible the class of circumstances contemplated - the range of matters to which the law has to apply.

The fact is that generality in the "language of law" (the manner statutory provisions are expressed) makes it possible for the law to cover as much as possible the classes of circumstance or persons contemplated, but at the same time, it makes indeterminacy (open

[5] Ibid.

[6] M. D. A. *Freeman, Lloyd's Introduction to Jurisprudence* 8th ed. (London) p.1557

texture) to set in when the provisions of the law (statute) are to be applied to some circumstances or persons. That is, it becomes indeterminate in certain situations whether or not the provisions of the statute should apply. This happens because the legislature never found it convenient or necessary to specify all conceivable situations to which the statutory provisions will apply. And indeed, it is impossible to be specific concerning all future situations to which a statutory provision will apply.

A legal rule or principle expressed in statutory provisions applies to plain cases which occur in similar contexts, without any doubt. Such plain cases constitute the paradigm situations for which the rule or principle was intended. However, it happens that from time to time, new cases emerge, in relation to which it becomes doubtful whether or not the rule or principle should apply. What creates such doubt is that the new cases share the features of the paradigm cases and also incorporate other novel elements. It is for the court to determine which of these sets of elements is so overwhelming to either make the rule or principle to apply to the situation or exclude its application. Even in this kind of scenario, the court is still involved in the "interpretation" of the statute.

By way of an illustration, a statutory provision (on safety standards for cinema houses) states that the occupiers of premises on which films are shown shall comply with certain safety regulations. The provision will apply unquestionably to all normal film houses. But when a new case emerges in which someone shows film in a cave, and he is served a notice by the local authority under the Film Act requiring him to comply with safety regulations in his "premises," an indeterminacy (open texture) will occur concerning the applicability of the relevant provision to the particular case. It will be the duty of the court to decide whether or not to assimilate a cave in the notion of "premises" for the purpose of the statutory provision in focus.[7]

The Nigerian court, just as its counterparts in other jurisdictions, is often faced with such situations, and how the court decides should be

---

[7] *Gardiner* v. *Sevenoaks* R.D.C. (1950) 66 TLR 1091.

prompted by the desire to do justice in particular cases. And one of the most important judicial functions is the interpretation of the statute.[8] In the process of interpretation of the statute, the court is assisted by certain principles, aids, and presumptions. The focus of this discussion will be on the mischief, literal and golden principles of statutory interpretation.

APPLICATION OF THE PRINCIPLES OF STATUTORY INTERPRETATION BY THE NIGERIAN COURT

As a former British colonial territory, Nigeria inherited the common law approach to the interpretation of the statute.[9] The courts in common law legal systems have developed and followed a number of conventions as a means of searching out the legislative intent[10] when faced with the task of interpreting of the statute. These include grammatical rules such as the *ejusdem generis* and the *expressio unius exclusio alterius* rules, various presumptions, and the three main principles of statutory interpretation – the mischief, literal, and golden principles. As indicated herein before, this chapter will focus on the three main principles. But it has been cautioned that it is wrong to give the impression that there are in existence three distinct principles of statutory interpretation because, according to some theorists, the three principles have been fused.[11] And according to another writer, the three principles are, to an extent, contradictory.[12] All that notwithstanding, our interest in this chapter is in how the Nigerian courts have been applying the principles.

The Mischief Principle

The earliest principle, the mischief principle, as it came to the known, was formulated in *Heydon's case* in 1584.[13] The principle was prevalent

---

[8] M.D.A. Freeman, *op. cit.*

[9] T. A. Aguda, "Bearing Faithful Allegiance to Law" *Nigerian Current Law Review"* (1995) pp.67-79, at 67.

[10] M. D. A. Freeman, *op. cit.*

[11] Ibid.

[12] Lord Templeman, *Jurisprudence: The Philosophy of Law* (London: Old Bailey Press, 1997) p.331.

[13] (1584) 3 Co Rep 7.

in the sixteenth century[14] and was dominant in case of law until the nineteenth century.[15] The classic statement of the principle is contained in Heydon's case, where the court laid down the criteria to be considered when interpreting statutes: the state of the common law before the statute was adopted, the mischief that the law did not provide for, the remedy appointed for that mischief, and the true reason of the remedy.

It may be necessary to point out that not all statutes are altering the common law in current times. Thus, the exact formulation of the criteria for the application of the principle needs alteration. However, whatever changes may become necessary in restating the criteria, they were approved by the Nigerian court in *Balogun* v. *Salami.*[16]

After considering the criteria for the application of the principle, the court is enjoined to interpret an ambiguous provision of a statute in such a way as to suppress the mischief and advance the remedy. In order to discover the previous mischief and the remedy intended by the statute sought to be interpreted, the court can consider some intrinsic aids such as the preamble, headings and titles, marginal notes, explanatory notes, and also previous statutes and case law dealing with the same matter.[17]

The Nigerian courts have applied this principle of interpretation of a statute in a number of cases. In *Akerele* v. *Inspector General of Police,*[18] the court had to interpret the word: "accuses" in Section 210(b) of the Criminal Code. The section provided that: any person who accuses or threatens to accuse any person of being a witch or having the power of witchcraft is guilty of a misdemeanour and is liable to imprisonment for two years. The accused in the instant case argued that the word: "accuses" in Section 210(b) meant making a formal accusation by information under oath.

This argument was rejected by the court, and Ademola J. stated:

---

[14] Templeman, note 12 *supra.* P.331
[15] Freeman, note 6, *supra,* pp.1555-1556
[16] (1963) 1 All N.L.R. 129.
[17] J. O. Asein, *Introduction to Nigerian Legal System* 2nd ed. (Lagos: Ababa Press Ltd., 2005) p.58.
[18] (1955) 21 N.L.R. 37

> It appears to me that the short history behind this chapter of the code is to prohibit indiscriminate accusations of witchcraft and to stop the practice of trial by ordeal and the like by making them punishable.

And bearing in mind this mischief which the statute was meant to cure, the court interpreted the section in the way it could advance the appropriate remedy. Accordingly, the court held that the section could not have contemplated a formal accusation under oath. Thus, in the circumstance, an oral accusation by the accused was sufficient and indeed, was what was needed to establish his guilt under the relevant section of the code.

The Literal Principle

The growth of parliamentary supremacy in England and other factors led to the development in the early part of the nineteenth century of the literal principle of interpretation of the statute. The literal principle emphasizes the intention of the legislature, and such an intention is assumed to be contained in the words of the statute.[19] According to this principle, if the words used in a statute are perfectly clear in meaning, then the court must apply those words in their literal and ordinary meaning, even if this leads to hardship for those affected by the statute, even if the court does not approve of the individual provision, and even if strict application leads to a highly unsatisfactory result.[20]

The literal principle of statutory interpretation has been applied in a number of cases in Nigeria, one of such being that of *Adegbenro* v. *Akintola*.[21] The case involved the interpretation of Section 33(10) of the Constitution of the then Western Region of Nigeria, which empowered the Governor to remove the Premier if "it appears to him that the premier no longer commands the support of a majority of the House of Assembly." The case went to the Privy Council on appeal, and it interpreted the words: "it appears to him" to mean that the judgment as to whether the premier no longer commands the support of a majority of the House was left to the Governor's assessment without any

---

[19] Templeman, note 12 *supra,* p.332

[20] Patricia Hirst and Michael Hirst, *Textbook on A Level Law* 2nd ed. (London: Blackstone Press Ltd., 1998) p.37

[21] (1962) 1 All N.L.R. 467

reference to what was happening in the House of Assembly. The court was not persuaded by the argument of the other party to the effect that the Governor's assessment as to whether the Premier no longer commands the support of a majority of the House members had to be based on a motion adopted by the House.

The literal principle also featured in the case of *Okumagba* v. *Egbe.*[22] The court, in the case, was to decide whether there had been a breach of Regulation 60(b) of the 1960 Parliamentary Regulations, which stipulated that every person who before or during an election knowingly or recklessly publishes any false statement of the withdrawal of a candidate at such election for the purpose of promoting or procuring the election of another person, shall be guilty of an offence.

The appellant, having been rejected as a candidate, changed his symbol to that of A, another candidate, and falsely told his supporters that A had withdrawn his candidature. He did that with the aim of inducing his supporters to vote for A's symbol, thereby swelling A's votes. The phrase "another candidate" in the relevant section could not implicate the accused, and the magistrate felt that the phrase should read "any candidate" in order to bring the conduct of the accused under the ambit of the law. But on appeal, the Supreme Court decided that the Regulation contemplated lying to help a different candidate, and the conduct of the appellant did not breach the relevant section. And commenting on the action of the magistrate, Bairamian, J.S.C. stated that: "amendment is the function of the legislature, and the courts cannot fill a gap which comes to light by altering the words of a regulation to make it read in the way they think it should have been enacted."

Another case that illustrates the hardship which may be associated with the application of the literal principles is that of *R.* v. *Bangaza.*[23] The statutory provision in focus here was Section 319(2) of the then Criminal Code, which prohibited the death sentence for any offender who had not attained the age of 17 years and was found guilty of

---

[22] (1965) 1 All N.L.R. 62
[23] (1960) 5 F.S.C. I

murder. The Supreme Court was of the opinion that the relevant age should be at the time of conviction and not at the time the offence was committed.

By following the literal principle, the court purports to emphasize the intention of the legislature. But considering the decisions in the cases discussed above, it is doubtful that the legislature intended such outcomes from the words they used. Regarding *Adegbenro* v. *Akintola,* it is difficult to accept that the legislature intended to give the Governor limitless power to remove the Premier on the ground of a lack of support of the House members without resources whatsoever to what was happening in the House.

Also, the decision in *R.* v. *Bangaza* could not have been in line with what the legislature intended; and this is confirmed by the fact that the relevant provision of the statute in focus was amended subsequently with a reiteration that the relevant age is the age at the time the offence was committed and not at the time of the conviction.[24] One can therefore say that in some instances of following the literal principle, it is not the "intention of the legislature" which the court is actually implementing. The word of caution is that the Nigerian court should exercise due care in applying this principle.

The Golden Principle

The golden principle of statutory interpretation, often attributed to Baron Parke in *Beckley* v. *Smith,*[25] though its origin could be traced back earlier,[26] was developed to temper the operation of the literal principle. According to Baron Parke in the cited case, it is a very useful rule in the construction of the statute to adhere to the ordinary meaning of the word used and to the grammatical construction unless that is at variance with the intention of the legislature to be collected from the statute itself, or leads to any manifest absurdity or repugnance, in which case the language may be varied or modified so as to avoid such inconvenience, but no further.

---

[24] The amendment was affected through the Criminal Justice (Miscellaneous Provisions) Act 1966.
[25] (1936) 2 M. & W 191; 150 E.R. 724.
[26] M.D.A. Freeman, note 6 *supra*, at 1556

However, the principle cannot be invoked for every imaginable inconvenience or absurdity.[27] But where there is a real ambiguity in the provision of a statute, the court is justified in departing from the literal principle of interpretation.

The golden principle is an off-short of the literal principle, and is to the effect that where the provision of a statute is capable of more than one meaning, the court should favour that meaning which will not lead to absurdity. If giving words of a statutory provision their plain meaning will lead to an absurdity, the court is right in interpreting them according to some other secondary meaning. The principle has been followed in some decisions in Nigeria.

In *R.* v. *Princewill,*[28] the accused was charged with the offence of bigamy under Section 370 of the Criminal Code, which provided that any person who, having married under the Marriage Act, contracts another marriage while the first is still subsisting shall be guilty of a felony and liable to imprisonment for seven years. The accused, having contracted a marriage under the Marriage Act when he was a Christian, later became a Muslim and went through a form of marriage with another woman while the first wife was still alive and the marriage still subsisted.

The question before the court was whether the accused had contravened Section 370 of the Criminal Code by his second marriage. The court held that the word: "marries" in Section 370 of the Criminal Code does not refer to contracting a valid marriage (as canvassed by the accused) but to going through a form of marriage known and recognized by law. To hold otherwise would negate the true intention of the legislature.

ATTITUDE OF THE NIGERIAN COURT

When faced with factors which call for interpretation of the statute in the judicial process, the court is often assumed to be trying to discover the intention of the legislature as it relates to the meaning of the words found in the statute; and the role of the court is generally said to be that

---

[27] J. O. Asein, note 17 *supra*, p.54
[28] (1963) 2 All N.L.R. 31

of declaring the law. However, it has been recommended that "the judiciary of this country must modify its approach to its interpretation of statutory provisions but more especially of constitutional provisions as well as judicial precedents if it must play a meaningful role in the desired political, social and legal development of the country." [29] Thus, it has been suggested that "we should not continue to perpetuate the 19th-century myth of a judiciary that simply interprets statutes or precedents in accordance with legal logic, but which need not concern itself with the deeper struggles and agonies of society."[30]

The review being canvassed by the learned writer is that, contrary to such position as taken by Bairamian JSC in *Okumagba* v. *Egbe*,[31] the court cannot fill a gap in a statutory provision in the judicial process in performing the duty of interpreting a statute; the court in some instances should be involved in a creative exercise which actually amounts to "filling the gap" in the statutory provision. One identifies with this view and recommends an attitude of "interpretative liberalism" by the Nigerian courts. The same position has been taken by other writers.

The conservative approach to judicial function – that the judge only declares the law and does not make law – is a product of the common law tradition.[32] In line with the conservative tradition, Lord Bramwell declared in *Hill* v. *East Indian and West Indian Government*:[33] "it is infinitely better to adhere to the words of an Act of Parliament and leave the legislature to set it right than to alter those words according to one's notion of an absurdity."

Having been a British colonial territory, Nigeria inherited the conservative common law approach to the interpretation of the statute. It has been asserted that this approach in Nigeria exhibits weakness against tyranny. Therefore, it is inadequate for the need of modern society; thus, a more dynamic attitude to the interpretation of the

[29] T. A. Aguda, "Bearing Faithful Allegiance to Law" Nigerian Current Law Review (1995) pp. 67-79, at 67.
[30] Ibid.
[31] (1965) 1 All N.L.R. 62.
[32] C. C. Nweze, "Judicial Sustainability of Constitutional Democracy in Nigeria: A Response to the Phonographic Theory of Judicial Function" in E. S. Nwauche and F. I. Asogwah (eds.) Essays *in Honour of C. O. Okonkwo* (Port Harcourt: Jite Books, 2000) p.227.
[33] (1884) 9 AC 448.

statute has been recommended for the Nigerian judges.[34] It is further argued that the Nigerian judge cannot afford the conservatism of the English judge if he is to faithfully serve his people and his conscience.[35] And it is noted that the English judge sees his task as one of interpreting the law and places implicit confidence in the good sense of the legislature and the Executive, and is not faced with tyrannical laws and the kind of political and social experience his Nigerian counterparts are faced with.[36]

A survey conducted by a researcher has shown that the Nigerian courts have only attained limited success in the direction of assuming the dynamic role in the interpretation of the law.[37] It is better for the Nigerian courts to incline themselves to the liberal approach to the interpretation of statute because, even in England, this approach has been adopted in different instances. In *Seaford Court Estates Ltd.* v. *Asher,*[38] the court (per Denning, L.J.) made it clear that when a defect appears in the act of Parliament, a judge cannot simply fold his hands and blame the draftsman.

In another English case,[39] the court (per Denning L. J.) indicated that finding out the intention of parliament in the process of interpretation of a statute is better done through filling in the gaps and making sense of the enactment than by opening it up to destructive analysis. Unfortunately, the House of Lords in England has been reluctant to accept the liberal approach to the interpretation of the statute, and the Nigerian Supreme Court still favours the conservative attitude.[40] But there are strong views in support of the liberal approach, particularly with respect to the interpretation of constitutional

---

[34] T. A. Aguda, note 29 *Supra.*
[35] Ibid.
[36] Ibid.
[37] C. C. Nweze, "A Survey of the Shifting Trends in Judicial Attitude to Fundamental Rights in Nigeria" in I. A. Umezulike and C. C. Nweze (eds.) *Perspective in Law and Justice (1996).*
[38] (1949) 2 K.B. 481.
[39] *Magor and St. Melons Rural District Council* v. *Newport Corporation* (1950) 2 All E. R. 1226, at 1236.
[40] J. O. Asein, note 17 *supra*, p.62.

provisions.[41] And in that regard, it has been asserted that the common law rules of interpretation may be inappropriate for Nigeria.[42]

It has been observed that the Nigerian courts, though generally favouring the conservative approach, are mindful of the objectives that constitutional provisions are intended to serve and have shown the readiness to adopt a liberal approach in their interpretation.[43] Indeed, in *Peoples' Democratic Party* v. *I.N.E.C,* [44] the Supreme Court of Nigeria restated some of the imperatives of constitutional interpretation, one of which is the need for a liberal and purposive approach.

CONCLUSION

When the court is to assign meaning to a word in a statute or decide on the applicability of a statutory provision to the case before it, all in an attempt to promote justice, the court is involved in the interpretation of the statute. In Nigeria, the courts have applied the extant principles of interpretation of statute developed by the courts in England. Generally, the courts in Nigeria, following the attitude of the English court, have regarded their role mainly as that of interpretation of the law and not that of making law; thus, they incline themselves to the conservative approach to the interpretation of the statute. But in a few instances, the courts have seen the need to adopt the liberal approach when faced with the task of interpreting the statute,[45] particularly where a constitutional provision is in issue. One recommends that in every instance of interpretation of the statute, the Nigerian courts should follow the approach that will enhance the interest of justice and should not be reluctant to "fill the gap" in a statutory provision if such interest so demands.

---

[41] Example: B. O. Okere, "Judicial Activism or Passivity in Interpreting the Nigeria constitution," 36 ICLQ 789 (1987).

[42] J. O. Asein, note 17 *supra*, at 65.

[43] Ibid.

[44] (2001) 1 W.L.R. 1

[45] Example: *PDP and Anor* v. *INEC and Ors* (1999) SCNJ 297; *Bronik Motors Ltd.* v. *Wema Bank Ltd.* (1983) 1 SCNLR 296; *Peoples' Democratic Party* v. *I.N.E.C.* (2001) I.W.L.R. 1

Chapter 9

LAW REFORM AND GOVERNANCE IN NIGERIA

Emeka Iheme*

INTRODUCTION

In every society, laws are made to regulate human affairs in line with the prevailing social, economic and political realities, particularly the world-view of those in authority. Over time, inevitably, internal and external forces compel every society to undergo changes. Such changes include those brought about by new ideas and new technology (which lead to new types of goods and services as well as new relationships), external threats, and internal weaknesses. Again, sometimes the law on a given subject may not be quite clearly stated in the books, which leads to confusion, or may be scattered in several statutes, making it difficult for people to ascertain the exact position of the law.

Accordingly, there is usually the need for new laws to replace some old ones, for restatements that make the law clearer, and for laws that regulate novel phenomena. Law reform is the process of addressing this need. It "is the process of examining existing laws, and advocating [or making] and implementing changes in a legal system, usually with the aim of enhancing justice or efficiency."[1] Law reform is an integral part of the governance process. But what is governance? In very simple

---

* He is a legal practitioner and development consultant with substantial experience in legal and institutional reform as well as project cycle management in Commonwealth African countries.

[1] Rachel M. Gisselquist *Good Governance as a Concept, and Why This Matters for Development Policy* (UNU-WIDER Working Paper No. 2012/30, United Nations University Press, 2012) <http://wider.unu.edu/publications/working-papers/2012/en_GB/wp2012-030/> accessed on 13 February 2014.

terms, governance has been defined as "the process of decision-making and the process by which decisions are implemented (or not implemented)."[2] Since governance is the process of making and implementing decisions, an analysis of the *actors* and *structures* involved in the process is indispensable to an understanding of governance.[3]

Some actors in the governance process are within the orbit of the state (i.e., government officials and government departments or agencies) while other actors are outside the orbit of the state (e.g., individuals such as businessmen and businesswomen, lawyers, land-owners; organizations, such as chambers of commerce, religious groups, cooperatives, women's groups, tenants' associations, youth associations, international donors and international financial institutions). The main formal structures in the governance process are the cabinet and the legislature, while informal structures include "kitchen cabinets" and caucus groups within the legislature. While state actors lead and take responsibility for governance decisions, the decisions sometimes reflect the views or preferences that non-state actors overtly or covertly place before the state actors.

It is in the governance process that the decision whether or not to reform a particular area of the law is made, and it is also in the governance process that a new law (the product of law reform) is effectively or partially implemented or not implemented at all. Again, the law reform process can be used to achieve "good governance." While there can be no universally acceptable definition of the concept of "good governance,"[4] the following are some of the attributes that are now most commonly associated with good governance: citizens' participation, accountability, transparency, the rule of law, effectiveness, and efficiency. In this chapter, we shall discuss some institutions and issues associated with law reform and note some

---

2 See "What is Good Governance?" < http://www.unescap.org/pdd/prs/Project Activities/Ongoing/gg/governance.asp> accessed 12 February 2014>

3 Ibid.

4 See Rachel M. Gisselquist *Good Governance as a Concept, and Why This Matters for Development Policy* (UNU-WIDER Working Paper No. 2012/30, United Nations University Press, 2012) <http://wider.unu.edu/publications/working-papers/2012/en_GB/wp2012-030/> accessed on 13 February 2014.

remarkable instances of law reform in Nigeria, noting how law reform initiatives fit into the larger processes of governance. Finally, we shall draw some conclusions from our discussions and offer some recommendations for promoting law reform in aid of good governance in Nigeria.

INSTITUTIONS, ISSUES, AND INSTANCES

Law Reform Agencies

History and Role

We have noted that government officials and departments or agencies, as well as individuals and groups outside the government, may play a role in the law reform and governance processes. Thus, following a commitment made in the manifesto of a ruling party, the cabinet may push for reform in a given area of law (e.g., land law), or the President or a Minister may set in motion a process for the reform of the law in any given area that he or she strongly considers being needful of reform. Similarly, a trade association, religious group, or other civil society organization may lobby for reform in a particular area of the law. None of these persons or groups, however, is primarily concerned, and on a continuing basis, with the organized and systematic making of changes in various areas of the law. That concern is one that may be placed on the shoulders of a law reform agency, i.e., a public institution that brings together legal scholars and keeps them engaged, on a continuing basis, in the task of reviewing various areas of law and proposing reforms.

In each area of the law that they examine for reform, law reform agencies typically conduct research, consult widely with experts and stakeholders (i.e., those to be affected by the law and proposed changes in it) and prepare a report setting out recommendations for reform. The reform measures they propose may seek to repeal an existing law or laws or enact a new law or laws. Where a new law is proposed for enactment, its provisions or content may be entirely new or maybe a consolidation (i.e., the collection and restatement of the law on a given subject matter as contained in various existing statutes) or a codification (i.e., the collection and systematic presentation of the law on a given subject matter as contained in existing statutes as well as case law). Although many law reform measures lead to the enactment or repeal of a law by the legislature, a law reform measure may also be introduced in new subsidiary legislation or practice directions or rules of court, thus possibly dispensing with the need for any action by the legislature.[5]

In the United Kingdom,[6] the history of the establishment of a permanent agency to systematically review the law goes back to 1934, when the Lord Chancellor, Lord Sankey, set up the Law Revision Committee. The Committee members were judges, legal academics, barristers, and solicitors, and they worked part-time, usually meeting from time to time after court hours. After the outbreak of the Second World War in 1939, the Committee became moribund, perhaps because its work was not considered a wartime priority. It was not until 1952 that the Law Reform Committee, another permanent agency that functioned just like its predecessor, was established.

Better days were to come. In 1963, Gerald Gardiner, QC, a long-time member of the Law Reform Committee, and Dr. Andrew Martin wrote a chapter in a book, *Law Reform – Now,*[7] in which they argued that the need for law reform was enormous and could not be adequately addressed through the mechanism of a committee of part-time members. They recommended the establishment of a permanent body of full-time commissioners (high-level experts, not being civil servants) operating independently and assisted by legal staff. They also

---

[5] The Nigerian Law Reform Commission is now in the final stages of the preparation of Sentencing Guidelines. In December 2013, the Commission organized a workshop in Uyo, Akwa Ibom State, to review the draft of the Guidelines. The communiquй issued at the end of the workshop recommended that the Guidelines "should be issued as a practice direction by the Chief Justice of Nigeria and should serve for the states to adopt." See 'Law Reform Commission Calls for Training of Judges, Magistrates on Sentencing Guidelines' Daily *Times Nigeria* (Lagos, 6 December 2013) < http://www.dailytimes. com.ng /article/law-reform-commission-calls-training-judges-magistrates-sentencing-guidelines> accessed on 13 February 2014

[6] Permanent law reform agencies have been in existence in the United States since the 1920s. In 1925, the State of New Jersey set up the New Jersey Law Revision Commission. This was followed by the establishment of similar bodies in the states of North Carolina, New York and Louisiana. See 'Law Reform Agencies: The Emergence of an Idea' < http://www.justice.gc.ca/eng/rp-pr/csj-sjc/ilp-pji/lr-rd/page2.html > accessed 14 February 2014

[7] Gerald Gardiner and Andrew Martin (eds), *Law Reform – Now* (1st edn, V. Gollancz, 1963)

recommended that there should be a rule that Parliament should enact at least one Law Reform Act each year.

By an auspicious turn of events, Gerald Gardner was given the opportunity to actualize this vision when, in 1964, he was appointed Lord Chancellor (and became Lord Gardiner) in Prime Minister Harold Wilson's first administration. Not surprisingly, the same vision was set out in the government's *White Paper on the Creation of a Law Commission for England and Wales and a Law Commission for Scotland* in 1965 and subsequently embodied in the Law Commissions Act 1965, which established two law commissions, one for England and Wales and the other for Scotland. The establishment of the law commissions under the Act of 1965 opened a new chapter in the history of law reform agencies and inspired other Commonwealth countries to set up similar bodies. In Nigeria, the federal law reform agency, the Nigerian Law Reform Commission (NLRC), was established by law in 1979. Most states, if not all, also have law reform agencies. In order to deepen our understanding of law reform agencies from a Nigerian national perspective, we shall place the NLRC in the centre of the rest of our discussion.

The Nigerian Law Reform Commission – Establishment and Functions

The Nigerian Law Reform Commission Act 1979 established the agency. Section 2 of the Act provides that the members of the Commission shall be appointed by the President and shall consist of four full-time Commissioners, one of whom shall be designated as the chairman. The commissioners shall be persons who hold high judicial office or are legal practitioners of not less than twelve years standing or eminent scholars in law. A commissioner shall hold office for a term of five years which may be renewed once.

The National Assembly may terminate the appointment of a member on the grounds of misbehaviour or inability to discharge the duties of his office by reason of physical or mental incapacity; in the case of a commissioner who holds a high judicial office, the National Assembly may terminate the commissioner's appointment only if the commissioner ceases to hold the high judicial office. Each commissioner shall be paid such salaries and allowances as the President may, from time to time, direct, provided that the salary and allowances of the chairman shall not be less than such as are paid to a Justice of the Supreme Court of Nigeria. Except in the case of persons holding high judicial office, the chairman and the commissioners shall not, while holding office as commissioners, hold any other offices of emolument either in the public service or in any other service whatsoever.

Section 5 prescribes the functions of the Commission. Broadly, under the sub-section (1), it shall be the duty of the Commission to take and keep under review all Federal laws with a view to their systematic and progressive development and reform in consonance with the prevailing norms of Nigerian society, including, in particular, the codification of such laws, the elimination of anomalies, the repeal of obsolete, spent and unnecessary enactments, the reduction in a number of separate enactments, the reform of procedural laws in consonance with changes in the machinery of the administration of justice and generally the simplification and modernization of the law.

By the effect of sub-section (2), the Commission shall undertake, pursuant to any proposals for law reform which may be made or referred to it by the Attorney-General of the Federation or any programs approved by the Attorney-General (whether the proposals were referred to it by the Attorney-General or prepared on its own initiative), the examination of particular branches of the law and the formulation, by means of draft legislation or otherwise, of proposals for reform therein. Sub-section (6) provides that the Attorney-General of the Federation "shall lay before the President" any programs prepared by the Commission (i.e., areas of law that the Commission proposes to examine for possible reform) as well as any proposals for reform formulated by the Commission (i.e., the recommendations for reform made by the Commission after examining an area of the law).

The Act gives the Commission the power, for the purpose of the efficient performance of its functions, to obtain such information as to the legal systems of other countries as appears to it likely to facilitate the performance of any such function. The Act further provides for the appointment of a Secretary and staff for the Commission. While the Secretary holds office for a fixed period of five years, which may be renewed once, the staff are pensionable employees. Under section 12, the Commission is required to prepare and submit to the President, through the Attorney-General, annual reports on the activities of the Commission, and the Commission may, from time to time, publish general reports on its activities for sale to members of the public.

The Nigerian Law Reform Commission – Mandate and Independence:

A number of issues arise in the light of the foregoing provisions of the Act and the performance of the Commission since its establishment. Firstly, does the Act give the Commission enough independence to perform its duties? It is submitted that the Commission is sufficiently independent. The chairman (if not other commissioners as well) is entitled to reasonable remuneration, and a commissioner may be removed only by the National Assembly and on a specified, weighty ground. Although the Commission requires the approval of the Attorney-General (who, in turn, is required to lay it before the President) before it can examine and propose reforms to any branch of the law, this does not detract from its independence. As Justice Peter Gibson, a former Chairman of the Law Commission of England and Wales argued in respect of the position of that commission: "Whilst the Government has power under the Law Commissions Act to prevent the Commission from examining a branch of the law with a view to reform, it cannot and does not seek to dictate to the Commission what conclusions the Commission should reach. The very independence from Government means that the Government cannot be expected to find every recommendation of the Commission acceptable."[8]

The requirement that, apart from giving his or her own approval, the Attorney-General "shall lay before the President" any programs

[8] See Mr Justice Peter Gibson, 'Law Reform Now: The Law Commission 25 Years On' 1991 Denning Lecture< http://lawcommission.justice.gov.uk/docs/1991_Denning_ Lecture_Mr_Justice_Peter_Gibson.pdf > accessed 15 February 2014

prepared by the Commission as well as any proposals for reform formulated by the Commission does not detract from the independence of the Commission but will probably lead to undue delay. It is also important to keep in mind that the independence of a law reform agency is not exactly as important as the independence of the judiciary. For one reason, a law reform agency, unlike a court, does not make final and binding decisions but only recommendations for law reform which are still subjected to discussions and modifications in the course of the journey through the executive arm to the legislature. For another reason, many areas of the law are not politically sensitive, even though reforms in those areas will significantly promote the ends of justice. Thus, while independent judgment is undoubtedly required in the formulation of reform measures in such areas of the law as electoral law (which is politically sensitive), it is not of much consequence in the formulation of reform measures in areas such as civil procedure and criminal procedure (which are merely technical).[9]

The Nigerian Law Reform Commission – Challenges

The main challenges faced by the Commission are lack of funding and the low level of implementation of its recommendations for law reform. According to an official document,[10] the Commission's funding problem is so acute that it has, over the years, failed to organize a national workshop on its reform projects or to host a meeting of law reform agencies in Nigeria. Also, the Commission faces the problem of high staff turnover even as the government placed an embargo on staff recruitment for many years. As of the first quarter of 2014, the Commission had no website, and according to its Chairman, Professor Oserheimen Osunbor, it had neither adequate office space nor a well-

[9] Accordingly, we do not agree with the following view of another commentator: "All functions of the commission must be approved by the attorney general who in turn by virtue of section 5 sub section 6 must lay these proposals and programmes for reform by the commission before the president and not the national assembly who has the duty of enacting reforms. These provisions impedes the independence of the Commission to a large extent little wonder then that in the 33 years of its existence not much can be attributed to it as achievements." See Oparaku Nzoma Akun, 'The Process of Law Reform' [*NIJLD*] Vol. 1 No. 1 (2012) 102 < http://www.nials-nigeria.org/journals/legdraftOparaku%20Nzoma%20Akun.pdf > accessed on 15 February 2014

[10] The Commission's SERVICOM Charter < www.servenigeria.com/charters/justice-nlr.doc > accessed 15 February 2014

stocked library.[11] The Chairman also decried the low rate of the implementation of the Commission's law reform recommendations.[12] One must assume that the Chairman knew what he was saying. But in the absence of reports readily accessible to the public, it is difficult to ascertain the actual rate of implementation of the recommendations.

By contrast, the website of the Law Commission of England and Wales contains an implementation log,[13] setting out each of the Commission's reports and indicating whether it has been implemented (either wholly or in part) or rejected. On the whole, even without any obligation on the part of the government to accept the Commission's recommendations or on the part of Parliament to expedite the passage of such recommendations, over two-thirds of the law reform recommendations of the Law Commission of England and Wales have been implemented. In order to further improve on this impressive rate of implementation, three measures have been taken, two of them being introduced under the Law Commission Act 2009, which amended the Law Commissions Act 1965.

The first measure is that the Lord Chancellor is now required to table an annual report to Parliament on the proposals of the Law Commission that were implemented during the year and the proposals that were not implemented, including "plans for dealing with any of those proposals," and where any decision has been taken not to implement, "the reasons for the decision." The significance of this requirement, according to Lord Justice Munby, the Chairman of the Law Commission (2009-2012), is that it increases the transparency of the Government's approach to the work of the Commission and puts pressure on Government to respond to the recommendations of the Commission.[14]

---

[11] See 'Law Reform Commission Decries Poor Implementation of Proposals' *The Nigerian Observer* (Benin City, 23 January 2014) < http://nigerianobservernews.com/13012014/ news/news9.html#. UxRMwuNd WhE > accessed 15 February 2014

[12] Ibid.

[13] < http://lawcommission.justice.gov.uk/docs/implementation_log_311013.pdf > accessed 15 February 2014

[14] Lord Justice Munby, 'Shaping the Law – The Law Commission at the Crossroads' 2011 Denning Lecture <http://lawcommission.justice.gov.uk/docs/20111129_Denning_lecture_Lord_Justice_Munby.pdf > accessed on 15 February 2014

Considering that it will be an unmitigated waste of public funds for the Lord Chancellor to authorize the Commission to examine an area of law for reform only to fail to implement the recommendations and also fail to offer an explanation, this requirement is a sound *quid pro quo* for the requirement that the Law Commission's program must be approved by the Lord Chancellor.

The second measure is that the Act now requires the Lord Chancellor and the Commission to agree to a protocol on how the Government and the Law Commission should work together to achieve law reform in the most effective way. The Protocol,[15] which took effect on 29 March 2010, places obligations on both the Commission and the Government, probably the most significant being the requirement that where the Commission is considering including a project in a law reform program, the Commission will notify the Minister with relevant policy responsibility, and in deciding how to respond to the Commission, the Minister will bear in mind that, before approving the inclusion of the project in the overall program, the Lord Chancellor will expect the Minister to give an undertaking that there is a "serious intention" to take forward law reform in the specific area proposed. The third measure is a House of Lords procedural rule, introduced in 2008, which fast-tracks non-controversial Law Commission Bills.[16]

The Nigerian Law Reform Commission – Achievements

In spite of the enormous challenges faced by the Commission, it has successfully completed law reform work in a number of areas. For instance, the Commission did outstanding work in the areas of company law (which resulted in the enactment of the Companies and Allied Matters Act 1990) and the law of evidence (which resulted in the enactment of the Evidence Act 2011). The Commission's work in the area of criminal procedure includes the drafting of a bill on plea bargaining, and this bill is now part of the Administration of Criminal

---

[15] < http://lawcommission.justice.gov.uk/docs/lc321_Protocol.pdf > accessed on 15 February 2014

[16] See 'The Parliamentary procedure for uncontroversial Law Commission bills' Consumer Insurance Law Reform Briefing Note 3 <http://www.peterjtyldesley. com/files/Parliamentary_ Procedure_ for_Law_ Commission_Bills_Briefing_Note.pdf > accessed 15 February 2014

Justice Bill, which is currently before the National Assembly. In the absence of detailed reports easily available to the public, however, it is not possible to fully outline and appraise the work of the Commission.

Borrowing from Foreign Legal Systems

The Commission's power, under the Act of 1979, to obtain such information as to the legal systems of other countries as appears to it likely to facilitate the performance of its functions deserves to be discussed briefly. This provision expressly permits the Commission, in the performance of its duties, to feel free to borrow or adapt rules from foreign legal systems. The practice of adopting or imposing a foreign legal principle or system, which Alan Watson[17] has described as a "legal transplant," is a very common approach in law reform. While imperial powers have imposed legal transplants on subject nations, many nations have, over the centuries, voluntarily adopted laws from other countries. But Japan's adoption in 1896 of a Civil Code based on that of Germany and Turkey's adoption in 1926 of a Civil Code based on that of Switzerland are only two examples of independent nations voluntarily reforming their laws with legal transplants. In the 20th Century and in the increasingly globalized world of the twenty-first century, legal transplants remain common in spite of the concern that transplants may not be suited to particular local contexts.[18]

The State Law Reform Agencies

Many states have their own law reform agencies, and they are concerned with the reform of state law, while Nigerian Law Reform Commission is concerned with the reform of federal law. A few examples may be mentioned. The Lagos State Law Reform Commission was established by a state law enacted in 2007 and amended in January 2012. In March 2012, the Commission was constituted for the first time. It has set up a website and has developed a law reform policy and its roadmap. Abia State has a Law Reform and Review Commission, established by a state law enacted in 1999. Akwa Ibom and Kano states

---

[17] Alan Watson, *Legal Transplants: An Approach to Comparative Law* (Scottish Academic Press, 1974)

[18] See Otto Kahn-Freund, 'On Uses and Misuses of Comparative Law' [1974] 37 MLR 1

also have law reform commissions. The law establishing the Ekiti State Law Reform Commission was signed into law in February 2014. The agency in Jigawa State is known as the "Jigawa State Justice Sector and Law Reform Commission," and its mandate and activities seem to go beyond the usual scope of the mandate of LRA as it includes the training of traditional rulers in alternative dispute resolution methods.[19] Many of the state law reform agencies seem to face challenges similar to those that confront NLRC, principally inadequate funding and a low rate of implementation of recommendations.

Non-governmental Organizations

Many non-governmental organizations (NGOs) and other civil society organizations are engaged in advocacy for policy and legal reform. These organizations do their best to persuade the government to change particular laws or policies. In this way, they engage in very much the same kind of activities as law reform agencies and produce recommendations for law reform. In addition, even when they do not originate a law reform process, they often intervene to support or oppose the enactment or repeal of certain laws, depending on the interests they represent. The fact that they engage in lobbying is an important difference between these organizations and the law reform agencies, which are not expected to lobby for the implementation of their recommendations. Probably the most outstanding example of a law reform measure spearheaded by NGOs and which was enacted into law in Nigeria is the Freedom of Information Act 2011.

Notable Instances of Law Reform in Nigeria

The enactment of any legislation that enhances justice and efficiency in the legal system represents a step in law reform. But some instances of law reform stand out due to their very far-reaching effect. In Nigeria, such instances include the revision of the "received English laws" in the

---

19 See 'Jigawa gets justice reform commission' in *The Guardian* (Lagos, 13 March 2012) < http://nigeriatrends.com/jigawa-gets-justice-reform-commission/ > accessed 20 February 2014, and "Commission trains 1, 000 traditional rulers on ADR in Jigawa" in *Nigerian Tribune* (Ibadan, 23 October 2013) < http://www.tribune.com.ng/news2013/index.php/en/community-news/item/24588-commission-trains-1,000-traditional-rulers-on-adr-in-jigawa.html> (accessed 20 February 2014)

defunct Western Nigeria in the 1950s and the making and enactment of the following laws: the Penal Code in the defunct Northern Nigeria, the Companies and Allied Matters Act 1990 and the Freedom of Information Act 2011.

Law Revision in Western Nigeria

From the very beginning of the colonial period, English laws were "received" and thus made applicable in various jurisdictions in Nigeria. In the standard phraseology used in the enactments,[20] "Statutes of General Application that were in force in England on the first day of January 1900" were received into and made applicable. Since these provisions did not identify the applicable statutes by name but only provided a formula for identifying them, whether a particular English statute came within the category and was therefore applicable usually remained uncertain until the court, after a dispute had arisen, decided on the matter. To address this problem of uncertainty in the law, the government of the Western Region of Nigeria set up a Law Revision Commission chaired by Sir John Verity, whose tenure as Chief Justice of Nigeria had ended in 1954.

The Commission was mandated to examine the English statutes that could come within the description of "statutes of general application" (except in so far as repealed or replaced by local legislation) and draft new bills to incorporate them. The Commission was also mandated, in drafting the new bills, to incorporate or draw from certain post-1900 English statutes that had introduced changes to the pre-1900 statutes. The Commission's work was a notable restatement and modernization of the law. It resulted in the enactment of 21 laws by the legislature of the Western Region in 1958 and 1959.[21]

The drafting of what became the Property and Conveyancing Law 1959 (Western Nigeria) is a very remarkable aspect of the work of the

---

[20] See Interpretation Act, s 45 (applicable to the then Federal Territory of Lagos, now Lagos State; High Court Law of Eastern Nigeria, s 14 (applicable in the states of the defunct Eastern Nigeria); High Court Law of Northern Nigeria, s 28 (applicable in the states of the defunct Northern Nigeria).

[21] See G. Ezejiofor, 'Sources of Nigerian Law' in C. O. Okonkwo (ed), *Introduction to Nigerian Law* (Sweet & Maxwell, 1980) pp. 4-7 and A. O. Obilade, *The Nigerian Legal System* (Sweet & Maxwell, 1979) pp. 69-82

Commission. By adopting the English Property and Conveyancing Act 1925, which was itself the product of post-1900 law reform in England, the Commission modernized the law of property in the region.

Reform of the Criminal Law in Northern Nigeria

In the pre-colonial era, there were various systems of what, for want of a better term, could be described as customary criminal law in Nigeria. Under these systems of unwritten laws, deviant or heinous behaviour was punished and social order preserved. In the Muslim principalities of Northern Nigeria, a written system of criminal law (of the Maliki school of Islamic law), which had been developed over the centuries as part of the Islamic religion and way of life, was in force.

Upon the advent of colonial rule, the British authorities introduced a dual system of criminal law in Northern Nigeria. On one level, a Criminal Code, enacted into law in 1904, was enforced by British-type courts.[22] The Code was modelled on a code drafted in England by Sir James Fitzstephen in 1878 and intended to replace the common law of crime, but it was not enacted into law. Prior to its enactment in Nigeria, the Code had been enacted in the Australian State of Queensland in 1899. On the second level, under the policy of indirect rule, the colonial authorities allowed the native courts to continue to administer the customary system of criminal law (which included Islamic criminal law), and the native courts were exempted from applying the Criminal Code.

This duality meant that the same fact situation could lead to different outcomes, depending on the court in which a case was tried. For instance, since adultery is a crime under Muslim law but not under the common law, a person who committed adultery could face criminal charges in a native court but go scot-free if brought before a British-type court. Again, in cases of homicide, the Criminal Code – but not Maliki law - recognised killing under provocation as manslaughter (punishable by imprisonment) and not murder (punishable by death).

Accordingly, in Professor Okonkwo's striking illustration,

---

[22] In 1916, following the Amalgamation in 1914, the application of the Code was extended to Southern Nigeria. It is still in force in the southern states of Nigeria.

> it could therefore literally be a matter of life and death...whether an accused who killed under gross provocation was tried under Maliki law, where the finding would be murder, and the sentence death (if the deceased's relatives so desired it), or under the Code, where the maximum punishment would be imprisonment for life.[23]

On the whole, since Maliki law was widely-accepted as part and parcel of the life of a Muslim, popular sentiment in the predominantly-Muslim Northern Region was against the Code. In 1958, the Government of the Northern Region appointed a Panel of Jurists to review and advise it on the legal and judicial system of the region.[24] Among other things, the panel recommended the introduction of a unified system of criminal law with a code (based on the Penal Code of Sudan) that would be applied by all the courts and the restricting of the operation of Muslim law to issues of "personal law," such as marriage, divorce, and succession of Muslims.

Following the acceptance of the recommendations, the Government instructed its law officers to prepare a draft Penal Code. The draft Code was the subject of consultations and, after a number of revisions, was adopted and enacted into law. The Penal Code represents "a compromise between the reformers and the traditionalists,"[25] combining elements from both English law and Maliki law. For instance, while it recognizes provocation as a mitigating factor in homicide cases, it criminalizes the drinking of alcohol by a Muslim and adultery by anyone that is subject to native law and culture that regards adultery as an offence.

---

[23] C. O. Okonkwo, *Criminal Law in Nigeria* (2nd edn, Sweet & Maxwell, 1980) p. 6 Like all compromises, the Code and the larger reforms of which it was part did not satisfy everyone. See Justin Price, 'Criminal Law Reform in Northern Nigeria: Retrograde Legislation in Northern Nigeria?' [1961] 24 MLR 604-11 Mr. Price, a British barrister, had served as Magistrate and Acting Judge of the High Court in Northern Nigeria.

[24] The panel consisted of the following: Sayyad Mohammed Abdu Rannat (Chief Justice of the Sudan) (Chairman), Mr. Justice Mohammad Sharif (Chairman of the Pakistan Law Commission), Professor J. N. D. Anderson (School of Oriental and African Studies, London), Mallam Shettima Kashim (Waziri of Borno), Mr. Peter Achimugu (former Minister, Northern Region) and Mallam Musa (Chief Alkali of Bida).

[25] Ibid. p.10 For a detailed account of the consultative process that led to the adoption of the Code, see John N. Paden *Ahmadu Bello, Sardauna of Sokoto: Values and Leadership in Nigeria* (Hudahuda Publishing Company, 1986) pp. 205-213

Companies and Allied Matters Act

While inaugurating the newly constituted Commission in March 1987, the then Attorney-General of the Federation directed the Commission to immediately undertake the reform of company law in Nigeria, and the Commission acted accordingly. It invited memoranda from the public and subsequently prepared Working Papers (including the draft of new legislation), which were widely circulated and discussed at a workshop held in February 1988. Taking into account the inputs received at the workshop, the Commission prepared a report which it submitted to the Attorney-General. In order to ensure even more consultations, the Attorney-General set up a Consultative Assembly on company law, to which he passed the draft. The members of the Assembly were drawn from among lawyers and related professionals, representatives of government departments and agencies, and business associations.

The Assembly held meetings in 1988 and 1989 and submitted its report to the Attorney-General, following which draft legislation was promulgated into law as the Companies and Allied Matters Decree (now Act) 1990.[26] The Honourable Justice J. O. Orojo, who was the Chairman of the Commission during this period, has described the law as "the result of unprecedented mass and public consultation and input,"[27] and it is difficult to fault the description.

Freedom of Information Act

From colonial times, information about the business of government in Nigeria has always been restricted to government officials. Only bits and pieces of such information may be made public and only by duly-authorized senior officials. In fact, the practice was fully backed by the Official Secrets Act and the Civil Service Rules. As a result of the culture of secrecy, manifestly unjust or incompetent decisions or corrupt practices on the part of public officers could be shielded from exposure to the public and to the outcry that could lead to the taking of

---

[26] See J. O. Orojo, 'An Overview of the Companies and Allied Matters Decree, 1990' in E. O. Akanki (ed.) *Essays on Company Law* (University of Lagos Press, 1992) pp. 1-13.

[27] Ibid., at p. 4

corrective measures. As an important part of the efforts to improve the quality of governance in Nigeria, some non-governmental organizations (led by Media Rights Agenda) and journalists championed the introduction of a freedom of information legislation in Nigeria. Following preliminary efforts that began in 1993 and which included the preparation of draft legislation in 1995, these stakeholders were able to get four members of the House of Representatives in 1999 to table the Freedom of Information Bill in the National Assembly. In 2011, after many years of lobbying, the Bill was passed by the National Assembly and assented to by President Goodluck Jonathan.

Under the Freedom of Information Act 2011, subject to certain exceptions, every person has a right to apply for access to records, documents, and information kept by public institutions, and public institutions are required to proactively publish certain types of information.

Where an application for public information is refused, the applicant may go to court for an order to compel the public institution to disclose the requested information. Since the enactment of the Act, several departments and agencies of government have worked with donors and NGOs to organize training workshops aimed at changing the orientation of public officials and familiarizing them with the requirements of the new law. The Act has the potential of making public functionaries to act with greater circumspection as their actions could be exposed.

But this gain is now threatened in at least two ways. Firstly, it has been suggested by the Federal High Court bench that in order to make a proper application for public information, an applicant must show a specific interest in the information sought. This was in the case of *Paradigm Initiative Nigeria* v. *Reuben Abati*,[28] in which the Court relied on that ground to refuse to make an order compelling the defendant, a public officer, to disclose to the applicant-organization the information it applied for. The Court frowned at the provisions of the Act, which do not require a person who applies for information to show that he has

[28] Suit No. FHC/ABJ/CS/402/2013 (Before Mr. Justice Gabriel Kolawole) See *The Guardian* 25 July 2013

any specific interest in such information, stating that it creates "a situation where scarce public resources, time and energy are permitted to be squandered" in attending to such requests.

The Court went on to call on the National Assembly to undertake "a review of the Act so as to ensure that access to information is only made available to such applicants who genuinely need it for a specific purpose(s)."[29]

The applicant-organization has since appealed against the decision. If a higher court upholds the decision of the Court, the effect is the Act will cease to be an effective tool for ensuring free access to public information, which promotes transparency in governance.[30]

Secondly, some lawyers have suggested that the Act, being a federal enactment, is not applicable to the state governments and their agencies.[31]

The provisions of the Act have been re-enacted in Ekiti State as a state law, the Freedom of Information Law 2011. This much-applauded decision to re-enact the provisions as a state law was presumably informed by the view that the Act does not apply to the state government and its agencies. In a case now before the Federal High Court, the Government of Lagos State has argued that the Act, being a federal law, does not apply to it.[32] In view of its importance, one hopes that the case would go as far as the Supreme Court so that a very strong pronouncement would be handed down. If the courts decide that the Act does not apply to the state governments, no more than a few states will probably follow the example of Ekiti and re-enact the provisions as

---

[29] Ibid.

[30] For a critical analysis of the Federal High Court decision, see Edetaen Ojo 'FOI: Where His Lordship Got It Wrong' *Vanguard*, (Lagos, 6 August 2013) < http://www.vanguardngr.com/2013/08/foi-act-where-his-lordship-got-it-wrong/> accessed 24 February 2014

[31] See 'Lawyers Disagree over Freedom of Information Act' in *The Punch* (Lagos, 16 February, 2014) < http://www.punchng.com/news/lawyers-disagree-over-freedom-of-information-act/ > accessed 24 February 2014

[32] An NGO, the Socio-Economic Rights and Accountability Project (SERAP) instituted the case against the Government following the Government's failure to meet a request for information on how it spent a $90 million World Bank facility for the improvement of its schools. See 'Where FOIA Does Not Apply' in *Vanguard* (Lagos, 14 February 2014) < http://www.vanguardngr.com/2014/02/foia-apply/ > accessed 24 February 2014 and 'Lagos Not Bound by FOI Act, AG Tells Court' in *The Punch* (Lagos, 10 February 2014) <. http://www.punchng.com/news/lagos-not-bound-by-foi-act-ag-tells-court/ > accessed 24 February 2014

state law. In most states, therefore, the regime of restricted access to public information will continue.

The Importance of Implementation

The implementation of a law gives practical meaning to the law. Sometimes it is observed that a new law, the product of a law reform process, is not being implemented at all or to a meaningful extent. This could be a result of the lack of technical or administrative capacity to implement the law, or it could be the result of a lack of political will. Where the problem is one of lack of capacity, it may be successfully addressed through a program of capacity building and training. But where the problem is one of lack of the political will to implement the law (which raises the question of whether the making of the law itself was a genuine reflection of political will or a public relations gesture), the situation is more complicated, and there may not be many prospects of diligent implementation. In the latter situation, one comes to appreciate clearly that the law reform process is an integral part of the larger process of governance; in the latter situation, the long-term question arises whether the existing constitutional and legal order may be kept alive through reforms or whether it will atrophy and yield to the clean sweep of a revolution.

CONCLUSIONS AND RECOMMENDATIONS

From the foregoing discussion, we draw the following conclusions. Firstly, the law reform process is an integral part of governance and can be used to promote the attributes that are associated with the idea of good governance. Secondly, political will is the most important requirement for any successful law reform program. In the language of arithmetic, one may say that law reform is equal to ten per cent legal scholarship and ninety per cent politics. This does not mean that all law reform measures are, or would be, politically contentious; indeed, as already noted, reform measures in many areas of the law may not be contentious. It means that law reform can only lead to changes in the law and the implementation of those changes if the political leadership is supportive. Typically, the support of the Attorney-General is a key factor.

Thirdly, while law reform may be undertaken even without a permanent law reform agency, such agencies are quite useful for the important task of the systematic and ongoing reform of the law. The Nigerian Law Reform Commission (NLRC) is not being adequately funded, and this is probably the case with several state law reform agencies as well. Fourthly, as an important way of promoting improvements in the governance process, civil society organizations initiate or participate in law reform efforts. The role of civil society organizations in the making of the Freedom of Information Act remains a shining example.

Toward the goal of promoting law reform as part of the broader goal of promoting good governance, we offer the following recommendations. Firstly, our law reform agencies need to be better funded. However, the agencies should also make more creative use of the funding they receive. For instance, it is difficult to blame the failure of NLRC to maintain a website on lack of funding, considering that it is not very expensive to maintain one and also that a website will be very useful in its work. With a website, NLRC will not merely publicize its programs but will also be able to conveniently disseminate its working papers to lawyers and other stakeholders and receive useful inputs. Also, the internet can facilitate regular exchange of information between NLRC and the state law reform agencies, and this will enable them to learn from each other and accomplish more with available funding.

Secondly, in order to check the low rate of implementation of the recommendations of the law reform agencies, the measures introduced in the United Kingdom under the 2009 Amendment to the Law Commissions Act 1965 should be introduced in Nigeria through amendments to the statutes that establish the law reform agencies. The effect is that the government will be obliged to implement the recommendations or explain why the recommendations will not be implemented. Thirdly, as vehicles for citizens' participation in governance processes, NGOs and other civil society organizations need to be even more involved both in initiating proposals for new laws and in campaigns aimed at supporting or opposing legislative proposals in whole or in part, according to their persuasions. In this regard, they should ensure that they have access to expert guidance and also remember that the needful changes may be achieved, not through action by the legislature, but through other types of action, such as the introduction of subsidiary legislation by a Minister or the introduction of new rules of court or practice directions by a Chief Judge or the Chief Justice of the Federation.

As Lord Denning said in 1965, "Each generation has its duty to keep the law in conformity with the needs of the time."[33] The discharge of this duty in Nigeria requires political will, adequately resourced and well-managed law reform agencies, and virile civil society organizations engaged in law reform programs.

FOR FURTHER READING

Books

1. Gardiner, G. and Martin, A. *Law Reform – Now* (1st edn, V. Gollancz, 1963)
2. Gisselquist, R. M. *Good Governance as a Concept, and Why This Matters for Development Policy* (UNU-WIDER Working Paper No. 2012/30, United Nations University Press, 2012)
3. International Centre for Not-for-Profit Law and United Nations Development Programme, *The Role of Legal Reform in Supporting Civil Society: An Introductory Primer* (UNDP, 2009)
4. Watson, A. *Legal Transplants: An Approach to Comparative Law* (Scottish Academic Press, 1974)

Journal Articles

1. Kahn-Freund, O. 'On Uses and Misuses of Comparative Law' [1974] 37 MLR 1
2. Akun, O. N. 'The Process of Law Reform' [NIJLD] Vol. 1 No. 1 (2012) 102

Websites

1. South African Law Reform Commission http://www.justice.gov.za/salrc/
2. Law Commission of England and Wales http://lawcommission.justice.gov.uk/index.htm

[33] Quoted in Lord Justice Munby, "Shaping the Law – The Law Commission at the Crossroads", 2011 Denning Lecture, *op. cit.*

PART C

LAW ENFORCEMENT, SANCTIONS, AND REMEDIES

Chapter 10

ROLE OF COURTS IN THE APPLICATION AND ENFORCEMENT OF LAW IN NIGERIA

A. K. Anya, PhD*

INTRODUCTION

This chapter examines the role of courts in the application and enforcement of law in a secular state as well as a multicultural society, Nigeria. It has grown to become a striking reality in such a society, with multifarious rules of customary laws, which usually are divided and, therefore, experience a constant struggle over their public sphere. Nigeria is a constitutional democracy with a subsisting federal structure. There are, in place, both federal and state courts that are primarily vested with original jurisdictions in areas proper by it. Against this backdrop, the paper considers the fact whether courts make new laws in the process of interpreting the law as constitutionally vested unto it by virtue of section 6, Constitution of the Federal Republic of Nigeria, 1999. The author draws immensely from the regime of customary rules to buttress his arguments, and argues that the courts have a great role to play in the process of applying and enforcing the law. In light of the above, the paper maintains that the attainment of a judicial role is only possible through the process of 'judicialization' of both rules of courts and subsisting Legislations, Statutes, or Acts, as the case may be. Ultimately, the process of judicialization will redound in

* Associate Professor of Law-Dept. of Public & International Law, Igbinedion University College of Law, Okada, Nigeria.

judicial activism with concomitant normative advancements in customary rules regimes.

The court in Nigeria is a constitutional entity. For instance, section 6 of the Nigerian Constitution provides for the vesting of the judicial powers of the Federation in the courts.[1] Undoubtedly, it is the bounden constitutional duty of the court to apply and enforce laws in the entity - 'Nigeria.' The court system, as a matter of fact, is an integral part of the judicial system.[2] Consequently, the chapter will be *limited to the role of judges in the application and enforcement of laws in* Nigeria.

Significantly, early and contemporary jurisprudence did succeed in adopting the perspective that judges are the sole priests of the law, the repositories of its ancient rules and traditions.[3] This assertion is premised on the fact that decisions are distilled in a mysterious way by the judge after assessing the facts of the case before the courts and ultimately applying the law on the matter. In this way, the judge steadfastly declares fresh applications of the ancient rule or authority on the matter. It has also been argued in some quarters that judges in the process of applying the law have succeeded in creating new laws. This, as a matter of fact, is saddled with academic imputation. Judges may seem to make new laws in the process of applying the law but will ultimately have their judgment set aside on appeal if it is shown amongst others that they committed an error of law or fettered discretion. Significantly, the language of the law is not straightforward but complex. Therefore, judges, inclusive of lawyers, due to their training, enjoy the special privilege of interpreting the law to the envy of the uninitiated.

This chapter is therefore set to examine the role of judges in the process of interpreting the law and thereafter, consider their constitutional duty of application and enforcement of laws. Furthermore, the paper will consider the challenges to the realization of judicial activism or empowerment, particularly in a developing

---

[1] See particularly the Constitution of the Federal Republic of Nigeria, 1999 [hereafter CFRN).

[2] It should be noted that a typical judicial system is made up of 'magistrates and judges' and courts' officials.

[3] This however fails to account for the roles of traditional rulers and elders in council, in settlement of disputes under African customary rules and settings.

multicultural society. In doing this, the chapter will examine the emotive question of what is ultimately good (that is, justice) and demonstrate the fact that the idea of justice would continue to confront the human race, law, and the entire human society.

JUDGES AND LEGAL SOURCES

The hallmark of every legal system is the ability to accommodate authoritative sources of law, upon which new sets of facts could be determined. Consequently, legal sources have undoubtedly been regarded as the very core raw material of the judicial process.[4] For instance, such expressions like this is the law! What is the law? This is bad law! And etcetera collectively constitutes common interests expressed about the law. Therefore a venture to ascertain the validity of the legal sources used by judges and even lawyers in any legal system is worthy of commendation. Due to space constraints, there are three known sources of law: judicial precedents, legislations, and customary rules.

However, it should be noted that judicial decisions have the force of law.[5] This leads us to the issue of the validity of the legal sources employed in the judicial process. This is a very controversial regime. Arguments abound in support of the validity of legal sources of law. According to Salmond, 'the rule that judicial decisions have the force of law is legally ultimate and underived.' He regarded these ultimate principles as the grundnorms or basic rules of recognition of the legal system in that they constitute rules of laws. Though his theory is controversial, yet, it is helpful in appreciating the process of creation and change in the ultimate rule, being the basic rule[6]. On the other hand, Hart relates his theory to the rule of recognition. According to him, Acts of parliament and judicial decisions have the force of law in that they command recognition in the eye of judges, officials, and

---

[4] Lloyd's., *Introduction to Jurisprudence,* 8th ed. Freeman, MDA, (London: Sweet & Maxwell, 2008) Pp. 1532 , 1533. It is of importance to note Salmond's objection to the assertion that legal sources constitutes the very raw material. He argues that they are merely contingent and not necessary. See Salmond, *Jurisprudence,* 12th ed. Pp. 91, 92.

[5] See generally Stone Julius and the Pure Theory of Law (1965) p.117

[6] Salmond, *supra,* p.91.

private citizens. To ascertain the validity of these legal sources, there is a need to resort to the primary rule of recognition, identifiable by reference to certain criteria.[7]

THE DISCRETION OF JUDGES IN JUDICIAL DECISIONS

The pattern of couching of legislation creates room for judges to fill in the gap. This requires an exercise of discretion, considering the pedigree and qualification for the post of a judge prior to appointment. Classic positive law maintains that the rule-making authority must exercise discretion, and there is no possibility of treating the question raised by the various cases as if there were one uniquely correct answer to be found, as distinct from an answer which is a reasonable compromise between many conflicting interests.[8] Practically speaking, legislations or rules are normally open-textured. The only effect is that they are indeterminate. Consequently, Hart identifies three reasons for the state of indeterminacy of legislations, to wit: language choice, general standards of rules, and inherent indeterminacy in the common law system of precedent. In summation, the language has been more or less 'English.' English, as a matter of fact, is diverse. In fact, we live in a world of Englishness.[9]

For instance, in order to avoid speculations with regard to the interests of members of the family when the right of will-making is exercised, the Wills Law[10] was enacted. Besides the above, the power of the testator to dispose of property under the will is limited specifically by virtue of section 3 of the Wills Law. The section ironically provides:

Subject to any customary law relating thereto, it shall be lawful for every person to devise, bequeath, or dispose of, by his will executed in a manner hereafter required, all real estate and all personal estate, which he shall be entitled to, either in law or in equity, at the time of his death and which if not so devised, bequeathed and disposed of would devolve

---

[7] Hart, *The Concept of Law.* Pp. 100, 102

[8] Ibid.

[9] For instance, UK English, Canadian English, Australian English, US English, *et cetera.*

[10] 1958, now applicable in all former western states of Nigeria, inclusive of Delta, Edo, Ondo, Ekiti, Ogun, Oyo, and Osun.

upon their at law of him, or if he became entitled by descent, of his ancestor or upon his executor or administrator.

It should be noted that the above section re-affirms the right of Nigerians to whom it applies to make a will, but "subject to any customary law relating thereto..." This clause has attained a peculiar status in the process of interpretation by courts. The instant provision of this particular Wills Law places a bar on the exercise of power of a devisor to devise property in respect of which a testator had no disposable interest. The decision in *Oke* v. *Oke*[11] is illustrative. Here a testator devised a house he built on a parcel of land belonging to the family of his former wife. The question that came up for determination was whether the devise was effectual in law. It was held that the will operated subject to Section 3 of the Wills Law of Western Nigeria then applicable in the then Bendel State, and accordingly, it was ineffective to pass property that belonged to the wife's family which, according to the customary law of the Urhobo and Itsekiri, could not be disposed of even by the wife.

By this decision, the court is saying that the power of testacy is restricted to individually acquired property that the testator had the power to dispose of during his lifetime and, in the absence of a will, would have devolved on his heirs at law. This premise flows from the language of the court, particularly the lead decision of Elias C.J.N: "the power of the testator (under section 3(1) of the law) to devise his real or personal estates by will is limited by the extent, if any, to which its exercise is permissible under the relevant customary law."[12]

Some writers have suggested that "permissible under customary law" meant that customary law controlled the capacity of a person subject to the law to make a will. To this end, Emiola argued that the law, specifically referring to Section 3(1) of the Wills Law, would have been totally irrelevant since every Nigerian comes under some customary law that could have prevented him or her from making a will.

---

[11] (1974) 3 SC 1.
[12] At p. 450.

The apparent uncertainty in the language of the court in *Oke* v. *Oke*[13] was unequivocally clarified by the same court in *Lydia Lawal Osula* v. *Chief Saka Lawal Osula*,[14] wherein Ogundare, J.S.C. said: "the court below, that is, the Court of Appeal, is right in holding that the phrase is not a qualification of the testator's capacity to make a will but a qualification of the subject matter of the property disposed of or intended to be disposed of by will." The learned Justice Belgore identified such property as including the "seat" of a hereditary title or chieftaincy house, and "perhaps ...the paraphernalia of office."[15]

Apart from the Wills Law, Islamic law also places a restriction on the kind of assets that a person may not dispose of by will. Islamic law restricts the proportion of a man's estate that he can give away by will to just one-third of the whole. Therefore, gifts in excess of that value are invalid *pro tanto.*[16]

JUDGES AND, APPLICATION AND ENFORCEMENT OF LAWS IN NIGERIA

It has been argued that contemporary democratic reality in Nigeria is influenced by the growing role of courts in socio-cultural and intimate relationships[17] as well as responses to heuristic factors in society, as social and rights activists regularly utilise the judicial process in venting their grievances or articulating new paradigm of interests or still further, securing subsisting values as effective laws. The reason for this approach is not far to be fetched.

It dawns on observers of constitutional politics that this phenomenon of constitutional transformation manifests primarily in the enactment of bills of rights accompanied by powers of judicial review.[18] These normative provisions embedded in the constitution enabled and simplified the ability of those with limited access to the

[13] *Supra*, at note 11.
[14] (1995) 9 NWLR (Pt. 419) 259
[15] At p. 274.
[16] *Apatire & anor.* v *Akanke ors.* (1944) 17 NLR 149
[17] Anya K A., *Normative Ethics in the Nigerian Law*, 1st ed. (US & Nigeria: Research Centre for Pacific African and Nigerian Law, 2010) Pp. 75, 76.
[18] Leviatan Ofit., Judicial Activism and Religion-Based Tensions in India and Israel 26 (2003) No. 3 *AJICL*, Pp. 583, 584, quoted by Anya, *supra*, at p. 75

majoritarian-led government process to challenge socio-cultural and politically related issues, if any, through the courts.

Empirical observation accommodates the fact that the appeal of litigation has been particularly strong with secular and plural ethnic societies, inclusive of Nigeria, increasingly viewing it as a principal opportunity to mould the public sphere in accordance with diversified and individualized socio-political, socio-cultural, and moral preferences.

Nigeria belongs to the common law tradition, bestowing legal development primarily in the hands of courts of records. Against this backdrop, there is, therefore, the need to evaluate the efforts to achieve these perceived goals: of effectuating change and giving vent to social claims or securing values as laws through the judicial process, by examining its effects in the context of the socio-cultural, economic, and political developments in the country.

Toward this end, I shall endeavour by way of empirical analysis to fathom the judicial impact on the realization of 'suppressed' rules of customary law, bearing in mind the obfuscation effect of the received law and equity on the African rules of customary law, as a dying legal system in Nigeria. Recall that the British colonialists later made legislations primarily aimed at supplanting rules of customary practices adjudged barbarous and uncivilized.

These laws came in the form of the 'Repugnancy test,' 'Incompatibility test,' and 'Public policy test.' Coupled with these laws is the Evidence Act, requiring proof of rules of customary laws as fact (that is to say, as foreign law) before the alien and colonial courts. This approach will achieve the need to rectify the existing discriminatory practices and thus foster the advancement toward a more pluralist and egalitarian society. The analysis of the judicial contribution to generating and establishing authoritative resolution to socio-cultural and intimate relationships' claims and interests will assist in appreciating our target.

Judicial activism by the Nigerian Supreme Court evolved from a phase of initial restraint into extensive engagement in politically charged policy questions. The complex multicultural reality in Nigeria effectively negated the possibility of separating the underlying core values of rules of customary law and the alien sense of social justice and equity. Subsisting attempts to demarcate this relationship have resulted in a deeply polarizing social conflict.

Nigeria is a multicultural and plural society. Oftentimes, societies with multifarious rules of customary laws are usually divided and experience a constant struggle over the public sphere. However, there is an antidote. The classic liberalist approach for the resultant conflict has always been to separate the spheres of primordial sentiments, inclusive of intimate relationships and politics. The essence of ideological separation is to ensure neutrality among competing and contending claims and interests seeking for recognition as law in the legal and political system. The one should not be mixed with the other in order to avoid obliging complete victory to the views of the actors.

Furthermore, there is still the need to accommodate the champions of primordial and intimate relationships' claims and interests, activists. Such a need will operate to give vent to them from disabusing their minds of feelings of marginalization against the foreseeable triumph of political activists. It is obvious from a Marxian perspective that control of political power is bound to affect legal arrangement and the resulting quality of legislation as well as the appointment of public officials.

Politically charged disputes over primordial and intimate relationships have increasingly been played out in the judicial sphere, with human rights, social activists, and individuals attempting to effectuate a change in unfavourable governmental policies and practices through the courts. Resort to the judicial sphere is largely favourable apparently because the law is viewed as a mechanism of politico-economic and social reform, and consequently, the legal process is perceived as enabling the possibility for progressive change, to which society will defer.

Significantly, the legal process is perceived as capable of resolving social conflicts authoritatively in a way that advances social peace. What can be more enduring? A decision by an expert and impartial judiciary asserting constitutional principles ought to be more persuasive than a similar advancement by partial politicians. These perceptions are very well welcomed in a multicultural and plural society with smoking gun tendencies to resort to strife.

Socio-cultural and moral compromises are rare. Therefore, the only viable option is to resort to litigation. In the light of the above, judges become handy and inevitable. They must play a role in dousing the socio-cultural and intimate relationships generated tensions. These judicial roles must as a matter of fact, be accomplished through the instrumentality of the law. As Justice Elias rightly observed with respect to tasks of law in a developing society:

> ...Our customary laws are already showing signs of coalescence into an acceptable common body of rules in such areas as land tenure and inheritance, marriage and the family. The courts, concerned mainly with discovering underlying principles, apply to the disputes before them precedents established in similar situations elsewhere, unless there are special reasons to the contrary...If, as we have seen to be the case in Ghana, all our Judges were to be deemed to know the customary law so that there is no need to prove it as a fact, the process of unification would be so much eased.[19]

Different theories have been offered to explain this judicial empowerment phenomenon. Dworkin characterizes this as an inevitable development in an age of human rights advancement generated by the effects of WWII.[20] Shapiro argues the prominence of constitutional judicial review as 'a manifestation of a global distrust' of bureaucratic governmental and corporate power, endowing the legal process with the task of protecting individuals.[21] Another commentator explains that judicial empowerment should be understood as an attempt by threatened governing elites to delegate power to the courts as a hegemony-preservation mechanism.[22] It is in light of the above that effort will be made to consider a befitting role for judges in the socio-cultural sphere in Nigeria.

---

[19] Elias, T.O., *Law in a Developing Society* 1st ed. (UK: London University Press) Chp. 5

[20] Dworkin, Ronald., *A Bill of Rights for Britain* (1990): Dworkin, *supra*, *Taking Rights Seriously* (1978), quoted by Anya, at p. 80.

[21] Anya, *supra*, note 204.

[22] Anya, *supra*, note 205.

ROLE FOR JUDGES IN NIGERIA

The notion 'jurisprudence' is universally limited to 'legal philosophy,' which deals with law, its scope, functions, and principles as opposed to specific legal rules. Due to length constraints, we are going to limit our argument to the wide range of legal transactions routinely carried out by judges, more particularly in the realm of succession and inheritance causes and matters in Nigeria. I shall hinge my approach on the Nigerian common law and thereafter use it to canvass a role for synthesizing the received English law and customary rules of law, inclusive of Islamic law of the Maliki School, as well as the fundamental human rights contained in chapter four to the Nigerian constitution and other numerous instruments with an international flavour.

It is an axiomatic fact that subsisting legal philosophies in any given society are largely influenced by the social, economic, and political experiences of that society. Significantly, these heuristic changes introduced by social, economic, and political factors are nonetheless the products of interpretation and application of the laws subsisting in the society by judges, who incidentally are the high priest of the law.

For as a commentator rightly observed, we need to strive to show in most legal systems, and specifically in that of Nigeria, the activities of their judges are legally influenced by the very norms inherent in the system. The Judges, by their calling continuously influence the development of rules of customary law, as can be gleaned from the erudite opinion of Nwokedi JSC when he urged in the case of *Agbai* v. *Okagbue*[23] that:

> The doctrine of repugnancy in my view affords the court the opportunity of fine tuning customary laws to meet changed social conditions where necessary, more especially as there is no forum for repealing or amending customary laws...when however customary law is confronted by a novel situation, the courts have to consider its applicability under existing social environment.

---

[23] (1994) 9 NWLR (Pt. 368) 301

Previously, the Supreme Court in *Okonkwo* v. *Okagbue*[24] adopted the dictum of Lord Wright in *Laoye* v. *Oyetunde*[25] when the court stated:

> The Courts which have been established by the British Government have the duty of enforcing these native law and custom so far as they are not barbarous, as part of the law of the land.

It could conveniently be asserted that judges of courts of record have doggedly demonstrated in cases before them that barbarous rules of customary law in the regime of succession and inheritance causes and matters, just like in other regimes of the law, more particularly, involving intimate relationships, are doomed to be thrown into the garbage bin. This judicial approach was emphasized in *Uke* v. *Iro*,[26] where the court quickly condemned the Nnewi rule of customary law called '*Ili Ekpe*.' The court stated that:

> The '*Oli Ekpe*' custom of Nnewi is not consistent with the civilized world. The custom stipulates that a surviving brother of a deceased would be allowed to inherit the property of his deceased brother because the surviving wife has no son. This rule of customary law discriminates against a particular sex and therefore an affront even on divine laws. It is therefore repugnant to natural justice equity and good conscience. The court therefore, followed its earlier decision in *Mojekwu* v. *Ejikeme*.[27]

Significantly, learned Justice Tobi in *Mojekwu* v. *Ejikeme*, in interpreting the meaning of lineage, observed that:

> a lineage refers to a direct line of descent and one can only talk of extinction of a lineage when the line of descent is extinguished or wiped out in the sense that it is no longer in existence or it is dead. Where there are children or even grandchildren and great grandchildren, directly traced or traceable to the ancestor, it will be wrong to hold that the lineage is

---

[24] (1987) 4 NWLR (Pt.119) 234
[25] (1944) 10 WACA 4
[26] (2001) 11 NWLR (Pt. 723) 196
[27] Infra, note 21.

extinct, unless the generation gap is so wide that history and tradition cannot relate sociological contiguity...[28]

THE CHALLENGES TO JUDICIAL ACTIVISM

There have been far-reaching cries against the concept of judicial empowerment. This controversy has generated ample debate over what is or should be the proper role of courts in the socio-political system and over how far courts can intervene in socio-political matters.

Proponents of judicial activism emphasize the advantages of a system armed with strong judicial review. The judicial process (court) provides a system of checks and balances on governments that are otherwise free to do as they please. Furthermore, they can respond to socio-political and intimate relationships and societal problems that would remain unsolved by the executive or legislative arms and protect minority concerns regardless of majoritarian political trends.

As a matter of fact, critics of judicial activism raise conceptual arguments and empirical evidence against judicial empowerment. Arguing from a conceptual perspective, they emphasize the undemocratic nature of the judicial review, where an unelected and unaccountable body can veto the popular statutory or executive choice. Other critics advance the argument of the damaging effect of judicial activism on the socio-political culture of persuasion, as the incentive to turn to judicial solutions detracts from the importance of compromise and consensus-building characteristics of the socio-political process.

But above all, the principal empirical argument against judicial activism revolves around the assertion that 'judicial review does not make much difference one way or the other' because courts are 'regularly being more or less in line with what the dominant national coalition wants.' Gavison explains that this view is supplemented by comments about implementation deficiencies and work overload impairing the ability of the judicial process to provide fast and efficient solutions to conflicts.

---

[28] (2000) 5 NWLR [Pt. 657] 402

CONCLUSION

Carving a befitting role for courts in the enforcement and application of law in Nigeria is a challenging task. Arguments abound in support of judicial empowerment or activism as well as the challenges thereof. The fact remains that Nigeria is a developing country with a peculiar political arrangement. Whatever role is carved out for judges or courts must accommodate the country's multicultural and secular inclination. What matters most is the attainment of justice. Ensuring there is justice to the laws of the land as well as to the parties. It should not be forgotten that the socio-political, economic, and legal frameworks subsisting in Nigeria flowed directly from her colonial master - the United Kingdom.

This scheme of things ultimately deprived the country of a locally fashioned socio-political, economic, and legal framework that could by any stretch of imagination be termed indigenous. Strange enough, it could be maintained that the colonial legal heritage in Nigeria has stood in the way of societal development toward social justice and equity and will continue to be an impediment to a new social order in the country.

From a nomenclature perspective, every legal system is unique but differs in content.[29] The content is the amount of indigenous social justice and equity inherent in it. Comparatively speaking, a legal system is capable of adapting to new changes. The foundations of a legal system are the sources of the existence of the Courts of that system and of their authority.

Judges should accommodate the socio-political, economic, and legal considerations in the system in arriving at a decision. In reality, the underlying benign consideration was, in the past, deeply rooted in the legal system of the colonial master. These factors never reflected the

---

[29] Per Karibi Whyte J.S.C, "Customary Law of Succession in Nigeria and Wills Enactments 1993, All Nigeria Judges Conference Papers Pp. 161, 180 noting that: 'the sense of a legal system has no universally accepted definition. Much depends on the school of jurisprudence from where one has graduated….for example, a legal system is made up of all the commands issued directly or indirectly by the present sovereign of that system. On the other hand, the legal system of a particular society could be described as all the norms whose creation is authorized by the society's fundamental law of the land, that is to say, its grundnorm….Hart, that is, a system that is made up of all the legal rules which ought to be recognized according to the rule of recognition accepted by the judges and other law enforcement officials within the society.'

indigenous or colonized peoples' usages, ethos, cultures, ethics, political and economic structures, let alone their sense of social justice and equity.

Consequently, this anomaly created a divide as to what type of 'decision' judges reached. Flowing from *Mojekwu* v. *Ejikeme*,[30] the decision of the appellate court to recognize the rights and interests of the appellants was partly due to the realization of the fact that the evolving socio-political, economic, and legal considerations have been tilted in favour of accommodating females, not only as specie deserving recognition in their capacity as beings but a reflection of the new advancement in normative ethics in Nigeria. Let me quickly point out that this paradigmatic shift is accentuated by changes both in the substrata and superficial society as a whole.

Changes that normally take place in society occur heuristically. Cumulatively, they are pronounced and therefore slowly impact the society. These changes are value-laden and not free. They depict the underlying core values of the society. For instance, in *Uke* v. *Iro*,[31] the court was saddled with the issue of considering the equality of all sexes under the constitution. The court stated that the rights of all sexes are protected under the constitution, which is the organic law of the land; therefore, any assertion or argument that a woman cannot give evidence in relation to the title to land is oblivious of the constitutional provision which guarantees equal rights and protection of all sexes under the law.

Rules of customary law, as an organizing legal framework, regulate the lifestyles of those it affects. Impliedly, rules of customary law marriage contain an inherent custom that considers marriage as an exchange of goodwill. Flowing from the above is the utility or otherwise of 'wife inheritance' or, in sociological terminology, 'levirate marriage.' This type of marriage is customarily permissive, premised on the inherent customary value of protecting and caring for the widow, who may be too shattered and depressed to fend a living, and in some cases,

---

[30] *Supra*, note 21.
[31] *Supra*, note 19.

when the widow is *virgo intacta* and remains in the family for the continuation of a marital consortium with any fancied extended family member.

From a customary perspective, marriage is seen and considered as an exchange of goodwill between families. Levirate marriage is, therefore, customarily permissive because of the inherent family value of protecting and caring for the widow. Could it, therefore, be conveniently asserted that levirate marriage offends the constitutional provision on the exercise of the right to freedom from discrimination or infringes or restricts, if any, a widow's right? We may anchor our standpoint on what the court said in *Uke* v. *Iro*[32] to the effect that once a rule of customary law flies against decency and is not consonant with notions, beliefs, or practice of what is acceptable in a court where the rule of law is the order of the day, then such a rule of customary law should be disregarded, discarded and dismissed as amounting to nothing.

Justice Idigbe has argued that the status of human rights being regarded as fundamental and justiciable is by virtue of being contained in Nigeria's constitution and expressly stated to be so.[33] The learned Justice categorizes jurisprudence of rights in Nigeria as either or not fundamental, justiciable, and enforceable upon violation. A useful distinction between human rights and fundamental human rights was made sometime in the past that:

> It must be pointed out at this stage that these rights which are antecedent to the political society itself do not exist only in societies or states with written constitutions. However, unless their existence or continued existence is guaranteed under the state's constitution they cannot with reference to that political state or political society be described as fundamental rights. It is therefore my respectful view that a description of these rights as fundamental rights ought to be confined to state or political societies governed by written constitutions.[34]

---

[32] Ibid.

[33] Idigbe, C, 'Fundamental Rights Provisions of the Constitution' in the All Nigerian Judges Conference Papers, March 8-16, 1982 P.2.

[34] Ibid., at Pp. 8, 9.

Therefore the Nigerian constitutional provisions, especially Chapter IV on Fundamental human rights, are wide enough or portend to accommodate the provisions of the Convention on the Elimination of all forms of discrimination against women. Practically speaking, a victim, more particularly a female victim, can rely on the provisions of chapter four to enforce her claims, interests, and rights created under the Convention. This is so because the provisions of Chapter IV on fundamental human rights are similar to the provisions of the convention on the elimination of all forms of discrimination against women. The only foreseeable problem remains the issue of enforcement. To this end, I take the liberty to urge that the same rules of court applicable to the enforcement of fundamental human rights and the jurisdictional competence of the federal high courts be extended to applications for the enforcement of rights ordinarily contemplated by the convention on the elimination of all forms of discrimination against women.

Judges must push forward in giving legal stamp to socio-political interests and agitations in society. They must recognize that judicial decisions invariably bind the parties and guides others as to what is the position of the law. There may be subsisting opposition to the judgment, but it is effective in that it has been pronounced.

Chapter 11

ENFORCEMENT OF HUMAN RIGHTS IN NIGERIA

Nathaniel A. Inegbedion*

INTRODUCTION

By Statutory Instrument number 37 of 2009 and pursuant to the powers conferred on him by section 46, subsection (3) of the Constitution of the Federal Republic of Nigeria 1999 (called the CFRN 1999), the Chief Justice of Nigeria issued a new Fundamental Rights (Enforcement Procedure) Rules 2009 (called "the 2009 Rules"). The Rules were made to replace the old ones that became operational in 1979. The 2009 Rules also simplified the hitherto rigid procedure for the enforcement of human rights and gave access to justice to those who otherwise, due to the exorbitant costs of approaching the courts for judicial relief, would have been denied justice through public interest litigation. The application of the Rules is, however, circumscribed within the confines of the rights cognizable under chapter IV of the Constitution of the Federal Republic of Nigeria 1999. They do not, therefore, apply to the whole gamut of human rights. Perhaps this represents an important limitation of the Rules.

The enforcement of human rights in Nigeria must therefore be understood within the context of the 2009 Rules, at least from the perspective of the State, though there are sufficient materials for contending that in spite of the Rules, the whole gamut of human rights

* LL.B; LL.M; Ph.D; Associate Professor, Department of Public Law, Faculty of Law, University of Benin. Member, Council of Legal Education; Notary Public. Email: nathaniel.inegbedion@uniben.edu

may be enforced or more appropriately, protected outside the Rules and within the realm of international human rights law.[1] In this chapter, the concept of human rights, the evolution of human rights, their enforcement, and the jurisdiction of the courts will be examined in some considerable detail.

THE CONCEPT OF HUMAN RIGHTS

It has been asserted that the subject of human rights in the world must be one of humanity's greatest concerns on earth. That no one may question the yearning of humanity to achieve a society where human decency prevails and all persons are treated with respect and dignity due the human person. The striving has always been to attain a universal norm of fair, decent, and acceptable treatment for all individuals throughout the world.[2] "Human rights" may then be defined as representing the demands or claims that individuals or groups make on society, some of which are protected by law and have become part of the *ex lata* while others remain aspirations to be attained in the future.[3] A clearer picture of the subject within the context of this thesis is afforded by the definition of Cranston. According to him,

A human right is something of which no one may be deprived without a great affront to justice. There are certain deeds, which should never be done, certain freedoms which should never be invaded, some things which are supremely sacred.[4]

Ishay[5] simply defines "human rights" as rights held by individuals simply because they are part of the human species. They are rights shared equally by everyone regardless of sex, race, nationality, and economic background. They are universal in content. According to the

---

[1] See for instance, the case of *Fawehinmi* v. *Abacha* (1996) 9 NWLR [Part 475] 996; [1998] 1 HRLRA 541. See also the African Charter on Human and Peoples' Rights which was adopted on 27 June 1981 and entered into force on 21 October 1986. See also *Social and Economic Rights Action Centre and Centre for Economic and Social Rights* v. *Nigeria* (2001) AHRLR 60; *Socio-Economic Rights Accountability Project* v. *Federal Republic of Nigeria,* Suit No. ECW/CCJ/APP/09.

[2] Edward, D.R, "Judicial Enforcement of International Human Rights" [1994] 27 *Akron Law Review* (Nos. 3,4) 281.

[3] See Eze, O, *Human Rights in Africa, Some Selected Problems* (Lagos: NIALS 1984).

[4] Cranston, M "Human Rights: Real and Supposed" in D.D Raphael ed. *Political Theory and the Rights of Man* (Bloomington: Indiana University Press, 1967) at 52.

[5] Ishay, M. R., *The History of Human Rights* (California: University of California Press 2004) 3

author, across the centuries, conflicting political traditions have elaborated different components of human rights or differed over which elements have priority. That, in our day, the manifold meanings of human rights reflect the process of historical continuity and change that helped shape their present substance and helped form the Universal Declaration of Human Rights (UDHR), adopted by the General Assembly of the United Nations in 1948.

Donnelly[6] argues that the very term 'human rights' points clearly to their source: humanity, human nature, being a person or human being. He contends that just as legal rights have the law as their source, and contractual rights arise from contracts, 'humanity', 'human nature' or some such aspect of all persons would seem to be the source of human rights. The problem, of course, is to specify what 'human nature' means in this context and how it gives rise to rights. He proffers a solution to this problem by examining the classic theories, which to him, provide little illumination. According to him, Locke ultimately falls back on the divine donation: God, in His infinite wisdom and mercy, grants us natural rights; they are 'natural' in the sense that they are part of our divinely ordained human nature. He takes a 'constructivist' theory of human rights by contending that the source of human rights is man's moral nature, which is only loosely linked to the 'human nature' of basic human needs.

According to him, human rights are 'needed' for human dignity rather than health, and violations of human rights are denials of one's humanity rather than deprivations of needs. "We have human rights not to the requisites for health, but to those things 'needed' for a truly human life. He denies that God, nature or the physical facts of life give human rights to man, but rather, that human rights arise from human action. Human rights represent the choice of a particular moral vision of human potentiality and the institutions for realizing that vision. The human 'nature' that grounds human rights is a moral posit, an essentially moral account of human possibilities.

---

[6] Donnelly, J, *The Concept of Human Rights* (New York: St. Martins Press, 1985) at 27

While not unrelated to human nature studied by scientists, the relation is primarily negative: the scientist's human nature sets the 'natural' outer limits of human possibility; the moral nature that grounds human rights is a selection of one set of possibilities. The scientist's human nature says beyond this we cannot go. The moral nature that is the source of human rights says that beneath this we cannot permit ourselves to fall. In essence then, human rights doctrines rests on something very much like an equation of having human rights and being human.[7] Human rights do appear as a sort of self-fulfilling moral prophecy: 'treat human beings like human beings and you'll get a truly human, and more fully realized persons. Donnelly posits that the relationship between human nature, human rights and political society is thus 'dialectical'. Human rights shape political society, so as to shape man, so as to realize the possibilities of human nature, which provided the basis for these rights in the first place. Without human rights, the 'real' human being is almost certain to be split-alienated or estranged-from his (moral) 'nature'. This then helps to explain the familiar claim of the inalienability of human rights: one can no more lose one's human rights than one can lose one's human nature. The claim for the inalienability of human rights is not one of practical impossibility, but rather, a claim of moral impossibility; one cannot lose such rights and live the life of a human being.

Finally, Donnelly argues that it is widely believed that the concept of human rights emerged from the notion of natural law. That it is not even uncommon to find "natural law" used as a rough synonym for 'natural rights'. He asserts that in fact, though the two concepts are largely unrelated, natural law represents an approach to questions of -political order quite different from that of natural or human rights. This is particularly clear in Aquinas' theory of natural law and rights, perhaps the best developed and best known of the classic natural law theories.[8]

---

[7] Donnelly, J., *op. cit.,* at 33

[8] Donnelly, J., *op. cit.,* at 45.

THE EVOLUTION OF HUMAN RIGHTS

The aftermath of the two World Wars contributed immensely to the development of human rights. For instance, the Nuremberg trials and the offense of "crime against humanity" had a natural law coloration about them. Shortly after World War II, there was the UDHR which also had a distinct natural law coloration. The Declaration was made against the background of the rights abuses carried out during World War II.

The Declaration can be attributed to the rise of Nazi and Fascist dictatorships, the spread of totalitarianism, the appalling savagery of the massacre of millions of innocent people in the name of racial ideology, and the deliberate repudiation by large and powerful nations of all norms of morality and culture. The Declaration contains both civil and political rights (also referred to as First Generation Rights) and Economic, Social, and Cultural Rights (also referred to as Second Generation Rights). The First Generation rights derive primarily from the outcomes of the English, American, and French Revolutions. Belonging to this class are such rights set forth in Articles 2-21 of the UDHR, including freedom from racial and equivalent forms of discrimination, the right to life, liberty, and the security of person, freedom from slavery and involuntary servitude, freedom from torture and from cruel, inhuman and degrading treatment or punishment, etc.

The Second Generation rights are, in large part, a response to the abuses and misuses of capitalist development and its underlying, essentially uncritical conception of individual liberty that tolerated or even legitimized the exploitation of working classes and colonial peoples. The rights under this Generation can be found in Articles 22-27 of the UDHR, and they include the right to social security, the right to work and to protection against unemployment, the right to rest and leisure, including periodic holidays with pay, the right to a standard of living adequate for the health and well-being of self and family, the right to education and the right to the protection of one's scientific, literary and artistic production. The Declaration was not legally binding since it was a mere declaration of principles.

Human Rights in Modern Times

However, the provisions of the Declaration soon found their way into the Constitutions of several emerging independent states, including Nigeria. The declaration was soon followed up by two covenants on human rights, that is, the International Covenant on Civil and Political Rights of 1966 and the International Covenant on Economic Social and Cultural Rights of 1966. Third generations of rights, known as solidarity rights, which include the right to self-determination and the right to a clean environment, have also emerged. The second-generation rights, as they are contained under the 1999 Constitution of the Federal Republic of Nigeria, are regarded as non-justiciable in Nigeria; that is, the enforcement of these rights cannot be a subject of litigation in Nigerian courts.[9] In fact, they are not rights properly so-called but "objectives" and "principles" that the government is expected to meet. Under the 1999 Constitution, the Legislature is enjoined to make laws for the purpose of enforcing the provisions of chapter 2. In *Archbishop Okogie* v. *Attorney-General of Lagos State (supra),* while interpreting the provisions of s.4(2) of the 1979 Constitution, the Court of Appeal, Nasir, P had this to say:

> It is clear therefore, that the National Assembly has the duty to establish authorities, which shall have power to promote and enforce the observance of chapter II of the Constitution. Until such authorities are established, it will be mere speculation to say which functions they may perform or in which they may be able to enforce the provisions of chapter II.[10]

Nigeria is a member of the international community and a signatory to many international instruments and treaties. These treaties include the Convention on the Elimination of all Forms of Discrimination Against Women, Convention Against Torture, the African Charter on Human and Peoples Rights, the Universal Declaration of Human Rights (UDHR), the ECOWAS Court, the

[9] See *Archbishop Okogie* v. *Attorney-General of Lagos State* [1980] F.N.R 445 at 455. See also the *obiter dictum* of Fatai-Williams, A. (CJN) in *Attorney-General of Bendel State* v. *Attorney-General of the Federation & Ors* [1981] A.N.L.R 85 at 110.

[10] At 456.

Additional Protocol to the African Charter on Human and Peoples Rights on the Rights of Women. These instruments have clauses that enjoin a State Party, including Nigeria, to take legislative and other measures to protect the rights provided in the instruments.[11]

In spite of Nigeria being a signatory to all the above-mentioned international instruments, the protection of Economic Social and Cultural Rights (ESC Rights) protected by these instruments has not always been secured, particularly in Africa. One argument that has been advanced for this is that the underdeveloped nature of most African countries makes it difficult for the implementation of ESC rights, in the sense that emphasis is on economic development rather than the protection of ESC rights.[12] This argument brings to the fore the clash between civil and political rights and socio-economic or developmental rights. Osinbajo & Ajayi[13] posed the question: Is there a real conflict, or is the conflict a convenient excuse for authoritarianism? According to the authors, the response of the west has been to insist on the universality of human rights and to attempt, where possible, to punish human rights violations by economic sanctions of varying kinds.

In the light of Nigeria's position as a State/Party to these human rights instruments, it is untenable to persist in the judicial assertion that the ESC rights components of these treaties are unenforceable or not justiciable within the context of section (6), subsection (6) (c) of the CFRN 1999.[14] What is the scope of the rights protected by the Constitution of the Federal Republic of Nigeria 1999? Are the rights the entire gamut of human rights following the concept of the indivisibility of human rights, or are they limited?

[11] See Article 2(1) of ICESCR; Articles 2(a), 3, 6 of CEDAW; Articles 2(1) & 5 of CAT and Article 2(1) of the Protocol to the African Charter on Human and Peoples Rights' on the Rights of Women in Africa.

[12] See for instance, Osinbajo, Y & Ajayi, O. "Human Rights and Economic Development in Developing Countries [1994] 28 Int'l Law 727.

[13] Osinbajo, Y & Ajayi, O. *op. cit.* at 728.

[14] For further reading, see Okafor, O.C & Ngwaba, U., "Economic and Social Rights: A Century of Constitutional Subordination in Nigeria" in Azinge (ed.), *Nigeria: A Century of Constitutional Evolution 1914-2014* (Lagos, Nigerian Institute of Advanced Legal Studies, 2013) at 688-726 and Olanrewaju A.A., "Fundamental Objectives and Directive Principles of State Policy, Azinge (ed.), *op. cit.* at 378-425

THE NATURE OF THE RIGHTS PROTECTED UNDER CHAPTER IV OF THE CONSTITUTION OF THE FEDERAL REPUBLIC OF NIGERIA 1999

Sometimes referred to as civil and political rights, these are a class of rights that the state seeks to protect by enshrining them in the Constitution. While they are generally the same for all nations, they, however, vary in terms of details. The rights have major components of the UDHR; the International Covenant on Civil and Political Rights of 1976 (ICCPR) and, with particular reference to Africa, the African Charter on Human and Peoples' Rights (ACHPR). In Nigeria, they can be found in chapter IV of the 1999 Constitution and are called Fundamental Rights. Historically, it was not until 1957 that Fundamental Rights were accorded recognition in Nigeria by the Willink Commission, which recommended their inclusion in the 1957 Constitution.[15]

Since then, the Rights have been included in subsequent Constitutions of Nigeria. The rights are as listed below:

Section 33- Right to life;
Section 34- Right to dignity of human person;
Section 35- Right to personal liberty;
Section 36- Right to fair hearing;
Section 37- Right to private and family life;
Section 38- Right to freedom of thought, conscience, and religion;
Section 39- Right to freedom of expression and the Press;
Section 40- Right to peaceful assembly and association;
Section 41- Right to freedom of movement;
Section 42- Right to freedom from discrimination;
Section 43- Right to acquire and own immovable property anywhere in Nigeria;
Section 44- Compulsory acquisition of property.

[15] For a detailed reading of the history of fundamental rights in Nigeria, see Ukhuegbe, S., "The Formal Evolution of the Nigerian Bill of Rights: From the Willink Commission Proposal to the 1999 Constitution" in Azinge (ed.), *Nigeria: A Century of Constitutional Evolution 1914-2014* (Lagos, Nigerian Institute of Advanced Legal Studies, 2013) at 620-687.

Jurisdiction of Court

The High Court is vested with the jurisdiction to entertain cases dealing with the infringement of any of the rights contained in chapter IV, that is, sections 33 to 44.[16] Thus, section 46 of the Constitution of the Federal Republic of Nigeria 1999 (called "the CFRN 1999") provides that,

> (1) Any person who alleges that any of the provisions of this chapter has been, is being, or is likely to be contravened in any state in relation to him may apply to a High Court in that State for redress.
>
> (2) Subject to the provisions of this Constitution, a High Court shall have original jurisdiction to hear and determine any application made to it in pursuance of the provisions of this section and may make such order, issue such writs and give such directions as it may consider appropriate for the purpose of enforcing or securing the enforcement within that State of any right to which to which the person who makes the application may be entitled under this chapter.
>
> (3) The Chief Justice of Nigeria may make rules with respect to the practice and procedure of a High Court for the purposes of this section.

From the wordings of section 46, subsections (1) and (2), it appears that only a person whose fundamental rights have been abridged or infringed upon may apply to the court for the enforcement of his fundamental rights. That is, only a person who has the *locus standi* can benefit from the provisions of the section. A meddlesome interloper cannot proceed to court for judicial relief. It would appear that only a person whose fundamental right has been infringed upon may qualify to be ascribed as an aggrieved person in the context of section 46, subsections (1) and (2). The legal concept of *locus standi* requires that an individual who approaches the courts for legal redress must show that the legal injury he suffered is peculiar to him and is far

[16] See s. 46 of the CFRN 1999.

above that suffered by the general public.[17] In the case of *Abraham Adesanya* v. *President of the Federal Republic of Nigeria & Anor.,*[18] the Supreme Court held that to entitle a person to invoke judicial power to determine the constitutionality of legislative or executive action, he must show that either his personal interest will immediately be or has been adversely affected by the action or that he has sustained or is in immediate danger of sustaining an injury to himself, and which interest or injury is over and above that of the general public.[19] The facts of this case are that, in the exercise of his power under section 141 of the CFRN 1999, the then President, Alhaji Shehu Shagari, appointed Hon. Justice Ovie Whiskey, the then Chief Judge of Bendel State, as the Chairman of the Federal Electoral Commission, which appointment was subject to Senate confirmation. The Plaintiff, as a member of the Senate and during the Senate confirmation proceedings, unsuccessfully opposed the appointment. He then approached the court for a nullification of the appointment and which was nullified by the Court of the first instance. On appeal to the Court of Appeal, the Court referred the matter to the Supreme Court for its determination. The apex court had no hesitation in holding that the Appellant lacked *locus standi.*

---

17 See Garner, B.A: *Black's Law Dictionary* (7th ed., St. Paul, Minn: West Group, 1999). See also the cases of *Pam & Anor.* v. *Mohammed & Anor.* [2008] All FWLR 1868 (SC); *Lawal & Ors.* v. *Governor of Kwara State & Ors.* [2005]3 WRN 171; *A.G. Anambra State* v. *Chief Chris Uba & Ors.* [2005] 33 WRN 191 (C.A); *Ladejobi & Ors.* v. *Oguntayo & Ors.* [2005] 7 WRN 229 (S.C) and *Emezi* v. *Osuagwu & Ors.* [2005] 30 WRN 1 (SC).

18 [1981] ANLR (Reprint edition) 1.

19 Note however that in the later case of *Gani Fawehinmi* v. *Halilu & Anor* (1987) 4 NWLR [Part 67] 797 the Supreme Court rejected the narrow interpretation given to the legal principle and held that in cases of criminal prosecution, everybody is his brother's keeper and as such, everybody has a duty to ensure that criminals are brought to book. This was a case where the appellant instituted mandamus proceedings against the Attorney-General of Lagos State to compel her to decide whether or not she will prosecute the Respondents for murder and where she decides not to prosecute, to issue him with a *fiat* permitting him to prosecute the Respondents. The trial court struck out the suit of the Appellant on the ground that he had no *locus standi*, in accordance with the narrow interpretation given to the principle in the *Adesanya case*. That decision was upheld by the Court of Appeal. On further appeal to the apex Court, the Court gave a very wide interpretation to the principle by adopting the neighbour principle. In the words of the Court, "the power to initiate criminal prosecution whether by the Attorney-General or by a private prosecutor or other authority is a right in the broad sense. It is recognized by the laws and the Constitution of the Federal Republic of Nigeria 1979. It is in respect of the States recognized by section 191 of the Constitution and, in respect of the Federation; it is recognized by section 160 of the Constitution". This liberal approach to the principle of *locus standi* only applies in criminal proceedings and under the criminal procedure law of Lagos State. It does not in any way apply in civil proceedings or do away with the principle enunciated in the *Adesanya case* and the subsequent cases that followed it.

Enforcement of Human Rights under the Fundamental Rights Enforcement Procedure Rules 2009

The Fundamental Rights (Enforcement Procedure) Rules 2009 Rules prescribe in some detail that the procedure for the enforcement of fundamental rights is recognised under chapter IV of the CFRN 1999. The Rules redefined the meaning of "the person aggrieved" to include persons not otherwise envisaged by section 46, subsection (1) of the CFRN 1999 and thereby broadened the traditional concept of *locus standi* as previously understood in the *Abraham Adesanya case*. Thus, paragraph 3(e) of the preamble to the 2009 Rules provides that the Court shall encourage and welcome public interest litigations in the human rights field, and no human rights case may be dismissed or struck out for want of *locus standi*. Paragraph 3(e) defines an Applicant seeking to enforce fundamental rights to mean (i) anyone acting in his own interest; (ii) anyone acting on behalf of another person; (iii) anyone acting as a member of or in the interest of, a group or class of persons; (iv) anyone acting in the public interest; (v) an association acting in the interest of its members or other individual or groups.

The purpose of this paragraph, particularly paragraph 3(e)(iv), is obviously to do away with the narrow interpretation of *locus standi* given in *Adesanya's case* so that enforcement of fundamental rights may become easily more realizable. Whether this can actually be achieved remains to be seen. This is in the light of the express wording of section 46, subsections (1) and (2), which appear to restrict the application of chapter IV to only persons whose fundamental rights have been trampled upon and who are therefore entitled to approach the court for judicial relief. While it may be possible to employ public interest litigation in the actualization of environmental rights and economic, social, and cultural rights, which are not encapsulated in chapter IV, it is doubtful whether the same tool can be deployed to actualize the provisions of chapter IV.[20] While infringement of the category of rights

[20] For a detailed commentary on the applicability of public interest litigation in the enforcement of fundamental rights, see Inegbedion, N.A., "The New Fundamental Rights (Enforcement Procedure) Rules 2009 and Public Interest Litigation. Expanding the Frontiers of Human Rights Litigation" (2008) 9 *Nigeria Education Law Journal* (No.1) 157.

called ESC Rights and indeed Environmental Rights may affect large groups of persons or several communities in one fell swoop, the same cannot be said for the provisions of Chapter IV, which does not include ESC Rights; and Environmental Rights (these are captured by chapter II). To the extent that the 2009 Rules have expanded the scope of persons that can enforce the provisions of Chapter IV, they appear to conflict or be inconsistent with the express wording of section 46, subsections (1) and (2) and therefore have doubtful validity.[21]

Paragraph 3(e) of the 2009 Rules is a wholesale adoption of section 38 of the Republic of South Africa's Constitution 1996 on the same subject matter and is completely novel in our human rights jurisprudence. Similar provisions on public interest litigation can be found in the Constitutions of other countries. For instance, Article 199, sub-Article (1)(b) of the Constitution of Pakistan 1973 provides that, subject to the provisions of the Constitution, a High Court may, if it is satisfied that no other adequate remedy is provided by law, on the application of *any person*,[22] make an order, directing that a person in custody, within the territorial jurisdiction of the Court, be brought before it so that the Court may satisfy itself that he is not being held in custody without lawful authority or in an unlawful manner. Further, Article 50(1) of the Ugandan Constitution of 1995 states that any person who claims that a fundamental or other right or freedom guaranteed under the Constitution has been infringed or threatened is entitled to apply to a competent court for redress, which may include compensation. Under subsection (2), any person or organization may bring an action against the violation of another person's or group's human rights. The combined effect of the two provisions is to permit public interest litigation with a view to getting around the common law principle of *locus standi*.

The difference between the Constitutions South Africa, Pakistan, and Uganda, on the one hand, and that of Nigeria, on the other hand, is that in the former, the provisions for public interest litigation are

---

[21] See s. 1(1) & (3) of the CFRN 1999.
[22] Emphasis supplied.

contained in their Constitutions, while in the latter, they are contained in the 2009 Rules which are not of equal status with the CFRN 1999. The constitutionality of the provision for public interest litigation in the 2009 Rules is therefore very much in doubt.

The provision of section 46, subsection (1) has been interpreted to mean both the Federal High Court and the State High Courts have concurrent jurisdiction to deal with matters pertaining to the enforcement of fundamental rights.[23] Section 46, subsection (4) requires the National Assembly to make a law guaranteeing financial assistance for an indigent person whose right has been infringed.

Objectives of the 2009 Rules

The preamble to the 2009 Rules, under paragraph 3 thereof, sets seven overriding objectives of the Rules. The first objective is that it mandates the Court to expansively interpret the provisions of the CFRN 1999, particularly chapter IV, and the African Charter on Human and Peoples' Rights (called "the Charter"), with a view to advancing and realizing the rights and freedoms contained in them and affording the protections intended by them. The second objective is that for the purpose of advancing but never for the purpose of restricting the applicant's rights and freedoms, the court shall respect municipal, regional and international bills of rights cited to it or brought to its attention. These bills include the Charter (including protocols made under the Charter) and the Universal Declaration of Human Rights (called "the UDHR"). The provisions of the Charter are expansive enough to cover the UDHR, so that it becomes unnecessary to include the UDHR as one of the international bills that the Court is enjoined to respect. This is more so when it is observed that the UDHR is a mere declaration and therefore does not create any legal obligation and can best be described as a moral adjuration. Again, it is doubtful if the Court can accord any respect to any international bill of rights that have not been domesticated in accordance with the provisions of section 12, subsection (1) of the CFRN 1999.

---

[23] *Kalu* v. *The State* [1998] 64 LRCN 5397 (S.C).

Therefore, such respect can only be limited to international bills with domestic flavour. For instance, the United Nations Convention on the Right of the Child, which came into force on 2 September 1990 and was ratified by Nigeria on 19 April 1991, has been domesticated as the Child Rights Act.[24] Such references to the Convention must enjoy the respect of the Court. Other than the international human rights instruments that have been domesticated, it is difficult to comprehend in what circumstances the court is required to respect international bills that have not been domesticated. One is not unmindful of the decision of the Court of Appeal in *Gani Fawehinmi* v. *Abacha*.[25] In that case, the appellant was detained by agents of the State Security Services, whereupon, the appellant filed an action challenging his detention and seeking, *inter alia*, a declaration that the detention and continued detention of the applicant without charge constitutes a gross violation of his fundamental rights guaranteed under sections 31, 32 and 38 of the 1979 Constitution and Articles 5, 6 and 12 of the African Charter on Human and Peoples' Rights (Ratification and Enforcement) Act,[26] and is therefore illegal and unconstitutional. By a preliminary objection, the respondent challenged the jurisdiction of the trial court in view of the ouster provisions in the State Security (Detention of Persons) Decree No. 2 of 1984, under which the appellant was detained; the Federal Military Government (Supremacy and Enforcement of Powers) Decree No. 12 of 1994 and the Constitution (Suspension and Modification) Decree No. 107 of 1993. The preliminary objection was upheld by the trial court. At the Court of Appeal, the appeal was allowed. While allowing the appeal, the Court held that the provisions of the Charter are in a class of their own and do not fall within the classification of the hierarchy of laws in Nigeria in order of superiority as enunciated in *Labiyi* v. *Anretiola*.[27] Musdapher J.C.A opined that the learned trial judge acted erroneously when he held that the African Charter contained in cap 10 of the Laws of the Federation of Nigeria

[24] Cap C50 Laws of the Federation of Nigeria 2004.
[25] (1996) 9 NWLR [Part 475] 996; [1998] 1 HRLRA 541.
[26] Cap 10, Laws of the Federation of Nigeria 1990, now cap A9, Laws of the Federation of Nigeria 2004.
[27] (1992) 8 NWLR [Part 358] 139.

1990 is inferior to Decrees of the Federal Military Government. It is commonplace that no Government will be allowed to contract out by local legislation its international obligations. According to him, notwithstanding the fact that the African Charter was domesticated by the National Assembly in 1983, it is legislation with an international flavour, and the ouster clauses contained in Decrees No. 107 of 1993 or No. 12 of 1994 cannot affect its operation in Nigeria.

The pronouncement of Musdapher JCA that no Government will be allowed to contract out, by local legislation, its international obligations seems to suggest that once Nigeria is a State Party to an international treaty, then it is binding on the country. That pronouncement was made during the military regime and may not be in tune with the spirit of section 12, subsection (1) of the CFRN 1999. When that section is read along with section 1 of the CFRN 1999, it becomes crystal clear that without any domestication by the National Assembly, a treaty cannot be operationalized in Nigeria. Consequently, and in the light of the aforementioned provisions of the CFRN 1999, Musdapher's pronouncement must be treated with a great deal of circumspection.

Another objective of the 2009 Rules is that the court shall proactively pursue enhanced access to justice for all classes of litigants, especially the poor, the illiterate, the uninformed, the vulnerable, the incarcerated, and the unrepresented.

Paragraph 3(f) requires the Court to pursue the speedy and efficient enforcement and realization of human rights in a manner that is calculated to advance Nigerian democracy, good governance, human rights, and culture. Under paragraph 3(g), human rights suits shall be given priority in deserving cases, and where the question of the liberty of the applicant or any person is in issue, the case shall be treated as an emergency.

Mode of Commencement of Action

Unlike the 1979 Rules,[28] the 2009 Rules do not require the leave of court before an action for the enforcement of fundamental rights may

[28] See Order 1, Rule 2 of the 1979 Rules.

be commenced. All that is now required is that such an action may be made by any originating process accepted by the Court, which shall, subject to the provisions of the Rules, lie without leave of Court.[29] The current rules require parties to file written addresses that were completely absent under the 1979 Rules. The Applicant is required to file his written address along with his Application,[30] while the Respondent has five days from the date of service on him of the Applicant's Application to file his address which he may accompany with a counter-affidavit.[31] The Applicant has five days, upon receipt of the Respondent's address, to file any reply on points of law and may accompany it with a further affidavit.[32] Similar to the 1979 Rules, the 2009 Rules require the application to be supported by a Statement setting out the name and description of the applicant, the relief sought, the grounds upon which the reliefs are sought, and supported by an affidavit setting out the facts upon which the application is made.[33] The 1979 Rules require the application for the enforcement of fundamental rights to be brought within twelve months from the date of the happening of the event, matter, or act complained of. The new 2009 Rules specifically provide that such application shall not be affected by any limitation statute whatsoever.[34] The Application shall be fixed for hearing within seven days.[35] Under the 1979 Rules, Order 2, Rule 1(2) thereof, the motion or summons must be fixed for hearing within 14 days.

Interim Order

Under the 1979 Rules, it was the rule of practice, where applicable, to couple an *ex parte* application for leave to enforce the applicant's fundamental rights with a prayer for an interim order in order not to destroy the *res.* In the light of the abridgment of the process by the 2009 Rules, which have removed the requirement of leave, there is the real

[29] Order II, Rule 2.
[30] Order II, Rule 5.
[31] Order II, Rule 6.
[32] Order II, Rule 7.
[33] Order II, Rule 3.
[34] Order III, Rule 1.
[35] Order IV, Rule 1

danger that before all the parties are served, and the hearing is concluded, the *res* may be destroyed, thus foisting on the court a situation of complete helplessness or hopelessness. The 2009 Rules have sought to meet this possible danger by making separate provisions for *ex parte* applications.

Therefore, under Order IV Rule 3, where the Court is satisfied that exceptional hardship may be caused to the Applicant before the service of the Application, especially when the life or liberty of the Applicant is involved, it may hear the Applicant *ex parte* upon such interim reliefs as the justice of the application may demand. However, where the Order is made *ex parte,* an aggrieved party may, within seven days after the service of the Order or within such further time as the Court may allow, apply to the Court by motion to vary or discharge the Order.[36] The intendment of this provision is to, without waiting for the conclusion of the case, allow a party against whom the interim order was granted to apply to the Court for either the variation of the interim order or its discharge.

A possible scenario where the Order may be discharged is where the facts deposed to in the affidavit in support of an application for the interim Order are found to be false. The Court may, on notice to the party obtaining the Order, either refuse to vary or discharge it with or without imposing terms as to costs or security, or, as may seem just.

The mode of service of the court processes is substantially similar with that of the relevant court rules.[37] However, Rule 7 (c) of Order V is not contained in the Federal High Court (Civil Procedure) Rules 2009. It provides that the court process can be served by substituted means by delivery of the document to any senior officer of any Government agency that has office both in the State where the breach occurred and head office either in the Federal Capital Territory or elsewhere; service on the agency through its office in any state where the breach occurred.

---

[36] Order IV, Rule 6.

[37] See Order V. For the mode of service under the relevant High Court Rules, see for instance, Order 6, Rules 1-6 of the Federal High Court (Civil Procedure) Rules 2009; Order 7, Rules 1-6 of the High Court (Civil Procedure) Rules 2012 of Edo State; Order 7, Rules 1—12 of the High Court (Civil Procedure) Rules 2012 of Delta State. See generally, Nwadialo, F: *Civil Procedure in Nigeria* (2nd ed., Lagos: University of Lagos Press 2000) 251-284.

This provision is designed to remove the hardship that will arise if the normal mode of service on a corporation, by personally serving at the registered office of the corporation, was to be observed. In most cases, the registered office of the corporation may be far removed from the place where the breach of chapter IV was committed, at times involving hundreds of kilometres, thus putting the Applicant to some considerable hardship in terms of time lost and expense in effecting personal service. In the process, the legal injury being sought to be avoided may have been committed.

1.1 Preliminary Objection

The 2009 Rules provide that a Respondent may apply to the Court to strike out the suit or set aside the proceedings for want of jurisdiction[38] , which should be done by way of notice of preliminary objection. The notice must be filed along with the counter-affidavit to the main application.[39] On the date fixed for hearing, the preliminary objection shall be heard with the main application,[40] and where the Court does not decline jurisdiction, it shall go ahead to give its Ruling on the substantive application. The reason for taking the two applications together is to save time which is in consonance with one of the objectives of the 2009 Rules.[41]

1.2 Hearing of the Application

Order XII of the 2009 Rules deals with the hearing of the substantive application. The Order must be read along with Order II, which provides for the filing of written addresses. In terms of Order XII, the Application is heard based on the written addresses filed by the parties along with the court processes,[42] with either party given twenty minutes to present the oral arguments. The essence of the oral arguments is not to repeat what is in the written addresses but to address the Court on

---

[38] Order VIII, Rule 1.
[39] Order VIII, Rule 2
[40] Order VIII, Rule 4.
[41] See paragraph 3(f) & (g) of the preamble to the 2008 Rules.
[42] See Order XII, Rule 1

such matters, not in the written addresses, provided such matters came to the knowledge of the party after he has filed his written address.[43]

Upon the date fixed for hearing or for the adoption of their written addresses and either of the parties is absent, the Rules enjoin the Court to, upon its own motion or upon the application of the counsel for the party present, order that the addresses be deemed adopted provided the Court is satisfied that the party absent had notice of the hearing date.[44] This provision is similar to Order 18, Rules 9 (4) of the Court of Appeal Rules 2011, which provides that,

> When an appeal is called and the parties have been duly served with the notice of hearing, but if any party or any legal practitioner appearing for him does not appear to present oral argument even though briefs have been filed by all the parties concerned in the appeal, the appeal will be treated as having been duly argued.

In keeping with the overall objectives of the Rules,[45] one of which is the speedy disposal of applications for the enforcement of fundamental rights, the deemed adoption of written addresses is designed to avoid unnecessary delay which may be occasioned by an adjournment of the matter simply because one of the parties is absent in court.

Effect of Non-compliance with the Rules

Where at any stage in the course of or in connection with any proceedings that have, by any reason of anything done or left undone, been failure to comply with the requirement as to time, place or manner, or form, the failure shall be treated as an irregularity and may not nullify such proceedings except as they relate to the mode of commencement of the application or the subject matter is not within Chapter IV of the Constitution or the African Charter on Human and

[43] See Order XII, Rule 2.
[44] See Order XII, Rule 3.
[45] See paragraphs (f) & (g) of the preamble to the 2009 Rules.

Peoples' Rights (Ratification and Enforcement) Act.[46] Under the old 1979 Rules, non-compliance is not treated as an irregularity, but rather, it may be a ground for the court to strike out the action. In *Chukwuogor & Ors.* v. *Chukwuogor & Anor.*,[47] the Applicant failed to comply with the provision of Order 2, Rule 1(4) of the 1979 Rules that requires the Applicant to personally file an affidavit of service rather than the court Bailiff. The Court struck out the motion for enforcement of fundamental rights on the basis of non-compliance with this requirement.

An appeal to the Court of Appeal, Calabar Division was dismissed. Again, in the case, *Umoh & Ors.* v. *Nkan & Ors.*,[48] the Court of Appeal, Calabar Division held that non-compliance with the provision of Order 2, Rule 1(2) of the 1979 Rules, which required that the motion or summons must be fixed for hearing within 14 days after the leave to enforce the applicant's fundamental rights was fatal to the applicant's case and that the effect of the non-compliance was to divest the court of the jurisdiction to entertain the case. In this case, the Applicant filed the motion 16 days after the leave was granted, which was a clear two days after the expiration of the 14 days.

The Court consequently struck out the motion. The first ambit of the exception in Order IX of the new 2009 Rules is a statutory expression of the view the Courts have always taken on matters filed using the Fundamental Rights (Enforcement Procedure) Rules but which cause of action cannot be located within chapter IV of the 1999 Constitution or where the breach of fundamental rights is only ancillary to the main claim. In such cases, the Courts have always struck out the action. *Kelvin Peterside* v. *International Merchant Bank (Nigeria) Limited*,[49] the Court of Appeal held that a party could not, by operation of his own whims and caprices, expand the frontiers of constitutional rights beyond the anticipations of the Constitution as no person can read into the Constitution what is not there.

---

[46] Order IX
[47] [2007] All FWLR [Part 349] 1154 (C.A)
[48] [2001] 6 WRN 1 (C.A)
[49] (1993) 2 NWLR [Part 278] 712

According to the Court, Chapter IV of the Constitution does not give the Appellant the right to employment or to remain in the service of his employer in perpetuity or until the contractual age of retirement. In that case, the Appellant was employed as an Operations Officer, Accounts, of the Respondent in June 1982. He rose from this position to the rank of Manager in the treasury department of the Respondent. On 22nd September 1986, the Appellant received a letter of warning from the Respondent, which letter alleged some professional wrongdoings on the part of the Appellant. Nothing happened after this. On 5th February 1988, the Respondent, by another letter, dismissed the Appellant from her service.

This letter also alleged professional wrongdoing against the Appellant. The Appellant initially approached the Court through a writ of summons, but due to a change in counsel, the Appellant withdrew the action and filed another one for the enforcement of his fundamental rights on the ground that he was not given a fair hearing before his dismissal in accordance with section 33(1) of the then Constitution of the Federal Republic of Nigeria 1979.

The Court held that the action did not qualify as one for the enforcement of fundamental rights and dismissed the action. The decision of the Trial Court was upheld by the Court of Appeal.[50] This was followed up by the decision of the Supreme Court in the case of *Grace Jack* v. *University of Agriculture, Makurdi*,[51] where the apex court, *per* Uwaifo JSC, held that,

> It has been established by a number of decided cases by this court that an action for wrongful dismissal from employment cannot be brought under the fundamental rights procedure rules. Wrongful dismissal belongs to

[50] See also the case of *Geosite Surveys (Nig.) Ltd.* v. *Nwagbara* (2007) All FWLR [Part 386 742 (C.A); *F.R.N* v. *Ifegwu* [2003] 45 WRN 27 (SC); *Grace Jack* v. *University of Agriculture, Makurdi* [2004] 14 WRN 91 (S.C) and *Sea Trucks Nig. Ltd.* v. *Panya Anigboro* [2001] 10 W.R.N 78 (S.C). In the case of *University of Ilorin* v. *Anor.* v. *Oluwadare* [2006] 45 WRN 145, the Supreme Court adopted the same view. However, the *Oluwadare* case was not based on employment law but was determined on whether a university had the power to discipline a student for misconduct bordering on criminality. The Applicant in this case approached the Court for judicial relief through the *Fundamental Rights (Enforcement Procedure) Rules 1979.* The Court again adopted the same principle that the main claim of the Applicant is not one founded on breach of fundamental rights and as such, the Applicant ought not to have resorted to the Rules. The apex Court consequently dismissed the appeal.

[51] Supra.

> common law class of actions; whereas action for contravention or threatened contravention of a fundamental right belongs to a constitutional class of actions which is specially provided for. It follows that the appropriate procedure must be adopted in each class of actions. Where the main or principal claim is not the enforcement or protection of a fundamental right, the fundamental rights procedure rules are inappropriate.[52]

Order XIII must be read along with paragraph 3(e) of the preamble to the 2009 Rules earlier discussed above, which deals with public interest litigation. The Order is an extension of the said preamble. Rule 1 of the Order provides that any person or body who desires to be heard in respect of any Human Rights Application and who appears to the Court to be a proper party to be heard may be heard whether or not the party has been served with any of the relevant processes, and whether or not the party has any interest in the matter. This Rule is only applicable in cases where the Application has already been filed so as to permit persons who the court considers necessary to join as parties in the determination of the matter.

The Rule represents an elongation of the judicial definition of a "necessary party." In *Obasanjo* v. *Yusuf,*[53] the Supreme Court, while relying on a plethora of other authorities, held that the only rationale for a party to be joined in action is that he shall be bound by the verdict of the court, and it is reasoned that the matter in controversy cannot effectively and completely be settled in the absence of the party who shall be bound by it.[54] Thus, it is important that for a party to be joined as a co-Defendant, his presence must be necessary for an effectual determination of the matter. Rule 1 appears to have done away with this requirement irrespective of the interest of the party seeking to be joined.

Consequently, even where the matter can be determined without joining the party seeking to be joined, the Court may still order a

---

[52] At 107. See also the case of *Tukur* v. *Government of Taraba State* (1997) 6 NWLR [Part 510] 549, [1997]6 SCNJ 81; *Egbuonu* v. *Borno Radio Television Corporation* (1997) 12 NWLR [Part 531] 29.

[53] [2005] 20 W.R.N 1.

[54] See also the cases of *Oduola & Ors.* v. *Coke* [1980] 5 S.C 197; *Peenok Investments Ltd.* v. *Hotel Presidential Ltd.* [1982] 12 S.C 1.

joinder on the application of the party seeking to be joined. Rule 2 of Order XIII provides that *Amici curiae* may be encouraged in human rights applications and may be heard at any time if the Court's business allows it. Though this provision is commendable, it is doubtful if it will be frequently resorted to by the court in view of the urgency of most human rights applications. Thankfully, the Court has been given the discretion in this regard.

Transitional Provisions

The 2009 Rules abrogate the old 1979 Rules[55] and provide that all pending human rights applications filed under the old Rules may continue to be heard and determined as though they have been brought under the 2009 Rules.[56] Where, in the course of any human rights proceedings, any situation for which there is or appears to be no adequate provision in the 2009 Rules, the civil procedure rules of the Court for the time being in force shall apply.[57] This provision is an innovation of the 2009 Rules, which was absent in the old 1979 Rules. The result of such absence is that the courts have always treated the 1979 Rules as *sui generis.* Thus, in *Chukwuogor & Ors.* v. *Chukwuogor & Anor.,*[58] Omokri, JCA opined that,

> The Fundamental Rights (Enforcement Procedure) Rules are made by the Chief Justice of Nigeria in exercise of his power pursuant to the Constitution of the Federal Republic of Nigeria. They are peculiar Rules restricted to the enforcement by a citizen of his right under Chapter IV of the said Constitution. It makes no provision for the importation of any other rules of court for the enforcement of such rights. It is therefore clearly wrong for the lower court to fall back to the High Court Rules and purport to derive its power to extend time therefrom.

The pronouncement of Omokri JCA no longer represents the law in the light of the 2009 Rules. Consequently, any lacuna in the 2009 Rules can be filled by reference to the relevant High Court (Civil Procedure) Rules.

---

[55] See Order XV, Rule 1

[56] Order XV, Rule 3.

[57] Order XV, Rule 4.

[58] *Supra* at 1167.

USING INTERNATIONAL HUMAN RIGHTS INSTRUMENTS TO ENFORCE HUMAN RIGHTS

From the discussion above, one major limitation of the enforcement of human rights under the Fundamental Rights (Enforcement Procedure) Rules 2009 is that the Rules only apply to a category of rights specified under chapter IV of the CFRN 1999, otherwise known as the Civil and Political Rights. Consequently, the Rules exclude the provisions of Chapter II, which contain the ESC Rights. The provisions of chapter II enjoin the State to provide housing,[59] food,[60] health,[61] jobs,[62] education,[63] a clean environment,[64] right to development,[65] and cultural rights.[66] It would then appear that where these constitutional provisions are breached, the aggrieved person is left without a remedy under the 2009 Rules. This may be so within the Nigerian legal system.[67] But there is no reason why an aggrieved person should feel helpless and throw up their arms in total surrender. International Human Rights Law provides a leeway for the enforcement of this category of rights using the sub-regional and regional system of human rights. Two of such instruments are the Protocol establishing the ECOWAS Court, the African Charter on Human and Peoples Rights, which established the African Commission on Human and Peoples Rights, and the African Court on Human and Peoples Rights.

Sub-regional System

In January 2005, the Protocol setting up the ECOWAS Court was amended to permit persons to bring suits against the Member States. Beyond this monumental change, the Council of Ministers also took the

[59] S. 16 (2)(d)
[60] S.16(2)(d)
[61] S.17(3)(c),(d).
[62] SS. 16(2)(d); 17(3)(a).
[63] S. 18.
[64] S. 20.
[65] S. 16(1)(d)
[66] S.21.
[67] For criticisms of the non-justiciability of Chapter II of the Constitution, see Inegbedion, N.A., "The 1979 Constitution in Perspective" in Azinge (ed.), *Nigeria: A Century of Constitutional Evolution 1914-2014 op. cit.* at 299, 310-318.

opportunity to revise the jurisdiction of the Court to include the review of violations of human rights in all Member States. This revision made it clear that the sources of law to be applied by the Court under its original Protocol would include not only general principles of international law but also those in relation to human rights. The amendment also grants the Court jurisdiction over any disputes arising under agreements other than the Treaty between the Member States that so provide.

The revised Protocol also gave national courts of Member States the right to approach the ECOWAS court for a ruling on the interpretation of Community law. Previously, the language in the Protocol was unclear as to whether a Member State court could only seize the Community Court of a matter through the auspices of the national government. Since the amendment to the Protocol, the Court has received several cases from individuals and institutions of the Community itself. Notably, the jurisdiction of the Court has been invoked by Nigerian politicians complaining of the violations of their human rights in the determination of election outcomes.[68] In the case of *Socio-Economic Rights Accountability Project* v. *Nigeria*,[69] the Court delivered a judgment that required the Nigerian Federal Government and the Universal Basic Education Commission to provide as a right, free, quality, and compulsory basic education to every Nigerian child. The Court also asked the Nigerian government to ensure that the right to education is not undermined by corruption.

In *Socio–Economic Rights Accountability Project* v. *Federal Republic of Nigeria*,[70] the applicant, a non-governmental organization registered in Nigeria, claimed that the Government was responsible for violations flowing from the degradation of the environment in the Niger Delta. The applicant contended that the Niger Delta, rich in resources, plants, and wildlife had suffered decades of oil spills that destroyed the surrounding environment, reducing its farming and

---

[68] In the case of *Ugokwe* v. *Okeke* [2008] C.C.J.L.R 149, the Court held that no provision, whether general or specific, gives it the powers to adjudicate on electoral issues or matters arising thereof.

[69] Suit No. ECW/CCJ/APP/08/08 delivered on October 27, 2009.

[70] Suit No. ECW/CCJ/APP/09 delivered on December 14, 2012

fishing productivity for local communities. The spills impacted the communities' access to food and had a negative impact on their health. The applicant attributed the damage to the government's poor maintenance of infrastructure, human error, vandalism, oil theft, and conflict leading to poverty.

The applicant argued that as a result of these failures, the people of the Niger Delta were denied their rights to an adequate standard of living, clean water and environment, social and economic development, life, dignity, and human security. The applicant also claimed that the failure of the respondents to adequately remediate and address the environmental damage, their failure to monitor the human impact, and continued denial of information to the community amounted to violations of the ICESCR, ICCPR, and the African Charter.

With respect to remedies, applicants sought pecuniary damages of one billion dollars and an order directing the State to hold the oil companies responsible for their complicity in their human rights violation. Nigeria argued that the Court could not consider claims under the ICESCR and ICCPR and that the claim was barred by the three-year statute of limitations in Article 9(3) of the Court Protocol.

The Court held that although ECOWAS has not adopted a specific human rights instrument, the Court considers all international human rights treaties to which ECOWAS member states are parties in matters that come before it. The application of the three-year statute of limitation depends on whether the case was based on isolated acts or on persistent and continuous omissions. Here the failure of the State to prevent the damage and hold anyone accountable was a continuous one, and the Court found the application not to be time-barred.

The Court further held that while there were laws regulating the oil industry and safeguarding the environment, these laws were not accompanied by concrete measures aimed at preventing damage, ensuring accountability, or repairing the environmental harm that had occurred.

Thus, Nigeria had violated Articles 1 (state responsibility) and 24 (peoples' right to an environment favourable for development) of the African Charter. However, the Court noted that the applicant had failed to identify a victim who should benefit from the compensation they claimed and that granting compensation to individual victims would cause

It, therefore, dismissed the applicant's claim for pecuniary compensation. It ordered Nigeria to take all effective measures within the shortest time possible to ensure restoration of the environment, prevent the occurrence of further damage, and hold perpetrators of environmental damage accountable.[71]

Regional System

One important machinery for the implementation of the provisions of the African Charter on Human and People's Rights is the establishment of the African Commission on Human and Peoples Rights.[72] The membership, appointment, tenure, privileges, budget, and mandate of the Commission are contained in Chapter II of the Charter. Particularly, the Commission is given the mandate to,

1. promote human and peoples' rights and in particular;
2. to collect documents, undertake studies and researches on African problems in the field of human and peoples' rights, organise seminars, symposia, and conferences, disseminate information, encourage national and local institutions concerned with human and peoples' rights, and should the case arise, give its views to or make recommendations to government.[73]

Complaints about the violation of the provisions of the Charter are by Communications by States/Parties to the Charter[74] against one another. At the inception of the Charter, there was no provision for individual communication, which was only introduced by a Protocol to the Charter.

---

[71] For further reading on the human rights jurisdiction of the Court, see Karen J. Alter *et al,* "A New International Human Rights Court for West Africa: The Ecowas Community Court of Justice," *The American Journal of International Law,* vol. 107, 737

[72] See Article 30.

[73] For the other functions of the Commission, see Article 45 of the Charter.

[74] See Chapter III of the Charter.

Complaints are sent to the Commission under Articles 47 to 59. Particularly, Article 55 of the Charter empowers the Secretary of the Commission to make a list of the communications other than those of States Parties to the present Charter and transmit them to the members of the Commission, who shall indicate which communications should be considered by the Commission. A communication shall be considered by the Commission if a simple majority of its members so decide.

However, before communication is considered by the Commission for hearing, the issue of admissibility of the Communication must first be determined. Thus, under Article 50 of the Charter, the Commission can only deal with a matter submitted to it after making sure that all local remedies, if they exist, have been exhausted unless it is obvious to the Commission that the procedure of achieving these remedies would be unduly prolonged. Non-exhaustion of local remedies, where available, will render the Communication inadmissible within the terms of Article 56. Articles 47 to 54 state the procedure to be followed by States Parties to the Charter in bringing a complaint before the Commission.

The complaints are brought in the form of communications by one State against the other. However, an individual may also bring a complaint for a breach of any of the rights provided for by the charter under Article 55. Such communication by an individual shall be considered by the Commission if a simple majority of its members so decide.

Before communication by an individual can be entertained, it must satisfy the following requirements:

1. the communication must indicate the author even if the latter requests anonymity;
2. the communication must be compatible with the Charter of the Organization of African Unity[75] or with the present Charter;

[75] Now called the Constitutive Act of the African Union.

3. the communication must not be written in disparaging or insulting language directed against the State concerned and its institutions or the African Union;
4. the communication is not based exclusively on the news disseminated through the mass media;
5. the communication is sent after exhausting local remedies if any unless it is obvious that this procedure is unduly prolonged;
6. the communication is submitted within a reasonable period from the time local remedies are exhausted or from the date the Commission is seized of the matter;
7. the communication does not deal with cases that have been settled by these States involved in accordance with the principles of the Charter of the United Nations, the Constitutive Act of the African Union, or the provisions of the present Charter.

Article 55 is in tandem with the provision of Article 50, earlier referred to, on the exhaustion of local remedies. In determining the merit of a Communication brought by an aggrieved party, the Commission is mandated to draw inspiration from international law on human and peoples' rights, particularly from the provisions of various African instruments on human and peoples' rights, the Charter of the United Nations, the Constitutive Act of the African Union, the Universal Declaration of Human Rights, other instruments adopted by the United Nations and by African countries in the field of human and peoples' rights as well as from the provisions of various instruments adopted within the Specialised Agencies of the United Nations of which the parties to the present Charter are members.[76] The Commission shall also consider, as subsidiary measures to determine the principles of law, other general or specialized international conventions, laying down rules expressly recognized by member states of the African Union, African practices consistent with international norms on human and peoples' rights, customs generally accepted as law, general principles of

[76] See Article 60.

law recognised by the African States as well as legal precedents and doctrine.[77]

The import of the provisions of Articles 60 and 61 of the Charter just mentioned above is that an aggrieved party can approach the Commission for relief by relying on the provisions of the Charter and other international human rights instruments dealing with ESC rights. These provisions are contained in Article 15, dealing with the right to work; Article 16, dealing with the right to health; Articles 17 and 22, dealing with the right to education and culture; and Articles 21 and 24, dealing with the right to compensation for environmental degradation and a generally satisfactory environment respectively. Other international instruments that can be invoked in pressing a case before the Commission include the Universal Declaration of Human Rights (UDHR). Articles 16, 17, 23, 24, 25, and 27 of the Declaration are relevant here. Article 16 protects the right to marry and form a family for all men and women of full age. They are entitled to equal rights as to marriage, during the marriage, and at its dissolution. Article 17 protects the right to property and states that no one shall be arbitrarily deprived of his property. The rights to work and to a free choice of employment, to just and favourable conditions of work, and to protection against unemployment are fully protected under Article 23. Article 24 provides that everyone has the right to rest and leisure, including reasonable limitation of working hours and periodic holidays with pay.

Article 25 protects the right of everyone to a standard of living adequate for the health and well-being of himself and his family, including food, clothing, housing and medical care, necessary social activities, and the right to security in the event of unemployment, sickness, disability, widowhood, old age or other lack of livelihood in the circumstances beyond his control. The Article also provides that mothers and children are entitled to special care and assistance and that all children, whether born in or out of wedlock, shall enjoy the same social protection. Article 27 provides that everyone has the right freely to participate in the cultural life of the community, to enjoy the arts,

[77] Article 61

and to share in scientific advancement and its benefits. The Article also protects the intellectual property rights of everyone. The provisions of CEDAW, Additional Protocol to the African Charter on Human and Peoples' Rights on the Rights of Women, and Child Rights Act are some of the other international and local human rights instruments that can be deployed before the Commission by an aggrieved Nigerian in seeking the protection of ESC rights.

Where the Commission admits the Communication for its consideration, it may then determine the merits of the case. In doing this, the Commission is guided by the provisions of Articles 60 and 61 of the Charter. The Commission invoked the provisions of Articles 60 and 61 in its consideration of the case involving Nigeria in *Social and Economic Rights Action Centre and Centre for Economic and Social Rights* v. *Nigeria,*[78] which shares some similarities with the *Serap* case considered earlier.

The Communication alleged that the military government of Nigeria had been directly involved in oil production through the state oil company, the Nigerian National Petroleum Company (NNPC), the majority shareholder in a consortium with Shell Petroleum Development Corporation (SPDC), and that these operations have caused environmental degradation and health problems resulting from the contamination of the environment among the Ogoni people.

The Communication alleged that the oil consortium had exploited oil reserves in Ogoniland with no regard for the health or environment of the local communities, disposing toxic wastes into the environment and local waterways in violation of applicable international environmental standards. Further, the Communication alleged that the consortium also neglected and/or failed to maintain its facilities, causing numerous avoidable spills in the proximity of villages. The resulting contamination of water, soil, and air has had serious short and long-term health impacts, including skin infections, gastrointestinal and respiratory ailments, increased risk of cancers, and neurological and reproductive problems.

[78] (2001) AHRLR 60.

The Communication alleged that the Nigerian government had condoned and facilitated these violations by placing the legal and military powers of the state at the disposal of the oil companies. Further, the government neither monitored the operations of the oil companies nor required safety measures that are standard procedures within the industry. That the government withheld from the Ogoni communities information on the dangers created by oil activities and that the Ogoni communities have not been involved in the decisions affecting the development of Ogoniland.

The communication alleged that the Nigerian government condoned and facilitated these violations by placing the legal and military powers of the state at the disposal of the oil companies. The communication contained a memo from the Rivers State Internal Security Task Force calling for "ruthless military operations." The communication further alleged that the government has neither monitored the operations of the oil companies nor required safety measures that are standard procedures within the industry.

The government did not require oil companies or its own agencies to produce basic health and environmental impact studies regarding hazardous operations and materials relating to oil production despite the obvious health and environmental crisis in Ogoniland.

The government even refused to permit scientists and environmental organizations from entering Ogoniland to undertake such studies. The government also ignored concerns of the Ogoni communities regarding oil development and responded to protests with massive violence and executions of Ogoni leaders. Again, the communication alleged that the Nigerian government did not require oil companies to consult communities before beginning operations, even if the operations pose direct threats to the community or individual lands.

That in the three years preceding the presentation of the Communication, Nigeria's security forces attacked, burned, and destroyed several Ogoni villages and homes under the pretext of dislodging officials and supporters of the Movement for the Survival of Ogoni People (MOSOP). These attacks came in response to MOSOP's non-violent campaign in opposition to the destruction of their environment by oil companies.

Some of the attacks have involved uniformed combined forces of the police, the army, the air force, and the navy, armed with armoured tanks and other sophisticated weapons. In other instances, the attacks have been conducted by unidentified gunmen, mostly at night. The military-type methods and the calibre of weapons used in such attacks suggested the involvement of the Nigerian security forces.

The failure of the Nigerian government to investigate these attacks, let alone punish the perpetrators, further implicated the Nigerian authorities in the attacks. The Nigerian army admitted its role in the ruthless operations which have left thousands of villagers homeless. The admission is recorded on several memos exchanged between officials of the SPDC and the Rivers State Internal Security Task Force, who has devoted itself to the suppression of the Ogoni campaign. One such memo called for "ruthless military operations" and "wasting operations coupled with psychological tactics of displacement." At a public meeting recorded on video, Major Okuntimo, head of the Task Force, described the repeated invasion of the Ogoni villages by his troops, how unarmed villagers running from the troops were shot from behind, and the homes of suspected MOSOP activists were ransacked and destroyed. He stated his commitment to rid the communities of members and supporters of MOSOP.

Finally, the communication alleged that the Nigerian government destroyed and threatened Ogoni food sources through a variety of means. These included the participation in irresponsible oil development that has poisoned much of the soil and water upon which Ogoni farming and fishing depended; the destruction of crops and farm animals by the Nigerian security forces; the creation of a state of terror and insecurity that made it impossible for many Ogoni villagers to return to their fields and animals. The destruction of these food sources created malnutrition and starvation among certain Ogoni communities.

The consequence of all these allegations is, according to the communication, that Articles 2, 4, 14, 16, 18(1), 21, and 24 of the African Charter on Human and Peoples Rights have been violated.

Article 2 is a general provision that states that every individual shall be entitled to the enjoyment of the rights and freedoms recognized and guaranteed in the Charter without distinction of any kind. Article 4 states that human beings are inviolable. Every human being shall be entitled to respect for his life and the integrity of his person. No one may be arbitrarily deprived of this right. Article 14 provides for the right to property, while Article 16 states that every individual shall have the right to enjoy the best attainable state of physical and mental health. Article 18(1) states that the family shall be the natural unit and basis of society. It shall be protected by the State, which shall take care of its physical health and morals. Article 21 provides, *inter alia,* that all peoples shall freely dispose of their wealth and natural resources. This right shall be exercised in the exclusive interest of the people. In no case shall a people be deprived of it. Article 24 states that all peoples shall have the right to a general satisfactory environment favourable to their development.

In its response to the allegations, the Nigerian government submitted a *note verbale*[79] describing the actions taken by the government in respect of all the communications filed against it, including this one. As it concerns the present one, the *note verbale* admitted the gravamen of the complaints but went on to describe the remedial measures being taken by the new civilian government. These included establishing, for the first time, in the history of Nigeria, a Federal Ministry of Environment with adequate resources to address environment-related issues prevalent in Nigeria and as a matter of priority in the Niger Delta area; enacting into law the establishment of the Niger Delta Development Commission (NDDC) with adequate funding to address the environmental and social problems of the Niger Delta area and other oil-producing areas of Nigeria; inaugurating the Judicial Commission of Inquiry to investigate the issues of human rights violations. In addition, the representatives of the Ogoni people

---

[79] A *note verbale* is an unsigned diplomatic note. It is usually written in the third person and sometimes accompanies a diplomatic message or note of protest to further explain the country's position or to request certain action. See Garner, B.A. *Black's Law Dictionary* (7th ed., St. Paul, Minn: West Group, 1999)

have submitted petitions to the Commission of Inquiry on those issues, and these are presently being reviewed in Nigeria as a top priority.

After dispensing with the issue of admissibility in favour of the Communication, the Commission proceeded to examine its merits. In doing this, the Commission considered four levels of obligations or duties imposed as a result of a country being a State Party to an international human rights instrument, including the African Charter. These are the obligations to respect, protect, promote and fulfil these rights.[80] The obligation to respect entails that the state should refrain from interfering in the enjoyment of all fundamental rights; it should respect rights holders, their freedoms, autonomy, resources, and liberty of their action. As it concerns socio-economic rights, this means that the state is obliged to respect the free use of resources owned or at the disposal of the individual alone or in any form of association with others, including the household or the family, for the purpose of rights-related needs. The obligation to protect entails that rights holders are protected against other subjects by legislation and the provision of effective remedies.

The obligation to promote entails that the state should promote the enjoyment of all human rights. This can be done by making sure that individuals are able to exercise their rights and freedoms, for example, by promoting tolerance, raising awareness, and even building structures. The obligation to fulfil requires the state to fulfil the rights and freedoms it freely undertook under the various human rights regimes. It is a positive expectation on the part of the state to deploy its resources toward the realization of the rights and corresponding obligation to promote the rights.

In the light of the obligations and considering the largely undisputed facts as contained in the Communication, and applying such facts to the above-mentioned articles alleged to have been violated, the Commission found the Federal Republic of Nigeria in violation of articles 2, 4, 14, 16, 18(1), 21, and 24 of the African Charter on Human

[80] See generally, Eide, Al. "Economic, Social and Cultural Rights as Human Rights" in Eide, A, *et al* (eds), *Economic, Social and Cultural Rights: A Textbook* (London: Martinus Nijhoff Publishers 1995) 21-40.

and Peoples' Rights. The Commission consequently appealed to the Federal Government to ensure the protection of the environment, health, and livelihood of the people of Ogoniland by carrying out the following:

(a) Stopping all attacks on Ogoni communities and leaders by the Rivers State Internal Security Task Force and permitting citizens and independent investigators free access to the territory;

(b) Conducting an investigation into the human rights violations described above and prosecuting the officials of the security forces, NNPC, and relevant agencies involved in human rights violations;

(c) Ensuring adequate compensation to victims of the human rights violations, including relief and resettlement assistance to victims of government-sponsored raids, and undertaking a comprehensive clean-up of lands and rivers damaged by oil operations;

(d) Ensuring that appropriate environmental and social impact assessments are prepared for any future oil development and that the safe operation of any further oil development is guaranteed through effective and independent oversight bodies for the petroleum industry;

(e) Providing information for health and environmental risks and meaningful access to regulatory and decision-making bodies to communities likely to be affected by oil operations.

In the light of the appeal made by the Commission, the Commission urged the Federal Government to keep it informed of the outcome of the work of the following bodies:

(a) the Federal Ministry of Environment, which was established to address environmental and environmental-related issues prevalent in Nigeria, and as a matter of priority, in the Niger Delta area, including the Ogoniland;

(b) the Niger Delta Development Commission (NDDC) enacted into law to address the environmental and other social-related problems in the Niger Delta area and other oil-producing areas of Nigeria;

(c) the Judicial Commission of Inquiry inaugurated to investigate the issues of human rights violations.

The decision is revolutionary in the sense that it was the first time that the Nigerian state will be indicted through a quasi-judicial (the Commission is not a judicial body properly so-called and is at best a quasi-judicial body) means and at the international level, for failing to meet its obligations imposed by being a State Party to international human rights treaties.

ENFORCEMENT MECHANISM OF THE SUB-REGIONAL AND REGIONAL SYSTEMS

One major distinction between enforcing human rights before domestic courts and doing so through the sub-regional and regional systems discussed above is that while in the former, the decisions of the courts can be enforced using the State machinery to do so, in the case of the latter, such enforcement requires the cooperation of the concerned State/Party which is usually not forthcoming. As can be seen from the decision of the Commission in the *SERAC case,* the Commission only made an appeal to the Nigerian State to address the complaints in the SERAC Communication while at the same time urging the State to keep it informed on the outcome of the work of certain agencies of the government set up to address some of the human rights issues raised by the Communication.

There is actually no evidence that the government has taken deliberate measures to carry out the recommendations of the Commission in the SERAC Case or even in the other cases decided by the ECOWAS Court as they apply to Nigeria. The sub-regional and regional courts completely lack the ability to enforce their decisions, though it must be acknowledged that such decisions at least foist a moral burden on the State to implement them.

There are grounds to even canvass the position that the decisions of the Courts also create a legal burden on the State. Nwobike[81] argues that Nigeria has obligations under international human rights law

[81] Nwobike, J.C. "The African Commission on Human and Peoples' Rights and the Demystification of Second and Third Generation Rights under the African Charter: Social and Economic Rights Action Center (SERAC) and *the Centre for Economic And Social Rights (CESR)* v. *Nigeria*" 1 Afr. J. Legal Studies (2005) 129 at 132

arising from the provisions of treaties to which the country is a party to and rules of customary international law. The Commission is not restricted by the legal principles it may apply in the determination of cases before it. For instance, Article 60 of the Charter provides:

> The Commission shall draw inspiration from international law on human and peoples' rights, particularly from the provisions of various African instruments on human and peoples' rights, the Charter of the United Nations, the Charter of the Organisation of African Unity,[82] the Universal Declaration of Human Rights, other instruments adopted by the United Nations and by African Countries in the field of human and peoples' rights as well as from the provisions of various instruments adopted within the specialized agencies of the United Nations of which the parties to the present Charter are members.

Article 61 of the Charter also provides as follows:

> The Commission shall also take into consideration, as subsidiary measures to determine the principles of law, other general or specialised international conventions laying down rules expressly recognized by member states of the Organisation of African Unity, African practices consistent with international norms on human and peoples' rights, customs generally accepted as law, general principles of law recognized by African states as well as legal precedents and doctrine.

Further, the Committee on Economic Social and Cultural Rights, created by the International Covenant on Economic Social and Cultural Rights, has issued guidance on the nature of State Party obligations in General Comment No. 3.[83] Flowing from the General Comment,

---

[82] Now the Constitutive Acts of the African Union.

[83] See the Nature of State Party Obligations (Article 2, para. 1): 14/12/90 (General Comment 3) in *Compilation of General Comments and General Recommendations Adopted by Human Rights Treaty Bodies,* UN Doc/HRI/GEN/1/Rev.7 (May 12, 2004 at 15-18.

Economic Social and Cultural Rights impose three types of obligations on States: the obligation to respect, to protect and to fulfil.[84]

These represent the primary, secondary and tertiary levels of obligations. As earlier observed in consideration of the SERAC case, the obligation to respect requires States to refrain from interfering with the enjoyment of economic, social, and cultural rights. The obligation to protect requires States to prevent the violation of such rights by third parties, and the obligation to fulfil requires States to take appropriate legislative, administrative, budgetary, judicial, and other measures toward the full realization of such rights.

These obligations contain expectations of conduct and result. While an obligation of conduct requires action reasonably calculated to realize the enjoyment of a particular right, the obligation of result requires States to achieve specific targets to satisfy a detailed substantive standard.[85] Minimum core obligations ensure the satisfaction, at the very least, of a minimum level of each of the rights that is incumbent upon every State Party.[86] In the light of the foregoing provisions, therefore, Nwobike[87] therefore rightly argued that Nigeria is under an obligation to respect, protect and fulfil not only the rights guaranteed under the Covenants but also the African Charter in strict fidelity to the principle of *pacta sunt servanda* which provides that "every treaty in force is binding upon the parties to it and must be performed by them in good faith."[88]

One possible approach to remedy the problem of non-implementation or enforcement of the decisions of the international human rights courts is the use of diplomacy and the instrument of the African Peer Review Mechanism under the New Partnership for Africa's Development (NEPAD) system to monitor compliance. The Mandate of the APRM is to ensure that the policies and practices of participating states conform to the agreed political, economic, and corporate

---

[84] See the Maastricht Guidelines on Violations of Economic, Social and Cultural Rights, January 22-26, 1997, paragraph 6, http://www1.umn.edu/humanrts/instree/Maastrichtguidelines_.html (accessed May 31, 2005.

[85] Ibid. at para. 7.

[86] See para.10 of General Comment No. 3.

[87] Nwobike, P.C, *op. cit.* at 133. Footnote 17.

[88] See Article 26 of the Vienna Convention on the Law of Treaties.

governance values, codes, and standards contained in the Declaration on Democracy, Political, Economic, and Corporate Governance. The APRM is the mutually agreed instrument for self-monitoring by the participating member governments.

The mechanism requires countries to remedy the defects identified in the report of the mission sent to any particular country. The failure of any particular country to carry out the identified defects may, it is suggested, lead to that country not being able to access funds from international development partners and agencies until it remedies the identified defects. In the case of Nigeria, failure to comply with the decisions of the human rights courts may form a basis for the denial of Nigeria's development assistance and may lead to diplomatic isolation.

Such sanctions are likely to compel compliance with the decision of the Commission or indeed that of any of the United Nations human rights treaty bodies.[89] This is an effective strategy in getting around the justiciability problem in the enforcement of human rights in Nigeria. In the alternative, aggrieved parties may resort to the African Court on Human and Peoples Rights, which does not suffer from the drawback of the ECOWAS Court or the Commission.

PROTECTING ESC RIGHTS THROUGH THE AFRICAN COURT ON HUMAN AND PEOPLES' RIGHTS

One reason for the establishment of the African Court on Human and Peoples' Rights is to complement the protective mandate of the Commission. The African Court has jurisdiction over cases submitted to it concerning the interpretation and application of the Charter, the Protocol establishing it, and any other human rights instruments, provided that the subject matter of the opinion is not related to a matter being examined by the Commission.[90]

Access to the African Court is open to the Commission, the State Party, which has lodged a complaint to the Commission, the State Party against which the complaint has been lodged at the Commission, and

[89] For a detailed analysis of the concept and design of the APRM, see Kanbur, R. "The African Peer Review Mechanism: An Assessment of Concept and Design" www.people.cornell.edu/pages/sk145

[90] See Article 3 of the Protocol.

the State Party, whose citizen is a victim of the human right violation and African Inter-Governmental Organisations.[91] The African Court may entitle relevant Non-Governmental Organizations with observer status before the Commission and individuals to institute cases directly before it.

Within the European system of human rights, the European Court of Human Rights does not seem to suffer the drawback of a lack of enforcement mechanism. The responsibility for the execution of the judgments of the European Court of Human Rights is the duty of the Committee of Ministers of the Council of Europe.[92]

This provision has been adopted by Article 29 of the Protocol to the African Charter on Human and Peoples' Rights on the Establishment of an African Court on Human and Peoples' Rights. The Article, in sub-Article (1), provides that the parties to the case shall be notified of the judgment of the Court, and it shall be transmitted to the Member States of the OAU and the Commission. Sub-Article (2) states that the Council of Ministers shall also be notified of the judgment and shall monitor its execution on behalf of the Assembly.

The text of Article 29 must be read along with that of Article 30, which states that the States Parties to the Protocol undertake to comply with the judgment in any case to which they are parties within the time stipulated by the Court and to guarantee its execution. Nigeria ratified the Protocol on May 20, 2004, and deposited the instrument of ratification on June 9, 2004. The Protocol comes into force thirty days after fifteen instruments of ratification or accession have been deposited.[93] The Protocol has been ratified by 24 African States that are States Parties to it and has therefore come into force by virtue of Article 34(3) of the Protocol.

It is expected that the African Court on Human Rights will achieve a higher degree of success than the Commission in the light of the enforcement mechanisms provided in the Protocol establishing the

---

[91] See Article 5(1).

[92] See Article 46(2) of the European Convention on Human Rights which provides that the final judgment of the Court shall be transmitted to the Committee of Ministers, which shall supervise its execution.

[93] See Article 34(3) of the Protocol.

Court, which is very much absent from the Charter establishing the Commission. In the light of the self-imposed obligation to comply with the judgment of the Court, any State that fails to comply with the said judgment can always be compelled to do so by other States Parties at the level of the Council of Ministers. It is submitted that failure to do so may attract a variety of punitive measures open to the African Union, including international isolation.

CONCLUSION

Enforcement of human rights under the Fundamental Human Rights (Enforcement Procedure) Rules 2009 is limited in scope and, consequently, not far-reaching enough in human rights protection. The non-justiciability clause embedded in section 6 subsection (6)(c), which provides that the provisions of Chapter II of the CFRN 1999 are non-justiciable, is often cited as the legal justification for this limitation. This is an unduly rigid position that fails to recognize the concept of indivisibility of human rights long embraced by other jurisdictions. Further, there are materials to suggest that despite the non-justiciability clause, Chapters II and IV are justiciable and, consequently, enforceable.[94] In any case, Nigeria, being part of the international community, has obligations to ensure the full and maximum protection and enforcement of human rights she has freely subscribed to. Otherwise, it may be compelled to do so either through the African Court of Human Rights or by the international community. Consequently, the Country must not be fettered by the problem of justiciability and must bring its Constitution in line with its international human rights obligations.

---

[94] See Azinge, E: *Living Oracles of the Law and the Fallacy of Human Divination,* being a paper delivered at the 6th Justice Idigbe Memorial Lecture on June 20, 2008, at Akin Deko Auditorium, University of Benin, Benin City, Nigeria; N. A. Inegbedion, "The New Fundamental Rights (Enforcement Procedure) Rules and Public Interest Litigation: Expanding the Frontiers of Human Rights Litigation?" (2008) 9 *Nigerian Education Law Journal* (No.1) 157

Chapter 12

REMEDIES UNDER THE NIGERIAN LAW

S. Gozie Ogbodo *

INTRODUCTION

It is trite law that for every right, there is a remedy. A remedy, also known as relief, is the "means of enforcing a right or preventing or redressing wrong; legal or equitable relief."[1] Babalola itemises five forms of relief, namely: a) affirmative relief, which a defendant seeks in a counter-claim or cross-claim; b) coercive relief, which is an enforceable legal or equitable relief; c) alternative relief which is mutually exclusive of any other form of judicial relief, such as where a party seeks both specific performance and damages in action; d) therapeutic relief which requires the defendant to carry out remedial action in favour of the plaintiff; and e) interim relief which is granted before an order finally disposing of a request for relief.[2] Under Nigerian law, remedies are awarded based on the principles of common law and equity and statutory provisions. The type of remedy that may be available to a plaintiff who alleges that his/her right has been violated or breached would often depend on the nature of the right in issue and

* Dr. S. Gozie Ogbodo is a Senior Lecturer at the Faculty of Law, University of Benin. He also currently serves as the Assistant Co-ordinator of the Post-Graduate Programme of the Law Faculty. He lectures students in the undergraduate and graduate levels and supervises Ph.D students. Prior to joining the Law Faculty of the University of Benin, Dr. Ogbodo had taught as an Adjunct Professor at the prestigious Golden Gate University in San Francisco, California, United States of America. Dr. Ogbodo holds the Fellowships of the Public Policy Institute of the University of California, Davis, as well as that of the Annenberg School of Communication, University of Southern California. He has published extensively in both national and international journals. Dr. Ogbodo can be reached at gozieogbodo@yahoo.com.

[1] A. Babalola, *Election Law and Practice* (Ibadan: Afe Babalola, 2007)

[2] Babalola, *Election Law and Practice.*

which court has jurisdiction to entertain the matter.[3] In civil actions, the remedies could vary from specific performance to damages, depending on the area of law under which the action is instituted and the special circumstances of each case. This paper reviews the available remedies in civil actions under Nigerian law. The paper also provides an overview of possible sentences against a defendant who has been convicted for an offense under Nigerian criminal law.[4]

ADMINISTRATIVE LAW

Administrative law is that body of law that relates to: a) the discharge of public functions in administration and government, including the functions of public authorities, officers, and special tribunals; b) judicial review of the exercise of such functions; c) civil liability and legal protection of persons who purport to exercise such functions; and d) avenues through which aggrieved persons may obtain extra-judicial redress for the wrongful exercise of such functions.[5] The functions are exercised through the exercise of power, which may either be classified as administrative and judicial or executive, administrative, and judicial.[6] Beyond "reducing the areas of conflict between the administrative agencies of the state and the individuals," as suggested by some legal scholars,[7] administrative law could also reduce areas of conflict among the administrative agencies of the states.[8]

Administrative decisions are subject to judicial review, i.e., "[J]udicial scrutiny of questions of *vires* and jurisdiction of law and fact, the scope of the obligation to act fairly and to observe the rules of natural justice, and the principles that must be observed in the exercise of statutory discretion."[9] Under the 1999 Constitution of the Federal Republic of Nigeria, it is the superior court of record, particularly the

---

[3] Akintunde Emiola, *Remedies in Administrative Law* (Ogbomoso: Emiola Publishers, 2000).

[4] It is important to note that criminal matters are prosecuted by the States and do not involve any direct remedy for defendants, except under the Lagos State Criminal Procedure Act which prescribes remedies such as community service, and damages, for certain offences.

[5] *Halsbury's Laws of England*, 4th (Hailsham) Ed. (London: Butterworths, 1973), p.5, para 1.

[6] Emiola, *Remedies in Administrative Law.*

[7] B. O. Iluyomade and B. U. Eka, *Cases and materials on administrative law in Nigeria* (Ile-Ife: University of Ife Press, 1980).

[8] Emiola, *Remedies in Administrative Law.*

[9] J. M. Evans, *Judicial Review of Administrative Action by S. A. de Smith* (London: Stevens & Sons, 1980).

High Court, which is empowered to exercise the duty of judicial review.[10] In so doing, the court considers the legality of the administrative decision and the manner in which it was reached and not the correctness of the decision or its merits. Furthermore, the judicial review is not an appeal, and therefore, the court cannot substitute its judgment for the decision of the public body whose action is under review.[11] Judicial review will apply on the grounds of *ultra vires*, error of law or fact, breach of the principle of natural justice, and lack of jurisdiction.[12]

There have been various classifications used for remedies available under administrative law, including prerogative and ordinary remedies;[13] judicial and extra-judicial remedies; and administrative, common law, equitable, prerogative, and statutory remedies.[14] Prerogative remedies include prerogative orders and the writ of habeas corpus, while all other remedies are classified as ordinary. Judicial and extra-judicial remedies are broad classifications that may be further subdivided. An administrative remedy is a non-judicial remedy that requires the administrative body to rectify the wrong suffered by an aggrieved person or government authority by returning to the *status quo ante*, or making reparation for a loss or an injury already suffered by the aggrieved party as a result of the act or omission of the administrative body.[15] This could take the form of appeals and petitions,[16] tribunals and inquiries,[17] or ombudsman.[18] Although tribunals are not bound by the normal rules of proceedings that apply in courts, they are bound by the principles of natural justice, which are the rule against bias and the right to a fair hearing.[19] Otherwise, the

---

[10] Section 6.
[11] *Governor of Oyo State* v. *Oba Afolayan* (1995) 8 NWLR (Pt. 413) 292, 310.
[12] See further Emiola, *Remedies in Administrative Law.*
[13] Iluyomade and Eka, *Cases and materials on administrative law in Nigeria.*
[14] Emiola, *Remedies in Administrative Law.*
[15] Iluyomade and Eka, *Cases and materials on administrative law in Nigeria.*
[16] *Federal Board of Inland Revenue* v. *Azigbo Bros. Ltd.* (1963) NNIR 121.
[17] *Wilson* v. *AG Bendel State & Ors.* (1985) 1 NWLR (Pt 4) 572; *Garba & Ors.* v. *University of Maiduguri* (1986) ANLR 149.
[18] Emiola, *Remedies in Administrative Law.*
[19] *Legal Practitioners Disciplinary Committee & Ors* v. *Gani Fawehinmi* (1985) 2 NWLR (Pt 4) 300.

decision reached would be null and void.[20] Nonetheless, there are some exceptions to the rule on natural justice, such as where the right to a fair hearing has been waived by the defendant.[21] Furthermore, court decisions have established the importance of considering the merits of each case, and where the lack of the natural justice principle does not cause a material injustice, then the decision reached by the tribunal may not be set aside.

Administrative remedies are particularly useful where the administrative body has wide discretionary powers which oust the jurisdiction of the courts. For instance, by virtue of section 6(6)(c) of the 1999 Constitution of the Federal Republic of Nigeria, Chapter 2 of the Constitution on fundamental objectives and principles of state policy is non-justiciable and, therefore, outside the jurisdiction of the courts. In such a case, the options that are available to an aggrieved party would be either political or administrative rather than judicial.[22]

Damages

Damage is "a pecuniary compensation or indemnity which may be recovered in the courts by any person who has suffered loss, detriment, or injury, whether to his person, property, or rights, through the unlawful act or omission or negligence of another."[23] Damage is a remedy that is available both under common law and in statutory provisions. As a general rule, damages should be compensatory and not punitive; however, there are some exceptions to this general rule in the form of an award of exemplary or contemptuous damages to which different rules apply. Damages may be awarded either as a complete remedy in itself, in addition to, or as a substitute for some other remedies.[24] Furthermore, damages can be awarded as a remedy in actions for tort, contract, employment, and administrative law. In order

---

[20] *Adedeji* v. *Police Service Commission* (1967) 1 All NLR 67; *Wilson* v. *AG Bendel State & Ors* (1985) 1 NWLR (Pt. 4) 572; *Olatunbosun* v. *NISER Council* (1988) 2 NWLR 25.

[21] *Ariori & Ors* v. *Elemor & Ors* (1983) 1 NSCLR 1, 13.

[22] Emiola, *Remedies in Administrative Law.*

[23] H. C. Black, *Black's Law Dictionary* (USA: West Publishing Co., 1979).

[24] *Ibenwelu* v. *Lawal* (1971) 1 All NLR 23,26; section 8, Interpretation Act of 1964; Dr. Jacob Abiodun Dada, Judicial Remedies for Human Rights Violations in Nigeria: A critical appraisal (2013) 10 Journal of Law, Policy & Globalization 8.

to be successful in a claim for damages, the aggrieved party must show that there is a cause of action, i.e., that the act of the defendant constituted a breach of contract, a trespass, a breach of statutory duty, the deliberate misuse of public functions which leads to economic losses, or another civil wrong.[25] In the case of *Maharaj* v. *Attorney General of Trinidad and Tobago*,[26] for instance, the judicial committee of the Privy Council held that damages are an appropriate remedy for the breach of the constitutional right to liberty because the contravention had occurred in the past and "the only practicable form of redress was monetary compensation."[27]

Under administrative law, a plaintiff may be successful in a claim for damages where a public or administrative authority: a) commits a tort; b) fails or refuses to perform its obligations under a contract that it lawfully entered into within the powers conferred by the statutes establishing the authority; c) breaches a statutory or constitutional duty. Examples of torts for which public or administrative authorities may be liable for damages include negligence,[28] an escape of dangerous things from its land under the rule in *Rylands* v. *Fletcher*,[29] unlawful detention,[30] defamation,[31] assault,[32] and unlawful imprisonment.[33]

A public or administrative authority may also be liable for damages as a result of unlawful termination of a contract of employment.[34] In addition, section 42 of the 1999 Constitution of the Federal Republic of Nigeria guarantees protection against compulsory possession of any movable property or interest in immovable property, including by public or administrative authorities, except under a law that provides

[25] Evans, *Judicial Review of Administrative Action by S. A. de Smith.*
[26] (1978) 2 WLR 902.
[27] At pp. 911, 912. See also *Janundoo* v. *Att-Gen of Guyana* (1971) AC 972.
[28] *Gbolahan Okuneye* v. *Lagos City Council* (1974) 4 UILR 42; *Machine Umudje & Anor.* v. *Shell BP Petroleum Development Co. Ltd.* (1975) 5 UILR 115.
[29] (1866) LR 1 Ex. 265. See *Nigerian Electric Power Authority* v. *Mudariru Amusa & Anor.* (1976) 6 UILR 255.
[30] *Shugaba Abdulrahman Darman* v. *Minister of Internal Affairs & Ors.* (1981) 2 NCLR 459.
[31] *Sola Saraki* v. *Dr. J. D. Soleye* (1972) 2 UILR 271. It is, however, important to state that statements made in official communication can enjoy either absolute or qualified privilege. While an absolute privilege is a complete defence to an action for defamation, a qualified privilege may be eroded by malice.
[32] *Alhaja Abibatu Mogaji & Ors.* v. *Board of Customs and Excise & Ors.* (1982) 3 NCLR 552.
[33] *Andrew Ogor & Ors.* v. *E. Kolawole (Chief Magistrate) & Anor.* (1985) 6 NCLR 644.
[34] *Nigerian Ports Authority* v. *Ephraim Banjo* (1973) 3 UILR 313.

for the prompt payment of compensation. In action for breach of statutory duty, the public or administrative authority may be held liable for wrongful performance of the duty and not for a failure to perform.[35] An exception to this is where the plaintiff suffers a foreseeable pecuniary loss as a result of the defendant's refusal to perform the statutory duty.[36] On the other hand, where a statute specifies a remedy, recourse must be had to that remedy alone except where the statute is also interpreted to also confer on the plaintiff a right to sue for damages.[37]

Declaratory Judgement

A declaratory judgment "merely states a court's opinion on a question of law or declares the rights, existing or future, of parties."[38] It asserts the existence of a legal relationship without specifying any order to be carried out by or enforced against the defendant.[39] Although, as a general rule, a plaintiff who seeks an equitable remedy must prove irreparable damage and that the available legal remedies are inadequate,[40] the scope of declaratory judgments is very wide and available in almost all cases where a right exists,[41] whether the public or administrative authority has acted in a judicial, executive, or administrative authority, except where they are made inapplicable by statute.[42] The remedy is available in cases where the public or administrative authority in the exercise of statutory or delegated powers fails to comply with some conditions precedent to an effective exercise of the powers or fails to observe some procedural requirements in the process of exercising the powers.[43] The remedy may also be sought by a plaintiff who challenges the validity of an act of the legislature[44] or the

---

35 *Ibadan City Council* v. *Odulake* (1972) 1 All NLR (Part 2) 319.

36 *Wosilatu Adesina* v. *Tijani Oladokun & Anor.* (1972) 2 UILR 241; *Ibadan City Council* v. *Odulake* (1972) 1 All NLR (Part 2) 319.

37 Evans, *Judicial Review of Administrative Action* by S. A. de Smith.

38 Evans, *Judicial Review of Administrative Action* by S. A. de Smith.

39 *Chuke Arah Akunnia* v. *A-G. Anambra State of Nigeria & Ors.* (1977) ANLR 118.

40 Evans, *Judicial Review of Administrative Action by S. A. de Smith.*

41 *Eguamwense* v. *Amaghizemwen* (1993) 9 NWLR (Pt 315) 1, 20.

42 Iluyomade and Eka, *Cases and materials on administrative law in Nigeria.*

43 *Senator Adebayo Doherty* v. *Sir Abubakar Tafawa Balewa & Ors.* (1961) All NLR 604.

44 *A-G. of Bendel State* v. *A-G of the Federation & Ors.* (1981) ANLR 153.

decision or act of a public authority and seeks to have the act declared null.[45]

The main disadvantage of declaratory judgments is that they are not legally enforceable.[46] In addition, there are some legal hurdles that must be surmounted by a plaintiff who seeks a declaratory judgment. One of those hurdles is the issue of *locus standi* or legal standing. *Locus standi* is the legal capacity to institute proceedings in a court of law.[47] Based on the application of *locus standi*, it is only a plaintiff who has a legal interest that has been adversely affected that can sustain an action in a court of law, and if it is a public interest in question, the plaintiff must also prove that he/she has suffered more damage, above other members of the public.[48] The object of the rule is to bar "professional litigants" and "busy-bodies" without sufficient legal interests from gaining access to the courts.[49] Second, the courts have developed a mechanism for balancing the freedom of the citizen against the right of the executive, and although the existence of other remedies may not prevent the courts from issuing a declaratory judgment,[50] the courts will normally refrain from making a declaration where a statute introduces new rights and duties with specific remedies.[51]

Injunction

An injunction is a court order which is issued to restrain a person from pursuing a particular course of action or which compels a certain course of action.[52] There are different types of injunctions depending on the stage when it is issued in the course of action and the purpose. A perpetual injunction is based on "a final determination of the rights of the parties, and it is intended permanently to prevent infringement of a right and obviate the necessity of bringing an action after every such

---

[45] *Dr. O. G. Sofekun* v. *Akinyemi & Ors.* (1980) ANLR 153.

[46] *Tito* v. *Waddell* (No. 2) (1977) Ch. 106.

[47] *Senator Adesanya* v. *The President & Ors*, (1981) 2 NCLR 358.

[48] *Adesanya* v. *Presidnet & Ors.* (1981) 2 NCL 358; *Onyia* v. *Governor in Council & Ors.* (1962) 2 All NLR 174. Cf. *Gani Fawehinmi* v. *A-G. of Lagos State & Ors.* (1987) 4 NWLR (Pt. 67) 797.

[49] *A-G of Gambia* v. *N'Jie* (1961) 2 All ER 504; *Adesanya* v. *President & Ors* (1981) 2 NCLR 358.

[50] Section 6(6)(b) of the 1999 Constitution of the Federal Republic of Nigeria extends the powers of the courts "to all matters…and to all actions and proceedings."

[51] *Samuel Oyebanji Ogunsola* v. *S. L. Akintayo & Anor.* (1980) 2 OY SHC 425.

[52] Emiola, *Remedies in Administrative Law.*

infringement."[53] A mandatory injunction is "issued requiring some affirmative act rather than forbidding it."[54] Interim injunctions are issued to maintain the *status quo* for a short period of time which is sufficient to put the other party on notice.[55] An injunction will be granted where a plaintiff establishes the existence of a legal right that has been unlawfully violated and continues to be violated.[56] The threat of injury must be a real one[57] and not merely speculative[58] or prospective.[59] An injunction will not be issued in cases where the act being complained about has been completed[60] or where it will be impossible to enforce the court order.[61] Also, the courts will not issue injunctions in cases where there are other equally effective remedies available[62] or where specific remedies are provided.[63] The courts are reluctant to issue an injunction that they cannot supervise to ensure compliance.[64] An injunction may be issued in cases where a public officer carries out an act *ultra vires*, even where the officer does so as an agent of the government.[65] Conversely, no injunction will be issued against a constitutional exercise of statutory powers.[66]

PREROGATIVE REMEDIES

Prohibition

A prohibition is a court order which restrains a judicial authority or a person acting in a judicial capacity from pursuing a course of action

53 M. I. Jegede, *Principles of Equity* (Ethiope, 1981).

54 D. B. Dobbs, *Remedies* (West Publishing Co., 1973).

55 E. Malami, *Administrative Law* (Prineton Pub. Com., 2008).

56 *A. O. Ibenwelu* v. *Lawal* (1971) 1 All NLR 23.

57 *Leslie F. Tate* v. *The Senior Immigration Officer* (1962) LLR 73.

58 *Samuel Oyebanji Ogunsola* v. *S. L. Akintayo & Anor.* (1980) 2 OY. SHC 425.

59 *Emmanuel Ojo Wey* v. *Lagos Executive Development Board* (1959) LLR 20; *Akenzua II Oba of Benin* v. *Benin Divisional Council* (1959) WNLR 1; *Aderibigbe* v. *Secretary Oranmiyan Local Government & Ors.* (1980) OY. SHC. 707.

60 *Akenzua II Oba of Benin* v. *Benin Divisional Council* (1959) WNLR 1; *Aderibigbe* v. *Secretary Oranmiyan Local Government & Ors.* (1980) OY. SHC. 707.

61 *Ogunsola* v. *S. L. Akintayo & Anor.* (1980) 2 OY. SHC 425; *Tony Momoh* v. *President of the Senate & Ors.* (1981) 1 NCLR 105.

62 *Ibenwelu* v. *Lawal* (1971) 1 All NLR 23.

63 J. F. Gamer, *Administrative Law* (4th edition) (London: Butterworhs, 1974).

64 *Eshugbayi Eleko* v. *Frank Morrish Baddelely* (1925) 6 NLR 56.

65 Emiola, *Remedies in Administrative Law.*

66 *Eshugbayi Eleko* v. *Frank Morrish Baddelely* (1925) 6 NLR 56.

that may adversely affect the legal interests of another person.[67] The main object of an order of prohibition is to prevent the violation of fundamental rights[68] or the completion of a threatened unlawful act.[69] Therefore, an order of prohibition cannot be issued once the act has been completed.[70] An order of prohibition may be used to prevent the violation of fundamental rights of citizens that are guaranteed under sections 33, 34, 40, 41, 42, and 44 of the 1999 Constitution of the Federal Republic of Nigeria.[71] Similarly, an order of prohibition may also be used to prevent the unlawful acquisition of lands for public use.[72] The conditions for the grant of an order of prohibition may be summarized as follows: a) that there is a body of persons on whom power is conferred, b) that the power so conferred is legal, c) that the power is for the determination of issues, d) that in the process of determination of issues, the body also has a concurrent obligation to act in a judicial capacity, and e) that the applicant for the issue of an order of prohibition has been able to prove the body has exceeded its legal authority.[73] This mostly relates to the exercise of statutory powers of a judicial nature by a public authority.[74]

Certiorari

An order of certiorari is used to quash the determination or decision of an inferior statutory tribunal.[75] A tribunal is a body "outside the hierarchy of the courts with administrative or judicial functions."[76] A person's actions may also be subject to an order of certiorari issued by a superior court, where the act in issue is a duty of an office created by

---

67 Emiola, *Remedies in Administrative Law*; R v. Electricity Commissioners (1924) 1 KB 71; *Obadara & Ors.* v *President Ibadan* Grade 'A' Customary Court (1964) 1 All NLR 336.

68 *Shugaba Darman* v. *Minister of Internal Affairs & Ors.* (1981) 1 NCLR 7.

69 *Akanni & Anor.* v. *Chief Magistrate Ogbomosho* (1980) 2 OY. SHC 324.

70 *The State* v. *Chief Samuel Ajayi & Ors. ex parte Chief Daniel Ayinde* (1980) 3 OY. SHC 659.

71 Emiola, *Remedies in Administrative Law.*

72 See sections 1, 5, 28, 34, 36 of the Land Use Act of 1978, and the Public Lands Acquisition Act/Laws. See also *Mofolorunsho Adekunle* v. *The Military Governor, Lagos State & Anor.* (1975) 9 CCHCJ 1277; *Att-General of Oyo State* v. *A-G of the Federal & Ors.* (1983) 4 NCLR 496.

73 *R* v. *Electricity Commissioners* (1924) 1 K.B. 171.

74 *The Queen* v. *The District Officer Ibadan, ex parte Fagebo* (1955) WNLR 45.

75 Emiola, *Remedies in Administrative Law.*

76 Emiola, *Remedies in Administrative Law.*

statute.[77] In Nigeria, the Supreme Court of Nigeria, the Court of Appeal, the Federal High Court, the State High Court of each of the 36 states of the Federation, the Sharia Court of Appeal, the Customary Court of Appeal, and the National Industrial Court make up the superior courts of record.[78] It is important to state that an order of certiorari cannot be issued against the decisions of any of the superior courts,[79] and a judge of a superior court cannot be sued for acts done in the course of exercising his/her judicial duties[80] as the judge of a superior court.[81] For judicial officers in inferior courts to enjoy immunity, they must "act in good faith."

The jurisdiction of the superior courts to issue an order of certiorari cannot be ousted by "finality clauses" that are characteristic of military decrees, for instance.[82] In the case of *Alhaji Balarabe Musa* v.. *The Speaker, Kaduna House of Assembly*,[83] the superior court declined jurisdiction on the ground that its intervention would constitute interference with the internal affairs of the house of assembly. However, it is now settled law that the Constitution is the grundnorm and that the ouster of the jurisdiction of the courts would only be absolute where the constitutional requirements for the composition and qualification of the members of the committee have been complied with by the legislature.[84] Although an order of certiorari is purely discretionary, there is evidence from decided cases that the courts will issue the order where there is an error on the face of the order of the inferior court.[85] But where the error is neither fundamental nor tantamount to a miscarriage of justice, the superior court may correct it on the

---

[77] *The State & Anor.* v. *Senior Inspector of Customary Courts, In re Mrs. E. O. Ojo* (1975) 1 NMLR 277; *Head of the Federal Military Government* v. *Public Service Commission, ex parte Kubeinje.*

[78] Section 6(5) of the 1999 Constitution of the Federal Republic of Nigeria.

[79] However, an objection can only be brought in the form of an appeal. See *R* v. *Central Criminal Court Justices, ex parte London County Council* (1886) 17QBD 586, 602.

[80] *Fred Egbe* v. *Hon Justices Adefarasin (C.J.)* [Lagos] (1987) 1 NWLR.

[81] *Emmanuel Ogbe* v. *Chief Justice, East Central State & Ors.* (1972) 1 All NLR (Part 2) 153; *Shugaba Abdulrahaman Darman* v. *Federal Minister of Internal Affairs & Ors.* (1981) 2 NCLR 459.

[82] *The Queen* v. *The Governor in Council W.R. ex parte Laniyan Ojo* (1962) WNLR 62; *E. O. Lakanmi & Anor.* v. *Attorney General (West) & Ors.* (1971) 1 UILR 204.

[83] (1982) 3 NCLR 229.

[84] *Attorney-General of Bendel State* v. *Attorney-General of the Federation & Ors.* (1981) 1 FNR 179.

[85] *R* v. *Northumberland Compensation Appeal Tribunal ex parte Shaw* (1952) 1 KB 338.

application of the parties.[86] In addition, the order will be issued where the applicant shows that the tribunal either acted *ultra vires*,[87] in breach of the rule of law,[88] the authority acted without "good faith,"[89] or in breach of the principles of natural justice.[90] Where, however, the decision against which the order is sought is a nullity, an order of certiorari will not be issued by the courts.[91]

Mandamus

An order of mandamus commands a public authority to perform an ascertainable public duty at the request of a private person.[92] The following conditions are essential to the grant of an order of mandamus: a) the person or body against whom the order is sought must be responsible for performing a public duty, b) which is owed to the applicant, c) the applicant must have specifically requested the performance of the duty by the respondent,[93] and d) the applicant must show that the respondent has refused to discharge the requested duty. In some exceptional cases, the "mere fact of non-compliance with a duty" [94] may be sufficient for the award of an order of mandamus, including where the public authority is aware of "what the applicant expected it to do so that it might decide at its own option whether to act or not,"[95] "where the applicant has been substantially prejudiced by the respondent's procrastination,"[96] where the respondent places some conditions which must be met before the duty is carried out,[97] or where

86 *The Resident, Ibadan Province & Anor.* v. *Memudu Lagunju* (1954) 14 WACA 549.

87 *Safi Abike* v. *Kadiri Ajope* (1957) 1 WSCA 212.

88 *Adedeji* v. *Police Service Commission* (1967) 1 All NLR 1677; *Adeyemo* v. *Oyo State Public Service Commission* (1979) 1 OY SHC 83.

89 *The Queen* v. *Administrative Officer Onitsha* (1960) 4 ENLR 51.

90 *Dr. M. O. Alakija* v. *The Medical Disciplinary Committee* (1959) 4 FSC 38; *The State* v. *Chief Samuel Ajayi & Ors., ex parte Chief Daniel Ayinde* (1960) 3 OY SHC 659.

91 *Bello* v. *Lagos Executive Development Board & Ors.* (1970) SC 229/70; *R* v. *Officer Administering Eastern Nigeria* (1960) 4 ENLR 33.

92 *Shitta-Bey* v. *Federal Public Service Commission* (1981) 1 SC 40, 68.

93 *Layanju* v. *Araoye* (1959) 4 FSC 154.

94 Evans, *Judicial Review of Administrative Action* by S. A. de Smith, p. 556.

95 See *The Queen* v. *Chief Ozogula II, ex parte Ekpenga* (1965) 1 All NLR 265.

96 Evans, *Judicial Review of Administrative Action* by S. A. de Smith, 556.

97 Emiola, *Remedies in Administrative Law.*

the time within which the duty is required to be performed has elapsed.[98]

Writ of *Habeas Corpus*

The writ of *habeas corpus* is a judicial remedy that secures the release of a person who is being held in unlawful detention or who has been wrongfully imprisoned.[99] There are various forms of the writ of habeas corpus. The *habeas corpus ad testificandum* can be invoked to overcome physical obstacles set up by the authorities to prevent a prisoner from giving evidence.[100] The *habeas corpus ad subjiciendum,* on the other hand, is designed to secure personal liberty by affording the subject "an effective means of immediate release from unlawful or unjustifiable detention whether at a prison or in private custody."[101] Under the 1999 Constitution of the Federal Republic of Nigeria, section 35, every person is entitled to his personal liberty, and no one shall be deprived of such liberty except in accordance with a procedure permitted by law. Exceptions to this right include where the detention is in the execution of a sentence of imprisonment imposed by a court of competent jurisdiction,[102] where a person is required to be held for an infringement of a law or an order of a court,[103] or where the arrest was effected with a view to bringing the prisoner to justice for an offense which he/she has committed or is suspected to have committed.[104] The Constitution, however, provides for the restriction of an infant under the age of 18 years, if this is for the sake of the child's education or welfare,[105] as well as the restriction of a person who is suffering from infectious or contagious disease, or is of unsound mind, or suffers from an addiction to drug, alcohol, or vagrancy.[106]

---

98 *R* v. *Henley* v. *Revising Barrister* (1912) 3 KB 518.

99 *Commissioner of Police* v. *Agbaje* (1969) 1 NMLR 176; *Thomas Twangie* v. *Commissioner of Police (FCT)* [1985] HCNLR 784.

100 Iluyomade and Eka, *Cases and Materials On Administrative Law in Nigeria.*

101 *Commissioner of Police* v. *Chief A. M. F. Agbaje* (1969) 1 NMLR 176, 180.

102 Section 35(1)(a).

103 Section 35(1)(b).

104 Section 35(1)(c). However, the period of detention must not be longer than the maximum period of imprisonment prescribed for the offence.

105 Section 35(1)(d).

106 Section 35(1)(e).

In Nigeria, the States' high courts have the jurisdiction to issue a writ of habeas corpus based on an ex parte application that is supported by an affidavit deposed by the person restrained or by some other person acting on his/her behalf.[107] One main limitation of this remedy is, therefore, that a writ issued by a court will not be effective in the case of a prisoner who is outside the area of jurisdiction of the issuing court.[108] This might pose a challenge in Nigeria, where each state high court has an autonomous jurisdiction, unlike the case of England, for instance, where the king's rate was applicable all over his territory.[109] It has been suggested that this situation could be rectified either through: a) a statute, preferably the Constitution, specifying that once a writ has been issued by the court in the state where a prisoner is detained, it should be applicable throughout the country, or b) the courts should be empowered to issue a mandatory injunction to compel the authority detaining the prisoner to keep the prisoner within the jurisdiction of the court that has issued the writ.[110]

ELECTION LAW

Election petitions are often instituted before an election petition tribunal by a petitioner who is aggrieved by the procedure for the conduct of a given election. Election matters in Nigeria are regulated by the Electoral Act of 2010, and the Court of Appeal is the final appellate court for election matters. Based on the provisions of the Electoral Law, the following remedies could be either granted or refused, or partly granted, or partly refused.

Cancellation or Nullification of an Election

It has been established by a plethora of cases that the mere evidence of irregularities or malpractice in the conduct of elections is not a sufficient ground for the cancellation or nullification of a given

---

[107] High Court (Civil Procedure) Rules.

[108] *Tafa Adeoye* v. *Commissioner of Police* (1971) 1 NMLR 172.

[109] *R* v. *Cowle* (1759) 2 Burr 834; Emiola, *Remedies in Administrative Law.*

[110] Ibid.; ibid.

election.[111] The petitioner must be able to prove the allegation of malpractices or irregularities beyond a reasonable doubt and also establish that the malpractices or irregularities fundamentally affected the outcome of the election to enable the tribunal to nullify or cancel the result.[112] The tribunal is also empowered to make consequential declarations and inquire into unpleaded issues which it may deem necessary for the full and proper determination of the election petition.[113]

Where an election is declared void, the petitioner cannot benefit from the voided election by requesting to be declared as the winner except where the petitioner has requested for the annulment of the respondent's election and return (for the petitioner) and has established that the petitioner received a majority of lawful votes at the election.[114] Instead, a fresh election will be ordered by the tribunal in order to fill the vacancy which arises where there is proof of substantial fraud, such as bonus votes for parties or multiple results for one polling station.[115] A bye-election is specifically held to fill a vacancy outside the schedule for general elections. The need for bye-elections often arises in special circumstances, such as where: a) there is a vacancy caused by the death of the erstwhile office holder or elevation to a new office, b) resignation or c) where for any other reason, the office becomes vacant.[116] The 1999 Constitution of the Federal Republic of Nigeria provides for the Deputy Governor of a State to assume the office of Governor where the office of Governor becomes vacant by reason of death, resignation, or incapacity.[117] In such a situation, the need for a bye-election would

---

[111] *Okoroji* v. *Ngwu* (1992) 9 NWLR (pt. 263) 113 at 211; *Edonkumoh* v. *Mutu* (1999) 9 NWLR (Pt. 620) 633; *Buhari* v. *Obasanjo* (2005) 13 NWLR (pt. 941) 1; *Daggash* v. *Bulama* (2004) 14 NWLR (Pt. 892) 144.

[112] *Oshiomhole* v. *INEC* (2008) 5 N.W.L.R. (pt. 1080) 227, *Osunbor* v. *Oshiomhole* (2007) 18 N.W.L.R. (pt.1065) 32, *Osunbor* v. *Oshiomhole* (2009) All F.W.L.R. (pt.463) 1363 at 1404, *Osunbor* v. *Oshiomhole* (2009) All F.W.L.R. (PT.463) 1363, *Amaechi* v. *INEC* (2008) 5 N.W.L.R. (pt.108) 227.

[113] *Abdullahi* v. *Alewa* (1999) 5 NWLR (pt. 602) 196.

[114] *Professor Eric Aguma Opia* v. *Chief Felix Ovuodoroye Ibru & 2 Ors.* (1992) 3 NWLR (pt. 231) 658; *Ige* v. *Akinyemi* (1998) 7 NWLR (pt. 557) 281.

[115] *United Nigeria Congress Party & 4 Ors.* v. *Democratic Party of Nigeria & 1 Or.* (1998) 6 NWLR (pt. 553) 337.

[116] *Ike* v. *Ofokaja* (1992) 9 NWLR (Pt. 263) 42. In the case of *Sowemimo* v. *Awobajo*, a bye election was held on the 16th of January 1999, because the result of the elections held previously on the 9th of January 1999 was inconclusive due to complaints received against the results from 5 out of 6 wards.

[117] Section 191 of the 1999 Constitution of the Federal Republic of Nigeria.

only arise with respect to the office of the Deputy Governor. This also applies even where the Governor-elect did not take the oath of office before the vacancy occurred.[118] Furthermore, a bye-election cannot be ordered with respect to polling stations but for the whole constituency where the election was conducted.[119]

LAND LAW

Land law enjoys a peculiar characteristic as it encompasses some aspects of equity, common law, and statute. The equitable remedies to which a party may be entitled are discretionary as they depend solely on the facts of any given case.[120] The following are some of the major remedies which can be granted in a land law case.

Mesne Profits

Mesne profit is the "intermediate pecuniary value of premises between the time when a tenancy terminates and the time when the tenant yields up possession."[121] At common law, *mesne* profits can only be recovered from an occupier who is a tenant.[122] However, the Rent Control and Recovery of Residential Premises Law 1976, section 40(1) states that "[M]*esne* profits means the rents and profits which a tenant who holds over or a trespasser has or might have received during his occupation of the premises and which he is liable to pay as compensation to the person entitled to possession." Chianu (2010) however submits that "the inclusion of 'trespasser' in the above definition notwithstanding, it is indubitable that the Rent Control Laws apply solely to tenants, not to trespassers."[123] *Mesne* profit is measured by the "open market rental value of the property."[124] Therefore, where the rent is below the market

[118] *PDP* v. *INEC* (1999) 11 NWLR (pt. 626) 174.
[119] *Chikbo* v. *Bello* (1993) 1 NWLR (pt. 267) 109
[120] Diane Chappelle *Land Law* 5th ed. (Edinburgh: Pearson Education Limited, 2001) p. 16
[121] Professor Emeka Chianu, *Law of Landlord and Tenant* (Abuja: Law Lords Publications, 2010) 324. See also *Osawaru* v. *Ezeiruka* [1978] 6/7 SC 135, 139.
[122] *Omotesho* v. *Oloriegbe* [1988] 4 NWLR (pt. 87) 225.
[123] Chianu, *Law of Landlord and Tenant*, p. 325. Also see Chianu, *Law of Landlord and Tenant* for the debates and conflict in judicial authorities on the issue of whether a statutory tenant is liable for *mesne* profits.
[124] Chianu, *Law of Landlord and Tenant*, p. 329. See also *Swordheath Properties Ltd* v. *Tabet* [1979] 1 WLR 285; *Inverugie Investnments Ltd* v. *Hackett* [1995] 3 All ER 841.

value of the property, it is the market value that would be awarded as *mesne* profit.[125] Furthermore, under the Rent Control Statutes and the Recovery of Premises Law, the tenant who holds over is required to pay not only rent but profits received during the unlawful occupation of the premises as compensation to the person who is lawfully entitled to possession.

Compensation for Use and Occupation

Compensation for use and occupation may be awarded by the courts where a tenant or licensee is in possession of a property with the consent of the landlord, but both parties have not yet reached an agreement on the amount to be paid as rent.[126] The measure of damages in compensation for use and occupation is similar to that for *mesne* profits.

CONTRACT/COMMERCIAL LAW

Commercial law is the branch of law that regulates the relationship between buyers and sellers of goods in Nigeria. Commercial transactions are mainly regulated by the provisions of the Sale of Goods Act of 1893. A buyer who suffers breach of contract for the sale of goods by a seller would be entitled to damages already discussed above. Other remedies available include:

Specific Performance

Specific performance is an equitable remedy through which a person against whom it is issued is compelled to perform his/her contractual obligations.[127] It is a discretionary remedy that the courts will only grant under circumstances where it is just and equitable to do so.[128] Therefore remedy is usually not available where damages are adequate compensation,[129] and it only applies to executory contracts[130] such as

---

[125]See *Debs* v. *Cheico* (Nig) Ltd [1986] NSCC 837.

[126] *Oshinfekun* v. *Lana* [1958] WNLR 122.

[127] K. I. Igweike, *Nigerian Commercial Law: Sale of Goods* (2nd edition, Lagos: Malthouse Press, 2001).

[128] Section 52 Sale of Goods Act, 1893; *Stickney* v. *Keeble* [1915] AC 386 at p. 419; *British Nylon Spinners Ltd* v. *Imperial Chemical Industries Ltd* [1955] Ch. 37.

[129] *Simeon Obile* v. *J. A. Ohaka* [1974] ECSLR 164; *Beswick* v. *Beswick* [1968] AC 58 at p. 88; *LSPDC & Ors.* v. *Nigerian Land Sea Foods Ltd* [1992] 6 NWLR 243 at 257.

contracts for the transfer of property or sale of land as a result of the unique character and scarcity of land, [131] and a separation deed or other similar contract which is neither illegal, immoral, nor contrary to public policy.[132] However, specific performance will not be awarded for contracts that limit the personal freedom of one of the parties,[133] contracts for which the court is not capable of supervising the performance,[134] or contracts for the transfer of chattel, except the chattel is of a unique character or of special value to the claimant,[135]

Action for money had and received

Under the Sale of Goods Act of 1893, section 54, parties have the right inter alia to 'recover money paid where the consideration for the payment of it has failed.' This means that a buyer is entitled to recover the amount paid as a purchase price for goods over which the seller has no title[136] or where the seller fails or neglects to deliver the goods to the buyer.[137]

Damages for Non-delivery and Breach of Term

Specifically, under commercial law, section 51(1) of the Sale of Goods Act of 1893 states that "where the seller wrongfully neglects or refuses to deliver the goods to the buyer, the buyer may maintain an action against the seller for damages for non-delivery." The right of the buyer to obtain damages for non-delivery arises where the goods are not delivered or where the goods delivered by the seller are not in conformity with the contract and have been rejected by the buyer.[138] The remedy is not available where the goods were delivered late but ultimately accepted by the buyer. Furthermore, success in an action for damages for non-delivery is also dependent on the seller's "wrongful" neglect or refusal to deliver. The measure of damages for non-delivery is

---

130 *Wolverhampton & Walsall Rail Co.* v. *London & North Rail Co.* (1873) L.R. 16 Eq. 433 at p. 43

131 *Fakoya* v. *St. Paul's Church, Shagamu* (1966) 1 ALR Comm. 461.

132 *Wilson* v. *Wilson* (1848) 1 HLC 538.

133 *De Francesco* v. *Barnum* (1890) 45 Ch. 430.

134 *Powell Duffryn Steam Coal Co.* v. *Taff Vale Railway Co.* (`1874) LR 9 App. 331.

135 *Falcke* v. *Gray* (1859) 4 Drew 651.

136 *Akoshile* v. *Ogidan (XXXX)* 19 NLR 87; *Rowland* v. *Devall* [1923] 2 KB 500.

137 *Ebrabim Dawood Ltd* v. *Heath Ltd & Anor.* [1965] 1 Lyds Rep 512.

138 Igweike, *Nigerian Commercial Law: Sale of Goods.*

"the estimated loss directly and naturally resulting, in the ordinary course of events, from the seller's breach of contract."[139] In cases where there is an available market for the goods, "the measure of damages is prima facie to be ascertained by the difference between the contract price and the market or current price of the goods at the time or times when they ought to have been delivered, or, if no times was fixed, then at the time of refusal to deliver."[140]

The buyer is also entitled to damages for late delivery because the time of delivery is regarded as an essential element of most commercial transactions.[141] Where the buyer accepts goods that are delivered late, the Sale of Goods Act does not specify the measure of damages. However, under the common law, there is a prima facie rule that the measure should be "the value of the article contracted for at the time when it ought to have been delivered and at the time when it actually was delivered."[142] Furthermore, the buyer is entitled to damages for breach of a warranty by the seller, or where the buyer has elected or is compelled to treat any breach of a condition by the seller as a breach of a warranty.[143] The Sale of Goods Act also provides for the rights of parties to recover interest or special damages.[144]

The seller is similarly entitled to damages for the buyer's neglect or refusal to take delivery of goods where the property has been passed by the seller to the buyer[145] or damages for non-acceptance where the property has not passed from the seller to the buyer.[146]

Action for Detinue or Conversion

The buyer may maintain an action for detinue or conversion in cases where the seller neglects to or refuses to deliver the goods after property in the goods has been transferred to the buyer. The buyer may maintain the action against the seller or anyone who is in possession of the goods

[139] Section 51(2) Sale of Goods Act of 1893.
[140] Section 51(3) Sale of Goods Act of 1893.
[141] Section 11(1)(a) Sale of Goods Act of 1893.
[142] *Elbinger A.G.* v. *Armstrong* [1874] L.R. 9 Q.B. 473 at p. 477.
[143] Section 53(1) of the Sale of Goods Act of 1893. See also section 11(1)(a)(b).
[144] Section 54 of the Sale of Goods Act of 1893. See also *Hydraulic Engineering Co. Ltd.* v. *Mc Haffie* [1878] 4 QB 524 at p. 528 for the rationale for the award of special damages.
[145] Sections 37, 48(3), 49(1) of the Sale of Goods Act of 1893.
[146] Sections 49(2), 50 of the Sale of Goods Act of 1893.

at the material time.[147] However, the issue of the measure of damages in action for detinue and conversion is far from settled.[148]

Quantum Meruit

Quantum meruit is an equitable remedy which provides restitution for unjust enrichment.[149] *Quantum meruit* applies in cases where a contract of service cannot be completed.[150] It is considered to be reasonable compensation for services rendered in a quasi-contractual relationship and can be pleaded as an alternative claim in action for breach of contract, even where the contract is unenforceable.[151] The claimant for compensation, for breach of contract, on a *quantum* basis, must provide the parameters and necessary evidence with which the court can assess what is reasonable compensation on *quantum meruit* for the services rendered by the claimant until the time when the contract was terminated.

Action for the Price

A seller has a common law right to claim for the price of goods where the property in the goods has passed to the buyer, but the buyer refuses to or neglects to pay the seller for the goods.[152] The Sale of Goods Act of 1893 similarly provides that "where, under a contract of sale, the property in the goods has passed to the buyer, and the buyer wrongfully neglects or refuses to pay for the goods according to the terms of the contract the seller may maintain an action against him for the price of the goods."[153] The only exception to the rule under the Sale of Goods Act that the property on the goods must have passed from the seller to the buyer in order to sustain an action for the price is "where under a contract of sale, the price is payable on a day certain irrespective of delivery, and the buyer wrongfully neglects or refuses to pay such

---

[147] See section 52 of the Sale of Goods Act of 1893.
[148] See *France* v. *Gaudet & Ors* [1871] LR 6 QB 199.
[149] *Black's Law Dictionary*.
[150] *Panar Ltd* v. *Wagbara* [2002] 2 NWLR (Pt. 644) p. 207.
[151] *Black's Law Dictionary*. See also *SBN Plc* v. *Opanubi* (2004) 15 NWLR (Pt. 896) p. 437.
[152] *Scott* v. *England* [1845] 15 LJQB 43.
[153] Section 49(1) of the Sale of Goods Act of 1893.

price."[154] The unpaid seller has a lien on the goods or a right to retain the goods for the price while they are in his/her possession.[155] Where the buyer is insolvent, the seller has a right to stop the goods in transit after parting with possession.[156] In addition to other remedies, where the property in the goods has not passed to the buyer, the seller has the right to withhold delivery.[157]

Rescission

Rescission allows a party to set aside a contract under circumstances of fraud.[158] Under commercial law, the seller's right to rescind is the equivalent of the buyer's right to reject, and the seller may exercise this right in cases where:

- The buyer fails to provide a bank guarantee of payment as required by the terms of the contract agreed between the parties.[159]
- The buyer fails to provide a confirmed credit as required by the terms of the contract with the seller.[160]
- The buyer fails to pay at the agreed time or within a reasonable time afterward, and time is of the essence to the contract.[161]

Rescission is also available where there has been a fundamental mistake in a contract.[162]

LIST OF BIBLIOGRAPHY

Akintunde Emiola, *Remedies in Administrative Law* (Ogbomoso: Emiola Publishers Ltd, 2000).

Kingsley Ikem Igweike *Nigerian Commercial Law: Sale of Goods* 2nd ed. (Lagos: Malthouse Press Ltd, 2001)

J. O. Fabunmi *Equity and Trusts in Nigeria* (Ile-Ife: Obafemi Awolowo University Press Ltd. 2006)

---

154 Section 49(2) of the Sale of Goods Act of 1893. See further Igweike, *Nigerian Commercial Law: Sale of Goods*, pp. 214 – 217.

155 Section 39(1)(a) of the Sale of Goods Act of 1893.

156 Section 39(1)(b) of the Sale of Goods Act of 1893.

157 Section 39(2) of the Sale of Goods Act of 1893.

158 *Seddon* v. *North East Salt Co. Ltd.* [1905] 1Ch. 326.

159 *SSCCMO Ltd* v. *Soc Gen De Camp* [1956] 1 Lyds Rep. 290.

160 *Trans Trust SPRL* v. *Danubiarn Trading Co.* [1952] 2 QB 297; *Saproma SPA* v. *Marine & Animal Bye Products Corp.* [1966] 1 Lyds. Rep. 367.

161 *Ryan* v. *Ridley & Co.* [1902] 19 TLR 45.

162 *Solle* v.*Butcher* (1950) 1 KB 671.

Emeka Chianu, *Law of Landlord and Tenant* 2nd ed. (Abuja: LawLord's Publications, 2010)

Afe Babalola, *Election Law and Practice* 2nd ed. (Ibadan: Intec Printers Ltd. 2007)

M. C. Okany, *Nigerian Administrative Law* (Onitsha: Africana First Publishes, 2007)

I. E. Sagay, *Nigerian Law of Contract* 2nd ed. (Ibadan: Spectrum Books Limited, 2000)

Diane Chappelle, *Land Law* 5th ed. (Edinburgh: Pearson Education Limited, 2001)

Jacob Abiodun Dada, Judicial Remedies for Human Rights Violations in Nigeria: A Critical Appraisal, *Journal of Law, Policy and Globalization* Vol. 13 (2013).

PART D

JUDICIAL AND QUASI-JUDICIAL SYSTEM

Chapter 13

COURT SYSTEM IN NIGERIA: JURISDICTION AND APPEALS

Justus Sokefun[*] & Nduka C. Njoku[+]

INTRODUCTION

The legal system of a nation is critical to the maintenance of law and order in that nation. The legal order is the foundation upon which the peace, order, justice, and development of the nation depend. The Courts play a pivotal role in the organization and maintenance of the legal order. This applies to Nigeria. This chapter examines Nigeria's legal order, especially the hierarchy of Courts in Nigeria, the jurisdictional limits of the various courts in Nigeria, as well as the appellate system of Nigerian courts.

The Nigerian legal system is essentially a colonial heritage that springs from the British colonial rule in Nigeria. Undoubtedly, it is for this reason that Nigeria's legal system is patterned after the British legal system. However, there is a fundamental difference between Britain and Nigeria in relation to the political organization of the state; while Britain adopted the unitary system of government wherein powers of government are legitimately concentrated at the centre, Nigeria adopted the federal system of government by which governmental powers are constitutionally shared between the central government and federating entities.

Directly flowing from these differences in the political arrangements of the two countries is the fact that Nigeria's legal system

[*] Justus Sokefun, Professor of Law, School of Law, National Open University of Nigeria, Lagos, Nigeria

[+] Lecturer, School of Law, National Open University of Nigeria, Lagos, Nigeria

and, in particular, its court hierarchy ought to be different from that of Britain. This is not entirely correct, as Nigeria's court system retains

Some essential attributes of a court arrangement suited for unitary systems of government. Despite this seeming anomaly, Nigerian courts are creations of the constitution, and it is the constitution that donates the jurisdictional limits of the courts. The same is the case with the appellate system, which is also constitutionally and statutorily granted to litigants in Nigeria.

THE NIGERIAN LEGAL SYSTEM

The Nigerian Legal System is "the totality of the laws or legal rules and the legal machinery which obtain within Nigeria as a sovereign and independent African country."[1] During colonial rule, Nigeria's grundnorm was derived from the Queen in Parliament. This position dramatically changed when Nigeria became an independent state, and the constitution became the basic and fundamental law of Nigeria.

As a result of Nigeria's historical circumstances, Nigeria's Legal System is part of the common law system. Accordingly, the Nigerian Legal System has been significantly influenced by the British Commonwealth. As a result, the common law of England, the doctrines of equity as well as the statute of general application in force in England as of 1st January 1900 form an essential part of Nigeria's legal system. Furthermore, certain English statutes that have been received into our laws by local legislation form part and parcel of Nigeria's Legal System. Beyond these, Nigerian law includes domestic legislation, Nigerian case law, and customary law. The principles of judicial precedent and hierarchy of courts are primary and basic parts of our legal system, with the Supreme Court of Nigeria at the zenith of the court system.

Nigeria runs the adversarial system of court proceedings. In Nigeria, the presiding judge is both a judge of facts and the law.

Directly flowing from the above is that the major characteristics of the Nigerian Legal System are: (a) duality because it acquired principles

[1] C.O. Okonkwo, ed. *Introduction to Nigerian Law* (London, Sweet & Maxwell, 1980), P. 40 cited by J.O. Asein, *op. cit.*

of the Laws of England and the customary law of the various ethnic nationalities in Nigeria; (b) external influence, which is reflective of colonial past and Islamic religion in the Northern part of Nigeria; (c) diverse, because the various numerous ethnic nationalities in Nigeria have their customary law coupled with the common law and Islamic law; (d) *stare decisis* by which courts below are bound by decisions of courts above in the hierarchy, e) adversarial system by which the judge takes the position of a neutral umpire and the hierarchy of courts.[2]

THE JUDICIARY

Judiciary means "The branch of government responsible for interpreting the laws and administering justice."[3] The term 'judiciary' denotes the branch of government that is constitutionally responsible for interpreting the laws and administering justice, by the application of the rule of law, through duly constituted courts[4]. Judicial power means:

> the authority vested in courts and judges to hear and decide cases and to make binding judgments on them; the power to construe and apply the law when controversies arise over what has been done or not done under it.

Section 6(1) of the 1999 Constitution of the Federal Republic of Nigeria vests judicial powers of the Federal and State governments of Nigeria in the Courts established by the constitution. The section provides that the "Judicial powers of the Federation shall be vested in the courts to which this section relates, being courts established for the Federation." Section 6(2) of the 1999 Constitution provides that "Judicial powers of the State shall be vested in the courts to which this section relates, being courts established, subject as provided by this Constitution, for the State."

By Section 6(6) of the Section,

---

[2] J.O. Asein, *op. cit.*, p.5-7

[3] The Black's Law Dictionary, 8th edition, 2004

[4] *Anozia* v. *Attorney General of Lagos State* (2010) 15 NWLR (Pt. 1216) 207 at 237

> "The judicial powers vested in accordance with the foregoing provisions of this section-
>
> (a) Shall extend notwithstanding anything to the contrary in this Constitution, to all inherent powers and sanctions of a court of law;
>
> (b) Shall extend to all matters between persons, or between government or authority and to any person in Nigeria, and to all actions and proceedings relating thereto, for the determination of any questions to the civil rights and obligations of that person...

The primary role of the judiciary is the interpretation of the Constitution and the laws enacted by the legislature in resolution of justiciable live issues brought before the courts. The judiciary also has the role of administration of justice according to law. In exercise of this role, the fundamental values of fairness, impartiality, integrity, and incorruptibility are sacrosanct. It is through the instrumentality of administration of justice that law and order are maintained in the state. Law and order are the primary functions of any government. Another role of the judiciary that is not easily discernible is the role of checks and balances. By the power of judicial interpretation, the judiciary can declare activities of the executive and legislature unconstitutional, null and void, and of no effect. This is usually undertaken through the processes of judicial review.

The role of the judiciary in the exercise of governmental powers was exemplified in the case of *A.G. Abia State* v. *A.G Federation*.[5] In that case, the National Assembly enacted the Monitoring Allocation to Local Government Act 2005. The Act, among other provisions, sought to monitor financial allocation that accrued from the Federal Government Account to the Local Government. The 1st Plaintiff contended that it was the House of Assembly of the State and not the National Assembly that may make such laws. In that case, the Supreme Court held as follows:

---

[5] (2007) 2 SC 146.

> it is also important to bear in mind that the judiciary...Is the guardian of the Constitution charged with the sacred responsibility of dispensing justice for the purposes of safeguarding and protecting the constitution and its goals. The judiciary when properly invoked has a fundamental role to play in the structure of governance by checking the activities of the other organs of government and thereby promoting good governance and respect for individual rights and fundamental liberties and also ensuring the achievement of the goals of the constitution and not allow the defeat of such good intendments. It is the duty of the court to keep the government faithful to the goals of democracy, good governance for the benefit of the citizen as demanded by the constitution.[6]

In *Gadi* v. *Male*,[7] the court opined as follows:

> it is trite, the courts of law in this country, an indeed in all the civillised counties of the world, are the primary custodians of the constitution, nay the rule of law. The courts are inherently imbued with sacrosanct and far-reaching fundamental powers to preserve, interpret and uphold the constitution. Such far-reaching and fundamental powers as conferred upon the courts are traceable to the constitution and laws as may be enacted by the legislature, federal and/or state.[8]

THE STRUCTURE AND JURISDICTION OF NIGERIAN COURTS

Meaning of Jurisdiction

Jurisdiction is "a court's power to decide a case or issue a decree."[9]

Rules of Jurisdiction, in a sense, speak from a position outside the court system and prescribe the authority of the courts within the system. They are, to a large extent, constitutional rules. The provisions of the U.S. Constitution specify the outer limits of the subject-matter jurisdiction of the federal courts and authorize Congress within those limits, to establish by statute the organization and jurisdiction of the federal courts.[10]

---

[6] (2007)1 CCLR SC p.104 at 131

[7] (2010) 7 N.W.L.R. (Part 1193) page 225

[8] (2010) 7 N.W.L.R. (Pt. 1193)225 at 266.

[9] Bryan Garner, ed., Black's Law Dictionary, Ninth Edition, (West Publishing, 2009) p.297

[10] Flemming James Jr; Geoffrey C. Hazardy & Leubsderf, "Civil Procedure" s 2.1 and s.5 (5th Edition, 2001) cited by Bryan Garner, *op. cit*,. p. 927

Jurisdiction is essentially the authority that a court of law has to determine matters or issues which are litigated before it or to take cognizance of issues presented in a formal way for its resolution. The limits of jurisdiction are prescribed by the constitution or by the enabling statute under which the court is constituted. Jurisdiction may be extended or restricted by statutory enactments.[11]

The basis of jurisdiction of Nigerian courts is the Constitution of the Federal Republic of Nigeria. By virtue of the 1999 Constitution of the Federal Republic of Nigeria, all courts in the Nigerian federation derive their jurisdiction or competence from the constitution.[12] Nigerian courts, like other courts in democratic nations, are creatures of the statute based on the constitution. Their jurisdictions are based on statutes, and as a corollary, no court in Nigeria assumes jurisdiction without its enabling statute. Jurisdiction cannot be implied, and as a result, where there is no enabling state, there cannot be jurisdiction. When a court has no jurisdiction, it is a futile exercise for that court to embark on the hearing of a matter.[13]

Jurisdiction is so fundamental that it is a condition precedent to any action which calls for determination before the court. Jurisdiction is usually an important issue in matters before the court and therefore goes to the root of the whole action. Once the issue of jurisdiction is raised during proceedings before the court, it should be decided at the earliest stage of the proceedings in order to save time and before the merits of the case are considered and determined.[14]

The ingredients which must be present before the courts can assume jurisdiction have been decided by the courts:

"A court is only competent when –

a. It is properly constituted with respect to the members and qualifications of its members;

---

[11] *Adams* v. *Umar* (2007) 5 N.W.L.R. pt. 1133, 41 at 97

[12] *Osadebay* v. *A.G. Bendel* (1991) 1 N.W.L.R. Pt. 169 525 at pp. 557 – 558; *Din* v. *A.G. Federation* (1986) 4 N.W.L.R (Pt. 87) 147 at 171 .

[13] *Osadebay* v. *A.G. Bendel* p.57; A.G. *Federation* v. *Sode* (1990) 1 N.W.L.R. (Pt. 128) 500 at 503, 504, and 505.

[14] *Abubarkar* v. *Usman* (2009) 6 N.W.L.R. Pt. 1136 69 at pp. 93-94

b. The subject matter of the action is within its jurisdiction;
c. The action is initiated by due process of law; and,
d. Any condition precedent for the exercise of its jurisdiction has been fulfilled.

Non-compliance with any of the foregoing matter is a defect in competence which may be fatal to its jurisdiction."[15]

The parties to a dispute cannot confer jurisdiction on a court. In any event, where the court lacks jurisdiction, the parties cannot confer and vest jurisdiction on the court.[16]

The question as to whether a court has jurisdiction can be raised at any stage of the trial, even for the first time on appeal. If a court lacks the requisite jurisdiction to hear and determine an issue before, any step taken in relation to the matter is a nullity and void.[17] Lack of jurisdiction emphasizes the want of legal capacity and lack of competence in the court to hear and determine the subject matter before it. Lack of jurisdiction necessarily means that the court does not have the competence to exercise the judicial powers vested in the courts by s.6(6)(b) of the 1999 Constitution of the Federal Republic of Nigeria, and a decision or judgment made while lacking jurisdiction is null and void[18].

There is a clear difference between jurisdiction over the subject matter and procedural jurisdiction. While procedural jurisdiction could be waived by the affected party to the proceedings, that cannot be said of jurisdiction relating to the subject matter. For example, where the wrong procedure was adopted in commencing a suit and no objection to the procedure was timeously raised by the opposing party, the procedure based on such a wrong procedure is valid and cannot be overturned on the basis of lack of jurisdiction on the part of the court.[19] Directly following this principle is the fact that non-compliance with the rules of court, as against a statutory provision, may not necessarily

---

[15] *Shelim* v. *Gobang* (2009) 12 N.WL.R. Pt. 1156 403 pp. 455-456, *Madukolu* v. *Nkemdilim*
[16] *Adams* v. *Umar*,(*supra*) p. 115
[17] *Adams* v. *Umar* (*supra*) p. 115. *Madukolu* v. *Nkemdilim* (1962) 2 S.C.N.J. 341
[18] *Adams* v. *Umar* (*supra*) p.116
[19] *Adams* v. *Umar* (*supra*) p.116

result in the judgment given being set aside on the basis of the absence of jurisdiction.[20]

The importance of jurisdiction in the adjudicatory processes has always been emphasised by the courts. It is of absolute importance in judicial proceedings and the life wire of adjudication. "Where there is no jurisdiction to hear and determine a matter, everything done in such want of jurisdiction is a nullity."[21]

"Power of a court is derived from its enabling statute. It is the statute which creates the court that defines its jurisdiction. In other words, all courts of record are creatures of the constitution, as their jurisdiction is confined, limited and circumscribed by the constitution."[22]

The Constitution creates Federal and State Courts as well as Election Tribunals.

The Federal courts are – The Supreme Court, The Court of Appeal, the Federal High Court, the High Court of Federal Capital Territory, Abuja, The Sharia Court of Appeal of the Federal Capital Territory, Abuja, the Customary Court of Appeal of Federal Capital Territory, Abuja. The State Courts are the High Court of the State, the Sharia Court of Appeal, and the Customary Court of Appeal. The Election Tribunals are the National Assembly Election Tribunals, the Governorship, and Legislative Houses Election Tribunals.[23]

Supreme Court of Nigeria

Section 230(1) of the 1999 Constitution establishes the Supreme Court of Nigeria. It is the highest court in Nigeria and the court of last resort. It is situated in the Federal Capital Territory, Abuja. The Chief Justice of the Federation, who is the head of the judiciary in Nigeria, presides over the Supreme Court. The court consists of the Chief Justice of Nigeria and such number of justices not exceeding twenty-one as may be prescribed by the National Assembly. Ordinarily, the court is duly

---

[20] *Adams* v. *Umar* (*supra*)p.116
[21] *Shelim* v. *Gobang* (*supra*) p.452
[22] *Shelim* v. *Gobang* 452
[23] Section 6(5) of the 1999 Constitution (as amended)

constituted with not less than five justices of the court, except where it is exercising its original jurisdiction or a matter which involves a question of interpretation or application of the constitution or whether any provision relating to Fundamental Rights provisions of the constitution has been, or is likely to be contravened. In this regard, the court is duly constituted if it consists of seven Justices of the court.

The decision of the Supreme Court on any matter is final, and it is not subject to an appeal to any other person or body. This is, however, without prejudice to the power of the President or Governor of a State's exercise of the prerogative of mercy in appropriate cases. The decisions of the Supreme Court are binding on all other courts in Nigeria.

Jurisdiction of the Supreme Court

Original Jurisdiction of the Supreme Court

The Supreme Court of Nigeria has both original and appellate jurisdiction. The original jurisdiction of the Supreme Court is contained in Section 232(1) of the Constitution. It provides that "The Supreme Court shall, to the exclusion of any other court, have original jurisdiction in any dispute between the Federation and a State or between States if and in so far as that dispute involves any question (whether of law or fact) on which the existence or extent of a legal right depends."

Additionally, the National Assembly also has the power to confer additional original jurisdiction on the Supreme Court. The constitution precludes the Supreme Court from exercising original jurisdiction with respect to criminal matters.[24] The National Assembly has enacted the Supreme Court (Additional Original Jurisdiction) Act,[25] by which additional original jurisdiction was conferred on the Supreme Court. By section 1(1) of that Act, it is provided that in addition to the jurisdiction conferred upon the Supreme Court by section 232(1)[26] of the Constitution, the court shall, to the exclusion of any other court, have original jurisdiction in any dispute (in so far as that dispute

[24] Section 232(2) of the Constitution
[25] Cap S16, Laws of the Federation of Nigeria, 2004
[26] The Act erroneously makes reference to section 323(1)

involves any question whether of law or fact or in which the existence or extent of a legal right depends) between:

(a) The National Assembly and the President;
(b) The National Assembly and any State House of Assembly;
(c) The National Assembly and the State of the Federation.

In *Attorney-General of Abia State* v. *Attorney-General of the Federation,*[27] the Plaintiff brought the suit at the Supreme Court pursuant to the original jurisdiction of the Supreme Court. The complaint was in respect of the activities of the Economic and Financial Crimes Commission (EFCC) against the plaintiff. The Supreme Court struck out the suit for want of jurisdiction because EFCC is a corporate legal entity that can sue and be sued in its own name and not necessarily an agent of the first defendant. The court was of the opinion that the claim does not qualify as a dispute within the meaning of section 232 of the 1999 Constitution, not being a dispute between the Federation and the State.

In *Attorney General of Anambra State* v. *Attorney General of the Federation,*[28] the question for determination was whether the tenure of office of the governor of Anambra State is a dispute of such a nature that could legitimately result in the invocation of the original jurisdiction of the Supreme Court. The court struck out the suit and held that in order for the original jurisdiction of the Supreme Court to be invoked pursuant to Section 232 of the 1999 Constitution, there must exist a legal right on the part of the claimant, and the dispute or controversy must be one between the Federation and a State of the Federation. The court went further to hold that while it may be true that the Governor of Anambra State qua Governor might have been short-changed on the question of tenure, that fact does not, ipso facto, make such an issue one between Anambra State as an entity and the Federation. The suit, therefore, remains incompetent and ought to be struck out for want of jurisdiction.[29]

---

[27] (2007) 2 S.C. 146
[28] (2007) 5-6 S.C. 192
[29] *A.G. Anambra* v. *A.G Federation* (*supra*) at page 193

In *Attorney-General of Kano State* v. *Attorney-General of the Federation,*[30] the plaintiff brought a suit to the Supreme Court by invoking the original jurisdiction of the Supreme Court. The plaintiff's case, in the main, is a complaint against certain conduct of the Inspector General of the Police. The question arose as to whether the original jurisdiction of the Supreme Court was properly raised in the circumstance where the plaintiff's case is of an alleged wrongdoing by an officer of the Federation. The Supreme Court unanimously struck out the suit. The court held that in order for the original jurisdiction of the Supreme Court to be invoked pursuant to section 232 of the 1999 Constitution, the following pre-conditions must be met:

1. There must be a justiciable dispute involving any question of law or fact.
2. The dispute must be:

(a) between the Federation and a State in its capacity as one of the constituent units of the Federation; or,

(b) between the Federation and more States that are in their capacity as members of the constituent units of the Federation; or,

(c) between States in their aforesaid capacity, and the dispute must be one on which the existence or extent of a legal right in the aforesaid capacity is involved. That the plaintiff's claim did not satisfy these pre-conditions and, therefore, the invocation of the original jurisdiction of the Supreme Court in that case fails.

In *Attorney-General of Lagos State* v. *Attorney General of the Federation & Ors,*[31] the plaintiff brought the suit challenging the competence of the Federal Government to legislate and collect Value Added Tax in Nigeria. The claim was brought under the original jurisdiction of the Supreme Court. However, the Supreme Court struck out the case for want of jurisdiction because the claim related to the

---

30 (2007) 3 S.C., (Part 1) page 59

31 (2014) LPELR 22

revenue of the government of the Federation, which ordinarily falls within the jurisdiction of the Federal High Court. Accordingly, the invocation of the original jurisdiction of the Supreme Court for that purpose was misconceived.

Appellate Jurisdiction of the Supreme Court

The appellate jurisdiction of the Supreme Court of Nigeria is as provided in Section 233(1) of the Constitution. The appellate jurisdiction of the Supreme Court confers on the Supreme Court's exclusive jurisdiction to hear and determine appeals from the Court of Appeal. An appeal may either lie to the Supreme Court as of right or with leave of that court or the Court of Appeal. An appeal shall lie as of right from decisions of the Court of Appeal to the Supreme Court in the following cases:[32]

(a) Where the ground of appeal involves questions of law alone, decisions in any civil or criminal proceedings before the Court of Appeal.
(b) Decisions in any civil or criminal proceedings on questions as to the interpretation or application of the Constitution.
(c) Decisions in any civil or criminal proceedings on questions as to whether any of the provisions of Chapter IV has been, is being, or is likely to be contravened in relation to any person.
(d) Decisions in any criminal proceedings in which any person has been sentenced to death by the Court of Appeal or in which the Court of Appeal has affirmed a sentence of death by any other court.
(e) Decisions on any question –
(i) Whether any person has been validly elected to the office of President or Vice-President under the constitution.

---

[32] Ibid., section 232(2)

(ii) Whether the term of office of President or Vice-President has ceased.

(iii) Whether the office of President or Vice-President has become vacant.

(iv) Whether any person has been validly elected to the office of the Governor or Deputy Governor under this Constitution.

(v) Whether the term of office of a Governor or Deputy Governor has become vacant.

(f) Such other cases as may be prescribed by an Act of the National Assembly.

The Supreme Court of Nigeria, like similar institutions in other political systems,[33] epitomizes the Nigerian Judiciary.[34] It not only plays a significant role in constitutional matters but also fashions out the judicial policies affecting the political environment generally.[35] In the words of Graham-Douglas, 'although many rules and principles of law have survived to this day from decisions of courts of the first instance, it is more to the courts at the pinnacle of the judicial system that the glory of the dynamism in law creation must largely go.[36] It serves as the overseer of the judicial branch and is the master of the judicial house.'[37]

BASIC PRINCIPLES OF CONSTITUTIONAL INTERPRETATION

According to Ezejiofor, there are two broad approaches to constitutional interpretation. One is that which regards the constitution as an ordinary statute that must be interpreted by the same method of construction and exposition that the courts apply to other statutes.[38] It must be given a strict and literal construction, and the intention of the

---

[33] In the United States, the study of the judiciary as a political institution began with studies on the Supreme Court in the government. See Martin Shapiro, 'Political Jurisprudence', *Kentucky Law Journal* vol LII 1964 page 294

[34] Kuti, A.F.D., 'Law and Polity: The Supreme court Approach.' Benin City Law times Ltd. (1988, page 13

[35] Ogundere J.D. "The Nigerian Judge and His Court" Ibadan (1994) page 138s

[36] Kasumu A.B "The Supreme Court of Nigeria" 1956 - 1870

[37] Mojeed O.A. Alabi, "The Supreme Court in the Nigeria Political System" 1963-1997 page 10

[38] See the Supreme Court of Nigeria 1956-1970 edited by A.B. Kasumu page 69

makers of the constitution must be ascertained from the document itself and from no other source.

The other approach is that a constitution is different from an ordinary statute, even if enacted by a legislature, and so should be more liberally interpreted than an ordinary parliamentary enactment. It is a document within which a polity sets up the machinery of government. A constitution is meant to endure for ages and consequently to be adapted to the various crises of human affairs. Judges should therefore show 'judicial statesmanship'[39] in construing its provisions and should give little weight to purely formal and technical arguments. It should not be constructed in any narrow and pedantic sense and should be given not only to its letter but also to its spirit.[40] Aside from these two approaches, the courts have evolved other methods to impose restraint on the exercise of the power of constitutional interpretation, including:

(a) The courts will not adjudicate upon the constitutionality of legislation:

(i) In a friendly, non-adversary proceeding.[41] In other words, they will not write essays on constitutional interpretation for the benefit of private individuals[42], and unless the constitution expressly so stipulates, the courts will not render mere adversary opinion.[43]

(ii) On the complaint of one who has availed himself of its benefits.[44]

(iii) On the complaint of one who fails to show that he is or is about to be injured in its operation. In other words, a litigant must have a substantial interest in the case or controversy raised.[45]

(b) The Courts shy away from deciding upon the constitutionality of a choice.[46] Therefore, if it is possible to base the decision of a case on other grounds they will gladly refuse to pass an opinion on the

---

39 See Jennings J. Constitutional Interpretation' Harvard L.J. Vol. 51 (1937) page 37. See further the diction of Holiness J. in *Bain Peanut Co. of Texas* v. *Pinson* 282 US 499 at page 50

40 See Marshall CJ in *Mc Culloch* v. *Maryland* 4 Wheaton 316

41 *Muskari* v. *US* 219 US 346, *Central Bank of India* v. *Their Workmen AIR* (1960) SC 12 page 28

42 *Sharma S* v. *The Supreme Court in the India Constitution* 1959 dp 50 - 51

43 *Liberty Warehouse Co.* v. *Grannis* 273 US 70. In India the Supreme Court has constitutional power to render advisory opinion at the instance of the president. See Article 143.

44 *Gt Falls Mfg* v. *AG.* 124 US 581; *Main Sukh Das* v. *State of Up* (1953) SCR 1184.

45 *Massachusetts* v. *Mellon* 262 US 447; *Fair Clinld* v. *Hughes* 258 US 126. But in a definite and concrete controversy touching upon the legal rights of parties the court can render a declaratory judgment. See *Nashville Railway Co.* v. *Wallace* 288 US 249

46 *Burton* v. *United States* 196 Us 285

constitutional question. Similarly, they may decline to pass on the constitutionality of a question on the ground that it is 'political' in nature and so should be settled by the political organs of a state.[47] Again, whenever possible, they readily apply the principle of severability in order not to strike down the whole of the impugned legislation. By that device, the portion of it which is *intra vires* is allowed to operate.[48]

(c) There is a doctrine according to which every presumption is to be indulged in favour of the validity of the impugned statute.[49] The presumption is rebutted only if the statute is arbitrary or is an unreasonable attempt to exercise the authority vested in the stated in public interest.[50] The theory is that the legislature represents and presumably speaks for a majority of the electorate, and the idea of democracy presupposes that such a majority is entitled to have its will enacted into law. The legislature, it is said, should be trusted because its members have the experience and knowledge which are not available to the judges. Moreover, if mutual self-restraint is maintained, it is necessary for the maintenance of harmony between the judicial, executive, and legislative branches of government. And it is on the voluntary acceptance of this doctrine by the branches rather than on any other sanction that the smooth operation of the concept of powers depends.

The Supreme Court of Nigeria

Under the Constitution of the Federal Republic of Nigeria, 1999, the Supreme Court of Nigeria is established by section 230. The appointment of the Chief Justice of Nigeria and Justices of the Supreme Court, original jurisdiction, appellate jurisdiction, constitution, the finality of determinations, and practice and procedure are all provided for in sections 231, 232, 234, 235, and 236, respectively.

---

47 *Coleman* v. *Miller* 307 US 433; *Srikisham* v. *State of A.P. Air* 1957 Andih, Pra, 734

48 *R.M.D. Chairman Bougwalla* v. *Union of India Air* 1957 SSC 628; *Presser* v. *Illinois* 116 US 252

49 *Whitney* v. *California* 244 US 357 at 371; See also *Gitlow* v. *New York* 268 US 652

50 *Muglar* v. *Kansas* 123 US 623 page 661; *Northern Railway* v. *Clara City* 246 US 434 page 439 (1882) 7 App Cas 829, 839

Nigeria is a developing country, and in its period of gradual evolution to nationhood as one of the developed countries of the world, the Supreme Court has an important role to play. The main role of the judiciary or the Supreme Court is not to adhere to the out modelled and orthodox view that the duty of the court is merely to interpret the law relying essentially on the rules already existing in the legal system. This method will definitely lead to the law being sterile and totally divorced from its social milieu. The Nigerian Supreme Court can only serve the Nigerian society if it succeeds in promoting economic growth and the social well-being of the people, if it contributes toward the elevation of the moral values of Nigerian society, and if it attempts to unify the several ethnic communities into the Nigerian society, and above all, if it succeeds in evolving a common law for the country out of the existing bodies of law.

However, to do this successfully, the Supreme Court can only view the Constitution as a political document embodying the fundamental creed of the people, which, therefore, cannot be interpreted by the same canons of construction as appropriate to statutes or ordinary Acts of parliament. Any narrow or unilateral interpretation of the provisions of the constitution vital to its proper functioning must be avoided if the constitution itself is to have efficacy, and the political framework and the legal order established within it are to have stability and legitimacy.

This will be realized only if those who are called to dispense justice in the society, which must be democratic, are themselves part of the democratic system and are imbued with democratic ideas. Therefore, the Supreme Court and its judicial officers must be insulated from the undercurrents of partisan politics. As human beings, they may have their individual political beliefs, but they must divorce their professional personalities from partisan politics if they would be trusted to dispense justice without fear or favour.[51]

The Supreme Court of Nigeria, like its counterparts the world over, is the final arbiter in both civil and criminal matters and, as such,

[51] Asomugha E.M. "The Supreme Court: Rational, Precedent and Policy, And its Role in Legal Interpretation". *The Supreme Court of Nigeria*, Kasumu A.B (ed.) page 62

usually employs the best reasoning in reaching a final decision in matters before it because failure to do so will definitely spell doom for the rule of law and the relevant statute in question. In doing so, or in an attempt to reach a final and full non-appealable decision, the Supreme Court, in most cases, adopts either one or all the various rules of interpretation of statutes whenever it is confronted with such plight and, by so doing several constitutional problems had been laid to final rest. Even though these rules of interpretation of statutory provisions are not devoid of lacuna, it is more advisable and reasonable to adopt one where the subject of interpretation, that is, the provision of the statute, is capable of more than one interpretation. Attention shall be shifted now to the consideration of these various rules of interpretation of statutes through the cases in order to drive home the subject of discussion.

CANONS OF INTERPRETATION OF STATUTES

The general view is that the way the courts exercise power whenever a statute is challenged as entrenched in the constitution is to lay the article of the constitution which is invoked beside the statute being challenged and to decide whether the latter squared with the former. But surely, constitutional interpretations mean more than this. Matters which usually arise do not lend themselves to such an easy and precise treatment as envisaged by this assertion. A typical example is where an invoked constitutional provision may be capable of more than one interpretation, and the impugned statutory may also be susceptible to more than one meaning.

The present state of statutory interpretation suggests that there is some error in the judicial approach to the whole exercise. The fact is that statutes are destined to operate over indefinite periods of time, so they should be viewed in a continuum.[52] Hence, a court is expected to invoke whichever of the rules that produces a result that satisfies its sense of justice in the case before it. However, for ease of reference, the

---

[52] Ibid., at page 391

various cannons of interpretation of statutes have been divided into the following:

1. Referential Approach;
2. Purposive Approach; and,
3. Compromise Approach.

The Referential Approach

The Referential approach is further subdivided into two major heads as follows:

(a) Literal or Plain Meaning Rule;

(b) Golden Rule;

(A) Literal or "Plain Meaning Rule"

Judges frequently use the phrase "the true meaning" of words in the pursuit of their tasks. The most widely used cannon of interpretation, the so-called 'Literal or Plain Meaning Rule' is best summed up in *Abley* v. *Dale*,[53] in the following words:

> If the precise words used are plain and unambiguous, in our judgment, we (the courts) are bound to construe them in their ordinary sense, even though it leads, to an absurdity or manifest injustice.[54]

This age-long dictum has since been overturned by more cogent and reasonable opinions of different judges all over the world, inclusive of our own Supreme Court Judges. In essence, rigid adherence to this literal approach will inevitably result in a situation where the constitution cannot be adapted to the current needs of the society and may give rise to decisions completely out of step with the spirit of the constitution. This was the view of the majority of the justices of the Supreme Court in the celebrated case of *Akintola* v. *Aderemi*.[55]

The issue, in this case, was the interpretation of section 33(10) of the Constitution of the Western Region, which provided that the Government 'shall' remove the Premier 'if it appears to him' that the

---

[5353] (1851) 11 C.B. 378

[54] Ibid., at page 391

[55] (1962) 1 All NLR 442

latter no longer commands the support of a majority of the members of the House of Assembly. The question then was whether, pursuant to this provision, the Governor could remove a Premier on the basis of factors extraneous to the activities on the floor of the House or whether he could only do so only as a result of events in the House.

The court held that the Governor could not remove a Premier except in pursuance of an adverse vote on the floor of the House because the Constitution of the Region was framed in the light of the normal English constitutional practice and so should be interpreted in that light. According to that practice, said the court, the Queen could not remove a Prime Minister except as a result of an adverse vote in the House of Commons. It said, "for the interpretation of section 33(10) of the Constitution of Western Region, no precedent can be found, the meaning of the subsection and the scope of its application must be read in the light of the convention."

This is, however, interesting because there was no ambiguity and yet the court was prepared to take this step. Over the years, the present Supreme Court of Nigeria has adopted this literal or plain meaning rule in the interpretation of statutes in matters before it. Most recently, this rule was applied by the Supreme Court of Nigeria in the case of *Attorney General Ondo State* v. *Attorney General of The Federation & 35 Ors,*[56] where the court, in determining whether the court should adopt a narrow or broad interpretation approach in the interpretation of the provisions of the Constitution, Muhammed Lawal Uwais, CJN, while delivering the lead judgment, quoted with approval the dictum of Fatayi Williams, CJN (as he then was) in *Senator Adesanya* v. *President of Nigeria*[57] in the following words:

> The only true guide and the only course which can produce stability in constitutional law is to read the language of the constitution itself, no doubt generously and not pedantically but as a whole.[58]

---

[56] (2002) 6 S.C. (Pt. 1) 1 180

[57] (1981) 2 N.C.L.R. 358

[58] At page 374. S

There is an avalanche of authorities on the interpretation of certain provisions of the Constitution through the literal or plain meaning rule by the Supreme Court of Nigeria. Of recent is the judgment of Tobi, JSC in the *Federal Republic of Nigeria* v. *Anache*[59] where the learned justice, on the meaning of 'State' in section 15(5) of the 1999 Constitution, said:

> I think this court dealt with the issue in *A.G. of Ondo State* v. *A.G Federation* (supra) Uwaifo JSC, appropriately dealt with the issue when he said o page 392 of that report, the Federal Republic of Nigeria shall be a State based on the principles of democracy and social justice. It is clear that it is the Federal Republic of Nigeria, as a State, that is looked upon under the constitution to take steps, or perhaps to spearhead the policy, so I entirely agree with the above constitution. It cannot be otherwise. It can move a bit further. Section 14(1) which defines a State in terms of the Federal Republic of Nigeria is a sub-section in Chapter II of the Constitution on Fundamental Objectives and Directive Principles of State Policy. The word 'State' in section 15(5) immediately after section 14 in the same Chapter II of the Constitution on Fundamental Objectives and Direct Principles of State Policy cannot bear any other meaning. The Federal Republic of Nigeria, as a State, is wider in operational scope than the definition of government in section 318(1) of the Constitution, as it conveys the meaning in section 1 of the Constitution. Words used in proximate sections will be presumed to have the same meaning and will be so construed unless it is clear from the particular section that the word is used in a completely different meaning. This, he said, is a correct canon of statutory interpretation. From whichever side one looks at the coin, the construction placed on section 15(5) by Uwaifo, JSC is correct.[60]

In the same vein, Uwaifo JSC, in *Awuse* v. *Odili*[61] said, while construing the meaning of 'decision' in section 318(1) of the 1999 Constitution of State said:

> ...there was no comparable applicable provision which defined 'decision' in both the 1979 and 1999 Constitution in Sections 277(1) and 318(1) respectively which is:

---

[59] (1993) 7 N.W.L.R. (Pt 308) 7171
[60] Ibid at page 72-73
[61] (2004) 6 W.R.N. 24

> 'Decision' means, in relation to a court, any determination of that court and includes judgment, decree, order, conviction, sentence, or recommendation. That definition does not distinguish between an interlocutory decision and a final decision in an election petition.

Apart from the rule providing that words of a statute must be given its liberal meaning, it was also stated that provisions or sections should not be read in isolation from the other parts of the statute or constitution. In other words, the statute or constitution should be read as a whole in order to determine the intendment of the makers of the statute or constitution. This was the view of Uwais, CJN in *P.D.P.* v. *I.N.E.C*,[62] quoted with approval by Bulkachuwa JCA in *A.G. of The Federation* v. *All Nigerian Peoples Party*.[63] This view was also supported by the Court of Appeal in *Mwana* v. *U.B.N.*[64] Per Mohammed JCA when the respected Jurist said, *inter alia*:

> If the words of the stature are in themselves precise and unambiguous, no more is necessary than to expand those words in their natural and ordinary sense, as the words themselves in such case best declare the intention of the legislature.[65]

What the foregoing simply connotes is that the court should be careful in ascribing another meaning to unambiguous and clear words in the statute because an attempt to do so will frustrate and render useless the primary intendment of the legislature.

In summary, it has been shown that the plain meaning Rule has evolved many explanatory riders, sub-rules, and a host of presumptions of legislative intent into which it is not proposed to enter here. None of these presumptions is binding for a variety of reasons. Some of these are that:

1. there is no order of precedence between conflicting presumptions;
2. presumptions themselves are often doubtful, being the subject of contradictory judicial pronouncements;

[62] (2001) 27 W.R,N, 62
[63] (2003) 27 W.R.N. 62
[64] (2003) 28 W.R.N. 142
[65] Dias, "Jurisprudence" 173

3. in case of conflict with a presumption, a court may adopt an interpretation without referring to the presumption, and,
4. there is no means of resolving a conflict between a presumption and the purpose of a statute.

One could validly state that the Supreme Court of Nigeria, as the final arbiter in a conflict situation, had, through the cases, applied the above sub-rules, and with regard to the application of the literal rule of interpretation of the statute, the Supreme Court of Nigeria is a force to be reckoned with.

In the case of *Dapianlong* v. *Dariye*,[66] the Supreme Court of Nigeria, while interpreting the 1999 Constitution, held that:

> ...mere technical rules of interpretation of statutes are to some extent inadmissible in a way so as to defeat the principle of government enshrined in the constitution. And where the question is whether the constitution has used an expression in the wider or narrow sense, in my view, this court should whenever possible and in response to the demands of justice, lean to the broader interpretation unless there is something in the text or in the rest of the constitution that narrower interpretation will best carry out the objects and purposes of the constitution." See the case of *Rabiu* v. *The State.*[67]

In interpreting Section 232 of the 1999 Constitution, the Supreme Court held that:

> it is now well settled that the duty of this court and indeed, any other court, is to interpret the words contained in the constitution, and any statute in their ordinary and literal meaning. Certainly, it is not the duty of the court to go outside words used in a statute and import an interpretation which may be or is convenient to it or to the parties or to one of the parties.[68]

Again, the Supreme Court reinstated the principles guiding the interpretation of statutes when it held that:

---

[66] (2007) 4 S.C. (Part III) 118 at 176 and 177.
[67] (1980) 8-11 S.C. 130 at 148 - 149
[68] *A.G Kano* v. *A.G. Federation* (*supra*) at page 79.

> law should be given their correct and grammatical interpretation. The provision of law should be viewed in its simple form and interpreted within its ambit and no extraneous matters should be introduced into it to give it a meaning different from what the legislature intended it to be. If such happens, then the law will be wrongly construed, and its purpose will fall outside the intendment of the legislature.[69]

The Golden Rule

The proponents of the literal rule of interpretation of statute argue that as a cardinal rule of interpretation, the meaning of words used in a statute and the intention of the legislature enacting the words can be properly understood after full consideration of the whole statute. This is more so when construing the meaning of words used in any part of a written constitution. Thus, the courts have stressed that while the meaning of words used in a written constitution must be deciphered from the constitution itself, such meaning can best be obtained after reading the constitution as a whole so as not to defeat the intention of the framers of the constitution.

An appreciation of some of the difficulties inherent in the 'Literal Rule' led to a courteous departure styled the "Golden Rule." The corpus of this rule is that the literal sense of words should be adhered to unless this would lead to absurdity, in which case, the literal meaning may be modified. It contradicts the Literal Rule, according to which, as explained, the plain meaning has to be adhered to even to the point of absurdity. The difficulty of deciding when words are plain and when they are not already been mentioned. Presumably, for the purpose of the rule now being considered, the words, though plain, should not be too plain where the apparent, plain meaning would lead to a result too unfair to be countenanced.[70]

Lord Reid aptly put it in *Luke* v. *I.R.C* as follows:

> To apply the words literally is to defeat the obvious intention of the legislature and to produce a wholly unreasonable result. To achieve the obvious intention and to produce a reasonable result we must do some

---

[69] *A.G. Anambra* v *A.G. Federation* (*supra*) page 219-220.
[70] Ibid 173 – 174s

> violence to the words...the general principle is well settled. It is only when the words are absolutely incapable of a construction which will accord with the apparent intention of the provisions and will avoid a wholly unreasonable result that the words of the enactment must prevail.[71]

There exists a paucity of judicial authority in the application of the Golden rule of interpretation under the referential approach. Noteworthy also is the fact that the basis of the employment of this rule is premised on the fact that most of the cases in which the literal rule was applied had, at one time, or the other, a dose of the application of the Golden Rule of interpretation of the statute.

The Nigeria *locus classicus* on the application of the Golden Rule of interpretation of the statute was the case of *Chief Obafemi Awolowo v. Alhaji Shehu Shagari and others.*[72] The two major issues for determination, *inter alia*, before the Supreme Court, were:

- that the Election Tribunal misdirected itself in law in construing two-thirds of 19 states as 12⅔ instead of 13 states when in law and especially within the context of Section 34(1)(c)(ii) of the Electoral Decree 1977 as amended, a State being a corporate body or a legal person cannot be fractionalized;
- that the Election Tribunal misdirected itself when it held that the dominant requirement in the election is the number of votes cast in each of the States, two-thirds State would be synonymous with two-thirds of the total votes cast in that State and not the physical or territorial area of such State.

The Supreme Court, while enunciating on the canon of interpretation applicable to this situation, stated that:

> it is also relevant to point out that anybody called upon to interpret any kind of statute should not for any reason, attach to its statutory provision, a meaning which the words of the statute cannot reasonably bear. If the words are capable of more than one meaning then the person interpreting the statute can choose between these meanings but beyond that, he must not go....Where there are two possible meanings conveyed by words of a

---

[71] (1963) A.C. 557

[72] (1979) All N.L.R. 120

> statute, it is the most reasonable one that should be adopted. Where the other meanings lead to absurdity or evince internal contradiction, that meaning should be dropped for the first as the legislature never intends to be absurd or contradictory. The word "each" in the Sub-section (1)(c) of Section 34(a) qualifies a whole state and not a fraction of a State and to interpret it otherwise is to overlook, the disharmony between the word "each" and the fraction "two-thirds" Two-thirds of nineteen, to avoid any disharmony gives thirteen.[73]

From the foregoing, it could easily be deduced that if absurdity is considered at all, it is apparently judged as at the time when the statute was passed. It could also be noted that the rule is hardly suited to giving effect to social policies. The paucity of authority reflects the uncertainty of its application. This is to further substantiate the fact that the absence of a coherent set of rules of interpretation is best seen when judges adopt opposing canons in the same case. In a nutshell, the referential approach, which encompasses the Literal or Plain Meaning Rule and the Golden Rule, is usually interchangeably applied, but most often, reliance is placed on the Literal Rule of interpretation because of its flexibility, compared with the rigidity and uncertainty of the Golden Rule of interpretation of the statute.

The Purposive Approach

Statutes are generally of indefinite duration, and consideration of them in this way takes account of their changing functions and functioning. It has also been pointed out that words possess an inner core of agreed application surrounded by a fringe of unsettled applications. This is the corpus of the purposive approach in the arena of rules of interpretation which has the 'Mischief Rule.'

The Mischief Rule

The third main traditional rule of interpretation of the statute, which is also the earliest of all canons of statutory interpretation, and which has

[73] Ibid., page 122-124

been pitched under the tent of the purposive approach, is the Mischief Rule of Interpretation of Statute.

The corpus of this rule of interpretation was long laid down in the old *Heydon's case* in 1584, where it was unanimously resolved by Sir Roger Manwood that:

> For the sure and true interpretation of all statutes in general, be they penal, or beneficial, restrictive enlargement of the common law, four things are to be discerned and considered viz:
>
> (1) What was the common law before the making of the act.
> (2) What was the mischief and defect for which the common law did not provide.
> (3) What remedy hath parliament resolved and appointed to cure the disease of the commonwealth.
> (4) The true reason of the remedy and then the office of all the judge is always to make such construction as shall suppress the mischief and advance the remedy, and suppress subtle invention and evasions for the continuance of the mischief and 'pro commode,' and add force and life to the cure and remedy according to the true intent of the maker of the act '*pro bono publico*.'[74]

The Supreme Court of Nigeria had fully incorporated the foregoing statement of The English Court into our legal system. This approach may pose a danger of introducing greater uncertainty into law because the object of the statute is gotten by the perusal of the language of the statute in view of the previous laws and the general knowledge of the social conditions.

The Mischief Rule was restated in the Nigerian case of *I.B.W.A Ltd* v. *Imano.*[75] Karibi Whyte JSC while adopting the Mischief Rule of Statutory Interpretation in interpreting the provision of Order 5 Rule 6 of the High Court of Lagos State (Civil Procedure) Rules, 1972 and Order 2 and 5 of the old High Court of Lagos (Civil Procedure) Rules, in *Kolawole* v. *Alberto*[76] stated thus:

---

74 3 Co Rep 7a at 7b
75 (1988) 2 N.W.L.R. (Pt 85) 633
76 (1989) 1 N.W.L.R. (Pt. 98) 382

> It is a well-known principle of construction that where the legislator uses words different from those originally used, he is to be presumed to have intended a different meaning. Thus, the 1972 rule must be taken as an amelioration of the 1948 Rules, because whereas a Writ of Summons not served within twelve months does not become void under the 1979 rules because the phrase "no write shall be in force" in order 5 Rule 6 means no more than not to have effect for the purpose of service under the Old Rule, Order 2 Rule 5, a Writ of Summons not served within twelve months becomes void.[77]

However, in line with the foregoing, Belgore JSC laid the rule more emphatically in *Ugu* v. *Tabi*[78] thus:

> Whenever there is ambiguity, and the intention of the legislation is unclear as to the mischief the law is supposed to obviate, the court can look outside the statute for the aid of construction. The previous legislation repealed or amended, the mischief in the previous law sought to be cured by the legislature or lawmaker, and the history of the social, economic, and political changes that the legislature sought to address will come in handy as an aid to the construction.

More recently, Uwaifo JSC in *Attorney General of Lagos State* v. *Attorney General of the Federation & 35 Ors,*[79] while commenting on the power of the court to take into account relevant constitutional conference committees' discussion, recommendation, and resolution in determining the meaning of statutory or constitutional provision stated thus:

> This court is entitled to take account of and use such material or information which it considers will help it to determine the true intendment of a statutory or constitutional provision in a purposive interpretive approach; or, which will lead it to assess the correctness of a meaning it has, through the usual canons of interpretation, given to such a provision. This is particularly so of a provision which is either ambiguous or seems to have become controversial.

---

[77] At page 688

[78] (1997) N.WL.R. (Pt. 513) page 368

[79] (2003) 35 W.R.N. 97

The effect of all these prominent and landmark judgments of the Supreme Court is that the days when the courts would be hampered by the application of an appropriate canon of interpretation to statutory provisions. Nowadays, the courts lean more on the use and employment of the liberal rule of the interpretation where the application of any of the other rules would result in manifest injustice to either of the parties to the suit before it.

This was summarized by Obaseki, JSC, in *Attorney-General of Bendel State* v. *Attorney General of the Federation*[80] while noting that they are explicitly presented as being principles rather than rules. In fact, if they were to be read as rules, important contradictions between several of them would be immediately apparent. Therefore, they should be understood as complementary to each other rather than as rivals among which one was chosen. He said:

> In the interpretation and construction of our 1979 Constitution, one must bear the following principles of interpretation in mind:
>
> 1. Effect should be given to every word;
> 2. A construction nullifying a specific clause will not be given to the construction unless absolutely required by the context;
> 3. A constitutional power cannot be used by way of condition to attain unconstitutional result;
> 4. The language of the constitution, where clear and unambiguous, must be given its plain evident meaning;
> 5. The constitution of the Federal Republic of Nigeria is an organic scheme of government to be dealt with as an entirety; a particular provision cannot be severed from the rest of the constitution;
> 6. While the language of the constitution does not change the changing circumstances of a progressive society for which it was designed to yield new and fuller import to its purpose;
> 7. A constitutional provision should not be construed so as to defeat its evident purpose;
> 8. Words are the common signs that mankind make use of to declare their intention one to another, and when the words of a man express his meaning plainly and distinctly and perfectly, there is no occasion to have recourse to any other means of interpretation;

---

[80] (1981) S.C.1

9. The principles upon which the constitution was established, rather than the direct operation of the literal meaning of the words used, measure the purpose and scope of its provisions;
10. Words of the constitution are, therefore, not to be read with stultifying narrowness.

The above aptly summarizes the current approach to the interpretation of statutes where the present crop of Supreme Court Justices draws inspiration.

OTHER AIDS TO INTERPRETATION

Apart from the three major principles of interpretation hidden under the canopy of the Referential and Purposive Approaches, there are other maxims that aid statutory interpretations. They are hereunder discussed.

The *Ejusdem Generis* Rule

This rule is to the effect that where a list of specific items is followed by a general clause, the general clause is deemed to be limited to the things of the same kind as those specified. The relevance and importance of this rule were more expanded by the Supreme Court recently in the case of *Ojukwu* v. *Obasanjo*,[81] where Edozie, JSC, quoting from Maxwell on the Interpretation of Statutes[82] and also quoting with particular reference to the provisions of section 137(1) 1999 Constitution of the Federal Republic of Nigeria stated as follows:

> The *ejusdem generis* rule is an interpretation rule which the court applies in an appropriate case to confine the scope of general words which follow special words as used in a statutory provision or document within the genius of those special general words. In the construction of statutes, therefore, general terms following from particular ones apply only to such persons or things as are *ejusdem generic* with those understood from the language of the statute to be confined to the particular terms. In other words, the general words or terms are to be read as comprehending only things of the same kind as that designated by the preceding particular

[81] (2004) 7 S.C. (Pt. 1) 117
[82] 12th Edition, p. 287

expression unless there is something to show that a wider sense was intended.[83]

The use of extraneous factors to determine the meaning of legislative provisions has, by the foregoing decision, been accepted as a means of determining legislative intentions as may be contained in the relevant provisions of a statute. The major bone of contention in the above case was the interpretation of Section 137(1) of the 1999 Constitution of the Federal Republic of Nigeria, which has been so elected on two previous occasions. It further focused on the interpretation of the word "office" and "president" as contained in that section.

Succinctly put, it has been noted that the importation of the *ejusdem generis* rule is often because of draftsmen's intention to cover a wide range of similar circumstances, usually using two or three particular examples, to create a rule followed by a general expression like "or other places," "or other lawful purpose", etc. They mean to extend the operation of the law to all particular circumstances with the rule created.

The Blue Pencil Rule

The "blue pencil" rule is applied to sever a part of legislation that is good in the sense that it is valid from the part that is bad in that it is invalid. That is, the blue pencil is run over the part that is bad. If what remains of the impugned legislation, that is, that part that is good, can stand, then it is applied. But if what remains cannot stand on its own, the impugned legislation is declared invalid.

Although this rule is of English jurisprudence origin, it found favour in the Nigerian case of *Balewa* v. *Doherty*[84] where Lord Delvin's statement was quoted with approval. In the more recent case of *A.G. Abia State* v. *A.G. Federation*[85] Kutigi, JSC, while delivering the lead

[83] (2002) 5 S.C. (Pt. 1) 63
[84] (1963) 1 All N.L.R. 949
[85] (2002) 3 S.C. 106

judgment on some aspects of the Electoral Act 2001, which contravenes some provisions of the constitution, had the following to say:

> There is no special provision in the constitution giving to the court any power of interpretation greater than that which flows from the ordinary rule of construction. The question is, therefore, whether the good can be severed from the bad and so survives. Clearly, it cannot here be done under the 'blue pencil' rule. There is no excess which can be struck out...but where there is the slightest doubt about what parliament would have intended, their Lordships cannot speculate. They have themselves no legislative power and they cannot rewrite the Act.[86]

The corpus of the 'blue pencil' rule speculates that where certain sections of a statute have been impugned and declared null and void and are struck out, the good can be severed from the bad, and the Act can survive. In the above case, it was held that it is part of Part II and all of Part IV of the Act that was affected. The remaining Parts on National Register of Voters and Voter's Registration, Political Parties, Electoral Offenses, Determination of Election Petitions, and Miscellaneous Provisions could stand on their own without the affected parts.

In essence, the purpose of the blue pencil rule is to delete some aspects of a statutory provision that is not in conformity with the intendment of the legislature. But going by the above decisions of the Supreme Court, such attempts would make nonsense of the effects of the legislature who had thought and deemed it fit to include the seemingly offending provisions of the statute.

Therefore, the Supreme Court has been very careful in its application of this rule as, in most cases, it works injustice to the parties to the suit.

A cursory look into the foregoing methods of interpretation of statutes applied by the Supreme Court of Nigeria so far tilts to the new approach toward statutory interpretation, and this is referred to as the plain and ordinary meaning rule of interpretation of statutes. It is, however, noteworthy that certain changes have occurred in the judicial

[86] At page 164

formulation of the three rules discussed under the two approaches to interpretation mentioned earlier.

Presently, there is only one principle or approach, namely, the words of an Act are to be read in their entire context, in their grammatical and ordinary sense, harmoniously with the scheme of the Act and the intent of the parliament. This approach is essentially an ordinary meaning approach, but ordinary meaning in total context. Words in themselves do not exist *in vacuo*. They exist along with other words, which must all be considered in totality.

More recently, the Supreme Court, in *Okolie* v. *Legal Practitioners Disciplinary Committee,*[87] while interpreting Section 12(7) of the Legal Practitioners' Act which specifically provides that a person to whom a directive given by the disciplinary committee of the Body of Benchers relates may at any time within 28 days from the date of service on him of the notice of the direction appeal against the direction to the Supreme Court held that:

> The language of the provisions is clear and unequivocal as to which court the aggrieved person should file his notice of appeal. It is at the Supreme Court. Any interpretation to the contrary may lead to an absurd situation by which the appellant may be deprived of his right of appeal as he may not be able to successfully go to the Court of Appeal.[88]

In view of the foregoing, it is hereby suggested that the context in which a word is used is an important aid toward its interpretation. Bearing in mind that a series of criticisms have been levelled against the search for legislative intent whilst trying to interpret, such interpretation should be looked at from different angles. What the courts are doing when interpreting contemporary statutes may be different from what they do when interpreting old statutes. As for interpreting contemporary statutes, the Supreme Court usually feels the pulse of society. The justices, themselves, are part of the society, and

[87] (2005) 3-4 S.C. 49
[88] At page 94

they can bring a more realistic interpretation of the statute when interpreting a contemporary statute.

In the same vein, whether a statute is contemporary or medieval, or pre-medieval, the interpretation given to it by a judge cannot but be influenced by the personality of the judge, which personality will be influenced by the economic, sociological, political, and environmental factors affecting the judge. A typical example was the decision in the famous case of *Ryland's* v. *Fletcher* where the background and past experience of the judge clearly influenced his decision.

All these varying factors can adequately be taken into consideration whilst proposing the plain meaning rule, which will definitely meet modern realities and satisfy the end of justice since society itself is not static.

The Supreme Court has recently put the position succinctly in the most recent case of *Ojukwu* v. *Obasanjo.*[89] Uthman Mohammed JSC, while reading the lead judgment, commented on the interpretation of Section 137(1)(b) of the 1999 Constitution of the Federal Republic of Nigeria thus:

> Section 137(1)(b) of 1999 Constitution is very clear. Even a layman can understand the intention of the framers of that provision. In interpreting the provision of the constitution, the language of the constitution, where clear and unambiguous, must be given its plain evident meaning.

He went further to quote Uwais, CJN's statement on the guiding principle for interpreting the provisions of the constitution in *P.D.P.* v. *I.N.E.C.*[90] thus:

> It is settled that in interpreting the provision or section of a statute or indeed the constitution, such provisions or section should not be read in isolation of the other parts of the constitution, in other words, the statute or constitution should be read as a whole in order to determine the intendment of the makers of the statute or the constitution.[91]

---

[89] *Supra* at page 124

[90] (1999) 7 S.C. (Pt. 11) 30

[91] *Ojukwu* v. *Obasanjo* (*supra*) 30

In the final analysis, one could safely conclude that the Supreme Court of Nigeria, while exercising its constitutional role of interpreting the provision of the Constitution of the Federal Republic of Nigeria, 1999 as conferred on it by section 233(2)(b) of the 1999 Constitution, has effectively done so through the cases.

By the above submission, it could be seen that even the Supreme Court has, through the cases, directly and indirectly, held that the plain meaning rule should be adhered to in as much as it meets modern realities and conforms with the primary law as intended by the legislature or parliament.

THE COURT OF APPEAL

In the hierarchy of courts in Nigeria, the Court of Appeal is next on the line after the Supreme Court of Nigeria. The decision of the Court of Appeal is binding on all other courts below it. The Court of Appeal is composed of the President of the Court of Appeal and other justices of the Court of Appeal not being less than forty-nine.

Jurisdiction of the Court of Appeal

Like the Supreme Court of Nigeria, the Court of Appeal has both original and appellate jurisdiction. A careful examination of the constitutional provisions conferring jurisdiction on the Court of Appeal will reveal that the Court of Appeal is primarily a court of appellate jurisdiction. The original jurisdiction of the Court of Appeal is essentially limited to election petition matters.

Original Jurisdiction of the Court of Appeal

Section 239(1) of the Constitution provides for the original jurisdiction of the Court of Appeal. By the provisions of that section, the court of Appeal has exclusive original jurisdiction to hear and determine any question as to whether –

(a) Any person has been validly elected to the office of President or Vice President under the Constitution; or,

(b) The term of office of the President or Vice-President has ceased; or,

(c) The office of President or Vice-President has become vacant.[92]

Appellate Jurisdiction of the Court of Appeal

Section 240 of the 1999 Constitution provides for the appellate jurisdiction of the Court of Appeal. By that section, the Court of Appeal has exclusive jurisdiction to hear and determine appeals from the: (1) Federal High Court; (2) the High Court of the Federal Capital Territory, Abuja; (3) the High Court of a state; (4) the Sharia Court of Appeal of the Federal Capital Territory, Abuja; (5) the Sharia Court of Appeal of a State; (6) the Customary Court of Appeal of the Federal Capital Territory, Abuja; (7) the Customary Court of Appeal of a State; and, (8) a court-martial or other tribunals as may be prescribed by an Act of the National Assembly.

Appeals as of Right

Section 241(1) of the 1999 Constitution appeals lie as of right to the Court of Appeal from decisions of the Federal High Court or a High Court in the following cases:

(a) Final decisions in any civil or criminal proceedings before the Federal High Court or a High Court sitting at first instance;

(b) Decisions in any civil or criminal proceedings, where the ground of appeal involves questions of law alone;

(c) Decisions in any civil or criminal proceedings on questions as to the interpretation or application of this Constitution;

(d) Decisions in any civil or criminal proceedings on questions as to whether any of the provisions of Chapter IV of this Constitution has been, is been or is likely to be, contravened in relation to any person;

(e) Decisions in any criminal proceedings in which the Federal High Court or a High Court has imposed a sentence of death;

(f) Decisions made or given by the Federal High Court or a High Court –

(i) Where the liberty of a person or the custody of an infant is concerned;

[92] *Buhari* v. *Obasanjo* (No.3)(2004) 1 W.R.N. 1

(ii) Where an injunction or the appointment of a receiver is granted or refused;

(iii) In the case of a decision determining the case of a creditor or the liability of a contributory or other officers under any enactment relating to companies in respect of misfeasance or otherwise;

(iv) In the case of a decree nisi in a matrimonial or a decision in an admiralty action determining liability, and

(v) In such other cases as may be prescribed by any law in force in Nigeria

By Section 241(2) of the 1999 Constitution provides that nothing in the foregoing confers any right of appeal:

(a) From a decision of the Federal High Court or any High Court granting unconditional leave to defend an action;

(b) From an order absolute, for the dissolution or nullity of marriage in favour of any party who, having had time and opportunity to appeal from the decree nisi on which the order was founded, has not appealed from that decree nisi; and,

(c) Without leave of the Federal High Court or a High Court or of the court of Appeal, form a decision of the Federal High Court, or High Court made with the consent of the parties or as to costs only.

Appeals with Leave

In all other cases and subject to the provisions of section 241 and subject to the provisions of section 241 discussed above, appeals lie from decisions of the Federal High Court or a High Court to the Court of Appeal with leave of either the lower court or the Court of Appeal. In determining an application for leave to appeal in respect of any civil or criminal proceedings in which an appeal has been brought to the Federal High Court or a High Court from any other court, the court of Appeal may dispense with oral hearings and base its decision on the records of proceedings, if the Court of Appeal is of the opinion that the interests of justice do not require an oral hearing.

Section 243(1) and (2) of the 1999 Constitution provide for the exercise of the right of appeal from the Federal High Court, National

Industrial Court, or a High Court in respect of civil and criminal matters:

(a) In the case of civil proceedings at the instance of a party thereto, or with the leave of the Federal High Court or the High court or the Court of Appeal at the instance of any other person having an interest in the matter, and in the case of criminal proceedings at the instance of an accused person, or, subject to the provisions of the Constitution and any powers conferred upon the Attorney General of the Federation or the Attorney General of a State to take over and continue or to discontinue such proceedings, at the instance of such other authorities or persons as may be prescribed;

(b) In accordance with any Act of the National Assembly and rules of court for the time being in force regulating the powers, practice, and procedure of the court of Appeal.

(1) An appeal shall lie from the decision of the National Industrial Court as of right to the Court of Appeal on questions of Fundamental Rights as contained in Chapter 1V of this Constitution as it relates to matters upon which the National Industrial Court has jurisdiction.

By virtue of Section 243(2), the right of appeal is removed with respect to issues to which the National Industrial Court has jurisdiction to determine, except when human rights are implicated in the issues before the National Industrial Court. It is rather curious that the National Industrial Court became implicitly the court of last resort in respect of issues and matters for which it has jurisdiction.

Appeals from Sharia Court of Appeal, Customary Court of Appeal, and Code of Conduct Tribunal

By Section 244(1) of the Constitution, appeals lie as of right from decisions of a Sharia Court of Appeal to the Court of Appeal in civil proceedings with respect to any question of Islamic personal law which the Sharia Court of Appeal is competent to decide. This right of appeal is exercisable:

(a) At the instance of a party thereto or, with the leave of the Sharia Court of Appeal or of the Court of Appeal, at the instance of any other person having an interest in the matter, and,

(b) In accordance with an Act of the National Assembly and rules of court for the time being in force regulating the powers, practice, and procedure of the Court of Appeal.

Also, by Section 245(1) and (2) of the Constitution, appeals lie as of right from decisions of a Customary Court of Appeal to the Court of Appeal in civil proceedings with respect to any question of customary law and such other matters as may be prescribed and such other matters as may be prescribed by an Act of the National Assembly. Such right of appeal is exercisable:

(a) At the instance of a party thereto, or with the leave of the customary court of appeal or of the court of appeal, at the instance of any other persona having an interest in the matter; and,

(b) In accordance with an Act of the National Assembly and rules of court for the time being in force regulating the powers, practice, and procedure of the court of appeal.

By Section 246(1) of the 1999 constitution, appeals lie as of right to the Court of Appeal from decisions of the Code of Conduct Tribunal established in the Fifth Schedule to the Constitution. Similarly, appeals lie as of right from decisions of the National Assembly Election Tribunals and Governorship and Legislative Houses Election Tribunals on any question as to whether –

(i) Any person has been validly elected as a member of the National Assembly or of a House of Assembly of a State under the Constitution;

(ii) Any person has been validly elected to the office of Governor or Deputy Governor; or,

(iii) The term of office of any person has ceased, or the seat of any such person has become vacant.

Section 246(2) of the Constitution empowers the National Assembly to confer jurisdiction upon the Court of Appeal to determine appeals from any decision of any other court of law or tribunal established by the National Assembly. By Section 246(1) and (3) of the 1999 Constitution, the decisions of the Court of Appeal in respect of appeals arising from election petitions are final.[93]

The Court of Appeal, for administrative purposes, is divided into judicial divisions, each presided over by a Presiding Justice. However, the law recognizes only one Court of Appeal, and decisions of any of the judicial divisions are treated as decisions of the court.

For administrative convenience, the court is divided into judicial divisions, which sit in various parts of the country, namely, Abuja, Lagos, Enugu, Kaduna, Ibadan, Benin, Jos, Calabar, Ilorin, Port Harcourt, Owerri, Sokoto, Yola, Ekiti, Akure, and Makurdi.

THE FEDERAL HIGH COURT

There is a Federal High Court in each state of the Federation and the Federal Capital Territory. Each is made up of a Chief Judge and such other number of judges as the State House of Assembly or the National Assembly (in the case of the High Court of the Federal Capital Territory) may prescribe. The High Court of the various states has original jurisdiction over civil and criminal matters except for matters in respect of which any court has been vested with exclusive jurisdiction, making them the court with the widest jurisdiction under the constitution. The court is duly constituted with one judge. Each High court is divided into judicial divisions for administrative convenience.

Jurisdiction of the Federal High Court

Section 251 of the Constitution provides for the jurisdiction of the Federal High Court. It provides that notwithstanding anything to the contrary in the Constitution, and in addition to such other jurisdiction as may be conferred on it by an Act of the National Assembly, the

---

93 *Awuse* v. *Odili* (2004) 6 W.R.N. 1

Federal High Court has exclusive jurisdiction in civil causes and matters.

(a) Relating to the revenue of the Government of the Federation in which the said Government, its organs, or a person suing or being sued on its behalf is a party;

(b) Connected with or pertaining to the taxation of companies and other bodies established or carrying on business in Nigeria and all other persons subject to Federal taxation;

(c) Connected with or pertaining to customs and excise duties and export duties, including any claim by or against the Nigeria Customs Service or any member or officer thereof, arising from the performance of any duty imposed under any regulation relating to customs and excise duties and export duties;

(d) Connected with or pertaining to banking, banks, and other financial institutions, including any action between one bank and another, any action by or against the Central Bank of Nigeria arising from banking, coinage, legal tender, bills of exchange, letters of credit, promissory notes and other fiscal measures;

Provided that this paragraph shall not apply to any dispute between an individual customer and his bank in respect of the transactions between the individual customer and the bank.

(e) Arising from the operation of the Companies and Allied Matters Act or any other enactment replacing the Act or regulating the operation of companies incorporated under the Companies and Allied Matters Act.

(f) Any Federal enactment relating to copyright, patent, designs, trademarks and passing-off, industrial designs and merchandise marks, business names, commercial and industrial monopolies, combines and trusts, standards of goods and commodities, and industrial standards.

(g) Any admiralty jurisdiction, including shipping and navigation on the River Niger or River Benue and their effluents and on such other inland waterway as may be designated by any enactment to be an international waterway, all Federal ports (including the constitution and powers of the ports authorities for Federal ports) and carriage by sea.

(h) Diplomatic, consular, and trade representation;

(i) Citizenship, naturalization, and aliens, deportation of persons who are not citizens of Nigeria, extradition, immigration into and emigration from Nigeria, passports, and visas;

(j) Bankruptcy and insolvency;

(k) Aviation and safety of aircraft;

(l) Arms, ammunition, and explosives;

(m) Drugs and poisons;

(n) Mines and minerals (including oil fields, oil mining, geological surveys, and natural gas);

(o) Weights and measures;

(p) The administration or the management and control of the Federal Government or any of its agencies;[94]

(q) Subject to the provisions of the Constitution, the operation and interpretation of this Constitution in so far as it affects the Federal Government or any of its agencies;

(r) Any action or proceeding for a declaration or injunction affecting the validity of any executive of any executive or administrative action or decision by the Federal Government or any of its agencies; and,

(s) Such other jurisdiction civil or criminal and whether to the exclusion of any other court or not as may be conferred upon it by an Act of the National Assembly:

Provided that nothing in the provisions of paragraphs (p), (q), and (r) of this subsection shall prevent a person from seeking redress against the Federal Government or any of its agencies in action for damages; injunction, or specific performance where the action is based on any enactment, law or equity.

Section 28(3)(First Alteration) Act, 2010 grants additional jurisdiction to the Federal High Court. It provides that "Subject to the

---

[94] *University of Abuja* v. *Ologe* (1996) 4 N.W.L.R. 706

provisions of Section 254(1) and other provisions of this Constitution, the Federal High Court shall have jurisdiction to hear and determine the question as to whether the term of office of a member of the House of Assembly of a State, a Governor or Deputy Governor has ceased or become vacant."

It is clear from the wording of Section 28(3)(First Alteration) Act, 2010, which grants additional jurisdiction to the Federal High Court, that the jurisdiction granted by that section is not exclusive to the Federal High Court. Accordingly, the Federal High Court will share the jurisdiction granted by that section with a State High Court.

THE NATIONAL INDUSTRIAL COURT OF NIGERIA

Section 254A of the 1999 Constitution established the National Industrial Court. The National Industrial Court consists of the President and such number of Judges as may be prescribed by an Act of the National Assembly.

Jurisdiction of the National Industrial Court

S.254C(1) of the Constitution provides for the jurisdiction of the National Industrial Court. It provides that "Notwithstanding the provisions of sections 251, 257, 272, and anything contained in this constitution and in addition to such other jurisdiction to such other jurisdiction as may be conferred upon it by an Act of the National Assembly, the National Industrial Court shall have and exercise jurisdiction to the exclusion of any other court in civil causes and mattes:

(a) Relating to or connected with any labour, employment, trade unions, industrial relations arising from the workplace, the conditions of service, including health, safety, welfare, employee, worker, and matters incidental thereto or connected therewith;

(b) relating to, connected with, or arising from Factories Act, Trade Disputes Act, Trade Union Act, or law relating to labour, employment, industrial relations, workplace the Acts or any other enactment replacing the Acts or laws.

(c) relating to or connected with the grant of any order restraining any person or body from taking part in any strike, lock-out or any industrial action, or any action industrial action, or any conduct in contemplation or in furtherance of a strike, lock-out, or any industrial action and matters connected therewith or related thereto;

(d) relating to or connected with any dispute over the interpretation and application of the provisions of Chapter IV of this Constitution as it relates to any employment, labour, industrial relations, trade unionism, employer's association, or any other matter which the Court has jurisdiction to hear and determine;

relating to or connected with any dispute arising from national minimum wage for the federation or any part thereof and matters therewith or arising therefrom;

(f) relating to or connected with unfair labour practice or international best practices in labour, employment, and industrial relation matters;

(g)relating to or connected with any dispute arising from discrimination or sexual harassment at a workplace;

(h) relating to, or connected with. or pertaining to the application or interpretation of international labour standards;

(i) connected with or related to child labour, child abuse, human trafficking, or any matter connected therewith or related thereto;

(j) relating to the determination of any question as to the interpretation and application of any:

i. collective agreement;

ii award or order made by an arbitral tribunal in respect of a trade dispute or trade union dispute;

iii. award or judgment of the terms of settlement of any trade dispute;

iv. trade union dispute or employment dispute as may be recorded in a memorandum of trade union constitution, the constitution of an association of employers or any association relating to employment, labour, industrial relations, or workplace;

vi. dispute relating to or connected with any personnel matter arising from any free trade zone in the Federation or any parts thereof;

(k) relating to or connected with disputes arising from payment or non-payment of salaries, wages, pensions, gratuities, allowances, benefits, and any other entitlement of any employee, political or public office holder, judicial officer, or any civil or public servant in any part of the Federation and matters incidental thereto;

(i) relating to

i. appeals from decisions of the Registrar of Trade Unions or matters relating thereto or connected therewith;

ii appeals from the decisions or recommendations of any administrative body or commission of inquiry arising from or connected with employment, labour, trade union, or industrial relations; and

iii. such other jurisdiction, civil or criminal, and whether to the exclusion of any other court or not, as may be conferred upon it by an Act of the National Assembly.

(m) relating to or connected with the registration of collective agreements

(2) Notwithstanding anything to the contrary in this constitution, the National Industrial Court shall have the jurisdiction and power to deal with any matter connected with or pertaining to the application of any international convention, treaty, or protocol of which Nigeria has ratified relating to labour, employment, workplace, industrial relations or matters connected therewith.

It appears that Section 254C of the Constitution, which vested the National Industrial Court with jurisdiction, has altered the relationship between Nigerian municipal law and international law. This is because for an international treaty to become operative in Nigeria, such international treaty must be enacted into law by the National Assembly in consonance with the provisions of Section 12(1) of the Constitution. Section 12(1) provides that "No treaty between the Federation and any other country shall have the force of law except to the extent to which any such treaty has been enacted into law by the National Assembly." The purport of Section 254C of the Constitution is that international treaties relating to labour have a force of law in Nigeria upon ratification by Nigeria without first being enacted into law by the National Assembly.

THE SHARIA COURT OF APPEAL

There is a Sharia Court of Appeal for the Federal Capital Territory and any state that requires it. This court has appellate and supervisory jurisdiction in civil proceedings involving questions of Islamic personal law, which the court is competent to decide in accordance with the constitution. The court comprises of a Grand Khadi, and other Khadis as the National Assembly or State Houses of Assembly (as the case may be) may prescribe.

Jurisdiction of the Sharia Court of Appeal

Section 262(1) of the Constitution provides for the jurisdiction of the Sharia Court of Appeal. In addition to such other jurisdiction as may be conferred on it by the National Assembly, the Sharia Court of Appeal shall exercise such appellate and supervisory jurisdiction in civil proceedings involving questions of Islamic personal law. The Sharia Court of Appeal shall be competent to decide:

(a) Any question of Islamic personal law regarding a marriage concluded in accordance with that law, including a question relating to the validity or dissolution of such marriage or a question that depends on such a marriage and relating to family relationship or the guardianship of an infant;

(b) Where all the parties to the proceeding are Muslims, any question of Islamic personal law regarding marriage, including the validity or dissolution of that marriage, regarding a family relationship, a foundling, or the guardianship of an infant;

(c) Any question of Islamic personal law regarding a *wakf,* gift, will, or succession where the endower, donor, testator, or deceased person is a Muslim;

(d) Any question of Islamic personal law regarding an infant, prodigal, or person of unsound mind who is a Muslim or the maintenance or the guardianship of a Muslim who is physically or mentally infirm; or

(e) Where all the parties to the proceedings, being Muslims, have requested the court that hears the case in the first instance to determine that case, or any other question, in accordance with Islamic personal law.

THE CUSTOMARY COURT OF APPEAL

There is a customary Court of Appeal for the Federal Capital Territory and any state that requires it. This court has appellate and supervisory jurisdiction in civil proceedings involving questions of customary law and it comprised of a president and such number of judges as the National Assembly or State Houses of Assembly (as the case may be) may prescribe.

Jurisdiction of the Customary Court of Appeal

Section 267 of the 1999 Constitution provides for the Jurisdiction of the Customary Court of Appeal of the Federal Capital Territory. It provides that "The Customary Court of Appeal of the Federal Capital Territory, Abuja shall, in addition to such other jurisdiction as may be conferred upon it by an Act of The National Assembly exercise such appellate and supervisory jurisdiction in civil proceedings involving questions of customary law."

HIGH COURT OF A STATE

Section 270(1) of the 1999 Constitution established the High Court of a State. By subsection (2)(a) and (b), the High Court of a State shall consist of "a Chief Judge of the State and such number of Judges of the High Court as may be prescribed by a law of the House of Assembly of the State."

Jurisdiction of the High Court of a State

Section 272(1) of the 1999 Constitution provides for the jurisdiction of the High Court of a State. It provides that:

> Subject to the provisions of section 251 and other provisions of this Constitution, the High Court of a State shall have jurisdiction to hear and determine any civil proceedings in which the existence or extent of a legal right, power, duty, liability, privilege, interest, obligation or claim is in issue or to hear and determine any criminal proceedings involving or relating to any penalty, forfeiture, punishment or other liability in respect of an offense committed by any person.

CONCLUSION

The Nigerian legal and court system is anchored on the common law system. However, the structure, hierarchy, jurisdiction, and appellate system of Nigerian courts reflect Nigeria's federal political structure. In recent times, there have been considerable efforts in the creation of specialized courts with limited jurisdiction to deal with special and technical issues which require special skills and competencies. This trend is likely to continue as Nigeria continues to develop, and the need for specialized courts emerges.

Chapter 14

NON-COURT SYSTEM OF DISPUTE SETTLEMENT IN NIGERIA

Juliana Omolegho Okani*

INTRODUCTION

From time immemorial, men have brought their differences or disputes to an end in a number of ways. The numerous ways of dispute settlement may be satisfactory or unsatisfactory to the parties. Increasingly, those with disputes have sought alternative means of resolving them. This alternate means include the non-court system of settlement of the dispute which is also known as the Extra-Judicial dispute settlement mechanism.

The system is an outside court settlement in which the parties do not resort to court or litigation but rather employ non-adjudicatory means to amicably settle their differences. Disputes vary in nature and origin. The disagreement between the parties may have arisen from contractual, personal, communal, family/marital, religious, corporate, or industrial relations. All of these can be settled amicably by adopting a non-judicial/outside court system of resolving the dispute.

Settlement is the peaceful resolution of a dispute between disputants either by themselves or by the intervention of a third party.[1] Where they are willing and ready to resolve their differences without going to court, and the dispute is peacefully settled, the result is usually satisfactory.[2] Extra-judicial settlement of disputes may be lawful or

---

* LL.M (Benin), Lecturer, Faculty of Law, Benson Idahosa University, Benin city.

[1] For example: family, relatives, friends, associates or other persons voluntarily or mutually agreed to by them.

[2] *Agoaka* v. *Ejiofor* (1972) 2 ECSLR 109.

unlawful. Persons who brought their dispute for an out-of-court settlement, and the institution before which they come, are enjoined to observe the principle of fair hearing.[3] Legal and satisfactory methods of resolving disputes discussed in this chapter include:

a) Alternative Dispute Resolution (ADR);[4]
b) Multi-door Court System;[5]
c) Statutory settlement of trade disputes;[6]
d) Customary Law Arbitration;

Other methods of dispute settlement that are considered unlawful are:

a) Trial by ordeal;
b) Trial by battle;
c) Jungle justice or constitution of "Kangaroo Court";
d) Self-help.

ALTERNATIVE DISPUTE RESOLUTION: ARBITRATION, CONCILIATION, MEDIATION

Alternative dispute resolution comprises of Arbitration, Mediation, and Conciliation. The mechanism commonly known as ADR[7] is the term given to various methods of resolving disputes in lieu of the traditional adversarial litigation process. The essence of the ADR is to restore peace to disputing parties. The ADR is neither a judicial nor adjudicatory method of ending a dispute, but to qualify as arbitration, the process of arbitration must be conducted in a judicial manner. ADR is a legal, friendly, and satisfactory means of resolving disputes outside the regular court system. The person(s) to whom a reference to arbitration is made is called an arbitrator(s). At the conclusion of an arbitration proceeding and after a careful study of the evidence and arguments presented to the arbitral tribunal, it is obliged to set down a decision of

---

[3] *Audi alteram partem & nemo judex in causa sua (*which means first: to hear the other side, second not to be a judge in your own your own court).

[4] A system of settling disputes outside court/litigation process is ADR: Arbitration, Conciliation, and Mediation. They are regulated by Arbitration and Conciliation Act, Cap A 18, 2004.

[5] A court connected alternative dispute resolution, introduced through a partnership arrangement between Lagos State Government and the private sector initiative (security, justice & growth (SGJ) established in Lagos, Abuja, Kano and recently in Kwara.

[6] Statutory ADR is a procedure to settle disputes between employers and employees as provided in The "Trade Dispute Act"1976 now Cap T 18,2004.

[7] Ibid., n4.

the arbitration. This is called an "award".[8] We shall briefly examine each of the mechanisms.

Arbitration

Arbitration is an outside court settlement that requires the parties to a dispute to submit or refer the dispute to a person or persons known as arbitrator(s) for decision. It is an approved method of resolving a dispute without going to court. The practice of dispute settlement through the process of arbitration is not a new concept in Nigeria. Before the invasion of Africa by colonialists, Arbitration was in place as the first alternative dispute resolution mechanism to litigation. It was a well-known method of dispute resolution and was used for the settlement of all types of disputes.[9] Arbitral proceedings are not strictly a judicial process; therefore, they are not confined to the judicial realm but extend to the non-judicial system of resolving disputes. Where the parties decide to be heard in a judicial manner, it must be conducted in that manner. Arbitration may not be guided by formalities of judicial and rules of court (it is more of an informal process).

The evidence adduced by the parties may be oral or documentary. It can also take the form of maps, diagrams, or models to illustrate the property or thing in dispute. The provisions of the Evidence Act[10] do not apply to arbitral proceedings. An arbitral tribunal is expected to hear all the evidence which seems material, even if it is remote to the matter it is meant to settle. The legal effect is that if the tribunal admits evidence that ordinarily is inadmissible, its award is sustainable by the court. If, however, it rejects the evidence because it considers it immaterial, its award will be set aside.[11] The arbitrator settles the disputing parties' claims using principles of law, equity, and fairness. Arbitration has long been accepted as an alternative to a court settlement, particularly in the sphere of commerce and business.

---

[8] Section 25(2), ibid., n4.
[9] Idornigie, P.O., "Overview of ADR in Nigeria Arbitration," IJAMDM, (2007), Vol. 73, No.1, p.73.
[10] Evidence Act 2011.
[11] See *Nickall* v. *Warren* (1844) 6 Q.B.615, 618.

Arbitration has received a lot of approval because of its use to fast-track the pace of settlement of disputes. It is currently a means of facilitating the administration of civil matters in courts. As disputing parties resort to arbitration, the number of cases that go to court and are pending in court have greatly reduced. To further reduce the pressure on the courts, Multi-Door court system has been established in Lagos State, Abuja, Kano and most recently, Kwara. This multi-services and specialized administration of the justice system is also meant to reduce the congestion in the court, resolve disputes quickly and ensure that justice is delivered on time.

Meaning of Arbitration

Arbitration is the reference of a dispute or difference between not less than two parties for determination, after hearing both sides in a judicial or non-judicial manner by a person or persons other than a court of competent jurisdiction.[12] An exercise is not arbitration in the strict sense, if it does not answer to the above definition. An arbitration board appointed not to settle a dispute, but to merely determine the value of certain assets taken over by the government from certain companies, is not arbitration.[13] A person or persons to whom a reference to arbitration is made is called an arbitrator or arbitrators. His decision is called "award." Disputes that can be referred to arbitration must be justiciable issues which can be tried as civil matters. They must be disputes that can be compromised by way of accord or satisfaction.[14]

Types of Disputes for Arbitration

It is trite that criminal matters are subjects of public policy and, therefore, not to be referred to arbitration. An indictment for an offense of public nature is not a matter for arbitration. In *Q* v. *Blackmore*,[15] the defendant was indicted for non-repair of a public highway. The matter

---

[12] Halsbury's Laws of England, 3rd ed. Vol. 2 p. 2.

[13] Section 4, Ports (Amendment) Act 1969 See: *Nigerian Ports Authority* v. *Panalpina World Transport (Nig) Ltd & ors* (1974) 4 U.I.L.R 89.

[14] *Blake's case* (1606) 6 Co. Rep.436 in Ejiofor, G., *The Law of Arbitration in Nigeria*, (Lagos: Longman Nig., 2005) p16.

[15] (1850) 14 Q.B. 544.

was set down for hearing, and before the jury was empanelled, the prosecution and defendant agreed to refer the question of liability to arbitration. The arbitrator made his award to the effect that the defendant was guilty as charged and directed that he should pay the cost of reference to prosecution. The court held that the reference was illegal and therefore cost could not be recovered.

In *The Queen* v. *Harday*,[16] the court held that reference of an indictment for conspiracy and perjury to arbitration is illegal. Disputes that can be referred to arbitration must be issues that are justiciable and of a civil nature. They must be such that allow compromise. Examples are disputes about any real or personal property, breach of contract, or whether one or both parties have been discharged from further obligation to perform. Others are forms of a deed of separation between husband and wife. Compromise by either spouse in a suit for dissolution of marriage and other matrimonial actions are held not contrary to public policy or good morals and, therefore, with leave of court, could be referred to arbitration.

The court in *Absalom Ltd* v. *Great Western Garden Village Society Ltd* [17] held that "specific question of law, such as the construction of award, cannot be set aside merely because the decision is erroneous."

A common feature of arbitration is the mode of reference of matters to an arbitration process. The words by which the reference is made must be very clear and express so as not to import implied terms/interpretations.[18] The reference must sufficiently state that jurisdiction is conferred on the arbitrator. A typical arbitration clause may be set out as follows: "All disputes, differences or claims arising out of or in connection with or in relation to the contract shall be referred to a sole arbitrator." If a reference does not cover a claim, it may not be possible to arbitrate on it.

In common law, an agreement to refer a dispute to arbitration could be oral or in writing. Written agreements to arbitrate are exclusively governed by statutes, while oral agreements to arbitrate are

---

16 Ibid., p.529.

17 [1933] A.C. 592 p.607.

18 International Labour Organisation (ILO), Turin. A Training Package, (2002) p.10

regulated by the common law. The authority of the arbitrator appointed by the *parol* agreement can be revoked by either party at any time before the publication of the award. Customary arbitration is not regulated by the Arbitration and Conciliation Act.[19] Disputes arising from void transactions, such as wagering and gaming contracts cannot be referred to arbitration. Contrary to the legal position which limits the administration of criminal justice to criminal offenses, ADR is now being applied to criminal cases of treat to the security of life and property and the theft of huge sums of money looted by political office holders through plea bargaining.

The Value of Arbitration Agreement in Nigerian Statutes

Statutory arbitration arises out of a statute that provides that disputes in a particular sector must be settled as stipulated in the agreement clause. Some important investment statutes in Nigeria have introduced arbitration as a means of resolving investment disputes. This innovation is actually not peculiar to Nigeria, yet it has become a common feature to give legal and regulatory provisions to investment as it is in developing countries

Nigeria and other Third World capital-importing countries are considered high-risk investment climates by capital-exporting countries, and therefore, the latter seek to protect their investments by ensuring that settlement of disputes relating to foreign investments does not take place in the perceived high-risk capital importing host country. This may be attributed to the fact that legislations are not normally repealed on whims, as contracts are prone to cancelation, and such arbitration provisions are perceived as more secure in legislation than in contracts.

(1) Examples of Statutes that contain arbitration provisions in Nigeria include a) Petroleum Act[20] the clause stipulates thus:

(1) Any question or dispute in connection with any licence or lease to which this schedule applies between the Minister and the Licensee or

[19] Ibid., n3

[20] Regulation 41 which is part of the subsidiary regulator to the Act

Lessee (including a dispute as to payment of any fee, rent or royalty), *shall be settled by Arbitration* unless it relates to a matter expressly excluded from arbitration or expected to be at the discretion of the Minister - Public Enterprises (Privatization and Commercialization) Decree No. 28 1999

Section 270 of this law states:

> There is hereby established under this Decree an ad-hoc body to be known as the Public Enterprises Arbitration Panel (in this Decree referred to as "the Panel") which shall be responsible for Effecting prompt settlement of any dispute arising between an Enterprise and the Council or the Bureau.

(1)(c) Nigeria LNG (Fiscal Incentives, Guarantees and Assurances) Decree 1990

Section 22 states:

> In the event of any dispute in respect of a substantial matter arising from the provisions of the Decree, the aggrieved Shareholder(s) in the Company shall issue a letter of notification to Government formally notifying Government and the other shareholders of the dispute. The Government's representatives and one or more of the Company's Shareholders as the case may be, shall make serious efforts to resolve amicably such dispute. In the event of failure to reach amicable settlement within 90 days of the date of the letter of notification mentioned above, such dispute *may* be submitted to arbitration before the International Centre for the Settlement of Investment Disputes.

The Arbitration and Conciliation Act Cap 18, Laws of the Federation, 2004 shows that the Act contemplates only reference to arbitration agreed upon by parties. Section (1) states that every arbitration agreement shall be in writing contained (a) in documents signed by the parties; or (b) in an exchange of letters, telex, telegrams, or other means of communication that provides records of the agreement. Section 2 provides that unless a contrary intention is expressed, an arbitration agreement shall be irrevocable except by agreement of the parties or by leave of the court or a judge. This is only consistent with the fundamental and central understanding that the principles of arbitration rest upon an arbitral tribunal can only assume jurisdiction in a dispute between parties where such parties have freely consented to this. From the foregoing, it is obvious that arbitration provisions as they exist in our legislation are contrary to those very fundamental principles upon which arbitration thrives. The provisions are also incongruent with the Arbitration Act, which recognizes arbitration proceedings in Nigeria.

Capacity of Persons to Enter Agreement to Arbitrate

Capacity to enter into an agreement to arbitrate is co-extensive with the capacity to enter into contracts generally. Any person who is capable of entering into a contract may be a party to an arbitration agreement. A person, who has no capacity to contract *ab initio*, cannot enter into an arbitration agreement. Where the capacity to contract is qualified, the power to enter into an arbitration agreement is qualified to the same extent. An arbitration agreement made by an infant binds him only if it relates to the supply of necessaries or to a reasonable contract of service or otherwise for his benefit.[21] Apart from the circumstances mentioned, the agreement is voidable by the infant for as long as his infancy status last or within a reasonable time after attaining maturity. A married woman now has the capacity to enter into an agreement to arbitrate just like any other person *sui juris.* The parties are bound by the agreement.[22] In a formal or strict sense, arbitral proceedings are not a judicial process but are conducted in a judicial manner. The arbitrators receive the facts in dispute, intervene in an impartial manner by receiving evidence from disputants and their witnesses, consider the same and arrive at a decision (award). The award is binding on the parties.

---

[21] Sagay.I.E., *Nigerian Law of Contract* ed. (Ibadan: Spectrum Publishing, 1989) p.399.
[22] Section 1, Married Women's Property Law, 1958 Cap.76 Laws of Western Region of Nigeria 1959.

Where an agent duly recognized enters into an arbitration agreement on behalf of his principal, he does not become personally liable for the act performed. The operating principle is that which regulate agent/principal relationship in the Law contracts. The agent's authority may be expressed or arise by implication. Parties to the arbitration agreement are bound by it. An assignment is allowed where the subject is not of a personal nature. The concept of privity of contract applies in arbitration such that a third person who is not a party to the arbitration agreement or who is not an assignee cannot impose himself on the proceedings.[23]

An arbitration agreement can be enforced against a deceased party or the personal representatives. The death of a party does not preclude him from the obligation. Where the subject matter of arbitration is a tort arising from seduction, defamation, or inducement of a spouse to leave or remain apart from the other so as to claim damages on the grounds of adultery, the death of a party destroys the cause of action. On the contrary, the death of a party to an oral agreement revokes the authority of the arbitrator.[24]

Mediation

Mediation is the voluntary submission of a dispute to a third party, known as a mediator. It is a legal and statutory means to resolve disputes. Where disputing parties are unable to settle the dispute on their own through negotiation, they are enjoined to mediate. A mediator is usually a neutral person who takes an active part in trying to bring the dispute to an end. He is a person trusted and accepted by both parties to the dispute. His role is to help the parties reach a settlement. In mediation, parties must be willing to compromise on certain issues in order to attain a harmonious settlement. A mediator is free to use formal or informal means to achieve the goal. He does not suggest a solution to the parties. The settlements reached through mediation are not binding on the parties, and the mediator cannot compel them to reach a settlement. The contending parties are free to

[23] *Niger Progress Ltd.* v. *N.E. Lines Corporation* (1989) 3 NWLR (pt. 107) 68.
[24] Ibid., n8 p.6.

abide by the terms of settlement or resort to litigation for the enforcement of their legal rights. It is often used in settling political or boundary disputes. It is voluntary where he is mutually selected and acceptable by the parties. Mediation is statutory, where the parties are directed by a statute to invite or allow a third party to assist them in settlement of their differences.[25]

Purpose of Mediation

The purpose of mediation is not to judge or to hold one guilty and the other innocent; rather, it is to help the parties get to the root of their problems and devise their own solution. A mediator is free to introduce some special features to turn an adversarial win/lose situation into achieving a result.

A mediator helps people to talk to each other in ways that prevent misunderstandings. Ideally, people should emerge from the process feeling satisfied that their needs and interests have been taken into account. A mediator can help parties reach an agreement without questions and issues of admissibility. By so doing, parties in dispute can concentrate on what should be done in the future rather than punishment and revenge or delve into who is responsible for "what is a past."[26] Mediation, as a part of a broad range of processes designed as Alternate Dispute Resolution, is not intended to supplant court adjudication but rather to supplement it. Mediation is useful for resolving mini-dispute that never gets to court.[27]

Mediation: On Family Matters

Mediation plays a significant role in divorce proceedings.[28] The trend generally is to lessen court intervention in matrimonial matters.[29] Divorce itself is basically a paper exercise, and the majority of financial matters and matters relating to children. The consent of the parties is necessary for the intervention of a mediator. The 1990s (in England)

---

[25] Ibid., p. 45.

[26] Dorchester District Court Mediation Unit-in ILO Publication *ibid* n19 p.35.

[27] Standing Commit on Dispute Resolution: American Bar Association. *Ibid* 24 p. 35.

[28] Richard, W., and Akhtar, A., *Walker and Walker's English Legal System,* 10th ed.(New York: OUP 2008) p.469

[29] Ibid.

saw a general trend toward encouraging and requiring mediation in the context of family disputes. The same extended to children and a range of projects aimed to complement the judicial process.

The aim is to provide mediation as an alternative to the court process in child protection, fostering adoption, or handling cases between the parents, the careers, and local authorities.

Conciliation

Conciliation is a process whereby a neutral third party brings the disputing parties together in order for them to solve their problems. They inquire from the parties whether they are prepared to settle the dispute amicably. If the answer is positive, they then arranges a meeting with them. The conciliator's primary role is to keep the parties together, reduce their inflammatory rhetoric and tension, open channels of communication, and facilitate continued negotiations.[30] Conciliation involves not so much making suggestions to the two parties but rather providing a forum for discussion and procedural guidance to bring them together. The service rendered by a conciliator does not involve him unless both sides agree and not until internal procedures under the collective bargain have been exhausted.[31] A major difference between conciliation and arbitration is that the conciliator submits their opinion to the parties. They do not impose it on them. Outside the joint meeting, they may meet with each party separately to find out the point beyond which the party is not prepared to go. They conclude by drawing the terms of agreement/settlement, which for both parties to sign.

Benefits of ADR

It is primarily a voluntary process. It avoids the win-lose, with winner takes all culture of litigation, where relationships tend to be quicker and, in most cases, a less expensive mechanism for resolving disputes. It avoids the inflexibility and rigidity of court procedures. It provides a greater option for parties to conduct cases without legal representation.

---

[30] Defined by: American Arbitration Association in ILO Publications: ibid n26 p. 33

[31] Bowers, J. A., *supra* n23, p.520, TULR (c) A 1992 S. 210(1)

It creates greater opportunities for retaining control of a more congenial forum. Due to its consensual nature, it can offer a superior resolution than court judgments. It focuses on real needs rather than strict rights and obligations under the law. It is less easy for more powerful or wealthy parties to delay and wear down the opposition.

Multi-door Court System

Constraints by congestion in the courts, and resolve for swift and effective judgment, can be achieved if litigation is not the sole legal dispute resolution apparatus for settlement of cases in Nigeria.[32] The multi-door system of settlement is a non-traditional method of dispute resolution whose aim is to give support to the development of commercial ADR mechanisms. It is a court-connected alternative dispute resolution mechanism. Presently, the program exists in Lagos, Abuja, Kano, and, most recently, Kwara State. The focus is to improve the legal and regulatory environment for the private sector economy through a quick and cheaper means of getting redress instead of cueing up in the conventional courts for a number of years.

December 2002, a case was successfully resolved in three hours as against the litigation it had gone through for over three years. The case study is reported thus:

> A client who was being accused of copying a handbag design consulted a legal representative. The handbags were seized as litigation commenced. The design was not registered and therefore technically her client's case was meritorious, indeed, there was a court precedent confirming this position. There is also precedent showing that it may take up to 10 years before the Supreme Court may rule on the matter. Applying ADR tactics, the lawyer met with the Claimant's counsel and suggested settling the matter out of court which he agreed to, provided her client pay compensation to his client. She informed her client that he had excellent prospects of success if the matter continued in court but as a businessman, her client sought a practical and speedy resolution to the matter. As a result, the matter settled and potentially lengthy litigation proceedings were avoided.[33]

---

[32] Kehinde, Aina., Initiated the public/private partnership on the multi-door courthouse option to expand the frontiers of ADR.

[33] http://www.google.com/#q=multi+door+dispute+resolution+division+nigeria Accessed 18 March,2014

Powers of the Court

Multi-door courthouse system is a court-connected settlement method where the High court judge can refer an existing case that he/she deems suitable for ADR. The cases so referred are known as "court referred cases." Once resolved, the terms of the settlement are sent back to the referring judge, who will endorse the settlement as a sealed order of the court. Under the multi-door dispute resolution system, parties or a party may apply directly to the Multi-Door Court for resolution of their dispute, with or without having first commenced action in court. This method is known as 'walk-in cases.'[34] If a walk-in case is resolved before the multi-door court, the terms of the settlement are also sent back to the ADR judge for endorsement, thereby giving it full legal weight as an "order" of the court.

An ADR Judge is a High Court Judge who has been appointed by the Chief Judge of the relevant state to oversee all matters that are brought before the Multi-Door Court. Their roles and powers vary from state to state, but all have the power to endorse agreements reached in cases that have come before the court, thus ensuring that any agreement reached is given the same status as full judgments of the High Court.

Features of Multi-door Courts

The ADR centres named Multi-Door Courts (MDCs) are independently run and managed but are attached to specific High Courts. They have the benefit of offering different services for resolving disputes in respect of cases that may or may not already be within the court system. It admits a court-referred case or a walk-in case. The multi-door court system does not require that the parties be legally represented.

Advantages of Court Connected Multi-door System

Under the multi-door system, distrust of new and unfamiliar processes can be reduced because of the involvement and oversight of the judiciary. It provides a fuller range of choices or doors for resolving

---

[34] Ibid.

disputes. For members of the judiciary, Multi-doors systems are a means of decongesting caseload for the judiciary, allowing them time to deal with other cases effectively, thereby increasing productivity and improving access to justice for litigants. MDCs provide flexibility in both avoiding and returning to litigation. Parties are given the opportunity to arrive at solutions that are mutually and commercially acceptable. Agreements can be recorded as judgments of the court and enforced through formal court mechanisms. It is cheaper and quicker than recourse to litigation. It is an attempt to maintain the relationship between the parties. Recourse to ADR mechanisms relieves pressure on the courts.

STATUTORY SETTLEMENT OF DISPUTES

Statutory arbitration arises out of a statute that provides that certain classes of disputes must be settled in line with its provisions. The mode of such settlement is initially consensual, but where settlement fails after complying with the preliminary steps, then the compulsory provisions may apply. The Trade Disputes Act (TDA)[35] is an example of a non-court settlement of disputes based on a statutory settlement procedure. The Act was established for the resolution of disputes or disagreements between employers of labour and their employees. The statutory procedure is exemplified by mediation, conciliation, industrial arbitration, and the exclusive jurisdiction of the industrial court on employment matters.

The Act enjoins the disputing parties to first meet with a view to resolve the trade dispute by existing (agreed) arrangement, if any.[36] If the attempt to settle the dispute by that means fail or if no such agreed means exist, the parties are to meet together under the presidency of a mediator mutually agreed upon by them with a view of amicable settlement of the dispute.[37] After exhausting the prescribed preliminary steps and the dispute is wholly or partly not settled, the Minister of

[35] TDA 1976, Cap 198 LFN 2004

[36] Section 3(1), ibid., n31, both parties shall endeavour to reach settlement by means of existing collective agreement which emanated from a collective bargaining process.

[37] Ibid., n31 section 3(2)

Labour is empowered to refer the matter for conciliation under a conciliator appointed by him as provided in the Act.

Notwithstanding the foregoing procedure, if the matter appears to the Minister as one for urgent attention, he may inform the parties or their representatives of the steps he proposes to take. They include conciliation as the first option or direct reference to the Industrial Arbitration Panel (IAP).

A duly constituted IAP will hear the parties and thereafter make its award (judgment) within the prescribed period of its constitution. The award is sent to the Minister, who is obliged to make it available to the parties. The panel is not to give the award directly to the parties. The parties are free to raise objections to the award if necessary. If there is no objection, the award is taken as a settlement of the dispute, and the terms are binding on the parties. Where some points in issue are yet to be settled, and notice of the objection to the award has been properly given, the Minister will refer the dispute or issues as not settled to the National Industrial Court (NIC), whose award on trade dispute matters is final and binding on the parties.

If the parties to the dispute are engaged in essential services, and reference to conciliation and arbitration would be considered inappropriate for want of time, the Minister shall refer the dispute directly to the National Industrial Court.

Customary Arbitration

Customary law arbitration is a method of settling disputes outside the court system. It is a recognized extra-judicial means of bringing a dispute to an end. The courts in Nigeria do recognize customary arbitration as part of our legal system, provided they satisfy the validity tests for enforcement of customary law. The test is hinged on: first, that the customary law is not repugnant to natural justice, equity, and good conscience; the second is that it is not incompatible either directly or by implication with any law for the time being in force, and third is that it is not contrary to public policy.[38]

---

[38] Obilade, A.O., *The Nigerian Legal System* (London: Sweet & Maxwell, 1986) p100.

In *Ohiaeri* v. *Akabueze*,[39] the Supreme Court affirmed the existence of customary arbitration as a process of dispute settlement in Nigeria. A distinctive feature of customary arbitration is that the agreement to resort to arbitration is oral. Its proceedings and decisions are not normally recorded in writing. Customary arbitration is still popular among people in the villages and in traditional institutions in cities. It is a method of settlement that is democratic in nature. The system is lawful and a valid mechanism of the non-court process. Its characteristic feature includes respect for tradition, fear of sanctions, and the effect of disobedience to decisions.[40]

In the words of Niki Tobi, JSC, the customary arbitration system is designed to ensure stability and peaceful co-existence of the people in the society and to ensure the maintenance of the rule of law and equity among citizens.[41] Customary arbitration is essentially a native arrangement whereby some selected elders of the community who are vast in the customary law of the place meet and take decisions on the matter before them in other to reach a settlement. Where parties submit to customary arbitration, they are bound by the decision. An arbitrary award of a customary arbitration is not a judgment of a court of law and, therefore, cannot be enforced unless it is pronounced upon by a court of competent jurisdiction. The court can only make a pronouncement if the award is specifically pleaded and proved during trial. As regards the question to the propriety of the constitution of the arbitration, Dean, C.J, said in *Asampong* v. *Kweku Amakua*[42] that: "by mutual consent, investigations by arbitrators at a meeting held in accordance with native law and customs and to which decision is reached, it is binding on the parties and the Supreme Court will enforce it."

Customary arbitration awards can create an estoppel, and any of the parties can invoke the plea. Karibi Whyte declared so in *Egesimba v.*

39 (1992) 2 NWLR (pt. 221) p.7.

40 Webster, J.B., and Bouhen, A. A., *The Revolutionary Years of West Africa Since 1800* (Lagos: Longman pub. 1967) p.102-103.

41 *Ufomba* v. *Ahucahoagu* (2003) 4 SC (pt 2) 65 @90.

42 (1932) 1 WACA, 192 @ p.20.

Onuzurike[43] when he held thus: if it is shown that they submitted to the arbitration and accepted the terms of the decision, the situation creates an estoppel.

Customary arbitration is applicable only to Nigerians. If the disputing parties are a Nigerian and a non-Nigerian, the English law will apply unless it can be shown that the application of that law will result in substantial injustice to either of the parties. The court will not ratify and enforce an arbitration award unless it is certain, final, reasonable, legal, possible of execution, and disposes of all differences submitted to arbitration. If the arbitral award is conditional or contingent upon a subsequent event, which may or may not happen, it is not a final award and, therefore, incomplete.

Islamic Customary Arbitration

Islamic law is the personal law of a Muslim. And it is acknowledged as all-encompassing, leaving no aspect of human life untouched. The law provides for arbitration as a mechanism for the settlement of disputes.[44] The provisions of the Quran and Hadith directs that "if two parties among the believers fall into a quarrel...make your peace between them with justice and be fair for; God loves those who are fair (and just)." The author further elicited thus, "If you fear a breach between them twain appoint (two arbitrators) one from his family and one from hers if they wish for peace God would cause their reconciliation for God had full knowledge and is well acquainted with all things."[45]

Legal Status of Customary Arbitration

Customary arbitration is one of the various methods of settlement of disputes which is legally recognized in Nigeria. This position is evidenced in the numerous judicial decisions reported under customary arbitration. Customary arbitration is binding on parties if they voluntarily submit to it. The position articulated by the Supreme Court

---

[43] (2002) 9-10 S.C. 1 p.19.

[44] Yusuf, A., Quran 4 verse 35 *The Holy Quran Text, Translation and Commentary* in Ibrahim, Imam., "Legal Regime of Customary Arbitration in Nigeria" No 1, 2002, p8.

[45] Ibid., Quran 5 v 9.

on customary arbitration is a sharp contrast to modern arbitration provisions as regulated by the Act,[46] or as contained in an agreement, especially a commercial agreement wherein once an award is made, it is final and binding on the parties.[47]

The court in *Ras Pal Gas Ltd* v. *FCDA*[48] per Katsina Alu JSC posits that "a valid award on a voluntary reference no doubt operates between the parties as a final and conclusive judgment." The position in arbitration law is that customary arbitration is not regulated by Arbitration and Conciliation Act,[49] neither is the scope limited to contractual agreement; rather, it is concerned with a traditional agreement based on respect for norms of a particular society. The legality of customary arbitration in Nigeria under the native law and custom or Islamic law, in order to have a binding effect on the disputing parties must possess some factors which the Supreme Court identified in the case of *Okereke* v. *Nwankwo*[50] as:

> a) Voluntarily submission of their dispute to non-judicial body, i.e., their elders or chiefs as the case may be for determination;
> b) The parties must indicate their willingness or refusal to be bound by the decision of the non-judicial body.

Advantages/Disadvantages of Customary Arbitration

The option of arbitration being a quicker, not too technical, and less cumbersome means of settlement is part of the reason parties resort to it as out of court system of settlement.

It has been established by writers[51] of repute that court litigation system in the resolution of disputes has the disadvantages of being time-consuming, expensive, and less friendly.

---

[46] Ibid.

[47] *Awosibe* v. *Okereke* (1992) 5 NWLR (pt 243) 514, the court held that a dissatisfied party may back out to show that he never believed there was a binding arbitration.

[48] (2001) 6 NSCQR (pt 1) 560 573

[49] Ibid., n4.

[50] *Okereke* v. *Nwankwo* (2003) 4 SC (pt1) 16 at 29.

[51] Gadzama, J. K., " Inception of ADR and Arbitration in Nigeria," NBA conference Abuja (2004), Aina, K., "Alternative Dispute Resolution (ADR), Solution to Court Congestion," (1997), Akanbi, M.M., *The Law of Arbitration in Nigeria*, (Lagos: Longman Nigeria Plc, 2007), Abdul, A.Y., "Arbitration in Nigeria: Problems, Challenges and Prospects," *Ilorin Bar Journal* (2002) Vol. 1.

Unlike Islamic arbitration, customary arbitration is not codified. Islamic arbitration has its laws contained in the Holy Quran.[52] Most people handling customary arbitration are not trained in arbitration; consequently, the procedure and the award may be faulted if appealed against in court. Similarly, a customary arbitration award cannot be enforced except upon the application of a party to court for it. This negates the advantage of customary arbitration for being quicker and less expensive.

Arbitration in Maritime and Insurance Industries

Arbitration is a viable extra-judicial means of settling disputes in the maritime industry and even matters of insurance. The maritime industry is not left out of arbitration proceedings. In the words of Agbakoba, "there is no better arena for disputes than the maritime industry with its floating interests."[53] The Nigerian maritime industry steadily generates its fair share of disputes. Resolution of the dispute is encumbered and often prevented by an ineffective court process, resulting yearly loss. Arbitration has been seen as a significant alternative strategy for a speedy and effective solution to peculiar disputes.[54]

The issues in this sector involve a ship, usually arising out of contracts for the carriage of foods by sea, but not excluding disputes from building of ships, sale or repair, and sometimes the sale of oil in the ship. Nigeria is not one of the big maritime powers; it is nonetheless involved in some shipping activities or contracts. Delay in court process can slowdown maritime business. To cut their losses, ship owners, in recent times, developed a mechanism for dispute settlement that dispenses of long court process. This means it is driven by the need to save time. It allows a ship owner who is slammed with a claim to settle the claim before it gets to court.

---

[52] Ibid., n 45.

[53] Agbakoba, O., "The use of Arbitration and ADR in Maritime Industry Disputes," *Journal of Arbitration* (2007), Vol. 2, No 1, p.11.

[54] Ibid.

The method has, in effect, succeeded in drastically reducing the number of maritime claims brought to court and thus decreased the losses occasioned by ship and cargo detention.

Arbitration clauses are often found in insurance policies, thus making arbitration a condition precedent to the insurer's liability. The clause usually stipulates that "any dispute claim must go to arbitration before it goes before a court of law."[55] Arbitration clause may refer to the issue of quantum of loss. In *Scott* v. *Avery*,[56] the court held that arbitration clauses in insurance policies are enforceable as conditions precedent, provided they are not intended to oust the jurisdiction of the court. The arbitration clause should clearly state the reference to arbitration.

UNLAWFUL/NON-PEACEFUL MEANS OF DISPUTE SETTLEMENT

Contrary to the lawful methods of settlement of disputes discussed above, certain persons or groups of persons may devise other methods which are considered unlawful and contrary to accepted legal norms to settle their disputes. In some extreme cases, when peaceful efforts have failed or are not encouraged, the dispute may escalate and result in the parties or their agents employing extra-judicial means with grave consequences. Nigeria as a nation recently witnessed a novel act of extra-judicial settlement of conflict when government and private sector employers were frequently forced to negotiation by pressure groups. Examples of such negative and unlawful practices are:

Customary Trial by Ordeal

This is an old and ancient practice of detecting wrongdoers by appealing to a deity (god) or a spirit which the people believe in to reveal to them the innocence or guilt of a person accused of an offense. This practice spans from requiring the accused to drink substances ranging from water which was used to bathe a corpse, a mixture of

---

[55] Agomo, C.K., "Insurance Law" in Akanki E.O.(ed) *Commercial Law in Nigeria* (Lagos: University of Lagos Press; 2007) p. 639.

[56] (1856) 5 H.L.C. 810.

native chalk, blood, herbs, etc., or requiring an accused to put his hand in the fire. If he gets burnt, he is deemed to be guilty of the offense and punishable according to the law. Trial by ordeal extends to binding a person and throwing him into the river. If he sinks, he is taken as guilty.[57] Trial by ordeal is crude and uncivilised. It is considered one of the worst forms of trials of human persons. It is a crime that has been abolished both in England and in Nigeria.[58]

Trial by battle

This is also an age-long practice whereby parties to a dispute appeal to a god to give victory to the right party and make the wrongdoer suffer defeat. The disputing parties thereafter engage in a fight it out. The result of the fight is considered to be the judgment of the god.[59] The practice is unlawful, uncivilised, and unacceptable in a decent and modern society. It was abolished in England after the case of *Ashford* v. *Thornton*.[60] A fight between two or more persons in Nigeria is a crime punishable under the Criminal Code Act.

Jungle Justice or Mob Action

This act is a form of self-help whereby a group of persons take laws into their hands and meet out "justice" on a suspect by lynching, burning, wounding, or killing the victim instead of handing him over to the police. The act deprives the victim opportunity for a fair trial. An innocent person may erroneously be labelled a criminal and sent to an early grave without judicial trial or due process by means of outside court settlement. In *R* v. *Aniogo*,[61] the accused was woken up by the cry of fellow villagers who were in pursuit of a thief that night. He came out of his house with a gun; saw a man running toward him ahead of a crowd. Suspecting the man to be the thief, he shot and killed him. The deceased was not the thief. The accused was convicted of manslaughter.

---

57 Malemi, E., *The Nigerian Legal Method*, 2nd ed. (Lagos: Princeton Publishing Co., 2012) p.268.

58 The practice was abolished in England in 1215. In Nigeria, its prohibition is expressly provided in sections 207-209, and 211-212 of the Criminal Code Act, Cap "C38", 2004.

59 Ibid., n5.

60 (1818) 106 E.R 149.

61 (1970) 1 ECSLR 43.

Self-help

Self-help is an act of settlement of dispute extra-judicially. It is prima facie unlawful unless the person has a lawful excuse in law to employ the means. An example of self-help that can receive justification is that which is employed in provocation or in self-defence. In *R* v. *Ebi*,[62] The accused had almost completed his building in his hometown when fighting broke out between two groups in the community. He had nothing to do with the fight. In the riot that followed, his building was substantially destroyed. He had to move most of his belongings to a neighbour's house. He returned the next day to inspect the damage on his property. While he was doing so, the warring parties resumed fighting and further damaged the building. In anger, he took his brother's gun, shot into the crowd, and killed one person. Acquitting him from the charge of murder, it was held that the killing was justifiable as it was done in defence of his property.

Extra-judicial means of recovering property, in the case of *Governor Lagos State* v. *Ojukwu*[63] was adjudged a wrongful act by the Supreme Court. The Title of a building at Ikoyi-Lagos was the subject of dispute between the parties. Defying an order of interim injunction stopping the defendant/appellant (Governor) from ejecting the plaintiff/respondent from the building, they resorted to self-help and took possession of the property by force. The State and its agents did not apply due process or observe the provisions of Rent Control and Recovery of Residential Premises Law. In the words of the Apex court, "no one is entitled to take possession of premises by a strong hand."[64]

The Supreme Court in *Agbai* v. *Okogbue*,[65] deprecating self-help, said that the doctrine stated in *Governor Lagos State* v. *Ojukwu* is not only applicable to government excesses and public authorities to check on the use and application of self-help, it is also applicable to individuals and private bodies for the same purpose. The court, in this

---

[62] (1936) 3 WACA 36.
[63] (1986) 1 NWLR pt.18 p 621.
[64] Ibid.
[65] (1991) 7 NWLR pt. 204 p.391

case, stressed the need for every person in authority to observe the rule of law.

Insurgence and Militia Attack

Attack by Niger Delta youths on persons, oil installations, and pipeline vandalisation was obviously a measure of self-help against the federal government and the oil companies for the neglect and exploitation of the region. The conflict was settled through contacts, meetings, dialogue, consultation, and lobbying. The group was finally granted amnesty.

The ongoing attack by the faceless "Boko Haram Sect" in Northern Nigeria is considered an extra-judicial means employed unilaterally by the insurgents and militia against the government. The reason for unleashing terror on Nigerians, expatriates, and public institutions resident in Nigeria is not defined and known to the ordinary man. Akpoghome examined whether the horrific activities of the group are that of non-state armed actors.[66] The acts of these bandits are not covered by the general framework for responsibility under IHL, but they have nevertheless committed atrocities that could give rise to prosecution.[67] It has been suggested that they be tried under domestic criminal law by the Terrorism Act.[68]

Exceptions to Self-help

Self-help is reasonably permitted and lawful in the circumstances of self-defence and defence of property. In self-defence, it is lawful and reasonable to defend oneself and persons whom one has a moral or legal obligation to protect or defend, using reasonable or commensurate force to avert, nullify or destroy any attack. The same rule applies to the defence of property. Self-help is reasonably permitted and lawful depending on the circumstances the defendant finds himself. Minor or light attacks will reasonably be repelled by minor force, while

---

[66] Akpoghome, T. U., "The Responsibility Of Non-state Actors To International Humanitarian Law In Northern Nigeria," *B.I.U Law Series*, (2013), Vol. 1, No. 1, p. 104.

[67] Ibid., p.84.

[68] Terrorism (Prevention) Act 2011.

deadly attacks will likely be repelled with severe force, which may result in the death of the attacker. In *State* v. *Okojie*,[69] a madman armed with a machete attacked people and injured them. A policeman shot and killed him. In a trial for the murder of the madman, the court held that the police had a legal duty to protect the public from the heinous attack by the insane.

FURTHER READING

Books

Akanki E. O., *Commercial Law in Nigeria* (Lagos: University Press, 2007).

Ejiofor G., *Law of Arbitration* (Lagos: Longman, 2005).

Fry G., *It's Good to Talk* 2006.

Malemi E., *Nigerian Constitutional Law* 3rd ed. (Lagos: Princeton Pub. 2012).

Malemi E., *Nigerian Legal Method*, 2nd ed. (Lagos: Princeton Pub. 2012).

Obilade A. O., *Nigerian Legal System* (London: Sweet and Maxwell 1986).

Sagay I. E., *Nigerian Law of Contract* 2nd ed. (Ibadan: Spectrum, 2002).

Ward R., & Akhtar A., *Walker & Walker English Legal System* 10th ed. (London: Oxford University Press, 2008).

Journals/Articles

Agbakoba O., Use of Arbitration & ADR in Maritime Industrial Disputes, *Journal of Arbitration* Vol. 2 No. 1(2007).

Akpoghome T. U., "Responsibility of Non-States Actors to International Humanitarian Law In Northern Nigerian," *B.I.U Law Series*, (2013) Vol.1, No.1, p.104.

Gadzama J. K., "Inception of ADR & Arbitration in Nigeria," *NBA Conference* Abuja, (2004).

Idornigie P. O., "Overview of ADR in Nigeria Arbitration." *IJAMDM* (2007).

[69] Unreported Auchi HC Charge No. HAU/16/ 76.

Chapter 15

JUDICIAL PERSONNEL: QUALIFICATIONS, APPOINTMENTS, TENURE, DISCIPLINE, AND INDEPENDENCE

Taiwo, Elijah Adew*

INTRODUCTION

The Constitution of the Federal Republic of Nigeria, 1999 (as amended) provides for the division of governmental powers among three organs of government, namely, the legislature, the executive, and the judiciary.[1] In terms of this Constitution, the judicial power of the Federation is vested in the courts of law listed in section 6 of the Constitution.[2] The section gives the judiciary the power to entertain

* Taiwo, Elijah Adewale, LLB, LLM, MPhil (OAU, Ile-Ife, Nigeria), LLD (NMMU, Port-Elizabeth, South Africa), BL (NLS, Lagos); Research Associate, Department of Public Law, Nelson Mandela Metropolitan University, South Africa; Professor of Laws & Head of Department of Private and Business Law, Afe Babalola University, Ado-Ekiti, Nigeria; Fellow of the Netherlands Institute for Advanced Study (NIAS), Wassenaar, the Netherlands; E-mail: equitabletaiwo@gmail.com.

1 The legislative powers of the Federation are vested in the National Assembly which consists of a Senate and a House of Representatives. The legislative powers of a State of the Federation are vested in the House of Assembly of that State. See the Constitution of the Federal Republic of Nigeria, 1999 (as Amended), s 4. The executive powers of the Federation are vested in the President and the Vice-President while the executive powers of a State are vested in the Governor and Deputy-Governor. See the Constitution of the Federal Republic of Nigeria, 1999 (as Amended), s 5(1) & (2); the President, Vice President, Governors and Deputy Governors exercise executive functions with the assistance of Ministers and Commissioners respectively. See the Constitution of the Federal Republic of Nigeria, 1999 (as Amended), s 6 for the judicial powers. This is a common feature of most democratic States. In this regards, see the Constitution of the Republic of South Africa, 1996 (as amended) for the Executive power (s 85 & s 125), Legislative power (s 43), and for Judicial power, (s 165); see also, the Constitution of the Republic of Ghana, 1992 (as amended), art 58 for the Executive power, art 93 for the legislative power, and art 125 for the Judicial power. See EA Taiwo, "Judicial Review of the Impeachment Procedure in Nigeria" (2009) 3(2) *Malawi Law Journal* 236-272, 237.

2 Those courts include, the Supreme Court, the Court of Appeal, the Federal High Court, the High Court of the FCT, a High Court of a State, the Sharia Court of Appeal of the FCT, a Sharia Court of Appeal of a State, the Customary Court of the FCT, a Customary Court of Appeal of a State, and such other Courts as may be established by the National Assembly or a state House of Assembly. Although other lower courts such as the Magistrates' Court, Customary Court and Area Court were not listed in s 6 of the

suits between persons or between governments or authorities and any person in Nigeria for the determination of any question as to the civil rights and obligations of that person.[3] The judicial power vested by the Constitution is wide as it covers all inherent powers and sanctions of a court of law, including judicial review of the acts of the other organs of government.[4]

Going by this constitutional arrangement, it is, therefore, submitted that one of the cardinal principles of the Nigerian Constitution is the separation of powers of the three arms of government.[5] Legislation, execution, and adjudication of disputes are vested in separate organs which are independent of one another in terms of their existence, functions, and personnel. It should be noted, however, that the judicial organ is placed with added responsibility as the guardian and protector of the Constitution. As such, whenever the executive or legislative arm of government exceeds its constitutional power or mandate, the judiciary, on a proper application to it, will curb such excessive powers and declare such an act a nullity.[6]

It is in this context that the judiciary is described as one of the crown jewels of the democratic system of government and, therefore, indispensable for a steady, upright, and impartial administration of the laws of a country.[7] It follows, therefore, that in any country, the judiciary has a great role to play as well as a great responsibility to discharge in the functions of a government.[8]

The adjudication of disputes is entrusted in the law courts, made up of judges appointed on the basis of possessing appropriate professional qualifications and experience.[9] This chapter is limited to discussing the qualifications, appointment, tenure, discipline, and

---

Constitution, however, s 6(4) (j) & (k) which recognises such other courts as may be authorized by law will include these courts.

[3] See s 6(6)(b) of the Constitution of the Federal Republic of Nigeria, 1999; see also, *Moses Oghenerume Taiga* v. *Nneka Mercy Moses-Taiga* [2012] 10 NWLR (pt 1308) 219, 240.

[4] Taiwo (n 1) 237.

[5] See *Ekpenkhio* v. *Egbadon* [1993] 7 NWLR (pt 308) 717, 744 (CA).

[6] See *Lekwot* v. *Judicial Tribunal* [1993] 2 NWLR (pt 276) 410; *DS Alamieyeseigha* v. *Federal Republic of Nigeria & 7 Ors* [2006] 16 NWLR (pt 1004) 1, 126.

[7] EA Taiwo and M Adigun, "The Judiciary and the Rule of Law" in JAA Ayoade, AA Akinsanya and OJB Ojo, (eds), *The Jonathan Presidency: The First Year* (University Press of America 2014) 137-175, 137.

[8] T Akinola Aguda, *The Judiciary in the Government of Nigeria* (New Horn Press 1983) 34.

[9] See BO Nwabueze, *Nigeria's Presidential Constitution 1979-83* (Longman Groups Ltd 1985) 20-21

independence of the judiciary. As such, other general issues relating to a court of law, such as the jurisdiction, constitution, composition, as well as practice, and procedure of each court, are outside the scope of this chapter. The chapter is divided into seven parts. Following this introduction is the second part which discusses the qualifications and appointment of judicial officers.

Parts three and four respectively discuss the role of the National Judicial Council and that of the Judicial Service Commission in the appointment of judges. Part five is devoted to discussing the tenure of office and discipline of the judicial officers, while part six is on the independence of the judiciary. The conclusion forms the last.

QUALIFICATIONS AND APPOINTMENTS OF JUDICIAL OFFICERS

The terms "judge," "justice," and "court" are often used synonymously and interchangeably, and they sometimes mean one and the same thing. The word "judge" is originally from the Latin word "*judex*." Under Roman law, *judex* means a private person appointed with the consent of the parties to try and decide a cause of action commenced before him. In the old English Law, it means a juror, which in this modern civil law becomes a judge. A judge is, therefore, a public officer appointed to preside and administer the law in a court of justice. He is the chief member of the court charged with the control of the entire proceedings before the court.[10] Judges are people learned in law and who are the final determiners of what the laws say about any particular set of facts or issues before them.

A judge conducts trials or presides over a court of justice; he determines controversies between parties based upon evidence and the legal argument presented.[11] He has the final say (subject to appeal) on any point raised in a trial before him. Although it is assumed that judges know all the laws, however, it is axiomatic that no judge is omniscient.[12]

---

[10] See D Pannick, *Judges* (Oxford University 1987) 143-147.

[11] SH Gifis, *Dictionary of Legal Terms* (4th ed., Barron's Educational Series, Inc. 2008) 277.

[12] JA Jolowicz, *Jolowicz on Civil Procedure* (Cambridge University Press 2000) 225.

One cannot, in reality, demand a judge a universal knowledge of all the rules of law in force in his jurisdiction. However, the society demands a judge a certain initiative on legal issues; above all, it demands that he has the ability to understand and evaluate legal reasoning put forward by the advocates and, for appellate judges, the reasoning of their colleagues of the lower courts or court below.[13]

In Nigeria, the term "justice" is used for the Justices of the Supreme Court and the Court of Appeal, while the term "judge," on the other hand, is used mostly for the presiding officer of other superior courts such as the High Court, the National Industrial Court, Customary Court of Appeal, and Sharia Court of Appeal (among others). Also, some inferior courts like the Area Courts and Customary Courts also adopt the nomenclature. The major courts enumerated in the 1999 Nigerian Constitution (as amended) are the Supreme Court,[14] the Court of Appeal,[15] the National Industrial Court,[16] the Federal High Court,[17] the High Court of the Federal Capital Territory,[18] the State High Courts,[19] the Sharia Court of Appeal of the Federal Capital Territory,[20] the Sharia Court of Appeal of States,[21] the Customary Court of Appeal of the Federal Capital Territory,[22] and the Customary Court of Appeal of States.[23] Apart from those specifically mentioned, the Constitution also provides for the recognition of such other courts

---

[13] Ibid.

[14] See s 230 of the Constitution.

[15] See s 237 of the Constitution.

[16] The Court is now included in the list of the Courts recognised under section 6 of the 1999 Constitution by virtue of the Constitution of the Federal Republic of Nigeria (Third Alteration) Act of 2010 (Act No. 3 of 2010. It was passed by the Senate of the National Assembly on 14 December, 2010, House of Representatives on 15 December, 2010, the report of approvals by the States Houses of Assembly was received on 8 February, 2011. The President gave assent to it on 4 March, 2011, a date when the Act commenced operation). The Act amended the original s 6 of the Constitution of the Federal Republic of Nigeria, 1999 to incorporate the National Industrial Court. (See s 2 of the Constitution of the Federal Republic of Nigeria (Third Alteration) No. 3, 2010). The Act provides for the establishment of the National Industrial Court. See s 2 of the Act No. 3, 2010; s 254A(1) of the 1999 Amended Constitution.

[17] See s 249 of the Constitution.

[18] See s 255 of the Constitution.

[19] See s 270 of the Constitution.

[20] See s 260 of the Constitution.

[21] See s 275 of the Constitution.

[22] See s 265 of the Constitution.

[23] See s 280 of the Constitution.

as may be established by the National Assembly or the States' Legislative Assemblies.[24]

In the performance of their functions, the judicial officers are expected to discharge their functions fairly, efficiently, and independently, without fear or favour. They are required to resolve disputes brought before them wisely, according to the law, so that the parties before them can see that they have had a fair trial. Thus, they are mandated by the law to give reasons justifying their decisions.[25]

Although judges stand in an enviable position in society, however, their task is not an easy one as they are always under the constant scrutiny eyes of lawyers, litigants, and the general public. Academics and social critics are also always on their toes criticizing errors in their decisions or making other comments as to the correctness or otherwise of those decisions. Thus, a judicial officer cannot afford to be negligent, indolent, or partial in the discharge of his functions.

To be able to perform his functions effectively, a judge is expected to have a high sense of duty, responsibility, commitment, discipline, intellect, integrity, probity, and transparency. He must know his onions; he must be honest and incorruptible. A judge must be current and up to date in his research with adequate knowledge of the law. Honesty and judicial rectitude is, thus, the insignia of a good judge.

A judge must not be reckless or be moved by private or personal motives, and neither must he be influenced by extraneous consideration in the discharge of his duties.[26] In this regard, Oputa rightly admonished that "the qualities of courage, honesty, and integrity required of judges are meant to ensure that they do not, either under pressure or of their own volition, yield their moral authority, and that they do not in the process of decision making allow themselves to be swayed from the part of truth and justice."[27]

---

[24] See s 4(a) & (b) & s 6(5)(j) & (k) of the Constitution.

[25] IE Sagay, SAN, "The Judiciary in a Modern Democracy," in IA Ayua, DA Guobadia and AO Adekunle, (eds.), *Nigeria Issues in the 1999 Constitution* (Nigeria Institute of Advanced Legal Studies 2000) 76-112, 86.

[26] See *Ikonne* v. *The Commissioner of Police & Anor* [1986] 4 NWLR (pt 36) 473, 496.

[27] Oputa, JSC, in a lecture titled "Access to Justice" delivered at the Obafemi Awolowo University, Ile-Ife, (1988) quoted in Sagay (n 25) 87.

The qualities of firmness and impartiality allow a judge to turn the wheels of justice objectively.[28]

A judge should be upright and unassailable in character; he must live above board in public and private life.[29] By the oath of office he has sworn to, he is to discharge his duties and perform his functions honestly to the best of his ability and without fear or favour.[30] This is because the judiciary is the hope of the hopeless, the defender of the defenceless, and the upholder of the rule of law. By the nature of the powers vested in it, the judiciary stands between the government and the citizens.[31]

In terms of the Nigerian Constitution, the appointment of judges rests largely on set rules and guidelines. Depending on whether the appointment is a Federal or a State Judge, the President or the Governor (as the case may be) appoints a judge on the recommendations of the National Judiciary Council (NJC). The National Judicial Council always receives advice from the Federal or State Judicial Service Commission (JSC) (as the case may be) on the person to be appointed a judge.[32] Having discussed the foregoing as background, the qualifications required for the appointment, as well as the process of appointment of judges into the respective courts in Nigeria, will now be discussed.

---

[28] Ibid.

[29] See EA Taiwo, "The Judiciary and Democracy in Nigeria: An Independent Messenger?" in JA Ayoade and AA Akinsanya (eds.), *Nigeria's Critical Election, 2011* (Lexington Books 2013) 249-282, 253.

[30] Thus, where it is shown that a party does not have confidence in the ability of a trial Judge to hold an even scale between the parties, and the judge feels that his integrity has been impugned or his impartiality called into question, it would be proper in the circumstance for the trial Judge to withdraw from further participation in the proceedings. See *Estisione H. (Nig.) Ltd & Anor* v. *Osun State Government & Anor* [2012] 14 NWLR (pt 1321) 540, 563-564; see also, *Secretary, Iwo Central Local Govt* v. *Adio* [2000] 8 NWLR (pt 667) 115.

[31] IB Lawal, "The Role of the Judiciary in the Crusade Against Corrupt and Unethical Practices in the Public Service" in AO Yusuf (ed.), *Issues in Justice Administration in Nigeria (Essays in Honour of Hon Justice S.M.A. Belgore, GCON)* (VGD International Ltd 2008) 249-274, 273.

[32] In appointing their judicial personnel, every country is admonished to be guided by the United Nations' Basic Principles on the Independence of the Judiciary which state: "Persons selected for judicial office shall be individuals of integrity and ability with appropriate training or qualifications in law. Any method of judicial selection shall safeguard against judicial appointments for improper motives. In the selection of judges, there shall be no discrimination against a person on the grounds of race, colour, sex, religion, political or other opinion, national or social origin, property, birth or status, except that a requirement that a candidate for the judicial office must be a national of the country concerned, shall not be considered discriminatory." See Para 10 of the Basic Principles, adopted by the United Nations' General Assembly in 1985.

THE SUPREME COURT OF NIGERIA

The highest court in the country is the Supreme Court of Nigeria. The Court came into existence on 1st October 1963 by virtue of Act No. 20 of 1963 as a successor to the then Federal Supreme Court, which had been in existence by virtue of the 1960 Constitution.[33] The 1963 Act provides for the establishment of the Supreme Court, which is composed of the Chief Justice of Nigeria and such number of other judges known as the Justices of the Supreme Court, not being less than five, as may be prescribed by law.[34] Under the current dispensation, the 1999 Nigerian Constitution (as amended) provides that there shall be a Supreme Court of Nigeria which shall consist of the Chief Justice of Nigeria and such number of justices of the Supreme Court, not exceeding twenty-one, as may be prescribed by an Act of the National Assembly.[35]

In terms of the provision of section 231 of the Constitution, the appointment of a person to the office of the Chief Justice of Nigeria (CJN) and other Justices of the Supreme Court (JJSC) shall be made by the President on the recommendation of the National Judicial Council subject to confirmation of such appointment by the Senate.[36] A person shall not be qualified to hold the office of Chief Justice of Nigeria or of a Justice of the Supreme Court unless he is qualified to practice as a legal practitioner in Nigeria and has been so qualified for a period of not less than fifteen years.[37] It should be noted, however, that in respect of appointments to the offices of the Justices of the Supreme Court, the President shall have regard to the need to ensure that there are among the holders of such office persons learned in Islamic personal law and person learned in customary law.[38]

---

33 See s 104 of the 1960 Constitution & s 111 of the 1963 Constitution. See also, AO Obilade, *The Nigerian Legal System* (Spectrum Law Publishing 1990) 170.

34 See also, s 210 of the 1979 Nigerian Constitution.

35 See s 230 of the 1999 Nigerian Constitution (as amended); see also, s 3 of the Supreme Court Act, (Cap S15), LFN, 2004.

36 See s 231(1) & (2) of the 1999 Constitution.

37 S 231(3) of the Constitution.

38 See s 288(1) of the 1999 Nigerian Constitution.

THE COURT OF APPEAL

The Court of Appeal was established on 1st October 1976.[39] It was then known as the Federal Court of Appeal. The Court was established to serve as an intermediate court between the High Court and other subordinate courts, and the Supreme Court. In terms of the earlier Court of Appeal Act, the Court was established with a President and at least twenty-one other Justices.[40] Under the 1999 Constitution (as modified by the revised Court of Appeal Act),[41] together with the President, the number of other Justices of the Court of Appeal shall be seventy.[42] Out of this number, not less than three Justices shall be learned in Islamic personal law, and while not less than three also shall be learned in customary law.[43]

The Constitution provides that the appointment of a person to the office of the President of the Court of Appeal (PCA) and other Justices of the Court of Appeal (JJCA) shall be made by the President on the recommendation of the National Judicial Council subject to the confirmation of such appointment by the Senate.[44] A person shall qualify for the appointment as President of the Court of Appeal or Justice of the Court of Appeal if he is qualified to practice as a legal practitioner in Nigeria for not less than twelve years.[45] Just like in the case of the Justices of the Supreme Court, it should also be noted that in respect of appointments to the offices of the Justices of the Court of Appeal, the President shall have regard to the need to ensure that there are among the holders of such offices, persons learned in Islamic personal law and person learned in customary law.[46]

---

[39] See the Constitution of the Federation, (the Constitution Amendment) (No.2), Decree No. 42, 1976.

[40] See s 1, Court of Appeal Act, (Cap. 75), LFN, 1990.

[41] See s 237(1) which establishes the Court under the current Constitution.

[42] See s 237(2) of the Constitution provides that apart from the President, the number of the justices shall not be less than 49. This has been modified by sec 1 of the Court of Appeal Act, (Cap C 36), LFN, 2004 which now increases the number to seventy. There is now a clamour that each State of the Federation should have a Court of Appeal, and if this is acceded to, the number of the Justices of the Court of Appeal will increase from time to time.

[43] S 237(2)(b) of the Constitution.

[44] See s 238(1) & (2) of the 1999 Constitution.

[45] S 238(3) of the 1999 Nigerian Constitution.

[46] See s 288(1) of the 1999 Nigerian Constitution.

THE FEDERAL HIGH COURT

The Federal High Court was initially established as the Federal Revenue Court in 1973.[47] The Constitution of the Federal Republic of Nigeria, 1979 changed the name from the Federal Revenue Court and renamed it the Federal High Court.[48] In terms of Section 249 of the 1999 Constitution, there shall be a Federal High Court which shall consist of a Chief Judge and such number of Judges of the Federal High Court as may be prescribed by an Act of the National Assembly.[49]

The appointment of a person to the office of Chief Judge of the Federal High Court shall be made by the President on the recommendation of the National Judicial Council, subject to confirmation by the Senate.[50] The appointment of a person to the office of a Judge of the Federal High Court shall be made by the President on the recommendation of the National Judicial Council.[51] A person shall qualify for the post of the Chief Judge or a Judge of the Federal High Court if he is qualified to practice as a legal practitioner in Nigeria for not less than ten years.[52]

HIGH COURT OF A STATE

By virtue of Section 270 of the 1999 Nigerian Constitution, each of the 36 States of the Federation shall have its own High Court consisting of a Chief Judge and such number of Judges as may be prescribed by a Law of the House of Assembly of the State. The appointment of a person to the office of the Chief Judge of a State shall be made by the Governor on the recommendation of the National Judicial Council, subject to confirmation by the House of Assembly of the State.[53] The appointment of a person to the office of a Judge of the High Court of a State shall be made by the Governor acting on the recommendation of the National Judicial Council.[54] A person shall qualify for the post of

---

[47] See s 1 of the Federal Revenue Court Act, 1973.
[48] S 230(2) of the 1979 Constitution.
[49] See also, s 228 of 1979 Constitution.
[50] S 250(1) of the 1999 Constitution.
[51] S 250(2) of the 1999 Constitution.
[52] S 250(3) of the 1999 Constitution.
[53] S 271(1) of the 1999 Constitution.
[54] S 271(2) of the Constitution.

the Chief Judge of a State or a Judge of the State High Court if he is qualified to practice as a legal practitioner in Nigeria for not less than ten years.[55]

THE HIGH COURT OF THE FEDERAL CAPITAL TERRITORY, ABUJA

The Constitution provides for the establishment of a High court of the Federal Capital Territory (FCT), Abuja.[56] The High Court of the Federal Capital Territory shall consist of a Chief Judge and such number of Judges as may be prescribed by an Act of the National Assembly.[57] The appointment of a person to the office of the Chief Judge of the High Court of the Federal Capital Territory shall be made by the President on the recommendation of the National Judicial Council, subject to confirmation by the Senate.[58]

The appointment of a person to the office of a Judge of the High Court of the Federal Capital Territory shall be made by the President on the recommendation of the National Judicial Council.[59] A person shall qualify for the post of the Chief Judge or a Judge of the High Court of the Federal Capital Territory if he is qualified to practice as a legal practitioner in Nigeria for not less than ten years.[60]

THE NATIONAL INDUSTRIAL COURT

Originally, the National Industrial Court (NIC) was established in 1976 for the purpose of dealing with trade disputes and collective agreements.[61] The Court consists of the President of the National Industrial Court and such number of Judges of the Court as may be prescribed by an Act of the National Assembly.[62] The appointment of a person to the office of the President of the National Industrial Court is

---

[55] S 271(3) of the Constitution.
[56] S 255(1) of the Constitution.
[57] S 255(2) of the Constitution.
[58] S 256(1) of the Constitution.
[59] S 256(2) of the Constitution.
[60] S 256(3) of the Constitution.
[61] See s 14 of the Trade Disputes Decree No.7 of 1976; see also, Obilade (n 33) 220.
[62] S 254A(2) of the 1999 Amended Constitution

made by the President on the recommendation of the National Judicial Council, subject to confirmation by the Senate.[63]

The appointment of a person to the office of a Judge of the National Industrial Court shall be made by the President on the recommendation of the National Judicial Council.[64] A person shall qualify for the post of the President and Judge of the Court if he is qualified to practice as a legal practitioner in Nigeria for no less than ten years and has considerable knowledge and experience in the law and practice of industrial relations and employment conditions in Nigeria.[65]

THE SHARIA COURT OF APPEAL

The Constitution provides for the establishment of a Sharia Court of Appeal of the Federal Capital Territory, Abuja,[66] and of a State.[67] The Court consists of a Grand Kadi and such number of Kadis as may be prescribed by the National Assembly or House of Assembly of a State as the case may be.[68] A Kadi is a scholar of Islamic jurisprudence, as such, may not necessarily be a legal practitioner. He must be knowledgeable in Islamic Personal Law.[69]

The 1999 Nigerian Constitution provides, however, that before a person can be appointed a Grand Kadi or Kadi, he must have been qualified as a legal practitioner for not less than ten years and has obtained a recognized qualification in Islamic law from an institution acceptable to the National Judicial Council.[70]

In the alternative, a Grand Kadi or Kadi must have attended and has obtained a recognised qualification in Islamic law from an institution approved by the National Judicial Council and has held the qualification for a period of not less than twelve years; and he either has

---

[63] S 254B(1) of the 1999 Amended Constitution.
[64] S 254B(2) of the 1999 Amended Constitution.
[65] S 254B(3)&(4) of the 1999 Amended Constitution.
[66] S 260 of the Constitution.
[67] S 275 of the Constitution.
[68] Ss 260(2) & 275(2) of the Constitution.
[69] See s 260 & 275 of the 1999 Constitution.
[70] See s 261(3)(a), s 276(3)(a) & s 288(2)(a) of the Constitution.

considerable experience in the practice of Islamic law or he is a distinguished scholar of Islamic law.[71]

The Grand Kadi of the Sharia Court of Appeal of the FCT shall be appointed by the President on the recommendation of the National Judicial Council, subject to the confirmation of the Senate.[72] The Grand Kadi of the Sharia Court of Appeal of a State shall be appointed by the Governor on the recommendation of the National Judicial Council, subject to the confirmation of the House of Assembly of the State.[73] The Kadis shall be appointed by the President for the Sharia Court of Appeal of the FCT on the recommendation of the National Judicial Council.[74]

The Kadis shall be appointed by the Governor for the Sharia Court of Appeal of a State on the recommendation of the National Judicial Council.[75]

THE CUSTOMARY COURT OF APPEAL

The 1999 Nigerian Constitution provides for the establishment of a Customary Court of Appeal of the Federal Capital Territory, Abuja,[76] and of a State.[77] The Court consists of a President and such number of Judges of the Customary Court of Appeal as may be prescribed by the National Assembly or House of Assembly of a State as the case may be.[78]

A Judge of the Customary Court of Appeal may not necessarily be a legal practitioner, but he must be knowledgeable in customary law. The 1999 Constitution provides that before a person can be appointed a President or Judge of the Customary Court of Appeal, he must be qualified as a legal practitioner for not less than ten years, and in the opinion of the National Judicial Council, he has considerable knowledge and experience in the practice of customary law.[79] In the

[71] S 261(3)(b) & sec 276(3)(b) of the Constitution.
[72] S 261(1) of the Constitution.
[73] S 276(1) of the Constitution.
[74] S 261(2) of the Constitution.
[75] S 276(2) of the Constitution.
[76] S 265 of the Constitution.
[77] S 280 of the Constitution.
[78] Ss 265(2) & 280(2) of the Constitution.
[79] See s 266(3)(a), s 281(3)(a) and s 288(2)(b) of the Constitution.

alternative, in the opinion of the National Judicial Council, he has considerable knowledge and experience in the practice of customary law.[80]

The President of the Customary Court of Appeal of the Federal Capital Territory is appointed by the President of Nigeria on the recommendation of the National Judicial Council, subject to the confirmation of the Senate.[81] The President of the Customary Court of Appeal of a State is appointed by the Governor of the State, acting on the recommendation of the National Judicial Council, subject to the confirmation of the House of Assembly of the State.[82] The Judge shall be appointed by the President for the Customary Court of Appeal of the Federal Capital Territory on the recommendation of the National Judicial Council.[83] In the same vein, the Judge shall be appointed by the Governor for the Customary Court of Appeal of a State on the recommendation of the National Judicial Coil.[84]

THE ROLE OF THE NATIONAL JUDICIAL COUNCIL (NJC) IN THE APPOINTMENT OF THE JUDICIAL OFFICERS

The National Judicial Council (NJC) and the Judicial Service Commission (JSC) play pivotal roles in the appointments and disciplines of the judicial officers in Nigeria. All the judicial appointments in Nigeria are made by the President or the Governor (as the case may be) on the recommendation of the National Judicial Council based on the advice of the Judicial Service Commission. As such, it is expedient to examine the compositions, powers, and functions of these two important bodies.

The National Judicial Council is made up of the Chief Justice of Nigeria (CJN), who is the Chairman, while the next most senior Justice of the Supreme Court serves as the Deputy Chairman. Other members are the presidents of the Court of Appeal. Five retired Justices selected by the Chief Justice of Nigeria from the Supreme Court or Court of

[80] S 266(3)(b) and s 281(3)(b) of the Constitution.
[81] S 266(1) of the Constitution.
[82] S 281(1) of the Constitution.
[83] S 266(2) of the Constitution.
[84] S 281(2) of the Constitution.

Appeal; the Chief Judge of the Federal High Court; five Chief Judges of States appointed by the Chief Justice of Nigeria from among the Chief Judges of the States and of the High Court of the FCT in rotation to serve for two years; one Grand Kadi to be appointed by the CJN from among the Grand Kadis of the Sharia Courts of Appeal to serve in rotation for two years; one President of the Customary Court of Appeal appointed by the CJN from among the Presidents of the Customary Courts of Appeal to serve in rotation for two years.

Others also include five members of the Nigerian Bar Association (NBA) who have qualified as legal practitioners for not less than fifteen years, at least one of whom shall be a Senior Advocate of Nigeria, appointed by the CJN on the recommendation of the National Executive Committee of the NBA to serve for two years and subject to re-appointment; and two other persons not being legal practitioners, who in the opinion of the CJN, are of unquestionable integrity. The Secretary of the Council, who shall be a legal practitioner, is appointed by the NJC on the recommendation of the Federal Judicial Service Commission. It should be noted that the five NBA members sit in the Council only for the purpose of considering the names of persons to be appointed a judge of the superior courts of records and nothing more. They do not sit when the Council is to discipline a judicial officer and other allied issues relating to the discipline of judicial officers.

The National Judicial Council exercises a number of power and functions, which include recommending to the President or the Governor (as the case may be) from among the list of persons submitted to it by the Federal or States Judicial Service Commissions or Judicial Service Committee (in the case of the FCT), for the appointment into the offices of the Chief Justice of Nigeria and Justices of the Supreme Court, President and Justices of the Court of Appeal, Chief Judges, Grand Kadi of the Sharia Court of Appeal, President of the Customary Court of Appeal, and Judges of all the superior courts of records in Nigeria.[85]

---

[85] See *Hon. Justice Raliat Elelu-Habeeb & Anor v The Hon Attorney General of Federation & 2 Ors* [2012] 13 NWLR (pt 1318) 423, 491 & 492-493.

Apart from the disciplinary power which is discussed below, other functions of the National Judicial Council include the power to collect, control, and disburse all monies, capital and recurrent, for the judiciary; advise the President and the Governors on any matter pertaining to the judiciary; appoint, dismiss and exercise disciplinary control over members and staff of the Council; control and disburse all monies, capital and recurrent, for the service of the Council; and deal with all other matters relating to the broad issues of policy and administration.[86]

It should be noted that what the Constitution allows NJC to do as far as the appointment of judicial officers is concerned is to merely suggest or to advise the President or the Governor as to whom he should appoint; it is silent on what happens if the recommendation is not followed. The pertinent issue is whether the Governor is bound by the recommendation of the NJC? Experience such as this can cause a crisis in the State judiciary if the Governor decides to appoint someone else other than the person recommended by the NJC.[87]

It is, therefore, becomes necessary to amend the relevant provisions of the Constitution to take care of such eventualities as to what happens if the President or the Governor, who is the final appointing authority, is not comfortable with the NJC recommendation and decides not to accept it.

THE ROLE OF THE JUDICIAL SERVICE COMMISSION/COMMITTEE IN THE JUDICIAL APPOINTMENT

Just like the National Judicial Council, the Federal Judicial Service Commission (FJSC), Federal Capital Territory Judicial Service Committee (JSC FCT), and the State Judicial Service Commission (SJSC) play pivotal roles in the appointments and discipline of the

[86] On the National Judicial Council, see generally, s 153(1)(i) of the 1999 Constitution as well as Item I, Part I, of the Third Schedule to the 1999 Nigerian Constitution.

[87] For instance, see the recent suspension of the newly sworn-in Chief Judge of Rivers State, Hon. Justice PNC Agumagu by the NJC for accepting the Office of the Chief Judge of Rivers State in place of Hon. Justice Daisy Okocha recommended by the NJC. See Nwannekanma Bertram, "NJC's Recommendation as Prerequisite for Chief Judge's Appointment" *The Guardian* (1 April 2014) 81-82.

judicial officers in Nigeria. To avoid repetitions, their respective powers and functions will be discussed together in this part. The FJSC shall comprise of the following members: the CJN, who sits as the Chairman; the President of the Court of Appeal; the Attorney General of the Federation; the Chief Judge of the Federal High Court; two persons who are legal practitioners and who have been so qualified for not less than fifteen years; and two other persons, not being legal practitioners, who in the opinion of the President are of unquestionable integrity.

The Commission shall have the power to advise the NJC in nominating persons for appointment in respect of the CJN, a Justice of the Supreme Court, the President of the Court of Appeal, Justices of the Court of Appeal, the Chief Judge of the Federal High Court, Judges of the Federal High Court, and Chairman and Members of the Code of Conduct Tribunal.[88]

The Judicial Service Committee of the FCT performs similar functions in respect of the appointment of judicial officers into all the superior courts of records in the FCT.[89] The Judicial Service Committee, FCT has in its composition, the following members: the Chief Judge of the FCT; the Attorney General of the Federation; the Grand Kadi of the Sharia Court of Appeal, FCT; the President of the Customary Court of Appeal, FCT, one person who is a legal practitioner and who has been so qualified for at least twelve years; and one person not being a legal practitioner, who in the opinion of the President is of unquestionable integrity.[90]

The State Judicial Service Commissions comprises of the following members: the Chief Judge of the State, who is the Chairman, the Attorney General of the State; the Grand Kadi of the Sharia Court of Appeal (if any); the President of the Customary Court of Appeal, (if any), two persons who are legal practitioners and who have been so qualified for at least ten years; and two persons not being legal

[88] Item E, Part I, of the Third Schedule to the 1999 Nigerian Constitution.
[89] See Part III, of the Third Schedule to the 1999 Nigerian Constitution.
[90] See Part III, of the Third Schedule to the 1999 Nigerian Constitution.

practitioners, who in opinion of the Governor is of unquestionable integrity.[91]

The Judicial Service Commission performs the function of recommending to the NJC, that is, the appointment of judicial officers into all the superior courts of records in the State concerned.[92] The State Judicial Service Commission also has statutory duty to recommend to the NJC for discipline, any erring judicial officer, including the Chief Registrar of the State Judiciary, Deputy Chief Registrar, or other subordinate officers of the State's Judiciary.[93]

Regarding the qualifications of the persons who are legal practitioners in the State Judicial Service Commission and the FCT Judicial Service Committee, one cannot understand the basis of the differentiation in the years of call to Bar, having regard to the facts that the two bodies recommend to the NJC, the appointments of judges of equal status and of coordinate jurisdiction. While the qualification for the FCT Committee is twelve years, that of the State Commission is ten years.

Having discussed the roles of both the NJC and Judicial Service Commissions/Committee in the appointment of judicial personnel, the next part is devoted to examining the tenure of office and discipline of judicial officers in Nigeria.

TENURE OF OFFICE AND DISCIPLINE OF THE JUDICIAL OFFICERS

The tenure of the judicial officers, remuneration, and conditions of service are adequately secured in Nigeria. In terms of the Constitution, the Chief Justice of Nigeria, the President of the Court of Appeal, the Justices of the Supreme Court, and the Court of Appeal shall hold office until they attain the age of seventy years. However, they may retire voluntarily when they attain the age of sixty-five years.[94] All other

---

[91] See Part II, of the Third Schedule to the 1999 Nigerian Constitution.

[92] See Item 6(a), Part II, of the Third Schedule to the 1999 Nigerian Constitution.

[93] See Item 6(b) & (c), Part II, of the Third Schedule to the 1999 Nigerian Constitution; see also, *Judicial Service Commission of Cross River State & Anor* v. *Dr (Mrs) Asari Young* [2013] 11 NWLR (pt 1364) 1 at 41.

[94] See s 291(1) of the Constitution.

judicial officers shall hold office until they attain the age of sixty-five years, but they may retire voluntarily when they reach the age of sixty years.[95]

In terms of the Constitution, the National Judicial Council (NJC) is saddled with the responsibility of disciplining the erring judicial officers. The Council is empowered to recommend to the President or the Governor (as the case may be) the removal from the office, judges of the superior courts of records. It also exercises disciplinary control over such officers.

It also has the power to appoint, dismiss and exercise disciplinary control over members of the Council.[96] In the same vein, the Federal and State Judicial Service Commissions, as well as the FCT Judicial Service Committee (as the case may be), are constitutionally empowered to recommend to the National Judicial Council the removal and discipline of the Judges/Justices of the Superior Courts of Records in the country.[97]

The tenure of office of the judicial officers is constitutionally guaranteed; as such, a judicial officer shall not ordinarily be removed from his office before his age of retirement. However, the President may remove the Chief Justice of Nigeria, the President of the Court of Appeal, the Chief Judge of the FHC, the Chief Judge of the High Court of the FCT, the Grand Kadi of the Sharia Court of Appeal of the FCT, and the President of the Customary Court of Appeal of the FCT from their respective offices acting on an address supported by a two-thirds majority of the Senate of the National Assembly stating that he be removed for his inability to discharge the functions of his office or appointment (whether arising from infirmity of mind or of the body) or for misconduct or contravention of the Code of Conduct.[98]

In the same vein, on the same account, the Governor may remove from their respective offices the Chief Judge of a State, the Grand Kadi

---

[95] See s 291(2) of the Constitution.

[96] See Item I, Part I, of the Third Schedule to the 1999 Nigerian Constitution.

[97] See Item E, Part I, of the Third Schedule to the 1999 Nigerian Constitution; Item C, Part II, of the Third Schedule to the 1999 Nigerian Constitution; and Part III, of the Third Schedule to the 1999 Nigerian Constitution.

[98] See s 292(1)(a) (i) of the 1999 Constitution.

of the Sharia Court of Appeal of a State, and the President of the Customary Court of Appeal of a State acting on an address supported by a two-thirds majority of the State House of Assembly.[99] Any other Judge or Justice of the superior courts of records other than the heads of the courts may be removed by the President or the Governor (as the case may be), acting on the recommendation of the National Judicial Council that the Judicial officer be removed for his inability to discharge the functions of his office or appointment (whether arising from infirmity of mind or of the body) or for misconduct or contravention of the Code of Conduct.[100]

Any exercise of the power to remove the Chief Justice of Nigeria, the President of the Court of Appeal or the Chief Judges of the State, Federal High Court, High Court of the FCT, Grand Kadi of the Sharia Court of Appeal, the President of the Customary Court of Appeal, must be based on: (a) inability to discharge the functions of office or appointment; or (b) inability to perform the functions of office arising from infirmity of mind or of the body; or (c) misconduct; or (d) contravention of the Code of Conduct.[101] Thus, the conditions specified under Section 292(1)(a)(ii) of the Constitution for the exercise of the power of removal must be satisfied before such power can be validly exercised by the President and the Senate or the Governor and the State House of Assembly (as the case may be).

The relevant case on this issue is *Hon. Justice Raliat Elelu-Habeeb & Anor* v. *The Hon Attorney General of Federation & 2 Ors.*[102] In that case, the House of Assembly of Kwara State, in the exercise of its legislative role, wrote a letter inviting the Chief Judge of Kwara State, Hon Justice Raliat Elelu-Habeeb, to appear at its plenary session with a view to exercising disciplinary control over her as the Head of the State Judiciary. She was away from her base at the time the content of the letter was communicated to her, which caused her to demand another date. The House of Assembly found the allegations against her

[99] See s 292(1)(a) (ii) of the 1999 Constitution.
[100] See s 292(1)(b) of the 1999 Constitution.
[101] See *Elelu-Habeeb* v. *Attorney-General, Federation* (n 85) 494-495.
[102] *Supra,* (n 85).

established and took steps to remove her as the Chief Judge of Kwara State in her absence. The notice of her removal was not communicated to her.

The 1st appellant (as the Plaintiff) reacted to the procedure adopted by both the Governor and the State House of Assembly to effect her removal and challenged the action at the Federal High Court, Ilorin. She claimed, *inter alia*:

> (1) (a) Declaration that by a combined interpretation of sections 4, 153, 292 and paras 20 and 21 of the Third Schedule, Part I of the Constitution, it is only the National Judicial Council (NJC) that has the exclusive power and authority to query, command, order or inquire into any complaint against her arising from or connected with the performance of her functions as a judicial officer and in her office as the Chief Judge of Kwara State or recommend to the Governor her removal as Chief Judge of Kwarate.
>
> (1) (b) An order setting aside, nullifying and putting away the decision of the 3rd and 4th defendant (Governor and the State House of Assembly) contained in the 3rd defendant's letter dated 4th May, 2009 and any other steps taken thereon in so far as it relates to the office of the Plaintiff as the Chief Judge of Kwara State, the same being inconsistent with sections 153, 197, 271(2) of the 1999 Nigerian Constitution and the 3rd Schedule thereof.

After hearing the parties on the originating summons and several preliminary objections of the defendants as to the jurisdiction of the court (taken together at the trial), the learned trial judge, in his judgment delivered on 23 July 2009, overruled the preliminary objections by dismissing them, he found in favour of the plaintiff and granted all the reliefs claimed. The defendants, being dissatisfied with the judgment, appealed to the Court of Appeal, Ilorin Division. In its split judgment of 4 to 1, delivered on 2nd July 2010, the Court of Appeal came to the conclusion that the trial Federal High Court lacked jurisdiction to adjudicate on the matter. In the same judgment, the court, however, proceeded to pass judgment on the merit of the case and arrived at the decision that the trial Federal High Court was right in its decision on the merit of the claims of the plaintiff and consequently affirmed it.

The 1st appellant (the plaintiff at the trial court) and the 2nd appellant (1st defendant at the trial court, the NJC) were not pleased with the decision of the Court of Appeal on the issue of jurisdiction of the FHC and appealed against it. The 2nd and the 3rd respondents also cross-appealed. Unanimously allowing the appeal and dismissing the cross-appeals, the Supreme Court held, *inter alia,* that although the Governor of a State has been vested with the power to appoint the Chief Judge of his State, the power is not absolute. He shares the power with the National Judicial Council, which recommends suitable persons, and the State House of Assembly, which confirms the appointment.

It is in the spirit of the Constitution in ensuring checks and balances between the three arms of government that the role of the Governor in appointing and exercising disciplinary control over the Chief Judge of his State is subject to the participation of the National Judicial Council and the House of Assembly of the State in the exercise to ensure transparency and observance of the rule of law.[103]

It held further that all the conditions or basis for the exercise of power to remove a State Chief Judge must be investigated and confirmed by credible evidence and placed before the Governor and the House of Assembly before they can proceed to exercise their power of removal granted by the Constitution. For example, the ground of removal for inability to perform the functions of office or appointment cannot be ascertained and confirmed by the Governor or the House of Assembly in the absence of any input from the NJC under which supervision the Chief Judge discharges his functions as a judicial officer and which body also directly responsible for exercising disciplinary control over the said Chief Judge.

The Court held that it is not difficult to see that for the effective exercise of the powers of removal of a Chief Judge of a State by the Governor and House of Assembly, the first port of call by the Governor on his journey to remove a Chief Judge of the State is the National Judicial Council which is equipped with the personnel and resources to investigate the inability of the Chief Judge to discharge the functions of

---

103 *Elelu-Habeeb* v. *Attorney-General, Federation* (n 85) 493.

his office, the subject of disciplinary action of removal through the Committee of the Council. And where the infirmity of the mind or body is involved, the services of a Medical Board to examine and submit an appropriate report on the Chief Judge to be affected could also avail the Council in the process of investigation.[104]

It should be noted, however, that on account of corruption and abuse of office, the NJC has on many occasions recommended to the President or the Governor of a State (as the case may be) the dismissal or suspension of judicial officers in recent times.[105] It is submitted, however, that to enhance the dignity of the office, it is a basic rule that once there is an allegation against a judicial officer, the affected officer should be given a fair hearing without delay. The initial hearing of the allegation should be conducted secretly, and the decision reached should as well be subject to an independent review.

The issue of corruption within the judiciary has become an open secret. The faceoff between the then Chief Justice of Nigeria, Katsina-Alu, and the then President of the Court of Appeal, Isa Ayo Salami, over the other's attempt to influence the empanelling or decision of the Court of Appeal on election petitions case pending at the Court of Appeal bring to fore, judicial corruption and the unfortunate "judicial politics."[106] No doubt, some manipulations do take place in the empanelling of justices to sit in important constitutional cases.

---

[104] Ibid., 494-495.

[105] At its sitting of 21 February, 2013 for instance, the NJC recommended the compulsory retirement of two Justices namely, Justice Charles Archibong of the Federal High Court, and Justice Thomas D. Naron of the Plateau State High Court for judicial misconduct. For Justice Naron, he was implicated as in the Osun State Election Petition Tribunal which he chaired. He was found to be in regular communication with one of the counsel in the petition, Kunle Kalejaiye, SAN. In the case of Justice Archibong, he dismissed the 26-count charge against Mr Erastus Akingbola, former MD of the defunct Intercontinental Bank Plc. without taking his plea. See Femi Falana, "Mukhtar and Anti-Corruption War in the Judiciary" *The Punch* (3 June 2013) 68 & 70; See also, the recent suspension of the newly sworn-in Chief Judge of Rivers State, Hon. Justice PNC Agumagu by the NJC for accepting the Office of the Chief Judge of Rivers State in place of Hon. Justice Daisy Okocha recommended by the NJC. See Bertram, "NJC's Recommendation as Prerequisite for Chief Judge's Appointment" (n 87) 81-82.

[106] See IA Salami, "CJN asked me to undermine Sokoto Gov Case" *The Punch Newspaper* (9 February 2011) 62; "Withdrawal of Suit: Civil Societies task NJC over Salami's Claim" *The Punch Newspaper* (19 February 2011) 4; "ASUU asks CJN to resign, threatens mass protest" *The Punch Newspaper* (15 February 2011) 9.

As such, it is not unexpected for politicians to want to influence the judiciary, but it is incumbent on the judiciary to manage the situation properly and not succumb to such pressure.

INDEPENDENCE OF THE JUDICIARY

Judicial independence is a universally recognized principle in democratic societies.[107] It is a prerequisite for a society to operate on the basis of the rule of law. It is essential for the purpose of maintaining public confidence in the judiciary.[108] Judicial independence is recognized in many international and regional human rights instruments as well as in several national constitutions. The concept of independence of the judiciary is of antiquated origin.[109]

The modern understanding of the concept owed much to the writings of John Locke and Montesquieu.[110] According to these scholars, established laws must provide for the right to appeal to an independent judge, and any society that fails to conform to this basic standard is in a state of nature.[111] Implicit in the concept of judicial independence is the doctrine of separation of powers which modern States have so strictly imbibed.[112] The main pillars of judicial independence are institutional and financial autonomy.[113]

The Universal Declaration of Human Rights (UDHR), 1948, provides for the right to a fair and public hearing before a competent, independent, and impartial tribunal established by law.[114] In the same vein, the International Covenant on Civil and Political Rights (ICCPR), 1966 also underscores the importance of judicial independence.[115] In 1985, the United Nations' General Assembly adopted the Basic Principles on the Independence of the Judiciary (the Basic Principles). Further, in 1989, the Economic and Social Council of the United

---

107 See S Rugege, "Judicial Independence in Rwanda" (2007) 19 *Global Business & Development Law Journal*, 411-425, 411.
108 Rugege (n 107) 411.
109 See Taiwo and Adigun (n 7) 156.
110 Ibid., 157.
111 See Baron de Montesquieu, *The Spirit of Laws*, 1748; John Locke, *Two Treaties of Government*, 1823.
112 See Taiwo and Adigun (n 7) 157.
113 Taiwo (n 29) 271.
114 See Art 19, UDHR.
115 See art 14, ICCPR.

Nations also adopted the Procedures for the Effective Implementation of the Basic Principles on the Independence of the Judiciary (the Procedures).

In the Procedures, States are enjoined to observe judicial independence by enshrining the Basic Principles into their Constitutions and domestic laws. The Basic Principles provide for the independence of the judiciary, which can be subsumed under the following heads: separation of powers, qualifications, selection and training, conditions of service and tenure, and discipline, suspension, and removal.[116] Independence of the judiciary should be adequately maintained with adequate security provided given the sensitive nature of the work of judicial officers.

Both government and the public should encourage good governance and independence of the judiciary.[117] Methods of appointment, status, and integrity of those to be appointed as judicial officers are critical in sustaining the independence of the judiciary. Honesty, credibility, and integrity should be the yardstick for appointment to the bench.[118] Candidates should be drawn from as wide a pool as possible. No one should be appointed a judge for purely political reasons when he or she is not otherwise fitted for the office.[119] As a mark of independence, a judge is expected to be impartial, patient, exhibit wisdom, prudence, and courage in the discharge of his duty. He should have the integrity of character and do the right according to the law.

Government, politicians, as well as the general public, should refrain from exercising undue influence and pressure on the judges. It is beyond dispute that to sustain a democracy in the modern world, an independent, impartial, and upright judiciary is a necessity.[120] What then calls for examination is how far the Constitution has made provisions in ensuring the independence of the judiciary. In order to be

---

116 Taiwo and Adigun (n 7) 157.
117 See Taiwo (n 29) 271.
118 "Honour and integrity are the two things which define a fine judicial officer alongside the grasp of the law." See Isa Ayo Salami, OFR, PCA (Rtd) vol. 3, No. 3, *The Capital Territory Law Review Magazine* 34.
119 See Taiwo (n 29) 271.
120 Aguda (n 8) 34.

able to perform its duties fearlessly and impartially, the Constitution attempts to grant the judiciary some amount of independence from the other two arms of government.[121] While other arms of Government, the Legislature, and the Executive, are elected, however, the Constitution provides for the appointment of the members of the Judiciary by a Judicial Service Commission (JSC) and the National Judicial Council (NJC).

To secure the independence of the judiciary, the salaries and allowances of the judicial officers are charged and paid out of the Consolidated Revenue Funds. Judges are also entitled to receive a pension for life upon retirement.[122] To also fortify the dignity of the judicial office, the Constitution provides that any person who has held the office as a judicial officer shall not, on ceasing to be a judicial officer, for any reason whatsoever, thereafter, appear or act as a legal practitioner before any court of law or tribunal in Nigeria.[123]

It should be pointed out that although the Nigerian Constitution guarantees the independence of the judiciary, that independence is, however, not total in the sense that the other two arms of government have some kind of influence and control over the judiciary, and this invariably impacts its independence. First, the judiciary lacks independence in so far as its recurrent expenditure is concerned.[124] Also, the appointment of a person to the office of the Chief Justice of Nigeria is made by the President at his discretion upon recommendation from the National Judicial Council, and the appointment is subject to confirmation of the simple majority of the Senate. As Aguda rightly submitted, one is at a loss as to the requirement of subjecting the appointment of the Chief Justice of Nigeria and other heads of Federal Courts to the Senate's confirmation since there is no such reciprocal power in the judiciary on the appointment of the Senate President.[125]

---

[121] See ibid 18.
[122] See s 291(3) of the Constitution.
[123] See s 292(2) of the Constitution.
[124] See Aguda (n 8) 22.
[125] Ibid., 22-23.

It should be noted that it is constitutionally required of a person appointed to any judicial office to declare his assets and liabilities and take the Oath of Allegiance and the Judicial Oath before he commences the functions of that office.[126] If this is not done, it is tantamount to a breach of the Code of Conduct of Judicial Officers as well as the Constitution. In the appointment of judicial personnel, both the National Judicial Council and the Federal and State Judicial Service Commissions play a pivotal role in the appointment and discipline of judicial officers in the country. As appointing bodies, they have the constitutional mandate to ensure that judicial appointments are based on merit and ensure that only persons of unquestionable character are appointed.

It is submitted that the NJC and the Judicial Service Commission should seek a more efficient way of appointing only competent persons to the bench. When judicial appointment is based on political consideration, there is bound to be manipulation, and departure from established principles or norms in order to please a section of the political class. It is submitted that the appointment of unqualified persons based on political consideration accounts for some of the poor judgments and conflicting decisions now coming from the various courts in Nigeria.[127]

Some of the judgments handed down by some judges are not only ridiculous but outrageously embarrassing. They seem to confirm the position that the various courts have been compromised or bought over.

In the same vein, although it is accepted that the Constitution vests in the National Judicial Council power to recommend judicial officers for an appointment, however, to secure the independence of the judiciary, NJC should not allow personal sentiments and other interests to influence its decision in terms of appointment and discipline of the judicial officers. For instance, the hasty suspension of the Rivers State

---

[126] See s 290(1) of the 1999 Constitution.

[127] In the election petitions cases for instance, the judgments in most cases are, at times, conflicting and opened to criticisms. See in this regard, *Babajide Omoworare* v. *Iyiola Omisore &ors* [2010] 3 NWLR (Pt.1180) 58; *Wamini-Emi* v. *Igali & 5Ors* [2008]11 NWLR (Pt.1097) 123, among others.

Chief Judge, Hon. Justice Peter N. Agumagu by NJC without a hearing sometime in March, 2014 erodes the independence of the judiciary rather than strengthening it. The Council gave four days to the embattled Chief Judge to show why he should not be removed as a judicial officer.[128]

It is submitted that by wielding the big stick against an innocent Chief Judge over a political or administrative tussle/dispute on whom to be appointed the Chief Judge of the State and who has the final say on such an appointment between the Rivers State Governor, Rotimi Amaechi, and the Rivers State House of Assembly, on the one hand, and the National Judicial Council, on the other hand, is to say the least, an abuse of power. This is so given that the embattled Chief Judge, Hon. Justice Peter N. Agumagu did not appoint himself to the post.

The stance of the Governor, which NJC should have rather investigated, is the claim that the embattled Chief Judge was the most senior judge in Rivers State at the time of his appointment. NJC should not misuse its power by eroding judicial independence by truncating the tenure of an innocent judicial officer over the battle for superiority between it and the State Governor.

As seen above, there is no doubt that the Nigerian Constitution has put in some measures to ensure and guarantee the independence of the judiciary in the country. As such, it is submitted that as a way of protecting the integrity of the judiciary, unless there is serious evidence of corruption and undue influence, the NJC, government, the public, and the political class are enjoined to avoid sentiments and should always appreciate and respect judicial officers. On its part, the government should not cow the judiciary by directly or indirectly punishing judicial officer(s) for delivering judgment against the ruling party, as it was the situation in the case of Hon. Justice Isa Ayo Salami, the former President of the Court of Appeal. On their part, Judges are also admonished to shun all forms of corruption and abide by the judicial oath, which forbids personal or political interest from influencing their decisions.

---

[128] Ebiri Kelvin, "Rivers Govt insists Argumagu is State's Chief Judge" *The Guardian* (3 April 2014) 1 and 2.

CONCLUSION

This chapter has discussed the qualifications, appointments, tenure, and discipline of judicial officers, as well as the independence of the judiciary. It is observed that the National Judicial Council, as well as both the Federal and State Judicial Service Commissions, play critical roles in the appointment and discipline of the judicial personnel. The President or the Governor of a State (as the case may be) appoints Judges based on the recommendations of the National Judicial Council, which also, in turn, acts on the advice of the Judicial Service Commission. As emphasized in this chapter, the quality of justice we receive in Nigeria depends, to a large extent, on the indiscretion of the National Judicial Council and the Judicial Service Commission on the quality of persons they recommend for judicial appointments.

As pointed out in this work, the Constitution places a bar or disqualification on certain persons from being appointed to judicial positions. In terms of the Constitution, no person shall be appointed into a judicial office whilst he is a member of the National Judicial Council or the Judicial Service Commission/Committee.[129] Such person shall remain so disqualified until a period of three years has elapsed since he/she ceases to be a member of the Council or the Commission.[130] The wisdom behind this disqualification/bar is commendable. The disqualification clause is to ensure that the appointment into a judicial office is transparent, made on merit, and is not in any way influenced on account of being a member of the appointing bodies.

Apart from the constitutional requirement that judicial appointments should be based on a minimum requirement of post-qualification legal experience, such as practicing or being employed as a lawyer in the area of teaching and research in law, it is strongly advised that the National Judicial Council should be guided in judicial appointments by other extra-constitutional qualities and abilities to wit: *(i) great intellectual capacity*, that is, high level of expertise in the

---

[129] See s 289 of the Constitution.
[130] Ibid.

chosen area or profession; ability quickly to absorb and analyse information; and appropriate knowledge of the law and its underlying principles; (ii) *personal qualities* which cover integrity and independence of mind; sound judgment; decisiveness; objectivity and ability and willingness to learn and develop quickly. Others include (iii) *the ability to understand and deal fairly*, that is, the ability to treat everyone with respect and sensitivity, whatever their background; and willingness to listen with patience and courtesy; (iv) *authority and communication skills:* the ability to explain the procedure and any decisions reached clearly and succinctly to those involved; ability to inspire respect and confidence; and the ability to maintain authority when challenged. Finally, (v) *efficiency,* which covers the ability to work at speed and under pressure; the ability to organize time effectively and produce clear, reasoned judgments expeditiously; and the ability to work constructively with others. If all these qualities are taken into consideration in appointing judges in Nigeria, it will go a long way to enhance the qualities and standards of judicial personnel in the country as well as the judgments coming out of the various courts."

Chapter 16

CORONER SYSTEM AND THE ADMINISTRATION OF CRIMINAL JUSTICE IN NIGERIA

E. O. Akingbehin*

The Constitution of Nigeria, amongst other municipal, regional, and international instruments, guarantees a citizen's right to life and prescribes a grave punishment for those who occasion a loss of others' lives, especially without excuse or justification. Yet, there has been wanton termination of lives by the day under sudden and unnatural circumstances. This has largely resulted in the legacy of impunity and lack of accountability for such deaths. The coroner system is aimed at determining the medical cause of death, allaying rumours or suspicion, and enabling society to be conscious of preventable deaths inter alia. The coroner system also enables the epidemiological units of hospitals and the relevant governmental agencies to have reliable data on how to prevent some sudden and unnatural deaths in society. However, the criminal justice administration in Nigeria is plagued by the ineffective implementation of the various coroner laws in the country, which, at best, have been described as dead letter laws. This paper, therefore, seeks to appraise the coroner system in Nigeria within the context of criminal justice administration. The writer beams a searchlight on the global history and development of the coroner system. The paper also analyses the practice and procedure of the coroner system in Nigeria with the assessment of the impact of the coroner system on the criminal

---

* E. O. Akingbehin, LL.B (Hons) Ife, LLM, Ph.D (Lagos) BL, Senior Lecturer, Department of Public Law, University of Lagos, Akoka, Yaba, Lagos, Nigeria.

justice administration. The chapter concludes, and the writer proffers recommendations for the way forward.

INTRODUCTION

A coroner system is a situation whereby an inquest is conducted by the state to unravel the circumstances surrounding a sudden and unnatural death of a person. A coroner's inquest is, therefore, an attempt by an independent body set up by the government to ensure that causes of unnatural or sudden death[1] are investigated and clarified through a transparent, independent, and formal procedure that provides ample opportunity to get to the root of the cause of death of any person.[2]

The Nigerian Constitution[3] seeks to guarantee a citizen's right to life by entrenching the necessary safeguards for the protection and preservation of human lives. It specifically forbids the act of anybody taking the life of another or subjection of a person to death except in certain justified and excusable circumstances.[4]

However, available statistics show that there has been a high degree of human rights violations since civil rule began in 1999, as several innocent lives have been lost to police brutality,[5] politically motivated killings, air crashes,[6] and terrorist attacks *inter alia*. According to

---

1 The English Court of Appeal, in interpreting the circumstances of unnatural death held in Touche's case that a woman's death could be regarded as unnatural after her blood pressure was left unmonitored following a caesarean section delivery. The court held further that where a person is suffering from a condition which if not monitored and treated in a routine way, will result in death and that treatment or monitoring is omitted, the coroner must hold an inquest, unless he/she can say that there are no grounds for suggesting that the omission was an affective cause of the death. See *RVHM Coroner for Inner London, Ex Parte Touche* (2001) 2.A.C. 810.

2 G. Akingbehin, "The Import of Coroner's Inquest in Addressing the Quest for Justice and Accountability in Extra-Judicial Killings: Lagos State in Perspective". Published in *Current Law Series*, a publication of the Faculty of Law, University of Lagos, Nigeria, Vol. 2, 2007, p.4

3 See Section 33 of the Constitution of the Federal Republic of Nigeria 1999 Cap C. 23 Laws of the Federation 2004 (As amended).

4 For example, death resulting from the execution of death sentence, or from the use of reasonable force for self-defence, or to prevent escape from lawful detention, or riot, insurrection, or mutiny. See S. 33 (1), (2) a – c CFRN 1999, ibid.

5 A. Ibidapo Obe, "Police Brutality: Dimensions and Control in Nigeria," *Essays on Human Rights Law.* Concept Publications, Lagos, 2005, p. 299

6 For example, the inquest into the Associated Airlines Crash, which occurred at the Murtala Muhammed International Airport, on the 3rd October, 2013, is currently being conducted by Mr. Tajudeen Elias, a Chief Magistrate Grade II, at Agege, Lagos State. It is saddening that 16 out of the 20 passengers on board died. The aircraft, which crashed few minutes after take-off, was flying to Akure with 20 persons, including crew members and the corpse of the late former Governor of Ondo State, Dr. Olusegun Agagu

Omogbehin,[7] about 289 deaths could be related to extra-judicial killings in the first three years of the life of the civilian administration.

It is rather worrisome that the government has not mustered the necessary political will to prosecute the law enforcement officers who arbitrarily kill innocent and helpless citizens. The government has also failed to take any credible and systematic step to institutionalize accountability in police service delivery, which has resulted in a large-standing legacy of impunity.

An inquest, therefore, is a means by which the state discharges its obligations to inquire into a death where there is an element of state responsibility, either for the death itself, the investigation of it, or both. This position was confirmed by the European Court on Human Rights (ECHR) in the case of *MCCAN* v. *United Kingdom,*[8] where the facts concerned the state's responsibility for and the investigation of the shooting of members of the provisional security forces, who were alleged to be planning to plant a bomb in Gibraltar. The ECHR was satisfied that the obligation to hold an effective official investigation had been discharged by the inquest.

Sequel to the foregoing, the coroner system is aimed at assisting the victims' families in getting justice and enhancing accountability for the extra-judicial killings and sudden and unnatural deaths. The coroner system is also aimed at determining the medical cause of death, allaying rumours or suspicion, and drawing attention to the existence of circumstances, which, if not remedied, might lead to further deaths, enabling society to be conscious of preventable deaths and also the preservation of the legal interest of the deceased's person's family, heirs and of other interested parties.[9] It is also important to underscore the fact that the conduct of a coroner's inquest, requiring autopsies, would enable the epidemiological units of hospitals and the relevant government agencies to have reliable data of reported deaths and enable

on board. See A. Adesomoju, "Air Crashes: FAAN Tells Coroner the Deficiencies in Rescue Operations" *The Punch Newspaper* 12 May, 2014, p. 77.

7 F. M. Omogbehin, "Licensed killers", a publication of the *Access to Justice*, August 2001, p. 42.

8 (1995) 21 ECHR 97.

9 F. Famoroti, "Coroner Law: The Controversy and the Need to Unravel Mysterious Deaths". See the *National Mirror Newspaper*, 29 November, 2012, p.8.

them to plan easily on how to prevent some sudden and unnatural deaths in the society.[10]

This chapter, therefore, aims to appraise the coroner system within the context of the criminal justice administration in Nigeria. It is divided into five parts. The first part introduces the topic whilst the second part attempts to beam a searchlight onto the global history and development of the coroner system. The third part delves into the analysis of the coroner system in Nigeria within the context of its practice and procedure, looking at the statutory and institutional framework. A critical appraisal of the impact of the coroner system on the criminal justice administration in Nigeria constitutes the thrust of the fourth part, whilst the paper concludes in the fifth part, and the author proffers suggestions for a way ward.

HISTORY AND DEVELOPMENT OF CORONER SYSTEM

The office of a coroner is a uniquely English institution. The class of privileges mentioned in English historical sources includes a grant of the coroner's office by the king to an English noble in the year 925. The post of a coroner dates from approximately the eleventh century, shortly after the Norman Conquest of England in 1066. The office of a coroner was formally established in England[11] to "keep the pleas of the crown."[12] It was during this era that the Justice in the Eyre was required to provide that three knights and one clerk were to be elected in every county, the appointment which included the coroner's duties.[13]

In 1887, a law was enacted in England requiring an inquest to be conducted whenever the coroner had reasonable cause to suspect violent or unnatural death. In 1888, the election of the coroners was abolished, and an "appointee" system developed.

---

10 F. Famoroti, "Coroner Law: The Controversy and the Need to Unravel Mysterious Deaths". See the *National Mirror Newspaper*, 29 November, 2012, p.8.

11 See Article 20 of the "Article of Eyre" of September 1194

12 The latin version is *Custo Placitorum Coronae* from which the word "coroner" is derived. The French version is *couronne.* It is important to underscore the difference between "holding the pleas" which was a judicial role and "keeping the peace" which was administrative task.

13 F. Moskof, Q. C. & J. Young, "The Roles of Coroner and Counsel in Coroner's Court". *Criminal Law Quarterly,* Vol. 30, 1987 – 88, pp. 193 – 196.

Scotland never had a coroner's system. She remained independent of England for a long time, and their system of law is more akin to that found on the continent. Wales inherited the English Coroner's System after the Edwardian Conquest of 1282. Before this period, the Welsh had their own system of law dating from about the ninth century. Ireland also acquired the English Coroner's system after the imposition of the Norman administration there from 1170. In later times, England exported her coroner system all over the world. Hence, the office of a coroner originated in Medieval England and has been adopted in many countries whose legal systems have, at some time, been subject to English or United Kingdom Law.[14]

The early American colonists brought the English system with them as early as 1600. The first record of an inquest was in New England in 1635, and the earliest mention of a physician in connection with the work of a coroner was in Maryland in 1860, where the coroner or his jury was authorised to require the attendance of a physician in cases of violent death.[15] In North Carolina, many countries ceased having coroners when the state judicial system was overhauled in the late 1960s, ending city jails and major courts. Paid medical examiners were appointed, with a requirement to be licensed physicians, often forensic pathologists or, in some instances, veterinarians or dentists, though most of the coroners have historically been morticians from local funeral homes.

It is not all American jurisdictions that use a coroner system for a medico-legal death investigation. While some are in medical examiner system, others are in a mixed coroner-medical examiner system. The terms "coroner" and "medical examiner" vary widely in meaning by the jurisdiction in the United States of America. In some states, additional functions are handled by the coroner. For example, in Louisiana, Coroners are involved in the determination of mental illness of living persons. Also, in Georgia, the coroner has the same powers as a county sheriff to execute arrest warrants and serve processes. However, in New

---

14 B. Knight, KBE, "History of Medieval English Coroner System".www.britannia.com /history/articles /coroner 1. html (Last accessed 24 March, 2014).

15 See G. Akingbehin, *op. cit.,* note 1 *supra.*

York City, the office of a coroner was actually abolished in 1915, though, prior to that time, possession of medical knowledge was not actually a requirement to be a coroner, a development that led to much abuse of the position.[16]

The first Coroner's Act in Upper Canada was enforced in 1850. Coroner or Medical Examiner Services in Canada are under the jurisdiction of provincial or territorial government within the public safety and security or justice portfolio, depending on location. These services are headed by a Chief Coroner and are supported by a team of coroners, with the assistance of other medical and law enforcement personnel. In Prince Edward Island and Ontario, all Coroners are, by law, physicians. However, in other provinces and territories with a coroner system,[17] coroners are not necessarily physicians, but they generally have legal, medical, or investigative backgrounds.[18] It is noteworthy, however, that the adoption of the coroner's law into Nigeria's legal system is the legacy of its colonial heritage of English Com Law.

CORONER SYSTEM IN NIGERIA: PRACTICE AND PROCEDURE

The recently enacted Coroner's System Law of Lagos State 2007 contains the statutory framework for the coroner system in Lagos State.[19] Coroner Law is also available in the statutes of other states in the Federation.[20] However, the experts are unanimous that the enforcement mechanism of the law is weak in Lagos State and almost moribund in the other parts of the country.[21]

---

16 Ibid.

17 These provinces and territories include British Columbia, Saskatchewan, Quebec, New Brunswick, North West Territories, Nunavit and Yukon.

18 See G. Akingbehin, *op. cit.,* note 1 , *supra.*

19 See the Coroner's System Law of Lagos State, signed into law by Governor Babatunde Fashola on the 14th August, 2007, though came into force on 18th May, 2007.

20 See for example, Coroner's Law, Vol. 1 Laws of Ogun State 2006, Coroner's Law, Cap. 36, Vol. 1. Laws of Oyo State, 2000. See also the Coroner's Laws, Cap. 34, Laws of Rivers State of Nigeria 1999 and the Coroner's Law, Cap. 36, Laws of Ondo State 2006. Some States like Osun and Ekiti States still retain the Western Region Coroner Laws of 1959, Cap 27. The States in the old Eastern Nigeria also still retain the Coroner Laws of Eastern Nigeria 1956.

21 F. Famoroti, "Coroner Law: The Controversy and the Need to Unravel Mysterious Deaths" *op cit,* note 10, p. 10.

On the qualification of a coroner, the Coroner's Systems Law of Lagos State[22] has now required that a person to be appointable as a coroner must possess a minimum of five years post-call experience, or if a magistrate, he must not be less than a Magistrate Grade 1. The 2007 Law also provides for the appointment of a Chief Coroner who shall be a judge of the High Court and shall supervise the coroners.[23] Also, the law provides for the appointment of a Chief Medical Examiner who is to supervise the District Medical Examiners. They shall be forensic pathologists, and their functions include the conduct of autopsies on the deceased bodies *inter alia*.[24]

Quite unlike in England, the coroner does not sit with the jury in Nigeria. At every inquest, the coroner shall take on oath such evidence as is procurable as to the identity, time, place, and manner of death of the deceased.[25] At, or before the first sitting of a coroner on a body, the coroner shall view the body or shall satisfy himself that the body has been viewed by an administrative officer, police officer, medical practitioner, or local government council official, and the coroner can thereafter issue an order authorising the burial of the body.[26] However, a coroner has the power to order the exhumation of a body that is buried without his/her view.[27] A coroner also has the power to issue summons and warrants to compel the attendance of witnesses before him.[28]

Inquests are not trials of persons alleged to have been responsible for the deaths of others, and it is not the job of the coroner to blame anyone for the death. Coroner's inquests are subordinate to trials, especially criminal trials, and an inquest must be put on hold during criminal proceedings.[29]

---

22 See Sections 4(1) of the Coroner's System Law of Lagos State 2007.
23 See Section 2(1) of the Coroner's System Law, ibid. This is similar to the position in Ontario, Canada. See F. Moscoff, Q. C. *et al*, *Op cit*, note 13 *Supra*, p. 191.
24 See Sections 7 and 11 of the Coroner's System Law of Lagos State *(*ibid*)*.
25 See Section 33 of the Coroner System Law, ibid.
26 See Section 31, ibid.
27 See Section 17, ibid.
28 See Section 32, ibid.
29 See Section 38, ibid.

Upon the conclusion of a proceeding, a coroner must return every inquisition together with the depositions and recognisances of the witnesses to the chief coroner in the judicial division in which the inquisition took place, and the registrar of the chief coroner shall take charge of the same.[30] The High Court judge, who is now designated as a chief coroner,[31] can then examine the record as to the correctness, legality, or propriety of any finding or verdict. However, where the chief coroner is not satisfied with any or whole of the proceedings, he may quash the verdict with or without ordering a new instruction.[32]

IMPACT OF THE CORONER'S SYSTEM ON THE CRIMINAL JUSTICE ADMINISTRATION IN NIGERIA

It is rather perturbing that the coroner's system, which is supposed to assist victims' families in getting justice and enhancing accountability for extra-judicial killings, has not been helpful due to a myriad of factors that impede its effectiveness. This has made writers describe the coroner law as a toothless bulldog, a smoke screen, and a mere window dressing.[33] It can then be said to offer a placebo rather than the much-needed panacea because a coroner cannot enforce any order or even adjudicate on a criminal matter over the perpetrators of a murder act. A lot of factors have been identified as militating against the effectiveness of the coroner's law.

The first factor that impairs the effectiveness of an inquest is premised on the fact that the rules of evidence which are regarded as germane to proof of liability or proof of rights in all courts, are not binding on the coroner.[34] It is submitted that the notion of justice is so tied to the notion that adherence to evidentiary rules is one of the safeguards of justice. Hence, how can it be said that a case is rightly and justly decided when it is fraught with the admission of inadmissible or irrelevant evidence or where oral evidence is replete with hearsay, or

---

30 See Section 44, ibid.

31 See Section 2, ibid.

32 See Section 44 (2) & (3), ibid.

33 G. Akingbehin, *op. cit,* note 2, *supra.*

34 See Section 34, ibid.

where documentary evidence is not proceeding from the proper custody? It is further contended that the rules of evidence are designed to secure justice by regulating the kind of and how evidence may be received and applied for the determination of cases and doing justice.

It follows, therefore, that overwhelming resistance would likely follow any attempt to accord the same evidentiary weight to the records of coroner's proceedings and the records of courts of justice. This is predicated on the ground that the evidence obtained in the coroner proceeding is not obtained, following strict rules. It must be realised that whether evidence is obtained through adversarial or inquisitorial mode is not the critical determination of whether facts are proven. The two modes may prescribe different ways of obtaining evidence, but this is not the same thing as suggesting that one is superior to the other. After all, Nigeria only adopted the adversarial system by accident of history.[35]

Another albatross of the coroner's system is the worth of the inquest. It appears such reports/inquests are not accorded any prominent recognition. The coroner law merely provides[36] that the inquest be transmitted to the chief coroner but fails to indicate what next to be done with the inquest, especially where the cause of death and the identity of the killer have been revealed. The poser that immediately calls for consideration is whether the evidence obtained in the course of coroner's proceedings should be accorded due value in subsequent litigation, in view of the fact that proceedings of an inquest are generally inadmissible at the trial for homicide.[37] Thus, when a person is either under arrest or accused of a crime at a coroner's inquest, any testimony that he or she gives cannot subsequently be used against him or her at a trial that stems from the inquest.[38] Hence on an

35 This is the legacy of the colonial heritage of English Common Laws.

36 See Section 44, ibid.

37 A. Atsenuwa, "Can Victims' Relatives Use Coroner's Evidentiary Records To Litigate Unlawful Killings?" Unpublished paper, presented at the Conference on Promoting Law Enforcement Accountability and Respect for the Right to Life, Using Coroner Procedure, on the 16th December, 2002 at Sheraton Hotel, Ikeja, Lagos, Nigeria.

38 www.co.adams.il.us/coroner/inquest.htm (last accessed 29 April, 2014)

indictment for homicide, neither the verdict of the coroner's jury nor the finding of the coroner can be used as evidence for any purpose.[39]

However, the rationale underlying this exclusion rule is that a person is not entitled to be represented by counsel at an inquest since it is merely a preliminary investigation. The practical consequence of allowing the coroner's verdict to be used as evidence during trial is that it would become the key piece of evidence in action. Thus, if this occurs, the judgment awarded in the case would probably end up being ratification of the coroner's verdict, thereby depriving the party action of his or her right to have "a day in court" with all the procedural safeguards.[40] Hence, what is the worth of an inquest?

The coroner's law[41] provides that the coroner's verdict, after due certification, shall be forwarded to the Attorney General, the Chief Coroner, the Chief Medical Examiner, and the Divisional Police Officer in the district of the inquest. Consequently, it would be inferable that, at best, the report/verdict will assist the Attorney General or the Divisional Police Officer, as the case may be, in preferring the appropriate criminal charges against those indicted in the report.

It is observed that the combination of sections 41 and 44 of the coroner's system law of Lagos State constitutes a rehash of the Coroner Laws of Western Region of Nigeria 1959, which allowed for preliminary inquiry by the Magistrates. The law requires the coroner to transmit his inquisition to the Chief Coroner upon the conclusion of the hearing, and the same law requires the coroner to forward his certified verdict to the Attorney General, Chief Medical Examiner, etc.

It is submitted that such verdict, which constitutes part of the inquisition, should be forwarded to the Attorney General and others by the Chief Coroner after exercising his power of review. The coroner should merely submit his report to the Chief Coroner for review.

In the wake of the enactment of the Coroner's System Law in Lagos State in 2007, there were a plethora of protests from the Muslim Community as regards some sections of the law that were perceived to

---

39 Ibid.
40 Ibid.
41 Section 41, Coroner's Systems Law, ibid.

be violative of the rights of the Muslims. The aspect of the law that was declared offensive is the section that requires that all dead bodies must go through an autopsy.[42] It is contended by the Muslims that autopsy constitutes the most dehumanizing way of treating the dead because Muslim corpses are held sacrosanct and must not even be delayed before burial.

Some Muslim organizations[43] also wrote the Lagos State Governor that certain provisions of the law contradicted the position of Islam that the corpse of a Muslim should be buried within 24 hours.

Delay in submitting autopsy reports by Forensic pathologists (medical examiners) is inevitable due to paucity in the number of such professionals in the country. In Nigeria, it was indicated that there are about 200 morbid anatomists in a country of more than 160 million people, thus, leaving a ratio of one million Nigerians to one of such experts, which is grossly insufficient.

It has been suggested that there should be more specialists in that field to augment the population of experts toward conducting autopsies within short periods.[44]

There have also been issues relating to conflicting forensic evidence, which has also whittled down the effectiveness of the whole coroner system. An example was the inquest of late Alaba Joseph's death, where divergent medical opinions were expressed by renowned pathologists.[45] Alaba Joseph, a former president of Mobitel (a Lagos-based telecommunications company), died on the 15th of September, 2005, in his company's premises while the court officials (bailiffs) accompanied by the police were trying to execute a receivership order against the company. His corpse was found in the parking lot with injuries only on the head in the form of holes. While the judgment creditor insinuated that the deceased must have committed suicide in order to avoid the shame of handing over the company to a receiver,

---

42 See Sections 15, 18, 26 and 27, ibid.

43 Some of the organizations were Muslim Rights Concern and Muslim Lawyers Association.

44 U. Ifionu, "Coroner Law: Double Trouble for Dead Body". *ThisDay* newspaper of 23 November, 2010, p.12

45 T. Amokeodo, "Joseph's Inquest and the Need for Truth". in *The Punch* newspaper of 28 November 2005, p.61.

the deceased family contended that he was shot by the gun-throttling policeman who accompanied the bailiffs. An autopsy was conducted by Professor John Obafunwa, a professor of forensic pathology, College of Medicine, Lagos State University (Now the University's Vice Chancellor), and his report revealed that Joseph died of craniocerebral and gunshot injuries.[46]

The Inspector General of Police thereafter set up a team of pathologists, led by Professor Williams Odesanmi of the department of forensic medicine, Obafemi Awolowo University, Ile-Ife, Nigeria, to conduct a second autopsy. However, the five-man team's report contradicted the first report by disclosing that the late Joseph died of misadventure, having suffered multiple fractures of the skull associated with lacerations of the brain due to a fall from a height.

In view of the contradictions in the two reports, the Chief Judge of Lagos State, Justice Ade Alabi, set up an inquest to look into the circumstances that led to the death of the Mobitel boss, and appointed Mrs. Ayo Odugbesan, a Chief Magistrate Grade 1, as the coroner.[47] The coroner ordered for a third autopsy so as to resolve the contradiction, and it was performed by pathologists from the Nebraska Institute of Forensic Sciences in the United States of America. Unfortunately, the team of experts could not arrive at a coherent conclusion because a lot of tissues in the skull that would have enhanced their decision were already missing.

The coroner, after taking the evidence of vital witnesses, including the pathologists in the case, eventually submitted her verdict, which aligned with the report of the first autopsy, that Joseph died of gunshot and was killed on the ledge, where his body was found. It is rather worrisome that since January 2006 when the coroner submitted her report to the registrar of High Court, in line with the provisions of the coroner's law, hitherto, no further step has been taken about the ascertained perpetrators of the dastardly and heinous act of killing. The Inspector General of police had persistently defied the Lagos Attorney

---

46 Y. Odunuga, "So, Who Killed Joseph?" *Saturday Punch Newspaper* of 4 February, 2006, p. 7

47 T. Amokeodo, "Mobitel Boss: Lagos Awaits Fresh Police Investigation". *The Punch* newspaper of 23 February, 2006, p. 10.

General's entreaties, requesting him to prosecute the culprits.[48] There is no gainsaying the fact that the cul-de-sac situation of this inquest has virtually rubbished the whole essence of the system. It is a travesty of justice.

Another example of a frustrating conclusion of an inquest was the one carried out on the death of Modebayo Awosika, a former employee of First Bank Plc, who was killed under controversial circumstances along Lekki-Epe road in Lagos in 2006. A coroner's inquest conducted under the new Lagos State Coroner's Systems Law 2007 revealed, in the verdict, that a police officer (Sgt Oyigie) was responsible for the brutal killing of the deceased.[49] The coroner court which was presided over by Philips Ojo, a Chief Magistrate, ordered that Oyigie, the killer cop, be produced in court for questioning and possible prosecution, an order which the Lagos State Commissioner of Police has flouted till date. It is consequently indubitable that the impact of the coroner system on the criminal justice administration in Nigeria is hardly credible.

CONCLUSION AND SUGGESTIONS FOR WAY FORWARD

This chapter has analysed the historical foundation of the coroner's system. It has also delved extensively into the practice and procedure of the coroner's system in Nigeria, especially in Lagos State. The writer has also identified the factors that are militating against the effectiveness of the law by submitting that the law remains a dead letter law, which has offered only a placebo instead of a panacea. The chapter also proffers some suggestions for ways out of the quagmire toward attaining justice and accountability for extra-judicial killings.

Against the backdrop of the militating factors which have eroded the values of the coroner system, the following suggestions are proffered.

1. The coroner's law should be amended to make the requirement of autopsy for sudden death optional. This will assuage the feelings of

---

48 K. Obasola, "Lagos Urges I. G. to Re-Investigate Death of Mobitel Boss," *The Punch* newspaper of 5 May, 2006, p. 11.

49 U. Ifionu, *op. cit.,* note 44 *Supra* p. 12

the embittered Muslim organizations, who perceive that the law is an affront to the sensibility of Muslim citizens.

In the Australian States and Territories, the Coronial jurisdiction is only attracted if the death falls within one of the listed number of categories.[50] It has also been held by the New South Wales Court of Appeal in the case of *Deitz* v. *Abernathy*[51] that the practice of making autopsy requirements compulsory is unlawful and that the coroner should consider each case on its merit and ought to take into account any objection that the family or religious organization may have to such a process. Nigeria should learn lessons from modernity.

2. The Government should make spirited and conscious efforts toward the massive training of experts in the field of forensic pathology. This chapter has shown that there is a dearth of these professionals and that it has resulted largely in the delays in the processing of autopsy reports, which has the effect of defeating the course of justice.
3. The position of the coroner system law that excluded a coroner from being bound by evidentiary rules is unjust to the status and worth of an inquest. Such exclusion has the effect of ridiculing the whole process. Thus, for an inquest to have legal credibility and status recognition, it has to be subjected to the avalanche of evidential rules on judicial proceedings.
4. The coroner system's law should make definite provisions on what becomes of a report/verdict submitted by the coroner to the chief coroner, especially where the report is satisfactory to the chief coroner. The coroner systems law[52] merely spelled out what happens if the chief coroner is not satisfied with the report of the coroner. The law is, however, silent on what happens if the verdict/report is

---

50 See G. Segal, "The Necessary Role of Autopsies in Cardiovascular Epidemiology," Hum. Path. 1998, December 29 (12) p. 1469.

51 (1996) 39 NSWLR 301. See also *Krantz* v. *Hand* (1999) NSWSC 342, where the court held that religious and other objections on the part of the family of the deceased should be taken into account. See sections 95-99 of the New South Wales Coroner's Act.

52 See Section 44, ibid.

satisfactory to the chief coroner. Is the prosecutorial action to be initiated by the police or the Attorney General, and how?

The present *lacunae*, as reflected by the late Alaba Joseph's inquest, is evidence of the failure of the system.

5. Both the Coroner's System Law and the Evidence Act[53] should be amended to accommodate the admissibility of an inquest report for the purpose of subsequent criminal action, especially where admissions have been voluntarily made. This also has the effect of serving as an estoppel for subsequent retraction of evidence.
6. The law should be further amended to increase the requirements for the qualification of a coroner. Considering the skill and experience required to conduct an inquest, which is even more herculean than a conventional judicial trial, because of its peculiar inquisitorial nature, it is suggested that a magistrate to be eligible as a coroner must not be below a chief magistrate. In the same vein, a legal practitioner, to be appointable, must possess not less than 10 years' post-call experience. It is noteworthy that the magistrates who conducted inquests in Alaba Joseph and Modebayo Awosika's cases were both chief magistrates with over twenty years post-call experience.

Consequently, it is only if the above suggestions are implemented that the quest for justice and accountability for extra-judicial killings, through the machinery of coroner's inquest, can be actualized within the context of our criminal justice system.

53 See Section 135, Evidence Act 2011, on the requirement of standard of proof in criminal.

PART E

LEGAL PROFESSION AND LEGAL EDUCATION IN NIGERIA

Chapter 17

ETHICS, PROFESSIONAL RESPONSIBILITY, AND DISCIPLINE

Dominic Asada*

INTRODUCTION

In 1989, the preamble of the code of conduct of lawyers in the European community that was formulated and approved read thus:

> In a society founded on respect for the rule of law, the lawyer fulfils a special role. His duties do not begin and end with faithful performance of what he is instructed to do so far as the law permits. A lawyer must serve the interest of the just as well as those whose rights and liberties to us trusted to assert and defend. It is the duty not only to plead the client's cause but to be his adviser[1]. A lawyer's functions... lay on him a variety of legal and moral obligation towards the client, the court and other authorities before whom the lawyer pleads his clients cause... the legal profession in general and each fellow, member of it, in particular, owes a duty to the public for whom the existence of a free and independent profession, bound together by respect for the rules made by the profession, as an essential means of safeguarding human rights in the face of the power of the state and other interests in the society.

This preamble is relevant to the legal profession of most jurisdictions, including Nigeria. In Nigeria,[2] the role of the legal practitioner is summed up in these words:

A lawyer shall uphold and observe the rule of law, promote and foster the cause of justice and a high standard of professional conduct

---

* Dominic Asada, is a Professor of law of the Faculty of Law, University of Jos and the current Deputy Dean of Law

2 See Rule 1 of the Rules of Professional Conduct for Legal Practitioner Nigeria, 2007

and shall not engage in any conduct which is unbecoming of a legal practitioner.

In order to be able to discharge the above responsibilities, the legal practitioner is allowed the luxury of certain rights and privileges. As a restraining mechanism however he is subject to certain codes of conduct and where is found wanting, the failure is said to amount to professional misconduct for which he is sanctioned under the prevailing disciplinary code.

The legal profession in every society occupies a vanguard position in ensuring the enthronement of egalitarianism and in the defence of citizens from the overbearing and tyrannical conducts of predators. It is in this regard that it cannot be overemphasized the relevance of a well thought out rules of professional ethics for the promotion of ethical standards in the practice of law and the adherence to code of professional responsibility and discipline in the legal profession.

The relevance of a code of conduct is always an important consideration where a group of people associate together in the form of profession. This is because codes of conducts assist in the reshaping or conditioning of behaviour and strengthening the lawyer's relationship with his client.

CONCEPTUAL CLARIFICATIONS

The expressions of professional conduct, ethics, and discipline are not defined in the rules or Act, but since an understanding of these concepts is of utmost importance, it is necessary as a preliminary approach to lay the necessary conceptual foundation by examining the concepts. The word ethics though a branch of philosophy, impinges on the province of law, which deal with normative principles.

Ethics is thus defined as: "Principles or standards of human conduct sometimes called morals… and by extension, the study of principles, sometimes called moral philosophy."[3]

The *New International Webster*'s *Comprehensive Dictionary* of the English Language[4] defined ethics as:

[3] Ethics", Microsoft (R) Encarta (R) 2009, (D.V.D), Redmond, W.A. Microsoft Corporation, 2008.

> The study and philosophy of human conduct with emphasis on the determination of right and wrong, one of the normative sciences; the basic principles of right action.

From the foregoing definition, it is glaring that ethics represents moral beliefs that influence people's behaviour and attitudes.

Discipline, on the other hand, entails the practice of making people adhere to rules, behaving or working in a controlled way, and sanctioning violators for violations. It has been said that:

> Discipline is the sole of an army; it make more numbers formidable; it procure success to the weak and esteem to all.[5]

It takes discipline to achieve orderliness. Discipline makes one live according to rules. It is a mechanism designed to achieve adherence to ethical rules and the enforcement of professional legal responsibility. Discipline is a binding force which holds a group of people, society or an association together professionally in the form of a code.[6]

The *New International Webster*'s *Comprehensive Dictionary of English Language* defines discipline in terms of "punishment for the sake of training; chastisement"[7] while, similarly, *Blacks Law Dictionary*[8] defines discipline to mean: Correction, chastisement, punishment, penalty, to bring order upon or bring under control.

As noted earlier, discipline may take the form of an administrative, civil or criminal mechanism to achieve obedience to ethical rules or behaviour and enforce professional responsibility. This is achieved through the instrumentality of disciplinary proceedings and the adherence to disciplinary rules or code of professional responsibility.

---

[4] The *New International Webster Comprehensive Dictionary of the English Language,* Encyclopedic Edition (USA: Typhoon Media Corporation, 2010 p. 426, see also *Black's Law Dictionary,* 8th Edition (USA: West Publishing Co p. 554 for a similar definition).

[5] See Oyedepo, O.D. "Exploits in Ministry" (Nigeria: Dominion Publishers) 2006, P. 240 quoting from a statement credited to former United States President George Washington. See also Terry, A; Giugni, D "Business Society & Law" (Australia: Harcourt Brace)

[6] Terry, A., Giugni, D "Business, society and law" (Australia: Harcourt Brace)

[7] See the *New International Webster's Comprehensive Dictionary of the English Language, op. cit,* p. 363.

[8] See *Black's Law Dictionary, op. cit.*

What determines the nature or outlook of ethical rules, disciplinary rules, and professional responsibility may vary from jurisdiction to jurisdiction and from profession to profession. But expectedly, there is likelihood of similarities in countries of common law jurisdictions and those of continental jurisdictions.[9]

Professional responsibility concerns the duties and responsibilities imposed by virtue of one's professional calling. In Nigeria, more than ever before, there has arisen the new challenge of reshaping the character and minds of the legal practitioner for positive contribution to National development. Nigeria is faced with new challenges today. These challenges concerns endemic corruption, serious economic inequality, alarming rate of poverty, the collapse of the value system, decline in morality, high level of criminality, inhibited access to law courts due to exorbitant legal fees etc.

There is no gain saying that considering the role of the lawyer and the legal profession in nation building he has tremendous role to play in tackling the above challenges. But sadly, however, lawyers have been fingered as culprits in bringing forth some of these challenges.[10]

THE ROLE OF A LAWYER IN SOCIETY

At various fora, the role of the lawyer has been emphasized. The lawyer's role was ably stated in the declaration of Delhi (1959) by the ICJ to the effect that "by virtue of his technical knowledge he has a special responsibility to translate into effective action the legitimate aspirations of the individual who made up the society and upon whose

---

[9] This is all the statutory and case law background of English and the American colonies before the American revolution. Most of the laws of England have tremendous influence over the laws of many English-speaking countries before independence.

[10] Lawyers have played negative roles in Elections and Electoral dispute resolutions: An example is the annulment of the June 12 1993 Elections reportedly won by late Bashorun MKO Abiola; After the 2007 general Elections observers noted that Elections were serious flawed. The then Elected President agreed that the Elections were not free and fair. When the Election was challenged the Supreme Court held that the Election was free and fair. Again, the Nigerian Bar Association boycotted courts for two days in protest against the flawed elections of e2007. Ironically, some lawyers went to the Election tribunal and courts to challenge the Elections or to declare that elections were free and fair. See generally Osita, N.A., "Oguno, PE" the Challenge of moulding the character and minds of law students for positive contribution to National Development ion Nigeria: The Role of legal methods and legal theory: in. Mozan, A.O. ed. Legal education in the 21st century. Proceeding of the 43rd Annual Conference of the Nigerian Association of Law Teachers (NALT),2010

fundamental rights and dignity a society under the role of law is here assumed to be based." Similarly, in the Nigerian case of *Williams* v. *Akintunde*[11] Pats-Acholonu, JCA (as he then was) observed that:

> ...the Attorney whose professional thoughts begin and end with his own private client is a pitiable mockery of what a great lawyer is and that only by taking part in the movement for the betterment of the law of the profession can he practice law in the grand manner, the only way it is worth practising.

The foregoing observations underscore the role and responsibility of the lawyer in a changing world.

As a member of the legal profession lawyers are prohibited from doing anything in the course of practice or permit another person to do on their behalf anything which compromises or imperils or is likely to compromise or imperil his ethical and professional responsibilities. Where he does so, he assumes full responsibility for the consequences.

LEGAL ETHICS/PROFESSIONAL RESPONSIBILITY

There appears be a little dividing line between ethics and professional responsibility. What appears to be the tiny dividing line is that while all professional conducts may be ethical, not all unethical conducts amount to professional misconducts. Some ethical conducts are mere etiquettes and take the form of attitudes or behaviour of legal practitioners in court developed over the years and intended to facilitate cordial relationship between the Bar and the Bench in the administration of justice. While some are governed by the rules of professional conduct for legal practitioner, no specific rules has been fashioned out by the Bar or under the direction of the judges. Such courtroom decorum, ethics, or etiquette concerns the dress and general comportment of counsel in court, the need to be properly robed or attired in a dignified manner in court appearances,[12] need for counsel

[11] (1995) 3 NWLR (Pt. 381) p. 101.

[12] Legal Practitioners conducting cases on their own behalf are not allowed to be robed or sit at the Bar. They are to appear like other members of the public. See rules 36 (F), 45(2); 36(d) of the Rules of Professional Conduct For Legal Practitioner, 2007 of Nigeria.

to conduct himself with decency and decorum and observe the custom, conduct, and code of behaviour concerning appearances, dress manners and courtesy; manner of addressing court, mode of citing law reports, reference to other counsel and counterpart cases, etc.

A breach of the above 'professional good manners' being established tradition and convention of the legal profession may not be regarded as dishonourable nor disgraceful. Thus sanction may take the form of expression of unpleasure or warning, though a serious breach of professional etiquette may be so grave or dishonourable to court to amount to professional misconduct. The manner of breach and the peculiar facts of every given case will always be relevant in gauging the seriousness of every breach.

Aside from the above situations, conducts ethics fall within the same compartment as those of professional conduct or responsibility. This article evaluates the role of professional Ethics or responsibility and discipline not only as a deterrent mechanism to keep the lawyer on his toes but also in ensuring that he fulfils his traditional role in contributing positively to shaping the social policy direction of his country:

BACKGROUND AND ORIGIN OF THE RULES OF PROFESSIONAL ETHICS/RESPONSIBILITY

In England there is no single code of conduct and etiquette regulating the legal profession since there are two separate branches of the legal professions, the solicitor and the advocate. In Nigeria, both professions are fused into one and though the legal practitioner is trained as a barrister, he practices both as a barrister and solicitor. In the past, the Nigerian legal practitioner relied heavily on the court directives, the provisions of the legal practitioners Act and the code of conduct and etiquette of the legal profession of England.

It was in 1967 that the first Rules of Professional Conduct in the legal profession was made. Between 1980 and 1992 and between 1982 and 2002, considerable efforts were made to revise the rules and make them up to date and a committee was set up for that purpose. The efforts, however, materialized in 2003 when the report was submitted, considered, and approved in the form of draft rules. It was, however, in 2006 that the draft rules were approved after a painstaking consideration and imputes were made by other members of the legal profession.[13]

Sources of the Rule of Professional Conduct for Legal Practitioners

The rules main sources are the Legal Practitioners Act 2004, decisions and directions of the courts; Rules of professional conduct adopted from other jurisdictions, decisions and directions of the disciplinary Committee and other rules considered by the Bar Council. The Legal Practitioners Act, 2004 tabulates what amounts to unprofessional conduct or professional misconduct.[14] The rules are the outcome of the amplification of the unprofessional conduct or misconducts dealing with infamous conducts in a professional respect that are inconsistent with the status of a legal practitioner. It must be pointed out that these rules are substantially drawn from those of United Kingdom, the Code of Ethics of the American Bar Association, the International Bar Association (IBA) Rules of professional conduct. These foreign rules are however of persuasive effect and not mandatory.[15]

The general purpose of the rules of professional ethics/conduct of the legal profession is encapsulated in rule 1. As stated in the rule,

> a lawyer shall uphold and observe the rule of law, promote and foster the course of justice, maintain a high standard of professional conduct and shall not engage in any conduct which is unbecoming of a legal practitioner…engage in any

---

[13] Previous Attorneys General who played critical roles in working on the draft rules which eventually metamorphosed into the substantive Rules are: prince Bola Ajibola, SAN; Chief O.C.J Okocha, SAN; Chief Bayo Ojo, SAN. But it was Chief Bayo Ojo, that actively ensured the project was completed in 2006 and approved by the General Council of the Bar. The commencement date of the Rules is 2nd, January, 2007. See the Federal Republic of Nigeria official Gazette No 11; Volume 94 of 24/1/2007 p. 657.

[14] The two words are used interchangeably. See S. 12 of The Legal Practitioner Act 2004

[15] In *Fawehinmi* v. *NBA* (1989) 2NWLR (pt 105) 495, *IBWA Ltd* v. *Imano (Nig) Ltd*; (1988) 3 NWLR (Pt 85) 633, court held in the former that for any omission in our rules of professional conduct , the remedy lies in amending the rules and not in filling the gaps and the latter case where the court held that where the local rules are not breached a lawyer will not be penalised for the breach of an English or foreign rule in respect of an Act which is not prohibited in Nigeria.

conduct that will bring unto disrepute the rule of law, the administration of justice or the honour and integrity of the legal profession and in particular shall not violate any rule of professional conduct; engage in illegal conduct involving moral turpitude or engage in any other conduct that conversely affects his fitness to practice as a legal practitioner.[16]

All other rules are designed to sustain the above rule. The rules encompasses the ideas and standards that legal practitioners are required to attain to fulfil their societal roles. As noted in the Edwards:[17]

> ... certain standards must be kept if the legal profession is to continue to command the respect of members of the public it is very much serves... we must set our faces against dishonesty and indiscipline by legal practitioner.

The Rules of professional conduct or ethics are designed to ensure the protection and preservation of the highest standard of professional ethics of the Bar and draws inspiration from international bar practices or values of the legal profession.[18]

Professional Conduct/Responsibility

The rules which essentially emanate from practice, traditions, values and specific requirements of the legal profession in Nigeria derive their inspiration from international best practices or values of the legal profession. The rules in their entirety enjoin every member of the legal profession not to do anything in the course of practicing or permit another person to do on his behalf anything which compromises or is likely to compromise his integrity or independence; his duty to court; standard of work; his good reputation or that of the profession; his duty

---

[16] See Rule (1), (2) of tap Rules of Professional Conduct for Legal Practitioners of Nigeria, 2007.
[17](1968) All NLR, 226 PC (Ademola, CJ.N at p. 232.)
[18] See *Ikeme* v. *Anakwe* (2003) 10NWLR (PT 829) 548

to act in the best interest of the client, etc.[19] The nature of these responsibilities may now be examined under various heads.

Responsibility to Client

There are two aspects of the relationship between the legal practitioner and client. In some situations, it is like that of an agent and a principal, while in some others, it is like that of an independent contractor. In the Nigerian case of *Afegbai* v. *A G. Edo State,*[20] the Court explained that a lawyer is a child of two worlds in relation to his client. While on one hand, he is regarded as an independent contractor and is thus mandated to adhere to the specific instructions of his client, the analogy cannot be interpreted to excuse the client from responsibility for wrong emanating from false instructions placed by the client at the disposal of counsel. This is especially the case where the lawyer acts within the scope of his authority.[21]

The relationship between a legal practitioner and his client is a fiduciary one which requires him to be honest and fair while acting with respect to his client. It amounts to professional misconduct for a lawyer to be dishonest or fraudulent while dealing with his client. This is where he fails to deliver clients' money, property, or making use of the same without authority;[22] fail to represent his client within the scope of his authority;[23] fail to show unflinching devotion and dedication to the cause of his client.[24]

The conflict of interest rule mandates the legal practitioner to observe the required standard of honesty and integrity to the client by making full disclosures. He must not put himself in a position where he

---

[19] See Akinjide, R Advocacy, Ethics and the Bar "in legal Ethics – lawyers Handbook, 6th edn (Abuja; Jide Olakunmi & Co) 2013, P. 167. (2001) 4 NWLR (pt 732) 425 SC.

[20] (2001) 4 NWLR(pt 732) 425 SL

[21]See *Edozien* v. *Edozien* ((1993) 1WLR (pt 732) 425, SC, *Mathew* v. *Minister* (1888) 20QB 141 where the courts restated that though counsel functions as an independent contractor, he has power to bind his client while acting within the scope of his authority, express or implied.

[22]See *NBA* v. *Ndukwe* (2006) 12NWLR (PT 2006) 427. In this case, counsel collected ₦25,000 on behalf of an old woman and failed to give her the money despite several demands. Counsel was convicted of the misconduct.

[23] Rule 15 of the Rules of Professional Conduct for Legal Practitioners 2007. A lawyer who while representing his client is in possession of information showing client to be fraudulent is required to of draw the client attention to it or report it to the court where client is adamant.

[24] A legal practitioner should not act for a creditor in a winding up petition where he is creditor or debtor

cannot serve the interest of his client because of his own personal interest or appear in matters where he runs the risk of compromising the position of his client,[25] purchase clients property except if done in good faith and for good consideration.[26] In order that the legal practitioner does not abuse his position of trust and to free himself from the presumption of undue influence, he is required when preparing or procuring the execution of a will under which he takes a benefit to ensure that the testator knew of or approved of the benefit or gift.[27]

Morality and law also disallow a legal practitioner who is an executor or trustee of the deceased estate from acting as solicitors to the estate. It is noted, however, that though this is unprofessional conduct, it is not infamous[28] under Rule 54 of the rules. Legal practitioners are not to accept gifts, compensations, commissions, rebates, or other advantages without the client's knowledge except with the client's permission after disclosures.[29] The rules also mandate the legal practitioner to advise his client against instituting speculative suits with no iota of merit and may be liable for offsetting the costs of the suit personally and refund to the plaintiff the total cost of filing the suit.

The conflict of interest rule also operates where a legal practitioner acts for two or more clients at the same time. Section 17(4) of the Rules of professional conduct discourages such practice except where the legal practitioner is prepared to obtain from each client the required consent after full disclosure.[30]

Other dimension to the Rule is the prohibition of a legal practitioner from accepting offered employment or representing

---

[25] A legal practitioner is not to appear before his relations. See rule 17 (5)

[26] In *Williams* v. *Frankline* (1961) All NCR 218 it was held that a legal practitioner who purchased clients property had discharged the duty of good faith once the price paid was reasonable and members of the clients family witnessed the transaction. See also *Mcmaster* v. *Byrne* (1952) ALL ER, 1324

[27] This principle is not captured under the Nigerian Rules of Professional Conduct Of Legal Practitioner, 2007

[28] See section 12 of the Legal Practitioners Act 2004

[29] Such benefits whether in cash or in kind are recoverable from the legal practitioner as secret profits

[30] See *Cocotto Poulos* v. *A.Z. & Co Ltd* (1965) LLR, 170 where the court held that: plaintiffs are at liberty to demand from the solicitor the repayment in full, all professional fees incurred on account of the case.

See also *Queen* v. *Ajagba* (1960) 5FS (238): Rule 17 (1) which mandates a legal practitioner to disclose to the client all the circumstances of his relationship with the parties and any interest in or connection with the controversy which may influence the client in the selection of the lawyer

successive clients where it is likely to affect his independent professional judgment except where he can adequately do so after full disclosure.[31]

Rule 6 provides that it is a misconduct for a legal practitioner to accept employment as a legal practitioner in a matter which he has previously investigated as a public servant. On this matter, section 39 (a) of the rules though specifically mentions advocates, would seem by implication to equally apply to all judicial officers. The constitutional provision of section 292(2) of the 1999 constitution of the Federal Republic of Nigeria is emphatic on this point as it prohibits legal practitioners from appearing before courts of judicial tribunals.[32] The rule is so strict that it extends to prohibiting partners in the law firm of former judicial officers.

Similarly, an advocate who has acted in respect of a matter previously before his elevation to the bench will be in breach of the rule if the accepts to sit over the trial of such case.[33]

Not all conflicts of interest arising from fiduciary relationships are dishonest in nature, though they may give rise to embarrassment. Such examples concern legal practitioners giving evidence in a case in which he acts, swearing affidavit evidence,[34] standing bail or surety for one client in a criminal matter in which he is involved,[35] and acting in a case in which he is a party.

The professional expectation of the legal practitioner is not an enviable one. Thus, he is required to perform his duty to his client diligently,[36] and is not immune from liability for damages attributable to negligence. He thus must perform its duties with due care and attention having been held out as someone possessing special skill. This duty has three segments, namely; contractual, tortious and fiduciary.

---

[31] See Rule 17(4), see also *Adesatan* v. *Thomas & Co* CCHCJ/3/72 where it has held that a solicitor that prepared a deed or mortgage for a former client, and held the power of Attorney in whom some court confidence was reposed by the client could not appear against the client in litigation that flowed from the former transaction for the purpose of setting aside the deed of mortgage

[32] See *Kehinde Adeniyi* v. *Balogun Adama* (1976) 40 D.H.C.I p 2

[33] See section 36(1) of the 1999 Constitution. Under this provision the judicial officer may be accused of bias

[34] See Rule 20 of the Rules of Professional Conduct 2007.

[35] See *Obadara* v. *The president, Ibadan West District Council Grade B customary court* (1958) WR N.L.R 110, where the Nigerian Supreme Court noted that it is undesirable of counsel to appear in a professional capacity in a case which he is a material witness.

See the Annual Statement of the General Council of the Bar in England (1933) p9

See also Rule 16 of the Rules of Professional Conduct 2007

The lawyer's albatross is occasioned by the fact that as the client retained, he is required to take a number of steps to fulfil the contract with his client; and may be liable for the tort of negligence on the principle of *Donoghue* v. *Stephenson*[37] and *Hedley Byrne & Co Ltd* v. *Hellers & Partners Ltd*,[38] since the client is in the contemplation of the legal practitioner. On the basis of the fiduciary relationship, he is required to make full disclosure of any interest in any matter that he is instructed and not to make a secret profit from any of the said instructions.

The duty of care and skill required of the legal practitioner is not an absolute one. He is required to display the level of skill and care that is reasonable in the circumstance. Though he cannot be expected to know all the law, it is within his competence to know where to find it.[39]

It is thus to be noted that where a legal practitioner fails to discharge his responsibility, and the client suffers thereby, he is liable to the client for the loss,[40] though he may be exempted from liability in the circumstances where he offers free service; where the negligence occurred in the face of court or tribunal while conducting proceedings.[41] But the immunity may be of no effect in Nigeria as the legal practitioner's disciplinary committee is at liberty to deal with or discipline such legal practitioner. Clients that suffer losses are also at liberty to bring against such practitioners' actions for damages. The nature of damages generally would depend on the particular transaction and the loss suffered.[42]

---

37 (1932) AC 562

38(1963) 3 All E.R. 575. It is important to note that the lawyers duty may discharged where he had insufficient time to discharge his responsibility or where the nature of work is imprecise thereby pulling him in a difficult situation to perfect the particular instruction. See generally Olakunle Orojo, "professional conduct of the legal practitioners in Nigeria" (Lagos: Mafix Books Ltd) 2008 pp. 179-180.

39 An area where the legal practitioner is expected to exercise his skill is provision for advice, avoidance of delay etc.

40 See section 8 of the Legal Practitioners Act 1975 now 2004

41 See section 9 (3) of the Legal Practitioners Act 1975, *Rondell* v. *Worseley* (1967) 3 All ER 993..

42 See Jackson Powell, Professional Negligence, and 1987. Most of the heads of damages which a legal practitioner may be liable to pay are: (1) loss of opportunity to defend or initiate proceedings, due to failure to take appropriate steps, and the matter becoming statute barred Diminution in value of property resulting from the lawyers erroneous advice or investigation, loss of financial advantage e.g. inability to recoup money loaned or loss in price or of earnings; liability to third parties, e.g. for additional rates on interest criminal liability e.g. where the crime is one of strict liability wasted expenditure, e.g. in lawyers' fees or in a aborted transaction incidental expenses; in difference and distress.

Rule 19 of the Professional Conduct for Legal Practitioners 2007 sets out the nature of communication with the client, which the legal practitioner may or may not reveal. Under section 19(1) and (2), legal practitioners are not to disclosure oral or written communications revealed to them by their client in the normal course of a professional engagement or reveal a confidence or secret of the client for his own advantage or to the advantage of a third party except with the client's consent or as permitted by law or in pursuance of court order or where the disclosure is to prevent the commission of crime by the client or the disclosure is necessary in order to collect his fees or defend himself against wrongful accusation.

The above rules emphasize the relationship between a legal practitioner and his client. The right to the secrecy of the confidence essentially belongs to the client. It is only he that can waive it.[43] The essence of the rule is that a client should be entitled to feel safe when making disclosures to his counsel. It is important to note that the responsibility continues even after disengagement. In *Minter* v. *Priest*,[44] Lord Atkin observed that the test for the protection of confidential information between a solicitor and client is whether or not it is professional communication of a confidential character for the purpose of legal advice or help in a counsel's line of legal responsibility.

Legal practitioners are enjoined to be in professional fellowship with one another and to ensure the observance of procedure and orderliness with one another, deal with each other in good faith as members of an honourable profession; not to directly or indirectly encroach upon the employment of another legal practitioner, observe strictly all promises, undertakings or agreements with other opposing

---

[43]See also section 170(1) and 173 of the Nigerian the Evidence Act which emphasises of the same duty of professional secrecy and privilege and the exceptional situations for disclosure. See also, the case of *Hon* v.. *Richard* (1975) 61CR. App. R. 128. In *Akintoye* v. *Omole* Suit No. HAD/10/75 of June 6, 1978 ,the defendant instructed X, a legal practitioner concerning a case without being aware x was already acting for the plaintiff. The defendant met the managing clerk and made disclosures after which the managing clerk took him to x who refused the brief. The court held that x duty of professional secrecy and privilege subsist and to hold otherwise is to defeat the object and purpose of the rule.

[42(a)](1930) AC. 558 p. 211.

[44] (1930) AC. 558 p. 211.

lawyers and not to take undue advantage of the predicament of the opposing counsel.[45]

As is common globally, a legal practitioner acting as an agent for another legal practitioner must perform such duties with utmost care and skill, while the principal's responsibility entails paying the fees of the agent legal practitioner. Though no special rules exist in Nigeria in this sort of agency relationship, the international code of ethics of the International Bar Association[46] provides a guide. Thus the basic responsibility of counsel in such a situation is to act with the utmost care, respect, cordiality, and good faith.

It is an act of professional misconduct for a legal practitioner to interview, communicate, or have any dealing with clients of another practitioner on the same matter without consent, except where the other practitioner fails to reply to previous letters.[47]

The rule applies in extension to cases where the opposing party is represented by counsel.[48] A legal practitioner is also an officer of the court who is required to act or conduct himself in a manner that may not obstruct, delay or adversely affect the administration of justice. As observed in *R* v. *O' Connel*, [49]

> ... the advocates of the Bar as well as the judge upon the Bench are equally ministers in that temple. The object of all equally should be the attainment of justice...

Thus a court of law under normal circumstances will not demand written authority from counsel appearing before it since he is regarded as an officer of court. He is a prior and perpetual retainer on behalf of truth and justice. All the facts and authorities at his disposal before the

---

[45] See Rules 16, 23, (1) & (2), 27(2), & (4) of the Professional Conduct For Legal Practitioner 2007.

[46] See Section 8 of Nigeria Legal Practitioner Acts, 2007; Rules 23, 27 and Rule 4 of the International Code of Ethics of the International Bar Association, 1988. Under Rule 19, a lawyer who engages a foreign colleague is responsible for paying the latter charges except there exist a contrary agreement.

[47] Rule 23(5) of the Rules of Professional Conduct For Legal Practitioners 2007 of Nigeria. It has been observed that it is not a breach of etiquette by the lawyer for the petitioner in a divorce proceedings to communicate directly with the respondent at the request of the petitioner where the respondent's solicitor refuses to pass on such information or communication. See generally, lung, professional ethics (International Bar Association) Book 111; see Rule 27(4) which prohibits such communication

[48] See *Anie* v. *Abdilamse* (1942) 8 WACA 67

[49] (1884) L.R. Lr 261 at p. 312

court are to enable the court to administer justice. He is not to mislead the court.[50]

Lord Denning, famously expounded the rule in *Rondel* v. *Wosely*,[51] thus: the legal practitioner must respect the court and treat it with dignity and honour,[52] notify the court of his intended absence, not ask for an adjournment on false grounds. Similarly, legal practitioners are enjoined not to: attempt to influence the court improperly, discuss a pending case with any judge unless the opposing party is present, fraudulently obtain money from a client on the pretext that it is meant for a judge, handle a legal matter without adequate preparation,[53] fail to appear in court, deal fairly and candidly while presenting his case,[54] honour his undertaking in court, make unfair, scandalous or unjustified allegations against a court, abuse court's process by unjustifiable litigation.[55]

One difficult problem that may arise in the course of a legal practitioner's professional responsibility is that of resolving conflict between the need to put in his best for his client and to discharge his duties to the court as an officer. This is where a client confesses to the commission of the crime. Rule 37(2) provides that the defending counsel shall be deemed to have given a solemn undertaking that he will personally conduct the defence if fees is paid. The court presumes the innocent of all accused persons until the contrary is proved. He is not, therefore, to refuse a brief to defend an accused because of his belief in the guilt of the accused person.[56] But he must not set up an affirmative defence.

---

50 *Controller of the Nigeria Prison Services* v. *Adekanye* (No 1) 92002) 15 NWLR (Pt 790) 318, SC; peat Marwick, in *Ogunde & Co* v. *Okike* (1995) 1WLR (Pt 369) 71 at pp 82 & 82; *Fawehinmi* v. *N.B.A* (WO1) (1989) 2 NWCR (pt 105) 494 at p. 523; *General oil Ltd* v. *Oduntan* (1990) 7 NWLR (Pt 163) 423 at p. 673.

51 (1967) 3 All E.R. 567 at p. 393 Lord Denning noted among other things that An advocate is a minister of justice just like a judge. He has a monopoly of audience in the higher courts.

52 Under paragraph 1(2) Supreme Court Practice & Procedure Order 1972, it is a disrespect for counsel who has notice of reserved judgment not to appear or be represented.

53 See. Rule 31(4) and (5) which provides that except where the opposing counsel fails or refuses to attend court the judge is informed of the circumstances, counsel must not disclose a pending case with a judge.

54 See Rule 16(1)(b)

55 See Rule 15(3) (b) which prohibits unjustifiable litigation

56 See generally rule 37(1) that deal with the duty and position of a solicitor who undertakes the defence of an accused person that has confessed to crime.

The legal practitioner is prohibited from engaging in acts that tend to give him an undue or unfair advantage in attracting legal business. Such acts or conducts are advertising and promotion as well as soliciting and touting. While the former is permitted on a general note, the latter is totally outlawed under the rules. Under Rule 39(1), a legal practitioner may engage in advertising or promotion provided it is fair and proper, complies with the rules, and is for the purpose of reaching clients. The general power to advertise is, however, limited if it is inaccurate or likely to mislead or likely to diminish public confidence in the legal profession or administration of justice or bring the legal profession into disrepute.[57]

For quite some time, the legal profession has witnessed some form of soliciting and touting among legal practitioners. These are soliciting for employment, soliciting for employment in court premises, soliciting for conveyance business, searching land registries for employment, instigating litigation, ambulance chasing, and undue association.[58] These practices are professionally reprehensible and a slap on the legal profession.

Professional Discipline of Legal Practitioners

The Legal Practitioner Act 2004 gives an indication as to what would constitute unprofessional conduct or professional misconduct. It states that they must relate to "infamous conduct in a professional respect" and offences incompatible with the status of a legal practitioner.[59] It is,

---

[57] See Rules 40 – 46 generally which deal with specific matters permitted. The use of Number plates, business cards, lawyers letter heads, endorsement of documents, signs and notices, change of address, telephone numbers, Directories etc.

[58] Touting lawyers are referred to "charge and bail lawyer." See generally Rule 47(1), (2) 47(2) (b) (c)

[59] Misconduct is not defined in the Act and under the Rules but in the *Black's Law Dictionary*, 7th Edition it is defined as a dereliction of duty, unlawful or improper behaviour. The expression infamous conduct in a professional respect is also not defined in the Act. But in *Allison* v. *General Council of Medical Education and Registration* (1894) IQB 750, it was interpreted to mean something disgraceful or dishonourable by one professional brethren of good repute and competency. Misconducts amounting to infamous conducts includes behaviour/conducts requiring a legal practitioner refunding money to clients or handing over of documents or any other thing. See section 12(2) of the Legal Practitioners Acts 2004 of Nigeria.

Offences incompatible with the status of a legal practitioner relate to fund related offences; offence against public justice, offences against the state and public offences against the person or individuals, sexual offence and offences against public peace. See especially section 12 (1) (b) of the Legal Practitioners Act of 2004 of Nigeria.

therefore, in relation to these that a legal practitioner is subjected to professional discipline in the event of professional breaches. These are where a member of the legal profession is adjudged by the disciplinary committee to be guilty of infamous conduct in any professional respect; is convicted by any court in Nigeria having the power to award imprisonment of an offence that is incompatible with the status of a legal practitioner or where a legal practitioner is fraudulently enrolled.

Court decisions[60] have indicated that the phrase 'infamous conduct' in professional respect is misconduct of grave nature whose effect is to erase the name of a practitioner from the register of members once it is shown that the practitioner, in the pursuit of his profession, engaged in a conduct that could be reasonably regarded as disgraceful or dishonourable by his professional brethren of good repute and competency.

An opportunity came for the Nigerian Supreme Court to interpret the meaning of "conduct in a professional respect" in *Re Idowu*: A legal practitioner[61] under the then Section 7(a) of the Legal Practitioners Act 1962. The court noted that an infamous conduct must be committed with professional respect; otherwise, it fails the test for culpability provided under the Act. The court observed pertinently that it is not enough that the legal practitioner is guilty of infamous conduct only, it must be such conduct arising out of or pertaining to his profession.

Though the Legal Practitioners Act does not draw a distinction between "unprofessional conduct and professional misconduct," it would seem that "unprofessional conduct connotes all manners of behaviours or misconducts exhibited by a legal practitioner that may not be infamous in nature, while professional misconducts are misconducts that are quite weighty in nature and would encompass

---

[60]See *Allison* v. *General Council of Medical Education and Registration* (1894) 1QBD 750; *Re solicitor* (1912) IKB 302; See also *Okike* v. *L.P.D.C* where the court adopted the same approach.

[61](1971) 1 All NLR 126. See also *Ex P. Meekam* (1965) N.S.W.R. 20 at p. 3. In that case the court while interpreting an enactment that was on all fours with section 12(a) of the Legal Practitioners Acts 2004 concerning the conduct of a medical practitioner said the expression must deals with conduct that is sufficiently related to the pursuit of the profession which would reasonable incur the strongest reprobation of professional brethren of good repute and competence.

substantially conducts connected with a legal practitioner professional activities."[62]

Unprofessional misconduct quite often manifests in criminal offences. Such offences as highway robbery, false pretences, fraud, offences against public peace and against the state, public individuals, sexual offences, and offences against public peace are incompatible with the status of a legal practitioner and may warrant striking such a practitioner's name off the role.

Before 1962, the Supreme Court Ordinance of 1872 first regulated the discipline of legal practitioners. The same position continued under the Supreme Court Ordinances of 1914 and 1917. Within this period, the Supreme Court exercised disciplinary powers over legal practitioners.[63]

The Legal Practitioner Ordinance of 1933 made a fundamental change in the discipline of legal practitioners as it created for the first time a legal practitioners committee to inquire into allegations of misconduct. An essential attribute of this committee is that it had the power to hear and conduct an inquiry into allegations of misconduct against any legal practitioner and report to the Supreme Court that had the final power to sanction such practitioner found wanting.[64]

The Legal Practitioner Act 1962, which followed, established two new bodies the legal practitioners' investigation panel and the legal practitioners' disciplinary Tribunal. While the former was charged with the duty of conducting a preliminary investigation into the misbehaviour of legal practitioners, the latter was charged with the duty of determining cases referred to it by the panel.[65] A series of

---

[62] Professional misconduct may entail the breach of undertakings, improperly borrowing money from or lending money to a client breach of rules, inexcusable negligence, deliberately misleading the court and betrayal of client's confidence. Unprofessional conduct on the other hand are those conducts that in all probability render him unfit to be an office court.

[63] Section 90 of the Ordinance of 1914 which regulated qualification, admission, enrolment, discipline for Barristers, advocates, etc. But the Supreme Court Ordinance, of 1917 did not provide for any disciplinary procedure.

[64] Under section 27(a) of the Ordinance the Supreme Court had power to admonish or suspend a legal practitioner. Under section 29(b) any judge of the Supreme Court could suspend a legal practitioner temporarily pending a reference to the Supreme Court.

[65] The Supreme Court was empowered under section 8(1) to take disciplinary measures against legal practitioner for infamous conduct in a professional respect. Similarly the Chief Judge is empowered under section 8(2) to exercise disciplinary powers.

amendments were made to the 1962 Act in 1968, 69, and 1971. The 1971 amendment paved the way for the establishment of the Legal Practitioners Disciplinary Committee to replace the hitherto Legal Practitioners investigating panel.

In 1975 the Legal Practitioners Act was enacted to incorporate the Act of 1962 together with all previous amendments to it. The 1975[66] Act provided for a disciplinary jurisdiction consisting of the Legal Practitioners Disciplinary Committee, the Supreme Court, and the Chief Justice.

Section 11 of the Act establishes the Legal Practitioners Disciplinary Committee as a Committee of the body of benchers. Under Section 11 (2), as amended by Decree No 21 of 1994, the composition consists of a chairman,[67] two Justices of the Court of Appeal,[68] two Chief Judges, two Attorneys General of a state, or two State Attorneys General; and four members of the Bar association who are not connected with the investigation of a complaint against legal practitioners for determination by the disciplinary committee.[69]

Section 10(1) of the Legal Practitioners Act states an essential aspect of the procedure for dealing with the discipline of erring legal practitioners thus:

> In any case where in pursuance of section 10(1) of the Act the disciplinary committee is of the opinion that a prima face case is shown against a legal practitioner, the Nigerian Bar Association shall forward a report of such a case to the secretary together with all the documents by the Nigerian Bar Association and a copy of the charges on which the Nigerian Bar Association is of the opinion that a prima face case is shown.

---

[66] Cap 207 of the Revised laws of the Federation 1990.

[67] The Chairman shall not be either the Chief Justice of Nigeria or a justice of the Supreme Court

[68] One of whom shall be the president of the Court of Appeal The procedure of the committee is regulated by section 5 or the legal practitioners disciplinary committee and it deals with: mode of presentation of case, fixing of hearing date; notice of hearing, hearing and rehearing, finding and direction of the committee publication of findings and directions, extension of time, keeping of exhibits etc.

[69] The procedure of the committee is regulated by section 5 or the legal practitioners' disciplinary committee and it deals with: made of presentation of case, fixing of hearing date; notice of hearing, hearing and rehearing, finding and direction of the committee publication of findings and directions, extension of time, keeping of exhibits, etc.

This is an essential requirement before charging a legal practitioner with an offence. Every party to the proceeding is entitled to be heard by the committee personally or through counsel of his choice.[70] The nature of the proceedings permits it to be held in private, but its findings and directions shall be pronounced in public.[71] Appeal against the decision of the disciplinary committee lies to the Supreme Court.[72]

The Supreme Court is empowered to give directions it considers appropriate after determining issues of guilt bordering on infamous conduct in any professional respect. And where it appears that a legal practitioner ought to be suspended from practice, the Chief Justice of Nigeria may suspend him from either with a view to the institute proceedings against such legal practitioner or while proceedings are pending, before the committee or before any court, after affording such legal practitioner an opportunity of making representations in the matter.[73]

The legal practitioner disciplinary committee or the Supreme Court is further empowered under Section 11 of the Legal Practitioners Act to give directions that have the effect of ordering the Chief Registrar of the Supreme Court to strike the legal practitioners name off the role of the register of legal practitioners in Nigeria; or suspend such legal practitioner from practice for a specific period of time or admonishing such legal practitioner as the case may be.[74]

Appeal against the legal practitioner's disciplinary committee lies to the Supreme Court.

CONCLUSION

This write-up has examined the ethical role and responsibilities of the legal practitioner in Nigeria, the nature of sanctionable conduct, and

---

[70]In *Okike* v. *LPDC* (2005) 15 NWLR (PT 949) (2006) 1 NWLR (PT 960) 67. It was held that a charge of professional misconduct is not by any standard a criminal charge but civil in nature.

[71] 13 of the Legal Practitioner's Disciplinary Committee rules 2004.

[72] Section 11 (7) of the Legal Practitioner Act, 2007.

[73] See section 13(1), (2) of the Legal Practitioners Act Nigeria, 1975.

[74] Striking of the role is for the most serious misconduct. This borders on disgraceful behaviour, fraudulent behaviour. Suspension on the other hand is meant for misconducts that are not of serious nature. The power exercised pursuant to section 12(1) and (2) include ordering the refund of money paid or the lending over documents or any other thing on the case may be.

the procedure for sanction as contained under the Rules and the Act. The analyses have shown the interrelationship between the three basic concepts of ethics, responsibility, and discipline in the regulation and control of the legal practitioner in order to ensure that he lives up to societal and professional expectations.

Chapter 18

LEGAL AID AND ADVICE IN NIGERIA

Joseph Ndubisi Madubuike-Ekwe*

INTRODUCTION

Legal aid is the provision of free legal services to persons who by reason of low income or circumstances cannot afford legal services.[1] Litigation is a very expensive thing and persons of insufficient means may find it difficult to retain the services of legal practitioners to prosecute or defend their matters to successful conclusion. For many people, a right to access the courts is meaningless unless they can get assistance from the state with the cost of litigation. The Nigerian Constitution provides legal aid to indigent persons.[2] As such, it is the role of the state to ensure that justice is accessible to all, irrespective of the person's financial or social background.[3]

The aim of this chapter is to discuss the provisions of the Legal Aid Act 2011 and the practice of legal aid and advice in Nigeria, and the various ways to improve its services. The chapter begins with a brief history of Legal Aid in Nigeria. It examines the rationale and legal basis for Legal Aid. It also discusses the current institutional structure of the Legal Aid Council, highlights some of the problems of providing Legal Aid services to the needy, and makes recommendations on how to ensure a robust and effective Legal Aid Scheme in Nigeria.

---

* Joseph Ndubisi Madubuike-Ekwe, S.J.D (GGU, San Francisco, USA), LL.M (Ile-Ife); BL.; LL.B (Hons) (UNN); Senior Lecturer and HOD, Public Law, Faculty of Law, Benson Idahosa University, Benin-City, Edo State Nigeria.

[1] Malemi, E., *The Nigerian Constitutional Law*,(Lagos: Princeton Publishing Co., 2006), p.414.

[2] 1999 Constitution of the Federal Republic of Nigeria (as amended), section 46(4)(b) as amended

[3] Beredugo, A.J., *Nigerian Legal System: An Introductory Text*, (Lagos: Malthouse Press Ltd., 2009), p.197

BRIEF HISTORY OF LEGAL AID IN NIGERIA

In Nigeria, legal aid began as an association of Public Defenders through the concerted efforts of notable legal luminaries such as Chief Chimezie Ikeazor, Debo Akande and Solomon Lar, and many others.[4] The intention of that group of lawyers was to provide free legal services to indigent suspects. The efforts of the association were recognized and given formal legal status by the government of General Olusegun Obasanjo (as he then was) in the Legal Aid Decree No. 56 of 1976,[5] which has now been effectively repealed by the Legal Aid Act, 2011.[6] The Legal Aid Act established the Legal Aid Council with a mandate to provide free quality legal services and advice to Nigerians who otherwise could not afford such services in the event of the violation of their rights.[7]

RATIONALE FOR LEGAL AID

Access to justice costs money, and just like any other commodity or service it is often those who can afford the cost that usually have access to it.[8] However, in an increasingly modern complex society, where the average individual is involved in multiple relations and transactions with others; political, economic, social, and otherwise, the services of a lawyer are essential, if not mandatory, to live a peaceful and liability-free life and to understand the increasing volume of complex laws and regulations encountered in the course of daily life, or in pursuing or defending a claim.[9]

The rationale for legal aid can be stated[10] as follows: Firstly, the prohibitive cost of litigation, either in terms of filing fees, counsel's fees, or other ancillary costs, make access to justice illusory to the average

---

[4]http://LegalaidCouncil.org.ng/index.php?option=com-content&view=article&id=79&itemid=70 Accessed 26th July, 2012.

[5]Malemi, E., *supra*, note 1, p.415

[6]Alli, Y., "Provide More Access to Justice for Nigerians, AGF Tasks Legal Aid Council" *The Nation,* June 23, 2012. p. 5.

[7] Ibid.

[8]Malemi, E. "The Challenges in Providing Legal Aid in Nigeria" (2005), Benin Journal of Public Law; Vol.3, p. 112.

[9] Ibid.

[10]Ogbu, O. N., *Modern Nigerian Legal System,* (Enugu: CIDJAP Publishers, 2002), p.336

Nigerian.[11] Secondly, there is the psychological barrier usually associated with the underprivileged due to the sense of fear, hopelessness, and unfamiliarity with the legal system. Thirdly, there is lack of awareness on the part of the average person in Nigeria as to his rights or the means of obtaining justice.[12] Fourthly, even a fairly educated person cannot understand the language employed in the drafting of legislation. The problem is compounded by our plural legal system, which encompasses the received English Law and customary laws. The idea of received English Law operating side by side with our indigenous laws alienates the underprivileged from the legal system.[13] People are, in many cases, deprived of the customary rules with which they are familiar, which should govern all aspects of their lives.[14]

THE LEGAL BASIS FOR LEGAL AID IN NIGERIA

The Nigerian Constitution is the legal basis for legal aid in Nigeria. Section 46(4)(b)(i) and (ii) of the 1999 Constitution (as amended) provides that:

> The National Assembly… shall make provisions
> (i) for the rendering of financial assistance to any indigent citizens of Nigeria where his right under this chapter has been infringed or with a view to enabling him to engage the services of a legal practitioner to prosecute his claim; and
> (ii) for ensuring that allegations of infringement of such rights are substantial and the requirement or need for financial or legal aid is real.

Clearly, this section imposes a duty on the National Assembly to appropriate funds for indigent persons for the prosecution of cases involving infringement of their fundamental rights. It should be noted that the National Assembly did not promulgate separate legislation for

[11] Ibid.
[12] Ibid.
[13] Ibid.
[14] Banire, M.A. "Legal Aid in the Administration of Justice in Nigeria" in Agbede I.O. (ed.) *Current Themes in Nigeria Law* (Lagos: Faculty of Law, UNILAG, 1997), pp. 55-57

this purpose. Rather the existing legal aid scheme was extended in 1994 to cover cases of alleged human rights violations.[15] The legal aid scheme is governed by the Legal Aid Act, 2011, which improved on the Legal Aid Act 1976.[16]

THE LEGAL AID COUNCIL (LAC)

The Legal Aid Council was established by the Legal Aid Council Decree No. 56 of 1976.[17] The Legal Aid Council is now regulated by the Legal Aid Act, 2011, which is:

> An Act to repeal the Legal Aid Act Cap L9, laws of the Federation of Nigeria 2004 in line with international standards and to provide for the establishment of legal aid and access to justice fund into which financial assistance would be made available to the Council on behalf of the indigent citizens to prosecute their claims in accordance with the Constitution and further to empower the existing Legal Aid Council to be responsible for the operation of a scheme for the grant of legal aid and access to justice in certain matters or proceedings to persons with inadequate resources in accordance with the provisions of this Act; and for related matters.[18]

Section 1 of the Act establishes the Legal Aid Council as a body corporate with perpetual succession that may sue or be sued in its corporate name and with a common seal.[19] Its primary responsibility is to provide legal aid, advice, and access to justice in respect of persons entitled thereto.[20]

The Legal Aid Council is administered by a Governing Board made up of the Chairman and the members; the Director-General of the Council; and such supporting legal and other staff engaged for the

---

[15]Ogbu, O. N. *supra* note 11, p. 337

[16] Ibid.; see Legal Aid Act, Cap L9, 2004; See also Malemi, E., *supra* note 8, p.114, Other statutes , which, prior to the Legal Aid Decree made provisions and still have provisions for limited legal aid are: The Criminal Procedure Act, C41, 2004, Section 352; The Criminal Procedure Code, Cap 30, Northern Nigeria 1963, section 186; The Supreme Court Act, Cap S15, 2004, section 28; The Court of Appeal Act, Cap 36, 2004, section 26, High Court Civil Procedure Rules of some states, for e.g. The Chief Judge of Lagos State has the power to grant Legal aid to an applicant who qualifies under Order 47 of the High Court of Lagos State (Civil Procedure) Rules 2004. ....

[17] As amended by Decree No. 22 of 1994

[18]Legal Aid Act, 2011, Explanatory memorandum.

[19] Legal Aid Act, section 1(2).

[20] Ibid. Section 1(3); See Asein, J.O, *Introduction to Nigerian Legal System*, 2nd ed., (Lagos: Ababa Press Ltd., 2005), p. 320.

purposes of the efficient performance of the duties and obligations of the Council under or pursuant to this Act.[21]

The Governing Board consists of the Chairman, who is appointed by the president and the following members:[22]

(a) representative of the Attorney-General;
(b) representative of the Federal Ministry of Finance;
(c) representative of the National Youth Service Corps Directorate;
(d) representative of the Inspector–General of Police;
(e) representative of the Comptroller-General of prisons;
(f) The Nigerian Bar Association, four representatives, one of whom shall be the General Secretary of that association;
(g) Representative of the Nigerian Labour Congress;
(h) Representative of women group providing free legal aid services;
(i) Two representatives of States sponsoring legal aid services;
(j) Representatives of civil society based organisations providing legal aid;
(k) Representative of the Nigerian Union of Journalists; and
(l) The Director-General.

The Council has a Director-General as the Chief Executive Officer, who is responsible for the day-to-day running of the affairs of the Council.[23] The Council is empowered to establish an office in each state of the Federation for the purposes of its services.[24] Each state shall operate three legal service units, namely, the Criminal Defence Unit, Civil Litigation Unit, and Community Legal Service Unit.[25] The President may give the Board directives of a general character or generally relating to particular matters with regard to its functions and which directions the Council shall carry out.[26]

---

[21] Section 1(4).
[22] Section 2(1).
[23] Section 4.
[24] Section 6(4); The Council is also empowered to establish a zonal office in each six geo-political zones of the Federation. Section 6(2).
[25] Section 6(5).
[26] Section 7; See Malemi, E., *supra* note 1, p.424.

The Act provides that the Council shall not in any way be liable to pay costs awarded against a person granted legal aid.[27] The Legal Aid Council maintains panels of Legal Practitioners willing to act for persons receiving legal aid for different purposes, for different courts, and for different districts in the country.[28] The Council also utilises the services of lawyers serving in the National Youth Service Corps (NYSC) free of charge except for a stipend and travelling allowance.[29]

The Council maintains a register of Non-Governmental Organisations and Law clinics that are engaged in the provision of legal aid or assistance to persons who are entitled to Legal Aid under the Act.[30] The Council may also partner with or otherwise engage the services of such organization in providing legal aid and assistance to indigent persons.[31]

The Council is empowered to conduct an inspection of prisons, police cells, and other places where suspected persons are held in order to assess the circumstances under which such persons are detained.[32] The Council may file an application in any appropriate court for the review of the case of any person who has been held in any place of custody without trial for a period exceeding the maximum provided by the Constitution.[33]

The Act makes provisions for miscellaneous and supplementary matters. These include the prohibition of disclosure of information furnished by any person to the Council.[34] It is an offense to do so, except with the consent of the applicant for legal aid.[35] The Council is required to make annual reports to the Attorney-General of the Federation regarding its operation and transactions and audited statements of accounts.[36]

---

[27] Section 10 (4).
[28] Section 14 (1).
[29] Section 16.
[30] Section 17 (1).
[31] Section 17 (2).
[32] Section 19 (1).
[33] Section 19 (5).
[34] Section 20 (1).
[35] Section 20 (2) and section 21.
[36] Section 22 (a) and (b); The statement of accounts must be audited in accordance with Section 13 of the Legal Aid Act, 2011.

THE SCOPE OF LEGAL AID

In defining the scope of legal aid and advice, Section 8(1) of the Act stipulates that legal aid should be provided in three broad areas, namely, Criminal Defence Service, Advice, and assistance in Civil Matters, including legal representation in court and Community Legal Services subject to the merits and indigence tests for the parties.[37]

Proceedings in connection with which legal aid may be granted shall be in respect of criminal matters specified in the Second Schedule of the Act. The Act establishes the Civil Litigation Service to assist indigent persons in accessing such advice, assistance, and representation in court where the interest of justice demands to secure, defend, enforce, protect or otherwise exercise any right, objection, duty, privilege, interest or service to which that person is ordinarily entitled under the Nigerian legal system.[38]

The Council is empowered to establish a Community Legal Service to ensure that individuals have access to services that effectively meet their needs.[39] Proceedings in respect of which Legal Aid may be given are specified in the Second Schedule of the Act as follows:[40]

> A. Proceedings in a court or tribunal (whether at first instance or on appeal) wholly or partly in respect of crimes of the following descriptions, or as near to those described as may be, respectively in any Criminal Code or Penal Code, that is to say:

	Criminal Code	**Penal Code**
1.	Murder of any degree.	Culpable homicide punishable with death.
2.	Manslaughter.	Culpable homicide not punishable with death.

---

[37] Section 8 (2).
[38] Section 8(3).
[39] Section 8(7).
[40] Legal Aid Act, 2011, Second Schedule; Section 8(2).

3. Maliciously or wilfully grievous hurt.	Wounding or inflicting bodily harm.
4. Assault occasioning actual body harm.	Criminal force occasioning actual bodily harm.
5. Common Assault	
6. Affray	
7. Stealing	
8. Rape	
9. Armed Robbery	

B. Aiding and abetting or counselling or procuring the commission of, or being an accessory before or after the fact to, or attempting or conspiring to commit, any of the offenses listed in paragraph A of this Schedule.

C. 1. Civil claims in respect of accidents including employee's compensation claim (under the Employee's Compensation Act, (Act No. 13 of 2010)].

2. Civil Claims to cover breach of Fundamental rights guaranteed under Chapter IV of the Constitution of the Federal Republic of Nigeria.[41]

3. Civil Claims arising from criminal activities against persons who are qualified for Legal Aid under this Act.

By Section 8(5) of the Act, Legal Aid consists of:

[41] The jurisdiction of the Council was enlarged in 1994 to cover breach of fundamental rights guaranteed under Chapter IV of the 1979 Constitution, now Chapter IV of the 1999 Constitution; See generally, Ogbu, N.O., *supra*, note 11, p.338.

(a) The assistance of a legal practitioner including all such assistance as is usually given to a private legal practitioner in the steps preliminary or incidental to any proceeding;

(b) Representation by a legal practitioner before any court; and

(c) Such additional aid (including advise) as may be prescribed.

The Act establishes a fund for the Council known as the Legal Aid General Fund for the activities of the Council.[42] The Federal and State governments,[43] philanthropic persons, and bodies are free to make contributions to this fund.[44]

ELIGIBILITY FOR LEGAL AID

The Act specifies that legal aid shall be granted to persons whose income does not exceed the national minimum wage.[45] However, the Board may, in exceptional circumstances, grant legal aid to a person whose earnings exceed the national minimum wage.[46] A person whose income exceeds ten times the national minimum wage may be required to make contributions toward the cost of legal services rendered on his behalf.[47] Guidelines on how to determine the means and needs of applicants are provided under the Act.[48] It is an offense for any person who is seeking or receiving legal aid or advice to furnish false information to the Council.[49]

However, legal aid is commonly granted to several categories of persons which includes low-income earners whose disposable income or capital fall within the financial limit prescribed by the Act.[50] Indigent persons,[51] other incapacitated persons, such as pensioners, prisoners, detainees, other kinds of inmates, for instance, inmates of a lunatic

---

42 Legal Aid Act, section 9(1).

43 Ibid., Section 9(1)(a) and (b).

44 Ibid., section 12(1)(a) and (b); see also Malemi, E., *supra* note 1, p. 424.

45 Section 10(1); The National minimum wage in Nigeria is ₦18,000.00 per month. See The National Minimum Wage (Amendment) Act, 2011, which amended the National Minimum Wage Act Cap. N 61 Laws of the Federation of Nigeria, 2004.

46 Section 10(2).

47 Section 10(3).

48 Section 17.

49 Section 21.

50 Section 10

51 1999 Constitution, section 46(4)(b)(i) as amended; *Udo* v. *State* (1988) 3 NWLR (Pt. 82) p.316 SC; *Udofia* v. *State* (1988) 3 NWLR (Pt. 84) p.533 SC; *Kim* v. *State* (1992)4 NWLR (Pt.233) p.17 SC.

asylum, destitute, financially stranded immigrants, and other persons who by reason of their circumstances have no earnings or are not earning a reasonable income.[52]

MODES OF LEGAL AID DELIVERY

The Legal Aid Council administers legal aid to applicants using several categories of lawyers. These are as follows:

Judicare System

A Judicare service is the provision of legal aid whereby an applicant for legal aid is assisted by an external legal practitioner who is to be remunerated by the Council.[53]

Salaried Lawyers

The LAC employs its own lawyers. These salaried lawyers are civil servants under the Federal government of Nigeria. They are usually required to attend to or complete a minimum number of cases per annum. They render legal services directly to applicants by personally attending to their legal aid needs.[54]

National Youth Service Corps (NYSC) Lawyers

These are lawyers who are on National Youth Service with the Council. In the one-year period of service with the Council, they render legal aid services to applicants as the Council may assign and direct. At the end of the service year, some may be employed by the Council whilst others move on to other sectors to continue with their lives.[55]

Non-Governmental Organisations (NGOs)

Section 17(1) of the Legal Aid Act empowers the Legal Aid Council to maintain a register of non-governmental organizations and law clinics that are engaged in the provision of legal aid or assistance to persons who are entitled to legal aid under the Act. The Council may partner with or otherwise engage the services of such organizations in a manner

[52] Section 10; See Malemi, E. *supra*, note 8, p. 114
[53] Malemi, Ibid, p. 116; Malemi E., *supra*, note 1, p.426
[54] Ibid.
[55] Ibid.

consistent with the mandate of the Council.[56] Some of these organizations include:

i. The Nigerian Bar Association;
ii. Civil Rights Groups;[57]
iii. Women Associations, such as the National Council of Women Societies (NCWS), The International Federation of Women Lawyers (FIDA);
iv. Religious bodies, such as Churches;
v. Network of University Legal Aid Institutions (NULAI) Nigeria.[58]

Access to Justice Schemes of State Governments

Some state governments such as Lagos,[59] Rivers, and the Bayelsa States have access to justice schemes under the Directorate of Citizens Rights of their respective States' Ministry of Justice. Where free and effective legal services are provided to members of the public who cannot afford to pay for such services.[60] The Directorate collaborates with Civil Society groups, the private Bar, and other interested parties to provide greater access to justice for the financially and otherwise disadvantaged and other vulnerable groups of the society.[61]

THE PROBLEMS OF PROVIDING LEGAL AID IN NIGERIA

Many factors undermine the objective of the Legal Aid Council of providing legal aid and advice to indigent persons across Nigeria. Some of these factors include:

---

[56]Section 17(3)

[57] Civil Rights Groups such as: Civil Liberties Organisations, Campaign for Democracy, Constitutional Rights Project, Committee for the Defence of Human Rights, Universal Defenders of Democracy, Shelter Rights Initiative among others.

[58]NULAI was established in Nigeria in 2003, by Professor Ernest Ojukwu, as a non-governmental, non-profit and non-political organization committed to promoting clinical legal education, legal education reform, legal aid and access to justice in Nigeria and the development of future public interest Lawyers. See http://www.nulai.org/.Accessed 8th August, 2012.

[59] See Beredugo, A.J., supra, note 4, p.200; See also Ade Ipaye, "Enhancing Justice Sector Reforms in Lagos State," *National Mirror*, 04/06/2012 at http://nationalmirrowonline-net/law-and-justice/law-justices-news/41447.html. Accessed 8th August, 2012.

[60]Ise-Oluwa, I. " *Nigeria: Lagos Government Establishes Citizens Mediation Centre*", *Vanguard*, April 10 ,2001 at http://allafrica.com/stories/200104100077.html Accessed 8th August, 2012.

[61] Vulnerable groups such as, low income earners, unemployed persons, unskilled or menial labourers, illegal aliens, refugees and so forth; See Beredugo, A.J., *supra*, note 61.

1. Inadequate funding: Inadequate funding by the government and private persons and organizations affect the Legal Aid Council adversely. It leads to so many other problems, such as:

a) Lack of essential infrastructure: The LAC lacks equipment, Utility Motor vehicles, motorcycles, electric generators, and little or no information technology. This makes it impossible to store and retrieve information that may help information dissemination in real time amongst LAC offices across the country.[62]

b) Poor remuneration of salaried lawyers and private legal practitioners who accept legal aid briefs. This leads to a high turnover of experienced lawyers and a loss of interest in the scheme.[63] Moreover, some court-appointed lawyers tend to be quite young, from small practices, have a smaller client base, and have fewer interactions with prosecutors. Thus, it may lead to more jail time and less justice for their clients.

c) Dearth of current and relevant law books, journals, and law reports which, of course, are *sine qua non* to the practice of law.[64]

d) Low publicity of the free legal services-
The few public enlightenment campaign programmes embarked upon by the LAC are insufficient to stimulate interest in the legal aid scheme in a predominantly ignorant and illiterate society.

2. **Delays in investigating crimes** by the police: Police lack the capacity to detect, prevent, arrest, investigate and prosecute crimes judiciously. It is not technically equipped to curb violent crimes. There is no national crime prevention strategy, weak community policing initiative, and limited coordination among law enforcement agencies. Poor training of officers and lack of infrastructures, such as patrol cars, radios, computers, and a good working environment, slows down the police in the investigation and disposal of cases. As Abdul Fatah Bakre, the South-West

---

62 Hassan Baba, U. A., "*An Overview of the State of Legal Aid Scheme in Nigeria: Pre-1999*", at http://www.ilagnet.org/jscripts/tiny-mce/plugins/filemanager/files/Antwerpen-2007/additions. Accessed 9th August, 2012

63 Ibid.

64 Ibid.

Zonal Director of the Legal Aid Council said recently: when people suffer deprivation, they often don't know where to go. In this part of the world, what obtains is arrest before investigation.[65]

The police do not bother to investigate crimes or complaints before arresting people, especially indigent suspects, who end up as awaiting trial inmates in the Nigeria prisons and overcrowded police cells.

3. **Delays in treating files** by the Director of Public Prosecutions (DPP). There are so many case files awaiting legal advice in the offices of the Directors of Public Prosecutions across the country. Evidence abounds of an acute shortage of manpower in DPP's offices, so much so that it takes years for legal advice to be issued if issued at all. Appearances of State Counsel to prosecute or defend cases for the State are no longer guaranteed as the lawyers are juggling too many cases in their offices. People accused of crimes are not getting adequate legal services. Cases could drag on longer, and there is a greater chance of appeals down the road. This leads to accused persons spending more time in detention than necessary.[66]

4. **Lack of Political Will** by the government to decongest the prisons, restructure the Police Force, and provide more resources to the Council.[67]
5. **Delays in the Administration of Justice**: The judiciary is not only the last hope of the common man; it is the only hope of government and concepts such as the rule of law.[68] However, the

---

[65] "*Legal Aid Council handles 6,500 cases,*" NAN, August 23, 2011.http://www.nangronline.com /section/judiciary/legal-aid-council-hanles-6500-cases. Accessed August 12th, 2012

[66] Ibid.

[67] See Speech delivered by J.B .Daudu SAN, President, Nigerian Bar Association at the world press briefing of the Nigerian Bar Association, Abuja, on 29th September 2010. http:www. Nba.org.ng/web/speech-delivered-by-jb-daudu-san-president-nigerian-bar-association-at-the-world-press-briefing-of-the-nigerian-bar-association html.Accessed 12thAugust, 2012.

[68] See Ogunleye, J. "A New Nigerian Judiciary is Necessary" at http://saharareporters.com/article/new-nigerian-judiciary-necessary-jiti-ogunye.Accessed 14th August, 2012.

judiciary has several operational difficulties, ranging from inadequate infrastructure, insufficiency of judicial and non-judicial personnel, debilitating delay in hearing and determination of cases and appeals, inadequate emolument, and lack of a reliable research resource.[69]

According to Hassan Baba, U., the former Director-General of the Legal Aid Council of Nigeria:

> The judiciary in Nigeria is today characterized by incessant delays and a backlog of cases in almost all courts, which problem is compounded by insufficient remuneration to judicial officers and personnel. Court facilities are lacking while material resources are almost non-existent. Few courts, if any, maintain a well-stocked library, which situation has seriously affected the quality of judgements delivered by the courts.[70]

All these problems slow down the administration of justice and lead to overcrowded prisons and police cells.

6. **Distant Offices**: Most offices of the Council are located in distant Federal and State Capitals, and their services and addresses are hardly advertised. Where the addresses are known, they are often located in exclusive parts of towns with little or no foot traffic, bus routes, and bus stops that serve people who need their services. As such, people are often unaware of the Council and its services.[71]

7. **The limited scope of legal aid and advice** available under the Act undermines the objective of the Council. Legal aid is not available for representation before administrative tribunals, and there is no organized way of funding lay representatives.[72]

---

[69] Ibid.
[70] See Hassan Baba, *supra*, note 64.
[71] Malemi, E., *supra* note 1, p.429.
[72] Peter, C., *Administrative Law*, 5th ed., (London: Oxford University Press, 2011), p.87.

8. **Lack of trust in legal aid lawyers**: Most people do not trust legal aid lawyers to deliver quality representation when their rights are trampled upon by the government. The perception is that since the legal aid scheme is run by the government and the lawyers are civil servants or private lawyers paid by the LAC, the lawyers may not represent them confidently against the government i.e. their employer.

9. **Prison Congestion**: The Nigerian prison is responsible for the confinement, reformation, and rehabilitation of awaiting trial persons (ATPs) and convicts. But the state of the Nigerian prison is appalling. There are no operational vehicles, especially the "*Black Maria,*" to convey ATPs to and from courts when due to answer to their charges, resulting in a backlog of cases in courts and ultimately prison congestion. Similarly, even when the vehicle is available, the driver would not convey the prison inmates without a "mobilization fee"[73] from the inmate's relatives and friends. Many legal aid clients are victims of these inadequacies of our prison system.[74]

RECOMMENDATIONS

While the Law on the legal aid scheme is commendable, there is no doubt that certain factors need to be improved upon if the goal of the Act is to be realised. These include:

I) Increase the scope of proceedings in respect of which legal aid may be given. For example, legal aid should be extended to administrative tribunals and to indigent politicians who may need it to protect the people's mandate.[75] It should be provided for indigent persons in every area of law.

---

[73]Mobilisation fee is a euphemism for "bribe" or "tip".

[74] See Hassan Baba, U. A., *supra*, note 64.

[75]Udeajah, G., *"Orji asks Legal Aid Council to Stop Services for robbers, others"*, at http://www.gbooza.com/group/nigeriapolitics/forum/topics/orji-asks-legal-aid-council-to. Accessed 10th August, 2012.

II) Increase public enlightenment campaigns to boost public understanding and acceptance of the legal aid scheme.

a. Public relations activities such as publicity events, photo-ops, or publicity stunts.[76]

b) Talk show circuits on television: a public relations spokesperson or a legal aid "client" does the circuit by being interviewed on television and radio talk shows with audiences that the LAC wishes to reach.

c) Direct communication with audiences instead of via mass media with, for example, printed or email newsletters.

d) Social media and social networking services such as Facebook, Twitter, etc.

e) Blogs.[77]

III) The office of the Directors of Public Prosecution (DPP) should be restructured for effective performance. There should be time frames for the completion of cases, and prosecutors should be closely monitored to avoid injustice to indigent suspects. Continued legal education for officers and employment of more lawyers to clear the backlog of cases, amongst others, is recommended.

IV) There should be more offices closer to the people in towns and villages along with adequate utility vehicles and motorcycles to traverse the bad roads in the country and to bring justice nearer to the people.

V) Federal and State governments should increase the funding of the Legal Aid Council and also encourage private persons and philanthropic bodies to donate funds to the Council in accordance with the Act.[78]

---

[76] See for e.g., Nurudeen Alimi, *"Legal Aid Council Sensitises Oyo People on Free Legal Service"* at http//www. Tribune.com.ng. Accessed 11th November, 2012.

[77] "Blog" is an abbreviated version of 'weblog', which is a term used to describe websites that maintain an ongoing chronicle of information It features a diary-type commentary and links to articles on other web sites, usually presented as a list of entries in reverse chronological order. Blogs range from the personal to the political, and can focus on one narrow subject or a whole range of subjects. See Word Press Codex, *"Introduction to Blogging" at http//www.codex.wordpress.org/ introduction_to_Blogging. Accessed 11th November, 2012.*

[78] "*Obasanjor allies support for Legal Aid Council*" at http://www.nigeriafirst.org/printer-3400shtml. Accessed 9th August, 2012.

VI) The Public Complaints Commission[79] should expand its Ombudsman services to the public.[80] Like the Legal Aid Council, its main function is to protect the citizens and any resident of the country from injustice that might result from administrative irregularities or malpractices. Thus the recent inauguration of the Public Complaints Commission by David Mark, the Senate president, is a step in the right direction.[81]

VII) The Nigerian Bar Association (NBA) should continue to lead in providing legal aid and advice to indigent persons. Article 4(d) of the Constitution of the NBA provides for:

> Establishment, maintenance and efficient operation of a system of prompt and efficient legal aid and assistance for those in need but who are unable to pay for same.[82]

It is in recognition of the leadership role of the NBA that the Legal Aid Act provides in section 2(1)(f) for four (4) representatives of the NBA, including its General Secretary, to be members of the Governing Council of the Legal Aid Council.[83] The NBA should not only fight for the independence of the judiciary, police, and prison reforms but also continue to encourage its members to provide free legal aid and advice to indigent persons.

CONCLUSION

This chapter has examined the provision of legal aid and advice in Nigeria to persons who by reason of low income or circumstances, cannot afford legal services. It highlighted the historical background and the constitutional basis of legal aid. It pointed out the challenges in providing legal aid, particularly the issue of underfunding of the Legal Aid Council and the inability of Nigerians to seek the assistance of the

---

79 Public Complaints Act, Cap. P37, Laws of the Federation, 2004.

80 Malemi, E., *supra*, note 8, p 123.

81 For The Record, *"You're Ombudsman of The Nation, Senate President to Commissioners," The Nigerian Observer,* 17 May, 2012, p. 23.

82 The Nigerian Bar Association (NBA) Constitution (Adopted at the delegates conference held in Calabar on 31st August, 2001) http://nba.org.ng/NBA_Constitution.pdf. Accessed 11th August, 2012

83 See Hassan Baba, U. A, *supra*, note 61.

LAC whenever the need arises. Finally, the chapter made recommendations, which, if implemented, will go a long way toward ensuring a robust and effective Legal Aid scheme in Nigeria.

PART F

SOME CONTEMPORARY ISSUES

Chapter 19

CONCEPT OF PLEA BARGAIN IN THE NIGERIAN LEGAL SYSTEM

Samuel Ojogbo*

INTRODUCTION

The concept of law and indeed legal system is based on relationships between parties and the need to protect persons and properties from injuries that may arise from the conduct of other persons. The importance of law to modern society cannot be overemphasized. It helps to ensure respect for rights and obligations. The sanctity of rights and obligations is a *sine qua non* for peace and order in society; the absence of law is invitation to anarchy.

In traditional Nigerian society, large-scale commerce and complex political arrangements were unknown. Since law and legal systems can only provide for known and experienced situations, the concept of law in traditional Nigerian society was rudimentary and simple, just enough to regulate the limited socio-economic and political environment.

The coming of the Europeans brought large-scale commerce, civilization,[1] and a legal system that emphasized rights and obligations. The civilization that followed from the colonization brought developments that were hitherto unknown to the traditional Nigerian society. Civilization also brought new crimes and increase in criminal

*Samuel E. Ojogbo, LL.M (Western Ontario) B.L, Lecturer Faculty of Law, Benson Idahosa University, Benin City, Edo State, Nigeria. Phone: 2348097924168, Email: samojogbolaw@yahoo.com; sojogbo@biu.edu.ng

[1] According to Professor Orojo, before the coming of the Europeans, first the Portuguese and later the British, trade in the area now known as Nigeria was restricted to internal trade in a rural and peasant economy. The exposure to international trade brought new products, Western culture and Western civilization to Nigeria. See J. O. Orojo, *Company Law and Practice in Nigeria* (Durban: Lexis Nexis; 2008) p.3

activities. The English legal system: "Received English Laws,"[2] the "Doctrines of Equity,"[3] and their complex justice administration process was introduced because what the colonialists met as the indigenous legal system were inadequate to deal with the socio-economic and political developments that followed from Western civilization. Even transactions involving Nigerians, which were unknown to customary law, became subject to the "Received English Laws."[4]

The Nigerian legal system is, thus, the laws of Nigeria, which include the customary law,[5] the received English law and the doctrines of equity, the courts, and the personnel involved in the administration of justice. Laws and enforcement processes make up the legal system, and the purpose is peace and order in society.

Law follows the development in technology, economics, and politics. This is the reason law is continuously reformed to respond to changes in technology, economics, and politics rather than initiate those changes.[6] The Nigerian legal system is no different. Since the coming of the Europeans, the Nigerian legal system has been in a continuous evolutionary process aimed always at bringing the law to meet the demands of justice in an ever-evolving socio-economic and political environment.

This chapter is concerned with the effects of socio-economic and political development on the Nigerian legal system. Currently, in the Nigerian political landscape, there are considerable challenges in the administration of justice, particularly in the criminal justice system, which the present legal regime did not envisage. Some of such challenges have taken a new turn since the return to civilian government in 1999. For example, the anti-corruption war has seen the

---

[2] Recieved English laws is used in this sense to include the common law of England and the statutes recieved into Nigeria otherwise called the statutes of general application.

[3] The Doctrines of Equity are the laws developed by the English Court of Chancery because of the rigidity of the common law. This is also a part of the received English laws.

[4] See *Okolie* v. *Ibo*, (1958) NRNLR 89.

[5] Customary Law includes the indigenous Customary Law and Islamic Law.

[6] P. G. Mahoney, "The Common Law and Economic Growth: Hayek Might Be Right" in M. B. Fox & M. A. Heller, ed., *Corporate Governance Lessons From Transition Economy Reforms* (Princeton: Princeton University Press, 2006) at 36

indictment of several top government officials since 2005,[7] and this has put added pressure on the legal system. There are suggestions[8] now that plea bargaining should become fully part of the Nigerian legal process. The issue of prison congestion occasioned by the tardiness and inefficiencies in the investigation and adjudication processes, apart from the corruption in the system, has given impetus to these suggestions.

In view of the above, this chapter will discuss the developments in the Nigerian political and socio-economic landscape, which have necessitated these suggestions for the full and proper introduction of the plea bargain concept into the Nigerian legal system. Part II will discuss the developments in the political and socio-economic life of Nigeria, particularly since the return of democratic governance in 1999, and the plea bargain deals that have set the motion for the plea bargain discourse. Part III will discuss the meaning, history, and nature of plea bargains. Part IV will discuss the practice of plea bargain and the legality or otherwise of the practice of the concept currently in the Nigerian criminal administration system, while Part V will discuss the desirability of the plea bargain concept in the Nigerian criminal justice administration system. Part VI, the concluding part, will discuss the possible benefits of the plea bargain concept to the Nigerian justice system and offer suggestions on the possible ways to properly and legally introduce the concept into the Nigerian legal system.

DEVELOPMENTS IN THE NIGERIAN LEGAL SYSTEM

Development in law is always a response to the development in the political and socio-economic environment. Developments of a legal system usually follow the same pattern. This is particularly true of Nigeria, where the Western civilization that resulted from the expansion in commerce necessitated the introduction of the English

---

7 See for example, *Chief Diepreye Solomon Alamiesieigha* v. *The Federal Republic of Nigeria* (2006) 16 N.W.L.R. See also *EFCC* v. *Lucky Igbinedion*, FHC/EN/6C/2008.

8 See the the paper presentation by Orbih F., "Plea Bargaining And The Anti-Corruption Crusade In Nigeria" at the law week of the Law Students Association (LAWSA), Benson Idahosa University, Benin City, Nigeria. On the 8th of May 2012. See also C. C. Ohuruogu, "Some Reflections On Adjudicating Corruption In Nigeria" in Prince O. A. Ikedinma, (ed.) *The Role Of The Judiciary In Nigerian Democratic Process: Essays in Honour of Justice Iche N. Ndu* (Lagos: Vox Nigeria Limited; 2008).

legal system into the country. The introduction of the English legal system started with the appointment of the first Consuls in 1849 by the British government, essentially to regulate the trade between the British merchants and the local merchants.[9]

As stated above, the concept of law is based on relationships between parties. Once there is a minimal level of socialization between persons, some conflict of interest will begin to manifest.[10] This was the case when the British merchants were exposed to the local merchants in the coastal parts of Nigeria in the early 19th century. There were conflicts between the foreigners and the indigenous merchants and attempts were made to settle these conflicts by the customary courts. However, this mode of dispute resolution according to Obilade was "strange to the British and other foreign traders"[11] and this resulted in the appointment of the first consuls in 1849.[12]

And because new challenges will always confront the human race, law reform will remain a continuous exercise in Nigeria as in other jurisdictions for the law to keep pace with political and socio-economic developments. It is not surprising, therefore, that identified deficiencies in the Nigerian criminal justice administration system have become a ground for suggestions for the introduction of the plea bargain concept.

New Challenges in the Politics and Socio-economy of Nigeria

Steady political and socio-economic development followed the emergence of Nigeria in 1914 under the management of the colonial government leading up to Nigeria's independence in 1960.[13] It is noteworthy that the Nigerian legal system witnessed tremendous development during this period.[14]

---

[9] Obilade A. O., *The Nigerian Legal System* (Ibadan: Spectrum Law Publishing; 1979) p. 18.

[10] See J. O. Igbokwe, The Course Outline for Nigerian Legal System, developed for the National Open University of Nigeria (NOUN), Department of Government and Public Policy, National Defense College, Abuja. At www.nou.edu.ng/noun/NOUN-ocl. Accessed 04/10/2012.

[11] *Supra,* note 9.

[12] Ibid.

[13] This chapter does not attempt to discuss the constitutional history of Nigeria, for a detailed account of Nigeria's constitutional development, see B. O. Nwabueze, *A Constitutional History of Nigeria* (London: Longman Group Limited, 1982).

[14] For a fuller and more colourful account of the development of the Nigerian legal system during this period, see A.O. Obilade, *Supra* note 9.

The full democratic experience came with the independent Constitution, which gave birth to Nigeria's Independence in 1960.[15] The steady march to democratic Nigeria meant that all the actors in the politics and economy of Nigeria were looking at developments in Nigeria to follow an uninterrupted democratic pattern. This was to change in January 1966, when the first military coup occurred in Nigeria.[16] The coup was partially successful[17] as a military government other than those involved in the coup formed the new military government. The second coup of July 1966 precipitated the Civil War, which was fought between 1967 and 1970.[18]

The developments in the Nigerian political and socio-economic environment after the Civil War created new situations that were not envisaged by the Nigerian legal system. For example, light weapons became readily available, and crimes such as armed robbery hitherto unknown in the Nigerian environment became commonplace.[19] The Military Government responded to these developments by enacting decrees establishing special tribunals to deal with the new era of crimes – the Robbery and Firearms (Special Provisions) Decree 1970[20] provides for the establishment of a special tribunal with respect to armed robbery and related offences, and firearms offences. So also did the Offences Against the Person (Special Provision) Decree of 1974[21] provide for the establishment of a special tribunal to try the offences of kidnapping, lynching, and other related offences. Most of these decrees provide for the death penalty upon conviction.

Another military coup led by the then Brigadier Murtala Muhammed occurred in 1975 and another in 1976 with the attendant

---

[15] *Supra* note 13 p. 29-61.

[16] This was the coup of the five majors in the Nigerian army led by Major Chukwuma Kaduna Nzeogwu. There main reason for the coup was corruption among the political class whom they called 10 percenters.

[17] It was partially successful because the officers that carried out the coup could not take over the rulership of Nigeria but their senior colleagues formed the central government under the leadership of Major General J. T. U. Aguyi Ironsi.

[18] See Nwabueze B. O., *supra,* note 13 at 161 – 200.

[19] Ibid., p. 215.

[20] No. 7 of 1970.

[21] No. 22 of 1974.

implications for the nation and its legal system.[22] However, it was the two later coups that set the tone for Nigeria's return to democratic rule in 1979 after more than thirteen years of military rule.[23] Unfortunately, the democratic experience, which began in 1979, otherwise called the Second Republic, was also terminated by another military revolution in December 1983[24] for the same reason that the First Republic was terminated – that the civilian government was corrupt and unable to maintain peace and security.[25]

The Military Government of Major General Muhammadu Buhari, which sacked the civilian government of Alhaji Shehu Usman Shagari in December 1983 was itself overthrown by another set of military officers led by then Major General Ibrahim Babangida in August 1985. Two other Military Regimes[26] and a period of interim government[27] followed before the return to democracy in 1999.

The Nigerian democratic experience from 1999, otherwise called the fourth republic, is the longest period of democratic experience since independence in 1960. The relatively long period of democratic rule has exposed the deficiencies in the Nigerian legal system. The two revolutions that terminated the past civilian governments in 1966 and 1983 identified corruption[28] as one of the reasons for the revolt, but there is no precedent arising from the efforts of those regimes on corruption matters.

It is worthy of note, however, that the government led by Major General Mohammadu Buhari made efforts to prosecute alleged corrupt politicians and recover their loots, but the war against corruption embarked upon by that administration was more political than legal.

---

[22] Murtala Muhammed as Head of State in 1975, set a time table for a return to democratic governance. This time table was duly followed by his predecessor in office, the General Olusegun Obansanjo who succeeded Murtala Muhammed after the Lt Col B. S. Dimka led unsuccessful coup that claimed the life of Murtala Muhammed.

[23] Yakubu J. A., *Constitutional Law in Nigeria* (Ibadan: Demyaxs Law Books; 2003) p. 483-487.

[24] Ibid.

[25] Ibid.

[26] General Sani Abacha, ruled between November 1993 and June 1998, and General Abdulsalam Abubakar who handed over to the civilian government on May 29, 1999 ruled between June 1998 and May 1999.

[27] Chief Ernest Shonekan was sworn in as the Head of the Interim National Government when Military President Ibrahim Babangida stepped aside on the 27th of August 1993 haven failed to declare the results of the elections of June 12, 1993 believed to have been worn by Chief M. K. O. Abiola.

[28] *Supra,* note 23.

The outcome of those trials did not leave the Nigerian legal system with any precedent.[29] Other efforts by various Nigerian governments, such as the creation of special bodies and laws specifically intended to fight corruption in public offices,[30] are undermined by corruption in the political system. As a result, the criminal justice system is left with no clear and effective means of addressing corruption, thereby leading to debates[31] on the legality or otherwise of the plea bargain option as a way of disposing of corruption cases.

As noted earlier, the criminal justice administration system in Nigeria is bedevilled by a myriad of problems, which has made justice delivery difficult. This is evident in the worrisome congestion in Nigerian prisons and delays in the prosecution process.[32] Further confirmation of the inadequacies in criminal justice administration is that out of the over forty thousand inmates in Nigerian prisons across the country, more than two-thirds (⅔) of them are awaiting trial inmates.[33] This is despite all the legislative and judicial efforts at ensuring efficiency in criminal justice administration through speedy trial of criminal cases. For example, the Constitution of Nigeria 1999 as amended provides, *inter alia*, that: "Whenever any person is charged with a criminal offence, he shall, unless the charge is withdrawn, be entitled to a fair hearing within a reasonable time by a court or tribunal."[34] This provision has received judicial support in the Supreme

---

[29] Buhari,s governemnet in 1984 set up Special Military Tribunal to try alleged corrupt politician. The government created a Special Decree for this purpose and against conventional wisdom appointed Military Officer to head the tribunal that was set up for that purpose. The tribunals sat behind closed doors and awarded ridiculous jail terms, sometimes prison terms above two hundred years were awarded against those found guilty. The result is that the process was reduced to a political trial and our criminal jurisprudence did not benefit from the outcome of that process.

[30] See for example, the Public Complaints Commission Act Cap P.37, LFN 2004, that established the Public Complaints Commission and the Code of Conduct Bureau and Tribunal Act, Cap. C.15 LFN 2004 that established the Code of Conduct Bureau and the Code of Conduct Tribunal.

[31] See the paper presentation by Orbih F., "Plea Bargain And The Anti-Corruption Crusade In Nigeria" at the law week of Law Students Association (LAWSA), Benson Idahosa University Benin City on the 8th of May 2012. See also Iyang U. K., http//topeadebayo//p.wordprocess.com/2012/03/27/the-legality-of-the-use-of-plea-bargain-in-the-nigeria-legal-system.

[32] J. Oshodi, "Reducing Prison Congestion in Nigeria" *The Punch* April 5th 2012 at www.punchng.com. Accessed 11/10/12.

[33] See the paper presentation by Chief Ferdinand Orbih SAN, "Plea Bargaining And The Anti – Corruption Crusade In Nigeria" at the law week of Law Students Association (LAWSA), Benson Idahosa University Benin City on the 8th of May 2012.

[34] Section 36(4), The Constitution of Nigeria 1999 as amended.

Court case of *Ari-Ori* v. *Elemo* where the court stated that an essential element of the fairness of trial is the speedy disposition thereof and that the speedy disposition constitutes a public right which an individual cannot unilaterally waive.[35]

The issues of prison congestion and the inadequacies in the criminal justice administration system apart;[36] the tardiness and inefficiencies in the investigation and the prosecution process as well as the high profile criminal defendants that have emerged from the political system and developments in the global political and socio-economic environment have foisted on the legal system other issues, such as terrorism, cyber-crimes and such other negatives that were not within the contemplation of the current legal system.

All the negatives highlighted above have exposed the need for improvement in criminal justice administration. Ohuruogu has aptly summarised the new challenges in the criminal justice system as developments in technology, prosecution, defence, and speedy trial.[37] According to the learned author, technology has rendered the Nigerian Evidence Act and most criminal laws obsolete. He also advocates the need for synergy between investigation and prosecution and adaptation to highly sophisticated forensic techniques and materials in this era of quality and high-net-worth defendants.[38] The emergence of these high-profile criminal defendants has brought attention to criminal law practice and pressure on the criminal justice system. This development has led to the exploration of the plea bargain option as a method of resolving criminal cases.

---

[35] (1984) 5 NLR 1.

[36] See Oshodi J., note 32.

[37] C. C. Ohuruogu, "Some Reflections On Adjudicating Corruption In Nigeria" in Prince Ikedinma O. A. (ed.) The Role Of The Judiciary In Nigerian Democratic Process: Essays in Honour of Justice Iche N. Ndu (Lagos: Vox Nigeria Limited; 2008) at 83.

[38] Some of the criminal defendants these days are former state governors and bank executives; See *Lucky Igbinedion* v. *EFCC*, FHC/EN/6C/2008; *EFCC* v. *Cecilia Ibru*, Vanguard Newspapers online, "Give Details of Property Recovered From Cecilia Ibru, Court Orders CBN at www.vanguardngr.com /2012/19/give-det. Accessed 05/10/2012..

THE MEANING, HISTORY, AND NATURE OF PLEA BARGAIN

There is almost a consensus in current scholarship that making the plea bargain concept a full part of the Nigerian system will improve criminal justice administration in Nigeria and make it more responsive to the demands of justice.[39] As noted earlier, the Constitution of Nigeria 1999, as amended, provides for speedy dispensation of criminal matters by a court or tribunal.[40] However, the fact that more than two-thirds of prison inmates in Nigerian prisons are on the awaiting trial list[41] makes the inefficiency of the criminal justice system obvious. A number of factors are responsible for the inefficiency of the criminal justice system – development in technology, tardiness, the inefficiency of investigation and prosecution, and the overwhelming influence and status of today's criminal defendants all combine to hobble the criminal justice system.

The plea bargain concept is not completely a new concept to the Nigerian criminal justice system. It has been employed in the resolution of a number of criminal cases involving government officials and business executives.[42] It is the selective application of the concept in the Nigerian system that has put the concept on the front burner in most national discourse and made it a subject of controversy.[43] Almost all sides to the controversy, however, agree that the concept is desirable. The point of controversy has been on the legality of the concept and its application.[44]

The deficiency in the legal system already noted above, occasioned by infrastructural decay and official corruption[45] has confronted the Nigerian legal system with issues in the administration of justice that must be addressed before the Nigerian legal system, especially the criminal justice system and indeed the national system can function

---

[39] See F. Orbih, *supra* note 22. See also Ohuruogu C. C. *Supra* note 24.

[40] Supra note 34.

[41] See F. Orbih, *supra* , note 22.

[42] See *EFCC* v. *Lucky Igbinedion* FHC/EN/6C/2008 & *EFCC* v. *Alamiesieigha*, (2006) 16 NWLR.

[43] See the speech by the former Chief Justice of Nogeria, Dahiru Musdapher CJN, at a worksop organised by the National Association of Judicial Correspondence (NAJUC) in collaboration with Open Society Justice Initiative (OSIJI) March 5th 2012. www.vanguardngr,com/2012/03/plea-bargain-cjn-slams-efcc/. Accesses 06/10/2012.

[44] See also f. Orbih note 34 and Ohuruogu C. C. note 37.

[45] Official corruption in this sense means corruption in public office.

efficiently. Most commentators are of the view that the plea bargain concept will help to resolve the identified inefficiencies in the criminal justice system especially issues of prison congestion and the tardiness in the prosecution process.[46]

Plea bargain, like most legal concepts, is not capable of a precise definition. In fact, there are as many definitions as there are authors on the subject. However, the definition in *Black's Law Dictionary* will be adopted in this chapter. Plea-bargaining, according to the *Black's Law Dictionary*, is:

> a negotiated agreement between a prosecutor and a criminal defendant whereby the defendant pleads guilty to a lesser offence or to one of multiple charges in exchange for some concession by the prosecutor, usually a more lenient sentence or a dismissal of other charges.[47]

This definition incorporates two things – an agreement which must be between a prosecutor and a criminal defendant and, the subject of the agreement – guilty plea by the defendant, in return for a concession by the prosecutor by way of sentence reduction or charge reduction. The benefit derivable from such arrangement is sentence reduction for the defendant and expeditious processing of the case with minimal cost to the state.[48]

History of Plea Bargain

The plea bargain concept does not have a particularly long and clear history. In fact, there is no precise reference to the time of its adoption, the origin, and the reason for the adoption in the jurisdictions where it all started - the United States and the United Kingdom. There is also no agreement on where the concept originated, but opinions favour the United States.[49] Some commentators hold the view that the concept

---

[46] See *supra* note 8.

[47] See *Black's law Dictionary*, 7th Edition at 1173.

[48] S. Oguche, "Development of Plea Bargaining in The Administration of Criminal Justice in Nigeria: A revolution, Vaccination against Punishment or Mere Expedience," *NIALS Journal of Law And Development*, Vol. No. 1 2011 at 53.

[49] O. Dirk, "Plea Bargain" The New York times magazine, September 29, 2002. www.nytimes.com. Accessed 07/10/201.

may have become part of the criminal justice system in the nineteenth century as prosecution moved from non-adversarial jury trial to adversarial trial.[50]

The rise of the adversary system, the involvement of lawyers and other professionals in the prosecution process, and the development of the law of evidence, according to Langbein, robbed the jury trial of the "wondrous efficiency" that has characterised it for years.[51] The complexities of the adversarial system which often leads to delays and high cost in criminal justice administration was said to be responsible for the introduction of the plea bargain concept.[52]

However, apart from the inefficiency of adversary system, the increase in criminal activities, which resulted from the birth of new crimes owing to the industrial revolution, also played a part in the choice of the plea bargain option.[53] The increase in criminal activities came with a concurrent increase in caseload. This development stretched the criminal justice system. The overwhelming caseload arising from the increase in criminal activities, created delays in the processing of the cases. These delays and the injustice that flow from such delays are some of the factors responsible for the exploration of the plea bargain option.

The non-adversary jury trial was adjudged swiftly such that the jury was able to try twelve to twenty cases per day.[54] The speedy dispensation of cases was possible under the system because the system was judge-dominated, and lawyers and other courtroom professionals were not involved with criminal trials.[55] Under this system, there was no need for plea bargain since the main reason for its practice is to achieve a speedy trial and a reduction in the cost of justice administration.

---

[50] J. H. Langbein, "Understanding the Short History of Plea bargaining," *Law & Society Review.* Vol. No. 2 261- 272 at 262.

[51] Ibid.

[52] Ibid.

[53] *Supra,* note 43 p. 58

[54] *Supra,* note 33 at 262

[55] Ibid.

Nature of Plea Bargain

Plea bargain are of two types – charge bargain and sentence bargain. The difference between the two is that charge bargain focuses on the charges against the criminal defendant while the sentence bargain is concerned with the sentence.[56] Charge bargain is simply an arrangement in which the prosecution agrees to press a less serious charge, which usually carries a lower punishment than what would otherwise be obtainable if the original charge was preferred and the prosecution was successful.[57] Sentence bargain on the other hand is the exchange of guilty plea by the defendant for the promise of leniency by the prosecution. In this case, the charge may not necessarily be different from the conduct with which the defendant is charged but the prosecution under this agreement recommends lenient sentence or minimal punishment.[58]

The classification of the two types of bargain into charge bargain and sentence bargain notwithstanding, there is no real difference between the two plea bargain types. This is because the result from the two types is the same – sentence discount or lighter punishment for the accused for the offence committed in consideration for pleading guilty.

This categorization of plea bargain, however, is only about the practice of the concept in the United States, where the concept is more widely in use, as only a charge bargain is permitted in other jurisdictions, such as the United Kingdom and Australia.[59] The practice of charge bargain in the United Kingdom admits of two modes. First is the practice where the prosecution may accept a plea of guilty to a lesser offence by the accused person. Second is where the prosecution may agree not to proceed on one or more of the counts in the indictment as consideration for a plea of guilty to the remaining charges.[60]

---

[56] *Supra* note 37.

[57] J. F. Parker, "Plea Bargaining" (1972) 1 *Am J. Crim. L.* 187 at 188.

[58] Ibid.

[59] S. R. Moody, & J. Tomps, "Plea Negotiations in Scotland," *Criminal Law Review*, Jan-Dec, (1983) 297.

[60] C. Oba, "Plea Bargain in a Developing Nigeria: Merits and Demerits" in A. O. Alubo *et al*, *Emerging Issues in Nigerian Law: Essays in Honour of Justice B. A. Adejumo* (Ibadan: Constellation Publishers; 2009) at 33.

THE PRACTICE OF PLEA BARGAIN AND THE LEGALITY OF THE CONCEPT IN THE NIGERIAN LEGAL SYSTEM

We have seen from the discussions in the preceding part that the plea bargain concept is a direct consequence of the chronic shortage of resources and manpower arising from caseload pressure on an overburdened criminal justice system. The concept, therefore, was just a way to relieve the pressure on the criminal justice system and bring justice to criminal defendants.

The plea bargain concept has become a necessity for the proper functioning of the criminal justice system, at least in the common law world, where the adversary trial system is the practice. In fact, some authors have argued that about 85 per cent of criminal cases in the United States federal system are resolved through the plea bargain arrangement.[61] In Nigeria, the concept has been used to resolve some high-profile criminal cases.[62] Despite the acknowledged usefulness of the concept, it has not been without criticisms.

In the United States, some commentators have argued that the plea bargain concept subverts the design of the United States Constitution, the 5th and 6th amendment viz.: the provision against self-incrimination and the right to fair trial by an impartial jury.[63] However, the major controversy over the concept, especially in the United States is not about its legality but about the benefit to criminal defendants and the fact that it is an easy course for criminals to escape justice by way of serious crimes receiving light sentences and possible conviction of innocent people.[64] Some commentators have also argued that that plea bargain is not a voluntary practice as it is enforced by "a substantial coercion from judges, prosecutors and even public defenders."[65]

---

[61] S. A. Smith, "The Plea Bargain Controversy" The Journal of Criminal Law and Criminology (1986) Vol. 77, No. 3 949 p. 949.

[62] See *EFCC* v. *Alameiesegha* (2006) 16 NWLR & *EFCC* v. *Lucky Igbinedion* FHC/EN/6C/2008.

[63] See *supra* note 61.

[64] M. M. Feeley, "Perspectives on Plea Bargaining," (Winter 1979) *Law & Society Review*, Vol. 13, No. 2, 199-209 at 202.

[65] John "The Impropriety of Plea Agreement: A Tale of Two Counties," *Law & Social Inquiry*, Vol. 1 (1994) 115-133 p.116.

In the Nigerian jurisdiction, there is almost a consensus[66] on the need to adopt the plea bargain option in the resolution of criminal cases. It is believed by most commentators in Nigeria, that the application of the concept will improve the efficiency of criminal justice administration in Nigeria.[67] However, the process of its introduction into the Nigerian legal system has become a source of unending debate amongst academics, practitioners and jurists.[68] While some argue that plea bargain "has no place in our law" and is therefore invalid,[69] others contend that plea bargain is part of Nigeria law. According to Odinkalu, "the claim that the plea bargain was never part of any Nigerian law until 2004 when the Economic and Financial Crimes Commission (EFCC)[70] was established is rather dubious."[71]

Those in support of the validity of the concept usually rely on Section 14(2) of the EFCC Act and Section 180(1) of the Criminal Procedure Act (C.P.A.)[72] The EFCC Act provides:

> subject to the provisions of Section 174 of the Constitution of the Federal republic of Nigeria, 1999 (which relates to the power of the Attorney-General of the Federation to institute, continue, takeover or discontinue criminal proceedings against any person in any court of law) the commission may compound any offence punishable under this Act by accepting such sums of money as it thinks fit, exceeding the maximum amount to which that person would have been liable if he had been convicted of that offence.

It has been argued that this provision and the Section 180(1), did not envisage plea bargain and that even if it did, the concept will be in

---

66 See F. Orbih, note 33, See also C. Oba, Note 60.

67 Ibid.

68 See Dahiru Musdapher CJN note 43, see also Dr. Odinkalu Chidi, www.vanguardngr.com/2012/03/plea-bargain-cjn-slams-efcc/. See also Iyang U. K. http//topeadebayo//p.wordprocess.com/2012/03/27/the-legality-of-the-use-of-plea-bargain-in-the-nigeria-legal-system.

69 See *supra* note 30.

70 EFCC will be used throughout this chapter to represent the Economic and Financial Crimes Commission

71 See www.vanguardngr.com/2012/03/plea-bargain-cjn-slams-efcc/.

72 C.P.A. is the Criminal Procedure Act. The short form C.P.A. will be used throughout this chapter.

violation of Section 36(4) 1999 Constitution as amended, which provides that: "whenever any person is charged with a criminal offence, he shall, unless the charge is withdrawn, be entitled to a fair hearing in public within a reasonable time," and also be a violation of Section 139(1) and (2) of the Evidence Act 2011.[73]

The controversy over the legality of the concept of plea bargain notwithstanding, it is clear that existing laws did not expressly provide for the concept, but it is arguable that some form of plea arrangements are conceivable under existing legislations.[74] Section 14(2) of the EFCC Act gives powers to the EFCC (subject the prosecutorial powers of the Federal Attorney-General) to compound cases arising under the Act. Implicit in this power is the power to settle criminal case and to continue and discontinue criminal cases. Arguably, the Commission can rely on this provision to enter a plea deal.[75]

Plea bargain can also be construed from the prosecutorial powers granted the Federal Attorney General under the Constitution 1999, as amended,[76] to institute, continue and discontinue any case in any court at any time before judgment. Prosecutorial discretion is the power of the prosecutor to enforce the law selectively.[77] Prosecutorial discretions, especially the unfettered powers granted the Federal Attorney General under Section 174 of the Nigerian Constitution could be safely relied upon to negotiate a plea deal.

The general acceptance of the plea bargain concept as an option for improving criminal justice administration makes it imperative that such an important aspect of the criminal justice administration is not left to conjecture. As stated earlier, no aspect of our laws permits or prohibits the practice of the plea bargain concept currently. However, it is submitted that for a concept as important as plea bargain to become fully part of our legal system, it must be clearly defined in our statutes.

---

[73] See *supra,* note 33.
[74] *Supra* note 37.
[75] Ibid.
[76] See Section 174 (1) Constitution of Nigeria 1999 as ammended.
[77] See *supra,* note 24 at 88.

THE DESIRABILITY OF THE PLEA BARGAINING CONCEPT IN THE NIGERIAN CRIMINAL JUSTICE SYSTEM

The daily problems in the social and economic life of Nigeria occasioned by population explosion and mismanagement by successive governments are also noticeable in the area of justice administration. There is chronic shortage of manpower and resources in the Nigerian criminal justice administration system and this has resulted in prison congestion[78] with a rising population of awaiting trial inmates.[79]

In most of the leading common law jurisdictions, the cost of administration is a major consideration in any plea-bargain discourse.[80] The problems already identified in the Nigerian criminal justice system are the same as the problems that have necessitated the adoption of plea bargaining concepts in other jurisdictions such as the United States and the United Kingdom – administrative considerations.[81] The situation in the Nigerian system is made worse by the pervading official corruption. It is, therefore, important to identify the benefits derivable from the plea bargain concept as a basis for its adoption into the Nigerian criminal justice system.

The process of relieving the Nigerian criminal justice system of the administrative pressure already identified will necessarily begin with improvement of the resources for criminal justice administration. This involves the provision of more facilities – courts, prison and other facilities and the massive employment of judicial and other personnel.

Nobody could hope for a massive allocation of funds to make the necessary provisions required to improve the criminal justice administration system in this era of dearth of funds, given the economic realities in the country. This means that an alternative means of justice delivery will be required to deal with the problems identified in our criminal justice system. One alternative that has worked in other jurisdictions is the plea bargain concept.

---

[78] J. Oshodi, Note 32.

[79] See F. Orbih, note 33.

[80] See S. J. Schulhofer, "Is Plea Bargaining Inevitable?" (March 1984) *Harvard Law Review* Vol. 97, No. 5, 11037-1107 at 1040.

[81] M. McConville, "Plea Bargaining: Ethics and Politics" (Dec. 1998) *Journal of Law and Society*, Vol. 25, No. 4, 562-587 at 564.

Apart from the issues of shortage of facilities and personnel in the Nigerian justice administration system, there is also the issue of corruption in the Nigerian political system. Now that Nigeria has run a full democratic course,[82] the nation is left with high profile corruptions cases, and the criminal justice system is expected to deal with these cases in a manner that will serve the interest of justice – justice for the Nigerian people who are the victims of corruption and justice for the defendants.

The pervasive corruption in the Nigerian political system has made justice administration difficult. Apart from a few cases of corruption that have been disposed through the plea bargaining process[83] other cases involving corrupt public officials and business executives have been stalled by fraudulent injunctions and other administrative bottlenecks.[84] This flux in the Nigerian judicial system is not good for criminal justice administration.

In view of the above, there is the need to explore new ways to move criminal justice administration forward and make the system more responsive in the war against corruption, especially concerning public officials and business executives. One way that may make our criminal justice system useful in dealing with issues of official corruption in this area is the proper adoption of the plea bargain concept through appropriate legislation and practice. This is the subject of the conclusion of this chapter.

CONCLUSION

It is obvious from the chronic shortage of manpower and resources that it is time for the plea bargaining concept in the Nigerian criminal justice system. The pervasive corruption in the political system makes the adoption of the concept imperative at this time. This is because of

---

[82]The first set of Governors and the first elected President in this democratic dispensation have done their full terms and handed over to a new set of elected leaders for the first time in Nigeria's history.

[83] Examples are *EFCC* v. *Lucky Igbinedion, EFCC* v. *Cecilia Ibru.*

[84] Examples are *EFCC* v. *Peter Odili and EFCC* v. *Erastus Akimgbola. Peter Odili's case* have particularly been stalled by a permanent injunction odered by the Federal High Court in Port Harcourt.

the successes recorded in the application of the concept in corruption cases.[85]

However, the adoption and the application of the concept advocated in this chapter is different from what is presently practiced in Nigeria as plea-bargain which has been criticized by legal professionals, jurists,[86] and prosecutors alike.[87] Plea bargaining is practiced in other jurisdictions to meet the end of justice – expeditious disposition of cases and the acceptance of responsibility of the act by the defendant.

The criticisms against the concept are acknowledged – serious crimes receiving light sentences and possible conviction of innocent people.[88] However, the advantages of the concept cannot be overemphasized – benefits to the prosecutors and the courts interested in speed and efficiency and the defendants interested in saving time and cost.

In advocating that the plea bargaining be made fully part of the Nigerian criminal justice system, this writer is not unaware that the concept is susceptible to abuse by the already corrupt political system. This is why a proper foundation for the introduction of the concept is advocated. The introduction of the concept will begin with the appropriate legislation that will make the concept applicable in all cases, unlike the selective application of the concept presently to cases of official corruption.

The concept is presently employed only by the EFCC to resolve criminal cases. The EFCC purportedly derives its power from Section 14(2) of the EFCC Act. Relying on the EFCC Act and any other legislation that purports to permit the application of plea bargain concept in Nigeria will limit the application of the concept. This is because the application of the concept under the EFCC Act is circumscribed – it is only applicable to offences listed under the Act.

---

[85] See note 42.

[86] See note 43.

[87] See See J. Ajani, Farida Waziri: The Unfinished Business, *Vanguard*, 27 November 2011 at www.vangaurdngr.com/2011/11/farida-waziri. Accessed 31 December 2012.

[88] M. M. Feeley, "Perspectives on Plea Bargaining" (Winter 1979) Law & Society Review, Vol. 13, No. 2, 199-209 at 202.

Therefore, only a clearly defined legislation will make the concept of a universal application in Nigeria.

The cases disposed through the plea bargain concept may not necessarily be satisfactory but they have been concluded and part of the loot recovered. This is what is required of the criminal justice system in a criminal trial of corrupt officials – recovery of all or part of the proceeds of corruption and punishment for the offenders. This is justice for society.

Chapter 20

TERRORISM IN NIGERIA: TRENDS, PROSECUTION, AND THE CHALLENGES

T. U. Akpoghome (Mrs)*

INTRODUCTION

This chapter will focus on terrorism in Nigeria, the trends, prosecution, and the challenges. This is due to the fact that the spate of terror witnessed in Nigeria between 1999 after the death of Ken Saro-Wiwa and 2014 following attacks by an Islamic sect, the "Boko Haram," is unprecedented. These attacks left many wounded and homeless and also accounted for the death of thousands of innocent Nigerians and some foreigners. On 26 August 2011, a suicide bomber drove through the gates of the United Nations (UN) headquarters in Abuja, the Federal Capital Territory of Nigeria, in a car strapped with a 100-pound bomb crashing into two security barriers near the building's reception area. The explosion tore through the UN building, leaving 23 persons dead and many injured. The Islamist group, Boko Haram, claimed responsibility for that attack and other attacks that came after that.[1]

These series of attacks have led to the displacement of thousands of Nigerians from their homes for fear of being victims. This chapter is divided into six sections. The first section will discuss the concept of terrorism, the second will examine the history of terrorism albeit briefly, the trends of terrorist attacks, the fourth will focus on

*LL.M, LL.B, BL. Lecturer, Department of Public Law, Faculty of Law, Benson Idahosa University, Benin City, Edo State. Ph:08065436545, 08056317472. E-mail: takpogho@biu.edu.ng, teremajor@gmail.com.

[1] These included the bombing of the Police Headquarters- Louis-Edet House; the bombing at the Eagle Square on 1st of October, 2010; the bombing of churches in Jos, Kano, Maiduguri, Yobe, the killings in Kaduna and the killings in the Southern part of Jos, Plateau State, and also the killing of several worshippers at the Deeper Life Church in Okene.

prosecution of terrorism in Nigeria, the fifth section will discuss the challenges in combating terrorism in Nigeria, the sixth will conclude the paper.

WHAT IS TERRORISM

Terrorism is not new, and although it has been used since the beginning of recorded history, it can be relatively hard to define. Terrorism has been described variously as both a tactic and strategy, a crime and a holy duty, a justified reaction to oppression, and an inexcusable abomination.[2] All criminal acts directed against a state and intended or calculated to create a state of terror in the minds of particular persons or a group of persons, or the general public.[3]

A definition proposed by Iran at an International Islamic Conference on terrorism reads thus: Terrorism is an act carried out to achieve an inhuman and corrupt (Mufsid) objective, and involving a threat to security of any kind, and violation of rights acknowledged by religion and mankind.[4]

Again the term has been defined as:

> ...anxiety-inspiring method of repeated violent action, employed by (Semi-) clandestine individual, group or state actors, for idiosyncratic, criminal or political reasons, whereby –in contrast to assassination- the direct targets of violence are not the main targets. The immediate human victims of violence are generally chosen randomly (targets of opportunity) or selectively (representative or symbolic targets) from a target population, and serve as message generators.[5]

In 2002, the European Union described terrorism as "...given their nature or context, (act which) may seriously damage a country or an international organization where committed with the aim of seriously intimidating a population."[6] India's Supreme Court in 2003, in the case

---

[2] International Terrorism and Security Research, "What is Terrorism". http://www.terrorism-research.com/. Accessed 24th July, 2013.

[3] League of Nations Convention

[4] 1987 International Islamic Conference on Terrorism.

[5] United Nations "Definition of Terrorism" http://www.web.archive.org/web/20071029121539/; http://www.unodc.org/unodc/terrorism-definition.html. Accessed 24th July, 2013.

[6] Article 1, Framework Decision on Combating Terrorism, 2002.

of *Madam Singh* v. *State of Bihar*,[7] described terrorist acts as the "Peacetime equivalent of War Crimes." In 2008, Bockstette Carsten, a German Military Officer serving at the George C. Marshall Centre for European Security Studies, proposed the following definition:

> Political violence in an asymmetrical conflict that is designed to induce terror and psychic fear (sometimes indiscriminate) through the violent victimization and destruction of non-combatant targets (sometimes iconic symbols).[8]

Section 2(c) of the Prevention of Terrorism Act 2011 of Nigeria defines terrorism as an act that involves or causes, as the case may be-

> An attack upon a person's life which may cause serious bodily harm or death; Kidnapping of a person; destruction of a government or public facility transport system, an infrastructural facility including an information system, affixed platform located on the continental shelf, public place or private property likely to endanger human life or result in major economic loss; the seizure of an aircraft, ship or other means of public or goods transport and diversion or the use of such means of transportation for any of the purposes in paragraph (b) (iv) of this subsection; the manufacturing, possession, acquisition, transport, supply or use of weapons, explosives or of nuclear, biological or chemical weapons as well as research into and development of biological weapons without lawful authority; the release of dangerous substance or causing of fire, explosion or floods, the effect of which is to endanger human life; interference with or disruption of the supply of water, power or any other fundamental natural resource, the effect of which is to endanger human life:

---

[7] *Madam Singh v. State of Bihar*. http://www.sacw.net/hrights/judgmentjehanabad.doc. Accessed 24th July, 2013.

[8] Bockstette, C "Jihadist Terrorist Use of Communication Management Techniques" (2008). http://www.marshallcentre.otg/mcpublicweb/McDocs/files/college/F-ResearchProgram/occpapers/occ-papers-20-en.pdf. Accessed 10th May, 2013.

A careful study of the above provisions would reveal that a comprehensive definition has been given to terrorism by the Act. The definition touched all foreseeable and future development that may be associated with terrorism in Nigeria.

Finally, the Economic and Financial Crimes Commission Act[9] defines terrorism as:

> (a) Any act which is a violation of the Criminal Code or the Penal Code and which may endanger the life, physical integrity or freedom of, or cause serious injury or death to, any person, any number or group of persons or cause or may cause damage to public or property, natural resources, environmental or cultural heritage and is calculated or intended to:
>
> i. intimidate, put in fear, force, coerce or induce any government, body, institution, the general public or any segment thereof, to do or abstain from doing any act or to adopt or abandon a particular standpoint, or to act according to certain principles;
>
> ii Disrupt any public service, the delivery of any essential service to the public or to create a public emergency, or
>
> iii Create general insurrection in a state;

These laws are complementary and can effectively be used to curb the dreaded act of terrorism. Apart from the aforesaid, it can be gleaned from the definitions that a lot depends on whose point of view is being represented. Terrorism has often been an effective tactic for the weaker side in a conflict. As an asymmetric form of conflict, it confers coercive power with many of the advantages of military force at a fraction of the cost. Due to the secretive nature and small size of terrorist organizations, they often offer opponents no clear organization to defend against or to deter. That is why pre-emption is considered to be so important. In some cases, terrorism has been a means to carry on a

[9] Section 46 of the EFCC Act, 2004.

conflict without the adversary realizing the nature of the threat, mistaking terrorism for criminal activity. Because of these characteristics, terrorism has become increasingly common among those pursuing extreme goals throughout the world. But despite its popularity, terrorism can be a nebulous concept.

Even within the United States Government, agencies responsible for different functions in the fight against terrorism use different definitions.[10] For instance, the United States Department of Defence defines terrorism as "the calculated use of unlawful violence or threat of unlawful violence to inculcate fear, intended to force or to intimidate governments or societies in the pursuit of goals that are generally political, religious, or ideological." Within this definition, there are basically three fundamental elements: violence, fear, and intimidation, and each element produce terror in its victims. Again, we can see from this definition that political, religious, and ideological factors can give rise to terrorism. The Federal Bureau of Investigation (FBI) states that "terrorism is the unlawful use of force and violence against persons or property to intimidate or coerce a government, the civilian population or any segment thereof, in furtherance of political or social objectives."[11]

Terrorism is a criminal act that influences an audience beyond the immediate victim. The strategy of terrorists is to commit acts of violence that draw the attention of the local populace, the government, and the world to their cause. The terrorists plan their attacks to obtain the greatest publicity, choosing targets that symbolize what they oppose.[12] The effectiveness of the terrorist act lies not in the act itself but in the public's or government's reaction to the act.

---

[10] International Terrorism and Security Research. Supra note 2, p 2.

[11] Ibid.

[12] For instance the bombing of churches by 'Boko Haram' is an indication that they want to Islamise the Northern part of Nigeria. Again the bombing of the UN building in Abuja was a direct message to the fact that 'Boko Haram' is opposed to anything western and to possibly draw foreign forces into Nigeria and make the country ungovernable.

HISTORY OF TERRORISM

The history of terrorism is as old as humans' willingness to use violence to affect politics.[13] This simply means that terrorism does not have its origin in the Nigerian State. It therefore becomes necessary that we present a brief history of terrorism as it were. As earlier stated, terrorism is as old as humans' willingness to use violence. The Sicarii were a first-century Jewish group who murdered enemies and collaborators in their campaign to oust their Roman rulers from Judea.[14] The Hashhashin, whose name gave us the English word "assassins" were a secretive Islamic Sect active in Iran and Syria from the eleventh century to the thirteenth century. Their dramatically executed assassinations of Abbasid and Seljuk political figures terrified their contemporaries. Zealots and assassins were not, however, really terrorists in the modern sense. Terrorism is best thought of as a modern phenomenon. Its characteristics flow from the international system of nation-states, and its success depends on the existence of mass media to create an aura of terror among many people.[15]

---

[13] Zalman, A. "History of Terrorism" http://www.terrorism.about. com/od/ whatisterr ris1/lp /DefiningTerrorism.htm. Accessed 29th July, 2013

[14] Ibid.

[15] Ibid, p 2. Terrorism comes from the reign of terror instigated by Maxmilien Robespierre in 1793, following the French revolution. Robespierre, one of the twelve heads of the new state, had enemies of the Revolution killed, and installed a Dictatorship to stabilize the country. This move he justified as necessary in the transformation of the Monarchy to a liberal democracy and states thus: "Subdue by terror the enemies of liberty and you will be right as founders of the Republic". Robespierre sentiment laid the foundations for modern terrorists, who believe violence will usher in a better system. While the characterization of terrorism as a state action faded, the idea of terrorism as an attack against an existing political order became more prominent.

The Rise of Non State Terrorism – 1950s

The rise of guerrilla tactics by non-state actors in the last half of the twentieth century was due to several factors. These factors include: the flowering of ethnic nationalism for example (Irish, Basque, Zionist), anti-colonial sentiments in the vast British, French and other empires and new ideologies such as communism. Terrorist groups with a nationalist agenda were formed in every part of the world. The Kurds, a distinct ethnic and linguistic group in Turkey, Syria, Iran, Iraq have sought national autonomy since the beginning of the twentieth century. The Kurdistan Workers Party (PKK) formed in the 1970's uses terrorist tactics to announce its goal of a Kurdish state. The Sri Lankan Liberation Tigers of Tamil Eelam are members of the ethnic Tamil minority. They use suicide bombing and other lethal tactics to wage a battle for independence against the Sinhalese majority government.

International Terrorism - 1970

International terrorism gained prominence in the late 60's when hijacking of aircrafts became a favored tactics. In 1968, the Popular Front for the Liberation of Palestine hijacked an El Al Flight. After twenty years precisely in 1988, the bombing of a Pan Am flight over Lockerbie, Scotland, shocked the world. The era also gave us our contemporary sense of terrorism as highly theatrical, symbolic acts of violence by organized groups with specific political grievances. The 1972 Munich Olympic bloody events were believed to be politically motivated. Black September, a Palestinian group, kidnapped and killed Israeli

In 1985, Air India Flight 182 flying from Canada was blown up by a bomb while in Irish airspace, killing 329 people, including 280 Canadian citizens, mostly of Indian birth or descent, and 22 Indians.[16] The incident was the deadliest act of air terrorism before 9/11 and the first bombing of a 747 Jumbo Jet, which would set a pattern for future acts of terrorism plots. The crash occurred within an hour of the fatal Narita Airport Bombing, which also originated from Canada, without the passenger for the bag exploded on the ground. Evidence from the explosions, witnesses, and wiretaps of militants pointed to an attempt to actually blow up two airliners simultaneously by members of the Babbar Khalsa Khalistan movement militant group based in Canada to punish India for attacking the Golden Temple.[17]

The April 19, 1995, Oklahoma City bombing was directed at the US government, according to the Prosecutor at the trial of Timothy McVeigh, who was convicted of carrying out the crime.[18] The bombing of the Alfred P Murrah Federal building in Oklahoma City claimed 168

---

athletes preparing to compete. Black September's political goal was negotiating the release of Palestinian prisoners. They used spectacular tactics to bring international attention to their national cause.

Munich radically changed the United States' handling of terrorism. Timothy Naftali a counter terrorism expert stated that "the terms counter terrorism and international terrorism formally entered the Washington political lexicon". Terrorist also took advantage of the black market in Soviet – produced light weaponry, such as AK - 47 assault rifles created in the wake of the Soviet Union Collapse in 1989. Most terrorist groups justified violence with a deep belief in the necessity and justice of their cause. Within this period, terrorism also emerged in the United State. Group such as the Weathermen grew out of the non-violent group students for a Democratic society. They turned to violent tactics, from rioting to setting off bombs, to protest the Vietnam War.

In the 1980s and 1990s, Islamic militancy in pursuit of religious and political goals increased, many militants drawing inspiration from Iran's 1979 Islamic Revolution. In the 1990s, well known violent acts that targeted civilians were the Sarin gas attack on the Tokyo subway by Aum Shinrikyo and the bombing of Oklahoma City's Murrah Federal Building. This period also saw the rise of what is sometimes categorized as single issue terrorism. If terrorism is the extension of domestic politics by other means just as war is for diplomacy, then this represents the extension of pressure groups into violent action. Notable examples that grew in this period are Eco-terrorism and Anti- abortion terrorism. In the Americas, the Contras were a Counter Revolutionary Militia formed in 1979 to oppose Nicaragua's Sandinista Government. The Catholic Institute for International Relations asserted the following about Contra operating procedures in 1987: "the record of the Contras in the field…is one of consistent and bloody abuse of human rights of murder, torture, mutilation, rape, arson, destruction and kidnapping". America Watch subsequently folded into Human Rights Watch accused the Contras of targeting health care clinics and health care workers for assassination; kidnapping civilians, torturing civilians, executing civilians, including children, who were captured in combat; raping women; indiscriminately attacking civilians and civilians houses, seizing civilian property; and burning civilian houses in captured town. The Contras disbanded after the election of Violetta Chamorro in 1990.

16 In Depth: Air India - The Victims, CBC News Online, 16th March, 2005.

17 Ibid.

18 Opening Statement of Prosecutor Joseph Hartzler in the Timothy McVeigh trial.

lives and left over 800 injured.[19] McVeigh, who was convicted of first-degree murder and executed, said his motivation was revenge for US government actions at Waco and Ruby Ridge.[20] There were series of attacks in the Middle East perpetrated by Hezbollah[21] and, Egyptian Islamic Jihad.[22] In the twenty-first century, the attacks of 11 September 2001 were carried out by Al Qaeda,[23] a terrorist group hiding in Afghanistan. The World Trade Centre[24] and the Pentagon were attacked in New York.[25] As a result of the attacks, the World Trade Centre Twin Towers completely collapsed, and 2,973 victims and 19 hijackers died.[26]

The United States responded to the attacks launching the War on Terror. Specifically, on the 7th of October, 2001, it invaded Afghanistan

---

[19] The Oklahoma City Bombing, 9-8-2004.

[20] The events at Waco and Ruby Ridge in 1993 was triggered by claims that the Branch Davidians religious sect, founded by David Koresh were believed to be involved in child abuse and sexual abuse as allowed by the doctrine of the church. The church established its headquarters at a ranch about 10 miles out of Waco, Texas. In 1993, the US Department of Justice report cites allegations of child sexual abuse. On 28th February, 1993, the Bureau of Alcohol, Tobacco and Firearms (BATF) raided Mount Carmel, the headquarter of the Davidian Church. The raid lasted for 52 days and resulted in the death of four FBI Agents and six Davidians. Shortly after the initial raid, the FBI and the Hostage Rescue Team (HRT) took command of the federal operation, since FBI has jurisdiction over incidents involving the deaths of federal agents. As the standoff continued, Koresh was injured by a gunshot wound which eventually led to his death. The church building caught fire and it was alleged that the fire was as a result of an incendiary weapon fired by the FBI (CS Gas = tear gas). This raid on Mount Carmel and the 1992 Ruby Ridge incident were cited by Timothy Mc Veigh and Terry Nicholas as motivations for Oklahoma City bombings. These terrorist acts were carried out on 19th of April 1995, to coincide with the second anniversary of the Waco assault.

[21] Hezbollah ("Party of God") is an Islamist movement and political party founded in Lebanon shortly after that Country's civil war in 1982.

[22] Egyptian Islamic Jihad (a.k.a Al – Gamaa Al Islamiyya) is a militant Egyptian Islamist Movement dedicated to the establishment of an Islamic State in Egypt. It was formed in 1980.

[23] Al Qaeda is an Islamic Jihadist movement to replace Western controlled or dominated Muslim countries with Islamic fundamentalist regimes. This organization was founded in 1988 by Osama bin Laden. In pursuit of its goal, Osama bin Laden issued a manifesto in 1996 that vowed violent jihad against US military forces based in Saude Arabia. On 7th of August 1998, individuals associated with Al Qaeda and Egyptian Islamic Jihad carried out simultaneous bombings of two US embassies in Africa which resulted in 224 deaths. On 12th of October, 2000, Al Qaeda carried out the USS Cole bombing, a suicide bombing of the US Navy destroyer USS Cole harboured in the Yemeni port of Aden. The bombing killed 17 US sailors. Al Qaeda's most well-known attack took place on September 11, 2001 when they bombed the twin Towers of the World Trade Centre and an attempted bombing of the Pentagon in the US. The World Trade Centre's twin towers completely collapsed resulting in the demise of 2,973 victims. The 19 hijackers also died in that attack. Osama bin Laden was finally killed by US forces in 2011, ten years after the bombings.

[24] "Bin Laden Claims Responsibility for 9/11. CBC News, October 29, 2004.Http:// www.cbc.ca /world/story/2004/10/29/binladen-message041029.html. Accessed 17th July, 2013.

[25] Terrorists Hijack 4 Airliners, Destroy World Trade Centre, Hit Pentagon: Hundreds Dead. CBC News. Ibid.

[26] Bin Laden Claims Responsibility. *supra* note 24.

to destroy the Taliban,[27] which had harboured Al-Qaeda terrorists. On 26th of October, 2011, the US enacted the Patriot Act, anti-terrorism legislation that expanded the powers of the US law enforcement and intelligence agencies. Many countries followed with similar legislation. After the September 11 attacks, there was the Moscow Theatre Siege, the 2003 Istanbul bombings, the Madrid train bombings, the Beslan School hostage crises, the 2005 London bombings, the 2005 New Delhi bombings, the 2008 Mumbai Hotel Siege,[28] and the 2011 Norway attacks. Also, in 2001, America saw the first act of bioterror with the 2001 anthrax attacks when letters carrying anthrax spores were posted to several American media outlets, and two Democratic politicians died. There were several fatalities.

TRENDS OF TERRORISM IN NIGERIA

The history and trends of terrorism in Nigeria date back to 1952 when there were several killings in Kano, Northern Nigeria, sponsored by misconstrued and misdirected politicians.[29] This has continued. On the

[27] The Taliban is an Islamic fundamentalist militant movement of Pashtun tribesmen. It ruled Afghanistan and its capital, Kabul, as an Islamic Emirate of Afghanistan from September 1996 to October 2001. It gained diplomatic recognition from three states: Pakistan, Saudi Arabia and the United Arab Emirates. The main leader of the Taliban movement is Mullah Mohammed Omar, and Kandahar is considered the birthplace of the Taliban. While in power, it enforced its strict interpretation of Sharia Law and leading Muslims have been highly critical of the Taliban's interpretation of Islamic law. The Taliban was also condemned internationally for their brutal repression of women. From 1995 – 2001, the Pakistani Inter-Service Intelligence and military were widely alleged by the international community to have provided support to the Taliban. Pakistan was accused by many international officials of continuing support to Taliban, but Pakistan claims to have dropped all support for the group since 9/11. Al Qaeda also supported the Taliban with regiments of imported fighters from Arab countries and Central Asia. The Taliban and their allies committed massacres against civilians, denied UN food supplies to 160,000 starving civilians and conducted a policy of scorched earth burning vast areas of fertile land and destroying tens of thousands of homes during their rule from 1996- 2001. Hundreds of thousands of people were forced to flee to United Front- controlled territory, Pakistan and Iran.

[28] The 2008 Mumbai attacks were more than ten co-ordinated shooting and bombing attacks across Mumbai, India's largest City, by Islamic terrorists from Pakistan. The attacks, which drew widespread condemnation across the world, began on November 26th, 2008 and lasted until 29th November, killing at least 173 people and wounding at least 308. See Friedman, T. "No Way, No How, Not Here" (2009) The New York Times. http://www.newyorktimes.com/2009/02/18/opinion/18friedman.html. Accessed 17th July, 2013. See also Indian Muslims Hailed for not burying 26/11 Attackers, Sify News, 19/02/2009. http;// www.sify.com/news/Indian-muslims-hailed-fro-not-burying-26-11-attackers-news-international-jegsNxehjhc.html. Accessed 17th July, 2013; Schifrin, N "Mumbai Terror Attacks: 7 Pakistani's charged-Action Comes A Year After India's Worst Terrorist Attacks:166 Die" (2009) http://www.abcnews.go.com/i nternational/mumbai-terror-attacks-Pakistanis-charged/story?id=9176592. Accessed 17th July, 2013.

[29] "History of Terrorism In Nigeria" http://www.newsflashes.com/world/africa/existence-of-internal-terrorism-in-Nigeria/ixzz21VBM2cEm. Accessed 24th July, 2013.

25th of December, 2009, Nigerians woke up to the news of a young man named Abdulmutallab who attempted to bomb an American-bound aircraft that he boarded from Amsterdam.[30] Prior to the 2009 incident, in 1986, a letter bomb was sent to Dele Giwa,[31] though an isolated case of bombing, the incident introduced terror within the media. In 2008, the Youths of Niger Delta region of Nigeria held the entire country hostage, following from perceived injustices. They kidnapped expatriates, shut down flow stations and bombed oil pipelines and installations. They called for a redress in the resource sharing formula and the establishment of true federalism in the country. They wanted the government to put an end to the marginalization and gross deprivation, and inequity in that region.

In 2009, the late President Musa Yar'Adua launched an Amnesty program which led to the disarming and reintegration of the youth. Today most of these youth are gainfully employed, and most of them are in universities under the President Goodluck Jonathans Federal Government Assisted Education Program. There are other groups that have existed at one point or the other in Nigeria, and they include: The Bakassi Boys, which terrorized the Eastern part of Nigeria by involving in extra-judicial killings; Arewa Peoples Congress (APC) held sway in the Northern part of Nigeria, their words were law; Oodua Peoples Congress (OPC) held the West to ransom, Egbesu boys also operates in the Niger Delta.

During the regime of the late General Sani Abacha,[32] there were a number of bombings, some of which were speculated to have been part of the elaborate security arrangement of the brutal regime to cause fear in the polity and give excuses to further adopt even more draconic stance to strengthen its hold on power.[33] Since 1999, there have been reported cases of bomb explosions mostly associated with the militant

---

[30] Aderounmu, A "Nigeria: From Regional Government to Terrorist Country" http://www.adernola.wordpress.com/2011/07/22/nigeria-forum-regional-government=to=terrorist-country. Accessed 29th July, 2013.

[31] Dele Giwa until his untimely and tragic demise in 1986 was the Editor in Chief of Newswatch Magazine. Till date, no one has been arrested or tried for that ugly incident which shook this nation, Nigeria.

[32] 1993 – 1998.

[33] S. N. Ifedigbo, "Terrorism In Nigeria: Beyond the Rhetoric. http://www.nigeriadial ogue.com/ 2011/ 10/05/terrorism-in-nigeria-beyond-the-rhetoric. Accessed 29th July, 2013.

groups in the Niger Delta.[34] The employment of bombs as instruments of terror became heightened on 1 October, 2010, at the 50th Independence Anniversary in Abuja. Cars were used to convey bombs to the Eagle Square venue of the event. It was reported that the movement for the Emancipation of the Niger Delta took responsibility for the act for which some persons are still on trial.[35]

On 26 August, 2011, an explosive-laden car driven by a suicide bomber smashed into the United Nations building in Abuja, killing 23 persons and many injured. The Islamic group called "Boko Haram," which had declared war on Nigeria State in an effort to bring to effect the adoption of extreme forms of Sharia law in the country issued a statement claiming responsibility for the attack. The group is reportedly founded in 2002 by Mohammed Yusuf; the name "Boko Haram" is intended to mean "Western education is forbidden" in Hausa language. Yusuf was killed by government forces in 2009, although he had instilled the group with extremist ideology, extolling a version of Islam where interaction with Western society is considered a sin. Boko Haram is a loosely organized grassroots insurrection against not only the Nigerian government but the traditional Muslim establishment as well.

The political goal of Boko Haram is to create an Islamic nation in the 12 northern states of Nigeria, eventually spreading to the rest of the country. The sect had always viewed Nigeria as a state ruled by unbelievers and made the government its main target even when a Muslim president was in power. After the killing of Yusuf in 2009, the group resurfaced in 2010 under new leadership, carrying out terrorist attacks, shootings, and bombings in the Northern part of the country, particularly Borno, Bauchi, and Jos, raiding police stations, churches, schools, conducting jailbreaks to free their arrested members. Some of their attacks include the bombing of military barracks in Abuja and Bauchi, the bombing of Police Headquarters in Abuja, the bombing of Churches in Yobe, Maiduguri, Jos, Bauchi Bayero University, Kano, Kaduna, and the Southern part of Jos in which a sitting member of the

[34] These bombings were mainly targeted at oil facilities and installations.

[35] This incident exposed the absence of structures to tackle this menace, no laws, poor intelligence network and a weak emerging management system.

Plateau state House of Assembly and a Federal legislator lost their lives in 2012.[36]

RECENT ATTACKS FROM THE SECT

Tuesday, January 14, 2014, the group, using a suicide bomber, killed 30 persons in Maiduguri, injured 50, and destroyed 10 vehicles;[37] on Tuesday, February 14, the dailies reported the Izghe Massacre, which led to the death of 146 civilians.[38]

On Tuesday, February 24, 2014, Nigerians were greeted by the news of the gruesome and senseless murder of 59 school children. The insurgents invaded the school premises at about 2 a.m. while the students were asleep in their hostels. They set the hostel ablaze before shooting and slitting the throats of some students that tried to escape through the windows. Some of the students were burned alive. The Secretary General of the United Nations, Mr. Ban Ki-Moon, expressed worries over the incessant killings and attacks on educational facilities and urged the government to bring the perpetrators to justice.[39]

Thirty-seven persons were killed in Adamawa on Wednesday, February 26, 2014.[40]

From the 2 to 4 March, 2014, The Punch reported that 87 persons lost their lives to different attacks carried out by the sect in Mafa and Maiduguri in Borno State.

On Friday, 14 March, 2014, The Punch also reported that gunmen attacked and killed 69 persons in Katsina.

Between the 22 and 23 March, 2014, another 90 persons lost their lives in Maiduguri and Benue, respectively.[41]

---

[36] In 2013, March 13, there was Kano Bus bombing which left 22 dead and 65 injured. May 7, 55 people killed in army barrack, police post. July 6, Yobe school shooting leaving 42 students dead. September 29, attack on College of Agric Gujba, Yobe State leaving 78 students dead, another 20 persons killed in Damaturu same day. 25 and 26 September another attack left 20 dead. October 26, 125 people killed in Borno and another 28 killed in Yobe. Nov. 3, Boko Hara attacked a wedding convoy in Borno killing the groom and 29 others.

[37] "Suicide Bomber Kills 30 in Maiduguri" *The Punch (*Wednesday, January 15 2014), p 2.

[38] Izghe is popularly known as Izghe Gwoza Local Government Area of Borno State. It was reported that the siege lasted for five hours in a village largely populated by Christians

[39] "Outrage as Death Toll reaches 59" *The Punch*, (Thursday February, 27 2014), p 2

[40] BBC News Hausa Service.

[41] Independent Television Main News, 7.30 pm Monday 24th March, 2014.

The 14 April, 2014, was a Black Monday as the Nigerians woke up to the news of a bomb blast at Nyanya, a suburb town in Abuja, the capital city of Nigeria. Official sources put the death toll at 72 and 124 injured, but eyewitnesses say the official figure is not reliable.[42] On Tuesday, 15 April, it was reported that the Boko Haram group had abducted over 270 school girls from Government Secondary School, Chibok in Borno, although 53 of them found some way of escape. The girls were said to be preparing for their Senior Secondary School Certificate Examination (SSSCE) when they were forcibly taken away by the gunmen around 3 a.m. The abduction has been described as a threat to girl child education and has been widely condemned.[43] This is less than 24 hours after the Monday bomb blast.

On the 1 May, 2014, at the Karshi Taxi Park, a few meters away from the Nyanya bomb blast spot in Abuja, there was another report from the media of an explosion believed to be a suicide attack, killing about 30 persons. This is barely three weeks after the Nyanya incident, not forgetting the fact that the abducted schoolgirls were yet to be rescued.

On the 5 May, 2014, the sect attacked and killed 300 people in Gamboru Ngala and also abducted 11 more girls in Warabe and Wala Communities in the Chibok Local Government Area of Bornu State.

It was reported on the 18 May 2014, that letters were written by the sect to some schools in Benue State that they would be attacked so that the sect could get schoolboys to marry the Chibok girls. The attacks were to take place on the 14 May. Although the attacks did not take place on the day in question, efforts have now been made by the government to beef up security in and around the schools.

On Saturday, the 17 May, 2014, the sect invaded the village of Dalwa-Masuba in Damboa Local Government Area of Borno State, killing 40 persons with so many injured.

---

[42] Dickson, P "Nigeria: The Nyanya-Abuja Bomb Blast and Casualty Figures" http://www.Iq4news.com/iq4news-nigeria/nigeria-nyanya-abuja-bomb-blast-and-casualty-figures. Accessed 15th April, 2014.

[43] "Nigerai: Abuja Bomb Blast, Abduction of Female Students Reported in Nigeria" http://www.panapress.com/Nigeria-Abuja-bomb-blast,-abduction-of-female-students-reported-in-nigeria-15906526-o-lang2-index.html. Accessed 15th April, 2014.

The same day, the sect attacked and killed 29 more persons in Ngurosoye village, Bama Local Government Area, Borno State. The insurgents fired a rocket-propelled grenade at the market in addition to shooting indiscriminately.

19 May 2014, the sect killed 24 persons in Kano.[44]

Tuesday, the 20 May 2014, twin bomb blasts/explosions at the Terminus Market in Jos, Plateau State, killed over 150 persons, with so many injured. Civilian properties were also destroyed in the attack.[45]

Thursday, 22 May 2014, 30 persons were killed by insurgents in three villages in Marte Local Government Area of Borno State. It was alleged that throughout the operation that lasted for about five hours, no security operative confronted the insurgents.[46] The sect also killed additional 19 persons in Alagarno in Damboa Local Government Area of Borno state.

Sunday, 25 May 2014, 24 persons were again killed by the insurgents. In addition, over 100 houses, vehicles, and shops in the market were burned in Kamuyya village, Biu Local Government Area of Borno State.[47]

Monday, 26 May 2014, 20 soldiers and 20 policemen were killed in Buni Yadi, Gujba Local Government Area of Yobe state. The same day, the insurgents killed 9 civilians in Chinene, Gwoza Local Government Area of Bornu State.[48]

Friday, 30 May 2014, the Emir of Gwoza, Alhaji Idris Timta, was killed by the sect.

Monday, 2 June 2014, 60 persons were killed in the Adamawa bombing.[49]

---

44 "Rescuers to Dig for Victims of Jos Bomb". http://www.news24.com.ng. Accessed 21st May, 2014.

45 Ibid.

46 " Boko Haram Kills 30 in Bornu Villages" *Punch* (Saturday, May 24, 2014) p 49. http://www.punchng.com. Accessed 24th May 2014.

47 "Boko Haram Kills 24 in Fresh Borno Attack", *Vanguard*, (May, 26th 2014) p 8. http://www.vanguardngr.com. Accessed 26th May, 2014.

48 "Boko Haram Attacks Police Station, Army Base" *The Punch* (May, 28th 2014) p 8. http://www.punchng.com. Accessed 28th May, 2014.

49 Channels TV News, 2nd June, 2014. In addition, 9 worshippers were killed on Sunday the 1st of June when the insurgents stormed a church at Attagara, Gwoza Local Government Area of Bornu State. On Tuesday the 3rd of June, about 100 persons were killed by insurgents in three border communities with Cameroon. Although official sources placed the number at 83, residents of the affected areas maintained that no fewer than 100 civilians lost their lives in that attack. On the 6th of June in a fresh attack by Boko Haram,

President Goodluck Jonathan inherited the Boko Haram problem and upon assumption of office in 2010, took several steps to attempt to solve the problem. A Special Joint Military Task Force (JTF) was set up, and Closed Circuit Televisions (CCTV) were reportedly installed throughout the Federal Capital Territory.[50] A committee was set up under the headship of Ambassador Usman Gaji Galtimari with the goal of dealing with Boko Haram.[51] In addition to these, the National Assembly in June 2011 passed a law on the prevention of terrorism.[52] The effectiveness and adequacy of these measures have been questioned as the attacks have continued.

In May 2014, the government of the United States, United Kingdom, China, France, and other African countries offered to help the government of Nigeria, and the offer of assistance was accepted by the Nigerian government. The United States and the United Kingdom have deployed Military troops to Nigeria, and France is assisting with intelligence. David Cameron, while addressing the British Parliament on the 7th of May, reiterated the fact that the fight against terrorism is a global fight and not for Nigeria alone. He noted that 'the act of abduction is pure evil and it shows that there are Islamist extremists who are against education, against progress, and against equality and we must look for them and get them anywhere they are.'[53] He also noted that Britain should be proud that they are assisting Nigeria by sending Military troops that are already in Nigeria training over 800,000 (eight hundred thousand) and about 600,000 (six hundred thousand) girls.[54]

over 45 persons were reportedly killed as a result of the attack on Bargari Local Government Area of Bornu State.

[50] After the Nyanya bombing in Abuja, it was reported that the ₦76 Billion Abuja Closed Circuit Television (CCTV) had been destroyed and stolen barely two years after the project was completed. Officials of various government agencies have been trading blames for their inefficiency. If the CCTV was working, it would have been easy to investigate this crime.

[51] Bartolotta, C. "Terrorism in Nigeria: The Rise of Boko Haram". http://www.worldpolicy .org/blog/2011/09/19/terrorism-in-nigeria-rise-boko=haram. Accessed 29 July, 2013.

[52] The Prevention of Terrorism Act, 2011.

[53] Channels News Track. 7 May, 2014.

[54] Ibid.

PROSECUTION OF ACTS OF TERRORISM

The Economic and Financial Crimes Commission Act in Section 46 gave a definition of terrorism; although terrorism was mentioned in the Act, the Act is primarily for the prosecution of economic crimes. Therefore acts of terrorism that are carried out in furtherance of the commission of Economic Crimes as defined in the Act are covered. The Prevention of Terrorism Act 2011 is specifically designed to tackle broader terrorism in Nigeria. A quick appraisal of the law will show that it is intended to prevent, prohibit and combat acts of terrorism, including the financing of terrorism in Nigeria. The Act also is to facilitate and promotes the effective implementation of the African Union (AU) Convention on the Prevention and Combating of Terrorism, as well as the suppression of the Financing of Terrorism.

The Act in Section 28 - 31 made provision for the prosecution of the act of terrorism. Section 28(1) provides:

> Subject to the general powers of the Attorney General of the Federation to institute and undertake criminal proceedings on behalf of the Federal Government of Nigeria, he may delegate his power to any agency charged with the responsibility of terrorist investigation to institute criminal proceedings against any person in respect of offenses categorized in this Act.

Here, investigation can be carried out by the National Security Adviser or the Inspector General of Police, and the interpretation section has listed the "Law enforcement agency" to include the Nigerian Police Force; Department of State Services; Economic and Financial Crimes Commission; National Agency for the Prohibition of Traffic in Persons; National Drug Law Enforcement Agency; National Intelligence Agency; Nigeria Customs Service; Nigeria Immigration Service; Defence Intelligence Agency; Nigeria Security and Civil Defence Corps (NSCDC); and any other agency empowered by an Act of the National Assembly. It is important to note that only the Nigeria Police Force, Economic and Financial Crimes Commission, and the Department of State Services can prosecute but other agencies listed can investigate.

Section 30 of the Act gave exclusive jurisdiction to the Federal High Court. The simple interpretation of this is that only the Federal High Court can hear and determine a case of terrorism. Section 30(1) reads: "The Federal High Court shall have the sole jurisdiction to try an offense and impose the penalties specified in this Act." This seems to be a departure from the usual trend where the Federal High Court will have concurrent jurisdiction with the State High Court. For instance, economic and financial crimes can be tried by both the Federal and the State High Courts, but specific issues listed in section 251 of the Constitution of the Federal Republic of Nigeria as amended are exclusively within the jurisdiction of the Federal High Court. The Federal High Court exercising exclusive or sole jurisdiction means that no other court in Nigeria can try any of the offenses specified in this Act.

In the case of *SSS* v. *Senator Mohammed Ndume and Alli Sanda Umar Konduga*[55] (the only case to have been prosecuted), a Chief Magistrate Court in Abuja assumed jurisdiction and convicted the second accused person on terrorism charges. Alli Sanda Umar Konduga (the second accused) was charged with terrorist activities – terrorist communication, threat messages to prominent Nigerians in Bornu State and other parts of the country. He pleaded guilty and was summarily tried and sentenced to three years imprisonment. The first accused pleaded not guilty to the charges.

From the provision of the 2011 Act, it would appear that the Chief Magistrate Court Abuja lacks the jurisdiction to hear and determine the case before it. One wonders the bases upon which the Chief Magistrate assumed jurisdiction as the likely outcome would be an appeal of the judgment to the Federal High Court, which would ultimately dismiss the case on the grounds that the Chief Magistrate Court lacks the jurisdiction to hear the case. The Chief Magistrate ought to have declined jurisdiction in the first instance. This brings the competence of some of our legal officers and legal system to question. Where a court lacks jurisdiction to hear a case, it is the duty of the judge or magistrate

[55] "Boko Haram: How SSS established case Against Ndume," *Vanguard,* November 27, 2011, p 5.

to *suo motu* decline jurisdiction, and the accused or defendants' counsel ought to have filed a preliminary objection on the issue of jurisdiction because it is very fundamental to the determination of any suit. Jurisdiction goes to the root of the case.

CHALLENGES IN COMBATING TERRORISM

Combating terrorism in Nigeria may be difficult as a result of widespread poverty, the lack of economic opportunities, and corruption among the political elite.[56] Thus, according to a Human Rights Watch Report,[57] corruption in Nigeria results in police abuse, human rights violations, lack of health care, and political violence. In its reports, Amnesty International[58] accused the Nigerian Police Force of hundreds of extrajudicial disappearances and killings each year, all of which have gone uninvestigated.[59] These factors of a failed development combine to create a climate of desperation in the people.

Most people have lost confidence and trust in the state institutions, and this has established the perfect recipe for the growth of extremism. Religion and globalization are also noted as other factors that may promote terrorism and pose a great challenge to the fight against terror. Religiously motivated terrorism is considered the most alarming terrorist threat today. Groups that justify their violence on Islamic grounds like Boko Haram, Al Qaeda, Hamas, and Hezbollah come to mind first. But Christianity, Judaism, Hinduism, and other religions have given rise to their own forms of militant extremism. This is believed to be a departure from any real religious precepts. Rather, these extremists manipulate religious concepts for their own purposes.

---

[56] The United States Secretary of State for Civilian Security, Democracy and Human Rights, Sarah Sewall noted that corruption is hindering Nigeria's efforts at ending insurgency in the North-East. She noted that the military must overcome entrenched corruption and incompetence if they must rescue the over 200 girls that were abducted by the sect. She further noted that despite Nigeria's $5.8bn security budget for 2014, corruption prevents supplies as basic as bullets and transport vehicles from reaching the front lines of the struggle against Boko Haram. On 24th of May, 2014 , the Nigerian Finance Minister, Okonjo-Iweala was accused by the service chiefs of delaying the release of defence votes. In a sharp reaction, the Minister noted that 'no budget will be enough to meet military demands, but I think the sector takes almost a trillion of the budget'. The Minister further noted that the military got N130bn in 4 months.

[57] Bartolotta, C. "Terrorism in Nigeria: The Rise of Boko Haram http://www.worldpolicy.org/blog/2011/09/19/terrorism-in-nigeria-rise-boko-haram. Accessed 29th September, 2013.

[58] 2009 and 2012 reports.

[59] Ibid.

Some scholars have tried to exonerate religion from the alleged criminality against humanity in the modern world via the instrumentality of terrorism and bloodbath conflicts. They opine that religion is not the problem of the modern world. Rather, it is an innocent victim of chance and circumstances.[60]

Globalisation and terrorism are two concepts that are intertwined. Although globalisation aids the development of state in economic, political, technological, and socio-cultural perspectives, it has been argued that globalization begets terrorism.[61] Cronin, for instance, has argued that the current wave of international terrorism, characterized by unpredictable and unprecedented threats from non-state actors is not only a reaction to globalization but is facilitated by it.[62]

The tools of globalization have become a veritable means for terrorists to carry out their activities successfully. This makes most terrorists ideological hypocrites.[63] It has been observed that the major instrument of globalization, such as mobile phones, the internet, mass media etc., have ensured that terrorist plans are executed with the same ease with which commerce is carried out among nations in the world.[64] Using technological advances in communication, these groups can easily contact and operate.[65] The use of information technologies like the internet, mobile phones, and instant messaging has extended the global reach of many terrorist groups.[66] One of the essential tools of globalization – the internet is used by insurgents, Jihadists, and terrorist organizations as a tool for radicalization and recruitment, a method of propaganda distribution, a means of communication, and ground

---

[60] Okoro, K. "Religion and Terrorism: A Socio-Historical Reconsideration" (2010), *Journal of Alternative Perspectives in the Social Sciences*, Vol.2, No. 2, pp 550 -576 at 559.

[61] Njoku, E.T "Globalization and Terrorism in Nigeria" (2011) Foreign Policy Journal. http://www.foreignpolicyjournal.com/2011/08/13/globalisation-and-terrorism-in-nigeria/. Accessed 17th July, 2012.

[62] Cronin, A.K "Behind the Curve: Globalization and International Terrorism" (2003) *International Security*, Vol. 27, No.3.

[63] Njoku, E.T., *supra* note 61

[64] Murphy, D "Activated Asian Terror Web Busted" (2002) Christian Science Monitor and Al Qaeda South Asia Reach, *Washington Post* as cited by Njoku, E.T. Supra note 61

[65] Ibid, p 8

[66] Pillar, P.R "Terrorism and US Foreign Policy" (2001) Washington D.C, p 47 as cited by Njoku, E.T., *supra* note 61

training.[67] It is sad to note that Nigeria is not taking any concrete steps to advance technologically like the other parts of the world.

Terrorist groups in Nigeria make use of information technology. The Boko Haram group which is against Western education, the groups in Niger Delta region like the Niger Delta Volunteer Force (NDVF), Movement for the Emancipation of the Niger Delta (MEND) Ijaw Youth Congress (IYC), and other groups have used the internet to communicate their responsibility for attacks on oil installations in Nigeria, for instance, the Boko Haram group which attacked worshippers during Christmas Eve church service in Suleja, Nigeria used the internet to communicate their responsibility for the attack.

Also, the perceived marginalization of some regions in Nigeria, such as the Niger Delta, gave rise to militancy. Politicians also contributed to the rise of terrorism in Nigeria. In order to satisfy their political goals and ambitions, they arm the youths for support and protection. After the elections, these youth are discarded while most of their arms are not retrieved, and they turn around to unleash terror on the populace.

CONCLUSION

Terrorism, as noted earlier, is not peculiar to Nigeria and must be given the attention it deserves if the menace must be curbed. It is good that there is a law on the prevention of terrorism, but no matter how good this piece of legislation is, it will amount to a fruitless effort if the provisions are not implemented. Nigeria has several laudable legislation, both international and national but always lacks the political will to implement these laws. Sometimes, crucial issues that will make the law effective are either left out or ignored. For instance, there is no provision for the protection of the fundamental rights of the accused persons in the 2011 Act, although Section 29(1) provides for witness protection, where the prosecuting agency is satisfied that the life of the accused is in danger. Protection of the fundamental rights and

[67] Ibid.

guarantees of the accused is necessary because an accused is deemed innocent until he is declared guilty by a court of competent jurisdiction.

Again, there is no provision on how to minimize or manage the consequences of terrorist attacks. There is a need to improve mechanisms on how to promptly respond to the immediate and long-term needs of victims of terrorism. The idea of vesting sole jurisdiction on the Federal High Court is not a very good one. Considering the number of cases pending in this court and the length of time it takes to dispose of cases, one would have expected that there should be a concurrent jurisdiction between the Federal and State High Courts, or alternatively, a special court should have been created to hear cases bothering on terrorism and related offenses. The supervisory functions of the judiciary in relation to investigations and prosecutions of terrorists are inadequate.

Finally, it is our earnest wish that this law will not go the way of others before it. Unless the Federal Government shows that it is capable of containing the current trend of insecurity in the country, the much-expected capital inflows will be a mirage. Some of the weak areas of the Act noted should be addressed to make the Act better. The government should make deliberate efforts to address some of the challenges noted in the paper, like training special intelligence squads in the military and police.

FOR FURTHER READING

1. Aderounmu, A "Nigeria: From Regional Government to Terrorist Country"http://www.adernola.wordpress.com/2011/07/22/nigeria-forum-regional-government=to=terrorist-country
2. Bartolotta, C., "Terrorism in Nigeria: The Rise of Boko Haram" http://www.worldpolicy.org/blog/2011/09/19/terrorism-in-nigeria-rise-boko-haram
3. Bockstette, C., "Jihadist Terrorist Use of Communication Management Techniques"(2008).http://www.marshallcentre.otg/mcpublicweb/McDocs/files/college/F-ResearchProgram/occpapers/occ-papers-20-en.pdf
4. Cronin, A.K "Behind the Curve: Globalization and International Terrorism" (2003) International Security, Vol. 27, No.3.

5. Ifedigbo, S.N "Terrorism In Nigeria: Beyond the Rhetoric. http://www.nigeriadialogue.com/2011/10/05/terrorism-in-nigeria-beyond-the-rhetoric
6. Okoro, K., "Religion and Terrorism: A Socio-Historical Reconsideration," (2010), *Journal of Alternative Perspectives in the Social Sciences*, Vol.2, No. 2, pp 550 -576 at 559.
7. Pillar, P.R., *Terrorism and US Foreign Policy*, (2001) Washington D.C.
8. Murphy, D., "Activated Asian Terror Web Busted," (2002) Christian Science Monitor and Al Qaeda South Asia Reach, *Washington Post*
9. Njoku, E.T., "Globalization and Terrorism in Nigeria," (2011), *Foreign Policy Journal.* http://www.foreign policyjournal.com /2011/08/13/ globalisation-and-terrorism-in-nigeria/
10. The Prevention of Terrorism Act, 2011
11. The Economic and Financial Crimes Commission (Establishment) Act, 2004
12. UN Office for Disarmament Affairs (UNODA), "Treaty on the Non-Proliferation of Nuclear Weapons," (NPT) http://www.un. org/ disarmament/WMD/Nuclear/NPT.
13. World Nuclear Association "Safeguard to Prevent Nuclear Proliferation," http://www.world-nuclear.org/info/inf12.html.
14. Zalman, A. "Types of Terrorism: A Guide to Different Types of Terrorism,"http://www.terrorism.about.com/od/whatisterroris1/lp/definingterrorism.htm.

Chapter 21

ELECTIONS AND ELECTION PETITIONS IN NIGERIA 1999 – 2014

Chinedu Akam Igwe *

INTRODUCTION

Election law is a combined interaction of constitutional law and political science. It involves politics of law and the law of politics. In this wise, politics of law refers to the political manipulation of law and legal process to achieve political purposes such as lobbying, cross-carpeting, anti-party activities, open letter writing,[1] instigation of internal political party crisis to undermine the party leadership, etc. On the other hand, the law of politics is the threshold issue of law regulating political processes such as the political party system, the nomination of candidates, general elections, election petition adjudication, etc. However, both in politics of law and the law of politics, the law is supreme and dictates the pace of both. This work deals with the law of politics and, in particular, Elections and Election Petition Tribunals within the Nigerian Fourth Republic.

MEANING AND TYPES OF ELECTION

Meaning of Election

Periodic election is healthy for democracy. This is because voting remains the primary means for most citizens to contribute to the

---

* Igwe, Chinedu Akam (LL.B, LL.M, BL), Lecturer, Department of Public and Private Law, Faculty of Law, Ebonyi State University, Abakaliki. E-mail:akamchiigwe@yahoo.com. 07031814067.

1 It is of common knowledge, the open letter writing criticism from the former President Olusegun Obasanjo to the sitting President Goodluck Jonathan and the reply thereto though both are members of the Ruling Peoples Democratic Party (PDP).

collective decision-making in a democratic polity. Thus, election is a central component of modern representative democracy. And for election to be democratic, it must be free and fair or be seen to have been so. Free election is one in which vote choices are made without coercion or undue influence of the voters, while fair election is an election in which candidates and voters alike participate on an equal basis.[2]

The word "election" is not subject to a definite definition. It is a process, not an event. First, election constitutes constituency delineation, accreditation, voting, counting and tabulation of votes, collation, and return. The legal concept of election denotes the whole process culminating in a return of a candidate with the required highest number of valid votes cast.[3] Merely voting in a polling unit is not an election but a poll.[4] Second, it means any election held under the Act and includes a referendum.[5]

An election under the Act is one in which the Electoral body is established,[6] voters[7] and political parties[8] are registered, publication of nominees of political parties[9], notices of election and poll are issued;[10] accreditation of voters, voting, counting, collation, and declaration of results are carried out in accordance with the letters of the Act. But election under the Act also means casting of votes by the electorates. This interpretation finds support from various provisions of the Act.

---

2 Sarah Binch and Bob Watt, *"Remote Electronic Voting: Free, Fair and Secret?" Political Quarterly*, January, 2004, P.4.

3 *INEC & Ors* v. *Onyembah E.C. Ray & ors* (2004) 14 NWLR (pt.892) 92 at P.123.

4 P.A. Onamade, *Advocacy in Election Petitions*, Phlade Co. Ltd., Lagos, 2007, P.2.

5 Section 156, Electoral Act 2010 (as amended). Referendum as a form of election can only be organised where the law permits it. E.g. on recall of National and State Assembly Members under sections 69 and 110 respectively of the 1999 Constitution (as amended). This is why it is difficult to subject the result of the on-going National Conference to referendum without legislative instrument from the National Assembly or amendment of the Constitution.

6 Section 153(1) (f) 1999 Constitution (as amended).

7 Sections 9 and 10, Electoral Act 2010 (as amended). Under the Act, registration of voters, updating and revision of register of voters must stop not later than 60 days before any election covered by the Act.

8 Section 222, 1999 Constitution (as amended); *INEC* v. *MUSA* 13 NSCQR 39 at P. 72.

9 Section 34 Electoral Act 2010 (as amended); *Osakwe* v. *INEC* (2005) 13 NWLR (pt.942) 446.

10 Sections 30 and 46, Electoral Act 2010 (as amended). The two sections require the Commission to issue notice of Election not later than 90 days before the date of election and notice of poll not later than 14 days before the date of election respectively.

For example, Section 46[11] mandates the Commission to "not later than 14 days before the day of the election" publish notice of poll. The word "election," as used in the above section and other provisions of the Act,[12] means no more than poll. Legally and strictly, a difference exists between an election and a poll, though it is conventional to refer to as election, the day voting takes place (polling day).[13]

Third, election also means "selecting of a person or persons for office, as by ballot."[14] It is the process of choosing by popular vote a candidate for a political office in a democratic government.[15] The vote is usually by an open secret ballot system.[16] Secrecy of the ballot is a fundamental principle of modern democracy guaranteed under the law, and the absence of it casts doubt on the electoral process.[17]

Types of Election

Primary Election

This is an election by voters of a ward, precinct, or other small district belonging to a particular political party of representatives or delegates

---

[11] Electoral Act 2010 (as amended).

[12] Sections 34, 35, 36, 38, ibid.

[13] Richard Price, *Parker's Law and Conduct of Elections*, Lexis Nexis, Butterworths, 2005, PP.1-2; *Hon Gozie Agbakoba* v. *INEC & 2 ors* (2008) 18 NWLR (Pt. 1119) 489 at. p.837 Paras D-E.

[14] *The New International Webster's Comprehensive Dictionary of the English Language*, Typhoon International Corp, U.S.A; Encychopaedic Edition, 2004, P.406.

[15] P.A. Onamade *op. cit.*, P.116; *Ojukwu* v. *Obasanjo & ors* (2002) 19 NSCQR 90 at Pp. 139-140

[16] Section 52(1)(a) Electoral Act, 2010 (as amended). The Act prohibits the use of electronic voting machine for the time being.

[17] Article 21(3), Universal Declaration of Human Rights, 1948; *McMahon* v. *The Attorney General* (1972) 1 R.69. Section 5(1), Ebonyi State Electoral (Amendment) and Other Related Matters Law No. 005 of 2010, provides for open voting system whereby voters queue behind the candidate of their choice in open and full glare of everybody. This provision undermines the secrecy of voting and therefore crude and undemocratic. It suppresses the free will of the people; the right to vote devoid of undue influence. It is against the universal democratic voting standard and offends *Article 21 (3) of the Universal Declaration of Human Rights, 1948* which guarantees periodic and genuine elections on the basis of equal suffrage and held by "Secret vote or by equivalent free voting procedures". In *Hon Peter Nwali* v. *Ebonyi State Independent Electoral Commission, unreported and suit No FHC/AI/CS/38/2013* ruling delivered on 20th September, 2013 per Hon. Justice M.A. Onyetenu J. of the Federal High Court, Abakaliki Judicial Division, the Court upon a Motion on Notice challenging the open voting system by way of Enforcement of Fundamental Rights, held that "fundamental right suit is not the appropriate procedure to challenge the law" and thereby dismissed the motion without hearing on the merit. This writer holds the contrary view with respect to the Judge. Fundamental right is an appropriate procedure to challenge section 5(1) (sic) although not the only procedure. I so advocate because *Article 21 (3) of the Universal Declaration of Human Rights 1948* provides for election my secret vote and *Order 3 Rule b (ii) of the Fundamental Rights (Enforcement Procedure) Rules, 2009* enjoins the court to advance and respect international Bills of Rights such as The Universal Declaration of Human Rights. I only think that this Bill either was not brought to the attention of the Court or the Court itself was not aware of it.

to a convention which is to meet and nominate the candidate of the party to stand for municipal or general election.[18] Primary election is the platform through which various political parties nominate candidates from amongst the members of the political party for sponsorship into various elective political offices at the general election.[19] Primary election is also known as the nomination of candidates for general election by political parties.[20] The Nigerian electoral law recognizes direct and indirect primary elections.[21] Both are affairs of political parties guided by the parties' constitutions/guidelines, subject to the Electoral Act and the overriding provisions of the Nigerian Constitution.

It is settled that courts of law cannot impose a candidate on a political party but are very much duty bound to interpret the law to ensure compliance by political parties in the exercise of their rights of sponsorship of candidates.[22] The court held categorically thus:

> ... the issue of nomination or sponsorship of an election candidate is within the domestic affairs of the political parties and the courts have no jurisdiction to determine who should be sponsored by any political party as its candidate for any election. The courts have no interest in who should be a candidate for any political party but are very much duty bound to interpret the law as made by the legislature so as to determine whether or not in the exercise of its rights of sponsorship or nomination, the political party has complied with the relevant provisions of the law laid out to regulate proper conduct so as to guarantee orderliness, peace and equity in the political area.[23]

It is obvious from case laws that the court lacks competence in the nomination of candidates by political parties. However, does the court

[18] B.A. Garner (ed.), *Black's Law Dictionary*, St. Paul, MINN, 7th ed., 1999, P.536.

[19] Sections 65 (2) (b) 106 (d), 131 (c), 177 (c) and 221, 1999 Constitution as (amended); *Onuoha* v. *Okafor* (1983) 2 SCNLR 244, *Dalhatu* v. *Turaki (*2003) 15 NWLR (pt.843) 316, *Ugwu* v. *Ararume (*2007) 12 NWLR (pt.1048) 365, *Amaechi* v. *INEC* (2007) 9 NWLR (pt.1040) 504, *Hassan* v. *Aliyu* (2010) 17 NWLR (pt.1223) 547.

[20] *Hon. Gozie Agbakoba* v. *INEC & 2 ors ., supra.*

[21] Section 87(2) Electoral Act 2010 (as amended).

[22] *Njideke Ezeigwe* v. *Chief Sir Benson Chuks Nwawulu & 2 ors* (2010) 4 NWLR (pt.1183) 159; *Mr. Augustine Omini Iwara* v. *Mr. Ubi Ettah Itam & anr* (2009) 17 NWLR (pt.1170) 337.

[23] *Mr. Augustine Omini Iwara* v. *Mr. Ubi Ettah Itam & anr. supra* at p.379.

lack the jurisdiction to determine the validity of a given nomination when disputed by candidates? The Supreme Court, per Onnoghen JSC, answered thus:

> ...the issue of validity of the nomination of the 1st respondent is not only irrelevant to the determination of the case but robs the Courts of the jurisdiction to determine the issue of validity of nomination of candidates of political party. So whether the nomination of the 1st respondent was conclusive as contended by the 1st respondent or inconclusive as contended by the appellant is clearly irrelevant.[24]

The above decision was rendered under the Electoral Act, 2006, which has been repealed. The Act then did not provide for the procedure for nomination of candidates by political parties, and therefore, there was no statutory provision on that requiring courts' interpretation. Hence, lack of jurisdiction by courts to determine the validity of the nomination. Presently, the nomination of candidates by political parties is governed by the Electoral Act.[25] Political parties must hold primaries for aspirants to all elective offices. It may be direct or indirect primaries. Direct primary means a primary election of a political party whereby all members of the party participate in nominating a candidate of the party for the general election.

On the other hand, an indirect primary election involves the following processes, namely:

(a) The Constitution and Rules of the Political Party shall:

i. Prescribe delegates of the party; and

ii. State clearly the procedure for the election of other delegates that are to vote at the Convention, Congress or Meeting;

---

[24] *Njideke Ezeigwe* v. *Chief Sir Benson Chuks Nwawulu & 2 ors supra* at p. 192. This decision is correct under the Electoral Act 2006 because the National Executive Committee of the Political Party was the final authority for resolving all disputes relating to the choice of candidates and for confirming the list of names of candidates for the party in any elective Public Officer in the Federation. Article 17.1, PDP Constitution 2009 (AS Amended). But the decision is no more relevant in view of section 87 Electoral (Amendment) Act, 2010 which provides for the procedure of Party Primaries. Nothing is domestic about Political Party activities in Nigeria under the current legal framework.

[25] Section 87, Electoral (Amendment) Act, 2010.

(b) A special Convention or Congress shall be held on specified date agreed by the National Executive Committee of the Party -

i. Where delegates shall vote for each of the aspirants;

ii. The aspirant with the highest number of votes at the end of the voting shall be declared the winner of the primary election; and

iii. The name of the declared winner shall be forwarded to the Commission.

Where there is one candidate, a special Convention or Congress must still be held on a specified date for confirmation of the aspirant before his name is forwarded to the Commission. In all cases of indirect primaries, political appointees at any level are not automatic delegates save where such a political appointee is also an officer of the political party.[26]

This provision has skewed discretion on the part of any political party in the conduct of primary election. Automatic or consensus candidate has been outlawed. Thus, even in the event of a single aspirant, a special Convention or Congress must be held for the confirmation of the aspirant. In view of the above provision, it is obvious that the court will have jurisdiction to determine the validity of the nomination of candidates – whether in the nomination of a particular candidate, the due processes of law as statutorily provided were followed.[27] The jurisdiction thereof is conferred on the Federal High Court, the State High Court, or the High Court of the Federal Capital Territory, Abuja.[28]

The jurisdiction of the court is subject to the proviso that it shall not grant an order to stop the holding of primaries or general elections or the processes thereof pending the determination of the substantive suit.[29] Although the above provision is meant to avoid sudden stoppage

---

[26] Section 87 (1) (2) (3) (4) (a) (i) (ii) (b) (i) (ii), (d) (i) (ii) (6) (7) (8) Electoral (Amendment) Act. 2010.

[27] Section 87 (9) ibid.

[28] Ibid.

[29] Section 87 (10) ibid.

of a scheduled election, it is submitted that the resultant effect of the above position of the law in conjunction with section 141 of the Act is injustice on the part of an aspirant who was lawfully nominated but unlawfully substituted. Such aspirant may succeed at the court and may later be declared the validly nominated candidate of the party. Meanwhile, the aspirant with whom he was wrongly substituted may have participated in the general election and declared the winner of the election. The wrongfully substituted aspirant cannot be declared as the winner of the general election even if he had specifically asked the court to so order. This is in view of Section 141 of the Electoral Act, 2010, which provides: "An Elector Tribunal or Court shall not under any circumstance declare any person a winner at an election in which such a person has not fully participated in all the stages of the said election."

It is contended that where an aspirant was nominated but wrongfully substituted; and the court declares him the validly nominated candidate of a given political party (even if the general election has been conducted and concluded without the physical participation of such candidate), the fact of the valid nomination of the said candidate inures him with the justifiable right to be declared the rightful person to occupy the office nominated for on the platform of the political party. The candidate did not participate in the general election on the ground of the unlawful and wrongful substitution meted out to him. Again, he is deemed to have remained the validly nominated candidate for the political party at all material times to the general election. More so, a political party cannot nominate two candidates at the same time for a particular office. It is one nomination and one candidate for a particular office over a given election.

It is strongly contended that once a court of competent jurisdiction declares a substitution wrongful, illegal, null, and void, the substitution is in law deemed not to have taken place. It was never done. Nothing happened. No substitution took place. The purported substitution was void and nullity.[30] The validly nominated candidate remained as such

---

[30] *Progressive Peoples Alliance & anr* v. *INEC & 3 ors* (2010) 12 NWLR (pt.1207) 70 at p. 94 where the court interpreted nullity to mean nothing, nothingness, that which has absolutely no legal force or effect.

and, in law, fully participated in the process leading to the return. He is, with respect, not caught by the legislative web of Section 141 of the Electoral Act, 2010. In any case, where a wrongfully substituted candidate is declared to assume office by court, his emolument begins to run from the day the court so declared him and not the day the House (in case of a legislator) was inaugurated. The rationale is that the Government cannot pay two "Members" for the same seat for the same period in question.[31] If it is an executive office, then from the date the candidate declared by the court took the Oath of Allegiance and the Oath of office.

General Election

This is an election that occurs at a regular interval of time. It is an election held in the Federation at large, which may be all at all levels, to select officers to serve after the expiration of the full terms of their predecessors.[32]

Bye-Election

This is an election held mainly to fill a vacant office that may occur as a result of death, resignation, impeachment, recall, or any other cause.[33] Any person elected through bye-election only holds office for the unexpired term of office of the last holder of the office. The election holds on the day appointed by the Commission within the statutory period.

Run-off Election

This is an election held "after a general election in which the two candidates who received the most votes neither of whom received a majority run against each other so that the winner can be

---

Rabe Nasiru v. *Sule Ali* Bindawa & 7 ors (2006) 1 NWLR (pt. 961) 355; *Mark Ogbeche Ukpo* v. *Gregory Nnaji & 3 ors* (2010) 1 NWLR (pt.1174) 175 at p. 202.

[31] *Njideke Ezeigwe* v. *Benson Chuks Nwawulu & 2 ors supra* at p.210.

[32] Section 156 ibid.; *Labour Party* v. *INEC* (2009) 6 NWLR (pt.1137) 315 at p.336. Sections 146(2), 191(2) 1999 Constitution (as amended)

[33] Any other cause could arise from the appointment of an elected public office holder into anther office and thereby create vacancy in the first office. Section 112(2) Electoral Act 2010 (as amended).

determined."[34] It may precede general or bye-election. It is conducted to choose between two candidates with the largest and second largest number of votes cast in the majority balloting but none with the required majority votes to be returned as elected.[35] It should be noted that where two or more candidates poll equal number of votes being the highest in an election none of the candidates shall be returned. Rather, a fresh election shall be conducted for the candidates on a date to be appointed by the Commission.[36]

(i) Electoral College

Electoral College is a body of electors or voters elected or nominated from each constituency to formally and finally elect the holder of an elective[37] office. The Presidential and Vice Presidential elections of the United States of America present a good example of an Electoral College system. It is a body of electors chosen from each state in the United States of America to formally elect the President and Vice President by casting votes based on popular votes. The number of electors is equal to the number of members of Congress.[38]

(vi) Referendum

Referendum[39] is a process by which a legislative act or a constitutional amendment proposal, or any important public issue is referred to the people for approval or rejection by popular votes.[40] In Nigeria, a referendum is only necessary where the law so provides.[41] And the conduct of the referendum is the responsibility of INEC. A referendum is one election without a political party platform.

---

[34] B.A. Garner (ed.), 7th ed. *op. cit.,* P.536.

[35] Section s134 (3), 179(3) 1999 Constitution (as amended).

[36] Section 70, Electoral Act 2010 (as amended).

[37] Section 13, Local Government Election Decree No 6 1996. This Decree was subsequently repealed and replaced with Local Government (Basic Constitutional and Transitional Provisions) Decree No 7, 1997.

[38] Article 11, Section 1, United States Constitution.

[39] Section 156 Electoral Act, 2010 defined election as including referendum.

[40] A. Appadorai, *The Substance of Politics*, Oxford University Press, New Delhi, 1975, Pp.376-377.

[41] Sections 69(b), 110(b) 1999 Constitution (as amended) and section 116(a)(b) Electoral Act 2010 (as amended).

ELECTION PETITION MATTERS: GROUNDS FOR ELECTION PETITION

Election and/or return at an election may be challenged by way of an election petition.[42] The petition shall complain of undue election or undue return. A petition must be predicated on the valid ground(s). Section 138(1)(2)[43] provides thus:

(1) An election may be questioned on any of the following grounds, that is to say-

(a) that a person whose election is questioned was, at the time of the election, not qualified to contest the election;

(b) that the election was invalid by reason of corrupt practices or non-compliance with the provisions of the Act;

(c) that the respondent was not duly elected by majority of lawful votes cast at the election; or

(d) That the petitioner or its candidate was validly nominated but was unlawfully excluded from the election.

(2) An act or omission which may be contrary to an instruction or directive of the Commission or of any officer appointed for the purpose of the election but which is not contrary to the provisions of this Act shall not of itself be a ground for questioning the election." The above represent the grounds for presentation of a valid petition. An act or omission which is contrary to an instruction or directive of the commission or its agent but in consonance with the provisions of the Act shall not itself constitute a ground for petition.[44]

---

[42] Election Petition shall hereafter be referred simply as "Petition"

[43] Electoral Act 2010 as (amended).

[44] In election petition matters, time is of constitutional essence. The Constitution regulates the time for the filing of the petition, hearing, judgment and appeal thereof. Thus, the petition must be filed within 21 days after the declaration of the election result. And the judgment thereof must be delivered in writing within 180 days from the date of the filing of the petition. Also an appeal against the judgment of the lower tribunal must be heard and disposed of within 60 day from the date of the delivery of the judgment of the lower tribunal. See section 285(5) (6) (7) 1999 Constitution (as amended). In *ANPP* v. *Alhaji Mohamned Goni.* (2012) 49 NSCQR (pt.1) 1, the Borno State Gubernatorial election was held on the 26th of April 2011. The ANPP candidate won while the PDP candidate lost. The latter filed petition on the 17th of May, 2011. The Election Tribunal dismissed the petition on the 12th of November, 2011 without a hearing on the merit. On appeal, the Court of Appeal allowed the appeal and ordered retrial on the merit by another Panel of Election Tribunal. The issue of time under section 285 arose for interpretation. The

The grounds shall hereunder be discussed *seriatim:*

(That a person whose Election in Question was at the time of the Election, not qualified to contest the Election[45]

This questions the qualification and disqualification of a candidate in an election in respect of elective offices established by the Constitution.[46] Qualification generally relates to citizenship, age, education, membership of a political party, and sponsorship by that party.[47] On the other hand, a candidate is disqualified if he is adjudged lunatic or otherwise declared to be of unsound mind, or he is under a sentence of death imposed on him by any competent court of law or sentence of imprisonment or fine for an offense involving dishonesty or fraud; he has been convicted and sentenced for an offense involving dishonesty or for contravention of Code of Conduct within a period of less than ten (10) years prior to the election; he is an undischarged bankrupt; he is a public servant of either of the federation or of any state who has not resigned, withdrawn or retired thereof thirty (30)

Supreme Court quoted section 285(6) 1999 Constitution (as amended) which provides: "An Election Tribunal shall deliver its judgment in writing within one hundred and eighty (180) days from the date of the filing of the petition" and held thus: "The above being the law, it follows that an Election Tribunal, in an election petition matter, must deliver its decision /judgment /ruling/order in writing within one hundred and eighty (180) days from the date the petition was filed. It means the judgment cannot be given a day or more or even an hour after the one hundred and eighty (180) days from the date the petition was filed". Per W.S.N Onnoghen JSC at p.31. The apex Court opined that the time fixed by the Constitution is like the rock of Gibraltar or mount Zion which cannot be moved. Thus, the Court cannot under any guise or circumstance enlarge the time. This simply means that once the time stipulated has elapsed, the court is robbed of the jurisdiction to continue to entertain the matter. The proper Order is to dismiss the petition without much ado. It is of some scholarship to state that section 285(5) 1999 Constitution as (amended) which provides in part that election petition shall be filed "within 21 days after the date of the declaration of result of the election" has obviated the much hitherto controversy over the time within which election petition shall be filed under the repealed Electoral Act, 2006. Specifically, section 141, Electoral Act 2006 provided thus: "An election petition under this Act shall be presented within 30 days from the date the result of the election is declared" while section 285 (5) is certain that the time begins to count "after the date of the declaration of result of the election", section 141 provided for "30 days from the date the result of the election is declared". The Supreme Court while interpreting the word "from" in section 141 in *Alhaji Mohammed Dikko Yusufe anr* v. *Chief Olusegun Aremu Okikiola Obasanjo & 56ors* (2003) 16 NWLR (pt.847) 575, *Hon. Gozie Agbakoba* v. *INEC & ors* (2008) 18 NWLR (pt.1119) 489 held that the date the result of the election was declared was exclusive. But the Court of Appeal in *Ogbebor* v. *Danjuma & anr* (2003) 15 NWLR (pt. 843) 403, *Action Congress* v. *Jonah David Jang* (2009) 4 NWLR (pt.1132) 475 opined that the day the result of the election was declared was inclusive even if took place at the last minute of the day.

[45] "Election" as mentioned under this ground refer to "poll"

[46] The offices are: offices of the President, Vice President, Governors, Deputy Governors, Members of the National and State Assemblies.

[47] Sections 65(1)(a)(b) (2) (a) (b) 106 (a) (b) (c) (d) 131 (a) (b) (c) (d) and 177 (a) (b) (c) (d) 1999 Constitution (as amended).

days before the date of the election; he is a member of a secret society, or he has presented a forged certificate to the Commission.[48]

We shall now turn to specific qualification and disqualification requirements.

(a) Citizenship: Every person is qualified for an election if he is a Nigerian. Citizenship of Nigeria may be acquired by birth[49] or registration,[50] or naturalization.[51] However, a person cannot contest election into the offices of the President, Vice President, Governor, or Deputy Governor unless he is a Nigerian citizen by birth.[52] Invariably, citizenship of Nigeria either by registration or naturalization does not qualify a person to stand election into the offices indicated above.

(b) Age Qualification: Age begins to count at birth. It varies from one elective office to the other. The age qualification for the offices of the President, Vice President,[53] Governor and Deputy Governor,[54] members of the Senate,[55] members of the House of Representatives,[56] and members of State Houses of Assembly[57] are 40, 35, 35, 30, and 30, respectively.

(c) Education Qualification: The minimum educational qualification is a school certificate or its equivalent. This means -

(a) Secondary school certificate or its equivalent, or Grade II teacher Certificate, the City and Guide Certificate; or

(b) Education up to secondary school certificate level; or Primary six school leaving certificate or its equivalent; and

[48] Sections 66 (1) (a-g), 107 (1) (a-g), 137 (1) (a-h and j) 182 (1) (a-h and j) 1999 Constitution (as amended). Note that sections 2, 8, 13 and 19 of the Constitution of the Federal Republic of Nigeria (first Alteration) Act, 2010 deleted sections 66 (1) (h).
[49] Section 25 (1) (a) (b) (c) 1999 Constitution (as amended)
[50] Section 26 (I) (a) (b) (c) (2) (a) (b), ibid.
[51] Section 27 (1) (2), ibid.
[52] Section 142 (2) and 187 (2), ibid.
[53] Section 131 (b), ibid.
[54] Section 177 (b), ibid.
[55] Section 65 (1) (a), ibid.
[56] Section 65 (1) (b), ibid.
[57] Section 106(b), ibid.

Service in the public or private sector in the Federation in any capacity acceptable to the Commission for a minimum of ten years, and

Attendance at courses and training in such institution as may be acceptable to the Commission for periods totalling up to a minimum of one year, and

The ability to read, write, understand and communicate in the English language to the satisfaction of the Commission; and

(c) Any other qualification acceptable by the Commission.[58]

The above represents the Constitutional minimum standard and qualification for election into elective offices. It is contended that under the requirement of Primary Six School Leaving Certificate or its equivalent and service in the public or private sector in the federation in any capacity acceptable to the Commission; and attendance at courses and training in such institutions acceptable to the Commission; and the ability to read, write, understand and communicate in English language to the satisfaction of the Commission all inure the Commission with the power to reject or disqualify any candidate where such service at the private or public sector of the federation or attendance at courses and training are unacceptable to the Commission; or if the Commission is not satisfied with the ability of the candidate to read, write, understand and communicate in English language. It does not behold on the court to determine what is acceptable to the Commission or when the Commission should be satisfied with the ability of a given candidate to read, write, understand and communicate in English Language. Conceded that the decision of the Commission thereof may be challenged in Court of law for a review, yet it is submitted that the Commission has the power to accept or reject candidates on that ground.

In view of the above, it is submitted that the proviso to Section 31 (1) Electoral (Amendment) Act, 2010 is inconsistent with the interpretation section of the Constitution. The said section provides:

---

[58] Section 318 (1), ibid.

"Every political party shall, not later than 60 days before the date appointed for a general election under the provisions of this Act, submit to the Commission, in the prescribed forms, the list of the candidates the party proposes to sponsor at the elections, provided that the Commission shall not reject or disqualify candidates for any reason whatsoever."

The Commission can reject or disqualify, where apart from the primary six school leaving certificate or its equivalent, other conjunctive[59] requirements are unacceptable to the Commission, or the Commission is not satisfied with the candidate's ability to read, write, understand or communicate in the English language.

In respect of the secondary school certificate, it is sufficient that a person sat for secondary school certificate examination even without obtaining the certificate.[60] It is enough that a candidate attended a secondary school and read up to the secondary school certificate class or level without passing or obtaining the certificate.[61]

Membership and Sponsorship by a Political Party

It is settled that only a political party and no other association can canvass for votes for candidates in any election.[62] The power to nominate and sponsor a candidate for an election is special preservation of a political party.[63] Such sponsorship is often accorded to those who, in the first place, are members of the political party and are nominated by such party. Hence, unless a candidate is a member of a political party and is sponsored by such party, he is not qualified to contest an elective office under the Constitution.[64] Independent candidacy is unknown to the Nigeria Electoral laws and processes.

---

59 *Saddiq Janro Bayo* v. *Don D. H. Njidda & ors* (2004) 8 NWLR (pt. 826) 544 at pp. 629-63-.

60 *Barrister Cyprian Chukwu* v. *Mr. Rogers Sam Icheoniro & ors* (1999) 4 NWLR (pt.600). 587 at 596.

61 *Supra* at p.598.

62 Section 221, 1999 Constitution (as amended).

63 *Njideke Ezeigwe c. Chief Sir Benson Chuks Nwawulu &* 2 ors *supra*; *ANPP* v. *Umar Abubakar T. Argungu &* 138 ors (2009) 17 NWLR (pt. 1171) 445; *Amaechi* v. *INEC supra*; *Ugwu* v. *Ararume supra.*

64 Sections 131 (c), 177 (c), 65 (2) (b) and 106 (d) 1999 Constitution (as amended).

Contravention of Code of Conduct

Conviction and sentence for an offense involving dishonesty within a period of less than ten years before the date of election disqualifies.[65] Where a person is found guilty of the contravention of the Code of Conduct, he shall be disqualified from membership of a Legislative House and from holding any public office for a period not exceeding ten years.[66] The Constitution established the Code of Conduct Bureau[67] and the Code of Conduct Tribunal.[68]

The jurisdiction of the Code of Conduct Tribunal is limited to the allegation of contravention of Code of Conduct for public officers as contained in the Constitution. However, a mere allegation of non-observance of the Code of Conduct does not *ipso facto* disqualify a person from vying for elective office during the election. Rather, it is a conviction by the Code of Conduct Tribunal that is a pre-condition for disqualification from contesting during the election.[69]

Employment in the Public Service

A person employed in the Public Service of the Federation or of any State who has not resigned, withdraw or retired from such employment thirty (30) days before the date of election is disqualified for election into any elective public office.[70]

Civil Service of the Federation means service of the federation in a civilian capacity as staff of the office of the President, Vice President, ministry or department of the Government of the Federation assigned with the responsibility for the business of the Government of the federation.[71] While public service of the federation means the service of the federation in any capacity in respect of the Government of the

---

[65] Sections 137 (1)(c), 182 (1) (e), 66 (1) (d), 107 (1) (d) ibid.

[66] Paragraph 18 (2) (b) Fifth Schedule, ibid.; *Ali Lawan* v. *Hon. Maina Yama & 4 ors* (2008) 9 NWLR (pt.877) 177 at pp. 138-139, paragraphs H-B.

[67] Section 153 (I) (a), 1999 Constitution.

[68] Item 15 (I) , Part I, Fifth Schedule, ibid.

[69] *Solomon Abiodun Sagaolu* v. *Independent National Electoral Commission* & 2 ors (1999) 7 NWLR (pt.612) 600.

[70] Sections 137 (1) (f), 66 (1) (e), 107 (1)(e) 1999 Constitution (as amended); Section 107 (1) (e) Electoral Act, 2010 (as amended).

[71] Section 318 (1) 1999 Constitution (as amended).

Federation, and includes service in the enumerated non-political offices in the Government of the federation.[72]

There are also public officers for the purpose of the Code of Conduct which includes political and non-political officer holders.[73] For the purpose of election, public officers for the purpose of Code of Conduct are irrelevant.[74] Again, elected political office holders are excluded from public officers for the purpose of resignation or withdrawal from office thirty (30) days before the date of the election. This is probably because they are not appointed by Federal Civil Service Commission, State Civil Service Commission, or Local Government Service Commission. Secondly, there must be continuity in government administration until a proper handover is made. The Court stated emphatically thus:

> If... the office of Chairman of Local Government Council and also of Councillors of same are taken as being part of the public service of the State and thereby making their occupants subject to resigning their appointments thirty (3) days to the election, a vacuum would be created with no transitional provisions in respect of the *interregnum* between the period of election and assumption of office of the new administration.[75]
>
> A person in the public service of the federation or state within the meaning of section 318(1) 1999 Constitution must disengage himself from service thirty (30) days before the date appointed for the election. The disengagement could be by way of resignation, withdrawal, or retirement.

Resignation means "the act or an instance of surrendering or relinquishing an office, right or claim. A formal notification of relinquishing an office or position."[76] The law is that once notice of resignation is given thirty (30) days to the election, the resignation is effective and good, whether the office to whom the resignation notice is addressed accepts it or not. In *Benson* v. *Onitiri*,[77] the court held that

---

[72] *Hon. Charles Ogbonnia Asogwa & 16 ors* v. *The Rt. Hon. Abel Chukwu & ors* (2003) 4 NWLR (pt.811) 540 at pp.574-576.

[73] Part II, Fifth Schedule, 1999 Constitution (as amended).

[74] *Anthony A. Dada* v. *Prof. Olusola* (Femi) *Adeyeye* & ors (2005) 6 NWLR (pt.920) 1 at p.21.

[75] S*upra* qt p.24.

[76] B.A. Garner, *Black's Law Dictionary*, 7th ed., 1999, p. 1311.

[77] (1960) SCNLR 177 at pp.189-190; (1960) 5 FSC 69; *Adefemi* v. *Abegunde* (2005) 15 NWLR (pt.895) I at p.28.

resignation takes effect from the date notice of resignation is given as there is absolute power to resign without the option to refuse the notice of resignation.

Would payment of one month salary in lieu of notice amount to valid disengagement from service? In *Mele* v. *Mohammed,*[78] the appellant contested and won election to Local Government Council in Borno State. The election was challenged on ground of the appellant's disengagement from Local Government Service of the State. The appellant paid one month salary in lieu of notice, disengaged from service thereof, contested and won the election. The disengagement was less than thirty (30) days to the date of the election. The Court of Appeal affirmed the tribunal's judgment and emphasized that the appellant did not pay one month salary in lieu of notice in good time to allow matters of his engagement thirty (30) days before the date of the election.[79]

It is clear that dismissal from civil or public service of the Federation or state does not disqualify from contesting election for offices created under the Constitution. This is because dismissal from service is not mentioned as a ground that disqualifies a candidate from contesting election. Thus, what is not expressly stated is deemed excluded.[80] This is imbedded in the Latin maxim *enumeration unius est exclusio alterius.*

Qualification and disqualification factors in respect of various offices are specifically stated in the Constitution. Dismissal from service – federal, state, local governments, or private is not any of those factors, notwithstanding the stigma in public fora such dismissal may portend. However, in respect of election into the Area Council under the Electoral Act, a person shall not be qualified to contest such election if he has been dismissed from the public service of the Federation, State, or Local Government Council.[81]

---

[78] (1999) 3 NWLR (pt.595) 425.

[79] *Mohammed* v. *Ibrahim* (1998) 6 NWLR (pt. 553) 553.

[80] *Babajide Omoworare* v. *Iyiola Omisore* & ors (2010) 3 NWLR (pt. 1180) 58; *Ehuwa* v. *Ondo State (2006)* 8 NWLR (pt. 1012) 544.

[81] Section 107 (1) (i), Electoral Act, 2010 (as amended).

That the Election was invalid by Reason of Corrupt Practices or Non-Compliance with the Provisions of the Act

Corrupt practices or non-compliance constitutes valid ground to challenge the election. Both are not the same. Corrupt practices are in the nature of the crime.[82] Non-compliance with the provisions of the Act relates to non-observance of the principles of the Act to the extent that would amount to conducting an election in a manner contrary to the principles of election by ballot system. The non-compliance must substantially affect albeit negatively the result of the election.[83]

The distinction between corrupt practices and non-compliance with the provisions of the Act lies in the fact that while corrupt practices are solely and wholly criminal in nature, allegation of non-compliance may just be civil. What constitutes corrupt practices is not defined in the Electoral Act or any other law in Nigeria. Electoral laws in the past employed the phrase "electoral malpractices."[84] The meaning and interpretation ascribable to that phrase is not different from corrupt practices. Electoral malpractices connote "illegal act done with a corrupt, fraudulent or sinister intention to influence the election in favour of a candidate."[85]

For a candidate to challenge election on ground of corrupt practices or non-compliance with the Act, the candidate must have participated in the said election and not otherwise.[86] Corrupt practices may include rigging, over voting, falsification of election result, thuggery, plural voting, impersonation of voters, under age voting among others.[87]

---

[82] *Alhaji Atiku Abubakar & 2 ors* v. *Alhaji Umaru Musa Yar'Asua* (2008) 36 NSCQR 231 at p.393.

[83] *General Muhammadu Buhari* v. *INEC & 4 ors supra* at p. 708.

[84] Ibrahim Isiyaku (SAN) "*The Electoral Act: Requirements of Proof in the Determination of Election Petitions*" in Dr. Kanem S. M.G. and A.M. Madaki (eds.), *Contemporary Issues in Nigeria Law, Legal Essays in Honour of Hon. Justice Umaru Faruk Abdullahi (CON)*, Private Law Department, Ahmadu Bello University, Zaria, 2006. p.255.

[85] B.O. Nwabueze, *Nigeria's Presidential Constitution* 1979-1983: *The Second Experience in a Constitutional Democracy*, Longman, 1985, p.401. quoted in Ibrahim Isiyaku (SAN), *"The Electoral Act Requirements of Proof in the Determination of Election Petitions"* in Dr. Kanem S.M. G et al (ed.). *op. cit.*. p.255.

[86] *Alhaji Atiku Abubakar* v. *Alhaji Umaru Musa Yar'Adua supra* at p. 284.

[87] Saraki v. Are *(1999)* 3 NWLR (pt.595) 409; *Etuk* v. *Isemin* (1992) 4 NWLR (pt. 236) 402.

That the Respondent was not duly elected by Majority of Lawful Votes cast at the Election

The plank of this complaint is that invalid votes were counted and recorded into various forms to the disadvantage of the petitioner and to the advantage of the respondent that was returned. The petitioner must plead the scores of all the candidates that participated in the election.[88] The candidate to be declared winner must have polled the highest number of valid votes cast at the election and,

(i) in case of the election of the President, has not less than one quarter of the votes cast at the election in each of at least two-thirds of all the state in the Federation and the Federal Capital Territory, Abuja,[89] and

(ii) in case of the election of a Governor, has not less than one quarter of all the votes cast in each of at least two-third of all the Local Government Areas in the State.[90] The votes cast for the candidates must be valid and lawful.[91]

(iii) That the Petitioner or its Candidate was validly nominated but unlawfully excluded from the election.

This ground avails a party who was in the first place validly nominated but did not participate in the election (poll).[92] A party that participated in the election (poll) but lost cannot lawfully and logically come under this ground.[93]

Parties to Election Petition

For a court or tribunal to exercise jurisdiction over a matter brought before it, it must be satisfied that it has the power and competence to adjudicate over the matter in respect of the parties before it.[94] The issue

---

88 *Chief (Dr) Ugwu N. Njam* v. *Chief Ken Nnamani & ors* (2006) 2 EPR 155 at p.172.

89 *Mohammad Buhari & anr* v. *Chief Olusegun A. Obasanjo & ors* (2005) 2 NWLR (pt.910) 24 at p.400; Section 134 (2) (a) (b), 1999 Constitution (as amended).

90 Section 179 (2) (a) (b), 1999 Constitution (as amended).

91 *Dr. Chris N. Ngige* v. *Mr. Peter Obi & ors(2006)* 14 NWLR (pt. 999) 1.

92 *Obasanjo* v. *Babafemi supra.*

93 *Abubakar* v. *Yar'A dua supra* at p.284. Strictly and legally speaking, substitution of a nominated candidate within a given political party primaries is different from unlawful exclusion from election. Exclusion from election is done by the Commission. This means both the nominated candidate and his political party did not participate in the general election.

94 *Ibrahim Idris* v. *All Nigeria Peoples Party* (2008) 8 NWLR (pt.108) 1 at p.101.

of *locus standi* is fundamental to the successful presentation of petition. In election petition, there are petitioner(s) and respondent(s).

Section 137(1) (2) Electoral Act, 2010 provides as follows:

(1) An election petition may be presented by one or more of the following persons -
(a) a candidate in an election;
(b) a political party which participated in the election.
(2) A person whose election is complained of is, in this Act, referred to as the respondent.[95]

For a party to validly institute an action in court, he must show that he has the *locus standi,* that is, the legal right to sue or institute the action. He must demonstrate the existence of sufficient legal interest which requires protection.[96] In a post-election matter, it is the right to file the petition in accordance with the law.

Petitioner(s)

In ordinary legal parlance, a person who instituted an action in court in a civil proceeding is called a plaintiff. In post-election matters, such a person in the election petition is called the petitioner. An election or return of a person at an election can only be questioned by:
(a) a candidate at the election; or
(b) a political party that participated in the election; or
(c) both such candidate and political party.[97]

A candidate in an election is not defined in the Act. The Court of Appeal in *Dr. (Mrs) Bukola Idayat Adebusuyi* v. *Hon. Babatunde Olugoye & ors*[98] held that a candidate could not be said to refer to a person "who had the intention to contest an election but who was not allowed to contest." This expresses the view that a candidate validly

---

[95] The quoted section is *in pari materia* with Section 133 (1) (2) Electoral Act, 2002 and section 144 (1) (2) Electoral Act, 2006.

[96] *Adesanya* v. *President, Federal Republic of Nigeria* (1991) 1 All NLR (pt.1) 1; (1981) 1 NCLR 358; *ANPP* v. *The Returning Officer, Abia South Senatorial District* & ors (2005) 6 NWLR (pt.920) 140 at pp.180-181.

[97] Section 137 (1) (a) (b) Electoral Act, 2010 (as amended).

[98] (2004) 1 NWLR (pt.854) 406 at pp.427-428.

nominated but unlawfully excluded is not a candidate for the purpose of presentation of election petition. On the other hand, the Court of Appeal in *Ibrahim Idris* v. *ANPP*[99] held that a candidate duly nominated by a political party but unlawfully excluded from the election qualifies as a candidate in an election and can present an election petition before the tribunal. The fact that the candidate was not voted for at the election is irrelevant. Again, in *Okonkwo* v. *INEC,*[100] the petitioner was validly nominated by his political party but unlawfully excluded from the 19th April 2003 gubernatorial election in Anambra State. He filed election petition for himself and on behalf of his political party. The petitioner contended that he is competent to present the petition on the basis of Section 134 (1) (d) Electoral Act, 2002, which provided:

> "(1) An election may be questioned on any of the following grounds;
> (a) …
> (b) that the petitioner or its candidate was validly nominated but was unlawfully excluded from the election."

The respondent submitted that the petitioner was neither a candidate in the election as he did not contest in the said election nor was he a political party that participated in the said election.[101] The Court held per Fabiyi JCA to *wit*:

> It appears glaring that he had no *locus standi* to personally file the petition since his main complaint is that he was validly nominated by his party to wit: Nigeria Advance Party but he was unlawfully excluded. Instead of allowing his party to question the election as dictated by section 134 (1) (a) of the Act, the appellant, who has no *locus standi,* filed the petition, 'suing for himself and on behalf of the Nigerian Advance Party,' that was not proper since a party who has no *locus standi* cannot sue for himself talk less of suing on behalf of another.[102]

---

99 *Supra* at p. 101; *P.P.A.* v. *Saraki* (2007) 17 NWLR (pt.1064) 453. (2006) 2 EPR 94 at pp. 137-138.
100 (2006) 2 EPR 94 at pp.137-138.
101 Section 133 (1) (a) (b), Electoral Act, 2002.
102 *Okonkwor* v. *INEC* (2006) 2 EPR 94 at pp.137-138.

A candidate at an election means a person who was duly nominated by his political party; whose name was submitted to the Commission, and the said name was published by the Commission; even if the Commission disqualifies such a candidate from the election, he does not cease to be a candidate for the purpose of filing an election petition.[103] A person who seeks or offers himself or is put forward by others for an office, privilege, or honour is a candidate at the election.[104] It means that the issue of candidature transcends contesting an election as a validly nominated candidate is inured with the right to present an election petition,[105] provided the candidate's political party did not participate in the election through another candidate.

It is submitted that where a candidate was validly nominated by his political party, and there is no court order disqualifying him from contesting the election, he is deemed to have fulfilled all the constitutional and statutory requirements for the purposes of election into the office concerned. Accordingly, an exclusion, albeit unlawfully, from contesting an election (supposedly by the Commission, which *ab initio* has "no power" to disqualify or to exclude a candidate from the election) ought not to be strictly construed to deny a candidate validly nominated but excluded from the right to present election petition as a candidate in the election. Valid nomination is part of the election, and a candidate validly nominated has taken part in the election except that he did not contest the poll as a result of unlawful actions of the Commission. It will amount to double punishment for a candidate unlawfully excluded to be deprived of access to court in his personal capacity except through his political party. What happens when the political party expels him or in any way denies him access to court through it? Then, the candidate will lose his case even without going to court. The decision of the Court of Appeal in *Ibrahim Idris* v. *ANPP*[106] is, with respect, better and ought to be followed subsequently. That is, a

---

[103] *Mr. Peter Okocha & anr* v. *INEC & 3 ors* (2009) 7 NWLR (pt.1140) 295. 308; *PPA* v. *Saraki* (2007) 17 NWLR (pt.1064) 453, (2006) 2 EPR 94; *INEC* v. *A.C.* (2009) 2 NWLR (pt.1126) 524.

[104] *Mr. Peter Okocha & anr.* v. *INEC & 3 ors supra* at p. 308.

[105] *INEC* v. *A.C.* (2009) 2 NWLR (pt. 1126) 524 at p.589.

[106] *Supra.*

candidate validly nominated but unlawfully excluded has the right to present a petition in person.

In *Chief Olusegun Obasanjo & anor* v. *Muhammadu Buhari & ors*[107] the Supreme Court affirmed the right of a candidate and the political party to present election petition jointly or severally and held that to participate in an election simple means to take part in no specific way either by the political party itself or through its authorized agent.

If a candidate validly nominated but unlawfully excluded does not qualify as a candidate in order to present election petition, can the same political party whose candidate was excluded from the election be said to have participated in the same election for the same purpose of presenting an election petition? It is submitted that if a political party that nominated a candidate and whose candidate was excluded from the election can present election petition because it has participated in the election, then the candidate so nominated and through which the political party participated can as well do so. Thus, political parties participate and win or lose election through their candidates validly nominated. Nomination itself is participation in the election. A candidate so nominated is a candidate in the election. Both the candidate in the election and his political party can jointly or separately present election petition.[108]

(Respondent(s)

The person who was returned at the election and whose election is being complained of, is referred to as respondent. If the petitioner complains of the conduct of an Electoral Officer, a Presiding Officer or Returning Officer, notwithstanding the nature of the complaint, the Commission shall be made a respondent and be deemed to be defending the petition for itself and on behalf of its officers or such other person.[109] Where criminal allegation is made against a Presiding Officer or Returning Officer, joining the Commission alone may not

---

[107] (2003) 17 NWLR (pt.850) 510 at p. 560.

[108] *Alliance for Democracy* v. *Peter Ayodele Fayose & ors* (2004) 8 NWLR (pt.876) 659.

[109] Section 137 (2) (3), Electoral Act, 2010 (as amended).

suffice. The Returning Officer or Presiding Officer should be joined in person to afford him the opportunity to present his defence. This is in consonance with personal liability for criminal conduct.[110] Again, Section 144(1) of the Electoral Act, 2010 contemplates joining the Electoral Officer, Returning Officer, or any other officer of the Commission as respondent in an election petition and being represented by a legal officer of the Commission.

Previously, where the petitioner complained about the conduct of an Electoral Officer, Presiding Officer, Returning Officer, or any other person who took part in the conduct of the election, such officers were deemed respondents and statutorily required to be joined in their official capacities as necessary parties.[111] Where a person is shown to have acted as an agent of the Commission, non-joinder of such person as a party to the petitioner shall not on its own void the petition if the Commission itself is made a party to the petition.[112]

Even police officers assigned the duty to ensure orderliness, peaceful and free conduct of an election but chose rather to assist in rigging the same election were made respondents to election petition.[113] This had made the number of respondents in an election petition too many.[114] It was such that a candidate that contested an election and lost was at one time joined as a respondent in an election petition.[115]

Where a court finds that a petitioner lacks the *locus standi* to present the petition, the appropriate order to make on preliminary objection is to dismiss the petition.[116] On the other hand, where a respondent that is statutorily required to be joined is not joined as such, all allegations made against such person in the petition shall be struck out.[117]

---

110 *Dr. John Okukayode Fayemi* v. *Olusegun Adebayo Oni* (2009) 7 NWLR (pt. 1140) 223.

111 *Chief Olusegun Obasanjo & 2 ors.* v. *Alhaji Mohammedu Dikko Yusuf & anr* (2004) 9 NWLR (pt.877) 144 at p.185.

112 Section 144 (2), Electoral Act, 2010 (as amended).

113 *Mohammadu Buhari* v. *Dikko Yusuf* (2003) 14 NWLR (pt.841) 446.

114 In *Alhaji Mohammed Dikko Yusuf & anr.* v. *Oluesengun Obasanjo & 56 ors supra,* where they were 57 respondents.

115 *Mohammadu Buhari* v. *Dikko Yusuf supra*

116 *Egwu* v. *Ike* (1999) 3 NWLR (pt.594) 189 at p. 204; *Egolum* v. *Obaasanjo* (1999) 7 NWLR (pt.611) 355.

117 *Chief Olusegun Obasanjo & 2ors* v. *Alhaji Mohammadu Dikko Yusuf, supra* at p. 185.

CONCLUSION

In view of space and time constraints, this chapter is by no means exhaustive of the elections and election petition matters within the Nigerian fourth Republic. It mainly x-rayed the concept of election, types of election, grounds for presentation of election petitions and parties to election petition matters. The issue of time for presentation of the petition and judgment thereto is given a cursory look at the footnote.

Chapter 22

PROHIBITION AND PROSECUTION OF CRIME OF KIDNAPPING IN NIGERIA

Ine Nnadi (Mrs)*

INTRODUCTION

Ever since the dawn of history, crime has been with us and it is no exaggeration to say that it is a product of society.[1] Of all the domestic crimes, the crime of kidnapping appears to be most deadly with international concern. It is a sphere of criminality that threatens the dignity of human person's liberty of mankind and international image of a nation. It has no respect for age, sex, colour and nationality. Its scope is massive hence the poor and rich are not safe.

There has been no day, month, or year since 2006 that kidnapping cases are not recorded in Nigeria. On 10 January 2006, militants kidnapped four foreign workers from an offshore platform and released them on 30 January 2006;[2] on 1 May 2007, the Movement for the Emancipation of the Niger Delta[3] kidnapped six expatriate workers from an offshore oil facility owned by Chevron. The group of six consisted of four Italians, an American, and a Croat;[4] on 9 September 2008, British oil workers Robin Barry Hughes and Matthew John Maguire were kidnapped along with 27 other workers when their vessel was hijacked by the MEND;[5] on the 16 April 2009, Julie Ann Mulligan,

---

*PhD, Senior Lecturer, HOD, Commercial Law, Faculty of Law, Imo State University, Owerri, Imo State.

[1] K. S. Chukkol, The Law of Crimes in Nigeria, Faculty of Law, ABU Zaria, 1988, P.1

[2] Ibid.

[3] Hereinafter called MEND

[4] Ibid.

[5] A Thomson Reuters Foundation services http://www. Alertnet. Org/thenews/newsdesk/L6194283. Htm Accessed on 11/11/2011.

a Canadian in Nigeria on a Rotary International Exchange was taken hostage, and 700,000 dollars was demanded before the hostage takers went down to 136,000 dollars before releasing her on 29 April 2009.[6] Also, in late October 2009, Elder Emmanuel Soludo, 78 years old, father of Professor Chukwuma Soludo, the former Governor of the Central Bank of Nigeria, was abducted for ransom;[7] on 16 October 2010, Dr. Stanley Uche, proprietor of Victoria Christian Hospital Aba, Abia State was abducted and murdered in spite of the payment of a ₦30,000,000 (Thirty million naira) ransom;[8] on 17 November 2011, two Americans and one Mexican sailor aboard the M/VC-Endeavour were kidnapped by militants.[9] Sometime in December 2012, Kamene Okonjo, the mother of the Minister of Finance and Coordinating Minister for the Economy, Dr. Ngozi Okonjo-Iweala was kidnapped from her home in Ogwashi-Uku Delta State by a gang of kidnappers and ₦3,000,000 (Three million naira) ransom was paid for her release.[10]

This story is endless and alarming. Kidnapping for ransom is part of a larger story. The current wave of kidnapping began with the abduction of expatriate oil workers by MEND in 2005 as means of alerting the world of the many years of injustice, exploitation, marginalization and underdevelopment of the Niger Delta Region. The apparent negligence and underdevelopment of the region have always been explained with limp reasons. The oil companies claim not to be responsible by virtue of the fact that they work for Nigerian Government and pay royalty to the government. Federal Government on its own blames the ministries constituted by it to tackle the problems of the region and the ministries blame the youths for disrupting projects.[11]

---

[6] Http: /www. Voanews Com/English/2009-04-21-voa 55 ctm Accessed on 3/5/2009.

[7] B. Anosike, *The Menace of Kidnapping in Nigeria: Credibility of the Federal Government & Judiciary on trial in the current Ogbuawa Case in Anambra* WWW. Elombah Com. Accessed on 13/11/2009.

[8] I.D. Odoh, *Kidnapping in Nigeria and its Root Causes* New Citizen Press, www. TNCP. NET. Accessed on 07/11/2010.

[9] Http: //www Kate Com. /News/gunmen–attack-shop-off-nigeria-coast-3-kidnapped.Accussed on 4/12/2011.

[10] Okolie I. *How Kidnappers of Okonjo-Iweala's Mum Killed 72-yr-old Woman*, www.vanguard ngr. Com. Accessed 12/2/2014.

[11] I.D. Odoh, *op. cit.*

Today kidnapping has turned into a lucrative venture with the youths at the centre of the pivot. This development is not healthy for our nation. With the increasing wave of kidnapping, it seems that law enforcement agencies and judiciary are relaxed on the issue. Hence the need to critically x-ray the prohibition and prosecution of the crime of kidnapping in Nigeria as well as the challenges faced in this respect.

MAJOR CAUSES OF KIDNAPPING

Kidnapping is not a magical phenomenon; rather, it is a product of society. Sometimes it is a response or revenge on society for its neglect of the welfare of the citizens. Thus, the following are some of the major causes of kidnapping in Nigeria:

a. unemployment amongst the youths;
b. insatiable quest for wealth syndrome that pervades the Nigerian society;
c. underdevelopment that paralyses the Nigerian economy;
d. marginalization of certain regions by the government;
e. environmental influence.

Crime of Kidnapping

Kidnapping is an aggravated form of false imprisonment, and perhaps that is why it is prohibited virtually in all jurisdictions in the world; Nigeria is not an exception. Thus, Section 364 of the Criminal Code Act[12] and sections 271, 273, and 274 of the Penal Code[13] provide for the crime of kidnapping. Section 364 of the Criminal Code Act states:

Any person who:

(1) Unlawfully imprisons any person, and takes him out of Nigeria without his consent: or

(2) Unlawfully imprison any person within Nigeria in such a manner as to prevent him from applying to a court for his release or from discovering to any other person the place where he is imprisoned, or in such a manner as to prevent

[12] Cap 38, Laws of Federation of Nigeria, 2004 as revised.

[13] Cap P3 Laws of Federation of Nigeria, 2004 as revised.

any person entitled to have access to him from discovering the place where he is imprisoned.

Is guilty of a felony and is liable to imprisonment for ten years.

The Criminal Code provides two forms of kidnapping: kidnapping out of Nigeria, which simply entails unlawful imprisonment of any person and taking him out of Nigeria without his consent, and kidnapping within Nigeria. In kidnapping within Nigeria, the following must be proved to *wit:*

Unlawful Imprisonment within Nigeria

Imprisonment means a total restraint of personal liberty of another. Thus, the restraint must be complete in the sense that, there would be no opportunity or avenue for escape. The opportunity or avenue for escape must be to the knowledge of the victim. Again, the restraint must be contrary to the law; hence there would be no justification in law for such conduct. The distance between where the victim was before the imprisonment and where he is imprisoned is immaterial provided it is within Nigeria.

Prevention

There must be evidence to show that as a result of the unlawful imprisonment, the victim was prevented from applying to a court for his release or from informing any other person where he is imprisoned, or persons entitled to have access to him are prevented from discovering the place where he is imprisoned. Thus, preventing the victim to have access to legal practitioner of his choice is sufficient proof of prevention from applying to a court for his release. The prevention must be complete as partial prevention though depending on the degree any not suffice.

A strict construction of section 364 of the Criminal Code Act shows that consent is a requirement only for unlawful imprisonment out of Nigeria. Thus, with regard to kidnapping within Nigeria, it is immaterial that the victim consented to the act. This interpretation looks absurd in the sense that it will be generally preposterous for an accused to be punished over an act consented to by the victim in such situations. Therefore it is submitted that the word *unlawfully* is wide enough to import the requirement of consent in Section 364(2) of the Criminal Code Act.

Under the Penal Code,[14] Section 271 deals with the crime of kidnapping of a male under fourteen years of age and a female under sixteen years of age, as well as an unsound person. It provides:

> Whoever takes or entices any person, under fourteen years of age if a male or under sixteen years of age if a female, or any person of unsound mind out of the keeping of the lawful guardian of such person without the consent of such guardian or conveys any such person beyond the limit of the state without the consent of someone legally authorised to consent to such removal, is said to kidnap such person.[15]

While Sections 273 and 274 deal with the crime of kidnapping of persons generally. Section 273 states:

> Whoever kidnaps or abducts any person shall be punished with imprisonment for a term which extend to ten years and shall also be liable to fine.

Section 274 provides:

> Whoever kidnaps or abducts any person in order that such person may be killed or may be so disposed of as to be put in danger of being killed, shall be punished with imprisonment for a term which may extend to fourteen years and shall also be liable to fine.

---

[14] Ibid.

[15] Section 273 provides punishment for the Crime of Kidnapping to the effect that whoever kidnaps or abducts any person shall be punished with imprisonment for a term which extends to 10 years and shall also be liable for fine. By virtue of section 274, if the victim was kidnapped or abducted in order to be killed or disposed of as to be put in danger of being killed the punishment shall be imprisonment for term which may extend to fourteen years and fine.

The Court of Appeal in *Yusuf* v. *State,*[16] where the accused were alleged to have killed an 8-year-old girl for money making ritual and were therefore arraigned in the High Court of Kwara State on 4 counts charge of criminal conspiracy to kidnap, criminal conspiracy to commit culpable homicide, kidnapping and culpable homicide, stated the ingredients of Section 271, of the Penal Code as follows;

a. The victim must be taken or enticed out of the keeping of his or her lawful guardian;
b. The victim must be under fourteen years of age if he is male or below sixteen years if she is female or a person of unsound mind.

With regard to Sections 273 and 274, the provisions are substantially the same, except to say that in Section 274, the *mens rea* of the accused at the time of kidnapping or abduction must be that the victim is killed or disposed of as to be put in danger of being killed. In both, there must be evidence of kidnapping or abduction[17] for conviction to be secured.

Comparatively, the provisions of the Criminal Code and Penal Code are substantially the same except to point out that the Criminal Code is wider in scope, but with regard to punishment, the Penal Code is broader. Be that as it may, a close survey of both codes reveals the following shortfalls:

a. A situation where an accused kidnaps or abducts a person with the intent to demand ransom was not taken care of;
b. A situation where an accused kidnaps or abducts a person with a threat to kill him, maim, or injure unless a particular act is done or refrained from being done, as a condition for the release of the person, was not taken care of;

---

16 (2012), All FWLR, Part 641, P. 1474.

17 Abduction means compelling by fraud or deceit any person to go from any place contrary to his will- Section 272 of the Penal Code.

c. A situation where the crime of kidnapping has been committed, and a person provides his building or place where the victim is kept was not taken care of;
d. A situation where one has fore-knowledge of kidnapping and fails to disclose same to the appropriate authority was not taken care of and;
e. A situation where one gives himself as volunteer to be kidnapped for any reason was not taken care of.

Thus, the narrow scope of the crime of kidnapping under the two codes made the Penal Law inadequate to take care of the new frontiers of criminality in the sphere of crime of kidnapping, as exposed above. This development perhaps caused an increase in the kidnapping business and elevation of same into merchandise. Hence, the crime of hostage taking was introduced as an extension of the crime of kidnapping with death sentence as punishment to checkmate this challenge by some states in Nigeria.[18] In Imo State, the Imo State Prohibition of Hostage Taking and Related Offence Act[19] provides for this crime. Sections 3 to 8 comprehensively provide different species of hostage taking or kidnapping. It states:

3. As from the commencement of this Law, any person who abducts another person or takes or keeps another person hostage with the intent to demand ransom is guilty of an offence and is liable on conviction to sentence of death.

4. Any person who takes another hostage and threatens to kill, maim, injure or cause panic in order to compel another person or a government organisation or a corporate body to do or refrain from doing any act as a condition for the release of a person taken hostage is guilty of an offence and is liable on conviction to sentence of death.

---

[18] Like Edo State, Enugu State, Imo State, Abia State *et cetera.*
[19] Laws of Imo State of Nigeria 2004-2010

5. Any person who wilfully or knowingly allows or permits a premise, building or place belonging or occupied by the person, which the person has control over for the purpose of keeping a person taken hostage is guilty of an offence and is liable on conviction to sentence of death. In the case of an artificial person, she is liable on conviction to a fine of ten million naira (₦10, 000,000).

6. A person who plans or conspires with another to take another person hostage is guilty of an offence and is liable on conviction to imprisonment for life without an option of a fine.

7. Any person who has foreknowledge of hostage taking and fails to disclose such information to any of the law enforcement agencies is guilty of an offence and is liable on conviction to fourteen (14) years imprisonment without an option of fine.

8. (a) Any person who gives himself to be a volunteer hostage for whatsoever reason shall be guilty of an offence and shall on conviction be liable to ten (10) years imprisonment without an option of fine.

(b) Any person who takes part in volunteer hostage keeping is guilty of an offence as contained in Section 3 of this Law.[20]

This provision is wide enough to take care of any sudden development that may crop up in the kidnapping business, as well as the ones pointed out above. The above provision is similar though wider, in contention with Section 212:1 of the America Model Penal Code that provides for crime of kidnapping. It states:

[20] This provision is similar to the states that introduced the crime.

A person is guilty of kidnapping if he unlawfully removes another from his place of residence or business, or a substantial distance from the vicinity where he is found, or if he unlawfully confines another for a substantial period in a place of isolation, with any of the following purposes:

(a) To hold for ransom or reward, or as a shield or hostage; or
(b) To facilitate commission of any felony or flight thereafter; or
(c) To inflict bodily injury on or to terrorize the victim or another; or
(d) To interfere with the performance of any governmental or political function.

1. A person, whatever his nationality, who in the United Kingdom or elsewhere
a. Detains any other person ("the hostage") and

b. In order to compel a State, international government organization or person to do or abstain from doing any act, threatens to kill, injure or continue to detain the hostages, commits an offence. A person guilty of an offence under this act shall be liable on conviction on indictment to imprisonment for life.
2. Proceedings for an offence under this Act shall not be instituted-
a. In England and Wales, except by or with the consent of the Attorney General; and
b. In Northern Ireland, except by or with the consent of the Attorney General for Northern Ireland.

Kidnapping is a felony of the first degree unless the actor voluntarily releases the victim alive and in a safe place prior to trial, in which case it is a felony of the second degree. A removal or confinement is unlawful within the meaning of this section if it is accomplished by force, threat or deception, or, in the case of a person who is under the age of 14 or incompetent, if it is accomplished without the consent of a parent, guardian or other person responsible for general supervision of his welfare.[21]

A situation where one gives himself to be a volunteer hostage for whatsoever reason was not taken care of by the American Model Penal law, and this gives more colours to the Nigerian Penal Law.

In England and Wales, hostage taking is an offence by virtue of the Taking of Hostage Act 1982. Sections 1 and 2 of the Act provide:

> Furthermore, Lord Brandom listed the ingredients of the crime to include taking or carrying away of one person by another, use of force or fraud, absence of consent, and without lawful excuse.[22]

PROSECUTION OF THE CRIME OF KIDNAPPING IN NIGERIA: CHALLENGES

Alarmed by the massive challenge on security posed by the pervasive wave of kidnapping in various parts of Nigeria, many States in the Eastern region for example ranging from Abia to Anambra and Enugu, have revamped their methods and strategies on stemming the menace. They have convened at the States Government Houses a countless number of meetings of their security teams[23] on effective measures and strategies. They have beefed up their funding on security matters and provided more equipment, more communication gargets, vehicle and other tools of policing, to the police command. They have even set up anew in some states, vigilante groups or revamped an existing one or augmented it.[24] All these notwithstanding, the crime of kidnapping is still prevailing with new frontiers. It then appears that prosecution of the menace is a mere illusion: as no record has shown that Nigerian

[21] W.R. Lafave, *Modern Criminal Law Cases Comments and Questions*, West Publishing Company, Minnesota, 1979, pp. 755-766.

[22] *R* v. *D*, (1984), AC. 778.

[23] The States Governors, Commissioners of Police, Directors of the Army, Air Force Security and Defence Corps, the Traditional Rules *et cetera*.

[24] Anosike B, *op. cit.*

Government and its agencies have achieved twenty percentage success in prosecuting the crime of kidnapping. Something must be wrong, it is either the measures set out to curb this crime are grossly inadequate or the agencies responsible for the prosecution are sabotaging the measures. Be thát as it may, we shall proceed to x-ray the challenges or constraints in the prosecution of crime of the kidnapping in Nigeria.

Lack of Investigation Apparatus

The police in Nigeria are poorly equipped to do proper investigation needed in curbing kidnapping. They lack modern and sophisticated communication equipment. A survey by the Constitutional Right Project shows that the following among others are lacking in most police stations in Nigeria to *wit,* telephone, fax machines, long-range radio communication, and pager.[25] The implication is that the police have to physically attend event or visit all necessary points to verify information or confirm incidents. Contact between police stations and check points in the cities and rural areas are almost non-existent, bearing in mind that most kidnappers operate from rural areas or have their hideout in rural areas. Most police stations both in urban and non-urban areas lack computer equipment making it virtually impossible for data to be stored or retrieved. Even Nigerian Police Headquarters in Abuja does not have data bank showing comprehensively particulars of prosecution of crime of kidnapping in Nigeria.

Furthermore, most police stations lack transport facilities, so the investigation of cases of kidnapping in most situations cannot take place at all or effectively in the absence of motor vehicles and motorcycles. They either hire vehicles or require the complainant to provide a vehicle for investigation. Also, such basic items like stationeries, files, pens, paper *et cetera* are lacking. They either use their personal money or require the complainants, suspects, or their lawyers to provide them with money for the purpose of buying those items for

[25] C. Nwankwo, *et al.*, The Failure of Prosecution CRP, Lagos 1996, P.19.

the recording of information[26] relating to an allegation of crime of kidnapping: Photographic, stenographic, and video cameras are virtually non-existent.[27] No police state command in all the states of Nigeria has a helicopter. It is exclusively reserved for Headquarters in Abuja, and it is not more than five. This development is an indication of unseriousness in the crusade against kidnapping in Nigeria.

Lack of Basic Training, Skill and Knowledge

Another constraint hampering prosecution of the crime of kidnapping is the lack of basic training, skill, and knowledge. Dimensions and sophistication of modern criminality with regard to kidnapping are undergoing exponential growth. In addition, with the emergence of the new crime of hostage taking, new methods of committing traditional crimes have developed particularly as regards the application of modern technology to them. Accordingly, no police force can afford to keep its staff-training program at the level of outdated technology for the purpose of tackling crimes perpetrated by means of state-of-the-art technology like hostage taking. Adeyemi. A.A. captured this when he observed that when an organized crime has a transnational dimension, it then requires special knowledge to appreciate its nature and scope and special skills to investigate it completely to a successful conclusion.[28] He further observed that the average Nigerian police personnel hardly understands the nature of organized crime, let alone its dimension.[29]

Use of Inexperienced Members of Nigeria Armed Forces and Security State Service

With the rapid growth of kidnapping in Nigeria, the Federal Government of Nigeria drafted men of the Nigerian Armed Forces and State Security Service to complement the role of the Nigeria Police

---

[26] U.U. Chukwumaeze, *Law Enforcement Agencies and the Administration of Justice in Nigeria: An Appraisal* in Nwebo O.C., *The Political Economy of Administration of Justice in Developing Society*, Versatile Publishers, Owerri 2004, P. 161.
[27] Nwankwo C. *et al., op. cit.*
[28] A.A. Adeyemi in U.U. Chukwuaeze, *op. cit.*, p. 163.
[29] Ibid.

Force in this regard. Accepted that this policy generally is commendable, but it has counterproductive value. These men are not trained for policing, let alone to carry out an investigation. For instance, soldiers are trained for combat in armed conflict: They have no knowledge of the investigation of crime. They lack the prerequisite skills for the job. Kidnapping is a very serious business that requires systematic planning and execution. It, therefore, requires a unit with basic training in this direction to check the same.

Police Prosecution

By virtue of Section 23 of the Police Act,[30] any police officer may conduct in person all prosecutions before any court whether or not the information or complaint is laid in his name. The Supreme Court in the *Federal Republic of Nigeria* v. *Osahon* [31] made it clear that a police officer can prosecute by virtue of Section 23 of the Police Act, Section 56(1) of the Federal High Court Act, and Section 174 of the Constitution of the Federal Republic of Nigeria as amended.

The police lack the requisite skill and education needed to appear before a court of record. A lawyer spends 5 years at the University studying substantive law and another year at the law school studying procedural law. These two schools prepare him for the proceedings in court. Despite that, the National Nigerian Bar Association has implemented the Continuing Legal Education Scheme, which is intended to keep lawyers focused and prepared with regard to court proceedings. On the other hand, police officers have no such training and are practically lost in the proceeding.[32]

There is nothing a police officer will achieve while prosecuting crime of kidnapping: in the first place, he does not know the ingredients of the crime; assuming but without conceding, that he knows, he is not trained on how to employ the rules of evidence to decipher the

[30] Cap P. 19, Laws of Federal of Nigeria 2004 as revised

[31] (2006), All FWLR, (Part 312), 1975.

[32] C.O. Chukwumaeze, *Power of Police Officers to Prosecute in Superior Courts: A critique* in U.U. Chukwumaeze, *et al*.(Ed), *Orient Law Journal* Vol. 1, NBA, Owerri Branch Owerri, 2013 p. 103.

testimony that prove the ingredients. The end result of this ugly situation is that the accused will be discharged.

In America, the police are considered the gatekeepers of the criminal justice system. Here police officers aid the Criminal Justice Process by making an arrest, obtaining information and evidence, writing reports, identifying suspects and witnesses, and providing testimony in court. Prosecutors are attorneys or solicitors trained for the work.[33] In Kenya, prosecuting counsel in the office of the Attorney General are qualified advocates of the High Court who have had legal training. The right of the police to prosecute is by virtue of delegated power from the Attorney General under Section 85 of the Criminal Procedure Code of Kenya. It is significant to note that under Section 14 of the Kenyan Police Act, the prosecution is not mentioned as one of the functions of the Police Force.[34]

Arbitrary Transfer of Police Officers

The unhealthy transfer of police personnel from their posts or out of the station to remote or sometimes far off new postings outside the area where they conducted an investigation or are prosecuting a case has a disruptive and sometimes stultifying effect on the investigation and prosecution of the crime of kidnapping. It is not uncommon in Nigeria for police personnel to be transferred from one post to the other, sometimes very far away, without notice and usually with immediate effect and definitely without regard to the nature of their work or continuity thereof. The implication is that handover and orientation is not normally done and several cases being investigated or prosecuted are abandoned or delayed. Where it is not abandoned, it sometimes leads to double jeopardy as a new officer assigned to investigate afresh and almost concludes the case not knowing where to start as a result of no handover and/or orientation from the former investigating officer or

---

[33] H.M. Nrobleski, and K..M. Hess, *Introduction to Law Enforcement and Criminal Justice* in C.O. Chukwumaeze, *supra* P. 101.

[34] Ibid., P.102.

commences afresh the arrest of suspects some of whom may have been granted bail or discharged.[35]

Investigating Style

The Nigeria Police Force, like any other police force in the world, becomes seized of a matter by means of a complaint. Its personnel then decide at that initial stage whether or not the complaint discloses a prima facie case. If it does, investigation starts. The starting point is usually to make contact with the prime suspect and commence investigation from that perspective. This style is wrong and should be changed as the suspect need not even know about the investigation until much later. This will certainly help to avoid the unnecessary frustration experienced by police personnel in the process of investigation, which may particularly arise where the suspect is virtually regarded as the prime source of information about the offence. Such a stance can lead to the unwholesome application of pressure on the suspect, such as inserting pins under his fingernails and broomstick into his penis, *et cetera*.

These are acts of desperation on the part of the exasperated policemen. The confessions extracted at the altar of such brutality are, of course, inadmissible,[36] thereby destroying the case at the early stage of the investigation. The crime of kidnapping is an organized crime, and its investigation needs to be detailed with patience. The police need to follow the suspects without them knowing and gather the basic information before arrest. This will give the police the needed evidence to prosecute the crime.

Corruption

It is no longer in doubt that corruption is one of the most devastating problems confronting Nigeria over the years. There is hardly any area of human endeavour that has not been affected by this malaise. Corruption has caused the nation a lot of international embarrassment. Apart from respectable Nigerians who are sometimes treated with scorn

---

[35] U.U. Chukwumaeze, *op. cit.*, p. 165

[36] Section 28 Evidence Act Cap E14 Laws of the Federation of Nigeria 2004 as revised.

and disdain outside, almost every year, the nation continues to make the list of the most corrupt countries in the world.

Prosecution of the crime of kidnapping has been marred with corruption right from the point of investigation to conviction. Majority of kidnapping cases are settled at the police stations between the police and suspects. Once the suspects are ready to play the game and speak the language of the police, which is corruption, the police will, right from the point of arrest, start laying a foundation for the release. Hence the case will be poorly investigated, laying foundation for no *prima facie* case for the suspect to answer. In certain cases, if the pressure is much, the police will poorly investigate the case by destroying the case at the investigation stage and later charge the same to the court. In the end, the court will discharge the suspect as a result of a lack of evidence connecting the suspect with the crime. Majority of the suspects arraigned in courts are those that failed to speak the language for one reason or the other.

From the police to the office of the Director of Public Prosecutions, where a lot of corrupt practices normally take place. At that level, some lawyers at the office are greatly influenced while writing their legal opinions in the case. Their influenced opinion may also influence the Director of Public Prosecutions toward dropping the charge against the suspects.

There is no obvious corruption on the bench with regard to the trial of kidnapping cases; this may be a result of the fact that in some cases, the judges themselves have been victims of the crime. Hence, the judiciary has to sit up in this regard in the prohibition and prosecution of the crime.

Delay in Trials

Constant delay in the trial of suspects in the crime of kidnapping has frustrated the justice in our Criminal Justice system. This delay is normally occasioned by incessant adjournments by lawyers without a time cogent reason(s). This adjournment takes up to 2 to 4 months. This development is capable of frustrating the proceedings, hence making the crusade against kidnapping a child play.

Witnesses' Indifference

In kidnapping cases, victims and witnesses are not willing to come and testify in court. They are either afraid that the cohorts of the accused persons may come after them and their families, or they are frustrated by the nature of the police investigation, or there is no protection for witnesses, let alone adequate protection made for their safety. Thus, in the absence of witnesses, the prosecution will definitely fail.

WAY FORWARD

Kidnapping has a compound and outrageous negative impact and effect not only on the victims but also on society as an entity and the international image of the nation. It makes a mockery of the right of the dignity of the human person and personal liberty: It reduces the economic, social, and cultural growth of the society: It blacklists the image of the society internationally. Perhaps, all of these informed the recent change of attitude toward the prohibition of the crime of kidnapping. Accepted that the abolition of kidnapping is impossible as since the dawn of history, crime has been with society, and kidnapping is not an exception, but this menace can be curbed. It is on the strength of this, the following recommendations are made:

(a) That police prosecution of crimes including the crime of kidnapping should be abolished with immediate effect. By extension Section 23 of the Police Act be amended to read:

Subject to the provisions of Section 174 and 211 of the Constitution of the Federal Republic of Nigeria 1999 (which relates to the powers of Attorney General of the Federation and of a State to institute and undertake, take over and continue or discontinue criminal proceedings, against any person before any court of law in Nigeria) any police officer who is a legal practitioner pursuant to sections 2(1) and 24 of the Legal Practitioners Act with at least 3 years' experience of court practice may conduct in person all prosecution before any court, whether or not the information or complaint is laid in his name.

Thus, being a legal practitioner is not enough for one to prosecute the crime of kidnapping; experience in prosecution is vital, and no one can ignore this.

(b) Periodic or monthly training of police officers on skills, knowledge, and innovations in investigation is further recommended. Experts both in Nigeria and abroad should be invited to conduct the training. This will afford the officers the opportunity to be abreast with the new development in the field of investigation.

(c) That the Federal Government, as a matter of urgency, provides investigating tools such as vehicles, helicopters, telephones, fax machines, long-range radio, computers, photographic, stenographic, and video cameras, *et cetera* to Nigeria Police Force. Each State Police Command should at least have 3 helicopters.

(d) A Police practice direction or policy should be introduced to the effect that police officers in investigation units shall not be transferred within 5 years in that command except if there is a serious allegation of corruption or abuse of office and evidence whereof is overwhelming. Two (2) months' notice of transfer shall be given to the police officer to enable him to hand over properly.

(e) Seminars, lectures, and workshops on curbing delay in criminal proceedings should be organized periodically for lawyers, magistrates, and judges.

(f) The Federal Government agencies as well as its personnel, should be re-positioned with more strength, powers, ideas, and innovations to fight corruption. The EFCC and ICPC should be restructured to have autonomy so that they can carry out their duties without fear and without the influence of the Federal Government.

A lot of people are idle and cannot find a sustainable means of livelihood. Job creation should be attended to adequately to ensure that many people are gainfully employed by the government.

CONCLUSION

Kidnapping, as can be seen, is a major problem in Nigeria - one capable of endangering stability, peace, security, social, economic, and political development and undermining the value of democracy and human rights, as well as breaking the cord that binds humanity together. To this end, prohibiting and prosecuting the crime of kidnapping becomes a priority in Nigeria, and same requires concerted efforts, exchange of experience, and a certain degree of standardization, bearing in mind that the body of laws in existence is adequate to curb this virus, but implementation is the major challenge. The rate of kidnapping is so alarming that Nigeria will lose a whole generation or more if nothing is done urgently. It is on the strength of this that all recommendations in this work were made, and we strongly believe that if they are implemented with the utmost sense of responsibility and honesty devoid of bias, influence, and compromise, Nigeria will be free from kidnapping and its attendant consequences.

Chapter 23

PROSECUTING ECONOMIC CRIMES IN NIGERIA

Frank Asogwah*

INTRODUCTION

Corruption and all other forms of economic crimes are the major causes of breakdown in the Nigerian system. Even a toddler in Nigeria knows these crimes are the reason governance and development have failed in the country. These crimes have dislocated the country's economy. They have severely battered her image abroad. They undermine democracy and security and adversely affect education. This chapter attempts to find out why, in the face of comprehensive laws on the subject in the country, the responsible agencies find it hard if not impossible to prosecute economic crimes in Nigeria. The chapter identifies some of the problems associated with the prosecution of these offences and recommends the abolition of plea bargain procedure in the prosecution of economic crimes. It urges the independence of law enforcement agencies from political interference, and recommends that a special court be set up for these crimes for greater efficiency. The chapter solicits the cooperation of lawyers for quick dispensation of justice; and recommends continuing education for investigators and prosecutors to eschew shoddiness and ineptitude and to make them versed in human rights protection and methods of law enforcement.

* Professor of Law and Dean, Faculty of Law at the Enugu State University of Science and Technology, Agbani

Lastly, the chapter calls on the general public to avoid unrestrained diatribe on the law enforcement agencies and their staff.

Quite a lot of people have written on general and specific matters on economic crimes in Nigeria[1] such that it may be wondered whether anyone can say anything new again on the subject. But economic crimes have continued to eat deeper and deeper into the socio-political fabric of the country, necessitating constant comment. Laws, like the Criminal Code,[2] Penal Code,[3] Corrupt Practices and other Related Offences (ICPC) Act,[4] the Economic and Financial Crimes Commission (EFCC) Act,[5] etc., have been passed to curb the menace of economic crimes, yet the problem is still very much on the ground. This author thinks that there are endemic and systemic problems associated, not with the letters of the law as they are, but with the prosecution of economic crimes, which needs to be identified and addressed as a panacea for arresting the ugly trend. This category of crime has completely dislocated the Nigerian economy. It has battered the image of the country abroad. It undermines democracy and security. It affects education negatively, enthrones mediocrity, and impedes development in the country in sundry other ways. The author is worried that despite the foregoing negative effects of economic crimes in Nigeria, there are still many problems associated with its prosecution. This chapter

---

[1] See J. F. Olorunfemi, "Unbundling or Merger of the Economic and Financial Crimes Commission and the Independent Corrupt Practices Commission: Which Way?", in C. G. Nnona, *Law, Security and Democracy: Commemorative Essays of the University of Nigeria Law Faculty,* (ed.) (Enugu: Snaap Press Nigeria Ltd., 2013), pp. 209-247. See also F. I. Asogwah, and P. Okoli, *Economic Crimes and National Development,* (Enugu: Institute of Development Studies, University of Niggeria, Enugu Campus, 2008). See also F. F. Adegbie, and A. S. Fakile, "Economic and Financial Crime in Nigeria: Forensic Accounting as Antidote", *British Journal of Arts and Social Sciences* ISSN: 2046-9578, Vol.6 No.1 (2012) *©BritishJournal Publishing, Inc. 2012 http://www.bjournal.co.uk/BJASS.aspx.* Last assessed on 16th February, 2014. See also E. A. Owolabi, *Corruption and Financial Crimes in Nigeria: Genesis, Trend and Consequences,* (Lagos Business School, 2007). See also N. Ribadu, "Obstacles to Effective Prosecution of Corrupt Practices and Financial Crime Cases in Nigeria". Paper Presented at the 1st Stakeholders Summit on Corrupt Practices And Financial Crimes in Nigeria Organised by House of Representatives Committee on Anti-Corruption, National Ethics and Values at the International Conference Center, Trade Fare Complex, Kaduna, (Kaduna: EFCC Publication, 2004). See also F. Waziri, "Corruption, a Threat to Nigeria's Economy," Paper Presented at the Launch of the Anti-Corruption Revolution Campaign (ANCOR), South West, Lagos Airport Hotel 2009. See also A. A. Oworojori, and T. O. Asaolu, "The Role of Forensic Accounting in Solving the Vexed Problem of Corporate World" *European Journal of Scientific Research* Vol. 29 No. 2, (2009).

[2] Cap. C38 *Laws of the Federation of Nigeria (LFN),* 2004.

[3] Cap. 532 LFN 1990.

[4] Cap. C31, *LFN,* 2004.

[5] Cap. E1, *LFN,* 2004.

identifies these problems and suggests ways of solving them to leverage the prosecution of this crime with a view to curbing the menace.

The chapter is divided into four parts. Part 1 is this general introduction. Part 2 discusses the nature and effects of economic crimes in Nigeria. Part 3 identifies the problems associated with the prosecutions of these offences in Nigeria, while Part 4 gives a summary of the author's findings, makes recommendations, and concludes the chapter.

NATURE AND EFFECTS OF ECONOMIC CRIMES

In this part of the chapter, the author discusses the nature and effects of economic crimes in Nigeria. The discussion is divided into two sub-parts, with one dealing with nature and the other with the effects of economic crimes in Nigeria.

Nature

People talk about "economic crimes" without, perhaps, knowing exactly what this phrase means. The phrase "economic crime" is, not unexpectedly, one that lacks a dictionary definition. It would appear that the best offered in the present connection is a separate understanding of each word. For example, "economic" (used only before a noun) is connected with trade, industry, and the management of money.[6] "Crime," in its broad definition, means "illegal activity in general." A lay person can, therefore, have an idea of what economic crime is generally all about without being burdened with any technicality. Adegbie and Fakile call it "socio-economic evil."[7] In any case, because of obvious legal interests and implications, more definitions will be examined.

If economic crime is an illegal activity connected with trade, industry, and the management of money, then it means more or less the same thing as corruption. It would serve some salutary purpose to examine the word "corruption." Corruption has been defined as "dishonest, illegal, or immoral behaviour, especially from someone with

---

[6] *Longman Dictionary of English,* (3rd edn., 2001), p. 439.

[7] Adegbie and Fakile, *op. cit.,* p. 39.

power."[8] When this is compared with the definition of economic crime (although as separately defined), it is obvious that there is a common denominator dishonest and illegal activity with money. The two concepts involve using power in a dishonest or illegal way in order to get monetary advantage for oneself.

The *Black's Law Dictionary* defines corruption as "depravity, perversion, or taint; an impairment of integrity, virtue, or moral principle; especially the impairment of a public official's duties by bribery."[9] The same dictionary gives a second definition of corruption as "the act of doing something with an intent to give some advantage inconsistent with official duty and the rights of others; a fiduciary's or official's use of a station or office to procure some benefit either personally or for someone else, contrary to the rights of others."[10] The courts have equally defined corruption in *Biobaku* v. *Police*[11] and *Azie* v. *State*[12] as an act that deflects and sways someone from proper performance of his duty.

Corruption thus appears to be synonymous with economic crime as both connote a public officer's corrupt violation of assigned duties for pecuniary gain. The EFCC Act 2004 does not define economic crime *simpliciter*; it defines "economic and financial crimes." But the repealed EFCC Act No. 5 of 2002 did define "economic crime." Although the present 2004 Act defines "economic and financial crimes," the substance of the two definitions remains the same. Under the EFCC Act 2004, "economic and financial crimes" mean:

> The non-violent criminal activity committed with the objectives of earning wealth illegally either individually or in a group or organised manner thereby violating existing legislation governing the economic activities of government and its administration and includes any form of fraud, narcotic drug trafficking, money laundering, embezzlement, bribery, looting and any form of corrupt malpractices, illegal

---

8 Ibid., p. 306.
9 B. A. Garner, *Black's Law Dictionary*, (8th edn., USA: Thomson West, 2004), p. 371.
10 Ibid.
11 [1951] 20 NLR 30.
12 [1973 1 NMLR 251.

arms deal, smuggling, human trafficking and child labour, illegal oil bunkering and mining, tax evasion, foreign exchange malpractice including counterfeiting of currency, theft of intellectual property and piracy, open market abuse, dumping of toxic wastes and prohibited goods, etc.[13]

In earlier work, Frank Asogwah and Pontian Okoli[14] rightly observed that this definition is so wide that any other shade of economic crime, perhaps by way of suggested definition, may appear superfluous. They also noticed, beyond the multiplicity of meanings, that corruption is a thread that runs through all the economic crimes.[15] It is, therefore, pertinent to consider a statutory definition of corruption here. The ICPC Act 2000 defines "corruption" to include bribery, fraud, and other related offences.[16] It appears that there is no conflict between the definitions of economic crime and corruption. Clearly, the definition of economic crime is so comprehensive that the definition of corruption can be very conveniently subsumed under it. Thus, this chapter uses both terms interchangeably where the circumstances permit.

Effects

It must be stated at the outset that in as much as this chapter asserts that there is a high degree of economic crimes in Nigeria, it is not pretended that other countries of the world do not face the scourge. Nigeria is not an island of corruption. In February 2014, the media carried it that corruption cost the European Union about one hundred and twenty billion Euros (€120,000,000,000) annually. Consider the Watergate scandal that rocked the United States and actually dealt a fatal blow to the presidency of Richard Nixon.[17] Consider again the

---

[13] S. 46 of the EFCC Act, 2004.

[14] F. Asogwah and P. Okoli, *Economic Crimes and National Development,* (Enugu: Institute for Development Studies, University of Nigeria Enugu Campus: 2008), p. 5.

[15] Ibid.

[16] The ICPC Act, s. 2.

[17] G. Agbroke, "Nixonistic Obasanjoism", *ThisDay,* May 30, 2006, p. 64.

Enron scandal of allegations of unprecedented accounting fraud.[18] Corruption had become prevalent in Britain as early as the 1850s, which warranted the introduction of reform Acts; the Corrupt Practices Act of 1854; the Second Reform Act of 1867; and the Corrupt Practices Act, 1883.[19] Even China, which now prides itself as the bastion of honesty, had its own dose of corruption.[20] The recent conviction of popular Chinese politician Bo Xing on charges of corruption bears eloquent testimony that corruption is a global phenomenon. Most other developed and developing countries are battling with one form of corruption or the other.[21]

Is this chapter saying that because corruption exists in other countries of the world, it should not be combated in Nigeria? No. Corruption should be fought vigorously because it has far-reaching debilitating effects on Nigeria and Nigerians. Adegbie and Fakile observe rightly that these economic and financial crimes are the greatest threat to national economic development as the nation has nothing to show for its huge earnings from oil.[22] Asogwah and Okoli say the effects of economic crime in Nigeria are multifarious.[23] Igwenyi says that corruption dislocates the economy, thus:

> The greatest effect of corruption on the nation is in the area of economic dislocation. Taxes, profits and all other manner of revenue which ought to legitimately accrue to the government are diverted to private pockets and institutions. As a result, infrastructural amenities such as water, electricity, roads and other good things of life which ought to be provided for the average Nigerian cannot be provided. Rather those who have been in government and those still in government build edifices in the major cities,

---

[18] C. Thomas, "The Fall of Enron", *The Economist,* April 16, 2005, p. 77. Also see M. Duffy and J. F. Dickenson, "The Enron Effect", *Time,* June 5, 2006, who said that Enron was the 9/11 of the financial market.

[19] K.. B. Smellie, *Great Britain since 1688 A Modern History,* (USA: The University of Michigan Press, 1962), p. 179. See also *Encyclopedia Britannica,* Vol. III, 1981, p. 167.

[20] "Fake Chinese Feed Company Defrauds Nigerian Farmer", *ThisDay,* August 1, 2006, p. 38. See also Asogwah and Okoli, *op. cit.,* pp. 33-34.

[21] See S. Robinson, and V. Walt, "The Deadliest War in the World", *Time,* June 5, 2006, p. 35.

[22] Adegbie and Fakile, *op. cit.,* p. 38.

[23] Asogwah and Okoli, *op. cit.,* p. 34.

buy choice cars, install electric generators in their distant villages thereby presenting the institution of government as 419 enterprise.[24]

Another serious effect of economic crime in Nigeria is the fact that the country has a severely battered image at home and abroad. Nigerians fear surviving at home because of corruption, so they flee the country like lemmings for greener pasture. In the United States, for instance, a special law was enacted by Congress against Nigerian fraud. Moreover, they are several cases where reputable Nigerians have been treated with great disdain, mainly because of the country's record in the comity of nations. A lot of discriminatory treatment based on gross suspicion is meted out to Nigerians by foreign agencies. Interpol is said to organize annual conferences against Nigerian fraudsters. Metropolitan Police, London has a Special Fraud Office for Nigerians.[25] Travelling with a Nigerian passport has become akin to putting on wears bearing the inscription "I am a fraudster."

Economic crimes equally undermine democracy and security. This is so because when democratic institutions are not sound, good governance becomes perverted and impossible, which in turn engenders insecurity. Lewis Akpogena noted rightly that:

> Corruption poses a serious development challenge. In the political realm, it undermines democracy and good governance by flouting or even subverting formal processes. Corruption in elections and in legislative bodies reduces accountability and distorts representation in policy-making, corruption in the judiciary compromises the rule of law, and corruption in the public administration results in the unfair provision of services. More generally, corruption erodes the institutional capacity of government as procedures are disregarded, resources are siphoned off, and public offices are bought and sold. At the same time, corruption undermines the legitimacy of government and such democratic values as trust and tolerance.[26]

---

[24] B. O. Igwenyi, *Anti-Corruption Act The Obasanjo Legacy* (Abakalilki: WillyRose and Appleseed Publishing Coy, 2001), p. 11.

[25] N. Ribadu, "Implication of Economic and Financial Crimes on the Nation's Economy" (being a paper presented to Defence Adviser Conference in Abuja on the 10th of September, 2004), p. 2.

[26] L. Akpogena, "Political Corruption and Good Governance", *ThisDay*, April 25, 2006, p. 16.

Tied to this point is the fact that economic crimes make the polity highly susceptible to electoral malpractices such as election rigging. This sometimes leads to a vicious cycle of violence, civil unrest, and the enthronement of bad leaders and monumentally corrupt government. In the 2011 general elections in Nigeria, youth coppers working as *ad hoc* electoral officers and other citizens were massacred by people, especially in Northern Nigeria, who felt the elections were rigged. Since then, insecurity, violence, and the culture of bloodbath have not ceased in that region.

Economic crimes also have an effect on education. Merit would mean nothing, and there would be a celebration of mediocrity. This has far-reaching consequences. If merit is brushed aside, then intellectuals and intellectualism could take flight such that brain drain would be the inevitable result.

There are other effects of corruption, some of which are economic, including loss of government revenue, paralysis of state institutions, business failures, industrial collapse, massive unemployment, and of course, poverty. The next part of this chapter shall take on the problems associated with the prosecution of these crimes and the need to eradicate or at least curb the effect identified herein.

PROBLEMS ASSOCIATED WITH PROSECUTION

When one is asked to discuss problems associated with prosecuting economic crimes in Nigeria, one should balance the logic of the discussion by equally highlighting cases or situations when the law enforcement agencies have gone all the way out to pursue the justice of a case. To discuss the problem does not connote that the responsible agencies have not recorded remarkable achievements. The EFCC, for instance, has secured the conviction of economic criminals in landmark cases like *Anejemba* v. *Federal Republic of Nigeria,*[27] bordering on charges of advance fee fraud. The commission has also effectively prosecuted and secured the conviction of the appellants in *Nwude* v.

[27] [2004] 13 NWLR (Pt. 890) 268.

Federal Republic of Nigeria,[28] who were arraigned on an 86-count charge of conspiracy, receiving money by false pretence, transportation of money through unlawful activities, forgery, using of forged documents including the seal of the Federal Republic of Nigeria. *Nwude* was notoriously known as the world's biggest advance fee fraud case, involving the sum of two hundred and forty-two million dollars ($242m) from a Brazilian bank.

This notwithstanding, folks in Nigeria believe that the law enforcement agencies play the lion king when prosecuting economic crimes against the common man. But that the agencies are actually toothless bulldogs when faced with allegations of economic crimes levelled against politicians or rich and powerful citizens. How else would you consider a case like *Emmanual Ahmed* v. *Federal Republic of Nigeria,*[29] where the EFCC filed a 9-count charge against the accused person (a common man) out of which only count one was actually an economic crime. Counts two to nine were charges of bare forgery. The gist of the allegation against the accused person was that he forged documents including an identification card to show, falsely, that he was an EFCC detective and with the forged documents, he extorted money from a government employee.[30]

Counsel to the accused person raised preliminary objection to the propriety of the commission, instead of the police, bringing counts two to nine (forgery). The trial court dismissed the objection, which made counsel to file interlocutory appeal on the issue. In determining the appeal, the Court of Appeal invoked section 6(a) and (b) of the EFCC Act on the responsibility of the commission and the meaning of financial crimes respectively, which did not avail the court, as forgery is not listed therein as a financial crime.[31] Further, the appellate court invoked Section 7(1)(a) and (2)(f) of the EFCC Act on the special powers of the commission to conduct investigation into any offence committed in contravention of the EFCC Act or other law (including

[28] [2004] 17 NWLR (Pt. 902) 306.
[29] [2009] 13 NWLR (Pt. 1159) 536.
[30] Ibid., p. 553, paras. F-G.
[31] Ibid., pp. 550-551, paras. G-A.

the Criminal Code and Penal Code) relating to economic and financial crime. Yet this did not avail the court, for the offence of forgery under the Criminal Code or Penal Code is not an economic and financial crime.

At this juncture, one would think the only route open to the Court of Appeal was to hold that the police, and not the EFCC, have the competence to file counts two to nine. But the court would not do that; it then resorted to legal policy to vindicate the respondent's contention that forgery was an economic crime. According to Massoud Abdulrahman Oredola, JCA, who read the judgment:

> It is against public policy to have multiplicity of actions and *a fortiori* multiplicity of prosecutions. It will amount to subjecting the accused person to double jeopardy. In the instant case, it would amount to double jeopardy for the appellant to be prosecuted by the Economic and Financial Crimes Commission in respect of only count one of the charge against the appellant while the police will take up counts two to nine either in the same court or in another court.[32]

One should not mistake this ratio of the court as evincing sympathy for the accused person who the court would not like to suffer double jeopardy! It is doubtful whether the issue of double jeopardy did arise as counts two to nine on forgery are different crimes from counts one on economic crime. The above ratio is rather a determined effort by the court to see the charges against the accused person succeed. For, what a sympathetic court should have done, which was what the defence counsel wished, was for the court to declare that forgery was not an economic crime and the commission could not bring it. The court rationalized its view further when it said that:

> The likely scenario being painted is that one of the counts will be prosecuted by the EFCC while the police will take up counts two to nine. I do not think that such a scheme of things is reasonable nor neat enough. A situation where the prosecutor and an accused person will be shuttling between courts in respect of offences allegedly committed in the same

[32] Ibid., pp. 553-554, paras. G-B.

> transaction or in one fell swoop...Indeed, how this could be done without running afoul of the principle of not subjecting the accused person to double jeopardy is what I am yet to discern or fathom.[33]

To the mind of the court, "if the end result is prosecutable, then the means by which that end result was attained should be prosecutable too."[34] Finally, the court hit the nail on the head by invoking Section 10(2) of the Interpretation Act,[35] which provides that: "An enactment which confers power to do any act shall be construed as also conferring all such other powers as are reasonably necessary to enable that act to be done or are incidental to the doing of it."[36]

This case has been analysed in detail to show that the court and the prosecutor are able and willing to go to great lengths and espouse strenuous legal logic to prosecute economic crimes when they are minded to. Another case that exemplifies the willingness of the authorities to prosecute economic crimes is *Jolly Nyame* v. *Federal Republic of Nigeria.*[37] Here, the appellant was found in Abuja and arraigned at the High Court of the Federal Capital Territory (FCT) Abuja on a 41-count charge of appropriating monies belonging to Taraba State when he was governor of that state. The appellant contested the charge on the ground that the High Court of the FCT lacked the jurisdiction to try the case; that the prosecution lacked *locus standi* to prosecute the case since the money allegedly appropriated was the property of Taraba State; and that the appropriate court to entertain the case was the High Court of Taraba State sitting at Jalingo. The Supreme Court held, relying on Section 4(2)(b) of the Penal Code, that the High Court of the FCT had jurisdiction and the Federal Republic of Nigeria had *locus standi* to prosecute the crime, saying that a thief has no right in law to choose who prosecutes him and where.

But, it is a different ball game altogether when the authorities are unwilling to prosecute. So, what are actually the reasons that predispose

[33] Ibid.
[34] Ibid.
[35] Cap. I23 *LFN,* 2004.
[36] *Emmanuel Ahmed* v. *Federal Republic of Nigeria, op. cit.,* p. 551, paras. F-G.
[37] [2010] 7 NWLR (Pt. 1193) 344 SC.

the agencies not to prosecute these crimes? Economic crimes have adverse social, political, and economic effects on Nigeria, so why is it that these crimes are not being prosecuted as effectively as one may think desirable for such a cankerworm? Adegbie and Fakile posit rightly that "politicization and blackmail, constitutional immunity as stated in section 308 of the Nigerian Constitution, public apathy and doubtful attitudes toward anti-corruption work, and slow justice" are among the reasons.[38] Certainly, there are problems associated with the prosecution of these crimes. The country has made elaborate relevant laws against economic crimes. The problem is that the practical procedure of enforcement appears jinxed. The problems will include the unpalatable introduction of plea bargain procedure into the Nigerian criminal justice process, political interference, ineffective bench, corruption, and non-cooperation from the bar. Other problems associated with the prosecution of economic crimes in Nigeria, which shall be analysed in this part of the chapter, include a shoddy investigation by law enforcement officers, inept prosecution, and adverse criticism by the general public.

Plea Bargain

Plea bargain is a negotiated arrangement between a prosecutor and an accused person whereby the accused person pleads guilty to a lesser offence or to one of multiple charges in exchange for some concession by the prosecutor, usually a more lenient sentence or a dismissal of the other charges.[39] Keith Inyang gives a working definition of plea bargain as a:

> Device allowing accused persons – in person or by their legal counsel – to reach an accommodation with the prosecutor to enable them plead guilty in court to an offence of lesser gravity than the one (s) prosecutors wish to charge them with or with which they have already been charged or to one or more of a multiple of charges; an accused person may also agree to plead guilty to the offence with which they are charged, all in a bid for a

[38] Adegbie and Fakile, *op. cit.,* p. 39.
[39] B. A. Garner, *op. cit.,* p. 1190.

> lighter sentence than would/might have been given if the case had been prosecuted fully and conclusively.[40]

Plea bargain is an invention of the American legal process; it started by convention but having been accepted by the courts; it is now entrenched in their federal and state criminal procedure rules.[41] Plea bargain is recent, if not alien to Nigerian criminal procedure. Since its introduction into the country, it has been applied in the prosecution of some economic crimes, and it has led to unpalatable outcomes. Look at how Keith Inyang put the furore recently generated by the application of plea bargain in Nigeria:

> To many, the practice conflicts with their sense of justice for the betraying thieves of the public's finances or savings; it is incomprehensible to them how highly-placed thieves of many millions and billions of naira are allowed to get away with miserably small sentences in the name of plea bargain, while thieves of smaller sums or thieves of the same millions and billions of naira but without the high-level placement or connections bag the weighty sentences generally more commensurate to their offences. Consequently, many question the justifiability and legality of the practice, saying that it is alien to Nigerian statutes on criminal matters and downright unfair.[42]

Many people are opposed to the practice of plea bargains because it conflicts with what they believe to be fair and just.[43] They argue that it makes a mockery of the seriousness of justice; they further argue that a refusal to "save the time of the state and court" on the part of accused persons who protest their innocence and insist on a full trial could lead to retaliation against an accused person through the imposition of the most stringent punishments available or the filing of more serious (but true) charges than the prosecutor had initially proposed.[44] There is

---

[40] U. K. Inyang, "The Legality of the Use of Plea Bargain in the Nigerian Criminal Justice System", available at https://topeadebayollp.wordpress.com/author/tallp/March 27, 2012. Last assessed on 15th February, 2014.

[41] Rule 11, Federal Rules of Criminal Procedure (United States of America).

[42] U. K. Inyang, *op. cit.*

[43] See E. Onyema, "EFCC and Plea Bargain Issue in Nigeria: Matters Arising", The Crime Free & Peace Initiative. Available at https://topeadebayollp.wordpress.com/author/tallp/March 27, 2012. Last assessed on 14th February, 2014.

[44] T. Lynch, "The Case against Plea Bargaining": Cato Institute. Available at https://topeadebayo llp.wordpress.com/author/tallp/March 27, 2012. Last assessed on 16th February, 2014.

also the risk of sentencing innocent people or people against whom the evidence of the State would not stand, who are constrained to plead guilty just to avoid heavy sentences.[45] The then Chief Justice of Nigeria (CJN), Honourable Justice Dahiru Musdapher, said, "plea bargaining is a novel concept of dubious origin. It has no place in our law–substantive or procedural. It should never again be mentioned in our jurisprudence."[46] Musdapher added that plea bargain "was invented to provide soft landing to high-profile criminals who loot the treasury entrusted to them. It is an obstacle to our fight against corruption."[47] On a later occasion, Musdapher still commented on plea bargain, referring to what he called "the sneaky motive behind its introduction into our legal system, or its evident fraudulent application."[48] He went on to say:

> You will see also that plea bargain is not only a flagrant subordination of the public's interest to the interest of 'criminal justice administration,' but worst of all, the concept generally promotes a cynical view of the entire legal system.[49]

Those in favour of the practice point to the fact that agreements to plead guilty without having to go through a trial are effective in saving time, costs of prosecution and reducing the burden of the courts. In Nigeria, it has been argued that without the use of plea bargain in cases of corruption and embezzlement, only small amounts of money would have been recovered through the fines that would have been imposed by way of punishment.[50]

It is imperative to point out in the Nigerian context, the opposition to plea bargain from the street is primarily due to the fact that it seems to be used for only rich and powerful thieves and not even an option extended to every criminal. The fact that people steal money meant for the use of the general society is the chief reason behind the decay and

---

[45] Ibid.
[46] The *Nigerian Tribune* of 16 November 2011, p. 1.
[47] Ibid.
[48] *Vanguard* newspaper of 6 March 2012, p. 3.
[49] Ibid.
[50] U. K. Inyang, *op. cit.,* p. 2.

collapse of Nigeria as a country; as the absence of funds means social amenities and welfare programs cannot be provided. Consequently, the wrath of the people demands the rolling of the embezzlers' heads and not merely the slapping of their wrists. Similarly, those who make away with peoples' bank savings are not expected to get away lightly; the Nigerian people demand that the breach created in the public trust be filled up by the most appropriate and deserved punishment of their betrayers.

Plea bargain gained notoriety in Nigeria when it was first used by the EFCC in 2005 to settle the case of corruption against former Inspector-General of Police Tafa Balogun. It was later used that same year for ex-governor D.S.P. Alamieyesagha of Bayelsa State for embezzlement and Emmanuel Nwude and Nzeribe Okoli, who had defrauded a Brazilian bank. It has subsequently been used in the cases of former governor Lucky Igbinedion of Edo State for embezzlement (2008) and the case of Mrs. Cecilia Ibru, erstwhile managing director of the then Oceanic Bank, for abuse of office and mismanagement of funds (2010). The EFCC has generally defended itself on the basis of the provision of Section 14(2) of the EFCC Act 2004, which reads, *inter alia*:

> The Commission may compound any offence punishable under this Act by accepting such sums of money as it thinks fit exceeding the maximum amount to which that person would have been liable if he had been convicted of that offence.

It is also worth noting that some have declared that plea bargain has existed in certain statutes on criminal justice even before the enactment of the EFCC Act 2004. In this connection, they make reference to Section 180(1) of the Criminal Procedure Act in particular and conclude that the use of plea bargain by the EFCC is not something done in abstraction or without statutory precedents. Section 180(1) CPA provides:

> When more charges are made against a person and a conviction has been had on one or more of them, the prosecutor may, with the consent of the

court, withdraw the remaining charge or charges or the court, of its own motion, may stay trial of such charge or charges.[51]

Others point to Article 37 of the United Nations Convention against Corruption (2003), which says that state parties should allow for the mitigation of punishment for accused persons who agree to give evidence of their corrupt acts in cooperation with prosecuting authorities.[52]

Neither the provision of the CPA nor that of the EFCC Act reproduced above supports the application of plea bargain. Keith Inyang demonstrates convincingly that the said provisions deal with the concept of compounding, not plea bargain.[53] Plea bargain constitutes the greatest clog in the wheel of the prosecution of economic crimes in Nigeria, as it sends a message to the citizenry either that the law enforcement agencies are unable to prosecute these economic criminals or that the system potentially condones such crimes. Plea bargain agreements do not meet the legal test required by section 138 of the Evidence Act 2011 and in fact, can sometimes be employed in a manner that could breach a fundamental right. Thus, plea bargain does not just hinder the prosecution of economic crimes, it also encourages people to commit the crime since the loots will eventually be shared and a lesser plea bargained.

Political Interference

A trend has evolved in Nigeria where, against the rule of law, laws are made or procedures set up to apply to some personalities differently from the way they apply to the entire citizenry. An instance is Section 52(1) of the ICPC Act 2000, which provides that when any allegation of corruption is made against the President, Vice-President, Governor, or Deputy-Governor, the Chief Justice of the Federation shall, upon a *prima facie* case, appoint an independent counsel to investigate the allegation. A report of his findings would be made to the National

---

[51] The only piece of legislation in the country at present that contains the phrase "plea bargain", with circumstances and rules on how to implement the practice is s. 76 of the Administration of Criminal Justice Law (2007) of Lagos State. Some wrongly content that s. 174 of the CFRN 1999 as amended, on the power of the AGF to discontinue criminal proceedings is a form of plea bargain.

[52] See U. K. Inyang, *op. cit.*, p. 5.

[53] Ibid.

Assembly in the case of the President or Vice-President and to the relevant House of Assembly in the case of the State Governor or Deputy-Governor. Perhaps, this provision is to bring anti-corruption law in line with the constitutional immunity of the stated personalities,[54] but it should be noted that these same personalities are the ones who, in most of the cases pilot the ship of economic crimes in the polity. The reports against them sought to be made to Parliament will fall into the hands of their cronies, who will simply accept gratification and sweep the allegation under the carpet. It will be simplistic to think that when immunity lapses at the cessation of office, these personalities will be prosecuted, for experience in Nigeria shows that even when they have left office, these personalities continue to be off the hook. Almost everyone who was in Nigeria between 1999 and 2007 knew that the administration of former president Obasanjo allegedly looted the national treasury, but seven years after they left office they still walk the streets free men. The same thing applies to the governors of his era, except James Ibori, whose conviction was with the gracious assistance of the British government.

As if to extend the political immunity to all and sundry, the Federal Government in early August 2007 directed the EFCC and other anti-corruption agencies to seek the approval of the Attorney General of the Federation (AGF) before embarking on the prosecution of those who allegedly offended anti-corruption law. The AGF is a politician appointed by the government of the day. Though it may be supported on the ground of the absolute prosecutorial powers conferred by the constitution on the AGF,[55] but, by this directive he was given a charter of liberty to block the prosecution of economic criminals in the good books of the government. Of course this directive caused a sharp divide between legal commentators and the general public. Commentators like Professor Itse Sagay and Olisa Agbakoba supported the directive on the ground that it will enable the AGF supervise the operation of the ICPC

---

[54] See s. 308 of the CFRN 1999 as amended.

[55] See ss. 174 and 211 of the CFRN 1999, as amended. See also *The State* v. *Ilori* [1983] 1 SCNLR 94 at p. 106, where Eso, JSC noted that the Attorney-General has at common law been a master unto himself, law unto himself and under no control whatsoever, judicial or otherwise, *vis-a-vis* his powers of instituting or discontinuing criminal proceedings.

and the EFCC and stop lawlessness on their part.[56] Among those who spoke out against the directive included Taiwo Osipitan, Ahmed Gafai and Funke Adekoya.[57] Uju Obuka generally assails the absolute prosecutorial powers of the AGF under the constitution.[58] Eventually, the AGF himself played down on the directive and the operatives continued their work independently.

Another area of political interference is the power of the President to hire and fire the Chairman of the EFCC and that of the ICPC. Amendment to the law is needed here to avoid a situation where the chairman would be inclined to owe allegiance to the President, who, in turn, could use the operatives as his personal tool of vendetta.[59]

Ineffective and Dependent Bench

Lawyers are trained to honour the bench, as it is not often that one sees a lawyer criticizing the bench. However, an Igbo proverb says that if the misdeed of a king becomes too obvious, his critics will wear masks and speak out against him. What else can one do but to most respectfully state that sometimes, some judgments or orders of certain courts leave one to wonder at the competence of the bench. Ineffective bench is one of the biggest challenges to the prosecution of economic crimes in Nigeria. The case of *Chinelo Nwaigwe & 16 Ors.* v. *Federal Republic of Nigeria*[60] illustrates this point. Here, the trial Federal High Court granted an interim forfeiture order against the assets of the applicants under Section 29 of the EFCC Act when the EFCC officials have not actually attached the said assets as provided by law. Of course, the Court of Appeal quashed the order on appeal on this ground, resulting

---

[56] See A. Adegbamigbe, "Aondoakaa's Death Wish for EFCC", *The News,* Vol. 29 No. 09, September 10, 2007, p. 30. See also Asogwah and Okoli, *op. cit.,* p. 189-190.

[57] Ibid.

[58] U. Obuka, "A Critique of the Absolute Prosecutorial Powers of the Attorney-General under the Constitution", in C. G. Nnona, *Law, Security and Democracy: Commemorative Essays of the University of Nigeria Law Faculty,* (ed.) (Enugu: Snaap Press Nigeria Ltd., 2013), pp. 326-345.

[59] See Ben Nwabueze, "Foreword", to C. G. Nnona, *Law, Security and Democracy: Commemorative Essays of the University of Nigeria Law Faculty,* (ed.) (Enugu: Snaap Press Nigeria Ltd., 2013), pp. xiii-xix. This vendetta issue was the mortal sin that was often committed by the EFCC under then president Obasanjo, especially as the 2007 elections drew near. It was generally believed that Obasanjo used the EFCC to scheme out unwanted candidates. See *Saturday Sun,* September 1, 2007, p. 8.

[60] [2009] 16 NWLR (Pt. 1166) 169 CA.

in a waste of two years of litigation time.[61] The application by which the interim order for forfeiture was granted by the trial court was incompetent since it was made without valid seizure of the property and assets in question. The court must be presumed to know that the first step, as provided by Section 28 of the EFCC Act, is for the EFCC operatives to attach any property or asset suspected to have been acquired by way of committing an offence under the Act and later apply to court for an interim attachment order. The court should not have allowed the EFCC to jump this simple and friendly procedure, thereby putting the cart before the horse. The slip in procedure wittingly or unwittingly allowed by the court led to the quashing of its order on appeal and a waste of two years of the time of the court and parties before it.

Outright allegations have at times been made that a judge took instruction from the executive to skew justice. A recent instance is the judgment of Evoh Stephen Chukwu J. of the Federal High Court sitting at Abuja on 14 February, 2014 in the case of *Federal Republic of Nigeria* v. *Dimeji Bankole*.[62] In this case, Bankole, former speaker of the House of Representatives, was arraigned on a 16-count economic crime charge totalling eight hundred and seventy-four million Naira (₦874m). The trial court acquitted him of all counts on the ground that the prosecution failed to make out a case against him. The rumour has raged across the country like wildfire that President Jonathan ordered the trial judge to skew justice in this case.[63] Another case against Dimeji Bankole on the charge involving a ten billion naira (₦10b) loan scam, which was allegedly obtained to fund the quarterly allowances of legislators, had earlier gone a similar way.[64] The trial judge acquitted him on the ground that the EFCC had not made out a *prima facie* case

---

[61] Ibid., p. 191, paras. C-D.

[62] The judgment was not reported. This author had not got hold of the suit number of the case as the time of writing (16th February 2014) and thus relies on the newspaper report thereof. See "Contract Scam: EFCC Vows to Appeal Bankole's Acquittal" *The Guardian,* Sunday 16, 2013, p. 4.

[63] See *The Guardian,* Sunday 16, 2013, p. 4.

[64] Ibid. Yet-to-be-confirmed information from political grapevine has it that the authorities are doing all these to launder Bankole and present him as People's Democratic Party (PDP) governorship candidate for Ogun State in the forthcoming 2015 general elections.

against the accused. Such is the problem associated with the prosecution of economic crimes in Nigeria.

Corruption

One may wonder how, after arguing in Part 2 of this chapter that economic crime means the same thing as corruption, this author returns here to say that corruption is one of the problems associated with the prosecution of economic crimes. Is it the same thing as saying that "A" is the problem associated with prosecuting "A"? It appears somewhat so! Corruption brings about a total breakdown of the system, including the legal system. When Law enforcement agents, judiciary staff, and other personnel involved in prosecuting economic crimes are allegedly corrupt, which is possible and indeed rampant in Nigeria, they pose a serious problem to this cause. Nuhu Ribadu, when he was the chairman of the EFCC, did not mince words to say that even judges get corrupt and subvert justice in economic crime cases. According to Ribadu:

> Corruption and financial crimes most often involve huge sums of money. Those who are beneficiaries of the crime are willing to share a little percentage of the proceeds with the judges. Once the judge takes the bait, the case fails *ab initio.* No evidence presented will sway him to the side of the prosecution. The evidential burden of proof beyond reasonable doubt is stretched to read "proof beyond every shadow of doubt" contrary to the long line of cases by the Supreme Court.[65]

In other words, Ribadu is saying that judicial corruption is a threat to the prosecution of economic crimes. Chinua Achebe had written in 1983 that corruption in Nigeria had reached an alarming proportion and that any person (obviously referring to then president Shehu Shagari) who thinks otherwise is either a fool, a crook, or else does not live in Nigeria.[66] Achebe was not alone in this view. Chukwudifu Oputa equally noted that:

---

[65] N. Ribadu, "Obstacles to Effective Prosecution of Corrupt Practices and Financial Crime Cases in Nigeria," *op. cit.,* pp. 5-6.

[66] C. Achebe, *The Trouble with Nigeria,* (Enugu: Forth Dimension Publishers, 1983), p. 46.

> In present day Nigeria, there is more stealing than before, more bribery and corruption; more white collar crimes like forgery and uttering. From a perspective, people engage in corrupt practices with such reckless abandon and impunity that it would appear that corruption is now institutionalised. Perhaps corruption is now a systemic or endemic problem in Nigeria.[67]

This comment made about four decades ago is still surprisingly true of Nigeria and her people. Law enforcement officers are not exempt from the list of Nigerians guilty of corruption, so you will see that in a good number of cases, corruption can indeed be one of the problems associated with the prosecution of economic crimes.

Non-cooperation from the Bar

The ordinary citizen wants to see lawyers as ministers in the temple of justice who help the court to get to the truth of matters before it, but this is not always the case. Lawyers cause a chunk of the impediments to the smooth prosecution of economic crimes in Nigeria. Lawyers are in the habit of making all sorts of frivolous interlocutory applications in court, especially when their clients have bad cases. *Jolly Nyame* v. *Federal Republic of Nigeria*[68] can illustrate this despicable practice. The appellant was found in Abuja and arrested and arraigned in July 2007 before the High Court of the Federal Capital Territory (FCT) Abuja on a 41-count charge of appropriating monies belonging to Taraba State when he was governor of that state.

The defence counsel filed a motion on notice on 10th October 2007 at the trial court seeking an order quashing all the 41 counts on the ground of want of jurisdiction and incompetence of the court to adjudicate the case as constituted. The defence counsel contended that only the High Court of Taraba State sitting at Jalingo had the requisite jurisdiction to try the case. The trial court dismissed the application for lacking in merit. Dissatisfied, the appellant appealed to the court of appeal, which also dismissed the appeal and affirmed the ruling of the trial court. Still dissatisfied, the appellant appealed to the Supreme

---

[67] C. A. Oputa, "Crime and the Nigerian Society", in T. O. Elias, *et al*, (eds.) *African Indigenous Laws* (Enugu: Government Printer, 1975), p. 1.

[68] [2010] 7 NWLR (Pt. 1139) 344.

Court, which equally dismissed the appeal and upheld the decisions of the courts below. The Supreme Court found, rightly, that Section 4(2)(b) of the Penal Code allows the High Court of the FCT to adjudicate over a crime if the accused person committed the offensive act or omission outside the FCT and afterward enters the FCT. He is, by such entry, liable to be tried for an offence of the same kind and is liable on conviction to the same punishment as if the offence had been committed at the FCT.[69] Defence counsel knew or is presumed to know of this principle of law, yet he wasted three years of the time of court in frivolous applications and appeals that lacked merit.

Good enough, Section 40 of the EFCC act provides that an application for stay of proceedings in respect of any criminal matter brought by the Commission before the High Court shall not be entertained until judgment is delivered by the High Court. This provision targets those lawyers who, when the case is going against their client, file a notice of appeal and seeks to arrest the trial proceeding with an application for stay. To a large extent, Section 40 bars lawyers from playing the "stay game" in economic crime cases. Commenting on Section 40, Gani Fawehinmi noted that:

> What pains lawyers most is that they cannot frustrate the effectiveness of the EFCC by seeking an order to stay proceedings in the High Court while interlocutory appeals are filed with the sole purpose of delaying justice in the matter pending before that High Court against the person accused of economic crimes.[70]

Such is the problem associated with the prosecution of economic crimes in Nigeria. Even lawyers who are supposed to be on the vanguard for justice are the ones who turn around to frustrate it.

Shoddy Investigation by Law Enforcement Officers

Investigation of allegation of crime stands between arrest and prosecution. It is in the course of investigation that the law enforcement

---

[69] Ibid., pp. 395-396, paras. A-D; 423-426, paras. D-E.

[70] G. Fawehinmi, "Between NBA and the EFCC", *The Guardian,* September 5, 2006, p. 15.

agencies gather relevant and material evidence with which to prove their case beyond reasonable doubt. Shoddy investigation leads to unsatisfactory prosecution and poses a problem to the system. This is another major problem associated with the prosecution of economic crimes in Nigeria. Adegbie and Fakile opine rightly that some economic crimes "involve document or subjects that are very technical requiring a well-schooled investigator to unravel."[71] Often, the EFCC or other prosecutors will rush to court when they have not completed investigation into a matter. This leads to filing and unendingly amending and re-filing counts and charges. In *James Ibori & Anor.* v. *Federal Republic of Nigeria,*[72] for instance, the Commission filed a 103-count charge and later amended it to a 129-count charge. Sometimes the prosecutor will file a charge and come to court without having any iota of evidence to prove the counts therein.

Inept Prosecution by Law Enforcement Officers

Those who commence economic crime proceedings in court are lawyers, yet one wonders at the level of ineptitude exhibited by some of them. With due respect to professional colleagues, one wants to think that some prosecutorial blunders committed by prosecutors of economic crimes are not just a result of ineptitude but a deliberately committed blunder aimed at ambushing the justice of the case. Adegbie and Fakile are rightly of the view that a "good case can be destroyed by the incompetence of a prosecuting counsel, who either is professionally incompetent or again has compromised himself in order to defeat the counsel."[73]

Three cases can illustrate the point. The first is *James Ibori & Anor.* v. *Federal Republic of Nigeria & 3 Ors.*[74] Here, on 13th December 2007, the accused person was charged with 129 counts of money laundering and sundry other crimes committed against the property of Delta State in Delta State, when the first accused person was governor of that state.

[71] Adegbie and Fakile, *op. cit.,* p. 39.
[72] [2009] 3 NWLR (Pt. 1128) 283 CA.
[73] Adegbie and Fakile, *op. cit.,* p. 39.
[74] [2009] 3 NWLR (Pt. 1128) 283 CA.

Instead of commencing proceeding in the Federal High Court sitting in Delta State; the EFCC instituted the action in the Federal High Court sitting in Kaduna. The accused persons challenged the forum in a preliminary objection that was dismissed by the trial court. Then they filed an interlocutory appeal on the point which the Court of Appeal allowed and ordered the trial judge in Kaduna to transfer the case file to the Chief Judge of the Federal High Court for proper assignment.

Thus, by this dint of prosecutorial ineptitude, perhaps it was a deliberate act of forum shopping by the EFCC lawyer, the prosecutor caused twelve months of the court's time to be wasted[75] only for the matter to commence *de novo* in a new court. It was not as if the EFCC lawyer who filed the charge in Kaduna, instead of in Delta, did not know that Kaduna lacked territorial jurisdiction; he knew, but merely fumbled by omission or commission. The EFCC lawyer equally knew that an accused person should not be uprooted from the place of the alleged commission of the offence and be transplanted or supplanted in an entirely different location or venue for the sole purpose of arraignment and standing trial in criminal prosecution. The lawyer knew that Section 45 of the EFCC Act forbids forum shopping, yet he sought to prosecute the case as if it were with a shopping list with regards to what to buy and where specifically and when precisely it catches one's fancy.

The second case is *Chinelo Nwaigwe & 16 Ors.* v. *Federal Republic of Nigeria.*[76] This case illustrates how ineptitude can pose a problem to the prosecution of economic crimes. Here, the EFCC purported to act under Sections 28 and 29 of the EFCC Act to investigate the assets of the appellants arrested for offences under the Act and obtained interim forfeiture order against the said assets. The appellants were supposed to be cronies of then governor Chimaroke Nnamani of Enugu State.[77] The

[75] The interlocutory appeal ruling was delivered on 19th December, 2008.

[76] [2009] 16 NWLR (Pt. 1166) 169 CA.

[77] The assets sought to be attached were those of Chinelo Nwaigwe, Davie Nwaigwe, Rainbownet Nigeria Ltd., Cosmo 105.5 FM, Capital City Automobile Ltd., Renaissance University and Renaissance University Teaching Hospital. Others were Mea Mater Elizabeth High School, Rock City Group PLC, Jefferson LLC, Cookie LLC, and Rainbow Associates LLC. The commission in the instant case also forfeited assets of Ferguson Group PLC, Jasmine Holding Corporation LLC, Intercontinental Associates, C & C Project LLC and Elizabeth Group LLC.

commission fumbled in the prosecution in the sense that it sought and obtained *ex parte* order of the trial court to forfeit the assets before actually attaching them. Whereas a combined reading of the relevant Sections 28 and 29 of the EFCC Act shows that the procedure to be followed is for the commission to attach the suspicious assets first before applying to the court for an interim forfeiture order. By sheer ineptitude, the prosecutor put the cart before the horse, warranting the Court of Appeal to set aside the interim forfeiture order. Now, one may ask: Did the EFCC prosecutor not know the right procedure to follow under Sections 28 and 29? Or did he know and deliberately fumbled to skew justice? Such is the problem! Good a thing, the Court of Appeal, per Hussein Mukhtar, JCA, who read the lead judgment in *Chinelo Nwaigwe,* restated the correct position of the law on this point for officers to follow in due course:

> The seizure of property by the EFCC is a necessary pre-condition to a competent *ex parte* motion for an order of forfeiture of property to the Federal Government. The word seizure used in section 29 of the EFCC Act refers to interim attachment recognised by the provision of section 28 of the Act being the only manner by which the EFCC is permitted to seize property suspected to be acquired through commission of economic or financial crime.[78]

The Court of Appeal allowed the appeal in *Chinelo Nwaigwe* because at the time the application for interim forfeiture of the assets was made by the trial court, there was no valid seizure of the property as provided by Section 28, as the trial court could not have granted an interim order for forfeiture of any property that had not been validly seized by the EFCC.

The last case is *Emmanuel Ahmed* v. *Federal Republic of Nigeria,*[79] where the prosecutor filed a nine-count charge against the accused person, who was arraigned on 1st August 2005. Only count one of the charge bothered on economic crime; whereas counts two to nine were merely charges of forgery, which the police could prosecute. The

---

[78] Ibid., pp. 175-176, paras.C-D.

[79] [2009] 13 NWLR (Pt. 1159) 536 CA.

defence counsel raised a preliminary objection to the propriety of the EFCC filing counts two to nine, which the trial court dismissed. Though the Court of Appeal dismissed the interlocutory appeal brought by the accused person on that point, the initial prosecution blunder had caused a three-year delay[80] in the time it took the court to decide this case. These and a lot more are ways problems are created to hinder the smooth prosecution of economic crimes in Nigeria.

ADVERSE CRITICISM BY THE GENERAL PUBLIC

Often it happens that the general public, which the law enforcement agencies are set up to serve, vilify the commission unnecessarily and dampen the spirit of its operatives to do a good job. There has even been a worse case where an EFCC operative was assassinated. On September 14, 2010, the head of the Forensic Unit of the EFCC, Abdullahi Muazu, was assassinated in Kaduna. He had been actively involved in the trials of several heads of banks.[81] Criticizing a government institution is certainly part of the exercise of the citizen's right to freedom of expression and the press,[82] but to launch a diatribe even at no cause against such an institution may pose a problem to the smooth performance of its statutory functions. Professor Ben Nwabueze has this to say about the EFCC:

> Look at the Act that the National Assembly has passed, the EFCC Act. Can you ever think that any independent National Assembly would pass the EFCC Act? The Act has destroyed the federal system in this country! We do not really have a federal system because of the EFCC, an agency of the federal government, taking over state governments, going to states and laying siege, everybody on the run because of EFCC! In a federal system! And yet the Act was passed by the National Assembly.[83]

---

[80] 20th January 2006 to 20th April 2009.

[81] "Gunmen kill EFCC's Forensic Team Leader in Kaduna". Available at http://www. International relations.house.gov/archives/109/rib051806.pdf15 September 2010. Last assessed on 4th January 2014.

[82] See s. 39 CFRN 1999 as altered.

[83] Interview with B. O. Nwabueze, *ThisDay,* April 11, 2006, p. 45. Cf. Interview with Prof. Ade Ipaye, *Daily Sun,* November 3, 2006, p. 34. He said: "EFCC is doing a good job, but reports indicate an increasing tendency to sacrifice due process. The end doesn't always justify the means.

A former president of the Nigerian Bar Association (NBA), Lanke Odogiyon, roundly criticized the EFCC and in much stronger terms, thus:

> Our position is that of zero tolerance to corruption and to that extent we support the Federal Government's war against corruption. While we acknowledge that the EFCC has succeeded in successfully prosecuting the war against corrupt persons and agencies, we condemn the use of the commission as an instrument of witch-hunting political opponents of the government. The EFCC has been sectional and selective in fighting corruption. While it turns blind eyes to brazen graft and looting of public funds by some people in government and those in the good books of the government, it has been hounding known political and business opponents of the government in power. The commission operates as if it is above the law, arresting and detaining people for weeks or months without charging them with any offence in court. It disregards court injunction – not to arrest and treats with disdain court orders to release those detained . . . We demand the re-organisation of the commission to re-orientate the staff personnel on citizen's rights and method of law enforcement.[84]

There may be those who do not criticize law enforcement agencies in such harsh words, and one may be invited to agree that in the long run, the views of those people will balance out with those of the others who peddle diatribes, but caution and moderation are advised when citizens talk about the affairs of agencies set up to protect them.

CONCLUSION

In all, this chapter finds that there are comprehensive laws prohibiting economic crimes; the problems associated with the prosecution of these crimes in Nigeria are basically procedural. These include the surreptitious introduction of plea bargain into the system, political interference, ineffective judiciary, corruption, non-cooperation from the bar, shoddy investigation, inept prosecution, and unnecessarily adverse criticism from the general public.

This chapter recommends that the plea bargain procedure in the prosecution of economic crimes should be abolished in Nigeria as a history of the series of abuse of the procedure in the country shows that

---

[84] *The Guardian,* September 5, 2006, p. 8

the country is not yet mature enough to operate the same. It urges the independence of law enforcement agencies from political interference as this violates the rule of law that the law should apply to everybody equally without regard to status or personality. A special court should be set up for these crimes, where judges should be specially trained and tested for stronger integrity for greater efficiency. The chapter solicits the cooperation of lawyers to forsake playing their games of technicality in the prosecution of economic crimes for quicker dispensation of justice. It recommends continuing education for investigators and prosecutors to eschew shoddiness and ineptitude and to make them versed in human rights protection and methods of law enforcement. Lastly, the chapter calls on the general public to avoid unrestrained diatribe on the law enforcement agencies and their staff as this may dampen their spirit and kill the incentive to do a good job.

If the recommendations made in this chapter are taken, the law enforcement agencies will have been re-positioned to curb the menace of corruption that constitutes the cog in the wheel of progress. The agencies will have been reinforced to protect national and foreign investments in the country with the result that they will imbue the spirit of hard work in the citizenry and discourage ill-gotten wealth. If the problems identified in this chapter are solved, the law enforcement agencies will have been equipped to identify illegally acquired wealth and confiscate it; help to build an upright workforce in both public and private sectors of the economy; and contribute to the global war against economic crimes.

PART G

OUTLINE OF PROCEDURAL/ADJECTIVAL LAWS

Chapter 24

SHIP REGISTRATION AND ARREST PROCEDURES IN NIGERIA

Gbadebo Anthony Olagunju*

INTRODUCTION AND HISTORICAL OVERVIEW OF SHIPPING IN NIGERIA

Nigeria is an emerging maritime country located on the west coast of Africa. The most populous Black country, Nigeria, is bordered on the north by Niger and Chad, on the east by Cameroon, on the west by the Benin Republic, and bounded on the south by the Gulf of Guinea and Equatorial Guinea. It has a total area of 923,766 square kilometres, of which the land area consists of 910,766 square kilometres, while the balance of 13,000 square kilometres is water, with a total coastline of 853 kilometres.[1]

The land area spans over six ecological zones, ranging from the swampy coastal rain forest of the South to the semi-arid fertile grassland of the Eastern region, about 600 metres over the Northern region, and 300 metres over the Western region. The coastal southern regions are the low-lying grounds which are generally below 300 metres and are characterized by creeks and lagoons on both sides of the Niger

*LL.B, LL.M, Ph.D, Solicitor and Advocate of the Supreme Court of Nigeria. Senior Lecturer in the Department of Jurisprudence and International Law, Faculty of Law, Lagos State University, Nigeria. Formerly Visiting Research Fellow at the Max Planck Institute for Comparative Public Law and International Law, Heidelberg, Germany, and Fellow, Salzburg Global Seminar, Austria (Session 424: The World Trade Negotiations: The Politics of Economics and Trade). Email: debsontop@gmail.com; gbadebo.olagunju@lasu.edu.ng

[1] G. A. Olagunju, "States' Compliance with International Maritime Law: Case of Safety and Security in Tanzania and Nigeria," Unpublished PhD Thesis, St. Augustine University of Tanzania (SAUT), 2013, 251.

Delta. The main drainage systems are the Niger-Benue Rivers, Lake Chad, and the coastal river systems.[2]

The country's maritime history dates back to the fifteenth century when European explorers opened up maritime contacts with the geographical area (then, of course, not known as Nigeria) after discovering rich natural resources in the west and central African regions, much needed at the time for their economic survival and the industrial revolution in Europe. Consequently, John d'Aveiro of Portugal opened up the Bight of Benin in 1485, paving the way for Captain Wyndham of Britain to land on the nation's coast much later in 1553.[3]

However, the real history of shipping and, consequently, port development in Nigeria started around the middle of the 19th century. Initial efforts at providing facilities for ocean-going vessels began with attempts to open up the entrance to the Lagos Lagoon. However, the constantly shifting channels in the bar at the entrance to the Lagoon, coupled with littoral drifts along the coast, made that difficult. The first major breakthrough, however, came in 1906 when dredgers were brought in to work at the bar. The same year, approval was given for the construction of the first length of the East Mole. With the construction of a railway from Lagos to Otta and then to the rock city of Abeokuta, there was easy transportation of stone needed for the construction of the mole. Thus, depths over the bar improved considerably as the entrance moles were pushed further seaward. On February 1, 1914, the first mail-steamer, S/S 'Akoko,' drawing 5.64 metres, entered the Lagos Harbour. Two months later, vessels began using the facilities provided at the customs wharf on Lagos Island. Meanwhile, a decision to develop the Apapa port had been taken earlier in 1913 for the construction of the first four deep-water berths of 548.64 metres long. This began in 1921, and by 1948, an additional 762 metres of berthage were constructed as a continuation - downstream of the first four berths.

---

[2] *Ibidem*, 252.
[3] *Ibidem*, 253

Also, about 41 hectares of reclamation behind the wharves were done to accommodate transit sheds, warehouses, and marshalling yards.[4]

Development of ports in the Eastern axis of the country began with the discovery of coal in Enugu, and by 1913, Port Harcourt was opened to shipping by Lord Lugard, the then Governor-General. The railway line from Port Harcourt to Enugu was completed three years later in 1916, and a berth for colliers was dredged out and constructed at the port as a place where loading could be effected. In 1927, four berths of 1,920 feet long were added to the existing one.[5]

In the period between 1927 and 1954, the concept of ports as an integral part of the social and economic development of a country had not been properly addressed, and so most port operations and management remained under the control of different Government departments like the Nigerian Railways Department, Public Works Department, etc. For example, the handling of cargo at the quays in Lagos and Port Harcourt was undertaken by the Nigerian Railways department; while the Marine Department was responsible for the maintenance of the harbour channel and the berthing of vessels; then a Port Engineer in the Public Works Department took charge of maintaining the quays.[6] In April 1955, the Nigerian Ports Authority was established, which took over from these various departments. Within the period 1955-60, the Authority added six berths of 943 metres to the existing ones in Lagos, and four berths with a total quay length of 506 metres were also added to that of Port Harcourt.[7]

In 1969, while the Nigerian Civil War was still on, the Federal Government (through the NPA) acquired the ports of Warri, Burutu, and Calabar hitherto operated by private entrepreneurs.[8] Immediately after the Civil War, the Lagos port, which was the only port in operation (as the Port Harcourt port had been shut down during the

---

[4] See Nigerian Ports Authority: Our History, available at: https://www.nigerianports. org/history .aspx?id =241 (Accessed 26 January 2014).

[5] Nigerian Ports Authority: Our History, *Supra*, note 4

[6] See G. O. Osoba, "The Nigerian Seaports and the Maritime Industry: A Critical Review" in Dele Badejo (ed), *Maritime Transportation in Nigeria*, Rex Charles Publication, Ibadan, 1998, 84,

[7] Nigerian Ports Authority: Our History, *supra*, note 4

[8] Warri Port was formerly owned by Holts Transport; Burutu by UAC; and Calabar by five operators among which were M/S Palm line Agencies Limited and Elder Dempster Agencies.

war), started experiencing serious congestion, both in cargo and ship calls, due to the rise in the level of imports. Particularly at the time, the Federal Government had imported 20 million tonnes of cement, out of which 16 million were for the Ministry of Defence alone, when the total capacity of all existing ports in the country put together was just 6.5 million tonnes of general cargo per annum.[9] As a result, by the middle of 1975, vessels waiting for berthing spaces had reached a record figure of 455, inclusive of 300 vessels carrying bags of cement.[10] This period (1970-75) can, therefore, rightly be described as a major turning point in the history of port development in Nigeria.

On October 14, 1977, the ultra-modern Tin Can Island port was commissioned, and two years later, both the new Warri port and the new Calabar port were commissioned.[11] The Tin Can Island Port Complex today is an amalgam of Roro and Tin Can Island Ports when both were merged in 2006 as a result of port reforms. Private terminal operators took over the terminals that year under a lease agreement. The development, modernization, and expansion of the Calabar Port were embarked upon under the 3rd National Development plan between 1975 and 1980 in order to make the Port facilities cope with the ever-increasing demand of the Nigerian economy. The new Port Complex consists of the following major operational areas: a total land area of 38 hectares; a total of Four Quays, each measuring about 215m long and 40m wide, decimated into six operational berths; 2 warehouses measuring 150m X 40m and 175m X 40m; operational area have been divided into two concessioned terminals.[12]

In the 1980s, the idea of a Federal Ocean Terminal, a deep seaport, planned to serve the transhipment needs of the sub-region, was conceived. It was originally designed to accommodate ships of 35,000 tons dead-weight and later to be expanded to take in vessels of up to

---

[9] See G. O. Olaore and A. Adeagbo, "Port Congestion: Causes and Control" in Dele Badejo (ed), *Maritime Transportation in Nigeria*, Rex Charles Publication, Ibadan, 1998, 136.

[10] See Nigerian Ports Authority, Our Historical background, available at: http://www.nigeri anports.org/ dynamicdata/OurHistory.aspx (Accessed 27 January 2014).

[11] On 16 and 19 June 1979 respectively. See http://www.nigerianports.org/ dynamicdata/ OurHistory.aspx (Accessed 27 January 2014).

[12] See Nigerian Ports Authority, Calabar Ports Complex, available at: http://www.nigerianports.org /AboutUsCalabarPort.aspx (Accessed 29 January 2014].

60,000 tons dead-weight. Construction work began in 1980 but was suspended in 1983. However, work was later resumed, and the construction of the first phase of the project was completed and commissioned in 1996. Known as the Federal Ocean Terminal, Onne, it is a multipurpose and ultra-modern seaport that is reputed to be the largest and first of its kind in Africa and is expected to handle exports from Nigeria's petrochemical industry.[13]

In all, there are six major operational seaports in Nigeria presently, comprising the following: Lagos Port Complex (LPC); Tin Can Island Port Complex (TCIPC); Rivers Port Complex (RPC); Delta Port Complex (DPC); Onne Port Complex (OPC); and Calabar Port Complex (CPC).[14] According to information from the Nigerian Ports Authority, a total of 4,837 vessels were recorded as entering all Nigerian ports in the year 2012, while 120,818,683 gross registered tonnages (GRT) were recorded for the same period.[15]

With six major seaports spread over the country and the volume of maritime traffic in Nigeria, the country can therefore be reasonably described as a major player in the maritime industry internationally. In fact, in a recent work, Oghojafor, Kuye, and Alaneme argued that since the commercialization of the Nigerian ports in 1992 and subsequent concessioning of same in 2007 or thereabout, activities at the nation's ports have considerably increased both in terms of cargo throughput and the number of vessels entering Nigerian ports, even though there are still a lot of inadequacies and inefficiencies.[16] Also, as noted by a learned maritime practitioner:

---

[13] *Idem*

[14] See Nigerian Ports Authority, Ports Operation, available at: http://www.nigerianports. org/portop eration.aspx (Accessed 12 February 2014).

[15] Which was in fact a decline from the 2011 figure of 5,232 and 122, 614,716 respectively. See Nigerian Ports Authority: Port Operation, Port Statistics, available at: https://www.nigerianports.org/ dynamicdata/ HQStatistics.aspx?id=178 (Accessed 30 January 2014) or Nigerian Ports Authority, Number and Gross Registered Tonnage (GRT) of Vessels that entered all Nigerian Ports: 2007-2012 pdf, available online at: https://www.nigerianports.org/dynamicdata/HQStatistics.aspx?id=178 (Accessed 30 January 2014).

[16] B. E. A. Oghojafor, O. L. Kuye and G. C. Alaneme, "Concession as a Strategic Tool for Ports Efficiency: An Assessment of the Nigerian Ports," *American Journal of Business Management* (2012), Vol. 1, No. 4, 214-222, particularly at 218-220. See also Nigeria Trade Hub News, "Nigerian Ports Record Increase Cargo Throughput and Vessel Traffic," available at http://www.nigeriatradehub.gov.ng /News/tabid/98 /entryid/154/nigerian-ports-record-increase-cargo-throughput-and-vessel-traffic.aspx (Accessed 12 February 2014).

> [N]igeria remains a significant shipping nation and the largest in cargo volume in the West African sub-region. Nigeria therefore remains a favourable jurisdiction for ship arrests and an enviable investment destination.[17]

It is for the above reasons that it is worthwhile to look at the laws of the country regulating the registration of ships and arrest procedures concerning ships entering those ports aforementioned or within the territorial waters of Nigeria.

REGISTRATION OF SHIPS IN NIGERIA

The registration of ships in Nigeria is handled by the Ship Registration Office, which was established by s.28(2) of the Nigerian Maritime Administration and Safety Agency Act, 2007. Prior to this date, the duty was performed by the Office of the Government Inspector of Shipping (hereinafter GIS), a ministerial department under the Nigerian Ministry of Transport. In 2002, however, the Office of the GIS was subsumed under the National Maritime Authority (hereinafter NMA), and by 2007, the latter was replaced by the Nigerian Maritime Administration and Safety Agency (hereinafter NIMASA).

The Ship Registration Office is vested with the power to enter ships into the Central Ship Registry created by Section 16(1) of the newly enacted Nigerian Merchant Shipping Act (hereinafter MSA) of 2007.[18] The office is also mandated to enter ships into the Special Register for Vessels and Shipowning Companies engaged in Cabotage created by Section 22 of the Coastal and Inland Shipping (Cabotage) Act, 2003.

Part III of the MSA deals with the registration and licensing of ships, and under it, Section 16(1) provides that "there shall be maintained a Central Ship Registry for registration and licensing of registry of ships." For the purpose of the Act, the ship is stated to

---

17 See Adedoyin Afun, "Ship Arrest- Recent Development in Nigerian Arrest Law," Paper Presented at the 8th Shiparrested.com Conference, Athens, Greece, June 2011, available online at: http://www.banwo-ighodalo.com/_downloads/SHIP%20ARREST%20-%20RECENT%20DEVELOPMENTS%20IN%20NIGERIAN%20ARREST%20LAW_BI_1111.pdf (Accessed 20 February 2014).

18 This Act repealed the Merchant Shipping Act, Cap 224 Laws of the Federation of Nigeria 1990. See S. 439 of the Act.

include any barge, lighter, or like vessel used in navigation in Nigerian waters, no matter how it is propelled.[19] However, no self-propelled vessel which is less than 15 gross tons shall be subject to registration.[20] In accordance with Section 18(1) of the MSA, which deals with "persons qualified to own a registered Nigerian Ship," the following guidelines are issued by the Nigerian Ship Registration Office under the authority of NIMASA concerning the registration of a vessel:

1. The applicant must be a Nigerian citizen;
2. If a corporate body, it must be registered under and subject to Nigerian laws and have its principal place of business in Nigeria;
3. Such other persons as the Minister of Transport may by regulations prescribe.

In addition, a formal letter of application for registration of the ship must be written by the owner of the ship or his agent accompanied with the following documents to the Ship Registration Office:[21]

a. Company's Particulars
i. Copy of Certificate of Incorporation
ii. Certified True Copy of Memorandum and Articles of Association
iii. Certified True Copy of Particulars of Directors (Form CAC 7)
iv. Certified True Copy of Allotment of Shares (Form CAC 2). Here, the company's share capital should not be less than twenty-five Million Naira (N25m).
v. The Company's Current Tax Clearance Certificate
vi. The Company's Bank Statement or Letter of Reference from the Bank
vii. Declaration of Ownership form (to be issued by the Ship Registry)[22]

[19] MSA, s. 16 (5)
[20] *idem*
[21] All correspondence should be addressed to: The Director General, Nigerian Maritime Administration and Safety Agency, Maritime House, 4, Burma Road, Apapa, P. M. B. 12861, G. P. O, Marina, Lagos, Nigeria. [Email: registrarofships@nimasa.gov.ng].
[22] See Nigerian Maritime Administration and Safety Agency: Services: Ship Registration, available at http://www.nimasa.gov.ng/service.php?id=30&type=sub&catId=8 (Accessed 19 January 2014).

Concurrently with submitting the application for registration, the ship owner is also expected to submit an application for a survey of the ship and issuance of certificate of tonnage measurement in order to facilitate the flag survey of the ship. To this end, the vessel particulars consisting of the following are required of him to furnish the Ship Registry:

i. Name of the ship
ii. Time and place of purchase of the ship
iii. Name of the Master of the ship
iv. Best particulars in respect of the tonnage, build, and description of the ship
v. Bill of sale or Builders Certificate (i.e., evidence of title to the ship)
vi. Condition survey report and tonnage measurement certificate as approved by the Minister
vii. Certificate of carving and marking note of the ship
viii. Call sign certificate
ix. Loadline certificate
x. Report of pre-purchase survey
xi. Deletion certificate (if vessel is flagging in from a foreign flag in order to avoid dual registration).[23]
xii. Certificate of approved plan issued by NIMASA (in case of a newly built vessel in Nigeria).
xiii. Vessel class certificate (applicable to conventional vessels only)
xiv. Evidence of insurance/P & I coverage
xv. Payment of registration fees[24]

In addition to the above, the ship owner is also required to furnish his particulars as follows:

i. Full names, addresses and occupation
ii. Evidence of ability or experience of the owner/purchaser to operate and maintain ship
iii. Logbook of the ship for the inspection of the Registrar of ships

---

[23] In order not to contravene Article 92 of UNCLOS 1982 which provides that ships shall sail under the flag of one State only and shall be subject to the exclusive jurisdiction of that State while on the high seas save only for certain exceptional cases expressly provided for in international treaties.

[24] See Nigerian Maritime Administration and Safety Agency, *Supra*, note 22.

iv. In the case of second-hand tonnage, a bill of sale with warranty against liens and encumbrances from the sellers

v. Evidence of financial resources sufficient for operation and maintenance of the ship.[25]

After the submission of all the above, it is imperative for the applicant to liaise with NIMASA's survey unit for flag State condition survey and issuance of Certificate of Tonnage Measurement.

THE ARREST OF SHIPS UNDER NIGERIAN LAW: PRACTICE AND PROCEDURE

The arrest of a ship 'means the detention of a ship by judicial process to secure a maritime claim, but does not include the seizure of a ship in the execution or satisfaction of a judgment.'[26] The procedure for arresting a ship under Nigerian law is set out in Order 7, Rule 1(1) of the Admiralty Jurisdiction Procedure Rules (hereinafter AJPR) 2011. Under this rule, a claimant with "maritime claim" as enunciated in Section 2 of the Admiralty Jurisdiction Act (hereinafter AJA) may commence an *in rem* proceedings against a ship that is within the jurisdiction of the Federal High Court (hereinafter FHC), which is the only court vested with exclusive jurisdiction with respect to admiralty matters in Nigeria,[27] or where the ship is expected to arrive jurisdiction within three days of filing the application. Before the 14th of March 2011, when the new rules became operational, an application for arrest could only be made when a ship was within the jurisdiction of the FHC.[28] This was provided for under Order VII of the defunct AJPR of 1993. The new rule (2011) has therefore stretched the ambit of the order of arrest by the court from the ship within the jurisdiction to ships anticipated to be within the jurisdiction of the court. As mentioned earlier, the criterion for application is that the applicant must have a maritime claim as enunciated in the Admiralty Jurisdiction

---

[25] *Idem*

[26] Order 1 Rule 5 AJPR 2011

[27] For further reading on this, see C. N. Ojukwu, "Arrest and Detention of Ships and other Property in Nigeria," *28 Tul. Mar. L. J.* (2004), 249.

[28] That is, every open sea within twelve (12) nautical miles of the coast of Nigeria (measured from the low water mark or of the seaward limits of inland waters). See s. 1 (1) Territorial Waters Act, Cap. 75, Laws of the Federation of Nigeria (LFN) 2004.

Act of 1991. Under that Act, what constitutes a maritime claim can fall under either:

i. "Proprietary Maritime Claim" or

ii. "General Maritime Claim"

With regards to the first, this includes claims relating to the possession of a ship,[29] title to or ownership of a ship or of a share in a ship,[30] mortgage of a ship or of a share in a ship,[31] mortgage of a ship's freight,[32] claims between co-owners of a ship relating to possession, ownership, operation or earning of a ship,[33] claim for the satisfaction or enforcement of a judgment given by the Federal High Court or any court (including a court of a foreign country) against a ship or other property in an admiralty proceeding *in rem*,[34] or a claim for interest in respect of any claim as enunciated above.[35]

With respect to General Maritime Claim, this includes claims for damage done or received by a ship (whether by collision or otherwise),[36] claim for loss of life or personal injury sustained in consequence of a defect in a ship or in the apparel or equipment of a ship,[37] claim for loss of life or personal injury arising out of an act or omission of the owner or charterer of a ship; person in possession or control of a ship; and person for whose wrongful act or omission the owner, charterer or person in possession or control of the ship is liable; subject to certain exceptions in the Act,[38] claim for loss of or damage to goods carried by a ship[39] claim out of an agreement relating to the carriage of goods or persons by a ship or to the use or hire of a ship, whether by charterparty or otherwise,[40] claim relating to salvage (including life salvage of cargo or wreck found on land),[41] claim in

---

[29] S. 2 (2) (a) (i)
[30] S. 2 (2) (a) (ii)
[31] S. 2 (2) (a) (iii)
[32] S. 2 (2) (a) (iv)
[33] S. 2 (2) (b)
[34] S. 2 (2) (c)
[35] S. 2 (2) (d)
[36] S. 2 (3) (a) and (b)
[37] S. 2 (3) (c)
[38] See S. 2 (3) (d) (i) – (iii) and the exception as contained in 2 (4)
[39] S. 2 (3) (e)
[40] S. 2 (3) (f)
[41] S. 2 (3) (g)

respect of general average,[42] claim in respect of pilotage of a ship,[43] claim in respect of towage of a ship or an aircraft when it is water-borne,[44] claim in respect of goods, materials or services (including stevedoring and lighterage service) supplied or to be supplied to a ship for its operation or maintenance,[45] claim in respect of construction of a ship (including such claim relating to a vessel before it was launched),[46] claim in respect of the alteration, repair or equipping of a ship or dock charges or dues,[47] claim in respect of liability for port, harbour, canal or light tolls, charges or dues, or tolls, charges or dues of any kind, in relation to a ship,[48] claim arising out of bottomry,[49] claim by a master, shipper, charterer or agent in respect of disbursements on account of a ship,[50] claim for an insurance premium, or for a mutual insurance call, in relation to a ship, or goods or cargoes carried by a ship,[51] claim by a master, or member of the crew of a ship for wages or an amount that a person as employer is under an obligation to pay to another as employer whether the obligation arose out of contract of employment or by operation of law (including by operation of the law of a foreign country),[52] claim for the forfeiture or condemnation of a ship or of goods which are being or have been carried or have been attempted to be carried in a ship or for the restoration of a ship or any such goods after seizure,[53] claim for the enforcement of a claim arising out of an arbitral award (including a foreign award within the meaning of the Arbitration and Conciliation Act) made in respect of a proprietary maritime claim or any claim already referred to above,[54] and finally, a claim for interest in respect of any claim referred to above.[55]

---

[42] S. 2 (3) (h)
[43] S. 2 (3) (i)
[44] S. 2 (3) (j)
[45] S. 2 (3) (k)
[46] S. 2 (3) (l)
[47] S. 2 (3) (m)
[48] S. 2 (3) (n)
[49] S. 2 (3) (o)
[50] S. 2 (3) (p)
[51] S. 2 (3) (q)
[52] S. 2 (3) (r)
[53] S. 2 (3) (s)
[54] S. 2 (3) (t)
[55] S. 2 (3) (u)

The Application for Arrest

Once any of the above claims are ascertained, the claimant is required to bring his application by way of filing his writ of summons; statement of claim; motion *ex parte* disclosing a strong prima facie case for arrest of the ship;[56] supporting affidavit stating the nature of the claim and containing such facts that the ship is within the jurisdiction of the court, or is expected to arrive jurisdiction within three days and that the ship may leave the jurisdiction of the court at any time. The applicant/claimant is further required to provide the following: an Affidavit of Urgency; Indemnity in favour of the Admiralty Marshal for his expenses in effecting the arrest order; and an Undertaking as to damages in favour of the defendant(s).[57]

The Caveat Register

There is also a requirement under the new rule which states that before obtaining a warrant of arrest for a ship, a claimant shall be responsible for conducting a search of the Caveat Register to ascertain that there is no caveat against arrest in force with respect to the particular ship.[58] It should be noted that the old rule did not require the claimant to search the Caveat Register before obtaining a warrant of arrest of a ship, and so under that rule, it was possible for an applicant to obtain a warrant of arrest of a ship even with full knowledge of a caveat against such an arrest.[59]

OTHER FACTORS RELATING TO ARRESTS IN NIGERIA

Change in Beneficial Ownership

Under the new rules, a warrant of arrest may not be issued where the beneficial ownership of a ship has changed since the issuance of a writ

---

[56] For a discussion on the proper legal status of ex-parte order of arrest of ship or other property, see M. I. Igbokwe (SAN), "Recent Developments in Nigerian Maritime Litigation," Paper delivered at the NIMASA 4th Strategic Admiralty Law Seminar for Judges, Lagos, Nigeria, 5th December, 2012, available online at: http://www.mikeigbokwe.com/new1/RECENT%20DEVELOPMENTS%20IN%20NIGERIAN%20MARITIME%20LITIGATION.pdf (Accessed 28 February 2014)

[57] See L. F. Anga, "Ship Arrest in Nigeria," *Ship Arrests in Practice* (7th Ed.), ShipArrested.com, NetCorporate Manager 2012, 126-128, esp at 127. Available online at: www.interlegal.com.ua/en/.../ *Ship_Arrests_ in_Practice_7th_all.pdf (Accessed 15 February 2014)*

[58] See Order 7 Rule 1 (2) AJPR 2011

[59] See Adedoyin Afun, *Supra* note 17

of summons. This could be as a result of the sale or disposal of the ship by any court in the exercise of its admiralty jurisdiction.[60]

Indemnification of the Admiralty Marshal and Accounts on Expenditures

As mentioned earlier, the applicant for warrant of arrest must give a form of undertaking to the court to pay the Admiralty Marshal, on demand, an amount equal to the expenses incurred in effecting the arrest. Under the old rules, the Marshal was entitled to claim an amount not exceeding ₦5,000.00 as a deposit toward discharging this liability. The Marshal may make additional demands for interim payments on account of those fees and expenses. This amount became grossly inadequate as time went by in view of the inflation in the economy. Thus, in line with present-day economic realities, the new rules provide that:

> [t]he Admiralty Marshall may accept an amount of money not less than ₦100,000.00 and not more than ₦500,000.00 as deposit towards discharging the liability; and make more demands fortnightly for payment on account of those expenses.[61]

In the same vein, the Marshal is required to file returns/receipts on expenditures to the court within seven working days after the release of the ship.[62]

Order of Judicial Sale of Arrested Ship

Pursuant to Order 9, Rule 6(2) of the AJPR 2011, an arrestor (claimant) or any other interested party may apply to the court for an order of sale of an arrested ship where the ship owner fails to provide bail for the release of the ship or fails to enter appearance to the suit or where sufficient security has not been provided six months after the date of

---

[60] See Order 7 Rule 1 (4) AJPR 2011
[61] See Order 9, Rule 2 (a) and (b) AJPR 2011
[62] Order 9, Rule 2 (1) AJPR 2011

arrest. Once the order is granted by the court, the sale is to be carried out by the Admiralty Marshal, and all proceeds of sale shall be paid into an interest-yielding fixed deposit account in the name of the Marshal pending further orders of the court.

Compensation/Reparation for Frivolous Arrest

A radical departure from the old rules in the new rules is the issue of compensation for the frivolous or unwarranted arrest of a ship. While the old rules prescribe a maximum of ₦20,000.00 as reasonable compensation to the defendant for any loss, injury, or expenses that he may have sustained as a result of such arrest, attachment, order of sale, or injunction; the new rules recognize the economic importance of a ship to its owner(s) and the consequential loss which may occur as a result of frivolous/needless arrest has now made provision empowering the court to award damages which is reasonable in the circumstances to the defendant. Thus Order 11 Rule 2(a) and (b) of the AJPR 2011 provides:

> In any case in which an arrest order as aforesaid has been made-
>
> (a)If it afterwards appears to the court that the arrest of any defendant, or any order of attachment, sale, or injunction, or any warrant to stop the clearance of, or to arrest any ship, was applied for on insufficient grounds; or
> (b) If the suit in which any such application was made is dismissed, or judgment is given against the plaintiff by default or otherwise, and it appears to the court that there was no probable ground for instituting such suit, the court may (on the application of the defendant made at any time before the *expiration of three months from the termination of the suit) award against the plaintiff such amount as it may deem a reasonable compensation to the defendant* for any loss, injury, or expenses which he may have sustained by reason of such arrest, attachment, order of sale or injunction, as aforesaid.[63]

[63] Words in Italics for emphasis

It is submitted that this new provision will go a long way to curb the bringing of frivolous and/or vindictive applications for arrest orders and also prevent or at least minimize the abuse of the court process.

CONCLUSION

In this work, we discussed the historical overview of shipping as an important sector of the Nigerian economy. We also examined the mode of registering ships in Nigeria and how any ship, whether registered in Nigeria or not, may be arrested in Nigeria under the country's admiralty law, practice, and procedure. In conclusion, it may be added as a sort of advice, especially in the area of ship registration, that whilst the duty of ship registration continues to lie with NIMASA, the Agency under its Director-General should ensure speedy registration and try as much as possible to check administrative/bureaucratic bottlenecks and red-tapism that may delay or discourage applicants; and also check corruption within the system as the Agency is not immune from this menace currently plaguing the Nigerian social system. This will go a long way to attract private investors, much needed in this area and in the long run, benefit the Nigerian economy.

Chapter 25

ENFORCEMENT AND ARREST OF SHIP PROCEDURE

T. C. Nwano* & O. T. Umahi+

INTRODUCTION

The arrest of Ship Procedure in maritime transactions is the focus of this paper. It is the finding of the writer that clauses transferring power of sale with specifics on arrest to the mortgagee should be drafted, inserted, agreed and endorsed by all the parties in standard mortgage agreements, so much that upon the power of sale becoming arising and exercisable, ship arrest would become an excellent way of obtaining security for a claim and potent for a judicial sale of the vessel.

This chapter looks specifically at ship arrest and procedure in Nigeria. Focusing in particular on the factors which need to be taken into account when deciding whether arresting a vessel is the appropriate course of action and, if so, where such action should be taken. This work is divided into three parts, part one focuses on the arrest of ship generally, part two juxtaposes the mortgage security with the arrest procedure, and part three concludes the article.

PART 1

A ship-owner who wishes to obtain money may do so by borrowing money on the security of his ship, given the person who is prepared to

---

* Nwano Theophilious Chinedu, LL.M, LL.B, BL, Barrister & Solicitor of the Supreme Court and lecturer Faculty of Law, Benson Idahosa University, Benin City

+ Umahi Okechukwu Timothy, PhD (Manchester), LL.M (Manchester), LL.M (LASU), LL.B (Enugu), BL., Lecturer Faculty of Law, University of Nigeria, Enugu Campus.

lend him the money an interest in the ship as security for the loan, this commercial arrangement is known as mortgage. Mortgage has been defined by the Court of Appeal[1] as a conveyance of a legal or equitable interest in property as a security for the payment of debt or the discharge of some other obligations for which it is given.[2]

It is well known principle that a mortgagee has no liabilities against the third parties since the mortgagor remains the owner of the ship or the shares in it. The mortgagor or owner is free to continue operating and trading the vessel as a profit-making possession, provided that he does not act in such a way as to jeopardize or put at risk the ship as security for the mortgage loan and thus prejudice the mortgagee's position.[3]

The importance of the doctrine of the "ship as security" is emphasized by the custom and practice of every mortgage containing a personal covenant by the mortgagor to repay the loan.[4] However, as security, a vessel is not an ideal form of security, viz.:

1. one reason being that certain privileged claims can rank against the vessel in priority before those of a mortgagee;
2. being a floating object, it will disappear from and escape out of the jurisdiction of the courts whose aid the mortgagee may be entitled to seek;
3. as for the precarious nature of a ship as security, is its permanent exposure to partial damage or even total destruction through the perils of the sea;
4. it is also worth noting that if a further advance is given on the same security and a second independent mortgage has been effected and

---

[1] *Pharmatek Ind. Projects Ltd* v. *Trade Bank PLC* (2009) All FWLR (pt 495) 1678.

[2] See also the cases of *Intercity bank Plc.* v. *Feed and Food Farms Nig. Ltd & Ors.* (2001) 17 NWLR (pt. 742) 347. *Ahaneku* v. *Iheaturu* (1995) 2 NWLR (pt. 380) 758.

[3] It however depends on the circumstance of each case as what would amount to jeopardy is objectively ascertained and whether the owners jeopardize the security in the circumstance. The courts have come to this conclusion in a case where the mortgagor failed to repair the ship, so as to make her incapable of performing a chartered voyage. Also where he allowed the ship to be burdened by maritime liens for an unreasonably length of time (such conduct showed the reduced circumstances of the owner and such liens ranked in priority to the mortgage).

[4] Once a mortgage is always a mortgage. See also Section 57(1) MSA 2007.

registered in the intervening period, the latter may rank ahead of any further advance on the first mortgage.[5]

As the economic turmoil continues, it appears that ship arrest is once again a remedy of which creditors to the marine industry should be aware.[6] Ship arrest is an excellent way to obtain security for a claim and potentially prepare for a judicial sale of the vessel, should that become necessary. An arrest may be a suitable remedy for a variety of creditors, such as owners that need to repossess the vessel under the charter party, bunker suppliers that have not been paid, a bank that has terminated the loan facility and wishes to draw on its mortgage or crew members that have outstanding wages.[7]

The arrest of a vessel is part of the process by which an Admiralty Court gains jurisdiction over the subject matter of a lawsuit. These lawsuits are known as *in rem* actions meaning that the action is against a "thing" rather than a person.[8] Generally, the vessel itself is responsible for payment of liens, mortgages, or any other maritime lien that may arise. When the owner encumbers a vessel with a First Preferred Ship's Mortgage, it is the ship that guarantees payment rather than the owner.[9] However, the owner may separately contract by a personal promise to pay or another type of guarantee to be personally liable.

Legal Framework

An arrest of a vessel is the prerequisite for the court to establish jurisdiction. An arrest is a physical process by which, in the case of the United States, a U.S. Marshal goes aboard the vessel and physically takes charge of it. The Notice of Arrest must be posted on the vessel, a copy given to the master or person in charge, as well as to the owner. Also, the notice must be published in a newspaper authorized to publish legal

---

[5] section 323(2) MSA, 2007

[6] Davies(ed),*Jurisdiction and Forum Selection in International Maritime Law*, 283-320

[7] W. Tetley, Maritime Liens and Claims(2'edn, Les Editions Yvon Blaislnc., Montreal, 1998), pp, 977-78

[8] *The Beldis* (1936) P 51, 75-76 (EWCA); *Monte Ulia (Owners)* v. *Banco (Owners), The Banco* [1971]P 137, 151(ECWA), however, the House of Lords per Lords Steyn controversially adopted a more extreme proceduralist position, stating that 'an action in rem is an action against the owners from the moment that the Admiralty Court is seized with jurisdiction'.

[9] *Harmer* v. *Bel* (The Bold l3uccieugh)(1851)7 Moo PC 267;13 ER 884

notices. The actual notice must be given to all other lien holders who claim an interest in the vessel.[10]

Once seized, the court, through the marshal's service or substitute custodian, maintains possession of the vessel and the owner loses all control. To avoid this situation and its effect on commerce, the court will allow the owner to post a bond or other suitable security. Once the security is accepted, the vessel is returned to the owner and the litigation continues with the security as the subject of execution of judgment. Letters of undertaking are stipulations by the owner or his insurance company to appear and defend any claim that is made, just as if the vessel had been arrested. If a judgment is entered, the owner or the insurer must pay the judgment.[11] This amounts to stipulated jurisdiction for the admiralty court and prevents the disruption of the owner's business during the litigation. Once the Marshal has seized a vessel, he is obligated to preserve the vessel and its equipment. Generally, the custodian of a seized vessel should not interfere with the conduct of cargo and other operations normal to a vessel in berth unless directed so by court order. In the United States, the "Manual for United States Marshals" sets forth the obligations and duties of the Marshal and how he should perform them.'[12]

If a vessel is not released by the posting of security, the court may order an interlocutory sale. An interlocutory sale means a sale prior to the completion of the litigation and the entering of a judgment. As a general rule, the sale will not be allowed for four months. The rules provide for sale if the arrested property is perishable, liable to deterioration, or if the cost of keeping it is excessive or disproportionate. Regardless of whether the sale is interlocutory or a judgment sale, the purchaser at the auction does not have any right in the vessel until the sale is confirmed by the court. If a higher bid is received within three days by the court, the court has the option of voiding the auction and ordering a new sale. Once confirmation is received, the buyer receives a title that extinguishes all other liens and

[10] The Dictator [1892] p 304

[11] Section 4 High Court (Admiralty Jurisdiction) Act 1961.

[12] K.S, *Admiralty Law and Practice* (London :Butterworth Publications Ltd;1998) pp 107-8

provides him with a clear title. An "*in rem*" action resolves claims of all of the world against the vessel, and no lien for past debts can be created or asserted. The proceeds of the sale are paid into the court and are used to satisfy any expenses incurred by the keeping of the vessel and fees to the Marshal. The balance is paid to the claimants and any balance left over is paid to the owner. If the sums received are not sufficient to pay all claims, the claimants pay proportionately to the shortfall. Unless the claimant/plaintiff who seized the vessel acts in bad faith, the owner of the vessel may not recover damages due to the arrest or for loss of profits.[13]

CLAIMS FOR ARREST

A. any claim to the possession or ownership of a ship or to the ownership of any share therein;
B. any question arising between the co-owners of a ship as to possession, employment, or earnings of that ship;
C. any claim in respect of a mortgage of or charge on a ship or any share therein;
D. any claim for damage done by a ship;
E. any claim for damage received by a ship;
F. any claim for loss of life or personal injury sustained in consequence of any defect in a ship or in her apparel or equipment, or of the wrongful act, neglect or default of the owners, charterers or persons in possession or control of a ship or of the master or crew thereof or of any other person for whose wrongful acts, neglects or defaults the owners, charterers or persons in possession or control of a ship responsible, being an act, neglect or default in the navigation or management of the ship, in the loading, carriage or discharge of goods on, in or from the ship or in the embarkation, carriage or disembarkation of persons on, in or from the ship;
G. any claim for loss of or damage to goods carried in a ship;

[13] See Dicey & Morris

H. any claim arising out of any agreement relating to the carriage of goods in a ship or to the use or hire of a ship;
I. any claim in the nature of salvage;
J. any claim in the nature of to wage in respect of a ship or an aircraft;
K. any claim in the nature of pilotage in respect of a ship or an aircraft;
L. any claim in respect of goods or materials supplied to a ship for her operation or maintenance;
M. any claim in respect of the construction, repair, or equipment of a ship or dock charges or dues;
N. any claim by a master or member of the crew of a ship for wages;
O. any claim by a master, shipper, charterer, or agent in respect of disbursements made on account of a ship;
P. any claim arising out of an ad which is or is claimed to be a general average act;
Q. any claim arising out of bottomry;
R. any claim for the forfeiture or condemnation of a ship or of goods which are being or have been carried, or have been attempted to be carried, in a ship, or for the restoration of a ship or any such goods after seizure, or for *droits* of admiralty.[14]

NIGERIAN ARREST LAW

The new Admiralty Jurisdiction Procedure Rules (AJPR 2011)[15] was made by the Chief Judge of the Federal High Court of Nigeria[16] on 1st March 2011 and came into force on 14 March 2011. This is pursuant to Section 254 of the Constitution of the Federal Republic of Nigeria 1999[17] and Section 21 of the Admiralty Jurisdiction Act (AJA) 1991,[18] which empower the CJS.1;F to make rules of practice and procedure for the FHC and to carry into effect the objects of the AJA. Together, the AJA and the AJPR govern admiralty matters in Nigeria, with the FHC as the court of first instance. The admiralty jurisdiction of the FHC is well

14 Order 70 of the Rules of High Court 1980.
15 The New Rules
16 Justice Daniel Abutu, FCI Arb, (as he then was)
17 CAP C20 LFN 2004.
18 Cap. A5,Laws of the Federation of Nigeria(LFN) 2004

stated in the AJA,[19] whilst the AJPR provides the procedure for the exercise of its jurisdiction. Appeals from the FHC lie to the Court of Appeal and the Supreme Court.

The New Rules are the result of the review of AJPR 1993 (Old Rules), which became necessary to keep up with the demands in shipping practice; noting the dynamic nature of the shipping industry. Various issues have been addressed in the AJPR 2011, with new rules added to bring the AJPR in line with modern shipping practices. There is in total, 23 Orders in the New Rules, amounting to an increase from the 17 Orders in the Old Rules.

CRITERIA FOR ARRESTING A SHIP IN NIGERIA

The process of applying for the arrest of a ship requires that the claimant possesses a 'Maritime Claim' as defined in Section 2 AJA. This generally means that the claim must be a 'proprietary maritime claim' or a 'general maritime claim' as follows: Proprietary maritime claims include claims relating to the possession of a ship, title to or ownership of a ship, or a share in a ship, mortgage of a ship or of a share in a ship, mortgage of a ship's freight or claims between co-owners of a ship relating to the possession, ownership, operation or earning of a ship. Also, claims for the satisfaction or enforcement of a judgment given by the court or a court (including a court of a foreign country) against a ship or other property in an admiralty proceeding *in rem*.[20]

General maritime claims include claims for damage done or received by a ship (whether by collision or otherwise), claims for loss of life, or for personal injury, sustained in consequence of a defect in a ship or in the apparel or equipment of a ship as well as arising out of an act or omission of the owners or characters of a ship. Once the claimant has ascertained that his claim falls within the meaning of a Maritime Claim as listed above, he may shall commence proceedings against the ship at the FHC in the judicial division covering the port or area where the ship is located.[21]

[19] Sections 1, 3 and 5 AJA Cap. A5,Laws of the Federation of Nigeria(LFN) 2004
[20] Sections 2(2) of the Admiralty Jurisdiction Act Cap. A5,Laws of the Federation of Nigeria(LFN) 2004
[21] Sections 2(3) of the Admiralty Jurisdiction Act Cap. A5,Laws of the Federation of Nigeria(LFN) 2004

SHIP ARREST DEVELOPMENTS IN NIGERIA

The New Rules, in its bid to update the AJPR, have provided new provisions, thus changing the face of ship arrest in Nigeria. Some of the important provisions are discussed below.

Application for the Arrest of a Ship

The new procedure for applying for the arrest of a ship is a statute based in Nigeria.[22] With this, a claimant with a Maritime Claim may now commence in-rem proceedings against the ship once the ship is within the jurisdiction or expected to arrive in the jurisdiction within three days at the time of filing the application.

This amounts to a major improvement as the Old Rules[23] failed to state whether a ship must be within the jurisdiction of the court or not, before an application for the arrest of the ship can be made to the Federal High Court. The practice therefore was for a ship to be within the jurisdiction of the court. This was premised on the fact that the Federal High Court cannot arrest a ship not within its jurisdiction, i.e., every open sea within twelve (12) nautical miles of the coast of Nigeria or of the seaward limits of inland waters, and that the grant of required to be filed for the warrant of arrest of a ship remains the same as under the Old Rules: Writ of summons; statement of claim; motion *ex parte* disclosing a strong prima facie case for the arrest of the ship; supporting affidavit stating the nature of the claim, that the ship is within the jurisdiction of the court or is expected to arrive jurisdiction within three days, and that the ship may leave the jurisdiction of the court at any time. The claimant is also required to provide an Affidavit of Urgency; Indemnity in favour of the Admiralty Marshal for his expenses in effecting the arrest order; and an undertaking as to damages in favour of the Defendants.

The new procedure for applying for a warrant of arrest of a ship deals with the lacuna in the Old Rules which allowed claimants to lose their window of opportunity to arrest a ship for a claim, simply because

---

[22] This is set out in Order 7, Rule 1 (1) Admiralty Jurisdiction Procedure Rules 2011.

[23] Order VII of the Admiralty Jurisdiction Procedure Rules 1993

they have to wait for the ship to be within jurisdiction before applying for a warrant of arrest.

Caveats

As part of the new procedure for obtaining a warrant of arrest for a ship, the New Rules clearly state that the Claimant shall be responsible for conducting a search of the caveat book for the purpose of ascertaining whether there is a caveat against arrest in force with respect to that ship.[24] This puts an end to lacunae in the Old Rules that allowed a claimant to obtain an arrest order for a ship, knowing that a caveat against arrest exists. This was the practice simply because the Old Rules did not require the Claimant to search the caveat register before applying for a warrant of arrest of a ship, and where such a caveat exists, inform the court accordingly.

Although the Practice for Caveat against Arrest — Form C in the Schedule to the Old Rules provides that the Caveator undertakes to appear within 14 days of service of a writ commencing an action against a ship, the Caveat against Arrest issued in practice and accepted by the Registrar/Admiralty Marshal provides that the caveator shall in a suit involving the ship within three days of been served. The New Rules have amended (Form 8 in the Schedule to the AJPR 2011) and brought the rules in line with practice.

Change in Beneficial Ownership

The provisions of the New Rules provide that a warrant of arrest of a ship may not be issued where the beneficial ownership of the ship has, since the issuance of the writ of summons, changed as a result of a sale or disposal by any court exercising admiralty jurisdiction.[25] It is, however, the duty of the new owner to inform the Federal High Court of his ownership of the ship to prevent the arrest of his ship.

Custody and Sale of Ship under Arrest

As you would recall, the application for a warrant of arrest constitutes an undertaking from the Claimant to the Court to pay the Admiralty

[24] Order 7 Rule 1(2) Admiralty Jurisdiction Procedure Rules 2011.
[25] Order 7 Rule 1(4) Admiralty Jurisdiction Procedure Rules 2011.

Marshal, on demand, an amount equal to the expenses of the Admiralty Marshal in relation to the arrest. As such, the Admiralty Marshal was allowed under the Old Rules to accept from the Claimant an amount not exceeding ₦5,000.00 (Approx. USD$32.30) as a deposit toward discharging its liability, and the Admiralty Marshal may make more demands for interim payments on account of those fees and expenses. This amount is clearly not commensurate to the demands of the time.

Whilst advising claimants on the ship arrest practice in Nigeria, it is estimated that the Admiralty Marshal's weekly cost is ₦100,000.00 (Approx. USD$645.15). Taking note of the current realities, the New Rules now provided that the "Admiralty Marshal may accept an amount of money not less than ₦100,000.00 and not more than ₦500,000.00 as a deposit toward discharging the liability; and make more demands for payment on account of those expenses."[26]

The Admiralty Marshal is also required to file a return or receipts and expenditures to the Court within seven working days of the release of the ship.

Judicial Sale of a Ship

In light of the various ships that litter the waterways of Nigeria as a result of ship owners failing to provide bail for the release of vessels under arrest or entering an appearance in a suit, Order 9, Rule 6(2) of the New Rules now empowers the court on the application of the arrestor or other interested party order the sale of the ship where the bail or sufficient security has not been provided six months after the date of arrest.

The ship is to be sold by the Admiralty Marshal and the proceeds of sale paid into an interest-yielding fixed deposit account in the name of the Admiralty Marshal pending further orders of the court.

Reparation for Needless Arrest

One of the most notable changes to ship arrest practice under the New Rules is the issue of reasonable compensation for needless arrest.[27]

---

[26] Order 9, Rule 2 (2d) Admiralty Jurisdiction Procedure Rules 2011.

[27] This is addressed under Order 11, Rule 2 AJPR

Under the Old Rules, if it appears to the Court that the arrest of any defendant, or any order of attachment, sale, or injunction, or any warrant to stop clearance of or to arrest any ship was applied for on insufficient grounds; or if the suit in which any such application was made is dismissed, or judgment is given against the plaintiff by default or otherwise, and it appears to the Court that there was no probable ground for instituting such suit, the court may (on the application of the defendant made at any time before the expiration of 3 months from the termination of the suit) award against the plaintiff such amount, not exceeding the sum of ₦20,000.00, as it may deem a reasonable compensation to the defendant for any loss, injury, or expenses which he may have sustained as a result of such arrest, attachment, order of sale or injunction, as aforesaid.

The maximum sum of ₦20,000.00 for compensation for the needless arrest of a ship has been highly criticized for a few years. The frivolous and/or vindictive arrest orders obtained over the years by various claimants have been blamed on this provision as it does not serve as a deterrent.

The New Rules, understanding the economic importance of a ship arrest to a ship owner has provided the Court with the power to "award against the plaintiff such amount as it may deem reasonable compensation to the defendant for any loss, injury, or expenses which he may have sustained as a result of such arrest, attachment, order of sale or injunction."

Order 11, Rule 2 AJPR would definitely serve as a deterrent to false applications for arrest orders and prevent an abuse of the court process.

PART II

The second part of this chapter juxtaposes mortgages and the arrest of the ship, bringing out the salient necessities a mortgagee needs to pay attention to.

Historically, mortgagees have favoured judicial sale as a method of enforcement, but in recent times, they have appeared reluctant to arrest vessels and have sought to restructure loans wherever possible, notwithstanding the inevitable financial haircut. However, with time running out for many owners, mortgagees are again looking at judicial sale. It must be mentioned from the onset that a mortgagee needs to ask himself certain questions before deciding whether to arrest.

Is the Mortgagee Able to Arrest?

Where events of default exist, which may well include a payment default, a mortgagee will usually have little difficulty in crystallizing a right to arrest the mortgaged vessel. The statute[28] gives a mortgagee, whose mortgage is by deed and contains no contrary intention, a power of sale if the mortgage is due at law.[29]

A further consideration is whether the mortgagee has an agreement with either the owner or, more commonly, a charterer of the vessel which restricts its ability to arrest. If the vessel is on charter when the mortgagee wishes to take action, a clear conflict of interest will arise between the charterer and the mortgagee, the charterer generally wanting action to be deferred until the end of the charter period.

Outstanding Debts

This is extremely important when evaluating whether or not to arrest. If there are significant outstanding debts, especially if they threaten to rank ahead of mortgage claims, such as those having the status of maritime liens,[30] the judicial sale[31] may not be the best option.

Rank of a Mortgagee in the List of Priorities

Assuming the mortgagee is not prevented from arresting, he would be well advised to do a cost-benefit analysis at this stage.[32] In simple terms

---

[28] Section 125 of the Property and Conveyancing Law or Section 20 Conveyancing Act 1881.

[29] The mortgage is said to be due at law when the legal date for redemption has passed or an instalment of the principal is in arrears. See the case of *Intercity bank Plc.* v. *Feed and Food Farms Nig. Ltd & Ors.* (2001) 17 NWLR (pt. 742) 347. *Ahaneku* v. *Iheaturu* (1995) 2 NWLR (pt. 380) 758.

[30] Section 5(3) of the AJA, which involves claims of maritime lien, a maritime lien may be invoked against a ship, aircraft or property for (i) salvage, (ii) damage done by a ship, (iii) wages of master or member of the crew, and (iv) master's disbursement.

[31] See generally Sections 74, 75, and 76 of the Merchant Shipping Act, 2007.

[32] A necessary consequence of judicial sale is that the available money realised from the sale will be used to settle creditors, as often in maritime practice the available funds will not be enough to settle all the claimants, thus the age long principle of ranking in order of priority is followed in establishing who get paid first, etc., subject always to the amount of money remaining unutilized at every stage been enough to meet the next set of payment. See the cases of *Hallyon Isle* (1980 3) ALL E. R. 197, *Loannis Das Kalelis*

- is it worth arresting the vessel and selling her or is it better simply to allow the status quo to remain undisturbed? The second alternative is likely to be preferred only if the mortgagee is anxious not to incur a substantial write-off in respect of the outstanding indebtedness in the near future or if - exceptionally these days - the vessel is employed on a lucrative charter.

In evaluating these alternatives, a mortgagee should consider not just the potential sale price of the vessel as against the outstanding amounts due under the loan but also what portion of the proceeds of sale is likely to be paid to the mortgagee when at the end of judicial sale proceedings, the court determines priorities between competing claimants and orders the sale proceeds to be paid out of court in accordance with that determination.

When money from the sale of a vessel is paid into court, it does not necessarily get paid out entirely to the arresting party: The court determines priorities in accordance with local law and practice; where the mortgagee ranks in the list of priorities is a major consideration in determining whether the jurisdiction is a "favourable" one for mortgage enforcement. The system of priorities is not the same in every jurisdiction and local law advice should always be taken at an early stage.

A mortgagee may assume that the court's arrest expenses (e.g., security guard, port dues, etc.), which he must fund, and the court's commission on sale will be deducted first from the proceeds of the sale. Once the vessel is under arrest, there will be arrest expenses such as port charges, bunkers, fresh water, and other items. These costs will vary from one jurisdiction to another and will depend on the length of time between arrest and sale.

(1974) 1 Lloyds Rep. *De Lyrmas* (1978) 2 Lloyds Rep. 300. *De Conet* (1965) 1 ALL E.R. 956. Where the following ranking process was followed: 1, Statutory Court and other charges and cost. 2, Cost of arrest and sale of the *rex.* 3, Possessory lien created prior to maritime lien. 4, Maritime lien which rank *inter se* from salvage, collision, Damages, seamen and master wages. 5, Possessory lien and necessaries. 6, Registered mortgages and other Charges. 7, Statutory right in rem. 8, other creditors. Maritime liens are traditionally "common law" liens, though now recognized under statute, see Section 75 of the Merchant Shipping Act 2007.

Maritime Liens

The next important ranking will be maritime liens. English law recognizes only a limited number of maritime liens: crew wages, master's disbursements, salvage, and damage done by a ship.[33] The existence of a valid maritime lien may mean that the mortgagee recovers little or nothing because the amount successfully recovered by the maritime lien holders is close to, or even exceeds the sale proceeds of the vessel.

It is important, therefore, to ascertain as far as possible whether any maritime liens exist and if they do, whether they are covered by the vessel's insurances. This is not always easy to do if the owner is unwilling to co-operate since there is no system of registration of liens. Inquiries can be made in the market and of the club with which the

---

[33] Other jurisdictions notably the USA - recognize a greater number of maritime liens, and the following relative priority of competing claims can be used for guidance:

1. Expenses of justice. These are the claims associated with the administration of justice while the vessel is under arrest, or *custodia legis* . Such expenses include U.S. Marshal's fees, substitute custodian fees and other expenses necessary to preserve the ship while under arrest. See *The Poznan* , 274 U.S. 117 (1927*); Gen. Elec. Credit & Leasing Corp.* v. *Drill Ship Mission Exploration,* 668 F.2d 811 (5 th Cir. 1982). Although not considered liens, as seizure terminates the owner's ability to contract for services, these expenses are granted top priority and are founded in the philosophy that the preservation of the vessel, while under arrest, inures to the benefit of all claimants.
2. Seaman's wage claims, maintenance and cure, including liens for wages of the master. *Thorsteinsson* v. *M/V Drangur,* 891 F.2d 1547 (11 th Cir. 1990); *Chung, Yong IL* v. *Overseas Nav. Co. , Ltd.,* 774 F.2d 1043, 1049 (11 th Cir. 1985*); Fredelos* v. *Merritt-Chapman & Scott Corp. ,* 447 F.2d 435, 437 (5 th Cir. 1971).
3. Salvage and general average contribution. As between competing salvers, the most recent services provided to the vessel outrank earlier efforts. *Complaint of Ta Chi Na* v. *Corp.,* S.A., 583 F. Supp. 1322 (S.D.N.Y. 1984).
4. Maritime tort claims, including collision, personal injury, wrongful death, liability for cargo loss, and property damage caused by negligence. *Oriente Commercial, Inc.* v. *American Flag Vessel, M/V Floridian* , 529 F.2d 221 (4 th Cir. 1975); *European-American Banking Corp.* v. *M/S Rosaria* , 486 F. Supp. 245 (S.D. Miss. 1978). See also *Fredelos,* 447 F.2d at 437.
5. Pre-mortgage contract claims for necessaries such as services, fuel, dockage and supplies provided to the vessel, 46 U.S.C. §§31301(4), 31341 and 31342;
6. A valid preferred mortgage on a U.S. flag ship or a preferred mortgage on a foreign vessel whose mortgage has been guaranteed under Title XI of the Merchant Marine Act of 1936, 46 U.S.C. §§30101-31343.
7. Maritime contract claims, including claims by suppliers for necessaries and repairs pursuant to the Maritime Lien Act. *Fredelos* , 447 F.2d at 437; 46 U.S.C. §§ 31301(4), 31341, 31342.
8. A valid preferred mortgage on a foreign flag ship; 46 U.S.C. 31326(b)(2); *Sasportes* v. *M/V Sol de Copacabana* , 581 F.2d 1204 (5 th Cir. 1978).
9. State-created liens of a maritime nature. The Diane , 45 F. Supp. 510 (S.D. Fla. 1942).
10. Maritime liens for penalties and forfeitures for violation of federal statutes.
11. Preferred non-maritime liens including tax liens and judgment liens.
12. Maritime liens in bankruptcy. In Nigeria maritime lien is covered by statute see generally section 5(3) of the Merchant Shipping Act, 2007.

vessel is entered. A mortgagee may instruct an agent to contact the master to find out whether crew wages are in arrears.

The existence of claims having priority over mortgage claims may not become apparent until after the vessel is arrested and possibly after she is sold.[34] In practice, vessels arrested first by an unsecured creditor (other than one who is a maritime lien claimant) are usually released once he realizes that the outstanding indebtedness under the mortgage vastly exceeds the value of the vessel (as is invariably the case). The mortgagee will then take over the arrest.

Where to Arrest?

If a mortgagee has decided that he does wish to arrest the vessel, the next question is where to arrest. A common misconception is that the place of arrest depends on the vessel's flag. This is not the case. The ability to arrest depends on the physical location of the vessel. The Admiralty jurisdiction of courts in many ports may be invoked by issuing a claim and the vessel proceeded against arrested if that vessel is physically located within the territorial jurisdiction of the court.[35]

Tracking the vessel's movements may be necessary. A mortgagee may be aware of the vessel's trading pattern, if not her exact location. If he is co-operating, the owner may direct the vessel to a preferred port for arrest. If not, ship watch services can locate the vessel and identify her next port of call. A coordinated approach is desirable where there are several mortgaged vessels to be arrested.

In choosing a jurisdiction, it is generally prudent to take local legal advice regarding notices, local arrest and sale procedures, duration, expense, and priorities between the mortgagee and other classes of the claimant.

CONCLUSION

The AJPR 2011 has improved maritime practice in Nigeria. The rules were timely as they focused on current realities in the industry. Notwithstanding the problems that can arise, judicial sale is still a

---

34 In which case they, like all other claims, will stand against the sale proceeds held in court.

35 See Section 3 of the Admiralty Jurisdiction Act, CAP A5 LFN 2004.

common way for a mortgagee to realise the value of its security. The key benefit is that a bill of sale executed in Admiralty proceedings has the effect of transferring title to the vessel free and clear of all claims, liens and encumbrances. A bill of sale executed in one jurisdiction is generally recognised as having this effect by courts in other jurisdictions. This means that a buyer can purchase the vessel without concerning himself about pre-existing claims, including maritime liens. Consequently a mortgagee will usually not need to provide the buyer with an indemnity. Another alternative that has become utilized more recently by institutions which have a large investment in the shipping industry is to retain the ship and operate it as a going concern. This approach, which essentially hinges upon increases in shipping market rates, could ultimately produce a very huge outcome.

Chapter 26

FORMS OF BUSINESS ASSOCIATIONS IN NIGERIA

Halima Doma Kutigi (Ph.D)*

INTRODUCTION

The term, "Business" may be defined as the organised effort of an individual (or individuals) to produce and sell, for a profit, goods and services that satisfy society's needs.[1] A business seeks to make profit through individuals working towards common goals, which would vary based on the type of business and the business strategy being used. Regardless of the chosen strategy, a business must provide some sort of service or product that meets the needs of society in some way using agents like firms, government, charitable associations, etc.[2]. Business organization refers to all necessary arrangements required to conduct a business; it refers to all those steps that need to be undertaken for establishing relationships between men, material, and machinery to carry on business efficiently for earning profits.

It then follows that in every society, issues that pertain to business are very vital. However, the nature, organization, and framework that regulate business operations differ from one society to another. Nigeria is not an exception. This Chapter examines the different types of business arrangements in Nigeria, their formulation, and requirements for registration. The legal and institutional frameworks that regulate the operation of business in Nigeria are also discussed with emphasis on

* Faculty of Law, Nasarawa State University, Keffi; Visiting Lecturer, BAZE University, Abuja.

[1] Pride, Hughes and Kapoor, *Business* (12th edn, Cengage Learning, 2012) 10.

[2] Ibid.

innovations in the recently enacted Companies and Allied Matters Act, 2020.

THE GROWTH OF BUSINESS IN NIGERIA

The Nigerian society from pre-colonial era to date has thrived on various types of businesses between the different kingdoms that now form the country. In the past, the only occupations known to Nigerians were farming, hunting, fishing, and trading, which were all carried out on a small scale. Trade was generally restricted to internal commerce in rural peasant economies, although there was some trans-Saharan trade dealings between North Africa and the northern parts of Nigeria. With the advent of the Europeans, economic activities started to expand up to the period of the establishment of British Authority over Nigeria in the nineteenth century. The trade growth continued in the early twentieth century (with agriculture taking the lead) and it was at this point that the first company's regulation statute, that is, the Companies Ordinance, 1912 was promulgated. This growth of the economy was interrupted by World War I (1914-1918), after which there was a partial economic revival. This development was again disturbed by the economic depression of the 1930s and World War II (1939-1945). However, the second war came with some blessings, as it brought out the economic potential of many countries including Nigeria, not only to Britain but also to other Allied Powers.[3]

The dawn after World War II saw the institution of a Ten-Year Development Plan (1945-1955) for:

(a) Re-organising the handling and marketing of the agricultural primary produce of the country and the improvement of social welfare and economic facilities; and

(b) Developing commerce and industry in the country which led to the setting up of public corporations and boards on the one hand and on the other, the encouragement of private enterprise through

[3] Ibid, 4.

the provision of loans by Government Loan Boards for industrial and commercial development.[4]

The aim of development in commerce and industry was to create awareness of the existing opportunities in organized private enterprising in the country for its citizenry. However, due to the low availability of human capital at that time, many people were excited to take advantage of the offers by various government loan schemes. Beneficiaries of these loan schemes invariably began to form trade associations which later transformed to registered businesses and companies. This situation was accelerated by the rapid economic growth of the early 1950s when some measure of political power was conceded to the Nigerian people by the British Colonial System and became even more vigorous at Independence in 1960. Ever since, government has continued to make concerted efforts to encourage Nigerians towards private enterprise and participation in the economic activities of the country. One of such efforts found expression in the Nigerian Enterprise Promotion Act, 1972 as amended in 1977.[5] The purpose of this Act was to deliberately reserve for Nigerians certain portion and areas of the economy which they had capital and relevant experience to run effectively while ensuring that in other areas of the economy, Nigerians equally had access to opportunities of participating in such areas. Thus, in effect, the 1972 Act did not only prohibit foreigners (non-Nigerians) from starting certain reserved new businesses but it also compelled them to sell to Nigerians all their interest in any business listed in the First Schedule of the Act, and to transfer to Nigerians their interests in companies listed in the Second Schedule in excess of 40 per cent of the equity, or 60 per cent of business listed in the Third Schedule to the Act. Over a thousand companies were affected by this law, which had many companies

---

[4] Ibid.

[5] Ismaila Mohammed, 'The Nigerian Enterprises Promotion Decrees (1972 and 1977) and Indigenization in Nigeria' being a Thesis Submitted for the Degree of PhD at the University of Warwick, University of Warwick institutional repository<http://go.warwick.ac.uk/wrap> accessed 9/11/118.

transferring equity through private placement, and others being listed on the stock exchange.[6]

Expectedly at that time, most businesses carried out by foreigners were operated as companies which many Nigerians desired to run by themselves. Hence, the policy enunciated by the law came at what could be said to be the right time as that period witnessed an increase in the number of incorporated and registered businesses. Also, the effect of the 'oil boom' of the 1970s caused the phenomenal rise in the number of incorporated companies and businesses.

UNITS OF BUSINESS ORGANIZATION

A business can be organized in several ways, and the form of organization affects the legal and tax liability of the company and its owners. The most common units of business organization are discussed as follows:

Individual

This is the oldest and most common unit of business undertaking in Nigeria. It can be traced from pre-civilization era through colonial era, to this time. While this system may appear to be quite satisfying and indispensable to the social and economic need, it lacks assured continuity and so cannot easily attract capital for development of the business. More so, since there is no limit to the liability of the individual arising from his business, the business can readily be ruined.

Partnership

A partnership is 'the relation which subsists between two persons carrying on business with a view of profit.'[7] The law regulating the relation between partners *inter se* and between the partners and outsiders can be found in the various partnership laws of the States as supplemented by the common law. Often times an individual or a partnership may carry on business under a business name. Such name

---

[6] Vincent Ola, "Using Local Resources to Achieve Increase in Productivity", *Nigerian Business Digest* (Universal Publications 1979).

[7] See, Partnership Laws of Lagos State, 2003.

may be required to be registered under the Companies and Allied Matters Act CAP C20, Laws of the Federation of Nigeria (LFN) 2004, now repealed and re-enacted as CAMA 2020.

Co-operative Societies

In Nigeria, there are statutory provisions for the formation and registration of co-operative societies.[8] A co-operative society is an autonomous association of persons united voluntarily to meet their common economic, social and cultural needs and aspirations through a jointly owned and democratically controlled enterprise. It is a system where individuals pull funds together to either invest in a particular business for profit or to finance projects or businesses of their own. Unlike other types of businesses which have shareholders, cooperatives sell shares to cooperative "members," who then have a say in the operations and direction of the cooperative itself. The main difference in the process of becoming a cooperative, as opposed to the other types of businesses listed, is that the organization must create by-laws, have a membership application and have a board of directors with a charter member meeting. Examples of such cooperatives exist in almost every public institution in Nigeria where civil servants of a particular cadre level or department make monthly or annual contributions which they invest in a venture outside the office for profits of share what has been gathered at the end of the year, serving like a type of savings account. Most often members are allowed to take loans from such cooperatives with a very minimum percentage of interest. Similarly, most tribal and regional meetings also practice this type of business, popularly known as '*Adashi*' or '*Esusu*'.

Co-operative societies are advantageous in the sense that the registration process makes it a corporation with perpetuity, and with power to hold property and enter into contracts.

Statutory Corporations

These are corporations set up by the Government for the purpose of participation in the economic activities of the country. While some of

[8] Nigerian Co-operative Societies Act, 1993, re-enacted as the Nigerian Cooperative Society Act, 2004.

the statutory corporations are essentially for social services (for example, the Agricultural Credit Corporation which has grown into the Agriculture Banks and other loan and finance corporations), others are largely commercial, and generally operate like private corporations. Due to lack of sustainable success, some of these government owned business ventures have been, and are still being privatised.[9]

Quasi-corporations

Sometimes, certain unincorporated bodies are given some functions in the discharge of which they may own property or enter into contractual relations. Examples are the boards of governors of schools which are set up by statute but without incorporation. Although they have no distinct legal personality, they are in some circumstances given status analogous to that of legal persons.[10]

Registered Companies

This is by far the most important unit of business organization for modern economic activities, and even more so in a developing economy as Nigeria. This is due to its legal personality, perpetual succession, the opportunity for investment and raising capital, and the strict legal control and protection of members and creditors. The registered company has played and will continue to play an ever-increasing role in the development of the national economy.

FORMS OF BUSINESSES IN NIGERIA

An investor, who intends to commence any business in Nigeria, must first make a choice on the form of business having in mind the legal configuration that defines the rights and liabilities of participants in the ownership, control, personal liability, life spam and financial structure of the business. In Nigeria the different forms and structure of businesses undertaken can be classified into the following:

---

[9] See the Privatization and Commercialization Act, 1984.

[10] See *Taff Vale Railway Co.* v. *Amalgamated Society of Railway Servants* [1901] AC 426; *Andrew Thomas* v. *Local Government Service Board* [1966] NMLR 310; *Kpebimoh* v. *Board of Governors Ijaw TTC* [1966] NMLR 130.

Sole Proprietorship

Sole proprietorship is one of the most popular form of business not just in Nigeria but in the world, because it only requires a single person to create. It is the simplest form of enterprise as it is owned and managed by a single individual. A major feature of this form of business is the absence of legal or financial distinction from the owner, which means that the business owner is fully accountable for all the profits, liabilities and legal issues that the business may encounter. It is the form of enterprise where the owner is exposed to the greatest personal risks because the sole trader is personally responsible for all aspects of the business and bears unlimited liability to all debts and legal actions.

The good thing about a sole proprietorship is that there is no need to fill out any forms or go through any legal procedure before engaging in the business. However, the law in Nigeria allows for the registration of a sole proprietorship business name, so that another person doesn't trade in that same name. The discussion on registered companies will provide details of how this registration can be done in Nigeria. It should however be kept in mind that, depending on the type of goods or services the sole proprietorship intends to engage in, the sole trader or proprietor may be required to have specific qualification, license or certified documents.

Advantages of Sole Proprietorship

1. Sole proprietors have complete control of their business – a sole proprietor has only himself to answer to. His judgments (good or bad), is his own responsibility.
2. Ease of formation and dissolution as it costs relatively little to start.
3. Personal attention to consumer needs. In a sole proprietorship business, one generally finds the proprietor taking personal care of consumer needs as most proprietorships normally function within a small geographical area.
4. Equitable distribution of wealth. Sole proprietorship business is generally a small scale business, hence there is an opportunity for many individuals to own and manage small business units. This

enables widespread dispersion of economic wealth and diffuses concentration of business in the hands of few.

5. Profits from the business flow through directly to the owners' personal tax return.

Disadvantages of Sole Proprietorship

1. Sole proprietors have unlimited liability and are legally responsible for all debts against the business. Their business and personal assets are at risk since there is no distinction of both when it comes to satisfying liability.
2. Sole proprietors are mostly at a disadvantage when it comes to raising funds, as they are often limited to using funds from personal savings or consumer loans which in the long run could be injurious to both the business and the owner.
3. The sole proprietorship may have a hard time attracting high-calibre employees, or those that are motivated by the opportunity or prospect of owing a part of the business in the future.
4. Management limitations. The sole proprietor who is the sole owner doubles as the sole manager and cannot be a specialist in all fields. He is a jack of all trades and master of none.
5. Uncertainty of duration, since sole proprietorship business is linked with the life of the proprietor. Thus, illness, death or insolvency of the owner brings an end to the business. This reason further makes it difficult to attract high-calibre experts for fear of job security.

Partnership

A partnership is a voluntary association of two or more individuals carrying on business for the purpose of making profit as the result of such association. In forming a partnership, no real formalities are required. A partnership can be formed orally, in writing or by conduct (practice) – even though it is advisable to reduce all such agreements into writing.

According to Section 1(1) of the Partnership Act, 1890, a partnership is the relationship which subsists between persons carrying on business in common with a view to making profit. Only a maximum of 20 people can validly form a partnership in Nigeria, so a partnership with more than 20 persons is illegal. A partnership may involve any professional or commercial venture established with the motive or intent of making profit, even though the business does not have to actually make profits.[11] Thus, profit-making and profit- sharing are considered in law *prima facie* evidence of the existence of a partnership.

Akin to sole proprietorship, the law does not distinguish between the partnership business and its owners, i.e. the partners. A partnership business lacks legal capacity of its own, therefore, the partners are personally responsible for all the profits as well as all the debts and liabilities of the partnership unless it has crystallized into a registered company. Equality of equity is the rule in partnership unless otherwise agreed by the partners. As every partner is jointly and severally liable for the liability of the partnership, there is no separate legal responsibility for the partners. Thus, the basic or essential elements of partnership are: agreement, contribution of capital, sharing of profit, conflict resolution, dissolution of the partnership amongst others. As in the case of the sole proprietorship, if the partners use a name for the business established by the partnership other than their names, for it to remain exclusively theirs and avoid conflict with any other business name existing like that within their area of business, they will be required to register the name of the business with the CAC.

Advantages of Partnership

1. Partnerships are relatively easy to establish; however, time should be invested in developing the terms and clauses of the partnership.
2. With more than one owner, the ability to raise more funds may be increased or is higher.
3. Where the partners are all involved in one form of management or the other, it means decisions to be taken can be scrutinized better, since two heads are better than one.

[11] This clearly excludes non-profit organizations (such as associations, clubs, societies etc.).

4. Partnership can attract employees with valuable expertise or of high-calibre if the prospect of becoming a partner is made available. It is also a motivational booster for employees to ensure maximum productivity.
5. The business will in most cases benefit from partners who have complementary skills or expertise.

Disadvantages of Partnership

1. Partners are jointly and individually liable for the actions and inactions of the other partners.
2. Profit is shared between the partners. There is no 100 per cent return on profits for an individual in partnership.
3. Since decisions are often shared, disagreements can occur which could delay making or executing of critical decisions.
4. The partnership may have limited life span or duration; it may end abruptly upon the withdrawal or death of a partner.

Types of Partnership

a. **General Partnership:** Partners divide responsibility for management and liability, as well as the shares of profit or loss according to their internal agreement. Generally, equal shares are assumed unless there is a written agreement that states differently.

b. **Limited Partnership /Partnership with Limited Liability (LLP):** "Limited" here means that most of the partners have limited liability (to the extent of their investment) as well as limited input regarding management decision, which generally encourages investors for short term projects, or for investing in capital assets. LLP as a business structure is now recognised in Nigeria by virtue of the new Act[12]. It therefore positions the legal structures in Nigeria to operate with that of other provinces.

c. **Joint Venture:** Acts like a general partnership, but is clearly for a limited period of time or a single project. If the partners in a joint venture repeat the activity, they will be recognised as an ongoing

[12] CAMA 2020, Sections 746-810.

partnership and will have to file as such, and distribute accumulated partnership assets upon dissolution of the entity. This type of formation of business is used when the purpose of the joint venture between the parties is for a short term. One of it benefits is that it is relatively set up, and so eases the working relationship between the partners. Investors can make use of joint ventures where the business is in respect of a specific individual project with a limited period of time. The Nigerian National Petroleum Corporation has several joint ventures with private oil companies and some of her subsidiaries for the purposes of either executing a certain project or short term contractual relationship for certain services.

Registered Business/Company (Corporations)

Registered businesses/companies (also referred to as corporations or incorporated companies or bodies corporate), are businesses registered under the Nigerian Companies and Allied Matters Act (CAMA). A registered business is considered by law to be a unique entity, separate and distinct from those who own it. A Corporation can be taxed, it can be sued, and it can enter into contractual agreements. The owners of a corporation are its shareholders. The shareholders elect a board of directors to oversee the major policies and decisions. The corporation has a life of its own and does not dissolve when ownership changes.

There are different types of companies from which promoters can choose to incorporate depending on the content or substance of the business they wish to undertake. Factors that inform which choice a promoter would make include: whether the promoter wishes that the liability of the owners of the company be limited or unlimited; whether the goal of the company is to become a large company or grow as a small company; whether it intends to source for funds from the public; whether it intends not to make profits but still carry on business, *inter alia.*

Features of a Registered Business/Company as a Form of Business[13]

Legal Personality: The company is a legal person distinct from its shareholders. It has rights and obligations; it can hold property and contract in its own name and it can sue and be sued. The liability of the members may be limited, in which case they will generally not be liable for more than the amount remaining unpaid on their shares. With regards to business name and partnership, the liability is normally unlimited and personal:

i. Number of Members: A company may consist of a large number as desired. However, the minimum number of people that can set up a private company has been reduced to one by provisions of CAMA 2020 as opposed to the former minimum requirement of two people;[14]
ii. Perpetual Succession: this is a special advantage of a registered company and is likely to encourage investment in companies more than in partnerships;
iii. Management: Unlike partnerships, the management of a company is vested in the directors who are accountable to the shareholders at the general meeting. The directors alone will be liable for mismanagement, whereas a partner cannot escape liability for wrongs done by the partnership;
iv. Borrowing Powers: the company enjoys the special privilege of being able to issue debentures especially by way of floating charges, in other words, equitable charges on the assets of the time being, of a going concern. On the other hand, when an individual or partnership borrows on a security, it must be by a fixed charge on specific property and when the property is a chattel the relevant Bills of Sales Law must be complied with;[15]
v. Transfer of Shares: unlike a partnership, the shares of a company (especially public company) are freely transferable and the transferee becomes a member of the company of the company. The shares of a

---

[13] (n 1) 4-5.
[14] CAMA S.18 (2).
[15] See the Bills of Sales Law of Lagos State, 1973.

company may be quoted on the Nigerian Stock Exchange, thus providing an easy market for the shares;

vi. Taxation: while an individual carrying business either alone or in a partnership is taxed on the basis of personal income tax, a company is taxed under the Companies Income Tax Act, 1979[16] with different incidents.

Advantages of Registered Business/Company as a Form of Business

1. Shareholders have limited liability for the corporation's debts or judgments against the corporation.
2. Generally, shareholders can only be held accountable for their investment in stock of the company. (Note however, that officers can be held personally liable for their actions, such as the failure to withhold and pay employment taxes.
3. Corporations can raise additional funds through the sale of stock.
4. A Corporation may deduct the cost of benefits it provides to officers and employees.

Disadvantages of Registered Business/Company as a Form of Business

1. The process of incorporation requires more time and money than other forms of organization.
2. Corporations are monitored by federal, state and some local agencies, and as a result may have more paperwork to comply with regulations.
3. Incorporating may result in higher overall taxes. Dividends paid to shareholders are not deductible from business income; thus this income can be taxed twice.

REGISTRATION OF BUSINESS IN NIGERIA

One of the primary aspects of starting a business enterprise is registering the business to make it a legitimate entity. The Corporate

[16] CAP C21, LFN, 2004.

Affairs Commission is the Agency empowered by the CAMA[17] to register businesses in Nigeria. The categories for business registration under the Act are: Business Name, Incorporated Companies (which could be limited by shares, unlimited or without shares), and Incorporated Trustees.[18] The process and procedure for registration are also clearly stipulated in CAMA.[19]

Registration of Business Name

A Business Name is registered under Part B of CAMA. Businesses registered under this Part are normally Sole Proprietorships and ordinary Partnerships. Thus, Sections 18–587 of CAMA provide for the formation, registration, operation, liability for defaults and guiding regulations of Business Name.

Procedure for Registering a Business Name[20]

Step A: Reservation of Name

This is the first step prior to the registration of a Business Name in Nigeria. An investor is required to supply proposed alternative name options for the Business Name in the prescribed form to the Corporate Affairs Commission (CAC). The CAC will then determine whether or not any of the proposed names are available for use. Where any are deemed available and approved by the CAC, one of the options will be reserved for that particular investor for a period of sixty days to allow for registration.

Step B: Submission of relevant documents to the CAC:

These documents are approved reservation of name form, duly completed Business Name registration form, 2 (two) passport size photographs of each investor, and certificates of professional qualification where necessary.

---

[17] Pursuant to Part B of CAMA 2020.

[18] CAMA 2020, Sections 21- 26.

[19] Ibid S.41.

[20] It is to be noted that in line with the Commission's desire to ease cost of doing business in Nigeria, it has introduced online registration of all business organizations with the aim of starting and completing registration within 24 hours after the approval of the application of name reservation.

Step C: Payment of the prescribed fees and stamp duties at the bank desk at the CAC.

Step D: Registration and provision of Certificate.

Registration of Incorporated Companies

There are different types of incorporated companies in Nigeria. We have the limited liability companies which can either be private or public; the companies limited by guarantee, and the unlimited liability companies.[21] Sections 22 –563 of CAMA provide for the promotion, formation, incorporation, operation and structure of incorporated companies. CAMA also makes provisions for the financial health status, and winding up procedures where necessary.

Procedure for Registering an Incorporated Company

CAMA provides under Part B for the process of incorporating limited and unlimited liability companies,[22] and also companies limited by guarantee. The procedure is as follows:

Step A: Reservation of Name

An investor is required to supply proposed alternative name options for the Company in the prescribed form to the CAC. The CAC will then determine whether or not any of the proposed names are available for use. Where any are deemed available and approved by the CAC, one of the options will be reserved for that particular investor for a period of sixty days to allow for incorporation.

Step B: Submission of relevant documents to the CAC.[23]

The documents required to be submitted here include: approved reservation of name form, duly completed Incorporation forms, duly stamped Memorandum and Articles of Association (2 copies), certification of proficiency where required, and copies of means of identification of the directors.

---

[21] CAMA 2020 S.21.

[22] Ibid., S.25-35.

[23] Ibid., S.36.

Step C: Payment of the prescribed fees and stamp duties at the Bank Desk in the CAC

Step D: Incorporation and provision of Certificate

Registration of Incorporated Trustees

Incorporated Trustees are incorporated companies for non-profit organizations such as religious bodies, associations, and non-governmental organizations.[24] This type of company is provided for under Sections 823-850 of CAMA covering its formation, operation, structure as well as winding up. Notably, Incorporated Trustees with similar aims and objectives can now merge under CAMA 2020.[25]

Procedure for* Registering *Incorporated Trustees

CAMA provides under Part C for the procedure of incorporation of Incorporated Trustees as follows:

Step A: Reservation of Name

As stated previously, this is the first step prior to incorporation of any company in Nigeria.

An investor is required to supply proposed alternative name options for the Company in the prescribed form to the Corporate Affairs Commission. The CAC will then determine whether or not any of the proposed names are available for use. Where any are deemed available and approved by the CAC, one of the options will be reserved for that particular investor for a period of sixty days to allow for incorporation.

Step B: Submission of the following documents to the CAC

- The approved reservation of name form.
- Duly completed incorporation forms.
- Formal application for registration signed by the chairman and secretary.

[24] A non-profit organization is a business organization that is intended to promote educational or charitable purposes. The "non-profit" aspect comes into play in that any money earned by the company must be kept by the organization to pay for its expense, programs, etc. There are several types of non-profit organizations available, many of which can receive "tax exemption" status. This process requires filing paperwork, including an application addressed to the government to recognize the organization as a non-profit organization.

[25] Section 849.

- Extracts of minutes of general meeting appointing trustees and adoption of special clause in the constitution signed by the chairman and secretary. The extracts of minutes shall also list members present and the voting pattern.
- Two printed copies of the constitution.
- Trustees' declaration form duly deposed to by each trustee in the high court.
- Impression of the common seal of the association on the application form.
- Notice of the situation of the address of the association or any change therein.
- Payment of filing fees.
- Cuttings (or National Library certified copy) of publication page of 3 x 2 notice of application for registration in two daily newspapers one of which must circulate in the locality of the association and the other a national newspaper.
- The newspaper publication shall state the name and principal object of the association, the full names of the proposed trustees; and invite objections to the name, objects or persons stated as trustees of the association within 28 days of publication.
- Thumb prints by illiterate trustees or officers shall be accompanied by a jurat.

Step C: Payment of the prescribed fees and stamp duties at the Bank Desk in the CAC

Step D: Incorporation and provision of Certificate

OTHER REQUIREMENTS FOR COMPANY REGISTRATION IN NIGERIA

CAMA 2020 now excludes small companies from the requirement of having a minimum of two directors as required under the previous Act. This means that small companies can now be registered with one director; as is the case with shareholder.[26] CAMA requires every foreign

[26] A small company is defined under CAMA as a private company having an annual turnover of N 120,000,000 and net assets value of not more than ₦60,000,000. It has no foreigner as its members and where the company has a share capital, the directors hold at least 51% of the share capital.

company that intends to do business in Nigeria to register a separate entity in Nigeria for that purpose. Notwithstanding this requirement, the law creates instances where a foreign company can be exempted from the requirement of registration.

Every company after registration is required to disclose on its letterhead papers, the following:

- Name of the Company/Business Name
- Registered Address of the Company/Business Name
- RC Number/BN Number of the Company
- Names of Directors of the Company

Foreign Participation in Registered Business in Nigeria

Subject to the provisions of any enactment regulating the right and capacity of aliens to undertake or participate in the trade or business, an alien or a foreign company may join in forming a company.[27] Similarly, Section 17 of the Nigerian Investment Promotion Commission (NIPC) Act provides that a non-Nigerian, whether company or individual may invest and participate in the operation of any enterprise in Nigeria except those in the negative list mentioned above.

It is from these provisions that a foreigner is allowed to participate in business in Nigeria but subject to some enactments. Incorporation of a company in Nigeria by foreigners is a legal requirement[28] (although exemption from local incorporation may be granted by application for exemption directly to the Minister of Trade).[29] This is because incorporation gives the Nigerian company its own distinct legal personality, separate from that of its overseas parent company. Unincorporated branch operations or representative offices are not allowed, but it is possible to incorporate a limited liability company which will carry out activities only as a representative office of an overseas parent company. Therefore, every foreign company intending to carry on business in Nigeria must take all the steps necessary to incorporate as a Nigerian Company and until such incorporation; the

[27] CAMA S.74.
[28] Ibid.
[29] Ibid., S.80.

foreign company must not have a place of business in Nigeria for any purpose other than the receipts of notices and other documents related to its incorporation.[30]

Please note that foreign investors may own up to 100 per cent of any Nigerian business except in the Maritime sector as provided in the Nigerian Maritime Administration and Safety Agency, 2007 and the Internal Cabotage Act, 2003. Furthermore, foreign investors cannot fully own companies involved in: production of arms and ammunition; production of and dealing in narcotic drugs and psychotropic substances; production of military and paramilitary wears and accoutrements) and such other items as the Federal Executive Council may from time to time determine.

Accordingly, a foreigner is free to participate in the economy of Nigeria through two (2) major methods, i.e. Foreign Direct investment of Foreign Portfolio Investment.

Foreign Direct Investment

Foreign Direct Investment (FDI) is a measure of foreign ownership of productive assets, such as factories, mines and land. A foreigner interested in setting up business in Nigeria through Foreign Direct Investment may choose to register a business name as a sole proprietor (or partnership) subject to a business permit, he may wish to incorporate a company with other aliens or Nigerians. Where he is incorporating a company, he may do business in any area except the negative list mentioned in 6.1 above.

Foreign Portfolio Investment[31]

Foreign Portfolio Investment (FPI) is the entry of funds into a country where foreigners make purchases in the country's stock and bond markets. Thus, if an alien desires to invest in the shares of a company, whether public or private, he can do so through Foreign Portfolio Investment. Foreign investors desirous of trading in securities listed on the Nigerian Stock Exchange can do so without pre-investment

---

[30] Ibid., S.78 - 80.

[31] See the Investment and Securities Act, 2007.

approvals, but such transactions are subject to guidelines issued by the Nigerian Securities and Exchange Commission, and the Nigerian Stock Exchange itself.

Legal and Institutional Framework for Foreign Participation of Business in Nigeria

Legal Framework

Companies and Allied Matters Act (CAMA) 2020

A foreign company wishing to carry on business in Nigeria must be incorporated under CAMA before carrying on business in Nigeria.[32]

i. Nigerian Investment Promotion Commission Act[33]

Companies with foreign participation are required to register with the Nigerian Investment Promotion Commission (NIPC) on incorporation and obtain a 'Business Permit', prior to commencement of business. A minimum share capital of ₦10,000,000.00 (the equivalent of about £42,600 pounds sterling) is required for companies applying for a Nigerian Business Permit. Employment of non-Nigerians is subject to an 'Expatriate Quota Approval', which can be issued by the NIPC. Foreign companies intending to operate in the hydrocarbon sector will be required to obtain an additional permit from the Department of Petroleum Resources (DPR), the regulatory body responsible for oil & gas matters in Nigeria.[34] Monetary and non-monetary imports (e.g. plants and machinery) must be recorded by way of a certificate of capital importation through an authorized dealer, enabling a foreign investor to repatriate dividends or the proceeds of the sale of its investment in Nigeria, should the desire to do so arise.[35]

Procedure for Registration with NIPC

1. The company seeking registration with NIPC must first obtain the NIPC form 1. A non-refundable deposit of ₦10,000.00 must be paid and receipt obtained

[32] n. 29; though nothing stops a foreign company to sue in Nigeria without registration in Nigeria.
[33] NIPC Act, Chapter N117 LFN 2004.
[34] Ibid, S. 19(1)(2).
[35] Section 15 of the Foreign Exchange (Monitoring and Miscellaneous Provisions) Act, CAP. F3, LFN, 2004.

2. The form will be completed by the company and submitted at NIPC headquarters in Abuja or state Ministries of trade with the following:

- 2 copies of receipt for payment of ₦10,000.00
- Certificate of Incorporation
- The memorandum and articles of association of the company
- Receipts for payment of stamp duties on the authorized share capital of the company as at the date of application
- Tax clearance certificate of the applicant company
- Partnership (joint- venture) agreement where applicable
- Feasibility Report and project implementation program of the company for its proposed business
- Title deeds of land evidencing firm commitment to acquire requisite business premises for the company's operations.
- Training program for the Nigerian staff or personnel policy of the company, incorporating management succession schedule for qualified Nigerians.
- Names, addresses, nationalities and occupations of the proposed directors of the company including non-resident directors which should be marked NRD
- Job title designations of expatriate quota positions required, and the academic and working experience required for the occupations of such positions.
- Information brochure, if any, on the foreign partner
- Evidence of capital importation for wholly foreign companies.

Immigration Act

No person other than a citizen of Nigeria shall set up a business or participate in a trade or business in form of a partnership without the consent in writing of the Director of Immigration.[36] Thus, a foreigner is required to obtain 4 basic permits before he can set up or participate in any business in Nigeria. These are:

1. Entry Permit or visa;

[36] Section 8 of the Immigration Act, CAP. I1, LFN, 2004.

2. Expatriate Quota;
3. Business Permit;
4. Residence permit.

National Office for Technology Acquisition and Promotion Act

A foreigner or an Alien interested in the transfer of foreign technology into Nigeria must register all the documents or agreements involving the transfer of foreign technology with the National Office for Technology Acquisition Commission. A contract or agreement involves transfer of technology if it includes:

1. the use of trademarks;
2. the right to use patented inventions;
3. the supply of technical expertise in form of the preparation of plans, diagrams, operating manuals or any other form of technical assistance of any description whatsoever;
4. the supply of basic or detailed engineering;
5. the supply of basic or detailed engineering;
6. the supply of machinery and plant; and
7. the provision of operating staff or managerial assistance and the training of personnel

The application for registration of contracts and agreements must be done not later than 60 days from the execution or conclusion of the contract. The application must be addressed to the Director, National Office for Technology Acquisition and Promotion, and must be accompanied by such number of certified true copies of such contract and agreement and other related documents and information as may be specified in any particular case by the director.[37]

Institutional Framework

A very indispensable factor that every investor must consider is the relevant institutional framework or regulatory body. A regulatory body or agency is a public authority or government agency responsible for exercising autonomous authority over some area of human activity in a supervisory capacity. Regulatory agencies operate in the areas

[37] Section 5(1) -(3) National Office for Technology Acquisition and Promotion Act, CAP. N62, LFN, 2004.

of administrative functions; codification and enforcement of rules and regulations; and supervision or oversight for the benefit of the public at large.

Accordingly, any investor interested in starting a business in Nigeria must take steps to register with the necessary and relevant regulatory body. There are many regulatory bodies in Nigeria supervising different sectors of the economy. For instance, in the financial sector we have: Central Bank of Nigeria, Nigeria Deposit Insurance Corporation, Securities and Exchange Commission, National Insurance Commission, and Federal Inland Revenue Service; for the telecommunications sector we have the Nigerian Communications Commission (NCC); and for the oil and gas sector we have: Ministry of Petroleum Resources (MPR), Directorate of Petroleum Resources (DPR), and Nigerian National Petroleum Corporation (NNPC), to mention but a few.

NOTABLE INNOVATIONS INTRODUCED BY CAMA 2020

Undoubtedly, the purpose of enacting CAMA 2020 (which repealed CAMA 1990) is to reform the business landscape in Nigeria given its extensive innovations. Besides simplifying the process of registering businesses, other key modifications introduced by the Act particularly in relation to the subject matter of discourse include:

i. **Promotion of Technology:** The Act promotes the use of technology in the registration of businesses in Nigeria in a bid to improve efficiency and cut costs. Notably, this initiative has already been successfully initiated by the Corporate Affairs Commission.[38]

ii. **Authorised Minimum Share Capital:** The Act introduces a new authorized share capital threshold for companies seeking registration in Nigeria with the authorised share capital for Private companies not being less than ₦100,000; and Public Companies not being less than ₦2,000,000.[39]

---

[38] CAMA 2020 S. 31 (1), 34 (2).

[39] Ibid S. 27 (2).

iii. **Annual General Meeting:** Small companies and/or companies having single shareholders have been exempted from the mandatory requirement to convene and hold Annual General Meetings.[40]

iv. **Company Secretary:** Whilst the appointment of Company Secretaries is still mandatory for public companies, the appointment of same by Small or Single member companies is optional.[41]

v. **Paid Up Capital:** There is currently no provision under CAMA for a timeline within which the shareholders of a company should pay for shares allotted to them. However, the new Act stipulates that 25% of the issued share capital of a company must be paid up at all times.[42]

vi. **Use of Common Seal:** The mandatory requirement for each company to have a common seal has been abolished. Each company may opt to obtain a common seal and regulate its use and design through its articles of association.[43]

vii. **Beneficial Ownership:** The Act promotes transparency and removes ambiguity in the ownership and control of companies in Nigeria by mandating every member of a company to disclose the capacity in which they hold their shares, and if on behalf of another person i.e. the beneficial owner, disclose the identity of such owner. With sanctions prescribed for non-compliance.[44]

viii. **Auditing by Small Companies:** Small companies are now exempted from appointing auditors. Specifically, the Act provides that a company is exempted from appointing auditors if:

a. it has not carried on business since its incorporation; or in a particular financial year; or

b. the company's turnover is not more than ₦10m and its balance sheet total is not more than ₦5m[45]

ix. **Business Rescue Proceedings:** Provisions have been made for Business Rescue Proceedings which is targeted at rehabilitating financially distressed companies. These provisions seek to create an

---

40 Ibid., S. 238(1); compare with Section 213 of CAMA 1990.

41 CAMA 2020 S. 329 (1).

42 Ibid., S. 133.

43 Ibid., S.193(1) and 721(1)(b).

44 Ibid., S. 92.

45 Ibid., S. 356.

effective insolvency regime in Nigeria and has a dual aim: to save viable businesses, and to ensure that non-viable businesses can quickly exit the market, allowing deployment of assets to more productive firms.[46]

x. **Electronic Meetings**[47]

xi. **Object clause:** Whereas Section 27(1)(c) of the 1990 CAMA requires a company to state its object(s), Section 35 of the CAMA 2020 states that unless a company's articles specifically restrict the objects of the company, its objects are unrestricted.

xii. **Penalty for Carrying on Business without Registration:** It is now unlawful for any person or association of persons to carry on business in Nigeria as a company, limited liability partnership, or under a business name without being registered under CAMA. Any defaulting individual, corporation or every partner in the firm shall be guilty of an offence and liable on conviction to a fine (prescribed and determined in accordance to the Commission's regulations from time to time) of ₦200.00 for every day during which the default continues.[48]

CONCLUSION

Nigeria is a country with a lot of business opportunities, and her large population provides a huge market for any good business or product to thrive. The most important decision that any individual or group intending to start a business must make is how to structure the business, and the regulatory requirements involved. This chapter has discussed the different types of business structures in Nigeria while explaining the advantages and disadvantages of each structure. Factors that should inform the choice of business were identified to include: whether the promoter intends the liability of the owners of the company to be limited or unlimited; whether the goal of the business is to become a large company or grow as a small company; the tax obligations of the company; whether it intends to source for funds from

---

[46] Ibid., S. 402.

[47] Ibid., S241(2).

[48] Ibid., S.853.

the public; whether it intends not to make profits but still carry on business. The chapter also discussed the legal and regulatory framework for the operation of business in Nigeria, while outlining the procedural requirements for setting up each type of business structure. Significant improvements in the newly enacted CAMA 2020 were also highlighted to the effect that the new Act will ease the rigors of doing business in Nigeria, thereby making the country more attractive to investors. This will enhance the nation's economy as the projected inflow of new businesses will help it flourish, by creating more wealth and employment opportunities.

Chapter 27

OUTLINE OF THE LAW OF TORTS IN NIGERIA

I. O. Igwe*

BACKGROUND

The historical background of the law of torts dates back to after the Norman Conquest when a new procedure was adopted to allow the King's Courts to hear individual complaints.[1] Whenever a person felt that he had suffered an injury as a result of the wrongful conduct of another, he obtained from the King's officer known as the Chancellor a document called a writ.[2] The said writ had a set of forms which comprised; the statement in the form of complaint, a direction on the sheriff to summon the defendant to attend a hearing on the matter before the representative of the King. However, where occasions exist where there is no type of writ to accommodate a particular injury, the Chancellor was empowered to exercise his discretion and formulate a writ for that purpose.

As time went on, the Chancellor abused the said discretion. This attracted criticism and opposition that led to provisions of Oxford (1258)[3] which curtailed the powers of the Chancellor.

Although the law of torts is the creation of common law, statutes and judicial decisions have, in many ways, contributed to the development of the law of torts in Nigeria.

---

* I.O. Igwe is a Lecturer at Faculty of Law, Ebonyi State University, Abakaliki.

1. B.A. SUSU *Law of Torts,* (Lagos: CJC Press (Nig) Ltd, 1996), p.1.
2. Ibid.
3. Ibid.

THE CONCEPT OF TORT

The word "tort" is derived from the Latin word *tortus*, which means twisted. It could mean wrong. In French, it means "*J'ai tori*," which means I am wrong.[4] It is a legal wrong for which the law provides a remedy.

Winfield and Jolowicz explained that:

> Tortuous liability arises from the breach of a duty primarily fixed by law; this duty is towards persons generally and its breach is redressable by an action for unliquidated damages.[5]

According to J.W. Salmond, a tort is:

> A civil wrong for which the remedy is a common law action for unliquidated damages, and which is not exclusively the breach of contract or the breach of trust or other merely equitable obligation.[6]

In the same vein, Kodilinye and Aluko said that a tort is:

> A civil wrong involving a breach of duty fixed by the law, such duty being owned to persons generally and its breach being redressable primarily by an action for damages.[7]

The *Black's Law Dictionary* puts it thus; a tort is:

> A civil wrong, other than breach of contract, for which a remedy may be obtained usually in form of damages; a breach of a duty that the law imposes on persons who stand in a particular relation to one another.[8]

The Court of Appeal in the case of *Aigoro* v. *Commissioner for Land Housing Kwara State*,[9] held that:

---

[4] T.A. Omotayo & E.O.I Iyodeji, *Law of Tort*, (Lagos: National Open University of Nigeria, 2008), p.15.
[5] Winfield & Jolswicz, *Tort, 15th edn*, (London: Sweet & Maxwell, 1998), p.4.
[6] J.W Salmond,law on *Tort, 18th edn*, (London; Sweet & Maxwell, 1977), p.11.
[7] G.Kodilinye & O,Aluko, *Nigeria law of Torts*, (Lagos; Spectrum Law Publishers, 1999), p.I.
[8] The *Black's Law Dictionary 8th edn*, (U.S.A: Thomson West Business, 2004), p. 1526.
[9] [2012]11 W.R.N, 55 at 62-63.

> A tort or tortuous act is an act which causes harm to a determinate person, whether intentionally or not being the breach of a duty arising out of a personal relation or contract and which is either contrary to law or an omission of specific legal duty or a violation of an absolute right. A civil wrong for which the remedy is common law action for unliquidated damages and which is not inclusively the breach of a contract or that of trust or other merely equitable obligation.[10]

What emerges from the definition of tort above is that a tort is a breach of a civil duty imposed by law which breach is actionable in the form of unliquidated damage or injunction, among others.

THE SCOPE OF THE LAW OF TORTS

In a nutshell, the Law of Tort covers areas such as:

- Trespass to a person, which includes assault, battery, and false imprisonment;
- Malicious prosecution;
- Trespass to chattel, which includes conversion and detinue;
- Trespass to land;
- Negligence;
- Nuisance;
- The Rule in *Rylands* v. *Fletcher* (Strict liability);
- Liability for animals;
- Vicarious liability;
- Occupier's liability;
- Defamation;
- Deceit;
- Passing off;
- Economic torts such as injurious falsehood, interference with contract, among others.

[10] The *Black's Law Dictionary 7th edn,* (U.S.A: St. Paul Minn., 1999), p.1508.

Trespass to Person

Trespass to person includes unjustifiable interference with the body of another person. It is an intentional interference with the body of another person or his liberty. According to the *Black's Law Dictionary,* it is an unlawful act committed against another person. This includes assault, battery, and false imprisonment.

Assault

In criminal law, assault means more than attacking, beating, or hitting somebody. According to Section 252 of the *Criminal Code Act,*[11] assault is committed when:

> a person who strikes, touches, or moves or otherwise applies force of any kind to the person of another either directly or indirectly, without his consent, if the consent is obtained by fraud or who by any bodily act or gesture attempts or *threatens to apply force of any kind to the person of another* without his consent, in such circumstances that the person making the attempt or threat has actually or apparently a present ability to effect his purpose… (italics mine).

Assault is a crime and a tort. In tort, assault is an attempt to apply unlawful force to the body of another person whereby that other person is put in fear of bodily harm. According to Kodilinye, "any act which puts the plaintiff in fear that battery is about to be committed against him is an assault."[12] The *Black's Law Dictionary* puts assault thus:

> The threat or use of force on another that causes that person to have a reasonable apprehension of imminent harmful or offensive contact; that act of putting another person in reasonable fear or apprehension of an immediate battery by means of an act amounting to an attempt or threat to commit battery.[13]

---

[11] Criminal Code Act, Cap C10 Laws of the Federation of Nigeria, 2004

[12] G. Kodilinye & O. Aluko, *Nigeria Law of Torts op.cit*, p.12.

[13] The *Black's Law Dictionary, 7th edn, op.cit,* p. 109.

For a plaintiff to succeed in the case of assault, he must establish that the defendant threatened to apply force on him and that the threat of the defendant actually put him in reasonable fear of immediate battery. See the following cases:

R. v. *St George;*[14] *Innes* v. *Wyhe;*[15] *Stephen* v. *Myers;* [16] *R.* v. *Ireland & Burston;*[17] *Tuberville* v. *Savage;* [18] *Hurst* v. *Picture Theatres Ltd;*[19] *Agbonavbare* v. *Ogbebor*[20]

Battery

Battery is the application of force to the body of another person. The purpose of tort of battery is to protect the body of a person and its dignity from unlawful contact by another person. Everyone is entitled to be free from any intentional, negligent and undesirable physical contact. Instances of battery include spitting on a person's face, pouring water on a person, beating a person with a stick, setting a dog to attack a person, among others.

The plaintiff who wishes to succeed in an action for tort of battery must establish that there was an intentional application of force on him by the defendant. See the following cases:

Mogaji v. *Board of Customs,*[21] *Shugaba* v. *Minister of Internal Affairs,*[22] *Nwankwo* v. *Ajaegbo,*[23] *Afisi* v. *Aghakpe,*[24] *Oyakhiri* v. *Obaseki*[25]

False Imprisonment

A tort of false imprisonment is committed when a person is denied of his movement or liberty by another person without lawful justification. The purpose of this tort is to protect the fundamental right to personal

---

[14] [1840]173 ER 921.
[15] [1844]174 ER 800.
[16] [1838]172 ER 735.
[17] [1997]4 All ER 225.
[18] [1669] 86 ER 684.
[19] [1915]1 KB I.
[20] [2006]48 W.R.N, 105.
[21] [1982]31 NCLR 552.
[22] [1981]2 NCLR 459.
[23] [1978] LRN 230.
[24] [1987]1 QLRN 216.
[25] [1986]1 NWLR (pt 19), p. 735.

liberty and freedom of movement.[26] "Every restraint of the liberty of a free man is imprisonment although he be not within the walls of any common prison."[27] To establish false imprisonment, the plaintiff must prove that: there was a restrain and that the restrain was total. See *Bird* v. *Jones.*[28] The restrain for the shortest period of time is sufficient. It is not necessary to establish the use of force or physical contact by the plaintiff. It is not necessary for the person who is restrained to know at the material time that he was restrained. See the following cases:

UAC (Nig) PLC v. *Sobodu;* [29] *A.I. B. Ltd* v. *Asaolu;* [30] *C.O.P. Ondo State* v. *Obolo;*[31] *Aigoro* v. *Anebuwa*[32]

Malicious Prosecution

Malicious prosecution is the intentional setting up of criminal prosecution in motion against a person without legal justification. The Court of Appeal, in the case of *UAC (Nig) PLC* v. *Sobodu,*[33] held that:

> ...where a complaint or charge is made to the police and the defendant also instigates them to arrest the person complained against and make a formal charge against him before a Magistrate and prosecute him...then the liability is also for malicious prosecution because the police cannot be said to be allowed the freedom of action and the party making the complaint will be more damnified if the charge subsequently proves to be fabricated or if the person complained against his ultimately discharged by the Magistrate.

See the following cases:

David Inneh v. *Igumaka Aroegbon;*[34] *Chief Etiman Paying & Anor* v. *Adiaba Aliuah & Anor;* [35] *Balogun* v. *Amubikahun*[36]

---

[26] See sections 35 and 41 of the Constitution of the Federal Republic of Nigeria, 1999 (as amended).
[27] Edward Coke CJ *Statutes of Westminster II C.48.*
[28] [1848]7 QB 742.
[29] [2007]48 WRN 34 at 39.
[30] [2006]5 W.R.N. 35.
[31] [1989]5 NWLR (pt.120), p. 130.
[32] [1996] NWLR 87.
[33] [2007]48 WRN 34 at 39.
[34] [1952]14 WACA 73 at 74 or [1970]1 All NLR I.
[35] [1953]14 WACA 267.
[36] [1989]3 NWLR (pt 11), p.18 at 30.

The plaintiff must prove the following elements to enable him to succeed in an action for malicious prosecution:

(a) that he was prosecuted by the defendant, that is to say, the defendant set in motion against him, the law leading to a criminal charge;

(b) that as a result of the prosecution, the plaintiff was discharged and acquitted;

(c) that the prosecution by the defendant was completely without reasonable and probable cause;

(d) that the prosecution was a result of malice by the defendant against the plaintiff.

See the following cases:

Barau v. *Choba*;[37] *Horst Sommer & 2 ors* v. *Federal Housing Authority*;[38] *Abdullahi* v. *Raji*;[39] *Mandilas & Karaberies Ltd* v. *Apena*[40]

Trespass to Chattel per se

A chattel is a moveable property. It includes goods, articles, or personal property other than land and that which is attached to the land. The tort of trespass to chattel is aimed at the protection from wrongful and intentional interference with the articles, goods, or personal property in possession of another person. The tort of trespass to chattel protects the chattel of a person who has title, possession, or right of immediate possession against meddling, damage, destruction, diminution, conversion, detinue, or any interference by a person without lawful justification.

Trespass to chattel is actionable *per se*. This means that once the tort is committed, the plaintiff can succeed in court without proof of any damage. According to the court in the case of *Davis* v. *Lagos City Council*,[41]

The plaintiff is entitled to succeed… in trespass… there may be a trespass without the infliction of any material damage by a mere taking or transportation…

---

[37] [1989]1 NWLR (pt. 357),p.366.
[38] [1992]1 SCNJ 73 at 80.
[39] [1998]1 NWLR (pt. 534), p.481.
[40] [1969] All NLR 382 at 3.86.
[41] [1973]10 CCHCJ 151.

Trespass to chattel is divided into three. They include:

(a) trespass to chattel *per se,* without conversion or a detinue;
(b) conversion;
(c) detinue.

Trespass to Chattel

Trespass to chattel is any direct or unlawful interference with a chattel in possession of another person. It is designed to protect the following interest in personal property:

(a) the plaintiff's right to retain possession of his chattel;
(b) the plaintiff's interest in the physical condition of the chattel;
(c) the protection of the chattel against unlawful interference or any form of intermeddling .

The following acts constitute trespass to chattel:

(a) Taking a chattel away;
(b) Throwing another person's property away;
(c) Mere moving of the goods from one place to another;
(d) Scratching or making marks on the body of the chattel
(e) Killing another person's animal, feeding poison to it, or beating it;
(f) Destruction, or any act of harm or damage;
(g) Touching of chattel;
(h) Use, that is using without permission;
(i) Driving another person's car without permission;
(j) Filling another person's bottle with anything;
(k) Throwing something at the chattel;
(l) Damaging or causing any harm to a chattel, among others.

The following person may institute an action in trespass to chattel. They include owners, bailers, lenders, assignees, trustees, finders, custodians, caretakers, adverse possessors, executors, and administrators of estates, among others.

Conversion

Conversion is committed when one intentionally deals with chattel in such a manner as is inconsistent with the possessory right of another person.

According to J. Salmon:

> A conversion is an act...of wilful interference, without lawful justification, with any chattel in a manner inconsistent with the right of another, where that other is deprived of the use and possession of it.[42]

See the following cases: *Ihenacho* v. *Uzochukwu,*[43] *Boniface Anyika & Co* v. *Uzor,*[44] *Henry Stephens Eng. Ltd* v. *S.A. Yakubu (Nig) Ltd.*[45]

The following acts could constitute conversion. Taking, using, alteration, consumption, damaging, destroying, receiving, detention, wrongful refusal to return a chattel, wrongful delivery, wrongful sale or disposition of chattel, among others. See *Wema Bank PLC* v. *Osilaru,*[46] *Danjuma* v. *Union Bank Nig. (Ltd).*[47]

Detinue

Detinue is the wrongful detention of the chattel of another person. An action in detinue is a claim for the specific return of the current market value and consequential damages. For a plaintiff to succeed in an action for detinue, he must establish that either he is the owner of the chattel or that person has the right of immediate possession of the chattel. In *Kosile* v. *Folarin,*[48] the Supreme Court of Nigeria held, in addition to the above, that for a plaintiff to succeed in an action for detinue, he must show that there has been a demand on the defendant to return the chattel, but the defendant persists in keeping the chattel. See the following cases: *Ihenacho* v. *Uzochukwu,*[49] *West African Examination Council* v. *Koroye,*[50] *Davies* v. *Lagos City Council,*[51] *Steyer Nig Ltd* v. *Gadzama,*[52] *Stitch* v. *A.G. Federation,*[53] *Ordia* v. *Piedmont Nig Ltd,*[54]

---

42 See J. Salmond, *Law of Tort, op. cit,* pp. 97-98
43 [1997]2 NWLR (pt 487], p.257
44 [2006]41 WRN 175
45 [2009]41 WRN 43
46 [2008]4 WNR 160
47 [1995]5 NWLR (pt. 395), p.318
48 [1989]3 NWLR (pt 107), p.1.
49 *Supra.*
50 [1977]2 S.C. 45.
51 *Supra.*
52 [1995]7 NWLR (pt 407] p. 305.
53 [1986]5 NWLR (pt. 47), 1007.

Ajikawo v. *Ansaldo Nig. Ltd,*[55] *Umoru* v. *Ijumu L.G. Council,*[56] *NACENN (Nig) Ltd* v. *BEWAC Auto Production Ltd.*[57]

Trespass to Land

A tort of trespass to land occurs when a person intentionally interferes with the land in possession of another person. It could take the form of entry, staying in, or causing the object to come in contact with the land in possession of the plaintiff. The law also recognizes air space over the land as part of the interest of the person in possession of the land. This tort is designed to protect the possessory right of the person entitled to possession of land and keep such interest from any form of physical interference.[58] See the case of *Omotoye* v. *Co-op. Supply Ass.*[59]

Negligence

Negligence is an omission to do something which a reasonable man would do or doing something which a reasonable man would not do in the circumstance. It is the failure to exercise the standard of care that a reasonably prudent person would have exercised in a similar situation. It could also mean any conduct that falls below the legal standard established to protect others against unreasonable risk of harm.[60] It could mean carelessness.[61] See *Diamond Bank Ltd* v. *Partnership Investment Co, Ltd.*[62]

The plaintiff in a case of negligence must establish three elements to enable him to succeed. The elements are:

(a) that the defendant owed him a duty of care;

(b) that the defendant breached the said duty of care;

(c) that he had suffered damage resulting from the defendant's breach.

---

54 [1995]2 NWLR (pt. 379), p. 316.

55 [1991]2 NWLR (pt. 173), p. 359.

56 [2010]35 WRN 118.

57 [2011]27 WRN I.

58 See B.A. SUSU, *Law of Torts, op. cit.*, p. 52.

59 [2010]52 W.R.N.

60 *Black's Law Dictionray, 8th edn, op. cit.*, p.1061

61 Ibid.

62 [2010]13,W.R.N.I

According to Lord Alkin in the celebrated case of *Donogue* v. *Stevenson,*[63] "you must take reasonable care to avoid acts or omission which you can reasonably foresee that would likely to injure your neighbour." He continued and asked the question, "who is your neighbour?"

According to him:

> Your neighbour in law include those person who are so closely and directly affected by your acts, that you ought reasonably to have them in contemplation as being so affected when you are directing your mind to the act or omission that are called to question.

See the cases of *Osemobor* v. *Niger Biscuit,*[64] *Nigeria Bottling Co.* v. *Constance Ngonadi,*[65] *JAMB* v. *Nkeiruka.*[66]

The standard of care expected from one is that of a reasonable man of ordinary prudence. Examples: moral qualities and knowledge, skills, intelligence, age, and lunacy, among others. In medical practice, a doctor has no obligation to an accident victim on the roadside, but where he stops to render help, he is bound by the ethics to exercise a degree of reasonable care.[67]

Nuisance

The tort of nuisance is aimed at the protection of the land user from the inconvenience caused by his neighbours. It is a condition, activity, or situation that interferes with the use or enjoyment of land. Nuisance could be divided into private and public.

It is a private nuisance where the injury or interference affects the individual owner or occupier of land from the enjoyment thereof. See *Abiola* v. *Ijeoma,*[68] *Tebite* v. *Nigeria Marine and Training Co. Ltd.*[69] While it is a public nuisance where the injury or interferences affect the

[63] [1932] AC 532
[64] [1973] CC HCJ 71
[65] [1985]1 NWLR 739
[66] [2008]44 W.R.N. 92
[67] Rules of Professional Conduct for Medical and Dental Practitioners, Revised Edition, 1995
[68] [1970]2 All NLR 268
[69] [1971]1 ULR 432

whole people or part of people in a given area. See *Hong Kong Syn Fibre* v. *Ajibawo*,[70] *U.T.B Nig.* v. *Ozoemena*.[71]

In private nuisance, the injury or interference will be considered by a court in one or combination of the following facts:

(a) Whether there is physical injury or sensible material damage. See *Ige* v. *Taylor Woodrow (Nig) Ltd*.[72]

(b) Whether there is substantial interference with the use and enjoyment of the land. See *Abiola* v. *Ijeoma*.[73]

(c) The unreasonableness of the conduct of the defendant. See *Sedleigh-Denfield* v. *O' Callaghan*.[74]

(d) The malice or motive of the defendant.

(e) The utility of the act of the defendant.

(f) The duration of the harm or inconvenience.

(g) The practicability of the relief sought by the plaintiff.

(h) The carelessness of the defendant.

In the case of a nuisance, the following persons can sue:

(a) Any person who has or uses land or has an interest in land;

(b) An occupier or user of land;

(c) Any person who has a reversionary right in the land may sue if his reversionary interest in land is being or has been affected.

The Rule in *Rylands* v. *Fletcher*

The decision of the English Court in the case of *Rylands* v. *Fletcher*,[75] otherwise known as the rule in *Rylands* v. *Fletcher*, represents one of the strict liability areas in the law of torts. In this case, the appellant, who was a mill owner, engaged independent contractors to build a reservoir on his land to supply water to his mill. During the construction, the contractors found disused mine shafts and passages that, unknown to them, linked to the respondent's mines on the adjoining land. The contractors carelessly omitted to block the disused

[70] [2008]34 W.R.N. 153
[71] [2007]13 W.R.N. 125
[72] [1963] LLR 140
[73] *Supra*
[74] [1940]AC 880 at 908
[75] [1866] LRI. Exch. 265, Affirmed [1868) LR 2 h.l. 330.

shafts, and when the reservoir was filled with water, it escaped and flooded the respondent's mine, inflicting some damage. The respondent, who was the plaintiff at the lower court, sued for damages. The court, after reviewing the existing scope of tort, found that the defendants were not liable for trespass because the damage was not direct and immediate; nor for nuisance, because the damage was not due to any recurrent condition or state of affairs on their land; nor for negligence because the defendants had not been careless and they were not liable for the negligence of their independent contractors. However, Blackburn J. held that the defendants were still liable for damages. According to the learned judge:

> A person who for his own purposes brings on his land and collects and keeps there anything likely to do mischief if it escapes, must keep it at his peril, and...is *prima facie* answerable for all the damage which is the natural consequence of its escape.

On appeal, the House of Lords upheld the decision of the lower court and added that: "the thing which escapes and causes damage should be a non-natural user of the defendant land."[76]

For a defendant to be liable under this rule, the plaintiff must establish that:

(a) he brings and keeps a non-natural user on his land;
(b) he kept it on his land at his own peril;
(c) the thing escaped and caused damage.

See the cases of *NEPA* v. *Alli;*[77] *NEPA* v. *Akpata;*[78] *Umudje* v. *Shell B.P. Pet. Dev. Co. of Nigeria Ltd;*[79] *National Oil Chem. Market P.LC.* v. *Adewusi;*[80] *Oto Kiti Nig. Ltd* v. *Peter James Ltd.*[81]

Liability of Animals

Strict or absolute liability is generally known as liability without fault. The keeper of an animal or his agent, servant, or proxy having the

---

[76] Ibid.
[77] [1992]8 NWLR (pt. 259), p.279.
[78] [1991]2 NWLR (pt. 175), p. 536.
[79] [1976]11 SC.
[80] [2008] 29 W.R.N. 99.
[81] [2005]12 W.R.N. 158.

authority of the owner of the animal to keep or look after the same is liable for any damage done by it. The rule is that a keeper of any animal does it at his own peril and owes a duty of care to his neighbours not to allow the said animal to cause injury to them.

An animal in this context includes any living creature on land or in water but does not include human beings and plants. This is generally classified into domestic and wild animals.

However, for the purpose of tortuous liability, they are classified into livestock, dangerous animals, and non-dangerous animals. Examples of dangerous animals include wolf, baboon, wild dog, crocodile, snake, monkey, lion, tiger, leopard, gorilla, wild cats, and chimpanzee, among others.

An action brought against the keeper of a dangerous animal is called *scienter* action. These animals are wild in nature *ferae naturae.* According to Denman C.J., "A person keeping a mischievous animal with the knowledge of its propensities is bound to keep it secure at his peril."[82]

There are animals that are naturally tamed, *Mansuetae naturae,* for example: dog, cat, goat, cattle, horse, sheep, and pig, among others. The keeper of these animals will be liable for the act done by then if it is established that there was damage and that the animal in question showed evidence of propensity.

The liability for cattle trespass is a common law tort. According to Williams J:

> If I am the owner of an animal, I am bound to take care that it does not stray on to the land of my neighbour; and I am liable for trespass it may commit, and for the ordinary consequences of the trespass whether or not the escape of the animal is due to my negligence is altogether immaterial.[83]

Vicarious Liability

Vicarious liability deals with the legal basis upon which a party may bear the legal consequences of injuries or wrongs committed by another

---

[82] See *May* v. *Burdeth [1933] Times Report* 7th December.
[83] [1863] 143 E.R. 171, at 174.

person even though the former is free from personal blame. This is a result of one standing in a particular relationship with another. An example is the master and servant relationship.

Liability of the Master for the Act of the Servant

A servant is a person who works under the direct supervision and control of another person. According to Salmon:

> A servant may be defined as any person employed by another to do work to him on the terms that he the servant is to be subject to the control and direction of his employer. A servant is a person engaged to obey his employer's order from time to time.[84]

A master is one who has authority over the service of another. He supervises and controls the service of his servant. He will be liable for the tort of his servant if the servant commits the tort in the course of his employment. That is to say, if he expressly or implied authorized the place, time, and manner of doing the work for which the servant is employed to do. See *B.P.E.N. Ltd* v. *Roli Hotels Ltd.*[85] The master may not be liable for the tort of his servant where the servant acted in excess of the scope of his employment. In other words, where the servant is on a frolic of his own. The Supreme Court, while trying to distinguish the act within the scope of employment and the one outside the scope of employment, has this to say:

> I am clearly of the view that the trial judge overlooked the differences between an act which is an improper way of executing an authorised act which is the performance of an authorised act...the learned trail judge overlooked the clear difference between prohibition that limits or defines the mode of performance of a duty and one that limits or curtails the scope of employment...[86]

In this case, a lorry driver who was designated to carry goods took some passengers on board and, in the process, had an accident and injured the plaintiff. The trial court found the owner of the lorry liable

[84] J.W. Salmond, *op. cit.*, P.174.
[85] [2005]38 W.R.N. 96.
[86] See *Jarmkani transport Ltd* v. *Abeke* [1963] N;R 180.

for the action of the driver. On appeal, the Supreme Court reversed the judgment.

However, where a professional or skilled worker is engaged to carry out a specific assignment based on his professional expertise, the employer will not be liable for the tort of his professional servant committed in the course of executing the assignment. These groups of workers are often times referred to as independent contractors.

According to O.T. Abisoye:

> An independent contractor is a person who agrees to carry out and/or perform a specific duty or task or to produce a specific result for a fee and who in the performance of his work or duty is not subject to the direct control of employer and he is entitled to use his discretion in the mode and method of carrying out or performing his work.[87]

Despite the above general rule, an employer may still be liable for a tort committed by an independent contractor where he expressly or implied authorized or engaged the independent contractor to commit illegality; or where the independent contractor commits a strict liability tort - see the Rule in *Rylands* v. *Fletcher.*

Defamation

The tort of defamation has to do with an injury to the reputation of a person resulting from words written or spoken by others against him. See *Fayose* v. *Independent Comm. Network.*[88] A defamatory statement has the following effect:

(a) to lower the plaintiff in the estimation of right-thinking members of the society generally; or
(b) to expose him to hatred, corruption or ridicule; or
(c) to cause other persons to shun or avoid him; or
(d) to discredit him in his office, trade or profession or
(e) To injure his financial credit- see *Olaniyi* v. *Elero*[89]

---

[87] O.T. Abisoye, *Law of Torts II* National Open University *op. cit.,* p.75.
[88] [2012]19 W.R.N, p. 146 at 154-156.
[89] [2007]8 NWLR pt.1037) 517

The plaintiff who wishes to succeed in a tort of defamation must prove the following:

(a) there was a publication;
(b) the publication was false;
(c) the publication was either in writing or spoken;
(d) the publication was made to a person apart from the plaintiff and the defendant;
(e) the publication referred to the said plaintiff;
(f) the publication was made by the defendant. See the cases of *Iloabachie* v. *Iloabachie*;[90] *Guardian Newspaper & Anor* v. *Ajeh*.[91]

Failure to plead the actual word used in defamation is fatal to the plaintiff - see *Olaifa* v. *Aina*;[92] *Okafor* v. *Ikeanyi*.[93]

Defamation can be classified into two: they are: (a) the defamatory statement made in a visible permanent form such as a written or printed statement. Examples: photographs, films, paintings, circulars, letters, newspapers, and books, among others. This type of defamation is called Libel, and it is generally actionable *per se*; *(b)* the second type of defamation is slander. Slander is a defamatory statement, either spoken or by a gesture.

Deceit

Deceit is the act of intentionally giving a false impression. It is a false statement of fact made by a person knowingly or recklessly.[94] It is the intentional false representation of facts by someone which is acted upon by another person, and as a result, that other person suffers damages.

In order to succeed in the tort of deceit, the plaintiff must prove that:

(a) the defendant made a false representation of fact by words or conduct;
(b) that the defendant intended that the representation would be acted upon by the plaintiff;

[90] [2005]35 W.R.N.I.
[91] [2011]31 S.C. 234.
[92] [1993]4 NWLR (pt 286) ,p.192.
[93] [1970]1 NWLR (pt.100), p. 678.
[94] The *Black's Law Dictionary* 8th edn. *op. cit.*, p.435.

(c) that the plaintiff did act upon the representation and suffered damages;
(d) that the defendant knew the representation to be false or at least had no genuine belief in its truth. See *Onwudiwe* v. *F.R.N.*[95]

Economic Tort
The increase in economic activities all over the world has created room for actions arising from conduct that cause economic loss. These actions are, in law, called economic tort. They include: passing off, interference with contract, and injurious falsehood, among others.

Passing Off
Passing off is a common law tort. It is an act of representing one's own product as that of another in an attempt to deceive potential buyers. In the case of *Trebor (Nig) Ltd* v. *Associated Industries Ltd*,[96] the court held that the fundamental rule is that one man has no right to put off his goods for sale as those goods of a rival trader.

The main function of passing off is the protection of consumers against origin confusion. The following acts may amount to passing off:
(a) trading with a name resembling that of the plaintiff's trade name. See *Niger Chemist Ltd* v. *Nigeria Chemist*;[97]
(b) marketing a fake product as that of the plaintiff by using the plaintiff's label or design;
(c) marketing a product with a name resembling that of the plaintiff's goods;
(d) marketing products with the plaintiff's trademark;
(e) copying the plaintiff's advertisement, among others.

In the case of *Reckitt and Coleman Products* v. *Borden*,[98] the House of Lords adopted what they called the "Trinity Test" in establishing the ingredients of passing off. They are:

---
95 [2006]49 W.R.N.I.
96 [1972] NMLR. 60.
97 [1961] All NLR 180 at 182.
98 [1990] All E.R. 873.

(a) that the plaintiff must establish the goodwill or reputation attached to the goods or services in question and identify the circumstances under which the goods and services are offered to consumers. According to Lord Macnaghten in the case of *Commissioner of Inland Revenue* v. *Muller & Co's Margarine Ltd*,[99] goodwill is the benefit and advantage of the good name, reputation, and connection of a business;

(b) that the plaintiff must establish that there has been a misrepresentation by the defendant which caused or has potential of causing the members of the public to believe that the goods or services emanate from him;

(c) that the plaintiff must demonstrate that he has suffered or is really likely to suffer losses by the reason of the defendant's misrepresentation as to the source of the defendant's goods or services which seems to suggest that they emanate from the plaintiff. See *Int'l Tobacco (Nig) Ltd* v. *B.A.T (Nig) Ltd.*[100]

Injurious Falsehood (Trade Libel)

Injurious Falsehood occurs when someone publishes information that could be damaging to a trader's position or reputation. It is aimed at protecting the business's reputation.

To establish a tort of injurious falsehood, the plaintiff must prove that:

(a) the statements were untrue, and that it was not mere advertisement puff;

(b) the statements were made maliciously, that is, without just cause or excuse.

(c) the plaintiff had suffered damage. See *Schuike & Mayr UK Ltd.* v *Aikapharm UK Ltd.*[101]

---

[99] [1901] AC 217.
[100] [2009] 44 W.RN. 54.
[101] [1999] F.S.R 161.

TERMINATION OF TORTS

Everything that has the beginning must definitely have an end. Activities that gave rise to tortuous actions may be terminated in one way or the other. Examples of acts that may terminate torts include: lapse of time, death *res judicata,* abatement, injunction, award of damages, waiver of right by the plaintiff, among others.

Remedies in Torts

The popular legal maxim that says *Ubi jus ibi remedum*, that is, where there is right, there is remedy, plays an important role in the law of torts. Where tortuous liability arises, the remedy will always come in to compensate the victim of the tortuous act. These compensations take the form of damages, injunctions, restitution, account of profits, delivery up, claim for current market value, among others.

Damages is the monetary compensation ordered by the court to be paid to the plaintiff by the defendant for the wrong done to him. Injunction is an order of the court directing a party to refrain from doing an act or compelling him to do an act. See *Tegede* v. *Bamidele.*[102]

Defences in Torts

Trespass to Person

The defences to action for trespass to person include:

(a) self-defence;

(b) defence of property - a person may commit a reasonable trespass to a person such as assault, battery, or false imprisonment in order to protect his property or property of another person, which he has a moral or legal obligation to protect;

(c) consent of the plaintiff - *Volunti non fit injuria;*

(d) inevitable accident;

(e) judicial authority. In the process of exercising or executing a court order, warrant of arrest, prison sentence, among others, trespass to person may be committed with excuse. See *Onitiri* v. *Ojomo.*[103]

---

[102] [2005] 44 W.R.N. 33.

[103] [1954] 21 NLR. 19

Trespass to Chattel

The defences to action for trespass to chattel include:

(a) inevitable accident;

(b) *jus tertii,* that is a plea that the title or better title to the chattel rests in a third party - see *C.O.P.* v. *Oguntayo;*[104]

(c) subsisting lien. A lien is a right to retain the possession of a property until you are paid;

(d) subsisting bailment;

(e) limitation of time (statute bar) this is a plea to the effect that the time allowed by law for the maintenance of a specific legal action has expired;

(f) laches and acquiesces;

(g) estoppels;

(h) honest conversion.

Negligence

The defences of the tort of negligence include:

(a) *contributory negligence*: This means that the conduct of the plaintiff contributed to the harm or tort committed on him;

(b) *consent*: *Volenti non fit injuria*, what a person consented to does not amount to harm to him. The consent under this head must be genuine. It must not be obtained by fraud or deceit, among others. See *Ndubuisi* v. *Olowoke.*[105]

Nuisance

The following are defences for the tort of nuisance:

(a) Reasonableness of the act or omission. The defendant in action for the tort of nuisance may make a plea that the alleged act or omission was a normal or reasonable act to be expected in the locality and that there was no malice accompanying the act. *Tebite* v. *Nigeria Marine & Trianing Co. Ltd.;*[106]

---

[104] [1993]6 NWLR (pt 299), p.259

[105] [1997]1 NWLR (pt.429), p.62.

[106] *Supra*

(b) statutory authority. As a general rule, Government departments like Electricity Board, Water Co-operation, and Health officers, among others, are deemed to have a license to enter somebody's premises for the purpose of distribution of bills or inspections;
(c) Act of God (*force majeure);*
(d) Act of a strange;
(e) consent.

Strict Liability (Animal Liability)

The defence available to the owner or a keeper of an animal includes:

a) fault of the plaintiff;
b) contributory negligence;
c) consent;
d) act of the third party;
e) Act of God.

Defamation

Defence for the tort of defamation includes:

(a) Justification or truth - *Iloabachie* v. *Iloabachie,*[107] *A.I.B. Ltd* v. *Asaolu;*[108]
(b) Fair comment: fair comment is an impartial observation, opinion or criticism on a matter of public interest, current events or discourse.[109] This must be based on true facts that border on a matter of public interest. See *Idim* v. *African Newspapers Ltd,*[110] *Makinde* v. *Omaghomi,*[111] *Okolie* v. *Marinho;*[112]
(c) Privilege: the plea of privilege as a defence for damnatory action is designed to protect certain statements from legal action on the ground of public policy. This includes absolute or qualified privilege.

It is an absolute privilege where it involves any of the following statements:

---

[107] *Supra*
[108] [2006]5 W.R.N. 35
[109] O.T. Abisoye; *op. cit.*
[110] [1990] 3 NWLR (pt 139), p.392
[111] [2010] 35 W.R.N. 11
[112] [2006] 27.W.R.N.

i. statements made in parliamentary proceedings;
ii. report ordered to be published by the legislature and parliamentary papers;
iii. matters of state and communications between officers of the state;
iv. judicial proceedings;
v. communication between legal practitioner and client.

In this case, the maker of the statement is totally immune from any legal action. The situations where qualified privileges arise include:

i. statement made in self-defence;
ii. fair and accurate reports of proceedings, either judicial or legislative;
iii. statement made in the performance of a legal, moral or social duty;
iv. statement made between parties having a common interest;
v. statement made to the proper authorities in order to obtain redress for public grievances.

In any of the above statements, the maker is not totally immune from legal proceedings.

See *Willie* v. *Ibioke*,[113] *Independent Newspapers Ltd* v. *Idiong*.[114]

Economic Torts

Passing Off

The following are defences for the economic tort of passing off:

(a) that the plaintiff does not have *locus standi;*
(b) that the defendant's activities do not harm or are likely to harm the plaintiff's goodwill in the business;
(c) that the defendant is not using the name in the course of trade;
(d) that the plaintiff did not establish the existence of goodwill associated with the trade name, trademark or get-up in the course of trade;
(e) that the defendant is making honest use of the name or mark;
(f) that the plaintiff acquiesced in the defendant's use of name or mark;
(g) that it is not a common filed of activity;

[113] [2012] 52 W.R.N. 80
[114] [2011] 46 W.R.N. 99

(h) *Res judicata.*

Interference with Contract

The defendant may plead illegality or justification as a defence for interference with contract.

SUMMARY

The objectives of the law of torts may include:

(a) Compensation: Law of torts aim at compensating the victims of tortuous act;

(b) Protection of interests: Law of torts protects a person's interests in land and other property, in his or her reputation, and in his or her bodily integrity.

Chapter 28

OUTLINE OF PROPERTY LAW IN NIGERIA

P. E. O. Oguno* & Chineze S. Obi-Okoye**

INTRODUCTION

The chequered history and evolution of the land tenure systems in Nigeria has resulted in a complex web of conflicting laws, rules and practices which appear incongruent with international principles of good land governance. This work discusses the multiple sources of property law in Nigeria, highlighting the areas of conflict and hierarchy of such sources of law. The various legislations which regulate land administration are summarised with emphasis on the major provisions of the Land Use Act. The Act is criticised and recommendations made for land reform in Nigeria.

The word property has diverse meanings depending on the context in which it is used. It could mean ownership or title, such as when it is said that 'property in goods passes to the buyer immediately when a contract of sale is concluded.' Ownership here extends to an interest in the thing, which, although less than ownership, nonetheless confers certain rights on the holder, such as a right to use or make a profit from the thing. Secondly, it may mean the '*res*' or actual thing over which ownership and other lesser interests may be exercised such as goods, land etc. Property is, therefore, anything capable of being owned, whether tangible or intangible.[1] It is generally classified into two types:

---

* Oguno, P.E.O. Ph.D, Faculty of Law, Anambra State University

**Chineze S. Obi-Okoye, LLM Lecturer, Faculty of Law Nnamdi Azikiwe University, Awka, Anambra State.

[1] Oxford Dictionaries, http://www.oxforddictionaries.com/definition/english/property, accessed 26/2/14.

'real' and 'personal.' Real property is land and anything ordinarily growing on or affixed to it, as well as things artificially attached or erected on it, such as buildings and crops. Real property includes intangible rights that issue from interests in land. Personal property (referred to as 'personalty'), is anything other than land that can be the subject of ownership, including stocks, money, notes, patents, copyrights, and other intangible rights over tangible goods.[2]

Property law is the area of law that governs the various forms of ownership and tenancy in real property. It regulates rights in and over land and the processes whereby those rights are created, managed, transferred and terminated.[3] Land is peculiar because unlike other properties, it is immovable, transferable in its form and yet capable of being owned in different forms. Different interests may exist on land simultaneously and each interest is a right enforceable by each interest holder. This feature of land is encapsulated in the theoretical doctrine of estates to facilitate the division of various degrees of ownership and rights in land. For example, A may have a life estate over green acre with the fee simple reversionary interest falling to B; A may lease the same property to C for a term of years, and C, in turn, may mortgage his term of years to D, and at the same time, build a house on the land and let the property to E for a lesser term of years. Upon A's death, B (or his heirs) will not have the right to possession of green acre until C, D, and E's estates have come to an end. The estate of B, though futuristic, will be regarded as running consecutively with those of A and his tenants (C, D, and E), whose interests run concurrently.[4]

DEFINITION AND SCOPE OF LAND

Land remains the most valuable property in the life of man - the bedrock of all properties. It is a source of livelihood, employment and wealth, a foundation for shelter and a base for agricultural production. The majority of natural resources are extracted from land and it is one asset that *mutatis mutandi*, perennially appreciates in value irrespective

---

[2] BO Nwabueze, *Nigerian Land Law*, (Enugu: Nwamife Publishers Limited,1972) p 4.

[3] *The Free Dictionary*, http://legal-dictionary.thefreedictionary.com/Law+of+property, accessed 26/2/14.

[4] MP Thompson, *Modern Land Law*, (Oxford: Oxford University Press, 2012), p 272.

of economic conditions. The Common Law definition of land goes beyond the earth's surface and its subsoil to include all other objects attached to the earth's surface, such as trees, rocks, buildings, and other structures, whether naturally attached or constructed by man. The definition even extends beyond these to incorporate abstract rights and interests like incorporeal hereditaments, easements like rights of way and profits enjoyed by persons over the properties belonging to others.

In Nigerian jurisprudence, the Interpretation Act[5] describes land as '...including any building and any other thing attached to the earth or permanently fastened to anything so attached, but does not include minerals.' This is actually no definition at all because it merely gives a restricted list of what land includes, thus leaving room for conjecture as to whether other lesser interests, such as incorporeal hereditaments, may be classified as land. Where a land transaction is regulated by a statute or law, the definition used in that statute will govern the transaction, but where there is no such definition, the definition in the Interpretation Act will apply. The statute which adopts the extensive and all-inclusive Common Law definition of land is the Property and Conveyancing Law (PCL) 1959. Section 2 of the PCL defines land to include:

> ...the earth surface and everything attached to the earth otherwise known as fixtures and all chattels real. It also includes incorporeal rights like a right of way and other easements as well as profits enjoyed by one person over the ground and buildings belonging to another.[6]

Olawoye[7] describes land as '...including, the surface of the earth, the subsoil and the airspace above it, as well as all things that are permanently attached to the soil. It includes streams and ponds. On the other hand, things placed on land, whether made of the product of the

---

[5] Cap 123 Laws of the Federation of Nigeria (LFN) 2004. However, where a land transaction is regulated by a statute or law, the definition used in the statute will govern the transaction; otherwise, the definition in the Interpretation Act remains applicable.

[6] S. 2, Property and Conveyancing Law, Cap. 100 Laws of Western Nigeria, 1959.

[7] CO Olawoye, *Title to Land in Nigeria*, (Lagos: Evans Brother Ltd., 1974), p 38; E Colson, *The Impact of Colonial Period on the Definition of Land Rights in Colonial Africa*, (London: Oxford University Press,1971).

soil or not, do not constitute land.' It follows, therefore, that while a crop or tree is planted, it forms part of the land and is regarded as land, but as soon as it is cut and removed, it ceases to be land. In the same vein, where a building is standing it forms part of land, but where the building is demolished it ceases to be land. To be regarded as forming part of the land, a fixture must be permanently attached to the land, where the fixture is not of a permanent nature it is not land, and can be disposed of without affecting land.[8]

The *Quic quid* Maxim on Fixtures

Ownership of the developments on land where the development was made by persons who are not the real owners of such land has been a major issue in real property law. The Common Law principle *quic quid plantator solo solo cedit* (whatever is affixed to the soil, belongs to the soil), was formulated to address this issue. A chattel affixed to the land, as to become part of it, loses its character as chattel and passes with the ownership of the land. Thus, chattels are of a temporary nature, while fixtures remain permanent. Whether or not a chattel has been affixed to the land is a question of law for the judge to decide. The decision turns upon the particular circumstances of each case, and mainly but not decisively, the *degree of annexation* and *object of annexation.*[9] By the degree of annexation test, a chattel will rank as a fixture if it is united to the land or affixed to an object which is physically attached to the land. Mere juxtaposition or lying of an article, however heavy, does not *prima facie* make it a fixture. Under the object of annexation test, one must ascertain whether the chattel has been fixed for its use as a chattel or for the more convenient use of the land or building.[10]

The *quic quid* rule applies under Nigerian customary law but depends on the circumstances of the case. Where a person builds a house on land without the consent of the owner, and after the owner has protested several times, he will ultimately lose the property to the

---

[8] Ibid.

[9] EH Burn, J Cartwright, *Cheshire and Burn's Modern Law of Real Property* (18th edn, London: Oxford University Press, 2011), p 10.

[10] Ibid.

owner of the land at the suit of the owner as the maxim applies.[11] However, where the structure or building was erected with the permission of the owner of the land, the improvements remain the property of the person that constructed the building or structure. In fact, customary law allows the maker to continue using the building or structure as long as they remain on the land.[12] Niki Tobi summarized the judicial position thus:

Although judicial opinion on the issue is not uniform, there is more support of the opinion that the [*quic quid*] maxim applies in Nigerian Customary Law. It will be inequitable to contend otherwise. It would appear however that the maxim will not apply under customary law if improvements are made on the land with the permission of the owner of the land. In that case, customary law draws a clear distinction between the land and the improvement made thereon.[13]

CLASSIFICATION OF RIGHTS IN LAND

Rights in Land may be classified under three heads: Ownership, Possession and Incorporeal Rights. Ownership connotes the totality of rights and powers that are capable of being exercised over land. These include the right to make physical use of a thing, the right to make profit from it, whether in money, in-kind, or in services, and the power of management, including that of alienation which is the most conclusive way of demonstrating ownership.[14] Ownership, therefore, implies the fullest rights of enjoyment, management, and disposal over property, the owner's title to these rights being superior and paramount to any other rights that exist in the land in favour of other persons. The absoluteness of a right of the owner of the land is represented by saying that such right is 'Allodial".[15] A person cannot have allodial ownership of land in Nigeria because Section 1 of the Land Use Act of 1978

[11] *Osho* v. *Olayioye* (1966) N.M.L.R 329, *Ezoni* v. *Ejodike* (1964) All N.L.R 402.

[12] *Adebiyi* v. *Ogunbiyi* (1965) N.M.L.R 395.

[13] N Tobi, *op. cit. Cases and Materials on Nigerian Land Law*, (Lagos: Mabrochi Books, 1992) 2.

[14] *Nsirem* v. *Nwakerendu*, (1955) 15 WACA 71, BO Nwabueze, *Nigerian Land Law*, (Enugu: Nwanife Publishers, 1972), p.9); AM Olong, *Land Law in Nigeria*, (Lagos: Malthouse Law Books, 2012), p. 35.

[15] Allodial ownership is an English concept which vests all lands in England in the Crown. No individual in England has allodial ownership but rather a right of seisin (occupancy) over land which may be finite or infinite.

removed the same from individuals and groups and vested it in the Governors of respective states. Individuals are now only entitled to rights of occupancy.

Possession, on the other hand, is an incident of ownership and means actual physical use or occupation of land or the right to do so. Possession need not be based on a right to possess, as a person who takes up possession of land without a right to do so (an adverse possessor) can lawfully maintain a right to trespass against all except a person with a better title.[16] Though an adverse possessor may not be able to keep out the person with a better title, if he resists entry of such a person, the person with a better title will have to go to court to eject him from possession. The secured right of the adverse possessor flows from the presumption of law that the person in possession is presumed to have title to the property until the person with a better title is established and declared by a competent court.[17] In fact, if the real owner does not take any step for a period of time, the possessory right may ripen into a title for lapse of time (prescription) or by *laches and acquiescence* on the part of the real owner.[18] To determine which acts amount to actual possession, the Court will consider the circumstances of each case. For instance, clearing, cultivating, erecting fences and other demarcations on land, erection of survey pillars, and letting of premises to tenants have all been held to constitute possession.[19]

---

[16] *Buraimoh* v. *Bamgbose* (2009) MJSC (pt 1), 120, *Nwadiogbu* v. *Nnadozie* (2001) 6 SCNJ 161 at 167.

[17] *Ogunleye* v. *Oni* (1990) 2 NWLR (Pt 135) 745; *Ugoji* v. *Onukogu* (2005) 16 NWLR (Pt 950) 97 at 112 & 119.

[18] There are Limitation Laws for various states in the Federation, usually culled from the Limitation Act of 1882 – a statute of general application. These require that a law suit must be commenced within a specific period of time from when the injury or omission causing the damage or loss arose or occurred. The effect of not commencing a law suit or judicial proceeding within the period limited for bringing the law suit is that such a law suit or claim will be extinguished after the time limited for commencing the law suit has elapsed. For example, the Limitation Law CAP 118 of the Laws of Lagos State 1994 in Sections 16, 17, 19 and 21 state that 'Actions based on any legal instrument under seal especially where such legal instrument relates to an interest or charge on land, or the arrears of an annuity charged on an immovable property, or the enforcement of an arbitration award where the Arbitration Agreement is under seal, or the judgment of a competent Court of Law, etc., must be commenced (or where a judgment or award is to be enforced) within a period of twelve (12) years from the period when the cause of action arose or the judgment or award was entered.' See *Owhanda* v. *Ekpechi* (2003) 9 S.C. NJ 1 at p.14; *Okafor* v. *Idigo III* (1984) 5 S.C. 1 at p.36; *Regd. Trustees* v. *James* (1957) 2 NWLR (Pt. 61) 556 at p.567; and *Uka* v. *Irolo* (2002) 7 SCNJ 137 at pp 167 168.

[19] *Nissan (Nig) Ltd.* v. *Yaganathan* (2010) 4 NWLR (Pt 1183) 149 at 154; *Alhaji Akibu & 3 Ors.* v. *Azeez & Anor.* (2OO3) 1 SCNJ. 393, *Adeniyi* v. *Ogunbiyi* (1965) NMLR 395; *Nzekwu* v. *Nwakobi* (1962) 6ENLR 114.

An incorporeal right is that thing which has no physical existence but capable of being owned or possessed. Land is a corporeal hereditament because it is a physical object capable of being possessed. Incorporeal hereditaments on land would consist of incorporeal rights to the corporeal use and profit of land. In other words, those rights on land which though not capable of physical existence or possession, actually exist and are capable of being enforced in law. For example, the right to institute legal actions, the right to easements such as the right of way, the right to make profit by taking something from another person's land, etc. Incorporeal rights are of two types: those which give future possessory rights such as remainders and reversionary interests after a grant/lease and those such as easements that never entitle their owners to possession of land.[20]

MULTIPLE SOURCES OF LAND TENURE SYSTEMS IN NIGERIAN PROPERTY LAW

Land tenure, as a legal phenomenon, is a body of rules that governs access to land and the relationship between the holder of land and the community on the one hand or that between the holder and another party having a superior title. Land tenure systems are always community specific as they reflect particular social and economic outlooks; hence the land tenure system of one community may not be easily imported or adapted by another community unless they have similar customs and socio-economic beliefs.[21] The evolution of land tenure in Nigeria was a complex and dynamic process, involving the traditional political system, the modern legal system and the imported common law system. Conflicts over jurisdiction in land matters arose and still arise between individuals with different tenurial rights under different systems of land tenure.[22]

---

[20] IO Smith, *The Law of Real Property in Nigeria,* (Lagos: Lagos State University Press, 1995) p 26.

[21] CO Olawoye, 'Statutory Shaping of Land Law Administration up to the Land Use Act', in JA Omotola, *Essays on the Land Use Act, 1978* (Lagos: University of Lagos Press, 1982).

[22] PC Lloyd, *Yoruba Land Law,* (London, Oxford University Press, 1962), p 12.

Nigeria has three main sources of tenurial land systems: the received English laws, Statutory law, and Customary/Sharia law. These shall be explained briefly.

Customary Land Tenure Systems

When Britain made a colony and protectorate of Nigeria in the mid-twentieth century, the customary laws of various communities were the only recognizable systems of land tenure. These diverse systems can be grouped broadly into two. The first obtained in northern Nigeria where the colonial administration had placed all lands under the control and subject to the disposition of the Governor. This was on the basis that the Maliki Law operated by the Fulani over much of Hausaland in the nineteenth century conferred on the colonial conqueror's rights to the land of the conquered.[23] All in the North were managed by the Emirs in accordance with Islamic tenets and upon conquest by the British in the early twentieth century, the ultimate rights in the land held by the Fulani lands dynasty were transferred to the British Crown.[24]

Pieces of land legislation were introduced between 1902 and 1935,[25] which consequently metamorphosed into the Land Tenure Law enacted in Northern Nigeria in 1962.[26] The aim of the Law was stated to be 'to protect and preserve the right of the natives to the use and enjoyment of the land of the protectorate and the natural fruits thereof in sufficient quantity for the sustenance of themselves and their families,' but the real aim was to facilitate the easy dispossession of the natives from their land if and when the land was needed for other

[23] The British colonialists adopted a system of indirect rule in the North which was able to thrive because of the pre-existing policy of paternalism instituted by the Fulani dynasty after the Usman Dan Fodio jihad in the early 19th Century. See AR Mustapha and K Meagher K, *Agrarian Production, Public Policy and the State in Kano Region, 1900-2000,* (Crewkerne, Somerset: Drylands Research Working Paper 35, (2000).

[24] CK Meek, *Land Tenure and Administration in Nigeria and the Cameroons*, (London, HMSO, 1957)

[25] These include Native Lands Acquisition Proclamation 1900, the Native Lands Acquisition Proclamation 1903, the Grown Lands Management Proclamation, 1906, as amended, the Native Acquisition Ordinance 1917, the Niger Lands Transfer Ordinance 1916 and the Crown Ordinance 1918. In 1935, the Registration of Title Act of that year was enacted. This Act provided for the registration of land instruments recognized under the Act and was preceded by the Registered Land Act 1965 which was also enacted for the purpose of registration of titles to land.

[26] IO Smith, "Title to Land in the Former Federal Capital Territory of Lagos: Matters Arising", (1996) *Journal of Private and Property Law*, Vol. 25, 1 at 14-15.

purposes.[27] The interest that an individual could have in land was a right of occupancy, which could be statutory or customary. The statutory right of occupancy was one granted by the Governor, while the customary right of occupancy was derived by force of customary law.[28]

By contrast, in southern Nigeria, the traditional system recognized that land was owned by lineages or extended families. Individuals had only rights of use over such family land. The only land held at the Governor's disposal was that which had been expressly acquired for public purposes as State land.[29] This strategy enabled the government to free large expanses of land from the prevalent customary land tenure in the South, which restricts land ownership to the family and communal and individual.[30] The only control imposed by law on the lineages and other local land-holders was an obligation to seek the consent of the Government when rights were being conveyed to aliens[31] and to register changes in title.[32]

The Concept of Land under Customary Law

Whether in Northern or Southern Nigeria, land is considered by the people as having historical, cultural, social and spiritual significance above its economic value, ownership of land conferred community identity. The ideology guiding all types of customary land tenures in Nigeria is that land belongs not to human beings, but to God; humans

---

27 Ibid.

28 The law forbade alienation of a statutory right of occupancy without the consent of the Governor and distinguished between natives and non-natives in that where the alienation was to a native, it was unlawful but not void, but where a non-native was concerned, then the alienation was void *ab initio*. A native was defined in the law as a person where father belonged to a tribe in Northern Nigeria. Thus other Nigerians and aliens were classified as non-natives and are therefore subject to the some degree of discrimination.

29 The Public Lands Ordinance of 1876 (later re-enacted as Public Lands Acquisition 1917) empowered the Government to acquire land compulsorily for public purposes subject to the payment of compensation to the land owners. The land acquired becomes state (formerly crown) land, and therefore becomes property of the state. Some of these laws were regional such as the Grown Grants (Township of Lagos) Ordinance, No.18 of 1947, the Arotas (Crown Lands) Ordinance, No19, 1947, and the Glover Settlement Ordinance, No.21 of 1947. See also *Ajibola* v. *Ajibola* (1947)18 NLR 125; *Glover & Anor* v. *Officer Administering the Government of Nigeria* (1949)19 NLR 45.

30 See AEW Park, "A Dual System of Land Tenure: The Experience of Southern Nigeria" (1965) JAL vol.9 1.

31 The Acquisition of Land by Aliens Law, Cap 2, Laws of Eastern Nigeria, 1952. Meek, *op cit.*

32 The Land Registration Act Cap 99 LFN 1958 and the various regional Land Registration Laws. For the most part, these laws were ignored as very few land transactions were ever registered.

merely have the use of the land. This right of use belongs primarily to the ancestors, but is also for the living and the future generations.[33] This is why in most Nigerian societies, the position at the beginning of the twentieth century was that land was not sold. To sell land to a stranger or migrant was to render the security of the community concerned a hostage to fortune. Yet, the extensive labour migrations that colonialism set in motion could not go on without land being alienated from strangers and migrants. Whether in the urban or rural areas, transactions in land gradually emerged in all parts of the country. Thus, as the colonial era progressed, land alienation and sales not only grew in volume and geographical spread but also became the cause of considerable litigation and communal strife, often resulting in violent confrontation.[34]

Initial acquisition of land under customary law is accomplished by conquest or settlement on virgin land by a group or individual.[35] Thereafter, a hierarchy of authority and control over land is followed. At the apex is the community head, followed by the traditional (village) chiefs and then by family heads. Individuals are entitled to portions of communal land as a result of membership in a family or clan. Families ensure continuous use of the same land by individual members over time but for the purposes of ownership, the family or community is considered a unit until and unless the land is partitioned. As a result, absolute title to communal or family land can never be vested solely in the family or community head; neither the head nor a member of the family can alienate his or her own private property from family holdings.[36] Nevertheless, personal ownership of land is recognized if it is permitted by the relevant law and custom of that area. Evidence of

[33] RW James, *Modern Land Law*, (Ile-Ife: University of Ife Press, 1973).

[34] DA Guobadia and AO Adekunle (eds), *Ethnicity and National Integration in Nigeria: Recurrent Themes*, (Lagos: NIALS, 2004), pp 58 – 87.

[35] *Mora* v. *Nwalusi* (1962) 1 All NLR 681.

[36] However, where the head of family alienates the family property without the concurrence of the principal members the sale is voidable. It is voidable at the option of any member of the family. *Ekependu* v. *Erika* (1959) 4FSC 79. See also, *Lukman* v. *Ogunsusu* (1972) 1 All NLR (pt. 41), *Mogaji* v. *Nuga* (1960) 5 FSC 107. In the case of *Essan* v. *Faro* (1947)12 WACA 135, the court held where majority of the principal members of the family opposed a sale by the head of family, that the sale was invalid. *Ogunbanbi* v. *Abowaba* (1951) 3 W.A.C.A. 222, *Folarin* v. *Durojaiye* (1988) IN.W.L.R (pt. 70) 351.

the partitioning of family or communal land signifies an end to the communal or family ownership of that land.[37]

The customary law of land tenure is recognised by our laws and the High Courts are to 'observe and enforce the observance of customary law which is applicable and not repugnant to natural justice, equity and good conscience nor incompatible either directly or by implication with any law for the time being in force.'[38] The customary land tenure varies from one community to the other, and because it is unwritten law, it must be properly proved before the court as the acceptable law governing the particular situation.[39]

Land Tenure *Vide* the Received English Law

By virtue of the Foreign Jurisdiction Acts, 1896-1913, the British Government assumed powers to legislate on Nigeria. Pursuant to this, the English Common Law, the Doctrines of Equity, and the Statutes of General Application[40] that were in force in England on 1st January 1900 became enforceable in Nigeria. The received English land law consists of all case laws establishing common law doctrines and principles of English land law. It follows that the English Common Law rules relating to land tenures, disposition of real property, estates inheritance, perpetuities, and a number of others are applicable in Nigeria, as are doctrines of equity such as construction of wills, institution, and settlement of land, legal and equitable estates and interests in land and the doctrine of constructive notice and *bona fide* purchaser for value. Likewise, English laws pertaining to real property became applicable in Nigeria such as the Statute of Frauds 1677, the Wills Act 1837, Limitation Acts of 1882, Real Property Act 1845, the Partition Act 1868,

---

37 *Nwadiogbu* v. *Nnadozie* (2001) 6 SCNJ 161 at 167; *Ogunbanbi* v. *Abowaba* (1951) 3 W.A.C.A. 222, *Folarin* v. *Durojaiye* (1988) IN.W.L.R (pt. 70) 351.

38 Section 26 of the High Court of Lagos State cap 60, Laws of Lagos State of Nigeria.

39 Until judicially noticed, every customary practice is a question of fact which is required to be pleaded and proved by witnesses in any legal proceeding - *Olubodun* v. *Lawal* (2008) All FWLR (Pt. 438) p.1468; *Odutola* v.. *Sanya* (2008) All FWLR (Pt. 400) p. 780, *Amodu Tijani* v. *Secretary of Southern Nigeria* (1921) A.C 399 at 404.

40 Statute of general application are all the laws that were in force in England as at 1st of January, 1900. N Tobi, *Cases and Materials on Nigerian Land Law*, (Lagos: Mabrochi Books,1992) 2.

the Conveyancing Act 1881, the Settled Land Act 1882 and the Land Transfer Act 1887.[41]

The influence of received English law is dwindling because we now have local pronouncements of the Supreme Court and other courts of record interpreting these legislations to suit our local conditions. Also, a number of the received laws have been domesticated, (e.g. Property and Conveyancing Law 1958 of Western Nigeria which replaced the Conveyancing Act 1881). As a result, the received English law on property will no longer be applicable in those areas where the laws have been domesticated. Moreover, when the English common law and doctrines of equity are in conflict with local legislations and laws, the local legislations and laws will prevail.[42]

LAND TENURE UNDER NIGERIAN LAND LEGISLATIONS

Various municipal laws have a direct impact on property transactions in Nigeria, the most prominent being the Land Use Act (LUA) of 1978, which nationalises all lands in the country by vesting the ownership of same in the State via the Governors of constituent states.[43] The need for the promulgation of the Land Use Act was borne out of the necessity to harmonize the land tenure system in the country and regulate land speculation. However, the major thrust of the Act was to extend the northern system of land management to the whole country as a means of ensuring easier access to land for government and, ostensibly, for individuals.[44] Some of the more important provisions of the Act are indicated below:

- All land situated in the territory of each state in the country is vested in the Governor of the state. This means that no person can hold a fee simple, fee tail, or even a life estate in land in any state in Nigeria - private individuals are entitled to mere rights of occupancy over

---

[41] See *Young* v. *Abina* (1940) 6 W.A.C.A. 180; *Apatira* v. *Akande* (1944) 17 NLR 149; *Lawal* v. *Younan* (1961) 1 All NLR 245; *Green* v. *Owo* (1936) 13 NLR 43.

[42] *Ude* v. *Nwara* (1993) 2 NWLR (Pt. 278) p. 647.

[43] Land Use Act Cap L5 LFN 2004, section 1.

[44] IO Smith, *op cit* at 198.

land, and this is the greatest and highest legal interest a holder can have;[45]

- Land control and management, including land allocation in urban areas, come under the Governor of each state, while land located in rural areas becomes the responsibility of the various local governments. Only the Governor can declare parts of the state territory governed by him as an urban area by an order published in the state gazette.[46] The Governor and Local Government are respectively empowered to grant Statutory and Customary Certificates of Occupancy (C of O) for a definite term for rights of access to land under their control;[47]
- Land in urban areas is to be administered by a body known as the Land Use and Allocation Committee, which has the responsibility of advising the Governor on the management of urban land. Similarly, a Land Allocation Advisory Committee is provided to advise local governments in like manner;[48]
- The consent of the Governor must be secured for the transfer of a statutory right of occupancy through either mortgage or assignment. The consent of the Local government or that of the Governor in appropriate cases must also be obtained for the transfer of the customary right of occupancy.[49] However, land which had already been developed remained in possession of the person in whom it was vested before the Act became effective. For undeveloped lands, the maximum area that any person could retain in an urban area was one-half of a hectare, while in rural areas, it was 5000 hectares. Such retained rights are deemed to have been retrospectively granted by the Governor;[50]
- The Governor retains the right to revoke a right of occupancy for overriding public interest, public purposes and for breach of the

[45] Land Use Act, *op cit*, sections 1, 28 and 29. *Kachalla* v. *Banki* (2006) All FWLR (Pt. 309) p. 1420. Section 5(1); *Ezennah* v. *Attah* (2004) All FWLR (Pt. 202) p. 1858 at 1884.
[46] Ibid., Sections 2 and 3.
[47] Ibid., Sections 5 and 6.
[48] Ibid., sections 2(1) and (2).
[49] Ibid., sections 21 and 22, *Savannah Bank Ltd* v. *Ajilo* (1989) 1NWLR (pt. 97) p 305.
[50] Ibid., sections 34-36, *Abioye* v. *Yakubu* (1991) 5 NWLR (pt. 190) p. 130.

terms and conditions of a Certificate of Occupancy. Where a right of occupancy is revoked for the first two reasons listed above, the holder shall be entitled to compensation for the value of their improvements on the land. This implies state appropriation of land from families and communities without any compensation except for economic crops and erected structures.[51]

All this notwithstanding, Section 4 of the Land Use Act preserves the application of the State and Federal Property Laws with the proviso that they will 'continue to have effect with such modifications as would bring them into conformity with the Land Use Act or its general intendment.' As a result of this section, the following major property laws are recognised:

- the 1999 Constitution which in section 43 provides for the right of every citizen to acquire and own immovable property anywhere in Nigeria and leans against the taking away of proprietary vested rights without specific legal authority and the provision of compensation.[52] Section 315(5)(d) provides for the sanctity of the Land Use Act;
- the Property and Conveyancing Law (PCL) 1959 was enacted by the western region of Nigeria and requires all conveyances of land or interests in land for the purposes of creating any legal estate to be made by deed;[53]
- the Conveyancing Acts (1881, 1882) are English Statute of General Application applicable to States of the old Eastern and Northern Nigeria and a part of Lagos;[54]
- Stamp Duties Act/Laws (2004) – There is a Stamp Duty Act for every State which provide for remittance of stamp duties on land within the control of a given State to the State Internal Revenue Service.[55]

---

[51] Ibid., sections 28 and 29.

[52] Constitution of the Federal Republic of Nigeria 1999, section 44.

[53] Sections 77 – 97

[54] These statutes have been repealed and modernized in England and there is no justification for their being retained in our statute books in Nigeria. As Niki Tobi JCA (as he then was) stated in *Caribbean Trading Fidelity Corporation* v. *NNPC* (2002) 14 NWLR (Pt. 786) page 133, "English is English, Nigerian is Nigerian… theirs are theirs, ours are ours… We cannot therefore continue to enjoy this borrowing spree or merry frolic at the detriment of our legal system…"

[55] Stamp Duties Act Cap S.8 Laws of the Federation of Nigeria 2004, section 1.

- Registration of Titles/Instruments Laws: there are three principal systems of recording rights/ownership of land in Nigeria. These include private conveyances, registration of titles and registration of deeds. The Registration of Instruments Act of 1924 and the Registration of Titles Act of 1935 apply throughout the Federation though some states have enacted modified versions of the laws.[56] The major purpose of these laws is to guarantee titles that have been investigated and registered by the Registrar of Titles so that purchasers of land can rely on it in determining if the vendor has title to sell the property and the encumbrances that attach to the land. An unregistered registrable land instrument must not be pleaded in court and is not admissible to prove title;[57]
- Wills Act (Amendment) Act, 1852 and Wills Laws of Various States – These laws ensure a testator's freedom to dispose of interests in land in his will;
- Administration of Estates Laws of States – These laws regulate the administration of the estate of a deceased person who dies intestate or testate. The law substitutes local provision on intestate succession with English law on intestacy.

RESOLVING ISSUES ARISING FROM THE TRIPARTITE LAND TENURE SYSTEM IN NIGERIA

In view of the above mentioned land tenure systems in Nigeria, the problem had always been identifying the particular law governing a particular situation. In other words, can one apply Customary Law, Common Law/Equity and Nigerian Statutes interchangeably? Is it possible for instance, to convert a customary land holding to an English-type fee simple estate? The fee simple estate absolute in possession is the most superior title capable of being held in land in England but is different in its quality and content from the ownership structure under customary law because the customary interest merely

---

[56] For instance, the Registration of Titles Law 2003, Cap. R4, Laws of Lagos State and the Land Instrument Registration Laws 1924 adopted as Cap 62, Laws of Lagos State (Lagos)

[57] *Adesanya* v. *Aderonmu* (2009) 9 NWLR (Pt. 672) 370; *Olowoake* v. *Salawu* (2000) 11 NWLR (pt. 667) 127; *Ossai* v. *Nwajide* (1975) 4 SC 207.

confers possessory right so that it does not confer any attribute of ownership.[58] What this means is that since the two interests are different in quantum and quality, it would be impossible to convert one into the other.

As Tow J. observed in the case of *Balogun* v. *Oshodi*,[59] "I do not think that the equitable jurisdiction of the Court can be invoked to convert a mere customary right of occupancy into a freehold because the occupier purported to convey the freehold by means of an instrument drown in English form." In *Boulous* v. *Odunsi*,[60] the plaintiff claimed the title in fee simple over a parcel of land which he acquired under customary law. His title under customary law was voidable and would be voided at the instance of the family. He thereafter created a series of conveyances purporting to convert the land to a fee simple estate. The court held that it was not possible to convert such interest under customary law into an estate in fee simple.

The Land Use Act attempted to address this conflict by converting the occupier status of a customary tenant before the Act into a right of occupancy, which is the Nigerian equivalent of freehold.[61] Indeed, all titles in land prior to the Act were automatically converted into deemed rights of occupancy.[62] By this section, a customary land title is legislatively converted into a non-customary title. Moreover, the Supreme Court has held that the grant of a certificate of occupancy does not defeat a pre-existing customary right over land, although customary rights of occupancy may only be granted on the condition that there are no statutory rights of occupancy, which would automatically nullify the former.[63] Customary law also continues to govern the inheritance of both customary and statutory land rights.

---

[58] *Balogun* v. *Oshodi* (1929) 10 W.L.R 36 at 57.

[59] *Supra*

[60] (1959) 4 FSC 234

[61] Section 34.

[62] Sections 34 – 36, *Savannah Bank Ltd* v. *Ajilo (supra)*.

[63] *AG Nasarawa State* v. *AG Plateau State* (2012) AFWLR 630; *Akunne Bosa Mbanefo* v. *Mofunanya ACBU & Anor.* (2007) 1 SCNJ 179; *Raphael Udeze &Ors* v. *Paul Chidebe & Ors.* (1991) 1 SC 148.

THE NEED FOR LAND REFORM IN NIGERIA

To ensure that the Land Use Act would not be easily amended by subsequent governments, it was made an integral part of the Constitution.[64] This has proved problematic in the face of the dire need for land reform in the country based on numerous criticisms against the Act.[65] One major criticism is the large amount of discretion given to state governors under the Act, which is susceptible to abuse. For instance, some Governors use the provision requiring their consent for assignments or mortgaging as a means of raising revenue for their States through imposing heavy charges for granting such consent, thereby obstructing the development of an efficient land market and housing finance institutions in the country. To acquire control over larger expanses of land, Governors designate entire communities and local governments as urban land. Much agitation has resulted from the gross inconvenience of subjecting the closing of land transactions to the arbitrary whims of Governors who have been known to be negligent in living up to their responsibility of signing the necessary documents at various stages of transactions in land.

These inconveniences and delays in securing Statutory Certificates of Occupancy have discouraged Nigerians from registering their land transactions with the result that many land transactions either remain in the informal market or are falsely dated as having been concluded before March 28, 1978, the operative date for the Land Use Decree. The power of Governors and the Local Governments to revoke any right of occupancy over land for overriding public interest has also been used arbitrarily, as Governors are known compulsorily to acquire land for their personal interest. Consequently, there is increasing reluctance by both the Courts and the banks to accept the Statutory Certificate of

---

[64] Section 315(5)(d) of the 1999 Constitution.

[65] An Act of the National Assembly for the alteration of the Constitution other than creation of states, shall not be passed in either House of the National Assembly unless: i) The proposal is supported by the votes of not less than two-thirds majority of all the members of that House; and ii) Approved by resolution of the Houses of Assembly of not less than two-thirds of all the states. See section 9 (2) of the 1999 Constitution.

Occupancy as conclusive evidence of the title of the holder to the land or as adequate security in an application for a loan.[66]

These various weaknesses of the Land Use Act of 1978 have become the major grounds for agitations to have the Decree first, removed from being part of the Nigerian Constitution and second, subjected to thorough review so as to develop an efficient and effective system of land management in Nigeria.[67] A serious free market economy requires a land reform that recognizes the rights of individuals or communities to land, either freehold or for relatively long-term duration, and is prepared to document these rights in an appropriate fashion. It is recommended that a fee simple interest be once again vested upon those with customary rights in order to enable farmers to use land as collateral for loans for commercial farming. Again, independent land reform commissions should be established at federal and state levels to exercise some of the overbearing powers of State Governors under the Land Use Act. Reducing the inimical cost of stamp duties and levies for registration of titles and instruments would go a long way to ensure greater compliance in registering land transactions from citizens. A digitized system of graphical land registration would improve the accessibility of records, especially where all State Land Registries can access the central records as is done, for instance, in the Corporate Affairs Commission.

FURTHER READING

Burn E.H., Cartwright J., *Cheshire and Burn's Modern Law of Real Property* (18th edn, London: Oxford University Press, 2011).

Elias, T.O., *Nigeria Land Law and Custom*, (London: Oxford University Press, 1951).

---

[66] *Goldmark Nigeria Limited & Ors.* v. *Ibafon Company Limited* (Unreported) Suit No SC421/2001, decided on Thursday, 4th Day October 2012 by Olufunlola Oyelola Adekeye. JSC. See also *Olutola* v. *Federal College of Education (Technical) Asaba* (2010) 10 NWLR (Part 1201) page 1; *Obiuweubi* v. *CBN* (2011) 7NWLR (Part 1247) page 465; *Nsiegbe* v. *Mgbemena* (2007) 10 NWLR (Part 1042) page 364; *Kachalla* v. *Banki* (2006) 8 NWLR (Part 982) page 364; *Elegushi* v. *Oseni* (2005) 14 NWLR (Part 945) page 348; *Obikoya & Sons Ltd.* v. *Govt. Lagos State* (1987) 1 NWLR (Part 50) page 385; *Ogunbambi* v. *Abowaba* (1951) 13 WACA page 222.

[67] World Bank, *Doing Business 2010 Nigeria: Comparing Regulation in 183 Economies*, (Washington DC:, 2010).

Nwabueze, B.O., *Nigerian Land Law*, (Enugu: Nwamife Publishers Limited, 1972).

Olawoye, C.O., *Title to Land in Nigeria*, (Lagos: Evans Brother Ltd., 1974).

Olong A.M., *Land Law in Nigeria,* (Lagos: Malthouse Law Books, 2012).

Tobi N.,*Cases and Materials on Nigerian Land Law*, (Lagos: Mabrochi Books,1992).

World Bank, *Doing Business 2010 Nigeria: Comparing Regulation in 183 Economies*, (Washington DC:, 2010).

Chapter 29

OUTLINE OF NIGERIAN IMMIGRATION LAW

Ambrose O. O. Ekpu*& Abdulhakeem A. Tijani**

INTRODUCTION

It is trite under International law that a state has the prerogative to determine whether or not to admit foreigners into its territory[1] and the conditions for such admittance and stay in its territory. The power of a country to determine its national policy with respect of and to control the ingress and egress of foreigners into its territory is inherent in its internal sovereignty as an independent state. In this chapter, therefore, focus is geared toward the Nigerian national policies on the control of entry into Nigeria of persons who are not citizens of Nigeria for whatever reason. To this end, an attempt will be made at understanding some basic concepts, while the principal Nigerian legislation touching on the essentials of immigration and deportation will be highlighted.

DEFINITION OF IMPERATIVES

'Immigration,' according to Black's Law Dictionary, means the "act of entering a country with the intention of settling there permanently." However, in practical terms, immigration covers every act of a foreigner entering another country, the motive, and the length of stay irrespective. In line with this reasoning, an 'Immigrant' is defined

• Professor Ambrose, O.O. Ekpu is the Dean, Faculty of Law, Ambrose Alli University, Ekpoma, Edo State, Nigeria. Email Address of the author is aoekpu@aauekpoma.edu.ng

• Abdulhakeem A. Tijani is a Lecturer in Faculty of Law, Ambrose Alli University, Ekpoma.

[1] Harris, D.J., Cases and Materials On International Law, *(London: Sweet and Maxwell, 5th Edition; 1998) pg.* 526

under Section 52(1) of the Immigration Act[2] as "any person other than a citizen of Nigeria or person accorded immunity by reason of diplomatic status who enters or seeks to enter Nigeria." A person is described as a 'Prohibited Immigrant' if he is liable to be refused entry or to be deported under the law.[3]

Closely associated with the above under Nigerian immigration law is the term 'alien' which is understood as any person, not a commonwealth citizen[4] or a citizen of Eire.[5] The term "Resident," when used in relation to an alien, means a person entering and remaining in Nigeria for 56 days or more.[6] Meanwhile, a person may be a 'citizen of Nigeria' by birth,[7] registration,[8] or naturalization.[9]

LEGAL/REGULATORY FRAMEWORK ON IMMIGRATION

Immigration law in Nigeria is governed by the Immigration Act, together with the two subsidiary legislation made pursuant thereto,[10] and the Passport (Miscellaneous Provisions) Act[11] (the "Passport Act"). Whilst the Immigration Act deals, exhaustively, with all matters bordering on the entering and leaving of Nigeria by persons other than the citizens of Nigeria, the Passport Act only creates offences in respect of fraudulent practices on passport matters. The Constitution, particularly Chapter III and Section 41, is also relevant to the subject.

---

2 The Immigration Act, originally enacted as No. 6, L.N. 91 of 1963, with commencement date of 01/08/1963, now Cap I1, Laws of the Federation of Nigeria, 2004

3 Section 52(1) of the Immigration Act

4 That is a citizen of one of the countries constituting former British empire

5 It is the Irish name for the Island of Ireland and the sovereign state of the same name. See section 52(1) of the Immigration Act

6 See para. 2 of the Immigration (Control of Aliens) Regulations made pursuant to section 51 of the Immigration Act

7 Under section 25 of the Constitution of the Federal Republic of Nigeria, 1999 (as amended) (the "CFRN") , a person is a citizen by birth if he is born in or outside Nigeria, before or after independence and either of whose parents or grandparents is a citizen of Nigeria or belongs or belonged to a community indigenous to Nigeria.

8 Under section 26 of the CFRN, any person of full age and capacity born outside Nigeria any of whose grandparents is a citizen of Nigeria or any woman who is or has been married to a citizen of Nigeria may apply to be registered as a citizen of Nigeria, and if the President is satisfied that such person is of good character, has shown clear intention of his desire to be domiciled in Nigeria and has taken the prescribed oath of allegiance, such person will be accordingly registered.

9 Under section 27 of the CFRN, a person is a citizen by naturalization, if he is granted Certificate of Naturalization by the President, having satisfied the requirements prescribed under the section

10 The Immigration Regulations; and the Immigration (Control of Aliens) Regulations both made pursuant to section 51 of the Immigration Act

11 Enacted in 1985 and now Cap P1, Laws of the Federation of Nigeria, 2004

With respect to immigration regulatory agencies, the Director of Immigration[12] under the general direction of the Minister of Internal Affairs is in charge of administering immigration law in Nigeria, and he is assisted by various Deputy Directors of Immigration, as well as other Immigration officers.[13] The Immigration Act also provides for the office of the Chief Federal Aliens Officer for the control of aliens in Nigeria and to be assisted by such alien officers[14] as may be necessary for the discharge of his duties under the law.[15] The powers of the Chief Federal Aliens Officer are subject to the direction and control of the Director of Immigration.[16]

Other regulatory bodies/agencies include the Ministry of Internal Affairs,[17] Immigration and Prisons Services Board,[18] Nigerian Customs Services,[19] and National Drugs Law Enforcement Agency.[20]

APPLICATION OF THE IMMIGRATION LAWS IN NIGERIA

The Immigration laws apply to all persons in Nigeria as well as persons entering or leaving Nigeria, including transit passengers, persons under the age of 16, and those with dual nationality.[21] In other words, every person entering or leaving Nigeria for whatever duration or purpose is liable to be examined[22] by Immigration officers before entry or

[12] But currently designated the Comptroller General of Immigration

[13] This takes the meaning of any officer appointed for the control of immigration. See section 52(1) of the immigration Act; and including medical inspectors, Nigerian Customs Services Preventive Service, as well as, members of the Nigerian Police Force appointed for the control of immigration. See section 6(1) of the Immigration Act. See section 5(1) of the Immigration Act

[14] Means any person appointed for the control of aliens and includes an immigration officer. See section 52(1) of the Immigration Act

[15] See section 5(2) of the Immigration Act

[16] Ibid.

[17] Which is the supervisory Ministry on immigration matters

[18] Established by the Immigration and Prisons Services Board Act, Cap I2, Laws of the Federation of Nigeria, 2004; and mandated, under section 3(b) of the Act, to control and manage the administration of the immigration and prisons laws.

[19] Established by the Customs and Excise Management Act, Cap C45, Laws of the Federation of Nigeria, 2004; it is mandated, among others, to check travellers and their baggage, cargo and mail.

[20] Established by the National Drug Law Enforcement Agency Act, 1989, now Cap N30, Laws of the Federation of Nigeria, 2004; and mandated to enforce laws against the cultivation, processing, sale, trafficking and use of hard drugs.

[21] See sections 1(1), 3 and 37 of the Immigration Act

[22] The power to examine here includes power to search such person and any baggage belonging to him or under his control, save that a woman or girl can only be searched by a woman. This power also accommodates the powers to detain, for a period not exceeding 7days, anything found on such person during such search for the purpose of examining same and to subject an immigrant or transit passengers to medical exams or vaccination. See sections 2(2,3) and 3(2) of the Immigration Act

embarkation to determine whether or not such person has met travel, health, or other requirements. However, there exist few exceptions in this regard:

a) Ministers of the Federal Government or Commissioners of any of the State Government are not required to complete entry or embarkation cards on entering or leaving Nigeria;[23]
b) Those who enjoy immunity for both official and unofficial acts;[24]
c) Any person exempted by the Minister from certain requirements may not be compelled by immigration officers to satisfy same before entry or leaving Nigeria;[25]
d) Any person who has satisfied the immigration authority of his identity as a citizen of Nigeria or the holder of a valid travel document or an employee of the Federal Government or any State Government;[26]
e) A person with a valid travel document or in the employment of the Federal Government or any State Government shall not be prohibited from entering Nigeria; and
f) A citizen of Nigeria cannot be deported from or denied entry into Nigeria.[27] However, this provision may raise difficulties because, in another breadth, the law says that such person must satisfy an immigration officer as to his identity as a citizen of Nigeria.

It is the duty of every person entering or leaving Nigeria to report to an immigration officer for examination and to furnish him with such information in his possession as that officer may reasonably require.[28] It is, equally, the duty of the captain of a ship or commander of an aircraft that lands in Nigeria to supply the immigration authority with

[23] See section 1(2)(a) of the Immigration Act

[24] See section 1(2)(b) of the Immigration Act. These would normally be diplomats and Heads of Governments

[25] See section 1(2)(c) of the Immigration Act. However, once such person ceases to enjoy such exemption, he must notify the Director of Immigration in writing. The Director or the supervising Minister may subsequently determine whether or not to grant permit to such person to remain in Nigeria. See section 1(3-4) of the Immigration Act

[26] See section 1(2)(d) of the Immigration Act

[27] See section 1(2)(e) of the Immigration Act

[28] See section 2 (1-3) of the Immigration Act

separate lists showing disembarking and transit passengers,[29] and the immigration authority may, if it thinks fit, examine transit passengers as if they were immigrants.[30]

ENTRY REQUIREMENTS UNDER THE LAW

Any passenger who enters or leaves Nigeria by any means at and from any recognized port,[31] or every member of the crew thereof, is required to produce to an immigration officer for examination, landing or embarkation cards and other travel documents, and the immigration officer may require any document from such person for the purposes of the examination.[32] Travel documents for entry into Nigeria include, in any proper case, a visa and employment papers and an international certificate of health valid for such entry, and where a citizen of Nigeria is departing, include any visa, employment papers, and international certificates of health valid for entry into or travel through any other country, as the case may require.[33]

For this limited purpose, the following travel documents will be considered briefly:

a) Passport;
b) Visa/Entry Permit;
c) Residence Permit;
d) Business Permit; and
e) Work Permit

Passport

A passport is a license for the safe passage of anyone from one place to another or from one country to another. It is a certificate of identity and, prima facie of, nationality and, at the same time, a request from

[29] Every such list of disembarking and transit passengers to be supplied must show the surname of every passenger in full together with the initials of such passengers, the port at which he embarks and the port at which he intends to disembark. See para. 1 of the Immigration Regulations

[30] See section 3(1) of the Immigration Act

[31] Otherwise referred to as 'Port of Entry' means in respect of person landing from or embarking in an aircraft, any recognized airport where there are facilities for customs, health and immigration inspection, and in respect of persons landing from or embarking in a ship or otherwise arriving in or departing from Nigeria, means any place where there are like facilities. Section 52(1) of the Immigration Act

[32] See section 4(1) and section 2(a) of the Immigration Act

[33] See section 52(1) of the Immigration Act

one state to another to grant entry to its bearer. A passport is evidence of permission from a sovereign to its citizens to travel to foreign countries and to return to the land of his allegiance, as well as request to foreign powers that such citizens be allowed to pass freely and safely.[34]

A passport is defined under the Immigration Act as a travel document furnished with a photograph of such person and issued to him by or on behalf of the country of which he is a subject or a citizen and for a period which, according to the laws of that country, has not expired, and includes any other similar document approved by the Minister establishing the nationality and identity of the person to whom it refers to the satisfaction of an immigration officer.[35]

Possession of a passport is a *sine qua non* for the exercise of the right to travel out of the country. The right to own a passport derives from the right to enter and exit Nigeria as guaranteed by Section 41(1) of the Constitution, Article 12(2) of the African Charter on Human and People's Rights (Ratification and Enforcement) Act, and Article 13(2) of the Universal Declaration of Human Rights.[36]

Immigration laws and practices in Nigeria show that a person cannot enter or leave Nigeria without valid travel documents, which, for all intents and purposes, include a valid passport.[37] Any attempt, therefore, to seize the passport of a Nigerian, particularly by unauthorized government personnel, in the words of Ayoola JCA (as he then was), is a potent curb on the desire of such person to travel abroad and an evident clog on the exercise of his right of freedom of movement.[38]

There are various types of passports recognized under the Passport Act, to wit: Standard Nigerian Passport; Nigerian Diplomatic or official

---

[34] See *Agbakoba* v. *The Director, SSS* [1994] 6 NWLR (Pt. 351) 475 at 495-496H-A

[35] See section 52(1) of the Immigration Act

[36] See *Attorney General of the Federation* v. *Ajayi* [2000] 12 NWLR (Pt. 682) 509 at 537A; See also *Agbakoba* v. *The Director, SSS, supra,* at 496-497H-A

[37] See section 4(1)(a) of the Immigration Act and section 6 of the Passport Act. See also the decision of the Court in *Agbakoba* v. *The Director, SSS, supra,* at 496E-F

[38] *Agbakoba* v. *The Director, SSS, supra,* at 497D-E; see also *The Director, SSS* v. *Agbakoba* (1999)67LRCN 418 at 452-453H-C, *per* Uwais JSC

Passport; Nigerian Pilgrim's Passport; and Seaman's Passport or Seaman's Card of Identification.[39]

Also, for the purpose of examining the residency status of immigrants, a person is deemed to possess a valid passport if he produces for inspection with his passport a valid visa and a residence permit.[40]

It is an offence punishable on conviction by imprisonment for a term not exceeding one year for a non-Nigerian to hold a Nigerian passport or be in unauthorized possession of more than one valid standard passport[41] or submit multiple application forms to one or more passport offices with the intention of obtaining multiple passports; or unlawfully alter, tamper with or mutilate any passport or any page thereof; or knowingly make or cause to be made any false statement for purposes of procuring a passport for himself or another or conceal, fail or refuse to disclose to the proper authority the loss of a passport; or act as a broker for the procurement of a passport at or in the vicinity of any passport office or elsewhere; or forge or traffic in passport or hold or be in possession of any forged passport, knowing same to be forged; or, otherwise, attempt, aid, abet, counsel, procure, connive or conspire with anyone to do any of the above.[42]

It is equally an offence, punishable on conviction by imprisonment for a term not exceeding two years without the option of a fine, for any recommender or guarantor to knowingly sign any application form that contains any false declaration.[43] Also, to unlawfully assist an alien to procure a Nigerian passport attracts punishment, both for the person assisting and the alien assisted, on conviction to 5 years imprisonment without the option of a fine.[44] These offences are triable summarily in a Magistrate's Court.[45]

---

[39] See section 6 of the Passport Act

[40] See section 18(4)(a,b) of the Immigration Act

[41] A person will not be regarded as being in possession of more than one standard passport if he is in possession of any other type of passport. See section 1(3) of the Passport Act

[42] See section 1 (1-2) of the Passport Act

[43] See section 2 of the Passport Act

[44] See section 3 and 4 of the Passport Act

[45] See section 5(3) of the Passport Act

Finally, the Minister may, at any time, cancel or withdraw any passport issued, and all particulars of same published in the Federal Gazette, if the passport is obtained by fraud, has expired, such person unlawfully holds more than one standard passport at a time, or it is in the public interest to withdraw or cancel the same.[46] It has been held, and rightly so that the power granted to the Minister in this regard is not to be exercised arbitrarily but restricted to defined circumstances, as afore-enumerated.[47]

Visa/Entry Permit

Visa and Entry Permit are two terms that are often heard in the realm of immigration. Both may have meanings that are somewhat dependent on the jurisdiction or territory but basically, both have same significance and roles to play.[48] Although, under the Immigration Act, a visa is defined in terms of an impress or endorsement by any means on a travel document, purporting to be signed and dated by an officer appointed for that purpose by or on behalf of the Government of Nigeria, and authorizing entry into or transit across Nigeria subject to compliance with any special requirements prescribed by the immigration authorities at a port of entry, and valid for a specified time and for the number of journeys stated therein.[49] The term Entry Permit is used if the applicant for visa is resident in a commonwealth country.[50]

A visa can be as simple as a label or stamp placed on a blank page of a passport or to signify eligibility for entry into the border of a certain country. Alternatively, it can also take the form of a separate document (less common). There are various types of visas, depending largely on the purpose for which the journey is intended, and any variation of the visa with the purpose of the journey will render such a

---

46 See section 5(1,2) of the Passport Act

47 See *Attorney General of the Federation* v. *Ajayi, supra* at 536-537F-C; also *Agbakoba* v. *The Director, SSS [supra]*

48 Obtained from "the Difference Between Visa and Permit" on www.differencebetween.net accessed on 11/07/2014

49 See section 52(1) of the Immigration Act

50 Obtained from "Guidelines To Nigerian Immigration Laws and Procedure" posted on www.hg.org accessed on 11/07/2014

visa inappropriate for entry, leading to either a refusal of landing or deportation, as the case may be.

Also, depending on its type, a visa or entry permit application may be made to and issued, if satisfied, by the head of a Diplomatic Nigerian Mission abroad designated for that purpose in such country,[51] with or without reference to the Comptroller General of Immigration. Also, in the case of application made by government officials of other nations, personnel of United Nations and its agencies, personnel of the African Union and its agencies, persons seeking entry under any technical aid scheme, specially organized trade delegations, and persons specially invited by the Federal Government of Nigeria, the diplomatic mission will also issue the appropriate entry permit.[52] But, in the case of applications by persons seeking to take up employment in Nigeria, the diplomatic Mission is required to refer such applications to the Ministry of Internal Affairs.[53]

Recognised types of visas in Nigeria include the ordinary (which is further divided into transit,[54] single journey,[55] and multiple journey[56] visas), diplomatic,[57] and gratis courtesy[58] visas.

---

[51] Where no diplomatic Nigerian Mission is established in the country, such application may lie to the Government of such country (if there exists an agreement between Nigeria and the Government of that country to that effect) or such diplomatic mission as may be designated for that purpose by the Minister for External Affairs (if no such agreement exist). See section 9(2) of the Immigration Act

[52] See section 9(1)(b) of the Immigration Act

[53] See section 9(1)(d) of the Immigration Act

[54] A transit visa is issued to applicants who wish to pass through Nigeria to a further destination. It may be obtained at a Nigerian mission and is given for a period not exceeding seven (7) days without reference to the Comptroller-General of Immigration. Such person seeking this type of visa must be in possession of an express approval (visa or any form of permission) to enter a specified third country, as well as a confirmed ticket or sufficient funds to pay for any means of transportation appropriate to reach that country. A transit visa may also be given at the port of entry on the specific approval of the Comptroller-General of Immigration. A transit pass is normally issued whether in the former or latter case, and it takes the form of an endorsement by rubber stamp on the passport of the applicant, which shall contain particulars of the port of entry, the date of entry and the period the person is permitted to remain in Nigeria in transit. See para. 6 of the Immigration Regulations for further reading on this point

[55] Single Journey Visa is valid for a single entry into Nigeria and may be issued as: (a) Short Visit Visa; (b) STR Visa (Subject To Regularisation for Residence Work Permit); or (c) T.W.P (Temporary Work Permit). The Short Visit Visa is issued to applicants who require a single entry to Nigeria for the purpose of tourism, visitation or for brief business or meeting in Nigeria. This visa is also issued at a Nigerian mission abroad without reference to the Comptroller-General of Immigration provided that, the applicant who fills Form (1MM 22), is in possession of a return air ticket to and from Nigeria or an onward ticket for a further destination, together with a visa or any other acceptable form of permission to enter that country. In case a passenger arrives at the port of entry without a return ticket or onward ticket to a further destination but is otherwise found to be admissible, he/she may be required to deposit the appropriate amount for the purchase of such ticket as may be necessary to enable him/her return to his/her country of domicile, or proceed to a further destination.

These various visas have varying requirements for the grant.[59] The provisions on entry requirement, as it relates to visa application, do not

---

STR Visa (Subject to Regularisation) is the type of visa required by foreigners seeking to take up employment in Nigeria. Section 8(1) of the Immigration Act provides that no person, not being a citizen of Nigeria, may take up employment in Nigeria other than employment with the federal or state government without the consent of the Comptroller-General of Immigration. Section 33 of the Immigration Act further provides that an application must be made to the Comptroller-General by the prospective employer, in writing, confirming that he/she has a vacancy on the expatriate quota and at the same time stating the position in which prospective employee is to be employed and confirming acceptance of immigration responsibility. The employer company applies to the Nigerian embassy or consular office in the country where such intending employee/applicant resides, requesting that he (and his accompanying spouse/ fiancñe/children, if applicable) be granted STR Visa (subject to regularisation for residence work permit) when he arrives in Nigeria. In such application, the employer company undertakes to assume immigration and other responsibilities for the employee (and his accompanying spouse/ fiancñe/children, if applicable) in Nigeria. The STR Visa is issued at Nigerian mission without reference to the Comptroller-General of Immigration provided that the applicant presents specified documents. STR visa is normally given for 90 days without reference, during which an application must be made to the Comptroller-General of Immigration, to regularise the stay of the prospective employee, and the person may assume his employment only when such application is approved and a RESIDENCE WORK PERMIT granted.

Temporary Work Permit (T.W.P) Companies and organisations wishing to engage the services of expatriates for short period assignments are required to apply direct to the Comptroller-General in Abuja for visa/entry permits for such expatriates. This is the temporary work permit visa and it is not issued without reference to the Comptroller-General of Immigration. If such applications are submitted at the Nigerian missions abroad, they must be referred to the Comptroller-General of Immigration for approval. The visa is normally approved by cablegram sent through NITEL offices in Nigeria to the Mission from where it would be issued. The cost of the transmission is borne by the company/ organisation applying for the facility. The T.W.P Visa is given for a period not exceeding 3 months and may be extended for a further period, upon application to the Comptroller-General of Immigration who will determine the desirability of such an extension. The temporary assignments, which are eligible for such approval, include: (a) erection/installation work; (b) feasibility studies; (c) repairs of machinery/equipment; (d) auditing of accounts; and (e) research work, and such other assignments as may fall into this category. Obtained from "Immigration Procedure And Requirements" posted on www.nipc.gov.ng accessed on 11/07/2014.

[56] Multiple Journey Visa is normally issued to non-resident directors of Nigerian based companies and other foreign businessmen and women for the purpose of attending meetings and for other frequent visits to pursue business arrangements, or make consultations regarding investment projects and without reference to the Comptroller- General of Immigration by the Nigerian missions abroad for a period not exceeding 12 months, and may be for a specified number of journeys within the period granted. Both the single and multiple journey visas are also given in Nigeria to employees of companies/ organisations whose stay have been duly regularised, in order to enable then return to their employment whenever they travel out either for business or holidays. This is called return or re-entry visa. Applications for this must be made personally by the employee in Nigeria and not from outside the country. The application must be supported by the employer confirming that the employee is returning to his job, and reaffirming acceptance of Immigration responsibility on behalf of the applicant, as well as showing proof of the continued availability of the expatriate quota position to be occupied.

[57] Diplomatic Visa is issued to visiting Heads of State and their families, top officials of Government and their families, diplomats and their families, holders of United Nations Diplomatic Passport and Laissez passer, members of accredited diplomatic missions, members of international organizations, members of accredited international non-governmental organization.

[58] GRATIS COURTESY VISA is issued to persons who do not qualify for diplomatic visa, but who are foreign government officials travelling on official business. It may be granted in cases where it is considered undesirable to accede to an application for a diplomatic visa, but where it is desirable on grounds of international courtesy to facilitate a journey.

[59] For further reading on this point, visit www.portal.immigration.gov.ng

apply to persons already working in Nigeria but go abroad on leave or to transit passengers who remain in or in the vicinity of the port of entry for not more than 48 hours.[60]

Residence Permit

A non-Nigerian may take up residence in Nigeria if he has a residence permit issued to him by the Director of Immigration. In practice, this is usually issued by the Comptroller General of Nigerian Immigration and endorsed on any travel document as a combined expatriate and residence permit card (CERPAC).[61] Such applicant may be required to give security in such amount as the Minister may specify and to furnish such particular as the Director of Immigration may reasonably require of him before the grant is made.[62] The Supreme Court has held in *West Construction Company Ltd.* v. *Batalha*[63] that, by a combined reading of Sections 8(1) and 34(1) of the Immigration Act, the duty to apply for a residence permit is that of the employer, not the employee.

A residence permit may be issued subject to conditions such as the area in which the holder will reside, the business or occupation he is to engage in, the duration of stay, and the control of any activity which may offend the religious beliefs of any member of the community and provision of security.[64] Also, no residence permit issued to an alien will be valid for entry unless the holder is in possession of a valid visa or is otherwise exempted from that requirement.[65]

Note that the Minister may by order exempt any person from the requirement of the Act for entry or departure.[66]

Business Permit

A non-Nigerian desirous of setting up, taking over a business enterprise, either alone or in conjunction with another, practicing a profession, or registering or taking over any company with limited

60 See section 9(3) of the Immigration Act
61 Guidelines To Nigerian Immigration Laws and Procedure, Ibid.
62 See section 10 of the Immigration Act
63 [2006] 7 MJSC 184 at 211A-G
64 See para. 4(3) of the Immigration Regulations
65 See para. 4(2) of the Immigration Regulations
66 See section 12 of the Immigration Act

liability, is required to first obtain consent in writing[67] from the Minister of Internal Affairs enabling him to do so.[68] Application for Business Permit is made to the Ministry of Internal Affairs or the Nigerian Investment Promotion Commission (the "NIPC").[69]

Work Permit

For a company registered in Nigeria to be able to employ foreigners, it is to obtain what is described as an expatriate quota from the Ministry of Internal Affairs or the NIPC. This is done by an application in the registration particulars of the company, a tabulation of official staff positions in the company, specification of positions to be occupied by foreigners and Nigerians, and, if available, a list of the foreigners to hold specific positions. It is intended to restrict foreigners from taking up employment that Nigerians are ordinarily qualified to do.[70] There are two types of expatriate quota, to wit: Permanent Until Reviewed[71] and Temporary.[72]

Accordingly, a non-Nigerian may only take up employment in Nigeria, not being one with the Federal Government of Nigeria or any State Government, with the written consent[73] of the Director of Immigration, failure of which is an offence and upon conviction is liable to deportation.[74] It is the duty of an employer to apply for a permit to enable such a person to take up employment with him.[75]

Thus, in *Oilfields Supply Centre Ltd.* v. *Johnson (No. 2),*[76] the Respondent, an Australian, worked with the Appellant company as a managing director and without holding a work permit. In the ensuing

---

67 This consent is described in terms of Business Permit as provided under para. 3 of the Immigration Regulations

68 See section 8(1)(b) and (2) of the Immigration Act

69 Requirement for grant may be found in Bhadmus, Y.H., Bhadmus On Corporate Law Practice, (Enugu: Chenglo Limited, 2009), p. 95; for further reading see also Akinola, O.B., *Understanding Nigerian Corporate Law Practice With Ethical Issues,* (Enugu: Chenglo, 2010) Chapter 6, pgs. 79-94

70 See Guidelines To Nigerian Immigration Laws and Procedure, Ibid.

71 This is usually granted for the post of chairman of a company's board of directors or the managing director of a company. See Bhadmus, Ibid., pg. 94

72 This is granted for directors and employees of a company, for a maximum period of 5 years in the first instance and renewable for a further period of 2 years. See Bhadmus, Ibid.

73 This consent is described as Work Permit

74 See section 8(1)(a) of the Immigration Act

75 See section 34(1) of the Immigration Act; see also para. 9 of the Immigration Regulations

76 [1987] 2 NWLR (Pt. 58) 625

financial crisis that rocked the Appellant company, after its compulsory acquisition by the Federal Government, the Respondent instituted a winding up proceeding against the same. It was argued on appeal and further appeal to the Supreme Court that the Respondent could not properly institute such action against the company, having been in breach of the Immigration Act and not being a shareholder. The Supreme Court found that the purport of Section 8(1) of the Immigration Act is to protect certain businesses from exploitation by non-Nigerians and make sure that Nigerians are not at any disadvantage. The Court went further to say that the section imposes no penalty for failure to comply, apart from deportation. The Petitioner/Respondent, having not been deported, the whole transaction cannot be voided.

Also, the Court of Appeal in *Nico Oliver* v. *Dangote Industries Limited*[77] reiterated the position of the law as follows:

> Furthermore, the power being questioned is exercisable under section 34 of the Immigration Act, Cap. I1, Laws of the Federation of Nigeria, 2004, which deals with employment of immigrants. The appellant, with respect, is not the applicant for the work permit. It is the employer of an immigrant that is required to apply for work permit for its immigrant worker or employee and not the employee applying for the permit....

REGISTRATION OF ALIENS

Having satisfied the preliminary requirements for entry discussed above, all aliens are required to formally register their presence in Nigeria, within 21 days of arrival, at the immigration office closest to their place of residence or occupation.[78] It should be noted that for this purpose, all state immigration offices are representatives of the Comptroller-General of Immigration and may, accordingly, deal with aliens in this regard.[79]

---

[77] [2010] All FWLR (Pt. 506) 1858 at 1875-1876H-B

[78] See para. 8 of the Immigration (Control of Aliens) Regulations

[79] See *Attorney General of Canada* v. *Cain* (1906) AC 502 at 546

Prohibited Immigrants

The following persons are prohibited immigrants and, accordingly, liable to be deported:[80]

a) any person who is without visible means of support or is likely to become a public charge;
b) any idiot, insane person, or a person suffering from any other mental disorder;
c) any person convicted in any country of any crime wherever committed, which is an extradition crime;
d) any person whose admission would, in the opinion of the Minister, be contrary to the interest of national security;
e) any person against whom an order of deportation from Nigeria is in force;
f) any person who does not have a valid passport or is under the age of 16 without a valid passport and unaccompanied by an adult on whose valid passport his particulars appear;
g) any prostitute;
h) any person who is or has been a brothel keeper; householder permitting the defilement of a young girl on his premises; or allowing a person under the age of 13 to be in a brothel; or causing or encouraging the seduction or prostitution of a girl under 13; or trading in prostitution; or a procurer; and
i) a stowaway.[81]

SUNDRY MATTERS ON IMMIGRATION

A person may be prohibited from leaving Nigeria if it is in the public interest to do so; or the travel documents of such person are not in the proper order; or there is an unsatisfied order of a court of competent jurisdiction; or a warrant of arrest relating to that person.[82] This does not apply to those who enjoy immunity for both official and unofficial acts.[83]

[80] See section 18(1) of the Immigration Act
[81] See section 28 of the Immigration Act
[82] See section 36(1) of the Immigration Act
[83] See section 36(2) of the Immigration Act

An immigration officer may refuse a non-Nigerian entry into Nigeria if it appears to him that such person is a prohibited immigrant; or has no current/valid visa, residence, or other permit (if required); or on the advice of a medical inspector, it is undesirable for medical reasons to grant entry.[84]

Offences in connection with control of immigration, immigrant employers, and workers attract various penalties[85] in terms of jail term and fine, and are believed to be too lenient to serve the appropriate end of deterring offenders in this regard. Penalties also include deportation, as earlier discussed.[86]

All civil matters bordering on citizenship, naturalization, alien deportation, extradition, immigration into and emigration from Nigeria, passports, and visas are vested exclusively in the Federal High Court.[87]

CONCLUSION

In this chapter, a quick run-down of the immigration laws in Nigeria was made. Whilst the laws, on a surface assessment, seem quite elaborate, it was observed that penalties in the laws had over-lived their relevance hence a need for urgent reform to accommodate stiffer punishments if the laws are intended to serve the end of deterrence.

Furthermore, by the provision of Article 27(1) of the ECOWAS Treaty, citizens of member states are to be regarded as community citizens, and, accordingly, member states undertake to abolish all obstacles to the freedom of movement and residence within the community.[88] Again, Article 2 of the Protocol on Free Movement of Persons, Right of Residence and Establishment, 1979, restated the commitment that the community citizens have the right to enter, reside and establish in the territory of member states. Thirty-nine years after

[84] See section 50 of the Immigration Act

[85] See sections 46-48

[86] See also sections 20 and 21 of the Immigration Act on the point that a court on conviction may make deportation order and effect thereof

[87] See section 251(1)(i) of the Constitution

[88] Similar to the provisions of Article 59 of the revised ECOWAS Treaty, 1993, which provides that citizens of the community shall have right of entry, residence and establishment

its formation, Nigerian Immigration laws, like most others within the West African community, are yet to accommodate/implement this provision of the ECOWAS Treaty and its Protocol on Free Movement of Persons, Right of Residence, and Establishment, to which it had long assented. This also applies to other international treaties and conventions to which Nigeria is a signatory, such as the Geneva Convention on the status of a refugee, etc. It is humbly recommended further that a reform of the Nigerian Immigration laws should be made in this direction.[89]

[89] For further reading on this point, see Lifu, P.O., "International Law and The Problem of Aliens in Nigeria", *(Kogi State University Law Journal, Vol. 2 & 3, 2008-2009)* pgs. 27-48; see also Bappah, A.I., "ECOWAS Treaty And The Right To Free Movement of Persons In Nigeria", *(Justice Journal: 2nd Edition, 2011)* pgs. 156-173; Toyin, O.J., International Law and Organization In A Dynamic World, (Abuja: Joecryss Venture Nigeria, 2003) pp. 178-181; Ladan, T.M., Introduction To ECOWAS Community Law and Practice: Integration, Migration, Human Rights, Access to Justice, Peace and Security, (Zaria: Ahmadu Bello University Press, 2009)

Chapter 30

OUTLINE OF FAMILY LAW IN NIGERIA

Sam Ojogbo*

INTRODUCTION

The law of marriage and divorce in Nigeria, otherwise called family law, is an important part of the Nigerian legal system. The importance of family law to the legal system derives from its place as that aspect of the law that is concerned with the relationship within the small unit of the human community called the family. The society is a composition of families; hence, the family is usually called the nucleus of society. Therefore, any serious discussion on the Nigerian Legal System must incorporate family law.

Family law in Nigeria, like all other aspects of Nigerian law, has a peculiarity that reflects Nigeria's colonization by the British. Family law recognizes two systems: monogamous or common-law marriage[1] and polygamous or customary law marriage.[2]

Monogamous marriage has the imprint of the English law of marriage and divorce, and they have the same character and incidents. It is the marriage that was described by Penzance in *Hyde* v. *Hyde* as "...the voluntary union for life of one man and one woman to the

---

* Samuel E. Ojogbo, LL.M (Western Ontario) B.L, Lecturer Faculty of Law, Benson Idahosa University, Benin City, Edo State, Nigeria. Phone: 2348097924168, Email: samojogbolaw@yahoo.com; sojogbo@biu.edu.ng

[1] The monogamous marriage, the common law marriage, statutory marriage or marriage under the Act will be used inter-changeably throughout in this chapter. They all refer to monogamous marriage.

[2] Polygamous marriage, customary law marriage and native law and custom will also be used inter-changeably throughout in this cahpter to refer to polygamous marriage.

exclusion of all others."[3] It is important to note that the Nigerian Interpretation Act 1964[4] adopts this definition of monogamous marriage in Nigeria. Mainly the Marriage Act Cap M6 LFN 2004 and the Matrimonial Causes Act Cap M7 LFN 2004 regulate monogamous marriage in Nigeria.

Polygamous marriage or customary law marriage in Nigeria, on the other hand, is a customary law[5] institution. The customary law governs its character and incidents. The Nigerian customary law, however, does not have a documented history like the common law. Therefore, customary law marriage does not have a settled definition like the marriage under the Act,[6] as customary law marriage may be defined as a voluntary union for the life of one man to one or more women.

One major difference between monogamous and polygamous marriage in Nigeria is that polygamous marriage permits the marriage of one man to more than one woman at the same time,[7] while monogamous marriage does not permit the marriage to more than one wife at a time.[8] The MA permits marriage between customary law couples who wish to marry under the Act, but a customary law husband is forbidden under the MA[9] to contract a common law marriage with any other woman other than his customary law wife.

To discuss the Nigerian family law, therefore, this chapter is divided into four parts, including this introductory part. Part two will discuss marriage in Nigeria, while Part three will discuss divorce. Part four, the concluding part, will discuss some of the issues that arise from divorce, particularly the maintenance and custody of children.

---

[3] (1886) LR 1 P & D 130, 133.

[4] No. 1 of 1964 section 18, CAP 118 Laws of Nigeria 1959.

[5] We acknowledge there are two types of customary law in Nigeria – the indigenous customary law and the non indigenous (Islamic) customary law. The difference between the two types of customary law is not relevant and, therefore outside the scope of this chapter as customary law in this chapter is used to represent the Islamic customary law and the indigenous customary law.

[6] See the definition in *Hyde* v. *Hyde supra* note 3.

[7] Note that the marriage to one woman by a customary law husband does not make the marriage a monogamous marriage as long as the customary law husband retains the capacity to take more wives.

[8] The qualifying phrase here is one wife at a time. The common law husband is forbidden from taking more than one wife at a time but he could have several wives at different times as is the case with serial monogamy.

[9] Section 33 Marriage Act, Cap M6 Law of the Federation 2004 (MA). The acronym MA will be used throughout in this Chapter to represent the Marriage Act

THE MARRIAGE INSTITUTION IN NIGERIA

There are two systems of marriage in Nigeria – statutory marriage and marriage under native law and custom. Marriages, under the two systems, carry their incidents and create different rights and obligations. However, these rights and obligations are predicated on the existence of a valid statutory or customary law marriage. Therefore, a review of the two systems will be necessary to enable us to understand when a valid marriage has come into existence because divorce is only available to a couple in a valid marriage.

A. Customary Law Marriage

We have defined customary law marriage above as a voluntary union for the life of one man and one or more women. Customary law marriage, like customary law, is a way of life of a people, a mirror of accepted usage. It is a reflection of the habits and social attitudes of a particular society or ethnic community. Customary law marriage derives its validity from the accepted practice of the people. It is generally unwritten except for some judicially recognized and documented usages of the people modified in some circumstances by statute or rules on customary law made in pursuance of statutory injunctions.[10] The marriage is in accordance with the unwritten custom of each individual community. Although it is mostly unwritten, the system is established over a long period, and the rules are simple and settled so that the requirement for validity is not in doubt. It is polygamous and involves one man and one or more women.

There is no customary law marriage system that is universal to Nigeria. Every community operates a customary law marriage system relative to the individual community. However, there are essential similarities in the basic requirements for a valid customary law marriage across the different ethnic communities in Nigeria. Some of these requirements are:

(1) Capacity of the parties;

---

[10] See for example, Marriage, Divorce and Custody of Children Adoptive By-Laws 1958 of Western Nigeria.

(2) Consent of the parties and the consent of the parents of the bride, especially the consent of the father of the bride;
(3) Statutory prohibition;
(4) Prohibited degree of relationships;
(5) Payment of bride price; and
(6) Celebration of marriage.

These requirements are examined hereunder.

Capacity

One of the characteristics of customary law is its unwritten nature. Customary law marriage rules, like customary law is mostly undocumented. The result of this unwritten nature of customary law marriage rules is the absence of age prescriptions for customary law marriage. However, some local governments have exercised the powers to make declarations or modifications of customary law rules applicable to their areas of authority,[11] by fixing the marriageable age at sixteen years.[12] See the case of *Emeakuana* v. *Umeojiako*,[13] where the appellant and her father gave uncontroverted evidence that the appellant was about fifteen years when the marriage with the defendant was celebrated and the court held that the marriage was void because it contravened Section 3 (1) of the Age of Marriage law.

Consent

Two types of consent are required for a valid customary law marriage - consent of the parties and parental consent, especially the consent of the bride's father. Consent of the parties was held to be a condition precedent for a valid customary law marriage under Benin customary law in the case of *Osamwonyi* v. *Osamwonyi*.[14] See also *Agbeke* v.

---

[11] See the Local Government Law, 1976 (Anambra State), see also NA (Declaration of Biu Native Marriage Law and Custom) Order 164 NALW 9 of 1964.

[12] See Section 3 (1) Age of Marriage Law Cap. 6 of Laws of Eastern Nigeria, 1963, which renders void any marriage to any person under the age of sixteen.

[13] Suit No. AA/1A/76 (unreported) High Court Awka October 15, 1976.

[14] (1972) 10 SC 1; see also *Ogunremi* v. *Ogunremi and Ovie*, Suit No. M/10/71 High Court of Western State, Ekiti Judicial Division, Delivered 12, July 1971, where the court held that the consent of the parties was an essential requirement of an Ekiti (Yoruba) customary marriage & *Okpanum* v. *Okpanum* (1972) ECSLR p. 561 at 563.

Salawa Iyanda[15] where the Oyo native Court of Appeal held that the plaintiff (woman) could repudiate a marriage contract entered into with the defendant on her behalf by her parents.

Parental consent on the other hand is required and sometimes mandatory for the celebration of a valid customary law marriage. Parental consent in this case is the consent of the bride's father, or guardian who is in *loco parentis* to the bride. Parental consent, however, may no longer be a requirement in some states of the former Western Region.[16] Therefore, lack of parental consent, may not be fatal to a customary law marriage where the laws permit that it could be dispensed with. However, it must be noted that no customary law marriage could be successfully concluded without the consent of the father of the bride or head of the family where there is no father because there will be nobody to receive the bride price and bride price is fundamental to a valid customary law marriage.

Prohibited Degree of Relationships

Marriage between persons who are related either by blood or marriage ties is forbidden under customary law marriage. In Nigeria, the prohibited degree of relationships for customary law marriage is wider than that applicable under the MCA. It is forbidden under this system to marry any person with whom you share blood relationship or any form of affinity no matter the remoteness of the relationship.

Statutory prohibition

The Marriage Act prohibits marriage under customary law to any person who is party to an existing statutory marriage or monogamous marriage recognised by law.[17] See the case of *Onwudinjoh* v. *Onwudinjoh* where the subsequent customary law marriage by one Jeremiah to Chinelo, was held void by the reason of Section 35 of the Marriage Act because of the subsisting statutory marriage between

---

[15] Suit 5/58 Civil Record Book Vol. XII.

[16] The former Western Region, now divided into eight states, includes Lagos, Ogun, Ondo, Ekiti, Osun, Oyo, Delta and Edo State. In these states, the requirement of parental consent has been abolished by the Marriage, Divorce and Custody of Children Adoptive By-Laws, WRLN 456 of 1958

[17] *Supra*, note 9 Section 35.

Jeremiah and Agnes at the time he purportedly married Chinelo under the customary law.[18]

Bride price

Payment of bride price is an essential ingredient of a valid customary law marriage. However, like every other aspect of customary law, there is no standard regulation as to the nature and quantum of bride price. There is also nothing to determine when the bride price is due and payable. However, the father is the right person to receive the bride price. Where there is no father, the right devolves to the male head of the family. Where there is no father or his immediate successor, the guardian of the girl or a person in *loco parentis* becomes entitled to receive the bride price.

In *Okpanum* v. *Okpanum*[19] it was decided that part payment of bride price was sufficient for a valid customary law marriage. Before now, the bride price could take the form of labour by the suitor to the parents of the bride in addition to some gifts. These days, the bride price usually takes the form of some money and gifts. Apart from the regulations stipulating the quantum of pride prices, such as the provisions of the Limitation of Dowry Law 1956[20] applicable only in the former Eastern region, communities or even families fix their bride price. In these modern times, some families (mostly well-to-do and elitist families) ask for only a token as the bride price but what is not usually possible is a complete waiver of the bride price because of the primacy of the bride price to the validity of customary law marriage.

Celebration of the Marriage

The handing over of the bride to the bridegroom and his family is the concluding or final process in the customary law marriage. Until the celebration of the marriage, which culminates in the handing over of the bride, a valid customary law marriage has been contracted. In the

---

[18] (1957-58) 11 ERLR 1.
[19] (1972) ECSLR 561 at 563.
[20] Cap 76, Laws of Eastern Nigeria 1963.

case of *Beckley* v. *Abiodun,*[21] the courts held that no valid Yoruba customary marriage could be contracted without the formal handover of the bride.

B. Statutory Marriage

A statutory marriage is a marriage contracted in accordance with the provisions of the Marriage Act.[22] A valid statutory marriage must satisfy the six essential factors required for a valid statutory marriage as well as fulfil the formal requirements.[23] Unlike customary law marriage, the MA and the MCA regulates statutory marriage and any person purporting to marry under the Act must satisfy the provisions of the law as any infraction of the provisions of the Act may render the marriage void or voidable.

Essential Validity of a Statutory Marriage

There are six factors essential for a valid statutory marriage; the age of the parties, prohibited degree of consanguinity and affinity, parties must be unmarried, parties must be sane and they must freely give their consent, while parental consent is required in the case of a minor.

Age

According to the MCA, marriage under the Act is void if either party to the marriage is not of a marriageable age.[24] However, the MCA did not define the term "marriageable age." In the absence of a statutory definition of the age of marriage, the court may have recourse to the common law rule on the subject to determine when a party to a statutory marriage is of marriageable age. Under the common law, marriageable age is the age of puberty - fourteen years in the case of a boy and twelve years in the case of a girl.

---

[21] In the Matter of Marriage Ordinance, (1943) 17 NLR 59, see also *Ikedionwu* v. *Okafor* (1966-67) 10 ENLR 178.

[22] *Supra,* note 9.

[23] The six essential requirements for a valid statutory marriage are: age, prohibited degree of consanguinity and affinity, neither party must be already married, consent of the parties, parental consent and sanity.

[24] Section 3 (1) (e) Matrimonial Causes Act Cap M7 LFN 2004 (MCA). The acronym MCA will be used throughtout in this chapter to represent the Matrimonial Causes Act.

Prohibited Degree of Consanguinity and Affinity

Marriage under the Act is void if it involves persons who are within the prohibited degree of consanguinity or affinity.[25] Before the Matrimonial Causes Act came into effect, Section 33 (1) of the Marriage Act prescribed the degree of consanguinity and affinity and it is the Marriage Act that still governs marriages contracted before 1970. Under the Matrimonial Causes Act 1970, a marriage is prohibited if the woman is or has been the man's ancestress descendant.[26]

Neither Party Must Be Already Married

Marriage under the Act is a marriage of one man to one woman to the exclusion of all others. As a result, any person who is already married under the Act or native law and custom is precluded from contracting another statutory marriage with another person.[27] Any marriage contracted in defiance of this rule is void, and it is an offense punishable by terms of imprisonment under the Matrimonial Causes Act and the Criminal Code.[28] Section 33 (1) MA forbids marriage to a party involved in a subsisting marriage under customary law. However, the same parties to a customary law marriage are permitted under the Marriage Act to contract a subsequent statutory marriage.

Consent of the Parties

The consent of the parties to a statutory marriage is fundamental for the validity of the marriage. The consent must be free, devoid of vitiating elements such as duress, fraud or misapprehension, which may render the marriage voidable.[29]

Parental Consent

Where either party to a statutory marriage, who is not a widow or widower, is under the age of twenty-one years, he or she must obtain

---

[25] Ibid., section 3 (1) (b).

[26] See the Act for a full list of those that are within the prohibited degree of consaguinity and affinity, see also Section 4 of the Act for exceptions to the rule with regards to the prohibited degree of affinity.

[27] *Obele Iniya* v. *Obele* (1973) 1 NMLR 155.

[28] Section 370 Criminal Code, prescibes seven years inprisonment and Sections 35 and 48 MA lay down five years inprisonment. See also *R.* v. *Princewill*, (1963) NNLR 54.

[29] Section 3 (1) (d) MCA.

the written consent of the father. However, if the father is incapacitated because of insanity or he is out of Nigeria, the mother will give the necessary consent subject to the soundness of her mind and her being in Nigeria. If both parents are unavailable for the reason of death, unsoundness of mind, or out of Nigeria, the guardian to the minor may give the necessary consent.[30] Any person who is giving the consent must sign it, and where the person cannot write or he is illiterate, he may affix his mark to the document in the presence of a High Court Judge or a Magistrate, or a Registrar or person of similar status.[31]

Sanity

According to Section 3(1)(d)(iii), it is necessary that parties to a statutory marriage are of sound mind. If one party is insane and therefore not mentally capable of understanding the nature of marriage contract, the marriage will be void *ab initio*.

Formal Validity of Statutory Marriage

Marriage under the Act requires more than just fulfilling the essential validity. It also requires the fulfilling of some formalities as laid down in the Marriage Act. For example, the Act requires intending parties to a statutory marriage to enter notice of the marriage.[32] The purpose is to give notice to the public of the impending marriage, thereby inviting any person who may have reasons to oppose the marriage to enter a caveat before the issue of the authority to marry – Registrar's certificate.

The Registrar's certificate authorizing the marriage is issued after twenty-one days and up to three months from the date of the notice where there is no objection to the marriage between the intending couple after the parties have satisfied the Registrar by affidavit of compliance in accordance with Section 11(1) of the MA. This is without prejudice to the powers of the governor to issue a special licence under Section 13 of the MA, authorizing the marriage if the parties satisfy him

---

[30] Section 18 MA.

[31] Section 19 MA. See generally Section 20 MA for those that may give consent, see also *Agbo* v. *Udo* (1947) 18 NLR 152, for the effect of parental consent and the absence of it on the validity of a statutory marriage.

[32] Section 7 & 8 Marriage Act.

by affidavit that there is no impediment to the proposed marriage between them.

One of the bases for a caveat against a proposed marriage is the existence of a customary law marriage between a party to the proposed marriage and a third party.[33] However, a party relying on the existence of a customary law marriage must prove its existence.[34]

The Registrar's certificate is not evidence of celebration of marriage and it does not confer a marriage status under the Act as decided in *Sofela* v. *Sofela*.[35] The parties to a statutory marriage, to acquire marriage status under the Act must proceed to celebrate their marriage in accordance with the provisions of the Act. There are essentially two ways of celebrating marriage under the Act – celebration in a licensed place of worship and celebration in a Registrar's office.

The governor of a State is authorised under Section 6 of the Marriage Act to licence any place of public worship in his state to be a place for the celebration of marriage in the State. It is only in such a place licensed for that purpose that intending spouses may celebrate a marriage that would be valid under the Act. Such a marriage must be celebrated with open doors and between the hours of 8:00 a.m and 6:00 p.m with at least two witnesses present and an officiating priest who must be a recognized priest of the denomination concerned, and the process must be carried out in accordance with the practice of that denomination.[36]

Celebration in a Registrar's office, on the other hand, shall take place with open doors between the hours of 10:00 a.m and 4:00 p.m in the office of the Registrar and in the presence of at least two witnesses with the Registrar presiding.[37] Apart from a licensed place of worship and a Registrar's office, a valid statutory marriage may also be celebrated under a special licence, which may permit the celebration in

---

33 Section 33 Marriage Act forbids any party to a subsisting customary law marriage from contracting a marriage with a third party under the Act while Section 35 of the Act prohibits a subsequent customary law marriage for a party married under the Act. See *Ogunremi* v. *Ogunremi* (1972) 2 ULR 466.

34 See *Olikagbue* v. *Olikagbue* suit No. M/1/68 (unreported) Benin High Court, 22nd September 1966. See also *Beckley* v. *Abiodun* (1943) 17 NLR 59.

35 (1976) 7 CCHCJ 1923.

36 Section 21 Marriage Act

37 Section 27 *id.*

a place other than a licensed place of worship.[38] A valid marriage may also be celebrated in a Nigerian Diplomatic or Consular Mission office abroad between parties, one of which must be a Nigerian citizen.

However, other forms of celebration, such as church marriages and church blessings that do not comply with the provisions of the Act do not constitute marriage under the Act. A common example of church marriage is a Roman Catholic Church marriage. It is usually a monogamous marriage performed in the presence of witnesses after the necessary banns of marriage have been published, and there are no objections against the union of the parties. The fact that a certificate is issued and that the marriage is monogamous does not make it a statutory marriage.[39]

DISSOLUTION OF MARRIAGE

There are two ways to contract a valid marriage in Nigeria – under the statute and under customary law. Whichever system the couple contract under, marriages are intended to last the lifetime of the parties. However, Nigerian marriage laws permit either party with a good cause to terminate the marriage.

The plurality of marriage systems in Nigeria is also reflected in the dissolution of marriages. Apart from the fact that different courts are seized with jurisdiction over matrimonial causes for the different types of marriage, the applicable rules and consequences of dissolution are also different. For example, the return of the bride price,[40] an essential requirement for the dissolution of a customary law marriage, is unknown to statutory marriage.

Dissolution of Customary Law Marriage

There are essentially three ways by which a customary law marriage may be dissolved – extra-judicially, judicially, or by death:

---

[38] Section 29 *id.*

[39] See the view expressed by Palmer on the validty of such Roman Catholic marriage in *Obiekwe* v. *Obiekwe* (1963) ENLR 196 at 199. See also *Setse* v. *Setse* (1963) GLR 155.

[40] Bride price and dowry will be used inter-changeably in this paper. They both mean the payment to the family of the bride in the process of a customary law marriage.

Extra-judicial Dissolution

This is the process by which a customary law marriage may be terminated without recourse to the court of law. Extra-judicial divorce may be unilateral or by the mutual agreement of the parties. The process of unilateral divorce begins where the husband evicts the wife from the matrimonial home with the intention not to allow her back or where the wife leaves the matrimonial home with the intention never to return. Such action by a customary law wife or a customary law husband will set a divorce process in motion. The refund of bride price will conclude the divorce process. Note that where it is the woman that leaves the matrimonial home, the bride price becomes immediately refundable but where the husband evicted her, the bride price becomes due only when she remarries or when she is able to pay.[41]

Judicial Dissolution

The customary courts have exclusive original jurisdiction in customary matrimonial causes.[42] Parties to a customary law matrimonial proceeding base their petition on reasons[43] rather than grounds, as is the case with matrimonial causes under the statute.

Although one of the reasons for the grant of divorce in a customary matrimonial cause is adultery, unlike matrimonial cause under the Act, adultery as a reason under customary matrimonial cause is applicable only with respect to the husband's case against the wife. In a customary matrimonial cause, divorce will readily be granted, and the refund of the price would be ordered once it is obvious that the parties to the marriage can no longer be reconciled or where one party is determined to see to the end of the union.[44]

---

[41] See *supra* note 19.

[42] See *Okpakpa* v. *Okor and Anor*, Suit No. 1/634/1969 9 (unreported) High Court Lagos 22 May 1970.

[43] Some of the reason for the grant of divorce in customary marriage matrimonial causes are as contained in the Adoptive By-Laws of Western Nigeria 1958: Betrothal under marriageable age; refusal to consumate the marriage; harmful diseases of a permanent nature which may impair the fertility of a woman or the virility of a man; impotence of a husband or the sterility of a wife; conviction of either party for a crime involving a sentence of imprisonment of five years or more; ill treatment, cruelty, neglect of either party by the other; venereal disease contracted by either party; lunacy of either party for three years or more; adultery; leprosy contracted by either party; desertion for a period of two years or more etc.

[44] See *Paul Okwueze* v. *Febisola Okwueze* , suit no. 1 CA/H/154/83 delivered 21, March 1985.

Dissolution By Death

Death constitutes dissolution of a customary law marriage only with respect to the customary law wife, as the death of a customary law husband does not bring a customary law marriage to an end. It is only the refund of the bride price rather than the death of a customary law husband that can terminate a customary law marriage. In *Amachree* v. *Goodhead*,[45] it was decided that after the death of a customary law husband, a customary law wife continued to belong to the customary law husband's family until the bride price was refunded.

When Customary Law Marriage Is in Fact Dissolved

The fact that the refund of bride price concludes the dissolution of a customary law marriage, whether it is dissolved judicial or extra-judicially or by death, [46] means that the issue of bride price is primary to customary matrimonial causes. It is important, therefore, to determine when a customary law marriage is, in fact, dissolved.

In the case of extra-judicial divorce, the courts have held in the case of the *Registrar of Marriages* v. *Igbinomwanhia*,[47] per Obaseki J., that separation does not constitute divorce under Bini customary law, and that customary law marriage can only be dissolved by the refund of bride price. Concerning judicial divorce, it was stated in the case of *Eze* v. *Omeke*[48] that a specific order dissolving any customary law marriage was unnecessary because it is the refund of the bride price that puts an end to the incidents of a customary law marriage. The implication is that a customary law marriage cannot be dissolved without the refund of the bride price.

Dissolution of a Statutory Marriage

The Matrimonial Causes Act regulates the dissolution of statutory marriage in Nigeria. MCA[49] provides for only one ground for the dissolution of marriage, namely, that the marriage has broken down

---

[45] (1923) 4 NLR 101.

[46] See *Registrar of Marriages* v. *Igbinomwanhia*, suit no. B/16M 22 (unreported) High Court, Benin, 5 August 1972. See also *Eze* v. *Omeke* (1977) ANSLR 136.

[47] See of *Registrar Marriages* v. *Igbinomwanhia* Ibid.

[48] See *Eze* v. *Omeke* (1977) ANSLR 136.

[49] CAP M7 LFN 2004.

irretrievably.[50] However, the provisions of factual situations in Section 15(2), which must be proved before marriage, can be held to have broken down irretrievably and appears to create the real grounds for the dissolution of marriage. This is because those facts situations are symptoms of a marriage that has broken down irretrievably. All a petitioner for matrimonial relief may need to prove to establish an irretrievable breakdown of marriage is one of the facts under Section 15 (2), as the petitioner is not required to prove an irretrievable breakdown.

However, apart from the grounds/facts as provided in Section 15 (2), Section 16(1) provides additional facts, any of which, if proved, would also constitute the fact in Section 15(2)(c), which is that the respondent has behaved in such a way that the petitioner cannot reasonably be expected to live with the respondent. It appears misleading to say that the MCA provides for only one ground for dissolution of marriage according to Section 15(1) MCA because a petitioner does not need to prove irretrievable breakdown but proof of the facts in Section 15(2) as evidence of the fact that the marriage has broken down irretrievably. Therefore, the real grounds for dissolution of statutory marriage are the grounds as provided in Sections 15(2) and 16(1) MCA, as decided by the Enugu division of the Court of Appeal in *Justin Obidi Megwalu* v. *Adline Njideka Megwalu*.[51] It was also stated in *Okojie* v. *Okojie*,[52] that under Nigerian law, a Court could not dissolve a marriage even though it has broken down irretrievably unless one of the facts under Section 15(2) is established to the satisfaction of the court.

Jurisdiction to Dissolve Statutory Marriage

Under the Matrimonial Causes Act, the basis for jurisdiction in matrimonial causes is domicile. Section 2(2) MCA provides that

---

50 Ibid., Section 15 (1).
51 (1994) 7 NWLR (Part 359) 730.
52 Suit No. WD/21/73 High Court of Lagos State, March 10 1976.

proceedings for a decree of the provisions in paragraphs a-f[53] may be instituted by any person domiciled in Nigeria. However, because domicile is fundamental[54] to the issue of jurisdiction, without which the court will not have the power to adjudicate the matter before it, it is important to understand what domicile is in matrimonial causes.

Domicile

Domicile is important, at least in the common law world, because it connects a person to the legal system of a given jurisdiction. It is the basis upon which a person may pursue a legal process, for example, matrimonial causes, succession, legitimacy, etc. Between married couples, the wife acquires the domicile of the husband upon marriage. This means that whenever the wife wishes to undertake matrimonial proceedings, she must do that in a court within the jurisdiction of the husband's domicile. The implication is that a wife who is normally resident in Nigeria cannot seek matrimonial relief in Nigeria where the husband has changed domicile by relocating to Ghana since the wife's domicile is tied to that of the husband.

To cure the problem of circumstances when a husband may deliberately change domicile to make it impossible for a deserted wife to seek matrimonial relief, the MCA under Section 7(a) provides that a deserted wife who was domiciled in Nigeria immediately before the marriage, or immediately before the desertion shall be deemed resident in Nigeria. Paragraph (b) also provides that a wife who is resident in Nigeria at the date of instituting proceedings under the Act and has been so resident for three years immediately preceding that date shall be deemed to be domiciled in Nigeria at that date.

(i) Jurisdiction and issue of forum court in matrimonial causes Section 2 (1) MCA provides:

---

[53] Proceedings that may be commenced by any person domiciled in Nigeria as provided by Section 2 (2) are a decree (a) of dissolution of marriage or (b) of nullity of a voidable marriage (c) nullity of a void marriage (d) judicial separation (e) restitution of conjugal rights (f) jactitation of marriage.

[54] *Bhojwani* v.. *Bhojwani* (1995) 7 NWLR (Part 407) p. 349.

> Subject to the Act, a person may institute a matrimonial cause under this Act in the High Court of any State of the Federation, and for that purpose, the High Court of each State of the Federation shall have the jurisdiction to hear and determine...

A literal interpretation of Section 2(1) above and Section 2(3)[55] appear to suggest that a party to a matrimonial proceeding may commence action before any state high court in the federation. The implication of such interpretation is that a spouse who lives and works in Benin, for example, may commence a matrimonial suit in Abia State High Court or any state of their choice in Nigeria. This was the view adopted by the court in *Victoria Adekanye* v. *Omosoba Adekanya,*[56] where the court refused the application by the respondent for a transfer of a suit commenced in Ibadan back to Lagos, where the couple lives and works.

However, the better view and current position of the law was the decision in *Adegoroye* v. *Adegoroye,*[57] where it was decided that Nigeria as a single domicile means that all the State High Courts constitute one jurisdiction for the purposes of matrimonial causes under the MCA. Consequently, the transfer of matrimonial proceedings from one State's High Court to the High Court of another state is permissible. Therefore, any matrimonial suit commenced outside the jurisdiction where the parties are normally resident will, on application by a party to the proceeding, be transferred to a forum court, thereby affirming that matrimonial suits can only be commenced in a forum court – the court that has jurisdiction where the couple normally lives and works. This view was followed in *Oladepo Folorunsho* v. *Elizabeth*

---

55 Section 2 (3) provides "For the avoidance of doubt it is hereby declared that any person domiciled in any State of the Federation is domiciled in Nigeria for the purposes of this Act and may institute proceedings under this Act in the High Court of any State whether or not he is domiciled in that particular State".

56 Suit No. 1/403 82 (Unreported) Ibadan Judicial Division, decided October 11 1983.

57 (1996) 2 NWLR (Part 433) 712.

Folorunsho.[58] The Matrimonial Causes Act, however, regulates only monogamous marriages.[59]

CONSEQUENCES OF DIVORCE

Marriage is a contract whereby the parties thereto enter into legal relations involving obligations. Thus, a valid marriage creates reciprocal rights and obligations for the parties. However, a marriage contract, although it has some features of ordinary civil or commercial contracts, such as the requirement of the consent of the parties, it differs from it in various ways. One of the many distinguishing features of a marriage contract is that it imposes obligations on the parties, which cannot necessarily be varied by agreement,[60] for example, the obligation of the husband to maintain his wife.[61]

Another peculiarity of a marriage contract is that an obligation under the contract is not restricted to the parties. For example, the obligation to maintain the children of the marriage, custody of the children, their welfare, and education are statutory rights and obligations recognized under the MCA.[62]

Apart from the non-restriction of marriage contracts to the parties thereto, another important peculiarity is that a marriage contract is not terminated by the dissolution of the marriage. In fact, issues of maintenance of the spouse and children of marriage and custody of the children of the marriage, which we now turn to in this concluding part of this chapter, are some of the ancillary issues that arise as a consequence of divorce.

Maintenance

There are two parties in a marriage relationship in whose favour a maintenance order may be made under the MCA[63] – a party to a marriage and children of the marriage.

---

[58] (1996) 5 NWLR (Part 450) 612.

[59] See section 69 MCA.

[60] Nwogugu E. I. *Family Law in Nigeria* Revised ed., (Ibadan: Heinemann Educational Books (Nigeria) Plc: 1990)

[61] Ibid.

[62] Section 70 (1) MCA.

[63] See Section 69 MCA.

A Party to The Marriage: Marriage as defined under Section 69 MCA includes any marriage contracted under the Act, which may be valid, void or voidable. The only marriages excluded by Section 69 are marriages contracted under the Islamic law and customary law. Therefore, any marriage contracted under the Act irrespective of the status raises the obligation of maintenance.

Children of the Marriage

Section 69 defines children of the marriage to include

(a) Any child adopted since the marriage by the husband and the wife or by either of them with the consent of the other.

(b) Any child of the husband and the wife born before the marriage, whether legitimated by marriage or not; and

(c) Any child of either the husband or wife (including an illegitimate child of either of them and a child adopted by either of them) if, at the relevant time, the child was ordinarily a member of the household of the husband and wife, so, however, that a child of the husband and wife (including a child born before the marriage, whether legitimated by marriage or not) who has been adopted by another person or other persons shall be deemed not to be a child of the marriage.

The Act is silent on a child born in lawful wedlock; however, it is obvious that a child born in lawful wedlock is a child of the marriage by the implication of the marriage between the father and mother.

The definition of a child of the Marriage under S. 69 (a) and (b) are quite straightforward, but the definition under S. 69 (c) has provided some challenges for the courts with respect to the definition of relevant time. However, the court in *May* v. *May*,[64] decided that the important factor was not the physical residency of the child with the spouses up to the time they ceased to live together but the existence of the relationship of being a member of the family at the material time. In *Osemabor* v.

[64] (1961) 2 FLR 383, 386.

Osemabor,[65] (1976) 4 CCHCJ 1215, the court found that the children of a wife by another man who lives with the family and were treated as integral members of the family were members of the family.

Maintenance under Customary/Common Law

The customary law wife does not have a right to maintenance upon desertion by or divorce from the husband. In *Adeleke* v. *Yinka*,[66] where a divorced woman applied to the court for maintenance for her and her child, the court declared that with regard to her maintenance, "payment of such an allowance to a divorced woman is contrary to native law and custom." However, the husband of a divorced or deserted wife may be required to pay for the cost incurred by his customary law wife for her maintenance and that of the child if the desertion or divorce took place when she is with a child or when she is pregnant.[67]

Unlike a customary law wife, a common-law wife has a right to maintenance under the "agency of necessity" principle. Where a husband deserts the wife or drives her out of the matrimonial home, he is obligated under the common law to continue to provide for her maintenance. Where, however, he fails to provide for the maintenance, he will be liable for the necessaries supplied to her. The wife is deemed his agent for the purposes of obtaining necessaries, but this is only applicable where the wife does not have the means of satisfying her necessary requirements. The husband, however, will only be liable for the necessaries supplied so that a supplier of luxuries will have no cause against the husband.

Maintenance under the Matrimonial Causes Act

The Matrimonial Cause Act provides for the maintenance of spouses and children of the marriage in Part IV of the Act. The courts have powers under the Act to make orders for maintenance of spouses, either pending proceedings or pending the disposal of proceedings.[68]

---

[65] (1976) 4 CCHCJ 1215. See also *Asomugha* v. *Asomugha* (1974) 4 CCHCJ 1419.
[66] Suit No. M/559/76 of 05/11/76 (unreported) Customary Court, Mapo, Ibadan.
[67] See *Adugba* v. *Anuku*, Suit No. 75/88 of 10/04 68 (unreported) Customary Court, Oturkpo.
[68] Section 70 (1) & (2) MCA.

Under the MCA, maintenance may be ordered against the wife or the husband of the marriage as the MCA did not make any distinction between the parties in a marriage. However, unlike in England, where the court in the case of *Calderbank* v. *Calderbank*[69] ordered maintenance against a wife, Nigerian courts still view maintenance from the common law perspective when they speak of a man's duty to maintain the wife as expressed by the Court of Appeal in *Nanna* v. *Nanna.*[70]

Factors Considered By a Court in Making an Order of Maintenance

The four factors relevant in determining when to make a maintenance order and how it should be assessed are as contained in Section 70(1): (i) means of the parties; (ii) earning capacity of the parties; (iii) conduct of the parties; and (iv) all other relevant circumstances.

The means of the parties have been held to include not only pecuniary sources but also assets.[71] The Nigerian Court of Appeal also approved the view that it is necessary to put in details of the means and earning capacity of the parties so that the court will have a factual and accurate basis for making a maintenance order.[72] However, it is the duty of the petitioner to show the means and the actual earning capacity of the respondent. The inability to fulfil these requirements was responsible for the award of only two pounds in *Achugbue* v. *Achugbue.*[73]

The earning capacity of the spouse refers to the actual and potential earning capacity of the spouse. This is why the court in *McEwan* v *McEwan,*[74] the court held that an order that the whole of a retired police officer's weekly pension be paid to the wife is not unreasonable.

---

69 (1975) 3 WLR 586.

70 (2006) 3 NWLR (Pt. 966) 1 at 12. See also *Oni* v. *Oni*, Suit No. M/52/70 of 27/01/71, High Court of Western State.

71 See *Rogers* v. *Rogers* (1962) 3 FLR 398.

72 See *Erhahon* v. *Erhahon* (1997) 6 NWLR (Pt. 510) 667.

73 Suit No. Uttc/21/70 of 26/11/70.

74 (1972) 1 WLR 1217.

Concerning the conduct of the parties, in the English case as decided in *Wachtel* v. *Wachtel*[75] Lord Denning stated that the guilt of a party does necessarily affect the order of maintenance, which would ordinarily be made in favour of the party. However, some grievous conduct, such as that of a wife who fired a shotgun at the husband after she was shut out of the house, has been taken into consideration in the making of an order for maintenance.[76] In Nigeria, the gravity of the misconduct of the applicant for an order of maintenance may affect the size of the maintenance order. The gravity of misconduct may actually affect the decision of whether or not the order will be made. This was the case in the case of *Okafor* v. *Okafor* where the wife's rejection of all reconciliation attempts contributed to the court's refusal to make a maintenance order in her favour.[77]

Section 70(1) has an omnibus provision – "all other relevant circumstances." In the case of *Nanna* v. *Nanna,*[78] the court stated that the relevant circumstances must be gathered by the court itself from the proceedings and evidence of the parties at the trial, as the claim for maintenance is not the same as a claim for special damages requiring strict proof. This leaves the courts with wide powers in dealing with the applications for maintenance under the MCA.

Custody

The MCA provides that "in any proceedings with respect to the custody, guardianship ... the court shall regard the interests of those children as paramount consideration..." The MCA did not provide for any standard to measure the interest of a child or children of the marriage in the award of custody of a child or children of the marriage. However, in dealing with cases with respect to the custody of the children of the marriage, Nigerian courts have followed the dictum by Karibi-Whyte J.S.C. in *Williams* v. *Williams*[79]– that age, emotional attachment to a particular parent, and inadequacy of facilities for education are some of the factors to be

[75] (1973) Fam 72.
[76] See *Armstrong* v. *Armstrong* (1874) 118 SJ 579.
[77] Suit No. O/6D/71.
[78] *Supra*, note 70 p.3.
[79] (1987) 2 NWLR 66 p.89.

considered in determining the interest of the child or children of the marriage.[80]

The important thing to note is the paramountcy of the interest of the child as tender age alone or excellent arrangement for the education of the child may not determine the grant of custody. Thus in the case of *Nanna* v. *Nanna*,[81] custody was granted to the mother of the children notwithstanding the observation by Abba Aji, J.C.A that "I have stated above the evidential account of the arrangement of the appellant for the well-being of the children."[82]

The courts have discretion based on the circumstance of every case to consider what will be the best interest of the child in the award of custody. However, this discretion must be exercised judiciously.[83]

80 See the case of *Damulak* v. *Damulak* (2004) 8 NWLR (Pt. 874) 151 p.170, where the tender age of the child-Muhammed was the main consideration for awarding the custody of the child to his mother because according to the court "the chil-Muhammed-must be presumed to be happier with the mother".

81 *Supra*, note 70 p.14.

82 Ibid., p.14.

83 *Odulate* v. *Odulate* (1975) 1 CCHCJ 1010.

www.ingramcontent.com/pod-product-compliance
Lightning Source LLC
LaVergne TN
LVHW052012200926
848481LV00005B/1472